REPRESENTATIVE ENGLISH COMEDIES

WITH INTRODUCTORY ESSAYS AND NOTES

AND

A COMPARATIVE VIEW OF

THE FELLOWS AND FOLLOWERS OF SHAKESPEARE

UNDER THE GENERAL EDITORSHIP OF

CHARLES MILLS GAYLEY, Litt.D., LL.D.,

*Professor of the English Language and Literature
in the University of California*

VOLUME III

THE LATER CONTEMPORARIES
OF SHAKESPEARE:

FLETCHER AND OTHERS

New York:

THE MACMILLAN COMPANY

LONDON : MACMILLAN & CO., LTD.

1914

PREFACE

In the second volume of this series the comedy of Jonson and others was considered. In this the history of the type is continued to the closing of the theatres in 1642, and six of the plays written by Shakespeare's later contemporaries are presented and discussed. Those of Dekker, Massinger, and Brome, since they were published during the lifetime of the authors, are reproduced from the original quartos. Those, on the other hand, of Middleton and Rowley, and Fletcher, which found their way into print only after their authors were dead, are, in conformity with the rule adopted for the series, presented in critical texts based upon collation of the quartos with other early editions; and, for reasons set forth by Sir A. W. Ward in his edition of Shirley's *Royal Master*, the same treatment has been accorded to that play. Neither *The Royal Master* nor Brome's *Antipodes* has been more than once before republished. They will, I think, be welcomed by the general reader, for the earlier editions are not always readily obtainable.

The next volume of this series, now well under way, will present the comedy of the Restoration. In reading the proofs of plays in this volume I have been assisted by my colleague, Dr. G. A. Smithson; and I return my hearty thanks.

CHARLES MILLS GAYLEY.

University of California,
    June 26, 1914.

CONTENTS

vii

Contents

A Comparative View

OF THE

FELLOWS AND FOLLOWERS OF SHAKESPEARE IN COMEDY

(Part Two)

By Charles Mills Gayley

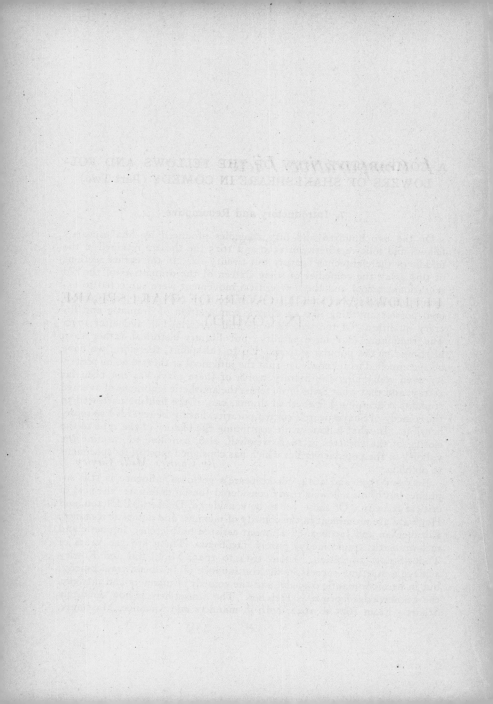

A COMPARATIVE VIEW OF THE FELLOWS AND FOLLOWERS OF SHAKESPEARE IN COMEDY (Part Two)

7. Introductory and Resumptive

OF the two hundred and fifty comedies produced by Shakespeare's fellows and followers between 1590 and 1625 the theatre retained in the middle of the eighteenth century but twenty-six. In the earlier sections of this essay the comedies of some sixteen of the dramatists of the old sensational school and the new critical movement were subjected to examination, and it was found that not more than ten of the plays considered possess anything like an artistic combination of dramatic and literary qualities. Of the ten, six were still performed in and after 1750. The remaining four have vitality; but literary-historical rather than histrionic in the popular esteem. Up to this point, therefore, we have been compelled to acknowledge that the judgment of theatre-going posterity even concerning the literary worth of these plays has not been far astray; and that what Swinburne terms the apathetic ignorance of average students concerning Elizabethan drama, can, if the field be narrowed to the comedy of Shakespeare's contemporaries, hardly be regarded as reprehensible. In what follows while continuing the history of the type to the closing of the theatres in 1642, we shall, also, continue to examine the validity of the popular verdict which has consigned most of its specimens to oblivion.

Between 1598 and 1614, Shakespeare's personal influence is still supreme; but of his fellows already considered Jonson dominates the field of critical comedy. Of those yet to be considered, Dekker, Middleton, and Heywood are prominent in the comedy of manners and domestic romance, Elizabethan and Jacobean; Beaumont assisted by Fletcher, in poetic and melodramatic tragicomedy, purely Jacobean. These are the years of Tudor-Stuart transition. From 1614 to 1625, Middleton and Rowley achieve a startling success in the continuance of Jacobean tragicomedy; but in heroic-romantic comedy, and the comedy of manners and intrigue, the acknowledged prince is Fletcher. The atmosphere is now definitely Stuart. From 1625 to 1642, both in manners and romance, Massinger,

Brome, and Shirley produce the earliest specimens of what has been called
our modern literary comedy, and prepare the way for the Restoration
comedy of manners. Following the lead of Massinger and Shirley, a host
of minor dramatists hastens the transition from early Jacobean tragicomedy to the heroic play. Till about 1614 the materials are sometimes
classical or Italian, or Spanish by way of translations, but still largely of
the soil, or of the inventive quality of the great Elizabethans; between
1614 and 1625 materials and method are increasingly of Spanish derivation; from 1625 to 1642 the materials are both of contemporary English
manners and of the French heroic romance, but the method is that of
students who have before them the printed works of the masters of Elizabethan comedy.

8. Popular Comedy to 1614: Romantic and Realistic—Dekker, Day, and Others

It would simplify matters if we could say that the imaginative romantic,
the social romantic, and the realistic, forms of comedy from 1599 to 1614
were developed historically in the order named; or that Heywood for
instance represented the first, Dekker the second, and Middleton the
third. But we cannot say these things, nor that each restricted himself to
one form, nor that they did not severally indulge in forms not here set
down. Dekker wrote comedies of all three kinds; Middleton, of the
second and third; Heywood, of the same. And Middleton and Heywood
wrote tragicomedies besides. Suffice it to remark that these dramatists
are alike in this, that while conscious of critical conventions, they wrote
neither with the fear of the dramatic unities before their eyes, nor with a
reverence for the didactic function of the "humour." Their common
and abiding aim was popular delight. Dekker's muse sends him forth,

> "Not where the lawes of Poetry doe call
> But as the storie needes."

Heywood acknowledges that he "comes short of that accurateness both in
Plot and Stile, that these more Censorious dayes with greater curiosity
acquire." And Middleton more than once frankly "breaks the stage's
law to-day of acts and scenes," and wishes to his "comic play-readers,"
anything but instruction—rather "venery and laughter."

In the year of Porter's disappearance from dramatic record, **Thomas
Dekker** was already the most important of the writers for the Admiral's
men. For Chapman had broken away in 1599; and Jonson, though he

wrote intermittently for Henslowe until 1603, had produced with the Chamberlain's in 1598, and was never identified with the Admiral's as closely as Dekker. Of the men who had been prominent in the Henslowe group during his connection with it, Jonson, in his conversations with Drummond of Hawthornden, expressed no high opinion: he said that Day and Dekker were "rogues," and again that Day and Middleton were "base fellows"; whereas he praised Beaumont and "loved" Fletcher, who had not been members of that group,—loved Chapman too, who had left it early. Dekker had written for the company maybe in 1596, certainly 1597; and we find him still writing for the companies which occupied the Fortune and the Rose till 1604. As distinguished from hack-work, mostly in the chronicle-ballad form of play and in multifarious collaboration, he produced as sole, or principal, author some ten comedies of interest to the historian of the drama. Four of these have literary as well as dramatic worth: *The Shomakers Holiday*, *Patient Grissil*, and the two parts of *The Honest Whore*. To the others I shall refer merely in passing.

If *The Pleasant Comedie of Olde Fortunatus* was Dekker's first essay in the comic field, and such it may have been,—for though the "whole history" is not assigned to Dekker till November, 1599, a first part is mentioned by Henslowe in 1596,—its treatment reveals a stronger tendency to the romantic than we should look for in a writer whose surest reputation was to be made in the comedy of contemporary manners. This old-fashioned piece is a product of the chap-book and folk-lore school on the one hand, and of the "moral" play upon the other; but, still, as Professor Lange in his essay upon Dekker says, "the poetic sweep and fire of *Fortunatus* give to this Romantic interlude an enduring place of itself." Into an ancient story of magic are introduced Virtue and Vice and the attendant Iniquity. But though the last of these comports himself as an excellent clown, and in his rôle of Irish costermonger talks the language of sheer realism, the interest of the whole is that of wonder and the fairy tale. It must have been to these qualities of the 'marvel,' rather than to any dramatic significance, that the play owed its run of twelve nights when as late as 1819 it was revived at Covent Garden with Mrs. Faucit in the part of Virtue. Those performances were of a spectacle; and in all of Dekker's work, no matter how true to contemporary mood and manner it becomes, there persists a flavour of the sentimental, or romantic, or spectacular.

This combination of qualities is found in admirably conceived proportion in the very pleasant comedy of the Gentle Craft, known as *The Shomakers Holiday*, for which Henslowe paid Dekker £3.0.0 on July 15, 1599. Professor Schelling's verdict will be accepted by all: "This is one of the earliest, as it remained one of the most successful, comedies specifically of London life. Indeed, among comedies of its class there is no purer nor merrier specimen, free as it is alike from the extreme of caricature into which this form of drama was soon to run and from unnecessary romance." Further consideration of the play, here, is needless, since it is carefully reviewed by Professor Lange in the edition which follows. It would be hard to controvert his conclusion that *The Shomakers Holiday* is "the best adaptation, before 1600, of romantic comedy to 'deeds and language such as men do use.'" [1] It was acted at Court, January 1, 1600, the *Fortunatus* having preceded it by four days. [2] As revived in the Greek Theatre of the University of California, some two years past, not only the humours of Eyre and the main romantic plot but the cleverly acted sentiment of the 'widowed' Jane and her recovered husband attested the dramatic vitality of the play.

The sentimental interest is again to the fore in *The Pleasant Comedie of Patient Grissil*, upon which Dekker, with the assistance of Chettle and Haughton, was engaged between October and December of the year in which the *Shomaker* was completed. The play is dramatically contrived, but its theme is of that intermediate sort that produces neither comic satisfaction nor tragic catharsis, but resentment. The literary qualities both of the humour and the pathos are indubitable; but the long continued persecution of the patient heroine, though of a poetic tradition much affected by the literature of chivalry, imposes so severe a strain upon the patience of the modern reader that one can with difficulty imagine even an Elizabethan auditor willing to subject himself more than once to the experience. While this is a romantic play of domestic life in a former age, it contributes, by anachronism, not a little to the portrayal of contemporary manners,—especially in the Welsh scenes of the comic counter-movement. The excellent caprices of Gwenthyan and the resulting agonies of her hen-pecked husband have been attributed to Chettle; but modern critics find in the Welsh dialect and the boisterous fun much more of Dekker. [3] Chettle's interest, discerned in his other dramatic productions, lay more in the emotional, the pathetic, the horrible. And his style lent itself more readily to the melodramatic than to the recital of the ludicrous. *Patient Grissil* deserves the attention of the student as an early forerunner of sentimental comedy.

And so, in marked degree, does Dekker's noblest and most serious contribution to the history of the romantic comedy of domestic life, *The Honest Whore*,—a play which, under any other name, would nowadays

---

[1] See, also, Miss Hunt's admirable criticism, *Thomas Dekker*, p. 58.
[2] Greg's *Henslowe's Diary* I, p. 116.   [3] Miss Hunt, *Dekker*, p. 60.

be in better odour than it is. If *Patient Grissil* revives the theme of the spotless, suffering motherhood, so tenderly presented in the Virgin plays of the old miracles, here is revived the complementary theme, elaborated with equal tenderness in the miracles and morals,—the theme of Mary of Magdala, the prototype in dramatic literature of the fallen woman who, by repentance flowering from sinner into saint, sweetens the lives of others with her own. Perhaps, in construction, both *Parts* of this play betray haste and the resulting crudity; and, perhaps, the realism and the dialogue of lechery and heartless indecorum are strong meat for the delicate digestion of the twentieth century; but, even though the drama may not now be capable of presentation upon the stage, I find in it the materials of perennial literature: fervour in the repentance of Bellafronte,—

> "When in the street
> A faire yong modest Damsell I did meet,
> She seem'd to all a dove (when I passed by)
> And I to all a raven;"

pathos in her struggles against poverty and renewed temptation; unquenchable laughter of close kin to tears, and an impressive dignity in her father, the faithful Orlando Friscobaldo, "whose heart-strings sure would crack, were they strained more"; and in general a fidelity to motive, a vigour of characterization, and a wholesome sentiment not easily to be matched outside of Shakespeare's best efforts in romantic comedy and tragicomedy. As a picture of contemporary manners the play is unsurpassed by any of that age. In 1604, just previous to its publication, Henslowe paid Dekker and Middleton £5.0.0 toward the acquisition of the *First Part* by the Admiral's, now Prince Henry's men. But the *First Part* was printed in 1604, as Dekker's only; of Middleton's style there is practically no trace, and of his dramatic method nothing but possibly the choice of disreputable life and situation as furnishing a plot of contemporary interest. In the *Second Part*, registered without author's name in 1608, and printed as Dekker's in 1630, Middleton had no hand whatever, so far as I can see. Here we have Dekker at his powerfulest and tenderest. And of this Dekker the eulogy bestowed by our last Titanic melodist is fully justified:—

> O sweetest heart of all thy time save one,
> Star seen for love's sake nearest to the sun,
>   Hung lamp-like o'er a dense and doleful city,—
> Not Shakespeare's very spirit, howe'er more great,
> Than thine toward man was more compassionate,
>   Nor gave Christ praise from lips more sweet with pity.

The five plays so far discussed have poetic value, but only one, and that the least dramatic, *Olde Fortunatus*, has been revived upon the public stage. *The Shomakers Holiday* and *The Honest Whore* are in every way superior and intrinsically better fitted for modern presentation.

Neither from the dramatic nor the literary point of view do Dekker's other comedies, whether of collaboration or of unassisted authorship, appeal to me as worthy of consideration. Historically, *West-ward Hoe* and *North-ward Hoe*, presented by the Paul's boys in 1605 and 1606, respectively, are pivotal. The former suggested a greater than itself in the citizens' comedy of contemporary manners, the *Eastward Hoe* to which I have already frequently referred; and the latter contributes to the biographical history of the drama by its somewhat amusing but utterly pointless ridicule of Chapman, as the "little hoary poet," Bellamont. In their intrigues of citizens' wives and of prostitutes, with gallants of a more elevated social standing, and in the pranks, which the wives, unrelievedly vulgar though providentially chaste, play upon their rakish husbands, these compositions are, on the one hand, the degenerate offspring of *Henry IV* and *The Merry Wives of Windsor*, and, on the other, brothers of the comedy of cuckoldry developed to its extreme, between 1604 and 1614, by Middleton. *West-ward Hoe* and *North-ward Hoe*, are, also, historically valuable as pictures of Jacobean morals and manners. They are mines of *realia* and *jeux d'esprit*. But the situations, conversations, and mirth are of that species of comic that passes by preference into unadorned indecency whenever a chance is offered; and in neither play does the intrigue achieve the dignity of the legitimate romantic. How any critic, who for a moment reflects what literature really is, can say that this stuff is "extremely good," I cannot conceive. As for dramatic value one has merely to set the plays side by side with any unquestioned dramatic masterpiece, not to say of Shakespeare, but of Jonson, Beaumont and Fletcher, and Dekker himself to realize their worthlessness. Indeed, it is inexpedient to be always judging the drama by its response to comparative tests, as literary historians and critics are prone to do. Once in a while it is as well to fall back upon the method of old fashioned judicial criticism, and ask, Is this art?

The title pages announce the authorship of *West-ward* and *North-ward Hoe* as by Dekker and Webster. The latter had been associated with Middleton and Heywood since 1602 in the composition of dramas of the tragic-historical and popular-chronicle type. He later mentions "Master Dekker," for his "right happy and copious industry," in the same breath with "Master Shakespeare"; and he probably regarded Dekker as in some sense his sponsor in the dramatic craft. Such was undoubtedly the rela-

tion between the two in 1604 when the former play was written. Webster was then but twenty-four years of age, had nothing but the *Induction* of *The Malcontent* to his undivided credit, lacked yet seven years of the maturity requisite for the production of his *White Devil*, and thirteen years of that which produced the *Duchess of Malfy*. I find but very little in the *North-ward* and *West-ward* that might not have been written by Dekker, nothing that differs in the intrigue from his infusion of violent dénouement and sudden force or, in the occasional intervals of merit, from his thrilling unexpected tenderness and his jovial bluntness, his odour of the city, his diction, his verse. Dr. Stoll whose searching investigation[1] renders further analysis unnecessary concludes that only "some slight undetermined part in the more colourless and stereotyped portions" may be assigned to Webster, and even that, under the shaping and guiding hand of Dekker.

Symons[2] and Stoll assign to Dekker the finest parts, also, of another citizens' comedy, *The Roaring Girle* or *Moll-Cut-Purse* (printed, 1611);[3] and although Sir Adolphus Ward thinks that "the bright vivacity which gives something like a charm to this strange figure may be confidently ascribed to Middleton's happier touch," it must be conceded that the astounding array of coincidences in construction and matter of plot, in quality, spirit, characterization, and definite turns of phraseology, between this play and Dekker's other comedies of manners, forces one to the conclusion that here, too, the author of *The Shomakers Holiday*, *The Honest Whore*, and the plays of *West-ward* and *North-ward* is the shaping force. Middleton talks bawdy all through the subplot of the seamstresses, Gallipot, Tiltyard, and Openwork, with their wittol-fashioned husbands and their woman-hunting gallants; Dekker writes the story of that historical celebrity "the wench, called Moll, mad Moll, or merry Moll" who, breeched as a Bohemian roisterer, keeps her 'roaring' to the windward of fornication, has "no humour to marry," swings a heavy hand and a keen rapier, sends her lustful gallant on a wildgoose chase to Brainford, assists the pair of honest lovers to their happiness, and concludes,

> "Perhaps for my mad going some reprove me;
> I please myself, and care not else who love me."

She is a salt breeze through the marshes; and she deserved her popularity

---

[1] *John Webster*, 72–76. See F. E. Pierce, *The Collaboration of Webster and Dekker*, 131 et seq., for an assignment of the slight Webster portions.
[2] *Cambridge Hist. Eng. Lit.*, VI, 71, 74.
[3] It may have been written as early as 1604–1605. Fleay, *Chron. Eng. Dr.*, I, 132.

on the stage with those who knew her off it. But the play, though fairly
well contrived, is after all what Middleton in his preface, headed "to the
comic play-readers—venery and laughter," calls it: a plot of "quaint
conceits and lecherous jests, dressed up in hanging sleeves." It is included
in this discussion merely as another instance of Dekker's contribution,
on the one hand, to the materials out of which social history may be re-
constructed, and, on the other, to the establishment of the realistic comedy
of contemporary manners. He was earlier in this field than Middleton;
and Dr. Stoll is probably justified in saying that "it was Dekker who
created this type of citizen play, imitating Shakespeare (*Henry IV* and
Merry Wives) in character and general scheme of plot, but adding the
specifically citizen spirit and London atmosphere." For though *Every
Man in his Humour*, and *Every Man out*, were also early in the field,
Jonson cared much more for the humour than for the man.

Another who cared for the humour more than for the man was **John
Day**. But the humour of this accomplice of the popular school, and mocker
of the critical, is not studiously contrived, grim, and purposeful like Jonson's but "loud from lips of boys brow-bound with May." It is whimsi-
cally romantic, light-heartedly satiric, indiscriminately bubbling, "out
of breath." Whether the fact that he was expelled from Caius College,
Cambridge, when he was but nineteen years of age, for stealing a book,
warrants us in assuming that he continued a "base fellow" and a "rogue"
all his life may be doubtful. "Honest" Ben Jonson thought there was
reason for so regarding him. But Ben hated the whole Henslowe tribe,
especially Dekker; and Day had joined the Henslowe dramatists in 1598,
five years after the untimely abandonment of his academic career, had
stayed with them for five years, and had written with Dekker, Chettle,
Haughton, and others no fewer than twenty-two plays, principally of the
fustian chronicle and folklore school that Jonson likewise detested. If
one could adopt the suggestion of Corney and Gollancz, that the author
of the Parnassus trilogy (1598–1602) was Day, the personal origin of Jonson's animosity would be evident: for in those plays both Jonson and his
future colleague, Marston, are sneered at. But the proof of Day's authorship cannot yet be considered conclusive.

That Day, however, was by way of glancing ironically at Jonson's
school of humours, appears beyond cavil not only in the title of his *Humour
out of Breath*, 1607–8, but in its mirthful burlesque of the Jonsonian method
run to seed. "Now to my business," says Octavio, the Duke of Venice
in disguise,—"Now to my business; I have a strange habit, and must cut
out a humour suitable to it, and humours are picked so near the bone,
a man can scarce get humour enough to give a flea his breakfast: but I

am a stale ruffian, my habit is brave, and so shall my humour be, and here comes one to give me earnest of it." Is not the Duke, Day himself, accepting with a swagger Jonson's opprobrium? Enter Aspero (the name under which Jonson had paraded in *Every Man out of his Humour*), asking of Octavio, "Thy profession?" *Octavio:* "A fool or a knave, choose you which." Again 'Asper' Jonson, beknaving him, "Dost know the duke of Venice?" "I am his right hand," replies 'Octavio' Day. "Tell him I hate him" (continues Jonson); "my name's Aspero."—To press the analogy further might be to hunt the March-hare after the fashion of well-intentioned students who have wildered themselves in the Forest of Stage Marvels; and in truth the play makes no persistent pretence of pursuing a personal allegory. Nor is it an allegorical burlesque of humours alone, but of extravagant romance and tragic absurdity as well. Such another romantic extravagance is the author's *The Ile of Gulls* (about 1605), a rainbow of airy fancy, insubstantial roseate loves, adventures, and purple passions, shifting hues of satire, personal and religious, gleams of vivacious, inconsequential wit. But the pillars of the iridescent arc lose themselves in muck. Perhaps, here too, the author (as Mr. Fleay suggests) is poking fun at Jonson, Chapman, and Marston. Of one thing we may be certain, his humours are not dramatic but Pickwickian. In *The Ile of Gulls*, Day laughs at three kinds of play beloved of idling auditors— the humours comedy, the unsavoury realistic, the fustian romantic. The *Ile* is inverted comedy: the interest is not in the creation of character or of plot, nor in the criticism of the manners mirrored, but in the *reductio ad absurdum* of comedy itself,—in the ironic parody of didactic humours, the subacid mimicry of libidinous realism, the mock-serious justification of fustian. The author is ridiculing not only overdone dramatic conventions but an audience sophisticated with popular delusions about art. In these comedies as in his *Law Tricks* (pr. 1608) Day is the literateur rather than the dramatist. He balloons across a popular Jacobean stage, patronized in those days of political and religious unrest by few people of serious mind; he balloons across the stage, and from a safe height, romantically blithe like a school boy with a pea-shooter, peppers away at giants and windmills, and occasionally hits a pigmy. His charm, as in his later allegory of *The Parliament of Bees*, is of capricious and jocund fancy, genial irony and melodious verse. That the theatre dropped his plays is not surprising. His claim upon the scholar's attention is literary and historical, not dramatic; and one cannot reproach the average student furnished with literature of perennial quality, or of more recent applicability, for ignoring him.

9. Popular Comedy to 1614: Middleton and Contemporary Manners

Thomas Middleton had made his début, with satirical pamphlets after the fashion of Thomas Nashe, and in 1596–1597 with an historical play of sensational folk-lore and crude farce of the Drayton-Munday style; and he had worked with these men and with Dekker, during 1602, on other plays of a like antiquated tragic kind. He broke away from Henslowe about the end of that year, and proceeded to write comedies for the Children of Paul's and the Queen's Revels' children at Blackfriars. For the former, between 1602 and 1607, he wrote two romantic comedies not primarily of contemporary manners; but, between 1604 and 1614, he devoted himself to the realistic comedy of London life. In, or about, 1615 he formed an association with William Rowley; and a maturer period of romantic comedy or tragicomedy, and of tragedy, ensued. Of his eight comedies of manners, three only have lasting dramatic and literary value,—and that for the scholar, rather than for the average student or the theatre; of his seven romantic comedies, only two. His higher genius is discovered in the more serious plays; and of these probably but one, *A Faire Quarrell*, had been written when Jonson, in the talks with Drummond (1619), pronounced him "not of the number of the Faithful," that is to say, of those faithful to poetry, "and but a base fellow." And it must have been because he, Middleton, could be judged only by comedies of manners that, in 1611, Webster omitted his name from the list of those whose worthy labours he cherished: Chapman, Jonson, Beaumont, Fletcher, Shakespeare, Dekker, Heywood.[1] He is called, as late as 1656, by one who also is regarding but his lighter works, the "squibbling Middleton." And when we come to the verdict of the present day, we find that the praise is all for plays written in, or after, 1615; and of the more serious kind. "If *The Changeling*," says Swinburne, "had not been preserved, we should not have known Middleton." But *The Changeling* was written between 1621 and 1623, and is a tragedy. "If *The Changeling, Women Beware Women, The Spanish Gipsy,* and *A Fair Quarrel* do not justify Middleton's claims to be considered a great dramatist," concludes Bullen in his Introduction to this author's works, "I know not which of Shakespeare's followers is worthy of the title." But *Women Beware Women* is a tragedy and, like the comedies of character and passion, the *Gipsie* and the *Quarrel*, was written after the beginning of 1615. It is, undoubtedly, by the products of his "graver and loftier genius" that Middleton's contribution to the vital drama must be appraised; and, in the field of ro-

[1] Preface to *The White Devil*.

mantic comedy, by *The Spanish Gipsie* and *A Faire Quarrell*. To these I shall revert in a later section.

Swinburne is probably the most enthusiastic of Middleton's admirers. Even in the earlier romantic comedies, *Blurt, Master-Constable* and *The Phoenix* he descries merit, "purple patches of poetry"; but the former betrays "rude and reckless composition, rough intrusion of savourless farce, bewildering combinations of incident, and far more bewildering fluctuations of character"; and the latter is "slight and sketchy, primitive if not puerile in parts." All readers will agree. Of the comedies of manners, according to his opinion and that of most modern critics, the best are *Michaelmas Terme*, *A Tricke to Catch the Old-one*, and *A Mad World, my Masters*. But of the last of these Swinburne concedes, "the matrimonial part of the catastrophe is something more than repulsive." And for the realistic plays, in general, this master of condemnatory epithet has nothing milder than the following,—"very coarse, very dull, altogether distasteful and ineffectual"; "of clumsy workmanship"; of "most lame and impotent conclusion"; of "unpleasant and extravagant quality"; of "sheer bewildering incongruity"; "ugly and unnatural"; "repulsive beyond redemption"; "preposterous beyond extenuation"; "crude and shapeless"; "heavy, empty and feeble"; "more stupid and offensive they could hardly be." To this condemnation by one who is otherwise a most effusive admirer, I need hardly add; but from sympathetic quotation of it I cannot persuade myself to refrain.

Michaelmas Terme is exempted by Swinburne from this sweeping reprobation as "an excellent Hogarthian comedy, full of rapid and vivid incident, of pleasant or indignant humour." Hogarthian, yes; excellent, no. It presents some excellent situations, as where after Quomodo's pretended death that usurer learns that his wife accounts herself "the happiest widow that ever counterfeited weeping," that she holds this the fittest season for a kiss from the country gull whom her husband had been cozening,—and that his son, Sim, is so ashamed of him that he'd rather be hanged than go to the funeral; and where Quomodo discovers that, duped even by his country-gull, he has signed away all his own property. But the previous process of ruining the seeming-innocent Easy, is both too facile in performance and too technical in legal terminology; and in the sub-plot of a seducer and country-wench there is, save for a few poetic lines, nothing to admire. As to the disguises upon which most of the humour turns they are with the exception of the central ruse, thin, unconvincing, absurd. Mr. Bullen finds that the play is "full of excellent fun,"—and "the reader has only himself to blame if he fails to find amusement." True, perhaps, so far as the selective reader is concerned; but the fun is manufactured with wooden machinery, and an audience would lose most of it for the creaking of the cogs. For Sir Adolphus Ward's opinion in such matters, as for Mr. Bullen's, I entertain a high respect; but I really cannot find that from the dramatic point of view "the general course of the play is cleverly contrived," or that it is "written with little coarseness." I began to count the pages that steam with coarseness but, though I am pardonably immune, deemed it wise to stop short of asphyxia.

The Mad World, my Masters is not in Swinburne's opinion, and he is right, "so thoroughly good a comedy as *A Tricke to Catch the Old-one*," still "it must be allowed to contain the very best comic character ever drawn by Middleton." The fun lies in a series of outrageous manœuvres by which an incorrigible scapegrace, Follywit, squeezes a living out of a "frolic grandsire," who intends to leave him a fortune at his death but takes good care, and no little pleasure, to postpone the occasion. "The prodigal grandfather, Sir Bounteous Progress, is," as Swinburne says, "perhaps the most life-like figure of a good-humoured and liberal old libertine that ever amused or scandalised a tolerant or intolerant reader." The main plot opens promptly and well; and it is cleverly connected, through Sir Bounteous' mistress, a courtesan, with the minor movement, in which a puritan wife indulges her passion for a gallant, appropriately christened Sir Penitent Brothel. Sir Bounteous is allowed to reveal his character with admirable naturalness of conduct and humour, and the various tricks by which, with the assistance of the courtesan, the rascally Follywit cozens his grandsire follow each other with fertility of device and most diverting success. Toward the close of the play the confusion of real and feigned comedy is piquant in the extreme. And, as usual with Middleton, the dialogue is both clever and spontaneous, and the satire quick and subtle, and of an effective wit. But the comedy is cheapened by an abundance of farcical unreality; and the barefaced monstrosity of the whole procedure stares you out of countenance, willing as you may have been to laugh it off as a lark,—a sheer unmoral, ludicrous irresponsibility. You think you are amused, till suddenly you find that what amuses you is fornication in the grotesque and then adultery; and, best caper of all, that the easiest way to make old Sir Bounteous "pay for his lechery," is to cuckold him of his mistress, and pass her on to the grandson by a process euphemistically sanctified as marriage. Through this highly edifying and genial arrangement young Follywit "makes amends for vice," and the courtesan is "made honest." There are some queer morals even in Skakespeare and Ben Jonson; but anything quite so unnatural as this inverted piety is far to seek. Judged merely as art, the thing is hideously undramatic. As for the verbal humour, it is normally porno-graphic; but it achieves the latrinal.

The fact is that only one of Middleton's comedies of manners and in-trigue is possessed of both literary and dramatic excellence; and that is so marred by vulgarity and by the moral, not to say artistic, obtuseness of the dénouement, that I doubt whether even it may be deemed to possess dramatic vitality. I refer to *A Tricke to Catch the Old-one*. Of course it was revived at the Restoration; but the stage has not known it for some two hundred years. As in *A Mad World*, the mirth lies in the outwitting of the older generation by the scapegrace younger, and in the turning of the tables upon avarice by the help of a compliant courtesan. And the moral is that policy is the best honesty and that, if only one be merry and consistently conscienceless, money and marriage, once attained, atone for previous pecadilloes from leasing to lust. Every one will agree with Swin-burne that this is "one of the best plays Middleton ever wrote," if ref-erence be had only to his comedies of the lighter kind. In construction it is by far his best: the threads more smoothly interwoven, the auditor more skilfully taken into confidence as to the 'parts' that the main char-acters are 'playing.' His debtors and vagabonds of the parish of All Hallows the Less, of creditor and usurer, host, drawer, prostitute, maid-servant, miser, and spendthrift,—his taverns and his village streets, his glimpses of Westminster Hall and of citizens' homes, and his "motions of Fleet Street and visions of Holborn,"—are all of the liveliest; and the fertility of comic device, as well as the lucidity, wit, and pertinence of the dramatic prose are worthy of admiration. But, though the major se-quence is well preserved, much of the minor stuff of character and incident is irrelevant. The Dampit-Audry scenes, for instance, are grimly vivid; but they best illustrate Middleton's inability to fit his panels of low life into the general frame. The names are all Jonsonian, and the humours highly inflated; but there are only two compendiously human figures in the play, those of Onesiphorous Hoard and his courtesan-wife. The play flowers into less obscenity than is usual with Middleton; but it is rotten at the root. Professor Matthews[1] views with distrust the generally re-ceived tradition by which this play is made the basis of Massinger's *New Way to Pay Old Debts*. The motifs may be similar but the conduct of each is distinct. Still, Middleton's comedies were a treasure-house of plot and device for ensuing dramatists; and it is not impossible that from the *Tricke*, Massinger derived a hint; as from *A Mad World*, Mrs. Aphra Behn derived one strand for her *City Heiress*, and Charles Johnson, another for his play of 1715, called *The Country Lasses*, or *The Custom of the Manor*.

[1] In his Essay preceding *The New Way*.

Middleton's remaining comedies of London life are devoid of literary significance in the nobler sense, and of that dramatic artistry which presupposes moral sanity. Their contemporary popularity was due to their ingenuity, to their impressionistic, and sometimes ironic, reproduction of a degraded stripe of manners and morals familiar to the audience and acceptable because of gay irresponsibility, to their smooth and natural dialogue, their grossly comic situations, their ribald jests, and their pervasive wit, sometimes subtle, more often cheap. But the dramatic ingenuity is of thieves set to catch their kind, or of disguises and other theatrical machinations, puerile, absurd, capable of diverting only the spectator who is fool enough to fancy that the *dramatis personæ* are possible and, therefore, greater fools than he. The portrayal of manners and characters is vivid. But the manners are not of England, or even of London, at the core. They are, as I have said, the manners of a theatre-haunting mob that recognized its image in the gallant, morbid with megalomania of sex, the drunkard, gambler, cozener, shopkeeping libertine and light o' love wife, strumpet, roarer, cuckold, wittol, and gull. And the characters are true to life, to the extent that they never divagate into a region of honour where the audience might lose its way. No wonder decent Jacobeans denounced the play-house, and modest women never frequented it. These comedies are cinematographs of immorality, not cast upon canvas with a view to the profit that may be derived from the pathetic or satiric exposure of frailty, but to the delight that attends the apotheosis of irreverence, wantonness and filth. The more successful the apotheosis, the greater the libel upon the genuine spirit of contemporary England. The spirit that showed itself in the continual condemnation of the stage by the great mass of puritans and by the city council of London, —the spirit that breathes in the non-dramatic poetry of the day, in the sweet unconscious joy of life, the pastoral innocence, of Browne of Tavistock, in the fervid verse of Giles Fletcher. This was the age of Florio's Montaigne, and Bacon's essays, of the elevated polity of Hooker and the forthright preaching of John Donne. In the year that the unspeakable *Family of Love* and the foolish *Your Five Gallants* were acting and printing, the separatist forefathers of the New England colonies were sailing for Amsterdam. *A Chaste Mayd in Cheape-side* and *Any Thing for a Quiet Life* were still freshly regaling the kind of London audience that liked that kind of thing in the year when the Puritans were leaving Leyden for the New World. The common people of that time did not like the concupiscent play, nor have we any proof that the literary classes hungered for it. It was popular in the atmosphere of Hampton Court, Greenwich, and Whitehall, but not immoderately desired. Between 1604 and 1625 only one of Middleton's London comedies is acted at Court, and that the least offensive, *The Trick*. But, on the other hand, three of his romantic comedies and the noble tragedy, *The Changeling*, have a hearing there, and, time and again, the best of Shakespeare, Jonson, Beaumont and Fletcher.

I have said that the London comedies are useful to the student of *realia*. They are useful to the student of *personalia* only with the qualification stated above. Their abiding service to comedy is that they stimulated wiser dramatists of a later day to photograph life and manners more genuinely representative of society; that they furnished hints of dramatic technique, and by their life-like dialogue helped to prepare the vehicle for realistic art. But none of them has set foot upon the stage since the century of its birth, nor have any of the numerous contemporary imitations of Middleton. Their names would but clutter the page. The theatre has let them die; and the average student may as well follow suit.

10. Popular Comedy of the Transition: A Panoramic Poet, Thomas Heywood

To classify the many-handed **Heywood** with one or the other group of Shakespeare's younger contemporaries is not an undertaking satisfactorily to be accomplished; for in the course of his long theatrical career from about 1594 to about 1648, he passed from company to company either as actor or playwright, and he had, according to his own statement as early as 1633, "either an entire hand or at least the main finger" in two hundred and twenty plays. Thomas was born in Lincolnshire, probably of gentle family; and he informs us that he was for a season at the University of Cambridge, and was then interested in dramatic performances of all kinds. There is some reason to suppose that the *Godfrey of Bulloigne*, acted by the Admiral's men in 1594, was his heroic grocer-drama better known under a later title as *The Foure Prentises of London, with the Conquest of Jerusalem*. He appears definitely as a playwright in Henslowe's diary for 1596,[1] and as connected with the Admiral's men; and on March 25, 1598, he engaged himself to Henslowe as a player at the Rose for two years. In 1599 his folk-historical tragedy, *Edward IV*, was entered on the Stationers' Registers, and played by Derby's men. He seems to have ceased playing with the Admiral's men in the same year; but, between August, 1602, and May, 1603, we find him again at Henslowe's theatre of the Rose, this time writing for the Earl of Worcester's men. During

[1] Greg, *Henslowe's Diary*, II, 284. For life and estimate, see Ward, *Hist. E. Dr. Lit.*, II, 550–589, and *Camb. Hist. Lit.*, VI, 92–120; also Fleay, *Chr. E. Dr.*, I, 276–306, and J. A. Symonds, *Heywood* (Mermaid Series).

this period he is mentioned sixteen times in connection with plays, sometimes with Dekker, Chettle and others as collaborators, sometimes alone. It is possible that the *Marshal Osric* performed by Worcester's men in 1602, was the earlier draft of his romantic tragicomedy afterwards known as *The Royall King, and the Loyall Subject.* On March 6, 1603, he receives full payment from Henslowe for his famous domestic tragedy, *A Woman Kilde with Kindnesse.* From 1603, on, he continues with Worcester's men, known after the accession of James I as Queen Anne's, and mention is made of him in various records, of 1604, 1609, 1612, 1616, 1617, as with them; and again in 1619 when he marched in the Queen's funeral procession. As late as 1634 he is listed as one of His Majesty, King Charles's servants. An anonymous comedy of contemporary manners, *The Wise Woman of Hogsdon,* which betrays some resemblance to his methods, has been assigned to the year, 1604. His romantic comedy, *Fortune by Land and Sea,* written with William Rowley, may have been produced before 1610; another romantic comedy, by Heywood alone, *The Faire Maid of the West* was printed in 1631, but savours of days much nearer the reign of Queen Elizabeth. His *English Traveller,* which even though a tragedy must, like *A Woman Kilde,* be mentioned here, for its influence upon romantic tragicomedy, was not printed till 1633; but it was acted a few years earlier. This is by no means a complete list of the extant plays of Heywood; but it is sufficient to serve as a basis for some brief appreciation of his services in comic drama. He continued his labours after 1630, and he may still have had a hand or "the main finger" in plays as late as 1648, when he passes out of historical record. In addition to his plays of chronicle history, mythology, comedy, tragedy and tragicomedy, and his masques and pageants, this amiable, versatile, and industrious writer poured forth odes, poetic "apologies," prologues and epilogues, poems heroic, didactic, and interminable,—translations of the classics, pleasantly discursive essays, a *Life of Ambrosius Merlin,* a history of Queen Elizabeth's earlier years, a *Lives of All the Poets,* and a *General History of Women.*

Difficult as it is to classify Heywood, it is not hard to indicate his services to various kinds of drama. He adjusted himself, even more variously than Chapman, to the fluctuating fashion of the day; but in two instances only, *A Woman Kilde with Kindnesse* and *The English Traveller,* did he produce dramas which in their age excelled others of their kind, and to the present day remain worthy of praise for their literary and their dramatic excellence. They are both domestic tragedies, but of that sentimental pathetic and, also, humorous quality which subserved the development of romantic tragicomedy. I cannot stay to describe either; but the forthright, sane and simple construction of the former, the tender pathos of the wife who falls, and is forgiven and then dies, the more than chivalrous nobility of her husband, the high relief of the *scènes à faire* and the distinction of the technique, cannot but have influenced the writers of *The Honest Whore* and *The Dutch Courtezan*, and may have been an example, in the choice of telling situations, to the author of the tenderest parts of *Philaster*, *A King and no King*, and *The Coxcombe*. Unfortunately, the nature of the supplementary action is such as to remove the play from possibility of revival at the present time. But in its own day it was vastly and deservedly popular; altogether the most successful of the series of domestic dramas produced between 1602 and 1607, which includes Joshua Cook's *How a Man May Chuse a Good Wife from a Bad*, the anonymous *Faire Maide of Bristow*, and *The London Prodigall*—pathetic comedies of no slight literary merit, but of historical rather than dramatic vitality.

The *English Traveller*, which, from the Prologue's repudiation of stage-allurements popular in the first two decades of the century, I take to be written much earlier than the date of publication, 1633, displays again the kindly humanity of its author, and in the conduct of the complication, not altogether dissimilar from that of *A Woman Kilde*, furnishes many a hint for writers of the sentimental novel and comedy of a later age. The hero in this tragedy of domestic life is not the wronged husband, though he does attain a moral dignity commensurate with his wife's heart-broken penitence, but the husband's friend, and wife's true lover, young Geraldine. No one has described the self-denying disposition of this youth better than Sir Adolphus Ward—a character "drawn with much grace and feeling; he is assuredly one of the truest gentlemen of Elizabethan drama." His devotion is of that exalted and ideal strain which we associate rather with the mediæval worship of *Dieu et ma Dame* than with the temperament of Jacobean play-lovers. But the theme, if not the domestic setting and the unadorned simplicity and pathos of the execution, is congenital with those of extravagant sensibility and chivalry affected by some Jacobean writers of tragicomedy whether earlier or of the same period,—Beaumont and Fletcher, Middleton and Rowley. Heywood did not originate the drama of the English home disrupted by passion, but he carried it to the highest development of which, in the first third of the seventeenth century, it seems to have been capable. The subplot here is much more humorous and less offensive than that of his preceding tragedy; but as a whole the *Traveller* does not equal *A Woman Kilde*. Nor, of course, does the early chronicle play of *Edward IV;* though, both in its rustic humour and its sorrowful story of faire Mistresse Shore, it foretells the course of Heywood's maturity in drama.

The other services of Heywood to comedy are mostly in the field of bourgeois valour and adventure; but they are rather of historical than of artistic permanence. The heroic tradesman's-comedy of *The Foure Prentises of London* (printed, 1610, but written about 1594) is of no more dramatic worth than one would expect of a rather prosaic playwright's earliest effort. But it was hugely popular with the guilds whose trades were adopted by the four heroes, sons of the impoverished "Earle of Bulloign"; and it has been a laughter for the gods ever since Beaumont, some thirteen years after its first appearance, burlesqued the crusading triumphs of the high-born prentises in the valours of his grocer's prentice, the Knight of the Burning Pestle. The ridicule does not seem to have cured Heywood of his penchant for the romance of bourgeois' prowess and travel. Unless *The Faire Maid of the West* is a revision of a play written by him during Elizabeth's reign (as historical setting and reference, literary style and allusion, might indicate) he is still continuing the romantic bourgeois theme as late as 1620. The opening scenes at the Sign of the Castle in Plymouth, where Spencer wooes Besse Bridges, the "taptresse,"—who has "a virtue but seldom found in tavernes,"—and slays a man for her and flies into exile, are a graphic cross-section of contemporary manners and speech. All that follows, however, in two long *Parts*,— how Besse as a skipper scours the ocean, seeking Spencer's body in the Canary Isles, how her fame grows great with Frenchmen and Dutchmen and Spaniards and Turks, and how in Barbary the lovers are reunited, only to be separated for further adventure—in which Besse triumphs by chastity and beauty over kings and minor princes,—is as fantastic a mélange as ever tempted the plebeian taste. But, even so, the play is not without savour. It has humour of idiosyncrasy and of situation, interest of intrigue and clever ruse, and a touch of sublimity in the climax.

Inchoate and overcharged with misadventure, hair-breadth escape and sensational shows of British luck and valour, as these dramas undoubtedly are, they furnished the middle and lower classes with a substitute for the more chivalric and erotic thrills, idyllic and palatial passions, with which the so-called dramatic romance was delighting the upper classes and the Court. If written in 1620, *The Faire Maid of the West* was of the period which produced the more high-toned *Spanish Gipsie* of Middleton and Rowley, and of about the date of Fletcher's *Island Princesse* and *The Pilgrim*, and Fletcher and Rowley's *The Maide in the Mill*, all dramatized romances of adventure and intrigue, fantastic arguments of patriotism, or love, man's honour or woman's virtue, and of the kind acceptable at Court. These are drawn from Spanish or Italian sources; Heywood draws his bourgeois romances from popular tales beloved by Londoners; and in the case of *The Faire Maid*, he pleased the Court as well. In the same vein are the much earlier *Fortune by Land and Sea*, wherein Rowley coöperated, and the much later *Challenge for Beautie*. Though, in these, courts be sometimes invaded, and princely personages appear, the romance is spiced with manners of the harbour, the little inn, the boozing comrade; and the turmoil of the sea, of pirates, wandering heroes and heroines, patriots and pages, of murders and duels and exile, all goes to prove the superiority of the English Middle and lower classes to the world beside in fearlessness and fortune.

If, in the plays of romantic wanderings as in those of domestic tribulation, the hearts and habits of the middle class are depicted with unerring touch, in the lighter comedy of contemporary manners called *The Wisewoman of Hogsdon* there is a commendable strain of the humour that characterizes the citizens' comedy of Dekker and Middleton during the first decade of the century. The play was probably written about 1604, and is not surely Heywood's,—but it displays his favourite combination of realism and the pathos of common life; and its vivid scenes, its bubbling goodnature, its rich assortment of queer characters,—the feather-pated Chartley, the blunt Boyster, the citizens' wives and the wise-woman herself, the knight and the stupid schoolmaster,—support the probability of his authorship. Save in the scenes presenting the heroine, Luce, and her honest father, it lacks however his *naïveté* and sentiment. It is too shrewd and tricky in characterization, too complex in the intrigue, and too witty in the repartee to be certainly regarded as of his sole authorship. In spite of incidental vulgarities, also not in Heywood's manner, the play is in the main wholesome. It is of the same fresh, racy, and original strain that produced the *Merry Devill of Edmonton* and *The Shomakers Holiday*. Though its dramatic career was not extended, it has a definite place in the history of the citizens' comedy. Possibly it suggested to Mrs. Cowley a scene in *Who's the Dupe?*

In the plays already mentioned, Heywood is abreast of the popular demand for chronicle tragedy or the drama of domestic sentiment, for heroic tradesman's comedy or the dramatized romance of adventure and swiftly varied sensation. And, if *The Wise-woman* and *The Fayre Mayde of the Exchange* (pr. 1607) are his, he kept pace with the demand for the comedy of London manners as well. In his *Royall King and Loyall Subject*, written probably as early as 1602, he was not only abreast, but in advance, of the heroic-romantic tragicomedy of Beaumont and Fletcher. As a herald of that kind of drama this effort of Heywood's, even if inferior in poetry and wit, is entitled to a place beside the contemporary *Gentleman Usher* of Chapman and the *Malcontent* of Marston. Here Heywood, contrary to his wont, uses an Italian source, and aims deliberately at transferring to English soil a fantastic tale of the patience of a military commander under the persecutions of an inhuman monarch. And, here, he anticipates by sixteen years, the far more famous, as more powerful and poetic, dramatization of the same theme by Fletcher, in *The Loyall Subject*.

Heywood's personality impresses the reader: he was industrious, hospitable to ideas, close to the heart of the people and of the theatre, careless of literary theories and of fame, generous in his estimation of his fellows. His scrutiny of mankind is, on the whole, sane, his speech kindly, and his dispensation of dramatic justice, charitable beyond that of the most of his peers. Not himself a master of poetic utterance and art, he had still the poet's sensitiveness to the simple, ever present and ever affecting, emotions, the poet's insight into the manners, aspirations, foibles of countryman and citizen,—especially into those of his beloved prentices and princes of London trade; and he coupled with a playwright's sense of what was dramatic an actor's knowledge of what would please the public,—yet not prostitute the stage. He had his finger on the pulse of the common people as none but Dekker among the later contemporaries of Shakespeare. His

> name has part with names of lordlier might
> For English love and homely sense of home.

Of the activities of the dramatic world in his long day, and of its successive fashions, except only in satiric comedy and high tragedy, his output presents a panorama. His services to the comedy of contemporary manners are of and for the period; his services to romantic comedy and the tragi-comedy of heroism and romance form as it were a bridge between the old sensational drama of the Henslowe group and the serious plays of Beaumont and Fletcher, of Middleton and Rowley. And from this point of view his *Royall King* deserves its place in literary history. He began to write before any of the dramatists just mentioned, and he outlived them all. But though two of his comedies, *Fortune by Land and Sea* and *The Faire Maid of the West*, have been recently revived by dramatic societies, and *The Wise-woman of Hogsdon* (perhaps by him) has literary as well as histrionic merit worthy of similar recognition, none of his contributions to the comic drama has survived upon the public stage.

11. The Predominance of Beaumont in the Beaumont-Fletcher Plays: 1607-1613

The collaboration of **Francis Beaumont** and **John Fletcher** is of especial importance in the history of the transition from Elizabethan comedy of character, humours, and romance to Jacobean tragicomedy and comedy of intrigue. The former, a son of Francis Beaumont of Grace-Dieu in Leicestershire, was born in 1584 or 1585. He began his career as a dramatist about 1606 or 1607; and he died in 1616. His activities save for one play written about 1614 or 1615, fall entirely within the period which opened with the accession of James I in 1603 and closed with Shakespeare's retirement from the stage in 1613. Fletcher, the son of a distinguished clergyman, afterwards Bishop of London, was born in 1579. He may have written plays before 1606–1607, but their identity has not been determined. After some seven or eight years of association with Beaumont and, probably, Shakespeare, he wrote alone, or with others, under conditions more and more distinctly Stuart in life, manners, literary and dramatic taste, until his death in 1625. The product loosely attributed to the twin-authors is representative not only of the culture of university men but of the social environment familiar to gentlemen in the conventional sense of that term. And the outlook of many of these fifty-three plays is Jacobean,—of the cosmopolitan, sensation-seeking, and pleasure-loving tone that distinguished the Court of the new King from that of Elizabeth. Comparing Beaumont and Fletcher with Shakespeare, Dryden says, "they understood and imitated the conversation of gentlemen much better, whose wild debaucheries and quickness of wit in repartee no poet can ever paint as they have done." And the plays of which Dryden is thinking were speedily more acceptable to the society of the seventeenth century than those of Shakespeare, because they catered to the demand, on the one hand, for a heroic and melodramatic tragicomedy violent in emotional conflict, rich in poetic colouring and phrase but never involved in expression, devised with technique of marvellous skill, replete with sudden surprises of situation, and adorned with gorgeous pageantry,—and on the other, for a realistic comedy of intrigue, brilliant in dialogue, novel in situation, and faithful to contemporary thought and manners.

Since the partnership of Beaumont and Fletcher has been the subject of many investigations,[1] and I have myself, elsewhere, discussed it at

[1] The most important are by Fleay, in *N. Shaksp. Soc. Trans.*, 1874; *Shakspere Manual*, 1876; *Engl. Stud.*, IX, 1886; *Engl. Drama*, 1891; Boyle, In *Engl. Stud.*, V, VII, VIII, IX, X, XVII, XVIII, XXVI, XXXI, 1881–1902; G. C. Macaulay, *Francis Beaumont*, 1883, and in *Camb. Hist. Eng. Lit.*, VI, 1910; Bullen, in *D. N. B.*, XIX, *John Fletcher*, 1889; Oliphant, in *Engl. Stud.*, XV, XV, XVI, 1890–92; A. H. Thorndike, *The Influence of Beaumont and Fletcher on Shakespeare*, 1901; O. L. Hatcher, *John Fletcher* (Chicago thesis) 1905; Alden, *The Knight of the Burning Pestle, etc.*, Introduction and Bibliography (Belles Lettres Series) 1910; Ward, in his *Hist. Dram. Lit.*, ii, 155–248, Ed. 1875; ii, 643–764, Ed. 1899; Schelling in his

length,[1] it will suffice here to recapitulate briefly the method of inquiry. Even such brief recapitulation is absolutely necessary, if the reader is to understand, at all, the respective services of these playwrights to comedy; for many of the excesses of Fletcher as well as some of his virtues have been, and are still, falsely reckoned to the account of his youthful associate.

I have spoken above of "the plays loosely attributed to Beaumont and Fletcher in common." The coöperation of Beaumont cannot by any *tour de force* be traced or conjectured in more than twenty-three of the fifty-three included in the "Works of Beaumont and Fletcher," that is to say in the two folios of 1647 and 1679. With regard to twelve of the twenty-three there is no certain historical proof that they were written before 1613 when Beaumont's dramatic activity practically ceased; and, with regard to eleven of the twelve, no generally admitted evidence that they preceded his death in 1616. To the separative criticism of the remaining eleven plays in which, according to external evidence, Beaumont could have had a hand, the verse-test seems to offer the best method of approach. Fletcher prefers the end-stopped line and feminine ending (sometimes triple or quadruple) and his rhythm is more anapæstic and therefore lyrical in its lilt than Beaumont's. The latter is chary of the feminine ending, and indulges in run-on lines. Though the verse-test is not of itself a reagent capable of precipitating fully the Beaumont and the Fletcher of the joint-plays it enables us to fix certain peculiarities of vocabulary, rhetoric, poetic or creative imagery, mental furniture and habit, moral and emotional insight and elevation, philosophical and religious outlook upon life, which, when taken in connection with the peculiarities of verse, discriminate the members of this literary partnership with somewhat convincing definiteness one from another.

For a careful discussion of the versification and vocabulary of these poets, I must refer the reader entirely to the works mentioned above and to my *Beaumont, the Dramatist*. Fletcher's rhetoric, as displayed in his own early work, and in the portions of the joint plays which verse and vocabulary show to be undoubtedly his, revels in iterations of thought, preferably by triplets, in the repetition of a sonorous word (as ' all '), in a plethora of adjectives and of nouns in apposition (triplets for choice), in tautology—spinning out the categories of a concept by 'division,' in corrective interruptions and parentheses, and in the elocutionary after-

---

Elizab. Drama, ii, 184–204, 526 (Bibliog.) 1908.   For Gen. Bibliog., see *Camb. Hist. Eng. Lit.*, VI, 492.
[1] In my *Beaumont, the Dramatist*, N. Y., 1914, from Part Two of which, Chapters XVI–XXVIII, most of this section and the next are condensed.

thought. He abounds in optatives. His figures are most frequently of winter and storm, heat and light, of trees in all their ramifications, blossoms and the destroying canker, of fever and ague, youth, desire, and the death by which one is "rocked to another world." He elaborates with prolixity commonplace mythological tropes. His diction is in general rather dramatic or conversational than philosophically poetic. Though he is a playwright of consummate craft, a pastoralist of fertile fancy, and a lyrist of delightful melody, the range of thought, as of observation, is narrow, the insight keen in superficialities alone, the sublimity theatrical, the pathos an article of *vertu* and the outlook worldly. His political views, as of the divine right of kings and the subservient loyalty of subjects, are conventional. Depth of moral conviction, his characters rarely display: "We are but our living coffins." Life, indeed, is kaleidoscopic, of impulses and sensations gorgeously tinted, or of weariness and disease coloured by opinion, error, dream,—but its figures are in either case an optical illusion, and its motive that of the hand that turns the tube. Life is sometimes of histrionic passion and peril, but generally of amusement. Its most strenuous amusement is love; and that is a predatory chase, or sentimental or hilarious. A few of his heroes are of noble habitude; most of them are graceless or reckless from choice. A few of his women are both concrete and virtuous: but most of the virtuous are unconvincing; and most of the concrete, libidinous,—at the best as sapient in vicarious immodesty as they are irresponsible in wit and seductive in personal charm. He delights in the piquancy of feminine word-play, the raillery of gallants, the boisterous humour of the mob. The atmosphere is of Jacobean gayety and excess; fetid when most real; when most imaginative, unmoral.[1]

The rhetoric of Beaumont, on the other hand, is sometimes of the repetitive order, but rather for word-play and irony than for mere expansion of the thought. His style, though sometimes appropriately syncopated as in dramatic conversation, is in the rhapsodical and descriptive passages both complex and balanced of structure. It is suggestive rather than enumerative; and when enumerative, then rather for mock-legal and other humorous ends than by way of redundant detail. Within the sentence, elocutionary quotations frequently occur. He is forever playing phrasal variations on 'little,' 'piece' and 'kind': "That little piece I hold of life"; "a kind of healthful joy." His heroines are assiduous to "grow acquainted" with their hearts. He uses more ejaculations than Fletcher but fewer optatives; and his exclamations run by preference into some figured hyperbole. So also his tropes, which are generally of the more creative species, metaphor, personification and metonomy, than of mere simile.

[1] For further discussion see Sections 15 and 16, below.

When not of elemental phenomena,—hills, caves, rocks, thunder, ice, they are frequently of the difference between man and beast. He is reminiscential of the country; his images of nature are sweet with April, violets, and fields of standing corn; and his pictures of idyllic beauty and content are known to all. From the world of books he borrows two metaphors, 'printing' and 'blotting' and he plies them with effective variety. He is powerful, if not fertile, in the use of vitalizing verbs. He personifies abstractions oftener than does Fletcher in those earlier years; and the personifications, again, run into hyperbole. Similarly noticeable is his faculty for "simple phrasing," for the elevated passion, sudden splendour, large utterance of brief sentence and single verse. With one scimitar-stroke of incomparable brilliance the unassuming beauty or sublimity, the simplicity, the pathetic irony, the heroism, or the horror, of a human life is cut upon the night of after-ages. In his composition, the purely poetic, sometimes operatic quality predominates over the narrative, dramatic or conversational. His philosophy is of destiny, of the frail divinity and fleeting breath of kings—and of meaner mortals alike, of man's distinctive property—reason, of the objective quality of evil, and of human weakness in the face of temptation, of conscience and its sensibility, and the efficacy of repentance. His most poetic themes are of the friendship of man for man, the whiteness of woman's innocence, the unselfishness of their love and their forgivingness, and the reverence due them from men who so little understand them. Prayer is to him a very present help. The sorrows of humanity spring from misapprehension, slander, unmerited pain. And for these the only solace is in death. That he invests with surpassing dignity and beauty. In the 'sleep' and 'peace' of the 'quiet grave,' Beaumont finds one of the two supreme realities of human destiny. The other he finds in the award of posterity: our virtues, "the world and memory" shall "sing to after times"; our sins "rise up for shame to after-ages."

Let us turn now to the eleven plays in which it is certain, or, according to a fair number of critics, historically possible that Beaumont and Fletcher collaborated, and try to reach some conclusion concerning the share of each author and his characteristics as a dramatist.[1]

Of the *Foure Playes in One*, published as by Beaumont and Fletcher in the folio of 1647, the last two, *The Triumph of Death* and *The Triumph of Time*, are, from the metrical point of view, undoubtedly Fletcher's, and have been assigned to him by all critics. The rest of these "Morall Representations" display neither the verse nor the rhetoric of Fletcher.

[1] For detailed information concerning dates of composition and evidences of authorship, consult *Beaumont, the Dramatist*, Chapters XXIII–XXVI.

On the basis of verse-tests Boyle assigns them to Beaumont. G. C. Macaulay says "probably," and adds the *Induction*. But Oliphant, taking into consideration also the rhetorical and dramatic qualities, gives the *Induction* and *The Triumph of Honour* to a third author, Nathaniel Field, and only *The Triumph of Love* to Beaumont. As to the *Induction* and *The Triumph of Honour* I agree with Oliphant. They are full of polysyllabic Latinisms such as Field uses in his *Woman is a Weather-cocke* (published 1611) and Beaumont never uses. The *Honour* is a somewhat bombastic, puerile, magical show written in manifest imitation of Beaumont's verse and rhetoric. As to *The Triumph of Love*, I go further than Oliphant: I assign at least half of it, *viz.*, scenes 1, 2 and 6, on the basis of diction, to Field. In scenes 3, 4 and 5, I find some trace of Beaumont's favourite expressions, of his thoughts of destiny and death and woman's tenderness, of his splendid poetic spontaneity, his sensational dramatic surprises; but I think these are an echo. The rural scene lacks his exquisite simplicity; and some of the words are not of his vocabulary.

Fleay's conjecture regarding the date of composition of the *Four Playes in One* is based upon an inaccurately dated reference. Fletcher may have written his *Triumphs* before the middle of 1610, Field did not make his contribution till after November 23, 1611. In my opinion the series was first performed about 1612, by Field's Company of the Queen's Revels' children at Whitefriars shortly after they had first acted *Cupids Revenge* at the same theatre.

Of the remaining ten plays in which according to historical evidence Beaumont could have collaborated, at least two furnish no material that can be of service in estimating his qualities. If *Loves Cure* was written as early as the date of certain references in the story, *viz.*, 1605–1609, it is so overlaid by later alteration, that, whether, as the textual experts guess, it be Beaumont's revised by Massinger, or Fletcher's revised by Massinger and others, or Massinger and Middleton's, or Beaumont's with the assistance of Fletcher and revised by Massinger, Beaumont for us is uncertain. Fleay, Oliphant, and others trace him in a few prose scenes, and in two or three of verse.[1] But where the rhetorical and dramatic manner remotely suggest him, or the metre has somewhat of his stamp, words abound which I find in none of his undisputed composition; and the scenes conjecturally ascribed to him reek with a vulgarity of which he was incapable. Little, indeed, bespeaks Fletcher. It is not unlikely, as G. C. Macaulay holds, that the play was written by Massinger, in or after 1622. As to that comedy of prostitution, with occasional essays on the special charms of cuckoldry, *The Captaine* (acted in 1613, maybe as

[1] II, 1, 2; III, 1, 3, 5; V, 3.

early as 1611, and by the King's Company), there is no convincing external proof of Beaumont's authorship. It is, on the contrary, assigned to Fletcher by one of his younger contemporaries, Hills, whose attributions of such authorship are frequently correct; and it speaks throughout more clearly of Fletcher than of any other dramatist. The critics are agreed, however, that it is not wholly his, and G. C. Macaulay in especial conjectures the presence of Massinger. The verse and prose of a few scenes[1] do not preclude the possibility of Beaumont's coöperation; but I find no vestige of his faith in sweet innocence, of his imaginative elevation or his dramatic quality.

The Woman-Hater, written during the spring of 1607, was entered on the Stationers' Registers, May 20, 1607, and published in quarto twice the same year "as lately acted by the Children of Paules,"—without indication of authorship in either case. It is an independent production of Beaumont, written while he was under the influence of Ben Jonson; but Fletcher has revised two or three scenes. The comedy is more distinctly of the "humours" school than any subsequent work of Beaumont save the *Knight of the Burning Pestle*. The manifestly exaggerated torments of Gondarino "who will be a scourge to all females in his life," the amorous affectation of Oriana, the "stratagems and ambuscadoes" of the hungry courtier in his pursuit of "the chaste virgin-head" of a fish, the zealous stupidity of the intelligencers, all borrow from well-known Latin originals or echo Ben Jonson. But the "humours" are flavoured with Beaumont's humanity, the mirth is his—genuine and rollicking. The satire is concrete; and the play as a whole, a promising precursor of that purple-flowered prickly pear, *The Knight of the Burning Pestle*.

Evidence, both external and internal, points, as I have elsewhere shown,[2] to the production of *The Knight of the Burning Pestle* between July 10, 1607 and some time in March, 1608, by the Queen's Revels' children, after the appearance of Shirley's *Travails of Three English Brothers*, which is alluded to, and before the Children had ceased to play as an independent company at Blackfriars. Though the verse is in many respects different from that which Beaumont employed in his more stereotyped drama, it displays in several passages his acknowledged peculiarity in conjunction with a diction and manner of thought undoubtedly his. The prose is generally of a piece with that of his other comic writing, as in *The Woman-Hater* and his scenes of low life in *Philaster, King and No King*, and *The Coxcombe*. Of the portrayal of humours, mock-heroic and burlesque, the same statement holds true. The subject and the mock-heroic purpose do not call for his usual dramatic vocabulary; but we

[1] IV, 5; V, 2, 4, 5.   [2] *Op. cit.*, Chap. XXIV.

recognize his "dissemble," his "carduus" and "phlebotomy" (compare *Philaster*), his "eyes shoot me through," his "do's." We recognize him in the frequent appeals to Chance and Fortune, in the sensational determination of Jasper to test Luce's devotion with a sword, and in the series of sensational complications and dénouements which conclude the romantic plot. In short, I agree with the critics[1] who attribute the play wholly, or chiefly, to Beaumont. Fletcher may have inserted a few verses here and there; but there is nothing in sentiment, phrase, or artifice to prove that he did.

The diversity of metrical forms is but an evidence of the ingenuity of Beaumont. He has used blank verse with frequent double-endings to distinguish the romantic characters and plot; as in the scenes between Venture-well and Jasper, Jasper and Luce. He has used the heroic couplet with rhymes, single and double, to distinguish the mock-romantic of Venturewell and Humphrey, Humphrey and Luce. For the mock-heroic of Ralph he has used the swelling ten-syllabled blank verse of Marlowe and Kyd, or the prose of Amadis and Palmerin; for his burlesque of the May-lord he has used the senarii of the antiquated interlude. For the conversation of the Merrythoughts and of the citizen-critics he has used plain prose; and for the tuneful ecstasies of Merrythought senior, a sheaf of ballads.

In spite of the assertion of Burre, the publisher of the first quarto, 1613, that both he and Keysar, who furnished him with the manuscript, could "confidently sweare" that *The Knight* was the "elder above a yeare" of *Don Quixote*,—meaning of the first English translation, Shelton's (1612),—and that he (Burre) had fostered that manuscript privately in his "bosome these two yeares," nearly every editor or historian who has touched upon *The Knight* informs us that it is undoubtedly derived from *Don Quixote*. They must mean, of course, from Shelton's manuscript-translation which was first circulated in 1609 or from the Spanish original of 1605. My determination of the date of *The Knight*, 1607–1608, if correct, renders the former supposition impossible; as to the latter, there is no evidence that Beaumont, or that Fletcher, for that matter, had a reading knowledge of Spanish.[2] Beaumont may, of course, have had information of Don Quixote, by hearsay. Other English dramatists allude to *Don Quixote* as early as 1607–8; and, indeed, it would be virtually

---

[1] G. C. Macaulay, Oliphant, Bullen and Alden.

[2] Of this I am assured by my colleague Professor Rudolph Schevill, who has made a special study of the plays and their sources. See his conclusions as stated in *Romanische Forschungen*, XX, 617 *et seq.* (1907), and in Murch's edition of *The Knight of the Burning Pestle*. New York: 1908.

impossible that any literary Londoner could have escaped the oral tradition of so popular and impressive a masterpiece two years after its publication.

All this supposition of derivation from *Don Quixote* is, however, so far as verbal indebtedness goes, or indebtedness for motifs, episodes, incidents and their sequence, characters, machinery, dramatic construction, manners, sentiments and method of satire, a phantom caught out of the clear sky. So far as the satire upon the contemporary literature of chivalry is concerned, when the ridicule is not of English stuff unknown to Cervantes, it is of Spanish material translated into English and already satirized by Englishmen before Cervantes wrote his *Don Quixote*. An examination, moreover, of *The Knight*, and of the *Don* in any version, and of contemporary English literature, reveals incontestibly not only that the material satirized, the phrases, and ideas come from works in English, but that even the method of the satire is derived from that of preceding English dramatic burlesques. So far as the specific conception of *The Knight* is concerned,—a satire upon the craze of London tradesmen for romances of chivalry and "bunches of ballads and songs, all ancient," and for bombastic dramas of knight-errantry and of the civic and domestic virtues and military prowess of prentices and shop-keepers, it is much more closely akin to the conditions and aspirations of contemporary Bow-Bells than to the madness of the Knight of La Mancha. Beaumont may have received from the success of *Don Quixote* some impulse provocative to the writing of his *Knight*, but the satiric conception might have occurred to him if *Don Quixote* had never been written; just as that other dramatic satire upon the dramas of folk-lore romance, *The Old Wives Tale* had occurred to Peele some fifteen years before *Don Quixote* appeared; and as it had occurred to the author of *Thersites* to ridicule upon the stage Greek tales of heroism and British worthies of knighthood and the greenwood, still fifty-five years earlier.

Peele, Jonson, Chapman, Marston, and Robert Anton in his *Heroical Adventures of the Knight of the Sea* (1600), had already satirized the literature of knight errantry before Cervantes' burlesque appeared in 1605. Similarly, in 1607, Beaumont conceives a drama burlesquing the citizen-devotees of the romances and ballads that are the fad in his day. Whether Beaumont had heard of *Don Quixote* or not,—and there is no doubt that he had,—there is, as I have said, nothing in *The Knight of the Burning Pestle* that in any way presupposes a working acquaintance with the burlesque of Cervantes. On the contrary, it has been proved by Professor Schevill in the article cited above, and following him, by Dr. Murch, in his edition of *The Knight*, that Beaumont's conception of the hero, Ralph, is fundamentally different from Cervantes' conception of Don Quixote; and they have demonstrated with a minuteness of chapter and verse that need not be followed here that the motives, machinery, characters, ideas and phrases, are, in so far as they have relation to romances of chivalry, drawn out of, or suggested by, English translations of *Amadis of Gaul*, the *Palmerins*, the *Mirrour of Knighthood*, and so on. This demonstration applies to the adoption of the Squire, the rescue of Mrs. Merrythought, the incident of the casket, the liberation of the barber's patients, the love-affairs, as well as the often adduced barber's basin and the inn-scene. Of the situations, there is none that is not a logical issue of the local conditions or the presuppositions of an original plot, whereas there are, on the other hand, numerous situations in *Don Quixote*, capable of dramatic treatment, that the Elizabethan playwright could hardly have refrained from adopting if he had used that story as a source.

The play is a satire, also, upon various chivalric dramas, such as Heywood's *Foure Prentises of London*, and bourgeois dramas, such as his *If you know not me, you know no body*, and dramas of romantic marvel like *Mucedorus* and *The Travails of The Three English Brothers*. It incidentally parodies with rare humour that well-worn delight of Londoners, Kyd's *Spanish Tragedy*. It pokes fun at their unsophisticated assumption of dramatic insight and critical instinct, and at their childish games and shows and military pomps. With all this satire of the main plot and of the spectator-gods in the machinery, the author has combined a romantic plot of common life—of Jasper, Luce and Humphrey—and a comic plot of humours in which Jasper's father, mother, and brother live as Merrythoughts should. He has produced a whole that in drama was an innovation, and in burlesque a triumph. The *Knight* was still an acting play in the last quarter of the seventeenth century. During the past thirteen years it has been acted by academic amateurs five times in America.

Our earliest record of *The Coxcombe* is of its presentation at Court by the Children of the Queen's Revels between Oct. 16 and 24, 1612. From a consideration of its relation, though not technical indebtedness, to Baudouin's French translation of *El Curioso Impertinente* and of the theatrical affiliations of the contemporary actors (whose names are preserved in the folio of 1679) I conclude that it was first acted between December 7, 1609 and July 12, 1610, or between November 29, 1610 and July, 1611; but I incline to the former alternative. If the date was earlier than January 4, 1610, the theatre was Blackfriars; if later, Whitefriars. Though the Prologue in the first folio, 1647, when the play was first printed, speaks of a revision, and the hand of a reviser, probably Massinger,—maybe, also of another,—appears, *The Coxcombe* is properly included among

Beaumont and Fletcher's works. In the commendatory verses to that folio, Hills and Gardiner speak of the play as Fletcher's, but all tests show that Beaumont wrote a significant division of it, the natural, vigorous, tender, and poetic sub-plot of Ricardo's desertion of Viola and his ultimate reclamation,—with the exception of two scenes and parts of two more. The exceptions are the first thirty-five lines of Act I, which have been supplied by some reviser; I, 3, in which, also, the reviser appears; I, 5, the drinking bout in the tavern, where some of the words (e. g. 'claw'd') bespeak Fletcher, and the gratuitous obscenity, Fletcher or his reviser; and Act II, 2, where Viola is bound by the tinkers and rescued by Valerio.[1] Perhaps, also the last thirty-six lines of Act III, 3, where Fletcher is discernible in the afterthoughts "a likely wench, and a good wench," "a very good woman, and a gentlewoman,"—and the hand of a reviser in the mutilation of the verse. The romantic little comedy of *Ricardo and Viola*, one-third of play as a whole, is so loosely joined with the foul portrayal of the Coxcomb who succeeds in prostituting his wife to his friend, that it might be published separately and profitably as the work of Beaumont.[2] It is well constructed; and it conveys a noble tribute to the purity and constancy of woman, her grace of forgiveness and her influence over erring man. When Viola speaks she is a living person, instinct with recklessness, sweetness and pathos. Few heroines of Elizabethan comedy have packed so much reality and poetry within so narrow a compass. Ricardo, too, is a creative study in the development of personality; and the rural scenes and characters are convincing.

In the main plot Beaumont had no hand whatever, unless, perhaps, in the prose of the trial scene at the end of the fifth act. It is Fletcher's; but in a few scenes his work has been revamped and—in verse as well as style—degraded by some reviser. Oliphant thinks that here and there Massinger may be traced,[3] and here and there, Rowley.[4] I should be sorry to impute any of the mutilations to the former. I think that the irregular lines, trailing or curtailed, the weak endings, the finger-counted syllables, puerile accentuation, and bad grammar have much nearer kinship with the earlier output of the latter. But of whatever sins of supererogation his revisers may have been guilty, the prime offence is Fletcher's,—in dramatizing the story at all. To make a comedy out of cuckoldry was not foreign to the genius of the Elizabethans; for the pru-

---

[1] Even here, as Oliphant has said, Viola's first speech is "pure Beaumont."
[2] His scenes are I, 4, 6; II, 4; III, 3—(to "where I may find service") IV, 1, 2, 7; V, 2; and the last twenty-seven lines of V, 3.
[3] I, 1, 2 *a* (to Antonio's entry); III, 1 *a* (to Servant's entry.)
[4] III, 2; IV, 4; V, 1, 3.

riency of it we can make historical allowance. But a comedy in which the
wittol-hero successfully conducts the cuckolding of himself is nauseating.
And that the wittol, his adulterous wife, and the fornicator should conclude the affair in mutual gratulation is, from the dramatic point of view,
worse even than prurient and nauseating: it is unnatural, and therefore unsuited to artistic effect. No amount of technical ingenuity on Fletcher's part
could have made his contribution to this play worthy of literary criticism.

Philaster was published first, in 1620, in a quarto which attributed it to
Beaumont and Fletcher. It had been acted by the King's company as
early as 1610; I think before July 12 and after December 7 of the year
preceding. With the exception of three scenes, two half-scenes and a few
insertions or revisions by Fletcher, the drama is Beaumont's. Fletcher's
scenes, as proved by rhetorical tests, and by metrical where they may be
applied, are I, 1 *b* (from the King's entry), II, 2 *b* (from *Enter Megra*),
II, 4 *b* (from *Megra above*), V, 3 and V, 4. The first part of Act II, 4, was
written by Beaumont; but Fletcher has inserted lines 14 to 29 [1] (from
Enter Arethusa and Bellario to "how brave she keeps him"). Similarly,
the first draught of Act III, 2 was Beaumont's; certainly lines 1–34
(*Exit King*), 105–112 (the opening of Philaster's long tirade), and 129–
173 (from Philaster's exit to the end). But beginning with Arethusa's
soliloquy, line 35, we find insertions marked by Fletcher's metrical characteristics, his alliterations, favourite words and ideas, tautological ex-
pansions, repetitions, interrogations, triplets, redundant "alls" and
"hows." The last three lines of that soliloquy are his:

> "Soul-sick with poison, strike the monuments
> Where noble names lie sleeping, till they sweat,
> And the cold marble melt;" [2]

and he has overlaid with his rhetorical triplets, his "alls," and "hows"
the genuine poetry of Philaster's accusation of Arethusa. "The story
of a woman's face," her inconstancy, the shadow-quality even of her
'goodness' soon past and forgotten: "these texts" Fletcher "to his last
hour" is never weary of repeating.

It will be observed that, in general, Fletcher's scenes are elaborative,
bombastic, verbally witty, conversationally easy; at times bustling, but
not vitally contributory to the business of the play. They comprise the
longest speeches of the King, Pharamond, Philaster, Megra and Bellario.
Some of these, such as the King's denunciation of Megra and her reply,
are wild, whirling, and vulgar rhetoric. The bawdy half-scene with its

---

[1] I follow the numbering of the *Variorum* edition.

[2] Fletcher repeats them almost word for word in *Wife for a Month*, Act I, 2,
lines 47–48.

maid of easy honour is his; the discovery of the low intrigue, the masque, and the mob-scene are his. They may display, but they do not develop, characters. They are sometimes fanciful, sometimes realistic; but they lack the pervading emotion, imagination, poetry of Beaumont. The play is two-thirds Beaumont; in fact, it is essentially his from the excellent exposition in the first act to the series of sensational surprises which precedes the dénouement in the fifth. The conception of characters and the complication are distinctive of that writer's plots: the impulsive, misjudged, and misguided hero, his violence towards the love-lorn maiden disguised as a page, and his unwarranted suspicion of the honour of his mistress. The subtle revelations of personality are Beaumont's,—the combination of idyllic, pathetic and romantic, the visualization, the naturalness of figure and setting, the vigour of dramatic progress, the passion, the philosophical insights, and the memorable lines. His too, are the humour of the rural sketches—the Country Fellow who has "seen something yet," the occasional frank animality, as well as the tender beauty of innocence.

The Maides Tragedy was acted at Court in 1612–1613, by the King's men; but it was known to the Master of Revels before October 31, 1611. It was presented by the King's also at Blackfriars, in all probability first toward the end of 1610, or in 1611. Published without name of author in the quartos of 1619 and 1622, it is first ascribed to Beaumont and Fletcher in that of 1630. Metrical tests, corrected by the rhetorical, show that Fletcher's contributions are limited to three scenes and two half-scenes,—II, 2, IV, 1 (as far as line 200 "Prithee, do not mock me "), the ten lines of V, 1, part of V, 2 (to *Exit Evadne*), and the perfunctory V, 3. The latter part, also, of Act IV, 1, from the entrance of Amintor (line 190), appears to have been drafted by Fletcher, and to have consisted of lines 190–200, 247–254, 260–262, and the conclusion, 263–285. But, between Amintor's supplication "Prithee do not mock me " (line 200) and Evadne's assertion of sincerity "I have done nothing good to win belief " (line 247).[1] Beaumont has inserted four speeches that convert a colloquy otherwise histrionic and mechanical into one of the tenderest passages of the play. And in five verses of Evadne's succeeding asseveration of reform, we find his sudden magic and his phrase:

> "*Those short days* I shall *number to my rest*
> (As many must not see me) shall, though too late,
> Though in my evening, yet perceive a will,—
> Since I can do no good, because a woman,—
> *Reach constantly at something that is near it.*"

[1] Numbering of the *Variorum*.

The remainder of this latter portion, from Amintor's entrance, belongs, in verse no less than in diction, to the scene as Fletcher originally wrote it. When to these two scenes we add the first and third of Act V, which as I have already implied are of no particular significance, and the second (to the death of the King), we have Fletcher's whole written contribution to this wonderful tragedy. In the murder of the King he displays his dramatic mastery of the grisly and shuddering; but though the scene is character-ized by the same rapidity of conversational thrust and parry as the Flet-cherian dialogue between Melantius and Evadne, it is, like it, marred in effect by violence physical rather than spiritual. Fletcher's tragic scenes excel not in portrayal of personality but in business; his contribution to Aspatia is not pathos but the embroidery of grief.

The volume and essential vitality are Beaumont's: the cruel desertion of Aspatia, her lyric self-obliteration and her desperate rush on fate; the artful revelation of Evadne's character; the innocent but shuffling hero, beloved by virgin and by prostitute alike, blinded by circumstance and besotted by loyalty to the lustful author of his wrongs; the spiritual ele-vation of Melantius; the pestilent King, and Calianax, the poltroon whose braggadocio is part humorous and part cunning, but all helpless and hope-less. These are Beaumont's; and his too, the wealth of dramatic situation and device; the deft exposition and the masque of the first act; the shrewd development of motive and the startling revolutions of the second and the third acts; whatever of tenderness or of more intricate complication the fourth displays—in fact all that is not palpable violence. His, the breathless suspense and the swiftly urgent, unexpected sensations that crowd the last scene of the fifth and crown the catastrophe; and his, the gleaming epigram and the poetic finality.

Though the tragedy of *Cupids Revenge* was printed in 1615 as the work of Fletcher alone, the publication was unauthorized, and the attribution is by a printer who acknowledges that he was not acquainted with the author. The quarto of 1630 assigns it correctly to Beaumont and Fletcher. The play is known to have been acted at Court by her Majesty's Revels' children of Whitefriars in January, 1611–12. The fact that the authors were at that time writing for the King's men does not preclude their com-posing a play for the Queen's children. It is not therefore necessary to date the writing earlier than 1611. Though the critics disagree concern-ing the precise division of authorship in nearly every scene, finding traces of alteration by Field, Massinger and others, they discern a definite sub-stratum of both Fletcher and Beaumont. It is unnecessary to specify the minor scenes in which Beaumont coöperated. The four which transfer the action from an atmosphere of supernatural caprice and sordid irresponsibility to the realm of character, moral struggle, pathos or passion, are by him.[1] In these his verse, diction, hyperbole, sudden splendour, suggestive characterization, are indubitable.

A King and no King was licensed in 1611, acted at Court December 26, of the same year, and published in 1619 as by Beaumont and Fletcher. Modern critics display singular unanimity in their discrimination of the respective shares of the composers. With only one or two dissenting voices they attribute to Beaumont the first three acts, the fourth scene of the fourth, and scenes two and four of the fifth. To Fletcher they assign the first three scenes of the fourth act, and scenes one and three of the fifth. The tests which I have already described lead me to the same conclusion. Beaumont's contribution is distinguished by a largeness of utterance and a poetic simplicity, a diversified and graduated characterization, a philosophical reach, a realism both humorous and terrible, and a power of dramatic creativity and tension, equal to, if not surpassing, any parallel elements or qualities to be found in the joint-plays. That dramatist rarely creates fixed or transparent character. Arbaces thinks that he is simple, single of nature and aim, as passionless as he is valiant; but he is in fact the creature of vainglory, hasty temper and wild moods, and his failure to fathom himself is part of his complexity. His sudden love for the woman whom he believes to be his sister, and the resulting horror of apprehension and conflict of desire, reveal him in many-sided dilatation and in swift succeeding revolutions of personality.

By a series of sensational *bouleversements*, and in a dramatic agony of suspense, we are keyed to the scene in which relief is granted: no kinship exists between the King who is now no King, and the princess who is now Queen. With the exception of a half-scene (Act IV, 2 *b*) of somewhat bustling mechanism and rant by Fletcher, the whole of the King's portrayal is Beaumont's; and with the exception of eighty lines written by Fletcher (Act IV, 1) of dramatic dialogue containing information necessary to the minor love-affair, the story of the innocent and most pathetic Panthea is also entirely Beaumont's. The Mardonius of Beaumont, in the first three acts and the fifth, is a fine honest, blunt, soldierly companion and adviser to the King; but when Fletcher takes him in hand (Act IV, 2) he degenerates into alliteration and rant. The Bessus of Beaumont whose "reputation came principally by thinking to run away," is Falstaffian or Zagloban; the Bessus of Fletcher is a figure of low comedy.

To Beaumont, who wrote three-quarters of the play, we owe, in the creation of *A King and no King*, one of the most intensely powerful dramas of the Jacobean period, one of the most popular in the age of Dryden,

[1] I, 3; II, 2; III, 2; IV, 1; V, 4.

and one of the most influential in the development of the heroic play of the Restoration. Though it be a spoiled tragedy, it is not, as many assert, an immoral tragicomedy. From the first the spectator may readily divine that the protagonists are not brother and sister. And the protagonists though enmeshed in the net of circumstance cease not to recognize the liberating power of self-denial.

The first quarto of *The Scornful Ladie*, entered S. R., March 19, 1616, assigns the play to Beaumont and Fletcher, and says that it "was acted with great applause by the Children of her Maiesties Revels in Blacke Fryers." The references in Act V to the Cleve wars show that it could not have been written before March, 1609. Its first production has been placed by some at Blackfriars before January 4, 1610; by others at White-friars in 1610–1611. I think, for reasons given in my *Beaumont, the Dramatist*,[1] that it was written between May 1613 and 1616, and first acted at the new Blackfriars in 1615–1616.

The commendatory verses of Stanley and Waller in the 1647 folio give the play to Fletcher; and the greater part of it is his. Beaumont has contributed the vivid exposition of Act I, 1 and 2, and the jovial posset-scene of Act II, 1, where Sir Roger's kindly pedantry is developed, and the minor love affair of Welford and Martha introduced. He contributed also Act V, 2, where the hero finally tricks his scornful mistress into submission. His Abigail of the earlier scenes is, to be sure, vividly vulgar and amorous. Fletcher takes her up and turns her into a commonplace stage lecher in petticoats; but Beaumont, in the fifth act restores her to womanhood by giving her something of a heart. The Scornful Lady of Beaumont's scenes is self-possessed and many-sided, introspective and capable of affection. In Fletcher's hands she is shrewd and witty but evidently constructed for the furtherance of dramatic business. The brisk but mechanical movement of the action, and the stagey characterization and more animated scenes are Fletcher's; also the manœuvres directed against the lady's attitude of scorn, except that by which she is overcome. This was a very popular play before the Restoration and after; and it held the stage till 1788. But, as Ward says, it is "coarse both in design and texture, and seems hardly entitled to rank high among English comedies."

These then, are the eleven plays from which one may try to draw conclusions concerning the respective dramatic qualities of Beaumont and Fletcher during the period in which collaboration was possible. In two of them, *Loves Cure* and *The Captaine* we find that Beaumont had no hand; and in *The Four Playes in One* but the suspicion of a finger. Two, *The Woman-Hater* and *The Knight of the Burning Pestle*, are, wholly or essenti-

[1] Chapter XXVI.

ally, of his authorship. The remaining six are the Beaumont-Fletcher plays. Still other plays in which certain critics think that they have found traces of Beaumont, assuming that in their present form they are revisions of earlier work, are *Thierry and Theodoret, The Faithful Friends, Wit at Several Weapons, Beggers Bush, Loves Pilgrimage, The Knight of Malta, The Lawes of Candy, The Honest Mans Fortune, Bonduca, Nice Valour, The Noble Gentleman, The Faire Maide of the Inne*. These I have carefully examined and can conscientiously state that in no instance is there for me satisfactory evidence of the qualities which mark his verse and style. When in any of the suspected passages the verse recalls Beaumont the style is not his, and *vice versa*. There is not one of them that bears his distinctive impress, nor one that might not have been written by Daborne, Field, or Massinger, or by any of half a dozen experts whose industry may have swelled the output of the Fletcherian syndicate. Nor is there concerning one of them definite information that it was written before Beaumont's retirement from dramatic activity.

12. The Dramatic Art of Beaumont and Fletcher: The Influence of their ' Romances '

Passing in review the qualities of Beaumont as a dramatist we find that in characterization he is, when at his best, true to nature, gradual in his processes, and discriminating in his delineation. He is melodramatic, at times, in sudden shifts of crisis but he is uniformly sensitive to innocence, beauty and pathos, appreciative of fidelity, womanly devotion, self-sacrifice and mercy, of romantic enterprise and the virile defiance of calumny, evil soliciting and tyranny; and he is contemptuous of their opposites. In the treatment of lust he is frankly Elizabethan rather than insidiously Jacobean. He portrays with especial tenderness the maiden of pure heart whose love is unfortunately placed too high, or crossed by circumstance. He distinctively appropriates Shakespeare's girl-page; and under his touch her grace suffers but slight diminution, and that by excess of sentimentality rather than by lack of individual endowment. For his love-lorn girls are integral personalities. His most virile characters are not the tragic or romantic heroes of the plays, but the blunt soldier-friends. It has been said that "there is scarcely an individual peculiarity among them." [1] But Mardonius never deserts his King, Melantius does. And neither the Mardonius nor the Melantius of Beaumont has the waggish humour of Beaumont's Dion. The romantic heroes are not so distinct in their several characteristics. The differentiation between them

[1] Thorndike, *Influence of Beaumont and Fletcher*, page 123.

lies in the dramatic motive. The tyrants of *Philaster* and *Cupids Revenge* are vociferous but shadowy forms; but the King of *The Maides Tragedy* is a thoroughly visualized monster, and Arbaces stands as an epitome of warring tempers and desires in a highly complex and concrete personality, absolutely distinct from any other figure on Beaumont's stage. In the construction of Evadne and Bacha a similar skill in evolution and individualization is displayed. Of his braggarts and poltroons Beaumont is profuse: the best are Bessus and Calianax, so far as they have not been reduced to horse-play by another hand. His Jonsonian humours are no more marked, nor better drawn, in the later plays, than in several characters of the earlier comedies. Of Beaumont's effectiveness in the description of country life, in satire, and in burlesque, enough has already been said.

It has been demonstrated that in technique the clear and comprehensive expositions of the joint-plays are generally his; that in the tragedies and tragicomedies the sensational reversals of fortune as well as the cumulative suspenses and reliefs of the closing scenes are in nearly all cases his; and that in tragicomedy the shifting of interest from the strictly tragic and universal to the more individual-pathetic, romantic and comic emotions is also in most cases his. What he was capable of in romantic comedy is shown by his 'Ricardo and Viola' episode. He cared much more for romance than for intrigue. He delighted in interweaving with the romantic and the sentimental that which partook of the pastoral, the pathetic and the heroic. And through the heroic and melodramatic the more serious plays pass into the atmosphere of Court life.

To the tragedies and 'dramatic romances' or tragicomedies of this partnership, Fletcher did not contribute one-third as much as his co-worker. He displays the dramaturgy of spectacular violence, the power of dramatic invective. But his aim is not the furtherance of interest by the unfolding of personality or of plot through the interplay of complicated motives or emotions, it is the immediate captivation of the spectator by rapidity and variety: by brisk, lucid and witty dialogue, by the bustle of action and the multiplicity of conventional device. Most of his scenes are stop-gaps, subsidiary to the main action, or complementary and explanatory. In the comedies of intrigue, on the other hand, assigned whether correctly or not to the collaboration, he bulks large. Conventional types of the stage or of the theatre-going London world—especially the fashionable and the Bohemian provinces thereof—owe their existence chiefly to him. Black-guards, wittols, colourless tricksters, roaring captains, gallants, debauchees, lechers, bawds, libidinous wives, sophisticated maidens who may boast of their virtue but not of virtuous thoughts,— all these pass in and out of the scenes which Fletcher wrote while Beaumont was still alive. And some of them thrust their faces into the romantic plays and tragedies written undoubtedly in partnership.

Symonds calls Beaumount and Fletcher the "inventors of the heroical romance." And lately it has been conjectured and maintained with no slight scholarship and skill [1] that the Shakespeare of *Cymbeline, Winter's Tale* and *The Tempest* was following the lead of the two younger dramatists in what is attributed to them as a new style of 'dramatic romance.' The argument is that *Philaster* (acted before October 8, 1610) preceded *Cymbeline* (acted between April 20, 1610 and May 15, 1611), and suggested to Shakespeare a radical change of dramatic method, first manifest in *Cymbeline*. And that five other "romances by Beaumont and Fletcher, *Four Playes in One, Thierry and Theodoret, The Maides Tragedy, Cupids Revenge* and *A King and no King*, constituting with *Philaster* a distinctly new type of drama, were in all probability acted before the close of 1611," and similarly influenced the method of *The Winter's Tale* and *The Tempest*, also of 1611. I have stated carefully my reasons for rejecting this theory in my study of *Beaumont, the Dramatist;* [2] and a recapitulation of them here would be futile because incomplete. I object, however, to the denomination of the six plays just mentioned as the dramatic romances of Beaumont *and* Fletcher, for in some of them Beaumont had no hand; and to the assumption that in any case Fletcher could, through the core of the group, *Philaster, The Maides Tragedy* and *A King and no King*, have influenced the method of Shakespeare's later romantic comedies,— for, so far as the essential peculiarity of romantic technique is concerned, Fletcher's contribution to those three plays was altogether immaterial. Shakespeare's indebtedness, if any, is to Beaumont. The apparent novelty in technique of the six so-called romances lies in the adaptation of the sensational qualities of narrative fiction to the conditions of tragic or comic drama; especially in the attempt to awaken interest and stir emotion by running up and down the gamut of sensibility: in tragedy, by adding the romantic thrill evoked by vicissitudes of fortune to the portrayal of character subjected to stress and strain; and in romantic comedy, by injecting the emotional situations and shocks characteristic of such tragedy. In the realm of tragedy this accentuation of the possibilities of suspense whether by Beaumont or any other, was novel merely in respect of degree. It could hardly have impressed the author of *Romeo and Juliet* and *Hamlet* as anything by way of astounding innovation. The Beaumont-Fletcher novelty, if any such appeared to Shakespeare's eyes, must have

---

[1] Especially by Professor A. H. Thorndike in his *Influence of Beaumont & Fletcher on Shakespeare*, 1901.

[2] Chapter XXVIII, *Did the Beaumont 'Romance' Influence Shakespeare?*

consisted in the transference of tragic suspense to the realm of romantic comedy with all its minor æsthetic appeals, and is consequently limited to the tragicomedies, *Philaster* and *A King and no King*. But can we conceive that the author of *Two Gentlemen of Verona*, *Measure for Measure* and *Pericles* found any such novelty in *Philaster* and *A King and no King?* I do not see that Shakespeare's *Cymbeline* and his later romantic dramas betray any consciousness of the existence of *Philaster* and its succeeding *King and no King*. Omitting the consideration of relative dates, I can say here, merely, that if in his later romantic dramas Shakespeare borrowed any hint of technique from Beaumont's 'romances,' he was but borrowing back what Beaumont had borrowed from him or from sources with which Shakespeare was familiar when Beaumont was still playing hide-and-seek with his brothers in Charnwood Forest. Shakespeare's later comedies are a legitimate development of his peculiar dramatic art. Beaumont's tragicomedies, with all their poetic and idyllic beauty and dramatic individuality, are technically novel only in respect of the employment of the sensational properties and methods mentioned above, in a heightened degree. Their characteristic, when compared with that of Shakespeare's last group of comedies is melodramatic rather than romantic. And what is most evidently not novel with Shakespeare in his later romantic comedies,—the consistent dramatic interaction between crisis and character,—is precisely what the 'Beaumont-Fletcher romances' do not always possess. Beaumont's characterization at its best, with all its naturalness, compelling pathos, poignancy, and abandon is lyrical or idyllic rather than dramatic; Fletcher's is expository and histrionic,—of manners rather than the man.

With regard to Beaumont it is marvel sufficient, that between his twenty-fifth and his twenty-eighth year of age, he should have elaborated in dramatic art, even with the help of Fletcher, so striking a combination of preceding models, and have infused into the resulting heroic-romantic type, such fresh poetic vigour and such verve of movement. His poetic virtues are his peculiar treasure; but the dramatic method of the heroic and romantic plays lent itself lightly to imitation and debasement. Not so much *The Maides Tragedy* and *A King and no King*, which respect the unities of interest and effect, as *Philaster*, *The Coxcombe* and *Cupids Revenge*, to which Fletcher's contribution of captivating theatrical 'business' and device is more considerable. Some of these plays, and some of Shakespeare's too, and of Marston's, Chapman's and Webster's because of similar qualities of method paved the way for the heroic play of the Restoration—a melodramatic development of tragicomedy and sentimental tragedy, in which philandering sentiment, strained and histrionic passion, took the place of romantic love and virile conflict, an affected view of life tinged crisis and character alike, an unreasoning devotion to royalty or some other chivalric ideal obscured personal dignity and moral responsibility, and the thrill of surprise was substituted for catharsis, whether tragic or comic. Upon the future of the comedy of intrigue and manners, Beaumont exercised no distinctive influence. In plays like *The Coxcombe* and *The Scornful Ladie*, it is the genius of Fletcher that dominates the scenes of lighter dialogue and comic complication.

Concerning the dramatic worth of the comedies to which Beaumont contributed, the verdict of literary criticism has been anticipated, though not continuously paralleled, by that of the play-going public. The longest-lived upon the stage have been the dramas of heroic-romantic cast. *Philaster*, played after the Restoration with success, enjoyed between 1668 and 1817, thirteen revivals,—the last at Bath on December 12 of the latter year, with Ward in the title-rôle and Miss Jarman as Bellario. In the revivals of *The Coxcombe* Beaumont's romantic sub-plot assumed the dominant position, and it was finally borrowed outright for a comedy called *The Fugitives*, constructed by Richardson and acted by the Drury Lane Company in 1792. With Palmer in the part of Young Manly (the Ricardo of the original), and Mrs. Jordan as Julia (*alias* Beaumont's Viola), the adaptation ran for a dozen nights or more. *A King and no King* was revived at least five times between 1660 and 1788. We are told by Davies that Garrick intended to revive it, taking the part of Arbaces, himself, and assigning Bessus to Woodward; but "his pleasure suffered diminution at every reading of it in the green-room; and he gave up his design." The most important of Beaumont's contributions to the comedy of intrigue is found in *The Scornful Ladie;* but it does not exceed four scenes of the play, and is there principally distinguished by a shrewd observation of contemporary thought and manners. This production was several times witnessed by Pepys; later, it was revived as a droll, and finally, as *The Capricious Lady*, by W. Cooke, had a run at Covent Garden. Since 1788, it has, however, not appeared upon the stage. *The Knight of the Burning Pestle* was revived after the Restoration with a new prologue spoken by Nell Gwynne; but since then its career has been purely academic.

13. The Theatrical Companies, 1614–1625

The most important acting companies between 1614 and the death of James I are the King's and the Lady Elizabeth's (after 1619 the Queen of Bohemia's). Of waning distinction are the old Admiral's or the

Palsgrave's, and Queen Anne's; and of temporary note, the Prince Charles's.[1]

In 1614 the Globe, which had been destroyed by fire in the preceding year, was rebuilt "in far fairer manner than before." The **King's men** continue to play there and at the Blackfriars until 1642. From 1614 till the time of his death in 1625, their chief dramatist is Fletcher; and during these years the company acts some dozen or more plays by him alone,— among them the very popular comedies of manners and intrigue, *The Mad Lover, The Wild-Goose Chase, The Chances,* and *Rule a Wife and Have a Wife;* the romantic comedies, *The Loyall Subject, The Humorous Lieutenant, The Island Princesse, The Pilgrim;* and the tragicomedy, *A Wife for a Month.* And it acts some twenty more written by Fletcher in collaboration. About 1614 Fletcher's most important associate after Beaumont's retirement, Philip Massinger, appears upon the scene, and the joint-work of master and disciple, *The Little French Lawyer, The Spanish Curate* and other long-lived plays, is in the hands of the King's men from 1616 on. During the same period Middleton gives them some of his more powerful tragedies and tragicomedies. They revive Webster's *Duchess of Malfy,* and they have occasional contributions from Jonson, Field and Rowley. The only other company that at any season during the period rivalled them at Court was the Lady Elizabeth's, but between January 1614 and June 1626 that company entertained royalty only ten times as compared with some fifty appearances of the King's. As to actors,—the King's from 1617 to 1619, when he retired, had Nathaniel Field playing second parts to Burbadge. In 1619 the latter died and Joseph Taylor, who had been with the Duke of York's (Prince Charles's) company in 1610, and the Princess Elizabeth's in 1611, replaced him, taking his Hamlet and the nobler figures in Fletcher's plays. In 1619, Heming, also, ceased acting, and his Falstaff fell to John Lowin, who in comedy filled the old "humour" parts of Ben Jonson and the new of Fletcher as well, such as the Belleur of the *Wild-Goose Chase,* and in tragedy took the second parts. Condell ceased playing about the same time as Heming, and was replaced by Richard Robinson and Thomas Pollard, the latter of whom played in many of the lighter comic rôles. From 1619 on Lowin and Taylor are actor-managers of the company.

Between 1614 and 1625 the **Palsgrave's men** are of altogether minor significance in the history of the drama. They do not appear at Court; and neither at the old Fortune, which was burned in 1621, nor at the new theatre of the same name, opened in 1623, do they act any plays of more

[1] See, in general, Greg, *Henslowe's Diary,* II (Commentary); Fleay, *Hist. Stage;* Murray, *English Dramatic Companies;* and the sources as cited by these writers.

than ephemeral popularity. After 1625, they appear, according to Mr. Greg,[1] to have lost the Palsgrave's patronage, and to be "known simply as the Fortune Company," till 1631.

Another old company, **Queen Anne's** (formerly the Earl of Worcester's) had been playing at the Curtain and the Red Bull, popular dramas principally of Dekker and Heywood. It continued, but evidently with waning favour, at the latter theatre until the Queen's death in 1619; save for a brief space in 1617 when it perhaps occupied the new private theatre in Drury Lane, called the Cockpit. In the five years preceding the Queen's death these men did not appear at Court. After 1619 they are called the Red Bull company; and, in 1622, the Players of the Revels at the Red Bull. During the latter period they have two or three of Massinger's plays, and one of May's (*The Heir*). But from 1619 on they are losing their best players to the Lady Elizabeth's (Queen of Bohemia's) and in 1625 to the King's and the new Queen's (Henrietta). After 1623 they have practically ceased to exist as a London company; and their dramatist of longest association, Thomas Heywood, transfers his services first to the Queen of Bohemia's, then to Queen Henrietta's men. In that year, beside the King's at the Globe and Blackfriars, the only companies recognized by the Master of the Revels, Sir Henry Herbert, as acting in London were the Palsgrave's, at the Fortune: the Prince's (Charles) at the Bull, and the Queen of Bohemia's at the Cockpit in Drury Lane.

The companies of Prince Charles, the second son of James I, and of his sister, the Princess Elizabeth, may be mentioned together; for, by their temporary amalgamation between 1614 and 1616, their leading writers, William Rowley of the former and Thomas Middleton of the latter, were brought into an association whence proceeded joint plays, *A Faire Quarrell*, (1615–1616), *The Changeling*, and *The Spanish Gipsie*. The **Prince Charles's men** were, perhaps, the continuators of the celebrated Queen's men (Queen Elizabeth's players) for whom Robert Greene used to write.[2] They were known in 1608 by the younger prince's appellation, as Duke of Albany's or Duke of York's, and were acting in 1610 probably at the Curtain; but after Charles, on the death of his elder brother Henry, 1612, became heir to the throne, they assumed the name of Prince's players. In this company Rowley was not only chief dramatist but, from 1610 on, a prominent actor and stockholder and, for some years on either side of 1616, manager. Though he may have acted with the Elizabeth's (Queen

---

[1] *Henslowe's Diary*, II, 98.

[2] It is conjectured by Schelling, *Elizabethan Drama*, 1: 495, n. 2, that the Duke of York's in 1610 took over the King's Revels' children, who had been Paul's children until 1607.

of Bohemia's) men about 1621–1623, and was with the King's in 1623–1624, he walked with the Prince's at the funeral of James in 1625. Other well known actors of the company were Joseph Taylor (who left them temporarily in 1611 and permanently in 1619) and Hugh Attawell. Between 1610 and 1622 the Prince's performed at Court fourteen times; but there is no proof that their plays were significant. Nor of their success in the City do we know much before 1614. Then they joined forces with the Elizabeth's men, and with them played, probably first at Whitefriars, and afterwards for a brief season at Henslowe's new theatre of the Hope, just opened on the Bankside. This amalgamation still continued on May 31, 1615, for on that date the manager, Rossiter, arranged for the building of a new theatre in Blackfriars where the two companies were to act. In that short-lived house they presented together Nathaniel Field's play, *Amends for Ladies*. After the partnership was dissolved, early in 1616, the Prince's men were the richer by, at any rate, one great play, Middleton and Rowley's *A Faire Quarrell*. During 1616 they may have occupied the Hope for a brief season. But from 1616 to 1623 they were again at the Curtain. During that period they played one or two of Middleton and Rowley's less notable productions. Between 1623 and 1625 they were at the Red Bull in Clerkenwell and there they acted a maiden play by Richard Brome and young Jonson (the son of Ben). They had also, between 1616 and 1625, some of Ford's and Dekker's lesser work. On the accession of Charles to the throne and his assumption of the patronage of the former King's men, they lost the name of Prince's players, and parted with several of their best actors, who joined the new King's company. After that they steadily sank in the scale. They are known in London as the Red Bull Company, and in the provinces as the 2 King Charles's; but their only title to historical notice is that in 1627 they were enjoined from acting Shakespeare's plays, which the original King's company continued to hold as its exclusive property.

Altogether the most successful company with the exception of the King's, and second only to it between 1614 and 1625, was the **Lady Elizabeth's**. It had sprung into existence as the Princess Elizabeth's in 1611 with some very good actors,—among them William Barkstead, Giles Carey, and Joseph Taylor. All of these had been Children of the Queen's Revels, and had been trained by such men as Philip Rossiter in plays of distinction, like *The Silent Woman* and *The Coxcombe*. In 1611–12 they played, probably at the Swan, Middleton's *Chast Mayd in Cheape-side*. In 1613 by amalgamating with Rossiter's Queen's Revels they gained, with others, the actor-dramatist Nathaniel Field; and they played during that year and the early part of the next, at the Swan or Whitefriars, productions of Fletcher and Daborne, and probably *The Honest Mans Fortune*, written by these authors in partnership with Field and Massinger. Between January 1612 and January 1614 they had been summoned to Court seven times, and had presented plays of distinction, Marston's *Dutch Courtezan*, and *Eastward Hoe*. About April 1614 came the further alliance with the Prince Charles's men, already mentioned; and in October of that year this third Elizabeth's company acted, at the Hope, Jonson's *Bartholomew Fayre;* and, in November, the same at Court. Though the association of these companies, continuing at Rossiter's new theatre in Blackfriars, did not last longer than February 1616 or thereabout, the partnership then commenced between Middleton, in whose earlier plays the best Elizabeth's actors had taken parts, and William Rowley of the Prince's men, lasted for many a year; and from it the Lady Elizabeth's company derived *The Spanish Gypsie* and *The Changeling*, acted at Court, in 1623 and 1624, respectively. In 1623 they had also the coöperation of Massinger, whose *Bondman* they acted that year at Court. That they were in high favour with the King as early as 1617 is attested by the fact that they, and not the King's own company, were chosen to attend him in a progress to Scotland. In, or after, 1619, on the death of Queen Anne, they were strengthened by the acquisition of Chistopher Beeston, one of the leading members of her company and of its predecessor the Earl of Worcester's, and before that a player in the Chamberlain's as early as 1598. The Princess Elizabeth's became Lady Elizabeth's after the marriage of the princess in 1613 to the Elector Palatine; and when, in 1619, she became Queen of Bohemia, the designation changed again, and accordingly, though the older name was frequently used. Where they played between 1616 and 1619 we do not know; but maybe at "the Private House in Drury Lane." This was erected about 1615 and named at first from a Cockpit on the site of which it was built; but in and after 1617 it is called also the Phœnix. Between 1619 and 1625 they were playing there at least part of the time. When, in the latter year, Charles I came to the throne, Beeston and some other prominent members of the Queen of Bohemia's company became members of an aggregation formed under the patronage of the new Queen of England, Henrietta; as the Queen's Majesty's servants. Henrietta's men occupied the Cockpit; and what was left of the Queen of Bohemia's, Lady Elizabeth's, company continued under a new license a precarious existence, principally in the provinces, until 1632.

14. Romantic Comedy and Tragicomedy, 1614 to 1625: Middleton and Rowley

In *The Old Law* (printed, 1656 but, I think, written between 1614 and 1623), *A Faire Quarrell* (printed 1617), and *The Spanish Gipsie* (acted 1623), written by Middleton and Rowley, we encounter with relief qualities altogether different from those which form the special characteristic of Middleton's comedies of manners. The scene in the first and the last is foreign, Epirus, Spain; the subjects of all involve a high sense of honour; the main interest is in a conflict of principles; a distinction between right and wrong is in each case attempted to be made; the characters are constructed and developed with unaffected human sympathy,—they are capable of profound emotion and they awaken the emotions of reader and auditor. The plays are romantic to an exaggerated degree; they may be called tragicomic in so far as the personages in each come near death or near losing that which is dearer than life. Though by no means void of offense in the minor plots, these dramas are less offensive in manners and speech than those of Middleton's unassisted composition, and they are of much more artistic construction than his other comedies. The question at once arises, why the improvement? Is it due to Rowley's coöperation or to Middleton's growing maturity, or to both? Of this presently; a word first of the plays themselves.

The Old Law, is dated ordinarily 1599 because of a mention of that date in the play. But the mention may be purely dramatic. If the play was written about 1614–1616, as I think most probable, the "old law," to the effect that men of eighty and women of sixty are to be put to death as having passed the period of efficiency—'Oslerised' as the newspapers now express it,—would naturally be dated back to the previous century and the previous reign. The style is entirely different from anything that Middleton was writing in 1599. Rowley was then about fourteen years old, and Massinger, who is credited with some share in the composition, was sixteen. The likelihood is that Massinger's share, if he had any, was in revision; and that, not until after Middleton's death in 1627. There is no trace of Massinger in the style. The play is based, as we have seen, upon a conception far-fetched, and fraught with direful possibility, but at the same time capable of fine-spun romantic and highly humorous, delightfully grotesque, treatment. And, in spite of indecencies from which neither Middleton nor Rowley could shake himself entirely free, it is admirably executed. A pious son and his wife conceal their father from the operation of the "law" until a tattling neighbour betrays their secret. Then the law is reversed and falls with almost equal severity on youths under twenty-one unless they have proved themselves "mature in obedience, manners and goodness." The fun is irresistible; the pathos, natural; the poetry, at times eager and elevated; the situations, most dramatic; and the subplot, principally by Rowley, a screaming farce,—its protagonist, Gnatho, who wants to be rid of his old Agatha that he may marry again, an entirely novel, most refreshing, brisk and lifelike creation.

In *A Faire Quarrell*, the major theme is romantic in a higher degree because not at all grotesque. It is seriously imaginative, involving a conflict of filial devotion and personal honour, a conflict of maternal instinct and womanly pride. And the minor plot deals with the rehabilitation of a much tried and fiendishly tempted girl by marriage with the lily-livered youth who has wronged her. Captain Ager, the hero, has been most grossly insulted by a quondam friend who casts aspersion upon his mother's fair name. He prepares to fight but is held back by conscientious scruple: the aspersion may spring from better knowledge than his, from truth. Having overcome the scruple he is next held back from the duel by his mother's acknowledgment of sin,—a false acknowledgment wrung from her by fear lest her son may fall. He refuses to draw. The Colonel, his antagonist, flings "coward" in his teeth. That looses his weapon, and the Colonel is disarmed. The Colonel's duplicity is exposed; and the mother's artifice condoned. This is, in many respects, the noblest production of the authors, short of tragedy,—a romantic tragicomedy, somewhat of the Beaumont type. The characters of Ager and Lady Ager are loftily conceived; the conflicting claims are dramatically portrayed; the atmosphere quivers with passion; there is an ethical sensibility in the dialogue, and the emotions of pity and fear are profoundly stirred. Charles Lamb finds no word of praise too strong for the scenes in which Ager debates of right and wrong.[1] The play was popular in its own day; and I notice that, with *The Spanish Gipsie*, it is confirmed as the possession of the King and Queen's young company in 1639, and others forbidden to play it. But it is not one of the plays that survived upon the stage even in the eighteenth century. While it has admirable acting qualities, I question whether the Captain's scruples and his mother's apprehensiveness may not seem a bit theatrical; whether a son's alacrity to reason of his mother's honour and to question her, is not, even though exquisitely conscientious, somewhat repellent. In spite of the dramatic situations and the poetry, occasionally natural in pathos and superb in intensity, the characters sometimes appear to wander in a labyrinth of rhetoric. In the subplot the wronged girl, Jane, begins finely but straightway de-

[1] *Works* (1904), Vol. IV, *Specimens of the English Dram. Poets*, 114–115.

velops a vocabulary of abuse that detracts from sympathy. The intrinsic delicacy of her situation is further elbowed out by sordid farce and 'roaring.' And the *double entendres*, the excremental and lickerish wit, do much to spoil the artistic excellence of the drama.

The Spanish Gipsie is not so powerful a tragicomedy as *A Faire Quarrell.* The violent and pathetic premise calls for a painful conclusion; the play not only stops short of that but devotes itself to mitigating the irremediable. It is breezy and vigorous in movement and manners, romantic in motive, complication, and atmosphere, charming in its higher characters, and delightfully lifelike and comic in the lower. For these reasons it is included in this volume as representative of the best in romantic comedy that Middleton and Rowley have produced. Though, like the *Quarrell,* for a time a favourite upon the stage, it dropped out before the middle of the eighteenth century: perhaps, because the opening scenes savour too much of the criminal; perhaps, because the construction might have been more simple and compact. But as dramatic literature *The Spanish Gipsie* deserves to live. Since it has been edited with sufficient preface by my friend Butler Clarke, I need say no more. He was a lover of Spain and Spanish literature,—a scholar whose untimely death those who knew him well will not cease to lament.

The nobler qualities of conception, characterization, moral dignity, emotionality, and style which mark these plays as compared with Middleton's unassisted productions, inevitably suggest an inquiry into the manner of the collaboration from which they proceed.

Rowley's characteristics as poet and dramatist have been with sufficient definiteness determined by previous critics[1] from a study of his unassisted tragedy, *All's Lost by Lust,* the first three acts of *A Woman Never Vext,* which are admittedly his, and such parallelisms as occur in other plays with which he was associated. In verse accent, as in measure, he is clumsy, irregular, and still not altogether devoid of vigorous sweep and a native rise and fall of emotional melody that to some extent compensate for the lack of regulated cadence; in vocabulary, he is not rich nor varied, but forceful, with a kind of primitive directness and manliness. His figures of speech have no subtle or allusive quality; they are of the ordinary comparisons of nature and life, or drawn from the conventional stock of preceding drama. His rhetoric is that of the less cultivated class of society, and it runs easily into coarseness or violence. In his tragic scenes he is melodramatic; in his humours, given to stale and malodorous jests, puerile

[1] Especially by Miss P. G. Wiggin, *The Middleton-Rowley Plays,* Boston, 1897; by Professor E. C. Morris, *Middleton and Rowley* (Belles-Lettres Series), Boston, 1908; and by Dr. Ward, *E. Dr. dit.,* II, 540 *et seq.*

puns, buffoonery and boisterous laughter. But he has a charm, all his own, of whimsical drollery, and of extravagant magnanimity and romance not altogether unconvincing, because of the *naïveté* with which they are premised as possible and portrayed as actual. He understands what is humanly right in motive and action; he presents the elemental passions with no attempt at sophistication; and, if his scenes of tragedy are over-washed with gore, his scenes of pathos are pencilled with a rude simplicity and tenderness that make them sometimes more effective than the efforts of more highly gifted writers. If his comedy is broad, it is often inescapably humorous; if his serious themes are far-fetched, they are none the less vigorously imaginative; and if his characters, even his heroines, are ve-hement and, in moments of excitement, ammoniac beyond probability, they are none the less true to the finer instincts of womanhood: loyalty, chastity, self-sacrificing devotion.

In Middleton's earlier work, on the other hand, we have discovered no sense of manly honour, no reverence for women nor reason why they should be reverenced; almost nothing of elemental passion or of inspiring motive to action; no idealization of the shabby world that Middleton saw; we have found a cold realism,—at the best satirical; a cunning in plot con-struction,—at the best, of artificial intrigue. But his prose style is, while not dignified,—facile, witty, that employed by men and women of the upper level, or of the citizen class; and his verse is characterized by a melody and elasticity as far beyond Rowley's as are the subtlety of his diction and the play of his fancy.

With regard to the superiority of the Middleton-Rowley romantic dramas over Middleton's previous work two explanations based partly upon manner, partly upon date, of collaboration have been offered. Ac-cording to the first of these explanations, the improvement was due to a natural maturing of Middleton's view of life and art, and of his dramatic power, after 1614, when most of his realistic comedies were already written. According to this theory, the romantic dramas were composed by Middle-ton between 1614 and 1622; and Rowley's share was limited to a process of revision by which certain passages of a nature to appeal to the 'pit' were added. According to the other explanation, the superiority of the romantic dramas is due to the coöperation of Rowley in the whole course of composition. As to the former hypothesis it must be conceded even by its advocates that none of Middleton's unassisted comedies of manners written before 1614 displays the nobler characteristics of the Middleton-Rowley productions. Nor are they displayed in his still earlier popu-lar historic drama, *The Mayor of Quinborough;* nor in his early romantic comedies, *Blurt, Master Constable* (pr. 1602) and *The Phœnix* (pr. 1607), though the latter evinces some apprehension of the dignity of law.

To examine further the worth of this first hypothesis we must consider the sequence of the Middleton-Rowley plays. We have no historical evidence of collaboration with Rowley before the amalgamation in 1614 of Rowley's Prince Charles's company with Middleton's Lady Elizabeth's. That theatrical union was dissolved, as stated in the preceding section of this essay, about February, 1616; and our earliest fixed date of a Middleton-Rowley play is of the following year, when *A Faire Quarrell* was published "as it was acted before the King and divers times publicly played by the Prince his Highness Servants." The performance before the King may have been at Christmas, 1616–1617; the public acting may have been during the union of the companies; but the composition, if by collaboration, was not earlier than 1614. And that the composition is not a mere revision of Middleton by Rowley is indicated by internal evidence. For, though the main plot is from the hand of Middleton and the subplot from that of Rowley, the former is not of proportions adequate to constitute an acting play,—it is, however, of a nobility of conception characteristic of Rowley but not of Middleton's previous work; and the subplot, though not of vital importance to the main movement, is interwoven with it in a manner unlikely to have been executed by a mere reviser. To the main plot, moreover, Rowley contributes at least one scene; and in the minor there are distinct traces of Middleton's style.

Our next historical indication of the sequence of the Middleton-Rowley romantic plays is of a performance of *The Changeling*, a tragedy, by the Queen of Bohemia's company, before July 9, 1623; for on that date, according to Butler Clarke, *The Spanish Gipsie* was presented at the Phœnix, by the same company (until 1619, known as the Lady Elizabeth's) and it makes reference to the tragedy as already acted.[1] On January 4, 1624, *The Changeling* was presented at Whitehall, by the Queen of Bohemia's, that is to say, Middleton's old company. The play was first composed after the publication of a story called *God's Revenge Against Murder*, 1621. Between 1621 and 1623 Rowley was in close association with Middleton and the Queen of Bohemia's men. In 1623–1624 they both were associated with the King's company. It is much more probable that during this period, 1621–1624, they were planning and writing plays together than that Rowley was up to 1623 still with Prince Charles's men and at the same time revamping earlier productions of Middleton for the Queen of Bohemia's. A careful examination of *The Changeling* shows that it is from beginning to end the result of collaboration. The main plot, as in *A Faire*

---

[1] *Sp. Gip.* II, 1, 105.

Quarrell, is predominantly of Middleton's execution; but, as Miss Wiggin's analysis proves, the first scene and the last two of it are by Rowley. If Middleton was capable of writing unassisted the other powerful scenes of the main plot, is it likely that his original first and last two scenes were so weak that Rowley in a process of revision had to throw them out and substitute others? Aside from the execution,—the tricks of verse and prose, of dialogue and imagery in the major part of the main plot, markedly Middleton's,—the exaggerated romanticism and the elevated sentiment are such as we find in Rowley's, not in Middleton's unassisted, plays. They are due to the influence of Rowley. The minor plot, again, is Rowley's; but though crude, and in many respects, violent, it is necessary as relief, and is just the interweaving of mirth that Middleton would approve and that collaborators would have deemed advisable from the first.

Our next record in this Middleton-Rowley sequence is of *The Spanish Gipsie*, as, according to Butler Clarke,[1] "played for the first time at the Phœnix by the Lady Elizabeth's servants, July 9, 1623." This date is consonant with two references in the play itself to the "five camels and an elephant" sent by the King of Spain to James I, which arrived in London on July 5. Hitherto the earliest mention noted of the play has been Sir Henry Herbert's record, "upon the fifth of November (1623) at Whitehall, the Prince being there only, *The Gipsie*, by the Cockpitt company." Since our earliest quarto, that of 1653, tells us that *The Gipsie* had been acted at "the Private House in Drury Lane," Professor Morris in his admirable edition deems it [2] "likely that the play was first acted soon after 1614, when Middleton and Rowley came together, and before the Private House had become well known by its other names, the Cockpit or the Phœnix"; and he holds that the original play was by Middleton, and was revised by Rowley *circa* 1623, while they were again working for the same company. But the "Private House" is merely a generic name. The theatre had been called the Cockpit from the time of its erection, about 1615, and alternatively, the Phœnix, since its reconstruction late in 1617. No inference can, therefore, be drawn as to the date of the first acting from the use of the generic name in a quarto published at least thirty years after the event. I think that the play was written not long before its performance in 1623; and while I agree with Professor Morris's assignment of the major part, especially the serious verse, to Middleton, and of the tomfoolery of Sancho and Soto to Rowley, I hold with Miss Wiggin that from its inception the play was a product of collaboration. Middle-

---

[1] Who cites as his authority the Office-Book of Sir Henry Herbert. See *Critical Essay* on *The Spanish Gipsie*, below.

[2] *Op. cit.*, pp. XVII–XVIII, XLVII–XLVIII, 128.

ton's original plot would have been futile without the scenes in which Rowley is supposed to have revised Middleton almost out of existence; while Rowley's contributions, by way of supposed independent insertion, include a number of scenes that are integral parts of the play as a whole, and must have existed as such at the time of its first writing.[1]

All this goes to show that the second explanation suggested above is correct: the Middleton-Rowley plays are the result of collaboration in conception as well as composition. Their superiority is to be found especially in the conduct and characterization of the main plots; these are in execution the work of Middleton, but they are not the outcome of his unaided genius. The nobler conceptions of life, more reverent and poignant revelations of womanhood, the chivalrous ideals of manhood, the concernment with questions of love, honour and duty,—fine-spun and fantastic,—the extravagantly romantic situations and stirring emotions, highly imagined, originated with the selective taste, if not the inspiration, of Rowley. Inferior as Rowley's acquaintance may have been with the higher realm of social intercourse, with the language and manners of so-called gentlemen and ladies, boorish as he was in humour and boyish in wit, and untrained in the melodies of verse or the subtle *nuances* of conversation, he was superior in constructive vision and appreciative discrimination; he had insight into the beauty and mystery of life, and some respect for its sanctities. The plays with which his name is connected, whether written by him alone, as *All's Lost by Lust*, or in conjunction with others, as the *Birth of Merlin*, *A Cure for a Cuckold*, *The Maid in the Mill*, and *A Woman never Vext*, turn almost uniformly upon themes of fantastic romance. Even though he appears, when writing with another, generally to have restricted his effort of composition to the subplot with its portrayal of droll and boisterous life, it is but natural to infer that this uniformity of fantastic theme is due to his preference or influence.[2]

His capabilities in the handling of romantic and domestic situations are perhaps most definitely apparent in *A New Wonder*, *A Woman never Vext* (printed 1632). Though this may have originally been an old rhyming play, it is admitted that Rowley wrote the first acts as we now have them. The conception is paradoxical in the extreme, still romantic, and the pathos of the domestic situation is excellently reproduced. A wealthy widow has been so persistently fortunate—even in the decease of her husband— that she feels her moral development to be incomplete. To rectify her stunted and warped condition she marries a confirmed scapegrace,—enters

---

[1] For the assignment of scenes, see *Critical Essay* on the play, below.

[2] For confirmation, see Miss Wiggin, *op. cit.* and Arthur Symons, *Camb. Hist. Lit.*, VI, 77.

on a quest of sorrow. But even here she fails: Stephen, the scapegrace, re-
forms, administers his wife with love and her estate with skill, and even en-
dows with a competence the debtors' prison in which he once had reposed.
The collateral interest of the play is furnished by the waning fortunes of his
brother, Old Foster, and Old Foster's termagant wife; and by the dilemma
of young Robert Foster, true on the one hand to his father and mother, and
on the other devoted to Uncle Stephen,—whom, in their woe as formerly
in their weal, the old Fosters distrust and despise. Stephen, of course,
brings about the restoration of his brother's prosperity. The quest of
sorrow is indicative of Rowley's penchant for whimsical and, still, ideal
motives; the dilemma of Robert illustrates his fondness for romantic and
pathetic themes. The characters of the leading movement are exaggerated
in temper, but vivid, entertaining, and natural in tone. They are dramatic.
I find the widow's quest freshly and infectiously comic; the devotion of
Robert to his scapegrace uncle, tender and ingenuous; the reform of
Stephen, though sudden, not at all surprising, and evidently sincere. His
behaviour to his new-wed widow is charmingly considerate, even reverent.
It would be hard to instance, outside of the best Jacobeans, a picture
of more simple and gentle marital affection. The rages of old Dame
Foster, on the other hand, and the obstinacy of her husband are melo-
dramatic; and the jests of the clown and the witless country wooers of the
young girl, Jane, sorry and insipid. As an acting play, however, the *New
Wonder* appealed to posterity: it continued to be staged as late as 1824
when it appeared at Covent Garden in a revision by Planché.

Rowley's wit is rounded with a pun; his sense of humour does not
reside above the waist-band. But his drollery is unique, and kindly.
No better example than in the return of the sea-dog, Compass, in *The
Cure for a Cuckold* (c. 1618), to find his family larger by one than it should
have been, and his insistence upon fathering the "bye-blow." Here again
the major theme, with some degree of certainty attributed to Webster,
is paradoxically romantic: the heroine out of sheer whimsicality requires
that her lover shall kill his best friend.

Such themes were, of course, all the fashion with the Jacobean court,
and had been made the more acceptable by the practise of Marston and
Fletcher; later by that of Rowley in association with Fletcher, and of
Rowley's quondam colleague, Webster, who continued the tradition of par-
adox and violence in his *Devil's Law-case* (c. 1623),—a striking tragicomedy
of mingled poetry and intrigue. But Middleton had not been given to the
employment of such themes before he fell in with Rowley; and in none of
the plays written by him without Rowley's assistance does he show himself capable of developing them with poetic truth,—of sustaining the emo-

tions upon a level of genuine suspense, and the characters in an atmosphere of ethical plausibility. *Any Thing for a Quiet Life* (c. 1623), a comedy of manners and intrigue with a fantastic presupposition worthy of Rowley, is a marked example of what Middleton could perpetrate when writing alone, even after he had, with Rowley's inspiration and assistance, produced *A Faire Quarrell*. It is, as Ward remarks, "one of Middleton's hastiest performances"; and one of his nastiest,—crowded with foolery and poor in technique. His *More Dissemblers besides Women*, entered for the King's men in October 1623, and written about the same time as *The Changeling* and *The Spanish Gipsie*, tries again to combine romantic motive with comic intrigue. The aged Cardinal's reliance upon the professions of celibacy advanced by a lascivious nephew and a very passionate Duchess is dramatically presented, and the plot is ingenious; but the emotions are a cynical sham; the heart-ache of the minor movement is shot with a lubricity which Rowley at his worst could not have surpassed, and would certainly have relegated to less promising scenes; and the portrayal of gipsy-life is a nauseating instance of what Middleton made of romantic vagabonds when Rowley was not at the making. In his *Women Beware Women*, written, I think, after 1623, Middleton is similarly unrestrained. Here is a tragedy vividly conceived, and of masterly execution so far as technique of fusion, situation, and dialogue are concerned. The language far surpasses Rowley at his best and the manners bespeak one acquainted with the world of loftier station. But the materials are horrible; and the result, a nightmare of ignoble passion. The feelings of the reader are unrelieved by any of that purification that proceeds from tragedy sanely and sadly conducted. The outlines of lust are clear and cold, intolerably real, heartless. The comic ingredient, though ironic and relentlessly clever, is grim and offensive. The play lacks the fierce directness of fatality that characterizes *The Changeling* and Rowley's *All's Lost by Lust;* it lacks, also, the fellow-feeling for the humanly tempted and unfortunate, and all sensitiveness to ideals. Of the beauty of virtue, by which in *All's Lost by Lust* Rowley, though but a third-rate dramatist at the best, transmutes the pathos of Jacinta into sublimity, of the just emotion with which he dignifies the common-place betrayal of Margaretta, Middleton, unassisted, has no glimmering.

While Middleton and Rowley's *Old Law*, *A Faire Quarrell* and *The Spanish Gipsie*, and Rowley's *New Wonder* are of dramatic distinction sufficient to warrant a contemporary vogue, only the last has been revived upon the public stage in modern times, and only the second and third are possessed of intrinsic literary quality worthy of the consideration of the average student to-day. One other play of Middleton's, mentioned neither among his romantic comedies nor his comedies of manners, *A Game at Chesse* (1624), must always command the respect of the historical and literary reader not only as one of the earliest and most powerful of English dramas of political satire, but as poetry of original and serious import, and as comedy of superior force,—a force, however, which, so far as the stage is concerned, expended itself with the Spanish controversy to which it owed its existence.

15. Fletcher in the Comedy of Manners and Intrigue

Between 1604 and 1625, the year of his death, Fletcher produced without the assistance of any colleague fourteen plays of more or less comic quality. Four of these plays, *Monsieur Thomas* (*c.* 1607–11), *The Womans Prize* (*c.* 1610–15), *Wit Without Money* (1614), and *Rule a Wife and Have a Wife* (1624), are comedies primarily of manners. In them the plot proceeds rather from the characters and 'humours' involved than from external, and hence artificial, manipulation; and the interest is in the manners displayed rather than in a romantic element or in the intrigue as such. Four plays, *The Chances* (*c.* 1615), *The Mad Lover* (*c.* 1618), *Women Pleased* (1620), and *The Wild-Goose Chase* (1621) are comedies primarily of intrigue. In these the interest is occupied but slightly, if at all, by romantic activity or passion, and only adventitiously by the display of character through 'humours' and manners in general: it is held by a series of entanglements, usually of an erotic nature,—each cunningly devised, and so interwoven with the rest as to keep the auditor guessing. The *amours* are woman-hunts or man-hunts. The hunter of either sex is destitute of morals or clad in some pretence which the manners belie. The manners themselves, though purporting to be those of the day, are factitious or, at the truest, of a fashion-loving, theatre-haunting coterie utterly unrepresentative of the law-abiding and normal European of that or any other day. The other six plays contain something of a serious element. Four are romantic comedies: *The Loyall Subject* (1618), *The Humorous Lieutenant* (1619), *The Pilgrim* (1621), and *The Island Princesse* of the same year. While in each of these there is more or less of the 'humours' *motif*, and of the heroic urged almost to the verge of tragedy or pathos, the real interest is in the successful assertion of the individual in love, gallantry, chivalric devotion or patriotism, amid circumstances which inspire admiration or wonder. They have all been called tragi-comedies; but even though Fletcher might have classed them as such, they are logically varieties of romantic comedy. While each of them "brings some near death," there is in none of them real horror or real pathos for the spectator; and those elements are requisite to tragicomedy if it is to be regarded as a distinct type of drama. The name, tragicomedy, however may be applied to two plays which remain to be mentioned in this list, *The Faithful Shepheardesse* (1608), and *A Wife for a Month* (1624): the former because it has all the requisites of which its pastoral limitations will permit; the second because all it lacks of being a tragedy is the conclusion appropriate to the tragic conflict.

Of the comedies primarily of manners the first to challenge attention is *Monsieur Thomas* (c. 1608–1611)[1] based upon the *Astrée* of the Marquis D'Urfé. Concocted with clever ease, and furnished with varied devices appropriate to comic effect—sham sickness, disguisings, mouse-traps, dupers duped, street-frolics and mock-sentimental serenades, scaling ladders, convents, and a blackamoor girl for a decoy-duck,—it is conceived in a rollicking spirit and executed in sprightly conversational style. Sir Adolphus Ward says that "as a picture of manners it is excelled by few other Elizabethan comedies." I am sorry that I cannot agree: I call it low, or farcical, comedy; and though the 'manners' be briskly and realistically imagined, I question their contemporary actuality or their dramatic probability. Amusing scapegraces like the hero of the title-part have existed in all periods of history; and fathers, who will not have their sons molly-coddles; and squires of dames, like the susceptible Hylas. But manners to be dramatically probable must reflect the contact of possible characters in a definite period. And can any one maintain that the contact of these persons with the women of the play is characterized by possibility? or that these manners could, even in James I's reign, have characterized a dozen actual Londoners? Thomas, who assumes sanctimony for the purpose of vexing his father, and blasphemy for the purpose of teasing his sweetheart—racking that "maiden's tender ears with damns and devils,"—is no more grotesque than many a contemporary embodiment of 'humour.' But what of his contacts with the "charming" Mary who "daily hopes his fair conversion" and has "a credit," and "loves where her modesty may live untainted," and, then, that she may "laugh an hour," admits him to her bed-chamber having substituted for herself a negro wench? And what of the contacts with his equally "modest" sister, Dorothy, who not only talks smut with him and with Mary, but proclaims his fornication "fine sport" and would act it herself if she were a man? I fear that the much reading of decadent drama sometimes impairs the critical perception. In making allowance for what masquerades as historical probability one frequently accepts human improbabilities, and condones what should be condemned—even from the dramatic point

[1] For date and general discussion, see *Beaumont, the Dramatist*, Chapter VI.

of view. I have found it so in my own case. With all its picaresque quality, its jovial 'humours' and its racy fun, this play of the "charming" Mary and the "modest" Dorothy is sheer stage rubbish: its women contradict the dramatist's presupposition, it has no basis in the general life of the class which it purports to represent, nor in actual manners, in likelihood or poetry. Its basis is in the uncritical and, to say the least, irresponsible taste of a theatre-going Rump which enjoyed the spurious localization and attribution to others of the imaginings of its own heart.

The characters are well-grouped; and the spirit of merriment prevails. The reversals of motive and fortune, the recognitions, and the dénouement are as excellently and puerilely absurd as could be desired of such an amalgam of romance and farcical intrigue. Richard Brome, writing in praise of the author for the quarto of 1639, implies that the play was not well received at its "first presenting,"—"when Ignorance was Judge, and but a few What was legitimate, what bastard knew." That was before 1612 and the few might have cared more for Jonson's *Alchemist* or something by Shakespeare, or for Beaumont and Fletcher's *Philaster*. But, as Brome assures us, "the world's grown wiser now." That is to say, it had learned by 1639 "what was legitimate," and could believe that in Fletcher's *Monsieur Thomas* and the like, "the Muses jointly did inspire His raptures only with their sacred fire." But even as transmogrified by D'Urfey and others the play did not survive its century.

The Womans Prize or *The Tamer Tamed* (*c.* 1610–1615) is perhaps a comedy of 'humours' and intrigue as much as of manners; but since the intrigue is designed merely to purge Petruchio of his tyrannical temper, and the purging gives occasion for the portrayal of manners which purport to be genuine and of Londoners and country women, the classification is justifiable. All the more so, since the play forms one of a sequence of manners' comedies dealing with the feud between dictatorial husbands and 'curst' wives. The date has been set, from internal evidence, as early as 1604 and as late as 1615. I cannot persuade myself that the references to the siege of Ostend determine the earlier date. That siege was likely to be a subject of colloquial reference for twenty years after its conclusion. One of the minor characters, called Moroso, may very well be a reminiscence of Morose in Jonson's *Silent Woman* (1610), for, says Sophocles in the presence of Moroso (III, i), "I never will believe a silent woman, When they break forth they are bonfires." Fletcher's Moroso was probably attired to recall the singular appearance of Jonson's hypochondriac "with the huge turban of nightcaps on his head buckled over his ears" for, says the Petronius of *The Womans Prize* to Moroso, "Burn your Nightcap, It looks like half a winding sheet" (IV, i). In the same catologue of advice we find "contrive your beard o' the top cut, like Verdugo's"—and in Jonson's *Alchemist* (1610) we have mention of "his great Verdugoship" (III, ii). This name for a hangman is of rare occurrence. The coincidence of Jonsonisms in connection with a Jonsonian character of 1610 may indicate that date as the upper limit of composition for *The Womans Prize*. The play is a very amusing sequel to *The Taming of the Shrew*. Katherine is dead; Petruchio has just wedded a second wife, Maria; and Maria, deeming that the first wife "was a fool and took a scurvy course," is going to make a man out of the woman-taming monster. Her sister Livia and her cousin Bianca are of the same "faith," they'll "all wear breeches." By a series of rebellions, beginning with the barricading of her apartments against her husband, Maria drives the amazed Petruchio to a series of counterplots ranging from pretended illness to pretended death. When at that last she, instead of bewailing his loss, bewails with feigned tears "his poor, unmanly, wretched, foolish life," he rises from his coffin and capitulates. And she, having tamed the tamer, relents. The play is written with facile wit, irresistible humour, and a mastery of conventional characterization and theatrical device only less complete than that of *Rule a Wife*. Miss Hatcher has pointed out[1] that "the organizing motive" in this as in Fletcher's other pure comedies "is the interplay of two humorously conceived groups on the principle of action and reaction. The moment of suspense comes with every trick of the gay intrigues, and the constant reversal of fortune keeps expectation busy. The complication is thus rather linked than cumulative, and the interest is distributed throughout the play." If Beaumont had been still actively engaged in dramatic composition when this play was written, it would be difficult to understand how he could have failed to collaborate; for the theme, the conflict, the characters, some of the situations and humours, are precisely of the kind that he affected in comedy and that he had already attempted in *The Woman-Hater* and, more or less, in *The Knight of the Burning Pestle* and in his share of *The Scornful Ladie*. But there is no trace of his verse or style; nor of his judgment. Few of Fletcher's plays are more unrestrainedly ribald. Treating a Shakespearian theme he wallows in the trough that Shakespeare had avoided. Beaumont did not, indeed, prune all Fletcher's luxuriance during the period of their close association, as witness *Monsieur Thomas*, but I think still that this play was written after the younger poet's retirement to the country in 1613. Indeed the similarity of phrases in this play to those of *Wit without Money* (1614): the lines on "frippery" in III, i, of the former and II, v, of the latter, and on the armies in the air at Aspurg in I, iv, of the former and II,

---

[1] *John Fletcher*, Chicago: 1905, p. 97.

iv, of the latter;[1] as well as the mention of "craccus," a favourite brand of tobacco at that time (*cf.* Middleton's *Faire Quarrell*, IV, 1, of 1616), incline me to set the lower limit of composition at about 1615. Probably, as Fleay conjectures, it was one of the plays acted by the Princess Elizabeth's men between 1613 and 1616. When it was presented by two of the old Princess Elizabeth's players in 1633, its flavour proved too high for the stomach of even that Cavalier age: it had to be purged by the Master of the Revels of "foul and offensive matter, oaths, profaneness and ribaldry." The King and Queen "liked it" thus purged "very well,"—even better than *The Taming of the Shrew*, which they had seen two nights before. The *Tamer Tamed* was revived after the Restoration. Reduced to a farce, it was presented at Drury Lane in 1757, with Palmer in Petruchio and Mrs. Pritchard in Maria; and a still later alteration, never printed, is said to have been performed at Brandenburg House, as late as 1795.

Wit without Money (*c.* 1614), "deserves," as Dr. Ward has said, "to rank among the higher class of Elizabethan comedies in which character is drawn with originality and force." Here we have a play of London manners, pardonably true to life,—boisterous, to be sure, but of a coarseness merely of expression and of the habit of the time, and easy to be expunged without detriment to motive, humour, or action. The picture is of the comic aspects of idiosyncrasy in love; and the plot proceeds not by external device but from the exigencies of character and situation. Valentine, who has mortgaged his estate, and despises matrimony as much as he does money and will live by his wits, is as well drawn a personage of the 'humours' variety as many in the pages of Ben Jonson,—in general, more true to natural possibility and more genial in his satiric sallies. In the matter of love he is a playful Petruchio who comes prepared to mock but stays to adore; and his love-affair is contrived both to feed 'humour' and to purge it. The character of the conquering widow, Lady Heartwell, is captivatingly disclosed in the scene of her first meeting with Valentine. With her artistic accomplishments, her poetic and philosophical aspirations, her science of the male sex and apparent independence of its components, her comfortable fortune, her wit, and willingness to be won, she has an undeniably Shakespearian flavour,—not of Katherine the shrew, nor of Rosalind the coquette, but of the soil from which such women spring. Her sister, Isabella, is a teasing, resourceful maiden in love, not altogether unlike Beatrice in merriment, but with more "Come hither." Few prettier and more amusing instances of the inverted proposal are

---

[1] 'Dragons in Sussex, Sir, or fiery battles seen in the air at Aspurg.' Fleay, *Chr. Eng. Dram.*, I, 198, points to 'the Sussex serpent' as appearing in S. R., first, August 24, 1614.

discoverable in Elizabethan comedy than the early morning scene in which this sister on her way to church accidentally (?) meets the timid Francesco and accuses him of having impudence sufficient "being so near the church," to "provide a priest and persuade me to marry you!" Interest is heightened by the skill with which Lady Heartwell entraps her improvident and now impoverished woman-hater. The minor characters are life-like: especially the epigrammatic Shorthose, whether running up and down with one boot on—in the moment of domestic upheaval—or snoring his way to morning prayer in charge of Isabella. The action is comically varied; and the false alarm and bustle of impending travel go far to produce an appearance of breathless rapidity. The play was justly popular. I count six revivals of it between 1672 and its last performance, in 1757, at Covent Garden.

Fletcher reaches his climax as a dramatist of humours and manners in the play by which he is represented in this volume, *Rule a Wife and Have a Wife* (c. 1624). In the critical essay preceding the text, Professor Saintsbury has directed attention to the skill with which "the mixed and compound plot" is here presented. In *Monsieur Thomas, Wit without Money,* and *The Womans Prize*, the component plots are but superficially connected. But here, though the connection of the Perez-Estefania intrigue with that of Leon and Margarita lies merely in the external accident that Estefania is Margarita's maid, the intrigues are complementary in comic tone: the former of the duper duped by his clever wife is a foil to the latter of the termagant tamed by her wittol-seeming husband. And the two movements are dynamically welded by the usurious-amorous 'humour' of Cacofogo. In no play has Fletcher given stronger proof of his ability to captivate and amuse by the presentation of frankly impossible and totally unmoral, if not immoral, figures of the foot-lights; and in no comedy has he permitted his conflicting 'humours' so convincingly to work their own embarrassment, or so naturally and ludicrously to swallow each its own 'purge.' The situations, the ruses, the tables turned, the gayety, the dialogue make this a masterpiece of stage-craft. Swinburne calls it "pure comedy," Saintsbury, "a comedy of intrigue, pure and simple," but "cunningly blended" of acutely comic and farcical and serious. Since the interest is not chiefly in any external or preconceived intrigue but in the clash of 'humours' from which the intrigue proceeds and in the coat of many manners, by no means improbable, with which it is invested, I venture to rank it with the manners class. But that is a matter of no particular significance.

Only one other comedy written between 1616 and 1642, *A New Way to Pay Old Debts,* has seen so brilliant a career. Of great popularity during those years, *Rule a Wife* was revived no fewer than twenty-one times between 1663 and 1829; and it is still regarded as an acting play. The irresistibly comic contrast between the assumed simplicity of Leon and his subsequent assertion of marital dominance has afforded scope to actors as different as Mills, Garrick, Edmund Kean, Warde, and Charles Kemble. The actresses, from Mrs. Barry down, who have presented the moods of Margarita have been surpassed only by those who have played the inimitably impudent Estefania—Mrs. Bracegirdle, Mrs. Cibber, Mrs. Pritchard, Mrs. Clive. The Copper Captain, writes Hazlitt in 1820, "is sterling to this hour." Betterton played him in 1683, Wilks in 1706, Woodward in 1756. "And his mistress Estefania", continues the critic above quoted, "died only the other day with Mrs. Jordan."

Of Fletcher's comedies, primarily of manners, three, at any rate, *The Womans Prize*, *Wit without Money* and *Rule a Wife*, have abiding literary and dramatic merit.

From plays of this kind it is but a step to those in which the interest is centred in the complication rather than in the 'humours,' manners, or personalities involved.

In *The Chances* (c. 1615) we have an intrigue of varied misadventure. The heroine has disappeared both from her lover, the Duke, and from her fire-eating brother, Antonio, who would pink the lover "in the wanton eye." A student of Bologna, Don Frederick, takes charge most willingly of the escaping Constantia and falls in love with her on sight; his comrade, Don John takes charge of a 'bundle' delivered to him by a nurse. Constantia and the contents of the bundle are entrusted by them to Gillian, their landlady, the mischief-maker and mar-plot of the play; and at Gillian's suggestion, the mother, for such Constantia is, and her recovered child of the bundle elude their student-protectors. These, meanwhile, are pursuing the Duke, and return with him to find that they are in for this fresh pursuit. So the intrigue progresses from mistake to mistake, and brawl to brawl, till through the agency of a sham magician, Gillian's kinsman, a solution is reached. A second Constantia, woman about town, has been injected into the plot; and love affairs of lower tone lend a farcical element to the play,—but well subordinated to the main movement. The heroine is one of Fletcher's few modest women; and, possibly on that account, she is but a shadowy centre about which the complication forms. The other characters are concrete but, with the exception of Antonio and Gillian, not distinguished by impressive qualities. The students are typical, care-free scapegraces; the magician, the courtesan, the minor personages that crowd the scene, bustle and divert as in a moving-picture. But the irascible 'humour' of Antonio has life; and the personality of the landlady breathes both life and manners. The manners of the rest are no truer to Bologna than to Petersham. The long-enduring popularity of the play,—for it was acted well into the nineteenth century, and even later included in editions of the best acting comedies,—is chiefly due to the skill with which the intrigue is conducted, the atmosphere of irresponsibility, and the witty dialogue. Based upon one of Cervantes' *Novelas Exemplares*, the drama is an excellent example of Fletcher's methods of adaptation. He has transformed the characters of a narrative into *dramatis personæ* by intensifying the motives of some, and by adding to the original number a few figures capable of prolonging the comic conflict. He has borrowed only such incidents as he could clearly visualize and has supplied others to increase the ludicrous effect. While thickening the complication, he has at the same time accelerated the movement. In their preoccupation with a central purpose, characters hurry from place to place, and with the same preoccupation the spectator hurries breathless but unwearied. In the latter half of the play Fletcher has increased the suspense of his original by cunning incitements,—farcical, mock-serious, and spectacular. He has also, for a wonder, given us one or two gentlemen, and suffered them to converse as such. The vulgarities of others, like Don John, and the inevitable wenching scenes might be purged without killing the play. So treated, *The Chances* could hold the stage to-day; but it is not literature. It has ingenuity and wit, but little poetry and no depth.

The Mad Lover (c. 1618) is a farcical-romantic woman-hunt. Written in the distinctive Fletcherian verse, it displays all Fletcher's extravagances of style at their most unrestrained; and it illustrates his idiosyncrasies as a dramatist at their liveliest and worst. The dialogue is brisk and vulgar; the intrigues are crowded and but loosely related; the dramatic tricks and conventional devices, numerous, varied, and cleverly designed to tickle the palate of an undiscriminating audience. Some of the characters, such as the Fool and the old rogue, Chilax, are well-drawn; but the principals are sophomoric, or repellent in design: the heroine, forward and shameless; the butt of ridicule, Memnon, a caricature of the bombastic braggart and enamoured idiot; and the rest of them, ecclesiastical and lay, steeped in the converse of the brothel. The plot is borrowed (by way of the Italian) from an old story suitable for a tragedy of lust; but Fletcher makes of it an extravaganza of intrigue, enlivened by cheap humour and invested in an hilariously immoral atmosphere of romance.

Women Pleased (1619 or 1620) is a loose-jointed contrivance, in which the superfluity of stage-worn characters—the usurer and his wanton wife, the lecherous suitors, the faithless gallants, the convenient maid-servant,— and of puerile disguisings, rope-ladders and bed-curtains,—is surpassed only by the vulgarity. The author has 'contaminated' three intrigues from Boccaccio with a romance from Chaucer's *Wif of Bathes Tale*. The naughty grace of the former is here smeared with smut, and the breezy humour of the latter sicklied with sentimentality. The women of the intrigue are 'pleased' with feculent jocosity, lying and adultery; those of the romance, with a cross-country love-chase and the untwisting of a riddle. By the latter feat the sappy hero, properly prompted, wins his princess, suitably divested of her disguise. By that resourceful maiden and the esurient servant, Penurio, and the realism of the morris-dancers and the country-side, the play is barely saved from bathos. This may be summed up as a comedy of intrigue in which mock-romantic men and women hunt each other with hircine intensity.

The Wild-Goose Chase (1621) is a comedy of intrigue in which the heroine hunts the hero, and the minor virgins are of the 'knowing' stripe of maidenly reluctance that "has a great mind to be married, . . . a grudging of good will that way, and would as fain be despatched." If written by G. Bernard Shaw it would be more witty, certainly more clean, and people would acclaim it as a convincing drama of the Life Force; but even as it is, it compares favorably with *Man and Superman*. The conversation in Hell between Shaw's Ana and Don Juan may be more philosophic than that in Paris of Fletcher's Oriana and Mirabel; but the Shavian characters are hardly less flamboyantly nude than the Fletcherian in their conception of sexual relations. While the Elizabethan Oriana is physically disgusted by the obscenity of her Mirabel's language, the Edwardian Ann Whitefield, to whose twentieth century ear obscenity is foreign, could hardly be figured as disgusted by anything, provided only she fulfilled her procreative destiny.

The best piece of characterization in Fletcher's play is Oriana's response to Mirabel's loathsome disdainer of feminine charm: "Are you not ashamed, Sir?" Anything, however, like genuine interest in her is negatived by the persistent *dementia* of her love-sickness. Her victim, "a travelled Don Juan" as Ward describes him, is one of the most repulsive gallants of English comedy,—of "insolent licentious carriage," a cad of most turbid water, manifestly not worth pursuit. Her associates in the man-hunt, the "airy daughters of Nantolet," Rosalura—"of a free behaviour," and Lillia-Bianca—"a little haughty, of a small body, and a mind well-mounted," are acutely differenced save in their surprising knowledge of matters which are not ordinarily supposed to be the subject of maidenly conversation. "Are not we alone and merry?" says Lillia to her sister,—"Why should we be ashamed to speak what we think?" And, unashamed, they think it with a vengeance. The success of the play

—and it was not only well received at its first acting and many times after, but was revived as late as the middle of the eighteenth century,—the success of the play proceeds not from the characterization but from the witty and the farcically complicated intrigue. By dint of endless disguisings and cleverly trumped up situations the tables are eight times turned with proper alternation upon hunters and hunted. Nor is the humour of these reversals confined to the relations of hero and heroine; it is as boisterous and effective in the cross-purposes of the daughters of Nantolet and their suitors-pursued. Fletcher is here reviving the method of that earlier comedy of intrigue, *The Scornful Ladie*, but with an inversion,—for that was a woman-hunt,—and with an abandonment of even the decency due to probabilities. The earlier play was coarse, especially in the scenes which Beaumont did not write; but the coarseness might be excised, and the plot suffer little. To cut the obscenity from Fletcher's unassisted *Wild-Goose Chase*, would be to cut out the vitals. Farquhar's experiment in *The Inconstant* (1702) for which he says he "took the hint from *The Wild-Goose Chase*" was not exactly successful. It should not, however, be adduced in evidence; for though the conception, the two leading characters, some of their speeches and some of the incidents are borrowed, the intrigue is radically altered, the dialogue is essentially Farquhar's and the interest is differently sustained. But even so the interest is inseparable from the vulgarity which distinguishes the theme. Commenting upon the recovery and publication of *The Wild-Goose Chase*, in 1652, Lovelace sets it beside the "emerald" of *The Mad Lover*, the "ruby" of *The Loyall Subject*, the "diamond" of *The Maides Tragedy*, as "one carbuncle that darkens all." It is "one carbuncle," but not of the mineral world.

In the comedies which I have classed as of intrigue, Fletcher deteriorates as he advances. The best was written while Beaumont was still living. And though, in *The Chances*, Beaumont did not coöperate, it is not unreasonable to conjecture that his superior judgment and restraining taste may have exercised some influence upon the author. With delightful certitude Hazlitt, speaking of the pure comedies in general, insists that *Rule a Wife*, *The Chances* and *The Wild-Goose Chase* "are superior in style and execution to anything of Ben Jonson's. They are, indeed, some of the best comedies on the stage; and one proof that they are so, is that they still (in 1820) hold possession of it." Concerning the first of these plays the verdict may be regarded as not without a grain of justice. *The Chances* has dramatic and conventional quality adaptable to the requirements of the modern stage, but its literary merits are slight. *The Wild-Goose Chase* is impossible.

16. Fletcher in Heroic-romantic Comedy and Tragicomedy

Of four romantic comedies written between 1618 and 1621, the three of which description immediately follows have value for the student of dramatic literature. *The Loyall Subject* (1618), based upon Paynter's translation of one of Bandello's tales, is, as the Master of Peterhouse has said, "spirited," distinguished by "ease of construction, naturalness of development, and variety of character," and worthy to be regarded as "one of Fletcher's masterpieces, exhibiting his chief gifts as a dramatist, within the limits to which they are restricted." But those limits are narrow at the best; and therefore, I cannot call the play "altogether admirable." Compared with the heroic-romantic dramas in which the authorship of Beaumont completely outshadows that of Fletcher, *Philaster* and *A King and no King*, this production is but second-rate. In mere stagecraft Fletcher, as usual, excels: the exposition is rapid and provocative of immediate curiosity. The twofold interest in romantic loyalty and romantic love is evenly sustained. But the "naturalness of development" is histrionic: it falls away if one questions for a moment the naturalness of the premises. The hero's spirit of loyalty is exaggerated, if not beyond probability, at any rate beyond common sense. When loyalty becomes maudlin, it not only loses elevation,—it ceases to convince. The action of this old general, Archas, in sending his daughters to a court that he knows to be corrupt, ruled by a duke whom he knows to be his foe, is motivated not in loyalty but stiff-necked idiocy. To be "drunk with duty" is admirable up to a certain point, but it is no longer dramatic when the hero "like a woodcock thrusts his neck i' the noose." The general's affection for his soldiers is inspiring and pathetic, but his Brutan severity towards his devoted and heroic son is delirious. In brief, we reject the presupposition underlying most of the loyal subject's actions; and we find that the conversions and pardons of the dénouement huddle what there was of natural in the development to an unnatural conclusion. Some of the characters, too, that give promise of great attractiveness proceed incontinently to alienate our sympathy. Why should the noble brothers, Theodore and Young Archas, deem it necessary to caution their sisters against the unchastity of court in language of the bawdiest smack? Viola and Honora know already that their sojourn with the Duke is to be as it were a week-end in a house of ill-fame. Did the dramatist imagine that this supererogatory indecency was justifiable as a foil to their decency? Or did he think that any audience, even Jacobean, could consider virginal purity so exceptional as to be abnormal? The sisters may appear to some over-wise,—the naïveté and humour of Honora's conquest of the Duke, forthputting and priggish and unmaidenly,—but it must be remembered that the twain are endowed with Fletcher's wit as well as with their own innocence. One of the few Fletcherian women who neither speak nor think wantonly, nor yet are assailed by licentious conversation, and who, while beautiful, are not, like Constantia of *The Chances*, shadows, but integral figures in the life of the plot, is the princess, Olympia. Her love for Young Archas disguised as Alinda has its reminiscence of Olivia's for Viola; and the reappearance of Young Archas in his proper guise inquiring the fate of his lost sister-self Alinda, finds its converse and inspiration in Beaumont's last scene of Aspatia. But this pretty love-affair, with the scenes in which Theodore displays his filial devotion and those that portray the devotion of the soldiery to Archas, is one of the most dramatic in the play. The literary quality is of the rhetorical strain to which heroic poetry lends itself. Though we hear the clamour of insurrection and the clash of arms, and see the effects of torture, the play is not genuine tragicomedy; for the conflict is factitious, and the suffering and the threatened death fail to awaken any semblance of apprehension or pathos. The play, as one might presage from its extravagant conception of loyalty, was popular after the Restoration; but, though altered and revived in the early eighteenth century, not even its cleverness and its diction could maintain it upon the stage to-day.

The Humorous Lieutenant (1619) has enduring vitality, though not because of its tragicomic presupposition. The wars and rumours of war are rhetorical or humorous; the devilish plans of the King upon the chastity of the heroine, predestined to failure; and the announcement of her death, a dramatic device which may impose upon the credulity of her noble lover but not upon an audience. In the manuscript of 1625 it is styled "a pleasant comedie"; and such it is, of 'humour' and romantic love, upon a background of the heroic. It is Fletcher's best comedy of the kind; one of the best of the later Shakespearian age. The conception of the Lieutenant, whose humour is to fight when he is plagued by loathsome disease and wench when he is well, is not original, nor the character of the hero Demetrius; but in the elaboration Fletcher has created them anew, surrounded them with other figures no less life-like, and set them in a plot, cunningly welded of comic, sentimental, and martial elements, and largely of his own invention. Though the interest is partly in a wanton intrigue, and the mirth grossly animal even when not bawdy, I think that the objectionable qualities are for one of a few times in Fletcher's career in comedy, not ineradicable. The wondrous charm, "matchless spirit," vivacity, and constancy of Celia render the machinations of Leucippe and her "office of concealments" futile,—so much dramatic realism to be accentuated or mitigated at the will of the stage manager,—and the alluring offers of the King are but so many instruments for his own defeat. I fear, indeed, that if the Lieutenant were not an indissoluble compound of hero, swashbuckler, shirker, and "stinkard," he would lose his savour. But the love of Rabelaisian humour is ingrained in the male of the species, and if the license be not nauseating, it is not necessarily damnable. This boisterous, pocky rascal who "never had but two hours yet of happiness," and who courts the battle-field to save him "from the surgeon's miseries," held the stage from the time of Condell, Taylor and Lowin, to that of Macready and Liston; and there is no reason why his vitality should not be perennial. There are few more ludicrous scenes in farcical literature than those in which, having drained a philtre intended to make Celia dote upon the King, the Lieutenant imagines himself a handsome wench of fifteen, wooes the King most dotingly, and kisses the royal horses as they pass by. The meeting and parting, the trials and reunion, of Celia and Demetrius constitute the most convincing and attractive romantic-pathetic love-affair in drama since Shakespeare ceased to write. Indeed, this "perilous crafty," spirited, "angel-eyed" girl, "too honest for them all," who so ingeniously and modestly shames the lustful monarch and wins her affianced prince, is not unworthy of the master. Nor is Demetrius. The play contains many genuinely poetic passages, and some of those lines of sudden beauty—"our lives are but our marches to the grave"—in which Beaumont abounded, and that Fletcher too rarely coined. With all the rankness of its humour, the comedy has such high literary and dramatic excellence that one cannot but regret the infrequency with which Fletcher produced that of which he was capable.[1] It enjoyed six revivals between 1663 and 1767. At Covent Garden, in 1756 and 1757, the part of Demetrius was taken by Barry, that of the Lieutenant by Shuter; and Peg Woffington made a great success in Celia. Ten years later, Woodward played Demetrius, and Mrs. Bellamy, Celia. And when, in January 1817, Reynolds, for the same theatre, condensed the five acts into three and interspersed them with music (not an improvement, said the critics), the rôles of Demetrius, the Lieutenant and Celia, were assumed respectively by no less actors than Macready, Liston, and Helen Faucit.

In *The Pilgrim* (1621) Fletcher makes use of an English translation, of the same year, of a French version of one of Lope de Vega's prose romances.[2] This is the cleanest, and one of the most vivacious, of the author's romantic

---

[1] For this analysis, and that of *A Wife for a Month*, below, see my *Beaumont, the Dramatist*, pp. 399–406.

[2] Rosenbach, as quoted by Schelling, *Eliz. Dr.* II, 208.

comedies. In altered form it held the stage through the seventeenth and eighteenth centuries, and down to 1812. With but a few excisions the original might be acceptably presented to-day. The scene is bathed in an atmosphere of romance; the exposition is a model of comprehensiveness, directness, and interest; the plot (not altogether de Vega's), delightfully fantastic; the runaway Alinda,—with her witty ingenuity and not too love-lorn heart,—and that "pretty desperate thing," her maid Juletta, worthy successors of the heroines of Arden. The tragic menace is but a scarecrow: every one knows that Alinda will rescue the pilgrim-lover from the outlaw-suitor. The disguisings are multitudinous, but the plot requires them; and they are so natural, and so transparent to everybody but those whom they should deceive, that even one in reading welcomes them. The romantic situations turn upon cunning and sometimes dainty devices, and the humorous upon a realism,—as that of the scenes in the madhouse, and the inveigling of the irascible father into temporary confinement,—not often surpassed in the age immediately following Shakespeare.

The *Island Princesse* (1621), is of little value to the student of comedy. As a play of the heroic type, it indicates, however, that Fletcher, when dealing with themes of serious love, valour, and religious constancy, was capable of elevated thought and eloquence, even sublimity of expression. But the rhetoric too frequently leaves us unmoved, because it is devoid of any semblance of vivid emotion. The author has visualized neither character nor conflict; and the reader looks in vain for the spontaneity, pathos, and compelling poetry with which Beaumont would have glorified material and environment of such romantic potentiality. The personages lack psychological shading; and the movement, though forthright, spectacular, and varied by histrionic surprises, could not, nowadays, hold an audience more than once. The bustling realism of the minor scenes and the cynical humour of Piniero supply some comic diversion. That bluff soldier, though he "talk but coarsely," is a shrewd observer of life and an amusing commentator; and his "lecture" of the "doors of Destiny" comes nearer the level of philosophical imagination than anything else in the play. That *The Island Princesse* enjoyed some popularity after the Restoration is proof rather of the poverty of the stage than of dramatic merit.

Of these romantic comedies, two, *The Humorous Lieutenant* and *The Pilgrim*, are in my opinion still possessed of dramatic vitality.

Passing to the two tragicomedies of Fletcher's sole authorship, one need but repeat concerning the earlier the verdict of lovers of literature. While *The Faithfull Shepheardesse* (1608) is of no value for the stage, intrinsically undramatic and morally cynical, it must always live as poetry;

and in the history of the pastoral drama it will occupy a place beside Jonson's *Sad Shepherd* and Milton's *Comus*. From *The Faithfull Shepheardesse* to *A Wife for a Month* (1624) is not so clearly from Hyperion to Priapus as one may think, for the former is but a subtly satiric lord of the morning. The latter is instructive in more ways than one: it illustrates Fletcher's skill in construction and his disregard of probability; his sense of moral conflict and his insensibility to moral beauty; his power to conceive characteristic situations and his recurrent impotence in the development of natural characters; his capability of noble sentiment and poetic expression and his beastly perverseness of fancy; his prostitution of art to sordid sensationalism. The story of the cumulative torments to which a lustful usurper subjects the maiden, Evanthe, whom he desires, and Valerio whom she loves, is graphically estimated by one of the *dramatis personæ*, "This tyranny could never be invented But in the school of Hell: earth is too innocent." Beside it Zola's *l'Assommoir* smells sweet; and a nightmare lacks nothing of probability. Ugly, however, as the fundamental assumption is: namely that the tyrant should permit a wedding on condition that at the end of a month the husband shall suffer death,—and with provision that, meanwhile, the honeymoon shall be surrounded with restrictions more intolerable than death itself; and incredible as is the contrivance of the sequel, kept a-going by the suppression of instinct and common sense on the part of the hero, and withheld from its proper tragic conclusion by a miraculous cure, an impossible conversion, and an unnatural clemency,—the plot is after all deftly knit, and the interest sustained with baleful fascination. But it would be difficult to instance in Jacobean drama a more incongruous juxtaposition of complication morally conceived and execution callously coarsened than that offered by the scene between Valerio and Evanthe on their wedding-night. In the corresponding scene of *The Maides Tragedy* (II, i), Beaumont had created a model: Amintor bears himself with dignity toward his shameless and contemptuous bride. But in Fletcher's play it is the woman who makes the advances; and she makes them not only without dignity, but with an unmaidenly persistence and persuasiveness of which any abandoned 'baggage' might be ashamed. And, still, the dramatist is never weary of assuring us that she is the soul of honour "mingled with noble chastity," and clad in "all the graces" that nature can give. In the various other trying situations in which Evanthe is placed it is requisite to our conviction of reality that she be the "virtuous bud of beauty": but the tongue of this virtuous "bud" blossoms into Billingsgate; she swears "something awful," and she displays an acquaintance with sexual pathology that would delight the heart even of the most rabid twentieth-century advocate of sex-hygiene for boys and girls in the public schools. Two or three of the characters, indeed, are nobly conceived and, on occasion, contrive to utter themselves with nobility. Valerio achieves poetry when he says of the shortness of his prospective joys:

> "A Paradise, as thou art, my Evanthe,
> Is only made to wonder at a little,
> Enough for human eyes, and then to wander from,"—

and when he describes the graces of spiritual love. And the Queen's thoughts upon death, though melodramatic, have something of the dignity of Beaumont's style. But otherwise the minds of the principal personages reflect not only the flashing current but the dead waters of Fletcher's thought. The passion, save for Valerio's, is lurid, and the humour latrinal. To sketch the bestial in narrative, however fleeting, is inartistic; to fix it on canvas is offensive; to posture it upon the stage is unpardonable. The last is practically what Fletcher has done here; and the wonder is that he appears to think that he is justifying virtue.

Fletcher has fancy, facile and fertile, and emotionality of word, rhetoric, and situation. But there is little pathos of character in Fletcher's unassisted plays, little of the tragic compulsion, sublimity, sudden imaginative splendour that dignify the creations of Beaumont; none of his moral earnestness, philosophical spontaneity and depth. When Fletcher's dramatic figures, moving with all the ease of well-oiled mechanism, are not manufactured, they are exogens proceeding by external deposit. They do not vitalize the plot, they exemplify it. They interest us and amuse; they hold us often in suspense,—but not in the suspense of motive, complex or subtle, nor of native uncertainty or probability. Their uncertainty is of dramatic device, crisis, and dénouement; their probability is of clever artifice, of manipulated narrative; and their passion is theatrical. His characters, in other words, are not of the world but of the stage. When the women of his comedies are virtuous they are, but too often, knowing; when vicious, disgusting. His men, when they are 'gentle,' are frivolous, fatuous or hypocritical, fantastically chivalrous or profligate; when base-born, they are unconvincingly bluff and honest, monstrously braggart and cowardly, or jocosely obscene. Of course, there are exceptions, as of instances already indicated; but though Fletcher's insight is shrewd, his judgment is seduced by clap-trap.

In dramatic dialogue he excels. It is witty, easy, natural beyond that of most of his predecessors and contemporaries. But with all its vivacity and its continual fillip to the action, it rarely reveals subtle hues and twilights of character. His humour, too, though frequently effective is boisterous rather than hearty. It is of the situation or the extravagant eccentricity: adventitious and better suited to the momentary amusement of the spectator, than to the delight of the reader.

Comedy should be of character. Fletcher's comedy is supremely of plot; and his plots are all 'business.' Here lies his strength as playwright,—in the hurry and thrill of crisis; here, too, his weakness and his vicious influence as comic dramatist. In tragedy, plot must be supreme; because plot means conflict, and conflict breeds passion. In comedy—high comedy—on the other hand, situation, sequence, and surprise exist not for the development of conflict but of that interplay of character by which the individual is adjusted to society; and not passion is bred nor mere curiosity of plot-interest, but "thoughtful laughter." In subordinating characterization and the comic catharsis of the individual to the fascinations of crisis and dénouement, Fletcher was setting an example which furthered the decadence of Elizabethan comedy. In tragicomedy, the lure of plot and passion has, of course, more warrant,—and in romantic comedy; but in none of his own plays of the more serious type, not even in tragedy, does Fletcher attain the level of the plays in which Beaumont collaborated; for, in spite of Fletcher's undoubted genius for dramatic "business," the qualities which lift the Beaumont-Fletcher plays to the region of high and enduring art are Beaumont's lyrical characterization and poetic poignancy, his vision of human sunsets and shooting globes of fire, and his large utterance of the earlier gods.

17. The Fletcher Syndicate, 1613–1625

After the cessation of Beaumont's activity Fletcher collaborated with others in eighteen comedies and tragicomedies. To thirteen of these Massinger contributed. In one or two Shirley is detected; Rowley in, perhaps, one; and other authors unknown in four or five. Much of the confusion which existed in the minds of readers and critics during the period following the Restoration, concerning the respective productivity of Beaumont and Fletcher, and the merits of each, is due to the facts that the quartos of individual plays in circulation were, as often as not, wrong in their ascriptions of authorship to one, or the other, or both of the dramatists; and that the folio of 1647, the more common source of information, lacked title-pages to individual plays and, save in one instance, prefixed no name of author to any play. The exception is *The Maske of Grayes Inne and the Inner Temple* "written by Francis Beaumont, Gentleman," which had been previously published in quarto as Beaumont's. In some half-dozen instances, Fletcher is indicated in the 1647 folio by Prologue or

Epilogue as author or author revised, and in general correctly, but otherwise the thirty-four comedies and tragedies here printed (exclusive of *The Maske*) for the first time, are introduced to the public by the general title-page, as if jointly "written by Francis Beaumont and John Fletcher, Gentlemen, . . . and now published by the authours originall copies." That the public should have been generally deceived is not surprising. Beaumont had a hand in but one of those plays, for certain, *The Coxcombe*. His presence is conjectured in two others, *The Captaine* and *The Four Playes*,—but in my opinion without confirmation.[1] Fletcher is sole author of eleven. Massinger appears, perhaps with others unknown, in one, *Loves Cure;* with Fletcher, in eight, and with Fletcher and others in five more. Field assisted in two or three. Rowley in at least one, maybe two. Among the other collaborators, actual or surmised, are Ben Jonson, Tourneur, Shirley, Daborne and Middleton. In at least five plays Fletcher had no share whatever.

The confusion is redoubled in the second folio, entitled "Fifty Comedies and Tragedies. Written by Francis Beaumont and John Fletcher, Gentlemen. . . . Published by the authors original copies, (etc.) 1679." There are fifty-three plays in the volume; the thirty-five of the first folio and eighteen previously printed but not before gathered together. The eighteen include five that are the joint product of Beaumont and Fletcher, *The Maides Tragedy, Philaster, A King and no King, The Scornful Ladie* and *Cupids Revenge;* two that are frequently regarded as their joint-products, but in which Fletcher had almost no part, *The Knight of the Burning Pestle* and *The Woman-Hater;* five of Fletcher's sole authorship; five in which he collaborated with others than Beaumont; and one, *The Coronation*, principally by Shirley. As in the 1647 folio, the only indication of respective authorship is to be found in occasional dedications, prefaces, prologues and epilogues. But, while in some half-dozen instances these name Fletcher correctly as author, and in two or three, by implication, correctly designate him or Beaumont, in other cases the indication is wrong or misleading. Where "our poets" are vaguely mentioned, or no hint whatever is given, the uncritical reader is led to ascribe the play to the joint composition of Beaumont and Fletcher. The lists of actors prefixed to several of the dramas afford valuable information concerning date and, sometimes, authorship to the student of stage-history; but the credulous would carry away the impression that Beaumont and Fletcher had collaborated equally in about forty of the fifty-three plays contained in the folio of 1679. Even the scholar of the Restoration rarely went back of the folios to the quartos; and the quartos, as I have said, are frequently wrong

[1] In both Fletcher was assisted by others.

in their attributions of authorship. Rymer includes *Rollo* among the
most applauded plays of the two greater poets, though it was not written
till after Beaumont's death. Dryden praises it, but with no inkling of the
fact that Massinger wrote as much of it as Fletcher, and that probably
other hands contributed as much as either. And in spite of the results of
modern criticism writers of to-day follow the old suit.[1] Dryden commends
Fletcher especially for the unraveling of the plot in *A King and no King*,
whereas the unraveling is part of Beaumont's preponderating share in that
play. Writing in 1668 or 1671, the same critic describes the folio of 1647
as the joint work of Beaumont and Fletcher; and cites by name, as their
productions in common, *The Chances*, *Rule a Wife*, *The Spanish Curate*,
and *The Little French Lawyer*, although none of these plays, save perhaps
the first, was written till after Beaumont's death, and in the last two Fletcher's associate was Massinger. Langbaine repeats the error; and so *ad
indefinitum*.

Of the plays in which Beaumont had no hand, produced in joint com-
position by members of the Fletcher syndicate, twenty-two are comedies.
In at least eighteen of these, as I have said, Fletcher coöperated; in thirteen
Massinger; and in eleven both. Of the twenty-two only nine, so far as I
have observed, were revived after the Restoration: in one, *The Night
Walker*, Shirley appears as reviser of Fletcher; in a second *The Maid in the
Mill*, Rowley was associated with Fletcher, and perhaps in a third, *The
Noble Gentleman*. The remaining six are by Fletcher and Massinger.
Two of them *The Custome of the Countrey* and *The Elder Brother* did not
long survive as acting plays. The others were still seen upon the stage
after the third quarter of the eighteenth century: *The Little French Lawyer*
as late as 1778; *The Prophetesse*, in 1784; *Beggers Bush* in 1815, and *The
Spanish Curate*, in 1840. A careful study of these four convinces me that
Massinger's contribution was fully as important as Fletcher's. In fact,
in all but *The Prophetesse*, the general design—that is to say, the main
plot and the conduct of the action—appears to be the work of the former.
Fletcher fills in the details of comic business, of lively but superficial
characterization and of intrigue.

For the purposes of our study, we may at once accept the verdict of
posterity by which *The Custome*, *The Night Walker* and *The Maid in the
Mill* were again speedily consigned to oblivion: the first and second are
offensive, and the third is weak. Of the thirteen comedies which did not
survive even the Restoration I shall presently mention two as worthy of

---

[1] *E. g.* Tupper on *The Relation of the Heroic Plays to the Romances of B. & F.* (*Mod.
Phil.* 1905). For more extended treatment of this subject, see my *Beaumont, the
Dramatist*, Part Two.

a better fate. The rest include certain in which the coöperation or revision of Field, Daborne, Tourneur, Middleton, Rowley, Shirley, and, as in the case of *Loves Pilgrimage*, Jonson, is determined or conjectured; but in spite of purple patches none of them is an indispensable contribution to the development of comedy or the enrichment of literature.

The six comedies longest retained upon the stage have the merit of representing the various trends of the syndicate in tragicomedy, romantic comedy and the comedy of manners; and at least three of them anticipate movements characteristic of the Restoration drama. *The Prophetesse*— in itself a worthless tragicomedy, with its romantic localization, elevated personages, perpetual emphasis upon strained sentiments of honour, valour, and love, its violent contrasts and its spectacular appeal—is a precursor, though by no means most representative, of the heroic play. *The Little French Lawyer*, a comedy of disjointed construction, but of keen and frequently amusing satiric intent, attains moderate historic merit in its ridicule of the sophisticated motives of honour which were to dominate the heroic play of Davenant and Dryden. *The Spanish Curate* carries forward the course of romantic comedy; but is historically notable for a subplot (manifestly by Fletcher) which, in its comic intrigue of shrewd device and witty dialogue, anticipates the comedy of manners of the succeeding age. *Beggers Bush*, also a romantic comedy, was to have a successor in comic extravaganza in *The Joviall Crew* of Brome; and, later still, as Professor Baker observes, in Gay's ballad opera of Polly and Captain Macheath. But it is to Fletcher's manipulation of the picaresque,—the vivid portraiture of the manners and humours of the wandering commonwealth,—and not to Massinger's thin romance, that the play owes its success. Of these four productions *The Spanish Curate*, alone, was possessed of qualities, both literary and dramatic, sufficient to justify a long and brilliant career; but even so, its mixture of lust and laughter is unlikely to be revived.

From the critical point of view we cannot altogether concur in the verdict of the theatre concerning the respective merits of the plays produced by the Fletcherian syndicate. Four other dramas in which Fletcher coöperated, have inherent vitality and power excelling those of *The Prophetesse*, *The Little French Lawyer*, and *Beggers Bush;* and they are of equal if not greater importance in the history of comedy. *The Knight of Malta*, to which Massinger and another, maybe Field, contributed, and *The Lovers Progresse*, in which Massinger's collaboration, or revision, is evident, definitely develop tendencies characteristic of the later heroic play. Not only are they among the most typical of Fletcherian heroic tragicomedies in their violent contrasts of passion and their delicate handling of ideals of chivalry, love, and self-sacrifice, they display splendour of elevated personage and circumstance and an eloquent but sophisticated dialectic concerning moral categories which clearly anticipate the efforts of Davenant and Dryden. I do not find that these tragicomedies were revived; but they are equipped with sentiment, romance and poetry of a high literary order; and the characterization and movement in both might be envied by many another play more fortunate in theatrical longevity. Two comedies of manners, also, though revived after 1660, have been neglected by the later stage: one romantic—*The Elder Brother*, the other satiric, *The Noble Gentleman*,—of quality superior to *The Little French Lawyer* and *Beggers Bush*, in either kind. They were adapted, the former by Colley Cibber, the latter by Sheridan Knowles, but with no outcome in continuance. In *The Elder Brother*, Fletcher and Massinger are paving the way for the comedy of sentiment, wit, and manners of Congreve, Vanbrugh, and Sheridan. The excision of vulgarity from the minor scenes would but enhance the romantic originality and comic freshness of a play in all essentials worthy to hold a modern audience. *The Noble Gentleman*, by Fletcher and another, maybe Rowley, licensed the year after Fletcher's death, is a revivification of the device of the *Induction* of the *Taming of the Shrew*, and of the action of *M. D'Olive;* but the later authors have carried the Shakespearian device into the main action, and have improved upon Chapman's technique in unity, dramatic irony, and comic surprise. The ambitious gull is no more life-like than Monsieur D'Olive, but he is a better pivot for the farcical whirl of delusion; and he is surrounded by a more cunningly diversified circle of tormentors. Here the dramatists are providing a model for Sheridan and his contemporaries in the manners comedy of mental delusion and practical joke; and here, again, the humorous characterization and incisive satire are of merit sufficient to warrant the revival of the play upon the modern stage.

Massinger's share in so large a number of the syndicate plays is determined by tests well-known to critics: a higher percentage of double endings than that employed by any other of his contemporaries but Fletcher; a higher percentage of run-on lines than even Beaumont's,—four times as high as Fletcher's; a greater ease, and at the same time variety, of metrical rhythm and of pause than are characteristic of either of those dramatists; an emphasis of light syllables and endings, and a habit of dividing the line between speakers that produces the impression of prose utterance. His repetitious phrases, figures, and literary allusions continually betray him. They have been listed by Boyle, Oliphant and other scholars. He is recognizable also in a lack of emotional spontaneity and of creativity in characterization; in his deliberate, argumentative and oratorical, style, and his moral earnestness; and no less in his vigorous and practical stage-craft. The presence of Rowley, Daborne, Field and others in what I have called the Fletcher syndicate is attested by evidence external and internal, not always definite in detail but in the mass convincing.

18. The Theatrical Companies, 1625–1642

Between 1625 and the closing of the theatres the London companies of actors are the King's, Queen Henrietta's, 1625, the new King's Revels, 1629, the Prince's (formerly the Palsgrave's) 1631, and Beeston's Boys, 1637.

The King's, now under the patronage of Charles I, took over some of the best actors from the company that he had patronized as Prince Charles; and, thus reinforced, they continued to play at the Globe and Blackfriars, under the leadership of Lowin and Taylor. Beside their old plays they were acting in the City those especially of Massinger: of the twenty written by him alone or in collaboration with others than Fletcher, between 1622 and 1636, only five or six were presented by other companies. As late as 1633 they are presenting new comedies from Ben Jonson; and from Ford they have recently had two striking dramas. Of the generation younger still, Jonson's "faithful servant and loving friend," Richard Brome, writes for them between 1629 and 1634, a long series of comedies. By 1636, that "limb of Fletcher, Davenant" has supplied them with seven plays; and minor writers, such as Glapthorne and Carlell are producing for them tragedies and tragicomedies of the heroic kind. Soon they are to have the coöperation of Mayne and Killigrew and of the last of the great dramatists of the pre-Restoration period, James Shirley. At Court, meanwhile, beside more modern plays they had continued to perform Shakespeare, Beaumont, Fletcher, Massinger; and they closed, at the outbreak of the Civil War, with *The Scornful Ladie* on Twelfth Night 1642. In the ten years preceding they had appeared before royalty at least a hundred times; and we have not the complete record. Not even their rivals, Queen Henrietta's men, had appeared more than one-third as often. From the primacy of Marlowe down, through Shakespeare, Fletcher, Massinger, Shirley, the company enjoyed a succession of masters of the drama such as no other company could boast. And of actors, as well. At King James's funeral in 1625, Burbadge was missing; but Heming and Condell of the older generation marched, and John Lowin and Joseph Taylor of the younger. These last, with Robinson and Pollard, were of the King's on Twelfth Night, 1642; and Lowin and Taylor in their issue of the folio of Fletcher's *Wild-Goose Chase*, 1652, still take pride in styling themselves "servants to his late majesty."

Queen Henrietta's company, which came into existence with the new reign, is second in importance only to the King's. Its manager was Christopher Beeston from the Queen of Bohemia's (the Lady Elizabeth's) company; and from the same company, as well as from the list of those who had belonged to Queen Anne's, it drew several of its principal actors. Its theatre was the Cockpit until 1637, when, surrendering that play-house to the newly organized Beeston's Boys, it joined the King's Revels at Salisbury Court. There, as Queen's men, this amalgamated body of actors performed till 1642. The Queen's had not only excellent players but a repertory by most of the best contemporary writers,—about twenty of Shirley's plays, five of Massinger's which had been written for the Queen of Bohemia's men, as many more of Middleton and Rowley's written for that company or the former Prince Charles's before 1624, one or two by Heywood and Webster written for Queen Anne's, and plays by Richard Brome, and by Davenport, Nabbes and other recent authors. A few also by Beaumont and Fletcher had descended to them; but they played only two of Jonson's and none of Shakespeare's. Between 1633 and 1639 they appeared at Court some thirty times.

When in 1629, the Salisbury Court Theatre was opened in Whitefriars it was occupied by a newly organized **King's Revels' company,** recruited partly from the Palsgrave's and Queen Henrietta's. Between 1632 and 1635 it played at the Fortune, but in the latter year returned to Salisbury Court. In 1637 it was absorbed into the Queen's company, which had removed to that theatre. Beyond the fact that the new King's Revels' men acted Shirley's comedy of *The Changes* and three of Richard Brome's plays, and that they appeared nine times at Court between 1631 and 1636, there is no evidence of their importance. They had, however, some well-known actors,—Wm. Cartwright, Sr., for instance, who had been an Admiral's man as early as 1602, Bourne (or Bird), and the eminent comedian, John Robinson.

In 1631 the Fortune company (formerly the Palsgrave's) regained something of its old prestige by passing under the patronage of the baby Prince Charles (afterwards Charles II). It is henceforth known as the **Prince's men.** Giving up the Fortune to the new King's Revels it played at Salisbury Court, till 1635. Between 1635 and 1639 it was probably at the Red Bull. In 1640 it closed its London career at the scene of its earlier triumphs in the day of Henslowe and Alleyn. The favour of these actors with the King, though at no time great, is attested by their accompanying him on a progress to Scotland in 1633; and by the fact that, between

1634 and 1639, they were summoned at least thirteen times to entertain the Court. Among their comedies were a few of Marmion's imitations of Ben Jonson, and of Nabbes's somewhat fresher presentations of London manners and intrigue.

Of much greater note, in a certain sense the legatee at the Cockpit of Queen Henrietta's men,—is the King and Queen's company of Children, established in 1637 and known commonly, from its manager, as **Beeston's Boys.** Through their organizer they form a link with the pre-Jacobean theatre, for Christopher Beeston had played with the Chamberlain's company, and with Shakespeare himself, in *Every Man in his Humour* at the Curtain in 1598. That was before the Globe was built. He had later been one of Worcester's company and one of the principal members of its continuator, Queen Anne's. After that Queen's death he had become a member of the Lady Elizabeth's, but since 1625 had been at the head of Queen Henrietta's. When the last mentioned company left the Cockpit to Beeston and his boys, it evidently vacated its right to a large number of plays that it had acted there. Forty-five of them are enumerated in an order of 1639, which forbids any company other than Beeston's to present them. From this list we derive most of our information concerning the repertory of the Queen's company, as given above. Beside fourteen plays of Shirley, including *The Example, The Young Admirall, The Grateful Servant* and *The Lady of Pleasure,* the list contains many other comedies of distinction, Fletcher's *Wit Without Money,* Beaumont's *The Knight of the Burning Pestle,* Massinger's *Bondman, New Way,* and *Great Duke of Florence,* Middleton and Rowley's *Faire Quarrell* and *Spanish Gipsie,* one or two by Dekker, and one by Green and Lodge. The Boys had, also, at least six of Brome's comedies,—among them *The Antipodes;* and something of the work of Nabbes, Marmion and Glapthorne. Their plays in the city, therefore, were up to date; and they acted occasionally at Court. But like the Children's companies of older time, they quickly got themselves into trouble by personalities offensive to royalty. In 1640 Beeston's son William, who had become manager, was dismissed. William Davenant took his place; and with Davenant we are embarked upon a new era. For, though the King and Queen's Young Company went out of existence with other companies in 1642, it, nevertheless, through its last director, its latest plays, and its theatre, constitutes a link between the earlier Stuart drama and the drama of the Restoration.[1]

[1] For materials of this section, see Murray's *English Dramatic Companies,* Fleay's *Hist. Stage,* and their sources.

19. The Beginnings of Modern Literary Comedy: Massinger, Brome, Shirley

Professor Neilson has laid just emphasis upon the consideration that, while the playwrights of the Elizabethan period had studied and imitated the products of preceding English dramatists, such study had for the most part been carried on in the theatre itself; but, that after the publication in 1623 of the first folio of Shakespeare, and indeed after that of the Jonson folio of 1616, playwrights could "brood over and assimilate the works of those and other masters"; and that, consequently, drama came from that time on to be regarded as literature, or at any rate, potential literature. Dramatists began to write "with a view to being read as well as heard." In dealing, therefore, with the works of Ford and Shirley, this scholar considers that "we are discussing not merely the last phase of Elizabethan theatrical activity, but also the first chapter of what may be called, in a special sense, modern dramatic literature." [1]

As the earlier conscious producers of modern literary comedy—for Ford's genius was predominantly tragic,—I should name Massinger, Shirley and Brome. These authors have been so fully discussed in the essays which follow that it remains for me but to emphasize their position in relation to the historical sequence of the type which we are considering. Massinger was only twenty years of age when James ascended the throne, and he died two years before the outbreak of the Civil War. Brome, from two to twelve years younger than Massinger, survived the Civil War, and died only in the year in which Cromwell assumed the title of Lord Protector. Shirley, but seven when Elizabeth died, wrote all his plays before the closing of the theatres in 1642, but he lived on to witness the revival of the drama under the Restoration. These three were dramatists exclusively of the early Stuart period.

The characteristics of Stuart comedy, as distinguished from that of the Elizabethan influence, have already defined themselves with growing clearness of detail in Middleton's irresponsible comedies of Jacobean London, in some of Chapman's and Marston's dramas, the later romantic plays of Shakespeare, the tragicomedies and romantic dramas of Beaumont and Fletcher and the earlier tragicomedies of Middleton and Rowley. Its characteristics in the heroic-romantic drama and the comedy of intrigue and of manners became increasingly obvious in the product of Fletcher's sole authorship after Shakespeare's withdrawal from the active management of the Globe.

Philip Massinger is the first important dramatist whose productions,

[1] *Camb. Hist. Lit.*, VI, 212.   Art. *Ford and Shirley*.

whether comic or tragic, of unaided authorship or in collaboration with men trained in the older school, are both distinctively Stuart in their characteristics and fall exclusively in the period following the cessation of Shakespeare's dramatic activity. Appearing first as joint-author, with Fletcher, Daborne and Field, of a play, perhaps *The Honest Man's Fortune*, about July 1613, for the Lady Elizabeth's company, he writes almost altogether for what may after that year be called Fletcher's company of the King's men, not only until Fletcher's death in 1625, but till his own. The elder dramatist during his supremacy, no longer inspired by Beaumont or restrained by Shakespeare, was producing not Elizabethan but Stuart comedy. And his company, at any rate from 1619 on, was for stage purposes a purely Stuart corporation. Of its principal actors not one, after that year, was of those mentioned in the license at the King's accession; and of the subordinate members, I think, only one, Nicholas Tooley, had played with the company during the reign of Elizabeth. Massinger, therefore, while in many respects indebted to his Elizabethan seniors in theatrical art, is, as Professor Matthews and others insist, not Elizabethan but Jacobean and Caroline. His London, his 'manners,' his political sentiment, his constructive art, and his inconsistencies of characterization, are of the Stuart stripe; and his apparently un-Stuart outbursts of moral elevation are of the genuine and nobler historical reaction of sterling Stuart England against the abnormalities of life and art that flourished in certain quarters to the detriment of the common weal.

Massinger is also our first conscious producer of modern literary comedy, in the sense above explained. Of his unassisted plays, all were written after the publication of the Jonson folio in 1616; and his earliest comedy, *The Bondman*, was composed in the year of the Shakespeare folio, 1623. That he studied the two great dramatists in the printed word appears from many a passage in his plays. At least seven of Middleton's comedies of manners, also, were at his hand in quarto form, and one of Middleton and Rowley's tragicomedies, and nearly all of Dekker's plays and of the joint compositions of Beaumont and Fletcher, when he wrote *The Bondman*. From Dekker and Field he had learned, in addition, by personal collaboration; but most of all from his "great friend" and master, John Fletcher. He is manifestly a student of English dramatic literature; and, with Shirley and Brome, an initiator of modern literary comedy. His distinctive qualities as a playwright, however, are not obscured but accentuated by what he derived from his predecessors. His oratorical style savours now of Shakespeare, and now of Jonson or Beaumont or Fletcher, but the political, moral, religious, and dramatic conviction is his own, and the resulting rhetoric is that of one who means not merely to be heard but read, and di-

gested. In romantic comedy or tragicomedy he continues the Fletcherian
emphasis upon situation, with its corresponding deficiency in vital characterization; but, though the persons of the play may, like those of Fletcher,
be histrionic rather than imaginatively real, the narrative movement is
at once more ample and simple, more continuous and effective. In the
comedy of manners he invigorates the realism of Middleton with something of Jonson's didactic insistency; but his portrayal of 'humours,'
while distinctly of the Jonsonian school, contributes more definitely to
the conduct of the plot. His women of intrigue have not much more heart
than Middleton's, his female monsters of lust, no more shame than Fletcher's; and, still, the heroines of *The Great Duke of Florence* and *The Maid
of Honour* shine with an effulgence not altogether devoid of Shakespeare's
nobility, and a tenderness nearly as thrilling as Beaumont's, quite as
natural as Dekker's.

As playwright of the King's company Massinger carried forward the
traditions of his predecessors in preëminence. Of the long theatrical life
of his plays, Professor Matthews has informed us: Shakespeare and Fletcher excepted, Massinger has been adjudged by posterity the most successful of the practical dramatists of the early seventeenth century. Of
his tragicomedies or romantic comedies, *The Bondman* continued to be
acted as late as 1779, *The Maid of Honour* as late as 1785, and *The Bashful
Lover* until 1798. Of his comedies of manners, the *City Madam* (altered
as *Riches*) survived in the theatre till 1822; and *The New Way to Pay Old
Debts*, acted before 1626 and written probably after July 1, 1625, so late
in the nineteenth century that it may be said still to hold the stage. At
least five other of his plays survived in adapted forms in the last quarter
of the eighteenth century. Fletcher's success, because of his larger productivity, may be regarded as more definitely approved by later theatrical
generations. If, however, we are to arrive at any just conclusion concerning the relative vitality of Fletcher and his two closest collaborators, Beaumont and Massinger, as practical playwrights, we must bear in mind that
of the four joint-comedies of Beaumont and Fletcher still presented upon
the stage in the closing years of the eighteenth century, *Philaster* and *A
King and no King* are predominatingly Beaumont's, and the two others,
The Coxcombe and *The Scornful Ladie*, in some salient merits his; also, that
in the four joint-comedies of Massinger and Fletcher, similarly surviving,
Massinger's share is as important as Fletcher's; and that in 1800 about
twice as many of Massinger's unaided comedies held the stage as of
Fletcher's. While Beaumont's *Philaster* lived in the theatre till 1817 and
Fletcher's *Rule a Wife* till 1829, Massinger and Fletcher's *Spanish Curate*
survived till 1840, and Massinger's *New Way* still lives.

As I have already said, the influence of Massinger upon the history of the drama has been in no slight degree obscured by the ignorance of Restoration dramatists and critics concerning his share in works which they ascribed loosely to Beaumont and Fletcher, or to Fletcher alone. But that Massinger's contemporaries were aware of his coöperation appears from Cockayne's statements of 1658 and 1662: "My good friend Old Philip Massinger with Fletcher writ in some that we see here" (i. e. in the 1647 folio); and "how came I, you ask, so much to know? Fletcher's chief bosome-friend [Charles Cotton the elder] informed me so." If Massinger or Fletcher had been living in 1647, the publishers of the folio could not so signally have misled the coming generation concerning the authorship of the "Beaumont and Fletcher" plays. Of the thirty-five plays of various kinds, there included, Massinger appears in at least fourteen; of the eighteen added in the folio of 1679 he appears in at least three.

To some it may seem forced to rank **Richard Brome,** who regarded himself as a mere "playmaker," of "a little wit, less learning, no poetry" among the earlier producers of modern literary comedy. But, though he wrote always with an eye to the audience,—too often with a sympathy for its coarse taste,—this most distinctive of the "Sons born of many a loyal Muse to Ben" was no mean scholar in letters, no unworthy prentice. In, at any rate, two of his comedies, *A Joviall Crew* (1641) and *The Antipodes* (1638), he displays the qualities that make for theatrical appeal, and couches his concepts whether whimsical, outrageously nonsensical, or romantic, in humble, unaffected, and frequently artistic, form. Though utterly unsentimental he can on occasion awaken pathos, as in *The Northern Lasse*, *A Joviall Crew*, and the romantic play, *Queen and Concubine*. He is a product of conscious study of the printed drama, as well as of the power that comes from careful observation of contemporary life and the conditions of the stage. He is in every way a dramatist of the literary transition.[1] On the one hand, he is a recipient: in romantic comedy, a disciple of Shakespeare, Fletcher and Massinger; in the comedy of manners, a follower not merely of Jonson's technique and his theory of humours, but of Dekker's idealism and pathos no less than of his genial portraiture of life. On the other hand, he is a transmitter, even an originator. Professor Baker has, in the essay preceding *The Antipodes*, significantly.indicated the relation of Brome's output to the later ballad-opera and farce comedy; and the line of descent, in the comedy of manners, through him to Wycherley and Vanbrugh, as through Shirley to Etherege and Con-

[1] See Dr. H. F. Allen, *Study of the Comedies of Richard Brome* (1912), and, more especially, Dr. C. E. Andrews, *Richard Brome: a Study of his Life and Works* (1913) for an estimate of his technical skill.

greve. His most popular play, *The Northern Lasse*, survived upon the stage till 1760; his best romantic comedy, *The Joviall Crew*, was played in opera as late as 1791. His best of humours and manners, *The Antipodes*, is from the literary as well as the dramatic point of view even more worthy of revival, and as such is presented in this volume.

James Shirley, too, is full of echoes of the masters of Elizabethan and Jacobean comedy. The discipline of the printed drama colours and regulates all that he has written, though it neither dominates his constructive ingenuity, the originality and faithfulness of his characterization, nor obscures the merit of his vivid, and still discriminating and effective, poetic style. In tragedy his indebtedness is most to Shakespeare, Beaumont and Webster; in romantic comedy of the more serious cast, to Fletcher, with whom, as Ward says, he betrays "a close affinity of genius,"—and also to Beaumont and the older masters, Shakespeare and Heywood; in the lighter and more realistic comedies of manners, to Jonson and Middleton. As a continuator of Jonson's minute and methodical technique, of Middleton's merry characterization and intimate ridicule of bourgeois types and ever recurring gulls, of 'delutherin' gallants and witful, deluded dames of fashion, and of Fletcher's high comedy figures, he produces, in such plays as *The Gamester* (1633) and *The Lady of Pleasure* (1635), what Professor Schelling has justly denominated "truer pictures of the better society of Carolan London than Middleton or Fletcher ever drew in their comedies of the London of King James." And it is precisely in the lucid presentation of "the whims and extravagances of high-bred ladies" and gentlemen, in the clean-cut situations, in the poise and polish, that he carried forward the movement which, culminating in Congreve, was yet prophetic of Sheridan and Goldsmith. By his devotion to Spanish ideals of gallantry, sentimental loyalty, and chivalry and to the French heroic-romantic elements of plot-interest in favour at the court of King Charles, he contributed to the movement by which the later Elizabethan tragicomedy was merged in the heroic play. But,

> A small clear beacon whose benignant spark
> Was gracious yet for loiterers' eyes to mark,—

in technique his influence was toward simplicity and restraint; and in morals, toward the earnest, often elevated, tone which characterizes Massinger.

His comedies are adequately discussed in the essay by the Master of Peterhouse which follows. The best in portrayal of manners, beside those mentioned above, are undoubtedly *The Wedding* (1626) and *The Example* (1634),—both of romantic vein to boot. The most noteworthy of serious, almost tragicomic, style are *The Gratefull Servant* (1629), *The Young Admirall* (1633) and *The Royall Master* (1638). Of his twenty-three extant comedies, not fewer than fourteen were played after the Restoration. In adaptation of whole or part, five survived well into the eighteenth century, —among them, *The Wedding* and *The Lady of Pleasure*. *The Gamester* was played in altered form by Garrick in 1757 and 1772; by others, as late as 1790 and 1806; and, as *The Wife's Stratagem*, by Poole, it still survived in 1827. Why *The Royall Master* with its superior ingenuity, variety of vivid portraiture, charm and force, was not among those long preserved by theatre-going posterity, I cannot understand. Many years ago Ward wrote of it, "judiciously edited, this play would be well fitted to grace the stage, to which I hope it may yet some day be restored." I trust that his own careful edition for this volume may hasten the day.

20. The Minor Writers: Transition to the Heroic Play

During the period 1625 to 1642 about one hundred and eighty-five comedies were produced, of which a hundred and forty are extant. But though several were revived after the Restoration, not more than a dozen, mostly by Massinger, Shirley and Brome, continued to hold the stage after 1760, and none is seen to-day. As to the comedies produced by the contemporaries of these authors, the verdict of the theatre is sustained by that of literary criticism. Of the minor sons of Ben Jonson,— May, Randolph, Mayne, Cartwright, Marmion,—the first three wrote a few comedies of manners and intrigue that had a more than temporary vogue: May, in 1620, *The Heir* and *The Old Couple;* later Randolph, *The Muses' Looking-Glasse* (which survived as *The Mirror* in 1756), and Mayne, *The City Match* (which reappeared as *The Schemers* in 1755). But taken in the lump these later comedies of contemporary life are either vile or vapid; they fail to combine tectonic and poetic art and are of no possible concern to any but historians of the drama. With regard to the initiators of that other form of writing, the heroic play, which after the Restoration Dryden, with his *Conquest of Granada*, was to carry to its highest artistic and popular possibility, as little need here be said. The heroic play has much to do with the history of melodrama, but with that of comedy, practically nothing. Its first specimens are an artificial and inflated development of the heroic plot of earlier Stuart tragicomedy. For dramatic conflict, sensational episode is substituted; and for characterization, the bombast of amorous ardour and valorous show. The heroic plays of Cartwright and Mayne, Glapthorne, Carlell and Davenant owe their elevated personages, romantic scene, political circumstance, marvellous and spectacular features of setting and device to such tragicomedies as *Pericles, Cymbeline, Two Noble Kinsmen, Philaster* and *A King and no King*; but their circumstance, motive, and atmosphere are sham, and they lack the romantic passion and the poetry of the earlier tragicomedy. Their themes of loyalty are of Beaumont's conception as exaggerated by Fletcher in the *Loyall Subject* or illustrated in Heywood's late revision of the *Royall King*,—of that conception run to drivel. Their sophisticated refinements of honour, heroic sentiment, and histrionic bravado, and their fantastic contortions of love as gallantry are a sickly reflection of Fletcher and Massinger in *The Knight of Malta* and *The Lovers Progress*, and of the Spanish and French sources of decadent romanticism. So, also, their heightened contrasts. In their grandiose morality and quibbling dialogue, they are the *reductio ad absurdum* of Massinger's vein; and in their melodramatic scenes of self-abnegation, they echo from afar the mode of Shirley writing to the taste of Henrietta Maria. Davenant with his *Platonick Lovers*, in 1635, caps the transition to the later efforts in this kind of Howard, Orrery, and Dryden.

21. Conclusion

At the beginning of this essay, in the preceding volume of this series, Swinburne's eulogy of the dramatic output of the fellows and followers of Shakespeare was quoted, and the question was asked, whether, so far as comedy is concerned, the eulogy can be justified: whether the fellows and followers of Shakespeare in the comedy of the half-century beginning 1590 were a "generation of giants and gods"; whether the estate created by them may be regarded as "rich and royal"; and whether one should "wonder beyond measure at the apathetic ignorance of average students in regard of the abundant treasure to be gathered from it." As preliminary to any reply it was emphasized that while the qualities of significance for life and of æsthetic worth are essential to the vitality of dramatic as of other literature, the paramount test of the drama is that of continuance upon the stage; and that the literary estimate, ethical, historical, or artistic should be employed as corrective of injustice due to caprices of dramatic fashion and vicissitudes of theatrical fortune. Otherwise the literary estimate would be merely expository of the drama in question, or explanatory of the verdict of generations of theatre-goers.

Dividing the half-century into two periods we have observed that during the former, which closed with the death of Fletcher in 1625, there were produced some two hundred and fifty comedies exclusive of Shakespeare's; that of the two hundred and fifty, somewhat over a half are still extant;

but that only twenty-six survived upon the stage in the middle of the eighteenth century; in 1825, five; and, after 1850, but one—*A New Way to Pay Old Debts*. In the light of the popular verdict, therefore, the apathetic ignorance of average students is not to be wondered at. And that the verdict is not altogether irresponsible would appear from the different treatment accorded by the public to Shakespeare's comedies. For up to 1850, theatre-goers, while dropping one after another of the two hundred and fifty comedies of Shakespeare's contemporaries, have persistently attended revivals of Shakespeare's plays; and at the present day they regard no fewer than sixteen out of his seventeen comedies as fixtures upon the stage.

Subjecting to a literary examination the non-Shakespearian comedies above mentioned which survived 1750 as acting plays, we have discovered that the verdict of the theatre-goers, so far favourable, is in large measure just. By the consensus of literary critics at least twenty of the twenty-six are of abiding worth. A few of these may, because of the change in social and moral conceptions or the requirements of modern technique, not again be publicly acted: as, for instance, Marston's *Dutch Courtezan*, Jonson's *Every Man in his Humour* and *Volpone*, and Fletcher and Massinger's *The Spanish Curate*. But the rest might with slight and judicious modification make money for the enterprising actor-manager,—Jonson's *Silent Woman* and *Alchemist*, Chapman and others' *Eastward Hoe*, Beaumont and Fletcher's *Philaster* and *King and no King*, Fletcher's *Tamer Tamed*, *Wit without Money*, *Rule a Wife*, *Chances*, *Pilgrim*, and *Humorous Lieutenant*, Massinger's *New Way*, *Maid of Honour*, *City Madam* and, perhaps, *The Bondman*. The remaining six of the twenty-six plays long approved by popular verdict, I for one, and, I imagine, most contemporary critics, would reject as unsuited for the modern stage. All of the twenty-six are of value to the student of dramatic history or construction, but a knowledge of these twenty is all that can be expected of the average student of the comedy produced between 1590 and 1625.

Turning from the plays of this period approved by popular acceptance to those which have been neglected by the stage, and applying the literary test as corrective of popular caprice and the vicissitudes of theatrical fortune, we have found that even for lovers of dramatic literature not more than eighteen others of the two hundred and fifty are of poetic or tectonic excellence adequate to yield abiding profit and pleasure. And even so, it must be conceded that their value is sometimes historical rather than primarily dramatic. These are the *Merry Devill of Edmonton*, *Englishmen for my Money*, *Two Angry Women of Abington*, *Shomaker's Holiday* and *Patient Grissil*, *The Honest Whore*, *All Fools* and *M. D'Olive*, *The Knight of the Burning Pestle, Bartholomew Fayre, A Trick to Catch the Old One, A Faire Quarrell, The Spanish Gipsie, A Wife for a Month, The Knight of Malta, The Lovers Progresse, The Elder Brother* and *The Noble Gentleman.* Not more than ten of these would essentially profit the average student.

In other words of the two hundred and fifty comedies written by Shakespeare's fellows and followers between 1590 and 1625, the lover of literature for its own sake will be content with some forty, and the average student with some thirty. As for the general reader who pretends to be neither a 'lover' nor a student, but desires to have a bowing acquaintance with the history of English comedy, I should say that he was doing well and profitably, if he read,—*Every Man in his Humour, Volpone, The Alchemist, The Silent Woman, Shomakers Holiday, The Honest Whore, Eastward Hoe, Philaster, King and no King, The Knight of the Burning Pestle, A Trick to Catch the Old One, A Faire Quarrell, The Spanish Gipsie, The Humorous Lieutenant, The Chances, A Wife for a Month, Rule a Wife, The Maid of Honour* (or *The City Madam*), and *A New Way.* The literary historian will, of course, wade through all of the two hundred and fifty that are extant; but that is a matter of honesty, not of literature or love.

Similarly, with regard to the comedies produced in the second period under discussion, from 1625 to 1642, we have found that the verdict of the theatre is in general valid for all but the specialist. Of the one hundred and eighty-five, the best are those which were still played in the eighteenth century; nine of which by Massinger, Shirley and Brome, have been already mentioned as of genuine power, dramatic and poetic. And though not more than one, or two, of them is likely to be revived upon the stage, they are invaluable to the lover of literature as well as the historical student. After 1625 the estate in comedy is rich in extent, but certainly not royal. If the average student or the general reader confine himself to *The Great Duke of Florence, The Bashful Lover, The Antipodes, The Gamester* (or *The Lady of Pleasure*), and *The Royall Master,* he is not to be reproached.

To conclude: during the half century there were produced about four hundred and thirty-five comedies,—an estate undoubtedly rich in abundance; and of these no less than forty enjoyed a life upon the stage lasting on the average one hundred and fifty years,—after all, something regal, numerically considered. But comparatively considered the product does not merit the encomium. What of the three hundred and ninety-five plays which the public speedily forgot? And what is a life of a century and a half for one-tenth of the output of all Shakespeare's fellows and followers when set over against a life of three centuries—still in its prime— for all but one of his seventeen comedies? The vitality of his fellows and followers is not the vitality which the public expects of a "generation of giants and gods." Of the half-hundred "giants" but eight are more than names to the general public a century after the period has closed. Three-quarters of a century later, but five, Jonson, Beaumont, Fletcher, Massinger, and Shirley still find a footing on the stage. And nowadays, if not Massinger, none. And when the popular verdict is appealed to the court of literary criticism, it is corrected in particulars but not reversed. Two-thirds of the comedies which a judicial estimate deems still worthy of the attention of the average student, if not of the actor, are those upon which the public had already set its seal of temporary approval. The remaining third, of the critic's choice, are preferred to those of popular vogue principally because of values historical or poetic rather than dramatic and histrionic. The total of the estate retained by the court of literary criticism is approximately the same as that retained for a time by popular favour: barely one-twelfth of the four hundred and thirty-five comedies of those fifty years. And about one-twentieth would suffice for the general reader who desires a bowing acquaintance with the history of comedy. The rest is but "weeds and briars of an under-wood" of plebeian imaginings and evanescent art. The generation that produced it was in numbers and energy gigantic, but in inspiration rarely divine. Nor more than three or four of the half-hundred comic dramatists that surrounded and succeeded Shakespeare attained with any degree of steadiness to the vision splendid and creative which posterity treasures. They are Jonson, Beaumont, Fletcher, and Massinger. A few others, intermittently, produced comedy that is also literature,—Dekker, Chapman, Marston, Middleton and Rowley, Shirley, and Brome; but little of their work in comedy is of that literary preëminence which commands the interest or respect of the English-speaking public of the present age,—still less of the public of other nationalities. Not more than a dozen of the four hundred and thirty-five comedies produced by the fellows and followers of Shakespeare between 1590 and 1642 are absolute literature; and the dozen are the work of three or four men. The rest are of historical interest, or of interest to the student of dramatic technique, or to the virtuoso who scours the woods for some fortuitous, poetic bloom. The apathetic ignorance of the average student in regard of this province of the English drama is not immoderately to be deplored. It is much more likely to be dissipated if the under-brush be cleared away, and that part of the overgrowth which is rotten and unsightly consigned to the flames, than if scholars continue to pretend that the whole forest is of magic worth. The remnant, not of doubtful import nor vicious luxuriance, will stand out compelling the admiration that it richly deserves.

Thomas Dekker

THE SHOMAKERS HOLIDAY
OR THE GENTLE CRAFT

*Edited with Critical Essay and Notes
by Alexis F. Lange, Ph.D., Professor
in the University of California*

CRITICAL ESSAY

Life.—Thomas Dekker was born in London about 1570 and died there, perhaps as early as 1632. Presumably he came of Dutch stock. Such scholarly training as his works disclose he obtained somehow in his native city. He may or may not have been an artisan's apprentice; but the lower middle-class, one cannot but conjecture, formed his early social environment. Other reasons apart, not one of his writings betrays any intimacy or instinctive sympathy with the upper social strata. His literary apprenticeship doubtless consisted in doing theatrical hack-work; "histories" and domestic tragedies, the latter especially, were probably his first marked successes in dramatic authorship. By January 8, 1598, he had become one of Henslowe's band of playwrights, and for nearly five years following there are not many months for which no contribution by him is recorded in Henslowe's *Diary*. His attack on Ben Jonson in 1601 attests the prominence he had achieved and undoubtedly added to his celebrity. In 1603 he was entrusted with a large part of the task of preparing the entertainment welcoming James I into London, and on several subsequent occasions with similar pageants in honour of new Lord Mayors. Other authentic data bearing upon his personal fortunes furnish little more than a sad record of failures to keep out of the debtors' prison.

Dekker's known literary career is twofold. From 1598 to about 1604 he is a dramatist chiefly. Henslowe's *Diary* registers nearly a dozen plays essentially Dekker's and more than a score written in conjunction with others. During the remaining twenty-eight or more years of his life he appears as a playwright sporadically; prose becomes his main resource. To this period belong, so far as is known, in the neighbourhood of fifteen dramatic productions, of which at least six are only partly his, while several of the rest seem to be recasts of early conceptions.

The following list gives, in the order of their publication,[1] the extant plays which may be definitely assigned in part or wholly to Dekker.

---

[1] Concerning the circumstances of their production, the time of acting, etc., see Fleay, *Eng. Dram.*, I, 115–137; and *Camb. Hist. Eng. Lit.*, VI, 57–65; Greg, *Hensl. Diary* and *Papers;* Hunt, *Thos. Dekker;* Small, *Stage Quarrel;* Stoll, *John Webster;* Pierce, *Webster and Dekker.*

Essentially Dekker's are—1600 *Shomakers Holiday*, *Old Fortunatus*,—comedies; 1602 *Satiromastix*—satiric comedy; 1604 *Magnificent Entertainment*—pageant, *Honest Whore*, Part I—tragicomedy; 1607 *Whore of Babylon*—political allegory; 1612 *If it be not good, the Divel is in it*—fantastic, semi-allegorical comedy, *Troja Nova Triumphans*—pageant; 1628 *Britannia's Honour*—pageant; 1629 *London's Tempe*—pageant; 1630 *Honest Whore*, Part II; 1631 *Match mee in London*—tragicomedy; 1636 *Wonder of a Kingdome*—comedy., Collaboration plays—1603 *Patient Grissill*—with Chettle and Haughton; 1607 *Sir Thomas Wyat*, *West-Ward Hoe*, *North-Ward Hoe*—with Webster; 1611 *Roaring Girle*—with Middleton; 1622 *Virgin Martir*—with Massinger; 1656 *Sun's Darling*—with Ford; 1658 *Witch of Edmonton*—with Ford, Rowley, etc.

The Shoemakers Holiday: Date and Authorship.—An entry in Henslowe's *Diary* attributes the *Shomakers Holiday* to Thomas Dekker.[1] Internal evidence confirms this. The same entry fixes the time of appearance. The manuscript copy was ready for the use of the Lord Admiral's players by July 15, 1599. The play had been written, we may be certain, during the six weeks unaccounted for otherwise between this date and May 30, when Henslowe paid in full for the collaboration drama *Agamemnon*. The first presentation doubtless took place immediately afterwards, in accordance with the usual practice at the Rose. The success of the piece won for it the distinction of a court performance, given on the night of January 1, 1600. *Old Fortunatus* had been played at Court a few days before on December 27.[2] During the early part of the new year both plays appeared in book form, each quarto being to all appearance a rather careful reproduction of an uncorrupted manuscript, although neither bears Dekker's name on the title-page.

The Literary Source, and the Construction of the Play.—

---

[1] Lent unto Samewell Rowley and Thomas Downton, the 15 of July, 1599, to bye a Boocke of thomas dickers, Called the gentle craft; the some of iii^{li}. *Diary*, ed. Greg, I, 110. According to a communication (*Shak. Soc. Papers*, IV, 110) by an anonymous writer concerning an unknown copy of the *Shomakers Holiday* in the possession of a nameless friend, Robert Wilson, the actor, had a hand in the production of the play. Fleay must be right in pronouncing the data communicated in this article a forgery. There is no evidence whatever to justify the coupling of Wilson's name with the play. Fleay's belief that it is not Dekker's either is too purely subjective to call for consideration. Fleay, *E. Dr.*, I, 124.

[2] Fleay, *H. S.*, 122.

There can be no doubt that the plot of the play grew out of materials and hints furnished by the three shoemaker stories in Deloney's Gentle Craft.[1] The last of these constitutes the main source. This story, a popular, Deloney mixture of history, tradition, and fiction, gives a realistically amplified account of "how Sir Simon Eyre being at first a shoemaker became in the end Mayor of London." Interspersed are two chapters of by-plot narrating the horseplay intrigues against one another of Eyre's journeymen, French John, Dutch Hans, and Nicholas the Englishman, rival suitors for the hand of Florence, one of Mrs. Eyre's maids. To the four chapters dealing with Eyre is owing the substance of the Eyre thread in the *Shomakers Holiday*. They are Dekker's warrant for making Eyre a shoemaker of Tower Street, and they account for the events assigned to his career—the hiring of a foreign journeyman, the lucky speculation, the entertainment at the Lord Mayor's house, the election to the offices of Sheriff and Mayor, and the banquet to the 'prentices in fulfilment of a boyhood promise. The group of merry journeymen in Dekker's comedy obviously parallels that of Deloney's by-plot. Hence is derived also Eyre's part in the wedding of Lacy and Rose,—Florence and Nicholas "being married by him out of his house with credit." Moreover, this by-plot contains the mediated Enoch Arden motif of the Jane-Hammon thread, only with circumstances reversed. John's wife, supposed to be dead, arrives in time from France to spoil her husband's plan of giving her a successor. Other correspondence there is none, with one notable exception,—the scene in which Hammon is "cozened," at an early hour, of Rafe's wife. This has its prototype in the practical joke whereby Nicholas frustrates the design of Hans and Florence to get married at midnight.

[1] Registered Oct. 19, 1597 as 'a booke called the Gentle Crafte intreating of shoomakers'; published 1598. The earliest extant copy (B. M.) bears the date 1648 and the title *The Gentle Craft*. Every indication points to this being essentially an unaltered reprint. Contents—the story of St. Hugh, chaps. I–IV; Crispine and Crispianus V–IX; Simon Eyre IX–XV. A 'Second Part,' not utilized by Dekker soon followed the first set of these very popular stories. The earliest extant edition of Part Two (B. M.) is of 1639. Both are reprinted in my edition of *The Gentle Craft by Thomas Deloney*, Palaestra, XVIII (1903).

For hints here and there or for inspiration, Dekker seems to have been indebted more or less directly also to *George-a-Greene*, *Frier Bacon*, *James IV*, *Every Man in his Humour*, and possibly *Henry V*.

The points at which these Eyre stories came to be knit with the romantic love-plot of the play have been indicated. The inception of the plot itself, however, as well as its most distinctive features, plainly resulted from the perusal of the Crispine and Crispianus legend as related by Deloney, while the tale of St. Hugh yielded at least the explanation of Lacy's skill in the use of St. Hugh's bones. Like Crispine and Crispianus, Lacy is of noble descent; like them he plies his trade under a court shoemaker (III, i, 84) and with fellows "as pleasant as their notes as they sit at their businesse." Crispianus is "prest" to a war in France, whence the background action and the common starting-point of the adventures of Lacy and Rafe. Crispine is sent for by the emperor's, Lacy by the Lord Mayor's daughter; love-making and shoe-fitting ensue in both cases. Ursula finds a refuge with Crispine's master; Rose escapes to Simon Eyre's house. The play ends, on a Shrove Tuesday, which Firk christens St. Hugh's Holiday, with the confirmation of the secret marriage by the king; in the story it is the emperor, who, to be sure, is Ursula's father, that sanctions the secret union of the lovers, 'whereupon there was great joy, and the shoemakers in the same town made holiday' in honour of Crispine and Crispianus.

Structurally subordinate, the Eyre element in the play is nevertheless the pivot of interest and must have been the organizing nucleus in the genesis of the plot as a whole. There is every reason to believe that the imagination of Dekker, the citizen and realistic playwright, came to be focused on the biography of Eyre. But this, he must have felt, was epic rather than dramatic. It might supply scenes and events too promising to omit but not a chain of dramatic action, except by doing open violence to the supposed facts concerning Eyre, "whose fame," Deloney asserts, "still lived in the mouths of many men." A very natural identification of Eyre with the shoemaker in the tale of Crispine and Crispianus suggested the main plot needed. Moreover, the love-story of Crispine and Ursula cannot have failed to appeal from the first to Dekker, the romantic poet who was soon to be busy with Fortunatus. But the process of creative fusion carried with it changes, some of them easily traceable. The scene of the main action shifted from Kent to London; and the time of Crispine and mythical French wars coalesced with the age of Henry V and Simon Eyre, which to the Elizabethan dramatist bore the features of his own day. Coincidently the figure of an earl of Lincoln arose to take the place of the King of Logria; of an Askew to take the place of Crispianus, the soldier, and of a Rowland Lacy to take that of Crispine who escaped going to the war through his love-affair with Ursula. The substitution of Rose for Ursula, and of the Lord Mayor of Deloney's story for the emperor, linked plot to plot and left room for a glimpse of the victor of Agincourt,[1] in a playful mood. But now a two-fold difficulty presented itself. The Lord Mayor held office for only one year; and without palpable absurdity Lacy's disguise could not be made to seem even that long. On the other hand, time had to be allowed for the rise of Eyre to affluence and office. Besides, the conditions of the interweaving of plots condemned the hero to comparative inactivity. The solution that occurred to Dekker consisted, so far as the Eyre story was concerned, in a rigorous compression, which involved even the untimely death of a number of aldermen, and in the development of another subsidiary plot to intensify the dramatic conflict and to swell the volume of plot interest.

As appears from the foregoing, the triplex thread of the play is not implicitly contained in the stories told by Deloney. It resulted rather from the selective coöperation of such external factors as Dekker's closeness to his public and the example of Ben Jonson, with Dekker's own trained aptitude for domestic themes and his interest in the social side of conduct. At all events, some of the requirements of plot technique aside, the fitness of Dekker's conception for the ends of a descriptive comedy of character and manners is unquestionable; not unlike in purpose to Chaucer's expedient of a pilgrimage, it afforded an excellent opportunity for representing dramatically a cross-section of community life from shoemaker's shop to Lord Mayor's mansion and nobleman's palace. In more than one important respect the concrete embodiment realizes just this type of representation. To be sure, the temptation to expand unduly the descriptive hints from the Eyre

[1] This slight anachronism mattered nothing, of course, to playwright or playgoer.

story proved too strong to be resisted. Accordingly, there is much in the shoemaker scenes that has little or no bearing on the triad of complication, itself but loosely held together and without concentric character and plot interest. At the same time the artisans rather crowd their "betters" in the picture of manners presented. The doings of the higher social groups become mere incidents in the epic of the Eyre of popular tradition. Nevertheless Dekker's transcript of actual London life is singularly comprehensive and many-sided, while belief in its fidelity to that life is compelled not only by its spontaneous vividness and the vital adaptation of stock devices but also by the sympathetic view of the social whole and the exhibition, in varying lights, of character through perennial social relations.

These notes of attitude and method give the *Shomakers Holiday* a distinct position among comedies of its own class and epoch. The accent falls on character; and this, action and social environment serve to reveal, not as isolated trait or abnormal tendency, but as a concrete whole in its living context. Eyre, for example, is humorous, consistently so; but the scenes that exhibit his oddities body forth likewise his substantial qualities as husband, master, man of business, citizen, and friend. He is an individual, but an individual with the impress of his occupation. One feels tempted to say with Mrs. Nickleby: "it is all in the leather." At any rate, would it not have been utterly at variance with received popular notions to have represented Eyre and his journeymen as tailors, for instance? *Mutatis mutandis* these remarks hold true for the chief representatives of the upper middle-class and the aristocracy. It is the class aspect of character, admirably brought out in the delineation of Otley and Lincoln, that is the source of the dramatic collision and eventually a potent factor in their comic undoing. The fundamental conception includes thus the established order. The levelling democracy of the heart becomes involved in a conflict with class interests and pride. In another country, several centuries later, the same motif was to take shape in *Kabale und Liebe;* Dekker's play, however, "purposed nothing but mirth," and while, significantly enough, no small part of the merriment is brought about by a shoemaker at the expense of an earl and a lord mayor, Dekker had no quarrel with society as organized.[1] Instead of accentuating social division and the provincialism of character caused by it, he dwells on the bonds of union. Differentiated as individuals modified by calling and station, the characters of the *Shomakers Holiday* share in being Londoners and Englishmen with common interests. In the foreground contrasting figures from the social extremes; in the background sketchy hints of other members of the same communal group; the whole set in the common national life and flooded with the sunniness of health and frolicsome spirits.

The Characterization.—In point of character-drawing the only personages inviting comparison between play and story are Simon Eyre and his wife. Concerning the historical Eyre, Dekker may have known what little we know and perhaps from the same source, his fellow-citizen John Stow. When he made enquiry for the Lord Mayor's name (not mentioned in Deloney's story), he can hardly have failed to gain information about the real Eyre too, "*honorandus famosus mercator,*" "*nobilis et potens vir,*" pious benefactor of the City and of her poor.[2] Patently not a man for the comic sock! It was different with the Eyre of City mythology, the hero of anecdote and tale of good fortune, and the popular, somewhat eccentric builder of Leadenhall, which perpetuated his memory and provided a stimulus for successive generations to fashion and refashion his biography and the image of his personality. There is nothing in the play, however, to show that Dekker drew from either of these sources directly; Deloney's novelistic attempt at blending both, and Dekker's first-hand knowledge of London

[1] As the *Whore of Babylon* shows, the more impersonal problems and the broader issues of history and politics lay entirely beyond his ken.

[2] Stow, *Survey* (1598), 80, 116-123 and the list of Lord Mayors and Sheriffs— Simon Eyre, 'sometime an upholster and then a draper,' built Leadenhall in 1419; was Sheriff of London 1434, Roger Otley, grocer, being Lord Mayor; became Lord Mayor 1445; died 1459 and was buried in the church of St. Mary Woolnoth. Later editions of Stow and Maitland's *History of London,* 1739, add a few details consisting chiefly of further illustrations of Eyre's public spirit and philanthropy. Dekker was probably familiar also with the memorial inscriptions over the porch and on the north wall of the chapel of Leadenhall, and on Eyre's monument in St. Mary Woolnoth. The other historic names of the play are—Otley, Scot, Askew, Lacy, Lovell. The last two—possibly all of them, of course—Dekker may have obtained from such a chronicle as Fabyan's.

character-types were sufficient to induce a reconception suitable for comedy. Yet it would be very strange indeed, if in reconceiving and reshaping the character of Eyre, Dekker was not in some measure directed, and limited as well, by living traditions of one sort or another. The shadowy outlines of Mrs. Eyre, on the other hand, anyone might fill in *ad libitum*.

In Deloney's crude but not unlife-like sketch Simon Eyre and his wife appear as a worthy, old-time, bourgeois couple, fond and proud of each other, thrifty, quietly ambitious, god-fearing and honest, though not above risking their good name by obtaining credit on false pretences. Modestly, and not without blushes of embarrassment, they adjust themselves to the ways of patrician society. Wealth and honour only deepen their sense of obligation to their fellow-men and their gratitude to God. Mrs. Eyre is right, however, in gently reminding her husband, when she has found her tongue again after their first supper in fine company, that next to God he may thank her. Without her ingenuity no argosy for him; and no shrievalty without her encouraging comment on his self-depreciation: others have been Sheriffs "whose wits have been as mean as your own." Anxious about his false modesty, and sure that " her mind would bear it well " to become a lady eventually, she sends a servant after him to the Guildhall to see whether he will accept if elected. The gown of office, she knows, will set off finely his handsome person, and a lady's costume, we must infer, assorts well with her own comeliness and demeanour. Not so in the playwright's portrait. A French hood, says Hodge, will make her look "like a cat out of a pillorie." Her speech and manners accord with the fact that Eyre took her "from selling tripes in Eastcheape." Greatness is thrust upon her. Social aspirations without cleverness lead to ludicrously futile efforts to act *comme il faut*. Thrift reappears as penny-wisdom, a sweet-tempered disposition to lecture as goodnatured nagging and scolding, which meets with grotesque abuse. She too believes that her husband is a thing of beauty but does well to add: "but let that passe too." In a word, from the view point of the relationship between the two conceptions Dekker's rendering is a capital plebeianized caricature designed after the stock pattern of a low-comedy shrew.

The germinal idea for the transformation of Eyre most probably came to Dekker through a legendary anecdote or two related by Deloney. The man who made good his boast of having a little table of extraordinary value by eating from his wife's lap answered far better to the image of a typical shoemaker and man of the people than the commercial and official Eyre. Whatever the process, a creative recombination of character-elements took place, resulting in "one of the merriest madcaps" in English comedy. To "silken fellows" he cannot but seem "a wilde ruffin," yet his claim of being a "man of the best presence" rests on substantial fact. All he lacks is grooming. The current of his physical life runs strong and swift, sweeping along a disposition in happy accord with the norms of existence. Work becomes mere play; to "speak bandog and bedlam" is a necessary outlet for surplus animal spirits. This elemental vigour and a clear conscience reinforce the flatcap's consciousness of individual worth. Deferential to those in authority, "serious, provident, and wise," when occasion demands, he brushes aside all social "flip-flap" when with friends, his King included. Being a member of the gentle craft he "beares a princely minde," manifested in chivalrous protection and large-hearted generosity. A shoemaker, he is a philosopher, of course. Enough for the day are the duties and pleasures thereof; "a pound of care paies not a dram of debt,"—a creed determined intellectually by a keen discrimination of values. His "madness" derives its humorous appeal in no small degree from the sanity of mind it discloses.

This temper of the principal character reflects the uniform mood of the whole play, which despite its obvious faults of execution is indeed a holiday of Elizabethan Londoners, truly perceived and happily reproduced by a humorist.

Dekker's Position in English Comedy.—In calling London "the mother of his life and the nurse of his being," Dekker acknowledged a relationship none of his more prominent brother-poets could have claimed with equal justice—had they cared to do so. Their formative years were interlinked with the country, or the court, or the universities. Dekker owed the moulding of his genius and personality largely to the City, as distinguished from the circles of the gently born or bred. Here his robust sense for full-bodied fact learned its first lessons; here his abounding vitality and social instincts made him a part of the stirring life about him; here suffering evoked his inborn kindliness and sobered gaiety into humour; here his temperamental optimism found goodness in unpromising corners. Original in assimilating, but scantily endowed with the reactive power that converted London into an illuminating symbol for a Shakespeare, Dekker's thought glided easily into the grooves of the City mind and his ethical views and standards took shape under the influence of communal spirit and bourgeois wisdom. Small wonder then, poet born though he was and idealist on one side of his genius, that his imagination should have turned into paths sanctioned above others in the poetics of the citizen playgoer during a period when no dramatic representations were more popular than the chronicle-play, the domestic tragedy, and the rough-and-tumble comedy directly descended from Morality and Interlude.

Such reconstructions are hazardous, no doubt; but it would seem to remain certain not only that Dekker entered the stream of English literature on the home side but also that the characteristic trend of his literary activity received its impulse as much from inner necessity as from the constant pressure of want. From first to last he is an Englishman, a Londoner, in attitude and sympathies. His feeling for Nature is genuine and fresh but her secrets are not a part of his inner life. The raw material of his versatile art is derived from every class of Elizabethan sources; the chief source, however, is domestic in consonance with Lanthorn Leatherhead's ideal: "your homeborn projects prove ever the best; they are so easy and familiar." Not infrequently the scene of action is laid at the court of foreign king or duke, but the simple theme and the vivid realism of its embodiment belong to the world Dekker knew best. Appealing instinctively to the many among whom he moved the classical and Italian contributions of the few became his only in naturalized forms. His prose presupposes the pamphlets of Nash and his plays the example of Marlowe, Greene and even Lyly, yet the direct influence of these predecessors on his imagination and method does not appear to have been very markedly formative, Greene's perhaps excepted. On the other hand Dekker's dramaturgy follows only too closely the vital but undifferentiated technique of the popular stage during the last decade or so of Elizabeth's reign. All his plays, regardless of date, bear out the statement that he must be regarded as a popular late Elizabethan dramatist whose dramatic method is essentially fixed by the time he ceases to be a playwright exclusively and turns to prose as well. If it were not for Friscobaldo, Dekker might have died immediately after the accession of James without serious loss either to his fame as a dramatist or to our knowledge of the nature of his work.

Dekker's services to comedy cannot be sought in construction and external form. Felicitously conceived themes born out of due season—this is in some degree descriptive even of the *Shomakers Holiday* and the *Honest Whore*. Original minor motifs and vital devices alternate with grotesque fancies and obsolete expedients. Masterly openings are offset by clap-trap dénouements. Effective scenes stand isolated or appear in incongruous juxtaposition. The style is often inchoate, slovenly, strained, and then again in delicate musical strength, inevitably expressive of tender emotion or of imaginative glances beyond the actual into the "statutes of eternity." In short, although Dekker had at times "poetry for anything," he frequently falls below less brilliant contemporaries in artistic workmanship. As Dekker well knew, "he is hoarse who always sings." Nor is the serenity of perfect mastery ever likely to be his who stands in daily fear of the Counter. The primary cause, however, lies deeper. It lies, for one thing, in the natural fluidity of Dekker's inspirations. His mobile fancy needed little prompting to shift the lines of the fundamental conception, pictorial to begin with, rather than deeply interpretative of essential relations and underlying causes. Action, characters, the tone or mood of the whole, were accordingly always in danger of Protean changes; and both movement and dialogue, in spite of their virile rapidity, of not making swiftly towards a fixed goal. This tendency was unfortunately not counteracted by any marked synthetic power of the more discursive sort. Where direct insight and imagination failed to create and to hold a concrete, complex unit, Dekker could not like Jonson or Massinger invoke the aid of logic. Nor did he have the resolute will requisite for excellence. It was far more his nature to "follow the humorous tide of his age" than to "swim like the sturgeon against the stream" of circumstance or impulse. Sane, cheerful, lovable he certainly seems to have been but not the man to fashion himself and to pursue his own pathway determined and steadfast.

This pathway, so far as comedy is concerned, lay clearly in the direction of the social comedy of humour. Dekker was not a "sharp-toothed dog." "No gall drops out of his quill." His comic method is not determined by judicial wit of any sort but by the blending of common sense and keen discernment of the ludicrous with fellow-feeling. And for this the serio-comic romantic drama offered the best available form of self-expression. But his genius as a whole fitted him especially for the enrichment and development of a particular species, a species for which actual phenomena supply both materials and postulates, social relations the motives, and character and manners the sources of laughter and tears. Chronicle-play and domestic tragedy had trained him in fidelity to fact or inherited tradition. The phases of human experience most intimately his were those provided by a large city; and in their appeal to his imagination ludicrous antics of chance, comic incident and intrigue, action in general, played a subordinate part. His leading interest centred in conduct,—but conduct arising not so much out of the relation of character to itself as out of family and communal relationships. The individual aspect of character is emphasized only in *Fortunatus* and in *If it be not good the Divel is in it.*

But Dekker's most characteristic qualification for the humorous treatment of the social aspects of character must be sought in his power to seize upon and to reproduce them in their context. Sketchy and unfinished, his pictures of "familiar London" nevertheless appear convincingly and artlessly true, mainly because of the masterly touches with which men and women are exhibited as individual participants in the varied vital unity of actual existence. Dekker never quite found himself as an artist. The promise of the *Shomakers Holiday* was not realized as was Jonson's explicit manifesto. *Every Man in his Humour* is therefore intrinsically and historically more significant in the history of comedy. Dekker is, however, fairly entitled to the credit of having produced in the *Shomakers Holiday* the best adaptation, before 1600, of the Romantic comedy to "deeds and language such as men do use."

The poetic sweep and fire of *Fortunatus* give to this romantic interlude an enduring place by itself and attest the kinship of its author with the poet of the *Midsummer-Night's Dream*. More persistently present elsewhere and of more direct bearing on comedy is Dekker's optimistic sympathy. It shows itself as a spirit of Bohemian good-fellowship, boisterous, coarse, healthy, magnetic. As pity it is his strongest passion, the transfiguring source of matchless scenes of pathos. Its range is limited but not by social barriers. The "laws of humanitie and brotherhood" are binding upon high and low alike. This attitude, at times strikingly like that of Charles Dickens, invests a Bottom and his fellows with a new interest. "The value of a diamond is not lessened by the roughness when it is uncut." "It can be no shame to gather a violet, growing close to the ground." Accordingly, Dekker's interpretation of the common and mean implies a precursory opening of a distinctly modern province of artistic motifs. A gentlewoman, though a shoemaker's wife and a seamstress, a Bellafront reformed through love like Victor Hugo's Marion Delorme, such conceptions, particularly in point of the prominence given to them, anticipate by many generations, the literary achievements of a later age.

If Dekker's idealistic tenderness comes out strongest in the delineation of womanhood, his men best exhibit the union of sympathy and the sense of the ludicrous. Scarcely one of them is merely the butt of ridicule. Ben Jonson is made the victim of very drastic sport but Dekker respects Ben Jonson and pays tribute to his genius. Tibaldo's callow love-fit is witnessed through the eyes of a sympathizing sister. The "patient man" has too much mercantile shrewdness to appear merely weak and henpecked. The fellow-feeling of real humour is reflected upon a Dutch journeyman or a French physician when impersonated, the one by a Lacy, the other by an Angelo Lotti. Dekker is partisan; he is straightforwardly moral. Catholics, Puritans, a paternal knave like Malevento, a selfish, riotous lord, the sensual self-deceivers of *If it be not good the Divel is in it*,—concerning these he is not simply non-committal, but his judgment is expressed without bitterness. In the larger view, including his prose, Dekker appears almost everywhere as a sane, cheerful spectator of life, making allowance for human frailty and possessing the humour that would not willingly dispense with the manifestations of incongruous humanity.

Dekker's greatest achievement as a dramatic humorist is the creation of Eyre and of Friscobaldo. In these two worthies his "happy and copious industry" produced not merely "stuffes rather slight to feede the eye with shew, than substantiall for enduring." The convincing interpretative realism with which they are presented, whole-brained, large-hearted men of Merry England both,[1] the unity of inner life and outward act; the skill with which oddities are related to the whole of character and this to environment, the absence of marks of effort and the presence of the subtle magnetism of personality—merits of characterization like these declare the true "maker" and invite comparison with the happiest inspirations of the English Thalia. Before 1600 the "mad shoemaker of Tower Street" has few competitors for the place nearest to Bobadill and Falstaff,—while Friscobaldo, a refined Eyre, ennobled by domestic grief, is still a source of special joy to the student of the last three centuries of English comedy. But Eyre and Friscobaldo claim attention aside from artistic excellence relative or absolute. Both are humorists in the narrower modern sense. They are whole in body and mind, and they live and act in agreement with the moral order of the universe. Strong in love of their kind as well as in feelings of selfhood, keenly sensible of harmless departures from the ideal or conventionally normal in others and in themselves, they rise above accidents of fortune or blows of fate, and play with the world of which they are a part—buoyantly, laughingly, tenderly. As humorists of this type they are not only life of Dekker's own life at its best but also creatures made in the

---

[1] Friscobaldo is Italian only in name.

image of his people, like Robin Hood or the Henry V of tradition. The thought seems warranted that characters such as Eyre and Friscobaldo are typical manifestations of Teutonic tendencies and ideals under wholesome conditions of freedom. Be this as it may, Dekker occupies an important position in the history of humour. No other imaginative figure of the Elizabethan drama represents better than Simon Eyre early attempts of the *Volksgeist* at humorous self-expression. Before the period of Goldsmith, no dramatic figure is more closely akin than that of Friscobaldo to those modern embodiments of humour which owe their being to the democratic spirit and universalized sympathy.

Previous Editions and the Present Text.—The edition of 1600 is the *editio princeps* (Q 1). Each of the other four quarto-editions (Q 2–Q 5), dated respectively 1610, 1618, 1631, 1657, is a reprint of its immediate predecessor [1] (see Warnke and Proescholdt's edition, Halle, 1886, V–VIII). In 1862 Fritsche (Fr.) published the first modern edition; Pearson (P) reprinted the play in 1873, *Dekker's Dramatic Works*, Vol. I; Warnke and Proescholdt (W.-P) first provided a good text; reproduced with modernized spelling by Rhys (R) for the Mermaid Series in 1887 and 1894. The present text is based on the *editio princeps*, which has been carefully re-collated with the other quartos. The changes made in the original text, save those prescribed for this series, will be found recorded in the footnotes. The arrangement of lines virtually coincides with that arrived at by the Halle editors. To them credit is chiefly due also for the division into acts and scenes as well as a number of stage directions, i. e. the matter enclosed in square brackets.

ALEXIS F. LANGE.

[1] The publisher of the first quarto was Valentine Symmes (Sims); of the next three, John Wright. The following extract supplies the external connection:—April 19, 1610. John Wrighte. Assigned over unto him from Valentyne Symms and under Master Waterson, Warden, his hand, a booke called the Shoomakers Holyday or the Gentle Crafte. Arber's *Transcript of the Stationers' Registers*, Lond. 1876, III, 194.

THE
SHOMAKERS
Holiday
OR
The Gentle Craft.

With the humourous life of Simon
Eyre, fhoomaker, and Lord Maior
of London.

As it was acted before the Queenes moft exellent Maiestie on New-yeares day at night laft, by the right
honourable the Earle of Notingham, Lord high Admirall of England, his feruants.

VIGNETTE

Printed by Valentine Sims dwelling at the foote of Adling
hill, neere Bainards Castle, at the figne of the White
Swanne, and are there to be fold.

1600

[The Persons of the Play[1]

THE KING.
THE EARL OF CORNWALL.
SIR HUGH LACY, *Earl of Lincoln.*
ROWLAND LACY } *his nephews.*
ASKEW
SIR ROGER OATELEY, *Lord Mayor of London.*
MR. HAMMON
MR. WARNER } *Citizens of London.*
MR. SCOTT
SIMON EYRE, *a Shoemaker.*
ROGER
FIRK } EYRE'S *Journeymen.*
RAFE
LOVELL, *a Courtier.*
DODGER, *Servant to the* EARL OF LINCOLN.
A DUTCH SKIPPER.
A BOY.
ROSE, *Daughter to* SIR ROGER.
SIBIL, *her Maid.*
MARGERY, *Wife to* SIMON EYRE.
JANE, *Wife to* RAFE.
Courtiers, Attendants, Officers, Soldiers, Hunters, Shoemakers, Apprentices, Servants.

THE SCENE: LONDON and OLD FORD.]

[1] First supplied by Fritsche, 1862.

TO ALL GOOD FELLOWES, PROFESSORS OF THE GENTLE CRAFT, OF WHAT DEGREE SOEVER.

Kinde gentlemen and honest boone companions, I present you here with a merrie-conceited comedie, called *The Shoomakers Holyday*, acted by my Lorde Admiralls Players this present Christmasse before the Queenes most excellent Majestie,[1] [and] for the mirth and pleasant matter by her Highnesse graciously accepted, being indeede no way offensive. The Argument of the play I will set downe in this epistle: Sir Hugh Lacie, Earle of Lincolne, had a yong Gentleman of his owne name, his nere kinsman, that loved the Lorde Maiors daughter of London; to prevent and crosse which love, the earle caused his kinsman to be sent coronell of a companie into France: who resigned his place to another gentleman his friend, and came disguised like a Dutch shoomaker to the house of Symon Eyre in Towerstreete, who served the Maior and his household with shooes:[2] the merriments that passed in Eyres house, his comming to be Maior of London, Lacies getting his love, and other accidents, with two merry Three-mens songs. Take all in good worth that is well intended, for nothing is purposed but mirth; mirth lengthneth long life, which, with all other blessings, I heartily wish you.

Farewell!

[1] Qtos., 'Maiestie. For'   [2] Qtos., 'shooes. The'

THE FIRST THREE–MANS SONG

O the month of Maie, the merrie month of Maie,
So frolicke, so gay, and so greene, so greene, so greene!
O, and then did I unto my true love say:
'Sweete Peg, thou shalt be my summers queene!

Now the nightingale, the prettie nightingale,   5
The sweetest singer in all the forrests quier,
Intreates thee, sweete Peggie, to heare thy true loves tale;
Loe, yonder she sitteth, her breast against a brier.

But O, I spie the cuckoo, the cuckoo, the cuckoo;
See where she sitteth: come away, my joy;   10
Come away, I prithee: I do not like, the cuckoo
Should sing where my Peggie and I kisse and toy.'

O the month of Maie, the merrie month of Maie,
So frolike, so gay, and so greene, so greene, so greene!
And then did I unto my true love say: 15
'Sweete Peg, thou shalt be my summers queene!'

THE SECOND THREE–MANS SONG

This is to be sung at the latter end.

Cold's the wind, and wet's the raine,
  Saint Hugh be our good speede:
Ill is the weather that bringeth no gaine,
  Nor helpes good hearts in neede.

Trowle the boll, the jolly nut-browne boll,   5
   And here, kind mate, to thee:
Let's sing a dirge for Saint Hughes soule,
   And downe it merrily.

Downe a downe, hey downe a downe, (*Close with the tenor boy*)
   Hey derie derie, down a down!   10
Ho, well done; to me let come!
   Ring, compasse gentle joy.

Trowle the boll, the nut-browne boll,
   And here, kind *etc.* [*as often as there be men to drinke.*
      [*At last when all have drunke, this verse:*
Cold's the wind, and wet's the raine,   15
   Saint Hugh be our good speede:
Ill is the weather that bringeth no gaine,
   Nor helpes good hearts in neede.

The Prologue

AS IT WAS PRONOUNCED BEFORE THE QUEENES MAJESTIE.

As wretches in a storme, expecting day,
With trembling hands and eyes cast up to heaven,
Make prayers the anchor of their conquerd hopes,
So we, deere goddesse, wonder of all eyes,
Your meanest vassalls, through mistrust and feare   5
To sincke into the bottome of disgrace
By our imperfit pastimes, prostrate thus
On bended knees,[1] our sailes of hope do strike,

---

[1] As a rule only the epilogue was spoken 'on bended knees.' A good illustration of like homage rendered off the stage is found in Hentzner's account (1598) of the Queen's progress through the Presence-chamber at Greenwich to her chapel—'Wherever she turned her face, as she was going along, everybody fell down on their knees.' *Shakspere's England. New Shak. Soc.*, Part I, Appendix II, LXXVI.

Dreading the bitter stormes of your dislike.
Since then, unhappy men, our hap is such,   10
That to our selves our selves no help can bring,
But needes must perish, if your saint-like eares,
Locking the temple where all mercy sits,
Refuse the tribute of our begging tongues:
Oh graunt, bright mirror of true chastitie,   15
From those life-breathing starres, your sun-like eyes,
One gratious smile: for your celestiall breath
Must send us life, or sentence us to death.

A PLEASANT COMEDIE OF

The GENTLE *Craft.*

[Act I. Scene I. *A Street in London.*]

Enter LORD MAIOR, LINCOLNE.

Lincolne. My Lord Maior, you have sundrie times
Feasted my selfe and many courtiers more:
Seldome or never can we be so kind
To make requitall of your curtesie.
But leaving this, I heare my cosen Lacie   5
Is much affected to your daughter Rose.[1]
   L. Maior. True, my good lord, and she loves him so wel
That I mislike her boldnesse in the chace.
   Lincol. Why, my Lord Maior, think you it then a shame,
To joyne a Lacie with an Otleys name?   10
   L. Maior. Too meane is my poore girle for his high birth;
Poore cittizens must not with courtiers wed,
Who will in silkes and gay apparrell spend
More in one yeare then I am worth, by farre:
Therefore your honour neede not doubt my girle.   15
   Lincolne. Take heede, my lord, advise you what you do!
A verier unthrift lives not in the world,
Then is my cosen; for Ile tel you what:
Tis now almost a yeare since he requested
To travell countries for experience;   20
I furnisht him with coyne, billes of exchange,
Letters of credite, men to waite on him,
Solicited my friends in Italie
Well to respect him. But to see the end:

     [1] Cf. the similar opening of *The Wonder of a Kingdome.*

Scant had he jornied through halfe Germanie,   25
But all his coyne was spent, his men cast off,
His billes imbezeld, and my jolly coze,
Asham'd to shew his bankerupt presence here,
Became a shoomaker in Wittenberg,[1]
A goodly science for a gentleman   30
Of such discent! Now judge the rest by this:
Suppose your daughter have a thousand pound,
He did consume me more in one halfe yeare;
And make him heyre to all the wealth you have,
One twelve moneth's rioting wil waste it all.   35
Then seeke, my lord, some honest cittizen
To wed your daughter to.
    L. Maior.   I thanke your lordship.
[*Aside.*] Wel, foxe, I understand your subtiltie.
As for your nephew, let your lordships eie
But watch his actions, and you neede not feare,   40
For I have sent [2] my daughter farre enough.
And yet your cosen Rowland might do well,
Now he hath learn'd an occupation;
And yet I scorne to call him sonne in law.
    Lincolne. I, but I have a better trade for him: 45
I thanke his grace, he hath appointed him
Chiefe colonell of all those companies
Mustred in London and the shires about,
To serve his highnesse in those warres of France.
See where he comes!—   50

Enter LOVELL, LACIE, *and* ASKEW.[3]

              Lovel, what newes with you?
    Lovell. My Lord of Lincolne, tis his highnesse will,
That presently your cosen ship for France
With all his powers; he would not for a million,
But they should land at Deepe [4] within foure daies.

---

[1] Familiar to Dekker's public as the home of Faustus. As to the influence of Marlowe's play on Dekker see Herford, *Lit. Rel. Eng. and Ger.*, 213, *et seq.*
  [2] So Q 2; Q 1 omits.   [3] In Qtos., stage-direction after 'you?'   [4] Dieppe.

Linc. Goe certifie his grace, it shall be done.   55

          Exit LOVELL.

Now, cosen Lacie, in what forwardnesse
Are all your companies?

 Lacie.   All wel prepar'd.
The men of Hartfordshire lie at Mile End,[1]
Suffolke and Essex traine in Tuttle Fields,
The Londoners and those of Middlesex,   60
All gallantly prepar'd in Finsbury,
With frolike spirits long for their parting hower.

 L. Maior. They have their imprest,[2] coates, and furniture;
And, if it please your cosen Lacie come
To the Guild hall, he shall receive his pay;   65
And twentie pounds besides my brethren
Will freely give him, to approve our loves
We beare unto my lord, your uncle here.

 Lacie. I thanke your honour.

 Lincolne.   Thankes, my good Lord Maior.

 L. Ma. At the Guild hal we will expect your comming.   70

          Exit.

 Lincolne. To approve your loves to me? No subtiltie![3]
Nephew, that twentie pound he doth bestow
For joy to rid you from his daughter Rose.
But, cosens both, now here are none but friends—
I would not have you cast an amorous eie   75
Upon so meane a project as the love
Of a gay, wanton, painted cittizen.
I know, this churle even in the height of scorne

---

[1] Cf. Brainworm's reference: 'He will hate the musters at Mile End for it, to his dying day.' *E. M. i. H.*, II. iii. Mile End Fields was the scene of the grand muster of London men in 1532, Stow-Strype, *Survey*, Bk. V, 451. Finsbury Fields and Tothill Fields were associated with martial exercises and sports. See Hodge's allusion to Finsbury, III, i, 58; Pennant, *Account of London*, 262; Walcott, *Memorials of Westminster*, 325. These names for east (Mile End), west (Tothill Fields), and north (Finsbury), emphasize the completeness of Lacy's preparedness.

[2] Not 'regimental badge or device,' as R. explains; but earnest money, specifically advanced for public service. Cf. lines 65 and 146 of this scene; and see *Notes and Queries*, first series, II, 106, seventh series, 253, 374.

[3] Qtos., 'No subtiltie nephew:'

Doth hate the mixture of his bloud with thine.
I pray thee, do thou so! Remember, coze, 80
What honourable fortunes wayt on thee:
Increase the kings love, which so brightly shines,
And gilds thy hopes. I have no heire but thee,—
And yet not thee, if with a wayward spirit
Thou start from the true byas of my love. 85
 Lacie. My lord, I will for honor, not desire
Of land or livings, or to be your heire,
So guide my actions in pursuit of France,
As shall adde glorie to the Lacies name.
 Lincolne. Coze, for those words heres thirtie Portugues,[1] 90
And, nephew Askew, there's a few for you.
Faire Honour, in her loftiest eminence,
Staies in France for you, till you fetch her thence.
Then, nephewes, clap swift wings on your dissignes:
Be gone, be gone, make haste to the Guild hall; 95
There presently Ile meet you. Do not stay:
Where honour beckons,[2] shame attends delay. *Exit.*
 Askew. How gladly would your uncle have you gone!
 Lacie. True, coze, but Ile ore-reach his policies.
I have some serious businesse for three dayes, 100
Which nothing but my presence can dispatch.
You, therefore, cosen, with the companies
Shall haste to Dover; there Ile meete with you:
Or, if I stay past my prefixed time,
Away for France; weele meete in Normandie. 105
The twentie pounds my Lord Maior gives to me
You shall receive, and these ten portugues,
Part of mine uncles thirtie. Gentle coze,
Have care to our great charge; I know, your wisedome
Hath tride it selfe in higher consequence. 110
 Askew. Coze al my selfe am yours: yet have this care,
To lodge in London with all secrecie;

---

 [1] Harrison, *Descr. Engl.*, 'Of forren coines we have all the ducats . . . . the portigee.' Nashe,—'great pieces of gold.' Worth about £4.10.0.
 [2] Qtos., 'becomes' or 'become.' Corrected by Malone.

Our uncle Lincolne hath, besides his owne,
Many a jealous eie, that in your face
Stares onely to watch meanes for your disgrace.   115
   Lacie. Stay, cosen, who be these?

Enter SYMON EYRE, *his* WIFE, HODGE, FIRK, JANE, *and* RAFE
with a peece.[1]

   Eyre. Leave whining, leave whining! Away with this whimpring, this pewling, these blubbring teares, and these wet eies! Ile get thy husband discharg'd, I warrant thee, sweete Jane; go to!

   Hodge. Master, here be the captaines.   120

   Eyre. Peace, Hodge; husht, ye knave, husht!

   Firke. Here be the cavaliers and the coronels, maister.

   Eyre. Peace, Firke; peace, my fine Firke! Stand by with your pishery pasherie,[2] away! I am a man of the best presence; Ile speake to them, and they were Popes.[3]—Gentlemen, captaines, colonels, commanders! Brave men, brave leaders, may it please you to give me audience. I am Simon Eyre, the mad shoomaker of Towerstreete; this wench with the mealy mouth that wil never tire, is my wife, I can tel you; heres Hodge, my man and my foreman; heres Firke, my fine firking journeyman, and this is blubbered Jane. Al we come to be suters for this honest Rafe. Keepe him at home, and as I am a true shoomaker and a gentleman of the gentle craft, buy spurs your self, and Ile find ye bootes these seven yeeres.   134

   Wife. Seven yeares, husband?

   Eyre. Peace, midriffe, peace! I know what I do. Peace!

   Firke. Truly, master cormorant, you shal do God good service to let Rafe and his wife stay together. Shees a yong new-married woman; if you take her husband away from her a night, you undoo her; she may beg in the day-time; for hees as good a workman at a pricke and an awle, as any is in our trade.   141

   Jane. O let him stay, else I shal be undone.

---

[1] pair of shoes; from *piece*; an ornament or patch set on shoe or garment. Cf. Cotgrave.

[2] senseless folk. Cf. 'gibble-gabble,' below; and Evans' 'pribbles and prabbles' in *M. W. W.*

[3] Q 1 punctuates 'Popes, Gentlemen, ... commanders':

Firke. I, truly, she shal be laid at one side like a paire of old shooes else, and be occupied for no use.

Lacie. Truly, my friends, it lies not in my power: 145
The Londoners are prest, paide, and set forth
By the Lord Maior;[1] I cannot change a man.

Hodge. Why, then you were as good be a corporall as a colonel,
if you cannot discharge one good fellow; and I tell you true, I
thinke you doe more then you can answere, to presse a man within
a yeare and a day of his mariage.[2] 151

Eyre. Wel said, melancholy Hodge; gramercy, my fine foreman.

Wife. Truly, gentlemen, it were il done for such as you, to
stand so stiffely against a poore yong wife, considering her case,
she is new-married, but let that passe: I pray, deale not roughly
with her; her husband is a yong man, and but newly entred, but
let that passe. 157

Eyre. Away with your pisherie-pasherie, your pols and your
edipolls![3] Peace, Midaffe; silence, Cisly Bumtrincket![4] Let
your head speake. 160

Firke. Yea, and the hornes too, master.

Eyre. Too soone, my fine Firk, too soone![5] Peace, scoundrels!
See you this man? Captaines, you will not release him? Wel,
let him go; hee's a proper shot; let him vanish! Peace, Jane, drie
up thy teares, theile make his powder dankish. Take him, brave
men; Hector of Troy was an hackney to him, Hercules and Termagant scoundrelles, Prince Arthurs Round Table—by the Lord

[1] The Lord Mayor and aldermen exercised large power of conscription. On
Easter Day, 1596, 'they took from out of the places of publick worship, during the
time of Divine service, the number of men requir'd [one thousand], who being
immediately arm'd, began their march the night after for Dover in order for their
embarkation to France.' Maitland, *Hist. London*, Bk. I, 170, after Stow, *Annals*,
1605, 1201.

[2] Hodge argues from Deuteronomy, XXIV, 50.

[3] Intensive repetition of the voc. of Pollux. Cf. Kemp's *Hunt after the Ballad-
maker* (1600), Arber's *Garner*, VII, 37. Used by Eyre for his wife's reiterated
phrases.

[4] Used again by Dekker, II, iii, 34, and in *Satiromastix;* also by R. Brome in the
beggars' song of the Jovial Crew. Cf. III, iv, 36. P.

[5] i. e. 'too soon to speak of horns; I have been married only some thirty-odd
years; we are still in our honey-moon.' W.–P. suggest—'again you interrupt me
too soon!'

of Ludgate [1]—nere fed such a tall, such a dapper swordman; by
the life of Pharo, a brave, resolute swordman! Peace, Jane! I
say no more, mad knaves.   170

Firk. See, see, Hodge, how my maister raves in commendation
of Rafe!

Hodge. Raph, thart a gull, by this hand, and thou goest [not.]

Askew. I am glad, good Master Ayre, it is my hap
To meete so resolute a souldiour.   175
Trust me, for your report and love to him,
A common slight regard shall not respect him.

Lacie. Is thy name Raph?

Raph.   Yes, sir.

Lacie.   Give me thy hand;
Thou shalt not want, as I am a gentleman.
Woman, be patient; God, no doubt, wil send   180
Thy husband safe againe; but he must go,
His countries quarrel sayes it shall be so.

Hodge. Thart a gull, by my stirrop, if thou dost not goe.
I wil not have thee strike thy gimblet into these weake vessels;
pricke thine enemies, Rafe.   185

Enter DODGER.

Dodger. My lord, your uncle on the Tower Hill
Stayes with the Lord Mayor and the aldermen,
And doth request you with al speede you may,
To hasten thither.

Askew.   Cosin, lets go.[2]

Lacy. Dodger, runne you before, tel them we come.—   190
This Dodger is mine uncles parasite,   *Exit* DODGER.[3]
The arrantst varlet that e're breathd on earth;
He sets more discord in a noble house

---

[1] Possibly merely one of Eyre's alliterative impromptues, more likely, however, a
nickname either for the new image of Lud on the east side of Ludgate, rebuilt 1586,
or for some character of the day. Sobriquets like Mad Shoemaker of Towerstreet,
Cocke of Westminster, Greene King of St. Martins—the last two from Deloney's
Gentle Craft, Second Part—must have had numerous analogues in fact.

[2] Q 2, 'Cousin, come lets go'; an unnecessary emendation. See Schipper, *Metrik*,
II, par. 164, and Abbot, *Shak. Gr.*, par. 507.

[3] The stage-direction follows 'thither' l. 189.

By one daies broching of his pickethanke tales,
Then can be salv'd againe in twentie yeares,   195
And he, I feare, shall go with us to France,
To prie into our actions.

 Askew.   Therefore, coze,
It shall behoove you to be circumspect.

 Lacy. Feare not, good cosen.—Raph, hie to your colours.

 Raph. I must, because theres no remedie;   200
But, gentle maister and my loving dame,
As you have alwaies beene a friend to me,
So in mine absence thinke upon my wife.

 Jane. Alas, my Raph.

 Wife. She cannot speake for weeping.   205

 Eyre. Peace, you crackt groates, you mustard tokens, disquiet not the brave souldier. Goe thy waies, Raph!

 Jane. I, I, you bid him go; what shal I do,
When he is gone? [1]

 Firk. Why, be doing with me or my felow Hodge; be not idle. 210

 Eyre. Let me see thy hand, Jane. This fine hand, this white hand, these prettie fingers must spin, must card, must worke; worke, you bombast, cotten-candle queane,[2] worke for your living, with a pox to you.—Hold thee, Raph, heres five sixpences for thee; fight for the honour of the gentle craft, for the gentlemen shoomakers, the couragious cordwainers, the flower of S. Martins, the mad knaves of Bedlem, Fleetstreete, Towerstreete and White chappell; cracke me the crownes of the French knaves; a poxe on them, cracke them; fight, by the Lord of Ludgate; fight, my fine boy!   220

 Firke. Here, Rafe, here's three twopences: two carry into France, the third shal wash our soules at parting, for sorrow is drie. For my sake, firke the *Basa mon cues.*[3]

 Hodge. Raph, I am heavy at parting; but heres a shilling for

---

[1] Qtos., lines 208–209, one line.

[2] Q 1 hyphenates also 'candle' and 'queane.' Eyre's grotesque appellation is suggested by Jane's white soft hands and delicate appearance generally. She is mere cotton padding, a cotton-candle. See *N. E. D.* The same expression occurs again III, i, but perhaps with a slightly different connotation, namely: tallow outside, cotton inside.

[3] Cf. vulg. French, *baisez mon culs (queue)*.

thee. God send thee to cramme thy slops with French crownes,
and thy enemies bellies with bullets.   226

Raph. I thanke you, maister, and I thanke you all.
Now, gentle wife, my loving lovely Jane,
Rich men, at parting, give their wives rich gifts,
Jewels and rings, to grace their lillie hands.   230
Thou know'st our trade makes rings for womens heeles:
Here take this paire of shooes, cut out by Hodge,
Sticht by my fellow Firke, seam'd by my selfe,
Made up and pinckt, with letters for thy name.
Weare them, my deere Jane, for thy husbands sake;   235
And everie morning, when thou pull'st them on,
Remember me, and pray for my returne.
Make much of them; for I have made them so,
That I can know them from a thousand mo.

Sound drumme. Enter LORD MAIOR, LINCOLNE, LACY, ASKEW,
    DODGER, *and* Souldiers. *They passe over the stage;* RAFE *falles
    in amongest them;* FIRKE *and the rest cry farewel etc., and so
    exeunt.*

[Act II. Scene I. *A Garden at Old Ford.*]

Enter ROSE, *alone, making a garland.*

[*Rose.*] Here sit thou downe upon this flowry banke,
And make a garland for thy Lacies head.
These pinkes, these roses, and these violets,
These blushing gilliflowers, these marigoldes,
The faire embrodery of his coronet,   5
Carry not halfe such beauty in their cheekes,
As the sweete countnaunce of my Lacy doth.
O my most unkinde father! O my starres,
Why lowrde you so at my nativity,
To make me love, yet live, robd of my love?   10
Here as a theefe am I imprisoned
For my deere Lacies sake within those walles,

Which by my fathers cost were builded up
For better purposes; here must I languish
For him that doth as much lament, I know,   15
Mine absence, as for him I pine in woe.

Enter SIBIL.

Sibil. Good morrow, yong mistris. I am sure you make that
garland for me; against I shall be Lady of the Harvest.[1]
Rose. Sibil, what news at London?
Sibil. None but good; my Lord Mayor, your father, and Maister
Philpot, your uncle, and Maister Scot, your coosin, and Mistris
Frigbottom by Doctors Commons, doe all, by my troth, send you
most hearty commendations.   23
Rose. Did Lacy send kind greetings to his love?
Sibil. O yes, out of cry, by my troth. I scant knew him; here
a wore a [2] scarffe, and here a scarfe, here a bunch of fethers, and
here pretious stones and jewells, and a paire of garters,—O, monstrous! like one of our yellow silke curtains at home here in Old
Ford House, here in Maister Bellymounts chamber. I stoode at
our doore in Cornehill, lookt at him, he at me indeed, spake to
him, but he not to me, not a word; mary gup,[3] thought I, with a
wanion! He passt by me as prowde—Mary foh! are you growne
humorous, thought I; and so shut the doore, and in I came.   33
Rose. O Sibill, how dost thou my Lacy wrong!
My Rowland is as gentle as a lambe,   35
No dove was ever halfe so milde as he.
Sibil. Milde? yea, as a bushel of stampt crabs.[4] He lookt
upon me as sowre as verjuice. Goe thy wayes, thought I; thou
maist be much in my gaskins, but nothing in my neather stockes.
This is your fault, mistris, to love him that loves not you; he

---

[1] See *harvest* and *harvest-queen, N. E. D.* The quotations there from Spenser and
Hall show that Londoners were familiar with this title as applied to a person.
Otherwise, Sybil's remark would apply, sportively, to the richly dressed and gar-
landed image which in many districts remained the only harvest-queen. Cf.
Hentzner's account (1598), *Journey in England,* ed. Walpole, p. 79.

[2] So Q 3 : Q 1, Q 2 omit.

[3] Cf. 1 *Honest Whore,* III, ii, where Mistress Fingerlock uses both 'marry gup'
and 'marry come up.'

[4] crab-apples.

thinkes scorne to do as he's done to; but if I were as you, Ide cry:
go by, Jeronimo, go by! [1]

    Ide set mine olde debts against my new driblets,
    And the hares foot against the goose giblets,
    For if ever I sigh, when sleepe I shoulde take,   45
    Pray God, I may loose my mayden-head when I wake. [2]

Rose. Will my love leave me then, and go to France?

Sibill. I knowe not that, but I am sure I see him stalke before
the souldiers. By my troth, he is a propper man; but he is proper
that proper doth. Let him goe snicke-up yong mistris.   50

Rose. Get thee to London, and learne perfectly,
Whether my Lacy go to France, or no.
Do this, and I wil give thee for thy paines
My cambricke apron and my romish gloves,
My purple stockings and a stomacher.   55
Say, wilt thou do this, Sibil, for my sake?

Sibil. Wil I, quoth a? At whose suite? By my troth, yes Ile
go. A cambricke apron, gloves, a paire of purple stockings, and
a stomacher! Ile sweat in purple, mistris, for you; ile take any
thing that comes a Gods name. O rich! a cambricke apron!
Faith, then have at 'up tailes all'. [3] Ile go jiggy joggy [4] to London,
and be here in a trice, yong mistris.   *Exit.* 62

    Rose. Do so, good Sibill. Meane time wretched I
Will sit and sigh for his lost companie.   *Exit.*

---

[1] From *The Spanish Tragedy;*—debased into current slang.

[2] The first couplet is printed as prose in Qtos.; the second in all but Q 5. For the
usual meaning of the proverbial formula in the first couplet cf.: 'But pardon them
and thou shalt me forgive, And quite each other all old debts and driblets, And set
the hare's head against the goose gyblets,'—Harington, *Orlando Furioso*, 1591, bk.
XLIII, stanza 136; also: 'Some foolish words she hath passed to you in the country,
and some peevish debts you owe here in the city; set the hare's head to the goose-
giblet, release you her of her words, and I'll release you of your debts, sir,' *A Trick
to Catch the Old One*, Middleton's Works, ed. Dyce, II, 78. Hence, according to
Sybil's application—'off with the old love, on with the new; an even exchange.'

[3] An old boisterous game at cards. 'Ruff, slam, whisk, uptails all, new cut,'
Poor Robin, 1757. Cf. *E. M. i. H.* I, iv, 81; and for 'roysterers,' *Satiromastix* (ed.
Pearson, I, 243).

[4] So *Satiromastix* (ed. Pearson, I, p. 221).

[Act II. Scene II. *A Street in London.*]

Enter ROWLAND LACY, *like a Dutch Shooemaker.*

Lacy. How many shapes have gods and kings devisde,
Thereby to compasse their desired loves!
It is no shame for Rowland Lacy, then,
To clothe his cunning with the gentle craft,
That, thus disguisde, I may unknowne possesse   5
The onely happie presence of my Rose.
For her have I forsooke my charge in France,
Incurd the kings displeasure, and stird up
Rough hatred in mine uncle Lincolnes brest.
O love, how powerfull art thou, that canst change   10
High birth to baseness,[1] and a noble mind
To the meane semblance of a shooemaker!
But thus it must be. For her cruell father,
Hating the single union of our soules,
Hath secretly conveyed my Rose from London,   15
To barre me of her presence; but I trust,
Fortune and this disguise will furder me
Once more to view her beautie, gaine her sight.
Here in Towerstreete with Ayre the shooemaker
Meane I a while to worke; I know the trade,   20
I learn't it when I was in Wittenberge.
Then cheere thy hoping sprites, be not dismaide,
Thou canst not want: do Fortune what she can,
The gentle craft is living for a man.[2]   *Exit.*

[1] First changed in Q 4 from 'barenesse' to 'basenesse.'
[2] 'And never yet did any know A Shooemaker a begging go.' (Deloney's *Gentle Craft*, dedicatory verses.)

[Act II. Scene III. *An Open Yard before Eyre's House.*]

Enter EYRE, *making himselfe readie.*

Eyre. Where be these boyes, these girles, these drabbes, these scoundrels? They wallow in the fat brewisse of my bountie, and licke up the crums of my table, yet wil not rise to see my walkes cleansed. Come out, you powder-beefe queanes![1] What, Nan! what, Madge Mumble-crust.[2] Come out, you fatte midriffe, swag-belly whores,[3] and sweepe me these kennels that the noysome stench offende not the noses[4] of my neighbours. What, Firke, I say; what, Hodge! Open my shop windowes! What, Firke, I say!   9

Enter FIRKE.

Firke. O master, ist you that speake bandog[5] and bedlam this morning? I was in a dreame, and muzed what madde man was got into the streete so earlie; have you drunke this morning that your throate is so cleere?

Eyre. Ah, well saide, Firke; well said, Firke. To worke, my fine knave, to worke! Wash thy face, and thou't be more blest. 15

Firke. Let them wash my face that will eate it. Good maister, send for a sowce wife, if youle have my face cleaner.

Enter HODGE.

Eyre. Away, sloven! avaunt, scoundrell!—Good morrow, Hodge; good morrow, my fine foreman.

Hodge. O maister, good morrow; yare an earlie stirrer. Heeres a faire morning.—Good morrow, Firke, I could have slept this howre. Heeres a brave day towards.   22

Eyre. Oh, haste to worke, my fine foreman, haste to worke.

Firke. Maister, I am drie as dust to heare my fellow Roger

---

[1] Q 1, 'powder-beefe-queanes.'
[2] So Qtos. 3, 4, 5; but Qtos. 1, 2, 'Madge-Mumble-crust.' A common reminiscence from *Ralph Roister Doister.*
[3] Q 1, 'Midriffe-swag, belly-whores.'
[4] So Q 3; Qtos. 1, 2, 'nose.'
[5] mastiff.

talke of faire weather; let us pray for good leather, and let clownes and plowboyes and those that worke in the fieldes pray for brave dayes. Wee worke in a drie shop; what care I if it raine?   27

Enter EYRES WIFE.

Eyre. How now, dame Margery, can you see to rise? Trip and go, call up the drabs, your maides.

Wife. See to rise? I hope tis time inough, tis earlie inough for any woman to be seene abroad. I marvaile how manie wives in Towerstreet are up so soon. Gods me, tis not noone,—heres a yawling!   33

Eyre. Peace, Margerie, peace! Wheres Cisly Bumtrinket, your maide? She has a privie fault, she fartes in her sleepe. Call the queane up; if my men want shooethreed, ile swinge her in a stirrop.

Firke. Yet, thats but a drie beating; heres still a signe of drought.

Enter LACY, *singing.*

Lacy. *Der was een bore van Gelderland,*
        Frolick si byen;   40
      He was als dronck he cold nyet stand,
        Upsolce [1] *se byen.*
      Tap eens de canneken,
      Drincke, schone [2] *mannekin.* [3]

Firke. Maister, for my life, yonders a brother of the gentle craft; if he beare not Saint Hughes bones; [4] Ile forfeit my bones; hees some uplandish workman: hire him, good master, that I may learne some gibble gabble; twill make us worke the faster. 48

Eyre. Peace, Firke! A hard world! Let him passe, let him vanish; we have journeymen enow. Peace, my fine Firke!

[1] Very likely only a misprint; i. e. 'ol' = 'al' was transposed or inserted by the compositor, who was doubtless not familiar with Dutch, into what was intended for 'upsee.' What Dekker wrote was probably: 'Upsee al se byen.'

[2] Q 1, 'schone'; other qtos., 'schene.'

[3] There was a boor from Gelderland,
        Merry they are;
    He was so drunk he could not stand,
        Dutch-full they all are—
    Now drain the cannikin,
    Drink, pretty mannikin!

[4] See Appendix *A.*

Wife. Nay, nay, y'are best follow your mans councell; you shal see what wil come on't: we have not men enow, but we must entertaine ever butter-boxe; [1] but let that passe.   53

Hodge. Dame, fore God, if my maister follow your counsell, heele consume little beefe. He shal be glad of men, and hee can catch them.

Firke. I, that he shall.

Hodge. Fore God, a proper man, and I warrant, a fine workman. Maister, farewell; dame, adew; if such a man as he cannot find worke, Hodge is not for you.   *Offers to goe.* 60

Eyre. Stay, my fine Hodge.

Firke. Faith, and your foreman goe, dame, you must take a journey to seeke a new jorneyman; if Roger remove, Firke followes. If S. Hughs bones shall not be set a worke, I may prick mine awle in the wals, and goe play. Fare ye wel, master; God buy, dame.   65

Eyre. Tarrie, my fine Hodge, my briske foreman! Stay, Firke! Peace, pudding broath! By the Lord of Ludgate, I love my men as my life. Peace, you gallimafrie! Hodge, if he want worke, Ile hire him. One of you to him; stay,—he comes to us.

Lacie. *Goeden dach, meester, ende u, vro, oak.* [2]   70

Firke. Nayls, if I should speake after him without drinking, I shuld choke. And you, frind Oake, are you of the gentle craft?

Lacie. *Yaw, yaw, ik bin den skomawker.*

Firke. Den skomaker, quoth a! And heark you, skomaker, have you al your tooles, a good rubbing pinne, a good stopper, a good dresser, your foure sorts of awles, and your two balles of waxe, your paring knife, your hand and thumb-leathers, and good S. Hughs bones to smooth up your worke?   78

Lacie. *Yaw, yaw; be niet vorveard.* [3] *Ik hab all de dingen voour mack skoes groot and cleane.* [4]

Firke. Ha, ha! Good maister, hire him; heele make me laugh so that I shal worke more in mirth then I can in earnest.

Eyre. Heare ye, friend, have ye any skill in the mistery of cordwainers?   84

---

[1] Dutchman.   [2] Good day, master, and you, goodwife, too.
[3] be not afraid.   [4] large and small.

Lacie. Ik weet niet wat yow seg; ich verstaw you niet.[1]

Firke. Why, thus, man: [*imitating by gesture a shoemaker at work*] Ich verste u niet, quoth a.

Lacie. Yaw, yaw, yaw; ick can dat wel doen.

Firke. Yaw, yaw. He speakes yawing like a jacke daw that gapes to be fed with cheese curdes. O, heele give a villanous pul at a can of double beere; but Hodge and I have the vantage, we must drinke first, because wee are the eldest journeymen. 92

Eyre. What is thy name?

Lacy. Hans—Hans Meulter.

Eyre. Give me thy hand; th'art welcome.—Hodge, entertaine him; Fyrk, bid him welcome; come, Hans. Runne, wife, bid your maids, your trullibubs,[2] make readie my fine mens breakefasts. To him, Hodge! 98

Hodge. Hans, th'art welcome; use thy selfe friendly, for we are good fellowes; if not, thou shalt be fought with, wert thou bigger then a giant.

Fyrk. Yea, and drunke with, wert thou Gargantua. My maister keepes no cowards, I tel thee.—How, boy, bring him an heeleblocke, heers a new journeyman. *Enter* Boy. 104

Lacy. O ich wersto you; ich moet een halve dossen cans betaelen; here, boy, nempt dis skilling, tap eens freelicke.[3] *Exit* Boy.

Eyre. Quicke, snipper snapper, away! Fyrk, scowre thy throate, thou shalt wash it with Castilian licour.—*Enter* Boy.—Come, my last of the fives,[4] give me a can. Have to thee, Hans; here, Hodge; here, Fyrk; drinke, you mad Greeks, and worke like true Trojans, and pray for Simon Eyre, the shoomaker.—Here, Hans, and th'art welcome.[5] 112

Fyrk. Lo, dame, you would have lost a good fellow that wil teach us to laugh. This beere came hopping in well.

Wife. Simon, it is almost seven. 115

---

[1] I don't know what you say; I do not understand you. Q 1, 'vestaw.'

[2] trillibub: tripe, anything worthless.

[3] I am to pay for half a dozen cans; . . . take this shilling, just tap freely.

[4] My smallest, my number five last and the last of those lasts—my last resort. Cf.: 'Her wast exceedin small, The fives did fit her shoo,' from *A Love Song* (about 1606), Ritson, *Ancient Songs etc.*, ed. Hazlitt, p. 348. Perhaps, also, a punning reference to one of the two games known as the *fives*—hand-tennis and a game at cards. [5] See Appendix C.

Eyre. Is't so, Dame Clapper dudgeon?[1] Is't seven a clocke, and my mens breakfast not readie? Trip and goe, you sowst cunger,[2] away! Come, you madde Hiperboreans; follow me, Hodge; follow me, Hans; come after, my fine Fyrk; to worke, to worke a while, and then to breakfast!   *Exit.* 120

Fyrk. Soft! *Yaw, yaw,* good Hans, though my master have no more wit but to call you afore mee, I am not so foolish to go behind you, I being the elder journeyman.[3]   *Exeunt.*

[Act II.   Scene IV.   *A Field near Old Ford.*]

Hollowing within.   Enter Warner *and* Hammon, *like Hunters.*

Hammon. Cosen, beate every brake, the game's not farre,
This way with winged feete he fled from death,
Whilst the pursuing hounds, senting his steps,
Find out his high way to destruction.
Besides, the millers boy told me even now,   5
He saw him take soile,[4] and he hallowed him,
Affirming him [to have been] [5] so embost
That long he could not hold.
Warner.   If it be so,
Tis best we trace these meddowes by Old Ford.

A noise of Hunters within; Enter a Boy.

Hammon. How now, boy? Wheres the deere? speak, sawst thou him?   11

Boy. O yea; I saw him leape through a hedge, and then over a ditch, then at my Lord Maiors pale, over he skipt me, and in he went me, and "holla" the hunters cride, and "there, boy; there, boy!" But there he is, a mine honestie.   15

Ham. Boy, God amercy. Cosen, lets away;
I hope we shal find better sport to day.   *Exeunt.*

[1] Because her 'mealy mouth' is as active and noisy as a beggar's clap-dish.
[2] conger-eel.   [3] Cf. III, i, 146.
[4] So Q 2; Q 1, 'saile.'   [5] Not in Qtos.

[Act II. Scene V. *Another part of the Field*.]

Hunting within. Enter ROSE *and* SIBILL.

Rose. Why, Sibill, wilt thou prove a forrester?

Sibill. Upon some,[1] no; forrester, go by; no, faith, mistris.
The deere came running into the barne through the orchard and
over the pale; I wot wel, I lookt as pale as a new cheese to see him.
But whip, saies Goodman Pinne-close, up with his flaile, and our
Nicke with a prong, and downe he fel, and they upon him, and I
upon them. By my troth, we had such sport; and in the end we
ended him; his throate we cut, flead him, unhornd him, and my
Lord Maior shal eat of him anon, when he comes.   9

Hornes sound within.

Rose. Heark, heark, the hunters come; y'are best take heed,
Theyle have a saying to you for this deede.

Enter HAMMON, WARNER, Huntsmen, *and* Boy.

Ham. God save you, faire ladies.

Sibil.   Ladies, O grosse!

War. Came not a bucke this way?

Rose.   No, but two does.

Ham. And which way went they? Faith, weel hunt at those.

Sibill. At those? upon some, no: when, can you tell?   15

War. Upon some, I.

Sibill.   Good Lord!

War.   Wounds! Then farewell!

Ham. Boy, which way went he?

Boy.   This way, sir, he ranne.

Ham. This way he ranne indeede, faire Mistris Rose;
Our game was lately in your orchard seene.

War. Can you advise, which way he tooke his flight?   20

Sibil. Followe your nose; his hornes will guide you right.

War. Thart a mad wench.

Sibill.   O, rich!

---

[1] 'Upon some, no' and 'upon some, I' seem to have been modish expressions of
assertion, formed after 'upon my word, my honour' etc. W.–P.

Rose.   Trust me, not I.
It is not like that [1] the wild forrest deere
Would come so neare to places of resort;
You are deceiv'd, he fled some other way.   25
    War. Which way, my suger-candie, can you shew?
    Sibill. Come up, good honnisops, upon some, no.
    Rose. Why doe you stay, and not pursue your game?
    Sibill. Ile hold my life, their hunting nags be lame.
    Ham. A deere more deere is found within this place.   30
    Rose. But not the deere, sir, which you had in chace.
    Ham. I chac'd the deere, but this deere chaceth me.
    Rose. The strangest hunting that ever I see.
But wheres your parke?   *She offers to goe away.*
    Ham.   Tis here: O stay!   35
    Rose. Impale me, and then I will not stray.[2]
    War. They wrangle, wench; we are more kind then they.
    Sibill. What kind of hart [3] is that, deere hart,[3] you seeke?
    War. A hart, deare hart.
    Sibil.   Who ever saw the like?
    Rose. To loose your heart, is't possible you can?   40
    Ham. My heart is lost.
    Rose.   Alacke, good gentleman!
    Ham. This poore lost hart would I wish you might find.
    Rose. You, by such lucke, might prove your hart a hind.
    Ham. Why, Lucke had hornes, so have I heard some say.
    Rose. Now, God, and't be his wil, send Luck into your way. 45

        Enter L. MAIOR *and* Servants.

    L. Mai. What, M. Hammon? Welcome to Old Ford!
    Sibill. Gods pittikins, hands off, sir! Heers my lord.
    L. Maior. I heare you had ill lucke, and lost your game.
    Hammon. Tis true, my lord.
    L. Maior.   I am sorie for the same.
What gentleman is this?   50
    Hammon,   My brother in law.
    L. Maior. Y'are welcome both; sith Fortune offers you

---

[1] Q 2; Q 1 omits.   [2] See Schipper, *Metrik* II, par. 164.   [3] Qtos. 2–5, 'heart.'

Into my hands, you shal not part from hence,
Until you have refresht your wearied limmes.
Go, Sibel, cover the boord! You shal be guest
To no good cheare, but even a hunters feast.　　55
　　Hammon. I thanke your lordship.—Cosen, on my life,
For our lost venison I shal find a wife.　　*Exeunt.*
　　L. Maior. In, gentlemen; Ile not be absent long.—
This Hammon is a proper gentleman,
A citizen by birth, fairely allide;　　60
How fit an husband were he for my girle!
Wel, I wil in, and do the best I can,
To match my daughter to this gentleman.　　*Exit.*

[Act III. Scene I.[1] *A Room in Eyre's House.*]

Enter LACIE, Skipper, HODGE, *and* FIRKE.

　　Skip. Ick sal yow wat seggen, Hans; dis skip, dat comen from
Candy, is al vol,[2] by Gots sacrament, van sugar, civet, almonds, cam-
brick, end alle dingen, towsand towsand ding. Nempt it, Hans,
nempt it vor u meester. Daer be de bils van laden. Your meester
Simon Eyre sal hae good copen. Wat seggen yow, Hans?[3]　　5
　　Firk. Wat seggen de reggen de copen, slopen—laugh, Hodge,
laugh!
　　Lacie. Mine liever[4] broder Firk, bringt Meester Eyre tot[5] det
signe un Swannekin![6] daer sal yow finde dis skipper end me. Wat
seggen yow, broder Firk? Doot it, Hodge. Come, skipper. *Exeunt.*
　　Firke. Bring him, quod you? Heers no knaverie, to bring my
master to buy a ship, worth the lading of two or three hundred
thousand pounds. Alas, thats nothing; a trifle, a bable, Hodge.　13
　　Hod. The truth is, Firk, that the marchant owner of the
ship dares not shew his head, and therefore this skipper that deales

---

[1] See Appendix *D.*　　　　　　　[2] Qtos. 2–5; Q 1, *wel.*
[3] I'll tell you what, Hans; this ship, . . . is all full, by God's sacrament, of
sugar, etc. Take it . . . for your master. There are the bills of lading. . . .
Eyre shall have a good bargain, etc.
[4] dear.　　　　　　[5] Qtos., 'lot.'　　[6] to the sign of the Swan.

for him, for the love he beares to Hans, offers my master Eyre a bargaine in the commodities. He shal have a reasonable day of payment; he may sel the wares by that time, and be an huge gainer himselfe.[1]   19

Firk. Yea, but can my fellow Hans lend my master twentie porpentines as an earnest pennie?

Hodge. Portegues, thou wouldst say; here they be, Firke; heark, they gingle in my pocket like S. Mary Overies bels.[2]   23

Enter EYRE *and his* WIFE.

Firke. Mum, here comes my dame and my maister. Sheele scold, on my life, for loytering this Monday; but al's one, let them al say what they can, Monday's our holyday.

Wife. You sing, Sir Sauce, but I beshrew your heart,
I feare, for this your singing we shal smart.

Firke. Smart for me, dame; why, dame, why?   . 29

Hodg. Maister, I hope, yowle not suffer my dame to take downe your journeymen.

Firk. If she take me downe, Ile take her up; yea, and take her downe too, a button-hole lower.   33

Eyre. Peace, Firke; not I, Hodge; by the life of Pharao, by the Lord of Ludgate, by this beard, every haire whereof I valew at a kings ransome, shee shal not meddle with you.—Peace, you bumbast, cotten-candle[3] queane; away, queene of clubs; quarrel not with me and my men, with me and my fine Firke; Ile firke you, if you do.   39

Wife. Yea, yea, man, you may use me as you please; but let that passe.

Eyre. Let it passe, let it vanish away; peace! Am I not Simon

---

[1] The increasing demand for articles of luxury, as well as Elizabeth's protective policy, especially the granting of monopolistic privileges to trading-companies guaranteed ready sales and high prices. Cf. Harrison's complaint, *Descr. Engl.* 131. Moreover, the abolition of the privileges of the Steelyard, followed by a warning to the resident Hanseatic traders to leave the kingdom before the end of Feb. 1598 (Loftie, *London*, II, p. 425), must have compelled more than one German 'marchant owner' to dispose of the cargoes of his argosies at great loss. Cunningham, *Growth of English Industry and Commerce*.

[2] So Q 4; Qtos. 1-3, 'Queries.' 'In Bridge ward, without, . . . standeth a faire church, called Saynt Mary over the Rye, or Overie, that is, over the water.' Stow, 333.   [3] Q 1, 'bumbast-cotton-candle-queane.'

Eyre? Are not these my brave men, brave shoomakers, all gentle-men of the gentle craft? Prince am I none, yet am I noblie borne, as beeing the sole sonne of a shoomaker.[1] Away, rubbish; vanish; melt; melt like kitchin stuffe.[2]   46

Wife. Yea, yea, tis wel; I must be cald rubbish, kitchin-stuffe, for a sort of knaves.

Firke. Nay, dame, you shall not weepe and waile in woe for me. Master, Ile stay no longer; here's a vennentorie of my shop tooles. Adue, master; Hodge, farewel.   51

Hodge. Nay, stay, Firke; thou shalt not go alone.

Wife. I pray, let them goe; there be mo maides then Mawkin, more men then Hodge, and more fooles then Firke,

Firke. Fooles? Nailes! if I tarry nowe, I would my guts might be turnd to shoe-thread.   56

Hodge. And if I stay, I pray God I may be turnd to a Turke, and set in Finsbury for boyes to shoot at.—Come, Firk.

Eyre. Stay, my fine knaves, you armes of my trade, you pillars of my profession. What, shal a tittle tattles words make you forsake Simon Eyre?—Avaunt, kitchinstuffe! Rip, you brown bread Tannikin;[3] out of my sight! Move me not! Have not I tane you from selling tripes in Eastcheape,[4] and set you in my shop, and made you haile fellowe with Simon Eyre, the shoomaker? And now do you deale thus with my journeymen? Looke, you powder beefe queane, on the face of Hodge, heers a face for a lord.

Firke. And heers a face for any lady in Christendome.   67

Eyre. Rip, you chitterling,[5] avaunt![6] Boy, bid the tapster of the Bores Head fil me a doozen cannes of beere for my journeymen.

Firke. A doozen cans? O, brave! Hodge, now Ile stay.   70

---

[1] See Appendix *B*.

[2] Cf. 'more greazie than a kitchen-stuffe-wifes basket,' Dekker, *Wonderfull Yeare*, Huth Library I, 140; 'they (i. e. chandlers) make them of all kinds of kitchen stuffe and other stinking baggage,' Stubbes, *Anatomy of Abuse*, in *New Shak. Soc.*, p. 49.

[3] Not white-bread but common. Tannikin (a diminutive of Anne, with pre-fixed *t*) was a colloquial name for Dutch-women. Cf. *Patient Grissill*, ed. Hübsch l. 1370.

[4] 'This East cheape is now a flesh market of Butchers . . . and such other as sold victuails readie dressed of all sorts,' Stow, *Survey*, 1598, p. 170.

[5] minced meat, sausage; addressed to wife,—also 'avaunt.'

[6] Qtos., 'avaunt boy'; wrong.

Eyre [*in a low voice to the* Boy]. And the knave fils any more
then two, he payes for them. [*Exit Boy. Aloud.*] A doozen cans
of beere for my journeymen. [*Re-enter* Boy.] Here,[1] you mad
Mesopotamians, wash your livers with this liquour. Where be
the odde ten? [*In a low voice to his wife.*] No more, Madge, no
more.—Wel saide. Drinke and to work!—What worke dost thou,
Hodge? what work?

Hodge. I am a making a paire of shooes for my Lord Maiors
daughter, Mistresse Rose.   78

Firke. And I a paire of shooes for Sybill, my lords maid. I
deale with her.

Eyre. Sybil? Fie, defile not thy fine workemanly fingers with
the feete of kitchinstuffe and basting ladles. Ladies of the court,
fine ladies, my lads, commit their feete to our apparelling; put
grosse worke to Hans. Yarke and seame, yarke and seame!   86

Fyrk. For yarking and seaming let me alone, and I come toot.

Hodge. Wel, maister, al this is from the bias. Do you remember
the ship my fellow Hans told you of? The skipper and he are both
drinking at the Swan.[2] Here be the Portigues to give earnest.
If you go through with it, you cannot choose but be a lord at least.

Firke. Nay, dame, if my master prove not a lord, and you a
ladie, hang me.   93

Wife. Yea, like inough, if you may loiter and tipple thus.

Firke. Tipple, dame? No, we have beene bargaining with
Skellum [3] Skanderbag [4] can you Dutch spreaken,[5] for a ship of
silke Cipresse, laden with sugar candie.   97

Enter the Boy *with a velvet coate and an Aldermans gowne.*[6] AYRE
puts it on.

Eire. Peace, Firk; silence, Tittle tattle! Hodge, Ile go through
with it. Heers a seale ring, and I have sent for a garded gown and

---

[1] Qtos. 1, 2. 'Heave you mad.'
[2] Of the two Swans mentioned in *Newes from Bartholomew Fayre* (quoted, Drake,
Shak. and his Times, II, 133) one at Dowgate, the other in Old Fish Street, the latter
was the more convenient to both the Thames and Tower street.
[3] Cf. Germ. *Schelm.* 'Schellum in Dutch, a theife,' marginal note on p. 349 of
A Strange Horse-race, Dekker's *Prose Works*, Huth Library, vol. III.
[4] John Kastriota. Cf.: 'Whoreson Scanderbag rogue!' *E. M. i. H., I*, iii, 20.
[5] This phrase is part of Firk's name for the skipper.
[6] See Appendix *D.*

a damask casock. See where it comes; looke here, Maggy; help
me, Firk; apparrel me, Hodge; silke and satten, you mad Philis-
tines, silke and satten.[1]   102

Firk. Ha, ha, my maister wil be as proud as a dogge in a dublet,
al in beaten damaske and velvet.

Eyre. Softly, Firke, for rearing of the nap, and wearing threadbare my garments. How dost thou like mee, Firke? How do I
looke, my fine Hodge?   107

Hodge. Why, now you looke like your self, master. I warrant
you, ther's few in the city, but will give you the wal, and come
upon you with the right worshipful.

Firke. Nailes, my master lookes like a thred-bare cloake new
turn'd and drest. Lord, Lord, to see what good raiment doth!
Dame, dame, are you not enamoured?   113

Eyre. How saist thou, Maggy, am I not brisk? Am I not fine?

Wife. Fine? By my troth, sweet hart, very fine! By my troth,
I never likte thee so wel in my life, sweete heart; but let that passe.
I warrant, there be many women in the citie have not such hand-
some husbands, but only for their apparrell; but let that passe too.

Enter HANS *and* Skipper.

*Hans. Godden day, mester. Dis be de skipper dat heb de skip
van marchandice; de commodity ben good; nempt it, master, nempt it.*

Aire. Godamercy, Hans; welcome, skipper. Where lies this
ship of marchandice?   122

*Skip. De skip ben in revere,[2] dor be van sugar, cyvet, almonds,
cambricke, and a towsand towsand tings, Gotz sacrament; nempt it,
mester: ye [3] sal heb good copen.*

Firk. To him, maister! O sweete maister! O sweet wares!
Prunes, almons, suger-candy, carrat roots, turnups, O brave
fatting meate! Let not a man buye a nutmeg but your selfe. 128

Eyre. Peace, Firke! Come, Skipper, Ile go aboord [4] with you.—
Hans, have you made him drinke?

---

[1] In Deloney's story Mrs. Eyre advises her husband to put on a doublet of tawny
satin, over this a cassock of branched damask furred round about the skirts with the
finest foynes, breeches of black velvet, a cap of finest black, a fair gown welted
about with velvet, and on the forefinger a great seal-ring of gold (ed. 1639, p. 44;
Lange's ed. *Palæstra*, XVIII, 68).

[2] river. Qtos., 'rouere.'   [3] Q 1, 'yo.'   [4] Qtos. 1, 2, 'abroade.'

Skip. Yaw, yaw, ic heb veale gedrunck.

Eyre. Come, Hans, follow me. Skipper, thou shalt have my countenance in the cittie. *Exeunt.* 133

Firke. Yaw, *heb veale gedrunck*, quoth a. They may well be called butter-boxes, when they drinke fat veale and thick beare too. But come, dame, I hope you'le chide us no more.

Wife. No, faith, Firke; no, perdy, Hodge. I do feele honour creepe upon me, and which is more, a certaine rising in my flesh; but let that passe. 139

Firke. Rising in your flesh do you feele say you? I, you may be with childe, but why should not my maister feele a rising in his flesh, having a gowne and a gold ring on? But you are such a shrew, you'le soone pull him downe.

Wi. Ha, ha! prethee, peace! Thou mak'st my worshippe laugh; but let that passe. Come, Ile go in; Hodge, prethee, goe before me; Firke, follow me.[1] 146

Fi. Firke doth follow; Hodge, passe out in state. *Exeunt.*

[Act III. Scene II. *London.—A Room in Lincoln's House.*]

Enter LINCOLNE *and* DODGER.

Li. How now, good Dodger, whats the newes in France?

Dodger. My lord, upon the eighteenth [2] day of May
The French and English were preparde to fight;
Each side with eager furie gave the signe
Of a most hot encounter. Five long howres 5
Both armies fought together; at the length
The lot of victorie fel on our sides.
Twelve thousand of the Frenchmen that day dide,
Foure thousand English, and no man of name
But Captaine Hyam and yong Ardington, 10
Two gallant gentlemen, I knew them well. [3]

---

[1] Ordinarily the oldest apprentice acted as usher to the master's wife. Cf. Massinger, *City Madam*, IV, iv.　　　　[2] Qtos. 1, 2, 'eighteene.'

[3] Probably as imaginary as Bobadill's description of the capture of Strigonium.

Lin. But Dodger, prethee, tell me, in this fight
How did my cozen Lacie beare himselfe?

Dodger. My lord, your cosen Lacie was not there.

Linc. Not there?   15

Dog.   No, my good lord.

Linc.   Sure, thou mistakest.

I saw him shipt, and a thousand eies beside
Were witnesses [1] of the farewels which he gave,
When I, with weeping eies, bid him adew.
Dodger, take heede.

Dodger.   My lord, I am advis'd
That what I spake is true: to prove it so,   20
His cosen Askew, that supplide his place,
Sent me for him from France, that secretly
He might convey himself thither.[2]

Lin.   Ist even so?
Dares he so carelessely venture his life,
Upon the indignation of a king?   25
Hath he despis'd my love, and spurn'd those favours
Which I with prodigall hand powr'd on his head?
He shall repent his rashnes with his soule;
Since of my love he makes no estimate,
Ile make him wish he had not knowne my hate.   30
Thou hast no other newes?

Dodger.   None else, my lord.

Lin. None worse I know thou hast.—Procure the king
To crowne his giddie browes with ample honors,
Send him cheefe colonell, and all my hope

Maybe, suggested, however, by Shakespeare's version of Holinshed's narrative, *Henry V*, IV, viii, 80–110. Lines 9–10, above, at least, appear to be a reminiscence. Cf. 'Sir Richard Ketly, Davy Gam, esquire: None else of name;' The hypothesis of a connection between Dekker's play and Henry V receives support from (1) the character given to the King, (2) the buoyant spirit of anti-French patriotism, and (3) Dekker's habit of availing himself promptly of the successes of rival playwrights. See Zupitza's remarks (Archiv. XCII, 104) on the relation of *Patient Grissill* to *M. W. W.*, and of the *Honest Whore* to *Othello*. It would follow, of course, that Henry V had been acted before July 15, 1599.

[1] So Qtos, 1, 2; other Qtos., 'witnesse.'

[2] Qtos., 'hither'; which may be defended on the ground that Dodger is reporting Askew's message.

Thus to be dasht! But tis in vaine to grieve,   35
One evill cannot a worse releeve.[1]
Upon my life, I have found out his plot;
That old dog, Love, that fawnd upon him so,
Love to that puling girle, his faire cheek't Rose,
The Lord Maiors daughter, hath distracted him,   40
And in the fire of that loves lunacie
Hath he burnt up himselfe, consum'd his credite,
Lost the kings love, yea, and I feare, his life,
Onely to get a wanton to his wife.
Dodger, it is so.   45
   Dodger.   I feare so, my good lord.
   Lincolne. It is so—nay, sure it cannot be!
I am at my wits end. Dodger![2]
   Dodger.   Yea, my lord.
   Lin. Thou art acquainted with my nephewes haunts;
Spend this gold for thy paines: goe seeke him out;
Watch at my Lord Maiors—there if he live,   50
Dodger, thou shalt be sure to meete with him.
Prethee, be diligent.—Lacie, thy name
Liv'd once in honour, now tis [3] dead in shame.—
Be circumspect.   *Exit.*
   Dodger.   I warrant you, my Lord.   *Exit.*

[Act III.   Scene III.   *London.—A Room in the Lord
Mayor's House.*]

Enter LORD MAIOR *and* MASTER SCOTTE.

   L. Ma. Good Maister Scott, I have beene bolde with you,
To be a witnesse to a wedding knot
Betwixt yong Maister Hammon and my daughter.
O, stand aside; see where the lovers come.

---

[1] An instance of omitted anacrusis. W.–P. propose to improve the line by reading 'more worse'!
[2] Qtos., 'end Dodger.'
[3] Not in Qtos., but required by metre and sense.

Enter HAMMON *and* ROSE.

Rose. Can it be possible, you love me so? 5
No, no, within those eie-bals I espie
Apparant likelihoods of flattery.
Pray now,[1] let go my hand.
  Hammon.   Sweete Mistris Rose,
Misconstrue not my words, nor misconceive
Of my affection, whose devoted soule 10
Sweares that I love thee dearer then my heart.
  Rose. As deare as your owne heart? I judge it right,
Men love their hearts best when th'are out of sight.
  Hamond. I love you, by this hand.
  Rose.   Yet hands off now!
If flesh be fraile, how weake and frail's your vowe! 15
  Hamond. Then by my life I sweare.
  Rose.   Then do not brawle;
One quarrell looseth wife and life and all.
Is not your meaning thus?
  Hamond.   In faith, you jest.
  Rose. Love loves to sport; therefore leave love, y'are best.
  L. Mai. What? square they, Maister Scot? 20
  Scot.   Sir, never doubt,
Lovers are quickly in, and quickly out.
  Ham. Sweet Rose, be not so strange in fansying me.
Nay, never turne aside, shunne not my sight:
I am not growne so fond, to fond my love
On any that shall quit it with disdaine; 25
If you wil love me, so—if not, farewell.
  L. Ma. Why, how now, lovers, are you both agreede?
  Ham. Yes, faith, my lord.
  L. Maior.   Tis well, give me your hand.
Give me yours, daughter.—How now, both pull backe[2]
What meanes this, girle? 30
  Rose.   I meane to live a maide.
  Ham. But not to die one; pawse, ere that be said.   *Aside.*

[1] Qtos., 'Pray now let.'
[2] Qtos., one line each to: 'Tis well . . . daughter.' and 'How . . . girle.'

L. Mai. Wil you stil crosse me, still be obstinate?

Hamond. Nay, chide her not, my lord, for doing well;
If she can live an happie virgins life,
Tis farre more blessed then to be a wife.   35

Rose. Say, sir, I cannot: I have made a vow,
Who ever be my husband, tis not you.

L. Mai. Your tongue is quicke; but M. Hamond, know,
I bade you welcome to another end.

Ham. What, would you have me pule and pine and pray, 40
With 'lovely ladie,' 'mistris of my heart,'
'Pardon your servant,' and the rimer play,
Rayling on Cupid and his tyrants dart;
Or shal I undertake some martiall spoile,
Wearing your glove at turney and at tilt,   45
And tel how many gallants I unhorst—
Sweete, wil this pleasure you?

Rose.   Yea, when wilt begin?
What, loverimes, man? [1] Fie on that deadly sinne!

L. Maior. If you wil have her, Ile make her agree.

Ham. Enforced love is worse then hate to me.   50
[*Aside.*] There is a wench keepes shop in the Old Change,
To her wil I; it is not wealth I seeke,
I have enough, and wil preferre her love
Before the world.—[*Aloud.*] My good Lord Maior, adew.
Old love for me, I have no lucke with new.   *Exit.*   55

L. Ma. Now, mammet, you have wel behav'd your selfe,
But you shal curse your coynes, if I live.—
Whose within there? See you convay your mistris
Straight to th' Old Forde! Ile keepe you straight enough.
Fore God, I would have sworne the puling girle   60
Would willingly accepted [2] Hammons love;
But banish him, my thoughts!—Go, minion, in!   *Exit* ROSE.
Now tel me, Master Scot, would you have thought
That Master Simon Eyre, the shoomaker,

---

[1] Qtos., What 'louerimes man?'
[2] So Qtos. 1–3. Q 4 'accept'; but, for construction as above, see *Coriolanus* IV,
vi, 35, and *Edw. III*, IV, v, 101. W.–P.

Had beene of wealth to buy such marchandize? 65
   Scot. Twas wel, my lord, your honour and my selfe
Grew partners with him; for your bils of lading
Shew that Eyres gaines in one commoditie
Rise at the least to ful three thousand pound
Besides like gaine in other marchandize. 70
   L. Maior. Wel, he shal spend some of his thousands now,
For I have sent for him to the Guild hal.

Enter EYRE.

See, where he comes.—Good morrow, Master Eyre.
   Eyre. Poore Simon Eyre, my lord, your shoomaker.
   L. Maior. Wel, wel, it likes your selfe to terme you so. 75

Enter DODGER.[1]

Now, M. Dodger, whats the news with you?
   Dodger. Ide gladly speake in private to your honour.
   L. Maior. You shal, you shal.—Master Eyre and M. Scot,
I have some businesse with this gentleman;
I pray, let me intreate you to walke before 80
To the Guild hal; Ile follow presently.
Master Eyre, I hope ere noone to call you shiriffe.
   Eyre. I would not care, my lord, if you might cal
Me King of Spaine.—Come, Master Scot.[2]

Exeunt [3] [EYRE *and* SCOT].

   L. Maior. Now, Maister Dodger, whats the newes you bring? 85
   Dod. The Earle of Lincolne by me greets your lordship.
And earnestly requests you, if you can,
Informe him, where his nephew Lacie keepes.
   L. Maior. Is not his nephew Lacie now in France?
   Dodger. No, I assure your lordship, but disguisde 90
Lurkes here in London.
   L. Maior.   London? ist even so?
It may be; but upon my faith and soule,
I know not where he lives, or whether he lives:

---

[1] Qtos. 1, 2, put after the question.
[2] Qtos., W.-P., and R. print lines 83–84 as prose; but cf. the short line I, i, 189:
'To hasten thither. Cosin, lets go.'
[3] Added in Q 4.

So tel my Lord of Lincolne.—Lurch in London?
Well, Master Dodger, you perhaps may start him;   95
Be but the meanes to rid him into France,
Ile give you a dozen angels for your paines:
So much I love his honour, hate his nephew,
And, prethee, so informe thy lord from me.
    Dodger. I take my leave.   *Exit* DODGER. 100
    L. Maior.   Farewell, good Master Dodger.
Lacie in London?   I dare pawne my life,
My daughter knowes thereof, and for that cause
Denide yong M. Hammon in his love.
Wel, I am glad, I sent her to Old Forde.
Gods Lord, tis late; to Guild hall I must hie;   105
I know my brethren stay my companie.   *Exit.*

[Act III.   Scene IV.   *London.—A Room in Eyre's
House.*]

    Enter FIRKE, EYRES WIFE, HANS, *and* ROGER.

Wife. Thou goest too fast for me, Roger.   O, Firke! [1]
Firke. I, forsooth.
Wife. I pray thee, runne—doe you heare?—runne to Guild hall,
and learne if my husband, Master Eyre, wil take that worshipfull
vocation of M. Shiriffe upon him.   Hie thee, good Firke.   5
Firke. Take it?   Well, I goe; and he should not take it, Firk
sweares to foreswear him.   Yes, forsooth, I goe to Guild hall.
Wife. Nay, when? thou art too compendious and tedious.
Firke. O rare, your excellence is full of eloquence; how like a
new cart wheele my dame speakes, and she lookes like an old
musty ale-bottle [2] going to scalding.   11
Wife. Nay, when? thou wilt make me melancholy.
Firke. God forbid, your worship should fall into that humour;—
I runne.   *Exit.*
Wife. Let me see now, Roger and Hans.

[1] Qtos. 1-2, omit.   [2] Because bottles made of leather were still in use.

H. I, forsooth, dame—mistris I should say, but the old terme so stickes to the roofe of my mouth, I can hardly lick it off.

Wife. Even what thou wilt, good Roger; dame is a faire name for any honest Christian; but let that passe. How dost thou, Hans?   20

Hans. Mee tanck you, vro.

Wife. Wel, Hans and Roger, you see, God hath blest your master, and, perdie, if ever he comes to be M. Shiriffe of London— as we are al mortal—you shal see, I wil have some odde thing or other in a corner for you: I wil not be your backe friend; [1] but let that passe. Hans, pray thee, tie my shooe.   26

Hans. Yaw, ic sal, vro.

Wife. Roger, thou knowst the length of my foote; as it is none of the biggest, so I thanke God, it is handsome enough; prethee, let me have a paire of shooes made, corke, good Roger, woodden heele,[2] too.   31

Hodge. You shall.

Wife. Art thou acquainted with never a fardingale-maker, nor a French-hoode maker? I must enlarge my bumme, ha, ha! How shall I looke in a hoode, I wonder! Perdie, odly, I thinke.

Roger [aside]. As a catte out of a pillorie [3]—[*Aloud.*] verie wel, I warrant you, mistresse.

Wife. Indeed, all flesh is grasse; and, Roger, canst thou tel where I may buye a good haire?

Roger. Yes, forsooth, at the poulterers in Gracious Street.[4]   40

Wi. Thou art an ungratious wag; perdy, I meane a false haire for my periwig.

Roger. Why, mistris, the next time I cut my beard, you shall have the shavings of it; but they are all true haires.

[1] reluctant to assist.

[2] Combining in one request the elevating features of two kinds of ladies' shoes, i. e. the corked shoe or slipper with a pad of cork inside rising towards the heel, and the shoe with a high wooden heel. Fairholt, *Costume*, II, 72; Drake, *Shakespeare;* Stubbes, *Anatomy.*

[3] The fronts of French hoods were depressed over the forehead and stood out in folds or flaps over the temples, whence Roger's comparison. Later on, l. 137, Eyre sees a resemblance to a 'shoulder of mutton.'

[4] Folk-etymology for Grass street, now Gracechurch street. 'Then higher in Grass street is the parish church of S. Benet, called Grasse Church, of the herb market there kept.' Stow.

Wi. It is verie hot, I must get me a fan or else a maske.   45
Roger. So you had neede, to hide your wicked face.
Wi. Fie upon it, how costly this world's calling is; perdy, but
that it is one of the wonderfull works of God, I would not deale
with it. Is not Firke come yet? Hans, bee not so sad, let it passe
and vanish, as my husbands worshippe saies.   50
Hans. Ick bin vrolicke, lot see yow soo.[1]
Roger. Mistris, wil you drinke a pipe of tobacco?
Wife. Oh, fie uppon it, Roger, perdy! These filthie tobacco
pipes are the most idle slavering bables that ever I felt. Out
uppon it! God blesse us, men looke not like men that use them.55

Enter Rafe, *being lame.*

Roger. What, fellow Rafe? Mistres, looke here, Janes hus-
band! Why, how now,[2] lame? Hans, make much of him, hees a
brother of our trade, a good workeman, and a tall souldier.
Hans. You be welcome, broder.
Wife. Pardie, I knew him not. How dost thou, good Rafe?
I am glad to [3] see thee wel.   61
Rafe. I would to God, you saw me, dame, as wel
As when I went from London into France.
Wife. Trust mee, I am sorie, Rafe, to see thee impotent.
Lord, how the warres have made him sunburnt! The left leg is
not wel; twas a faire gift of God, the infirmitie tooke not hold a
litle higher, considering thou camest from France; but let that
passe.
Rafe. I am glad to see you wel, and I rejoice
To heare that God hath blest my master so   70
Since my departure.
Wife. Yea, truly, Rafe, I thanke my maker; but let that passe.
Rog. And, sirra Rafe, what newes, what newes in France?
Rafe. Tel mee, good Roger, first, what newes in England?
How does my Jane? When didst thou see my wife?   75
Where lives my poore heart? Sheel be poore indeed,
Now I want limbs to get whereon to feed.
Roger. Limbs? Hast thou not hands, man? Thou shalt never

---

[1] I am merry, let's see you so.   [2] Q 1 omits 'now.'   [3] Qtos. omit 'to.'

see a shoomaker want bread, though he have but three fingers on
a hand.　　　　　　　　　　　　　　　　　　　　　80

Rafe. Yet all this while I heare not of my Jane.

Wife. O Rafe, your wife,—perdie, we knowe not whats become
of her.　She was here a while, and because she was married, grewe
more stately then became her; I checkt her, and so forth; away
she flung, never returned, nor saide bih nor bah; and, Rafe, you
knowe, "ka me, ka thee."[1]　And so, as I tell ye—Roger, is not
Firke come yet?　　　　　　　　　　　　　　　　87

Roger. No, forsooth.

Wife. And so, indeed, we heard not of her, but I heare she lives
in London; but let that passe.　If she had wanted, shee might
have opened her case to me or my husband, or to any of my men;
I am sure, theres not any of them, perdie, but would have done
her good to his power.　Hans, looke, if Firke be come.　　92

Hans. Yaw, ik [2] sal, vro.　　　　　　　　　　*Exit* HANS.

Wife. And so, as I saide—but, Rafe, why dost thou weepe?
Thou knowest that naked wee came out of our mothers wombe,
and naked we must returne; and, therefore, thanke God for al
things.　　　　　　　　　　　　　　　　　　97

Roger. No, faith, Jane is a straunger heere; but, Rafe, pull up a
good heart, I knowe thou hast one.　Thy wife, man, is in London;
one tolde mee, hee sawe her a while agoe verie brave and neate;
weele ferret her out, and London holde her.　　　　IOI

Wife. Alas, poore soule, hees overcome with sorrowe; he does
but as I doe, weepe for the losse of any good thing.　But, Rafe,
get thee in, call for some meate and drinke, thou shalt find me
worshipful towards thee.　　　　　　　　　　　105

Rafe. I thanke you, dame; since I want lims and lands,
Ile trust to God, my good friends, and my hands.[3]　　*Exit.*

Enter HANS *and* FIRKE, *running.*

Fyrke. Runne, good Hans!　O Hodge, O mistres! Hodge, heave

---

[1] help me, help thee. Cf. 'thou art pander to me for my wench and I to thee for
they cosenage: Ka me, ka thee, runs through court and country,' *Eastward Hoe,*
II, iii, 6.

[2] Qtos., 'it.'

[3] So Fr. and W.-P.—Qtos. I, 2 read 'Ile to God, my good friends, and to these my
hands.'　Qtos. 3-5, 'I'll trust to God, my good friends, and to my hands.'

up thine eares; mistresse, smugge up your lookes; on with your best apparell; my maister is chosen, my master is called, nay, condemn'd by the crie of the countrie to be shiriffe of the citie for this famous yeare nowe to come. And time now being, a great many men in blacke gownes were askt for their voyces and their hands, and my master had al their fists about his eares presently, and they cried 'I, I, I, I,'—and so I came away—   115

       Wherefore without all other grieve,
       I doe salute you Mistresse Shrieve.[1]

Hans. *Yaw, my mester is de groot man, de shrieve.*

Roger. Did not I tell you, mistris? Nowe I may boldly say: Good morrow to your worship.   120

Wife. Good morrow, good Roger. I thanke you, my good people all.—Firke, hold up thy hand: heer's a three-peny peece for thy tidings.

Fyrk. Tis but three halfe pence, I thinke. Yes, tis three pence, I smel the rose.[2]   125

Roger. But, mistresse, be rulde by me, and doe not speake so pulingly.

Firke. Tis her worship speakes so, and not she. No, faith, mistresse, speake mee in the olde key: 'too it, Firke', 'there, good Firke', 'plie your businesse, Hodge', 'Hodge, with a full mouth', 'Ile fill your bellies with good cheare, til thy crie twang.'

Enter SIMON EIRE, *wearing a gold chaine.*

Hans. *See, myn liever broder, heer compt my meester.*   132

Wife. Welcome home, Maister Shrieve; I pray God continue you in health and wealth.

Eyre. See here, my Maggy, a chaine, a gold chaine for Simon Eyre. I shal make thee a lady; heer's a French hood for thee; on with it, on with it! dresse thy browes with this flap of a shoulder of mutton, to make thee looke lovely. Where be my fine men? Roger, Ile make over my shop and tooles to thee; Firke, thou shalt be the foreman; Hans, thou shalt have an hundred for twen-

---

[1] First printed as verse by Fr.

[2] The threepenny silver coin of Elizabeth had the queen's bust and a rose on the obverse side. Not in general circulation. It was maundy money, and Mrs. Eyre is here affecting the attitude of almoner of the sovereign.

tie.[1] Bee as mad knaves as your maister Sim Eyre hath bin, and
you shall live to be Sherives of London.—How dost thou like me,
Margerie? Prince am I none, yet am I princely borne. Firke,
Hodge, and Hans!　　　　　　　　　　　　　　　　　　　　　144
　　Al 3. I forsooth, what saies your worship, Master [2] Sherife?
　　Eyre. Worship and honour, you Babilonian knaves, for the
gentle craft. But I forgot my selfe, I am bidden by my Lord Maior
to dinner to Old Foord; hees gone before, I must after. Come,
Madge, on with your trinkets! Nowe, my true Trojans, my fine
Firke, my dapper Hodge, my honest Hans, some device, some
odde crochets, some morris, or such like, for the honour of the
gentlemen [3] shooemakers. Meete me at Old Foord, you know
my minde. Come, Madge, away. Shutte up the shop, knaves,
and make holiday.　　　　　　　　　　　　　　　*Exeunt.* 154
　　Firke. O rare, O brave! Come, Hodge; follow me, Hans;
　　　　Weele be with them for a morris daunce.　　　　*Exeunt.*

[Act III. Scene V. *A Room at Old Ford.*]

Enter LORD MAIOR, EYRE, *his* WIFE *in a French hood,*[4] [ROSE],
　　SIBILL *and other* Servants.

　　L. Maior. Trust mee, you are as welcome to Old Foord
As I my selfe.
　　Wife. Truely, I thanke your lordship.
　　L. Ma. Would our bad cheere were worth the thanks you give.
　　Eyre. Good cheere, my Lord Maior, fine cheere! A fine house,
fine walles, all fine and neat.　　　　　　　　　　　　　　6
　　L. Maior. Now, by my troth, Ile tel thee, Maister Eyre,
It does me good and al my brethren,
That such a madcap fellow as thy selfe
Is entred into our societie.　　　　　　　　　　　　　　　10
　　Wife. I, but, my lord, hee must learne nowe to putte on gravitie.

---

[1] See III, i, 21.　　　　　　　　　　　[2] So Q 5. Other Qtos., 'mistris.'
[3] So Q 4. Qtos. 1, 2, 'gentle'; Q. 3, 'gentleman'.
[4] Qtos. 1, 2, 'Wife, Sibill in a French hood.'

Eyre. Peace, Maggy, a fig for gravitie! When I go to Guild hal
in my scarlet gowne, Ile look as demurely as a saint, and speake
as gravely as a justice of peace; but now I am here at Old Foord,
at my good Lord Maiors house, let it go by, vanish, Maggy, Ile
be merrie; away with flip-flap, these fooleries, these gulleries.
What, hunnie? Prince am I none, yet am I princely borne. What
sayes my lord Maior?   18

L. Maior. Ha, ha, ha! I had rather then a thousand pound,
I had an heart but halfe so light as yours.   20

Eyre. Why, what should I do, my lord? A pound of care paies
not a dram of debt. Hum, lets be merry, whiles we are yong; olde
age, sacke and sugar will steale upon us, ere we be aware.

L. Ma. Its wel done; [1] Mistris Eyre, pray, give good counsell
To my daughter. [2]   25

Wife. I hope, Mistris Rose wil have the grace to take nothing
thats bad.

L. Ma. Pray God, she do; for ifaith, Mistris Eyre,
I would bestow upon that peevish girle
A thousand marks more then I meane to give her,   30
Upon condition sheed be rulde by me;
The ape still crosseth me.   There came of late
A proper gentleman of fair revenewes,
Whom gladly I would call sonne in law: [3]
But my fine cockney would have none of him.   35
You'le prove a cockscombe for it, ere you die:
A courtier, or no man must please your eie.

Eyre. Be rulde, sweete Rose: th'art ripe for a man. Marrie
not with a boy that has no more haire on his face then thou hast
on thy cheekes. A courtier, wash, go by, stand not uppon pisherie
pasherie: those silken fellowes are but painted images, outsides,
outsides, Rose; their inner linings are torne. [4] No, my fine mouse,
marry me with a gentleman grocer like my Lord Maior, your

---

[1] The lord mayor's approving comment on the first three-men's song, which has
just been rendered. Cf. R.

[2] Qtos., lines 24–25 as prose.

[3] Scan: Whom glad(e)ly, etc.

[4] *Wonder of a Kingdome* (Pearson, p. 272): 'I regard no mans out-side, 'tis the
linings Which I take care for.'

father; a grocer is a sweete trade: plums, plums. Had I a sonne
or daughter should marrie out of the generation and bloud of the
shoe-makers, he should packe; what, the gentle trade is a living
for a man through Europe, through the world.   47

A noyse within of a Taber and a Pipe.

Maior. What noyse is this?

Eyre. O my Lord Maior, a crue of good fellowes that for love
to your honour are come hither with a morrisdance. Come in,
my Mesopotamians, cheerely!   51

Enter HODGE, HANS, RAPH, FIRKE, *and other* Shooe-makers, *in a
morris; after a little dauncing the* LORD MAIOR *speakes:*

Maior. Maister Eyre, are al these shoe-makers?

Eyre. Al cordwainers, my good Lord Maior.

Rose [*aside*]. How like my Lacie lookes yond shooe-maker! 55

Haunce [*aside*]. O that I durst but speake unto my love!

Maior. Sibil, go fetch some wine to make these drinke.
You are al welcome.

All. We thanke your lordship.   60

ROSE *takes a cup of wine and goes to* HAUNCE.

Rose. For his sake whose faire shape thou representst,
Good friend, I drinke to thee.

Hans. Ic bedancke, good frister.[1]

Eyres Wife. I see, Mistris Rose, you do not want judgement;
you have drunke to the properest man I keepe.   65

Firke. Here bee some have done their parts to be as proper as he.

Maior. Wel, urgent busines cals me backe to London:
Good fellowes, first go in and taste our cheare;
And to make merrie as you homeward go,
Spend these two angels in beere at Stratford Boe.[2]   70

Eyre. To these two, my madde lads, Sim Eyre ads another;
then cheerely, Firke; tickle it, Haunce, and al for the honour of
shoemakers.   *All goe dauncing out.*

---

[1] Dutch *vrijster* (from vrijen, to woo or court), miss or mademoiselle.

[2] Cf. '—to keep a custom that many hold, that Mile End is no walk, without a
recreation at Stratford Bow, with cream and cakes.' Kemp, *Hunt after the Ballad-
maker,* Arber's *Garner,* VII, 20.

M. Come, Maister Eyre, lets have your companie.   *Exeunt.*

Rose. Sibil, what shal I do?   75

Sibill. Why, whats the matter?

Rose. That Haunce the shoemaker is my love, Lacie,
Disguisde in that attire to find me out.
How should I find the meanes to speake with him?   79

Sibill. What, mistris, never feare; I dare venter my maidenhead to nothing, and thats great oddes, that Haunce the Dutchman, when we come to London, shal not onely see and speake
with you, but in spight of al your fathers pollicies steale you away
and marrie you.   Will not this please you?   84

Rose. Do this, and ever be assured of my love.

Sibil. Away, then, and follow your father to London, lest your
absence cause him to suspect something:
      To-morrow, if my counsel be obayde,
      Ile binde you prentise to the gentle trade.   *Exeunt.*

[Act IV. Scene I. *A Street in London.*]

Enter JANE *in a Semsters shop, working; and* HAMOND, *muffled, at
another doore; he stands aloofe.*

Hamond. Yonders the shop, and there my faire love sits.
Shees faire and lovely, but she is not mine.
O, would she were! Thrise have I courted her,
Thrise hath my hand beene moistned with her hand,
Whilst my poore famisht eies do feed on that   5
Which made them famish.   I am infortunate:
I stil love one, yet no body loves me.
I muse, in other men what women see,
That I so want! Fine Mistris Rose was coy,
And this too curious! Oh, no, she is chaste,   10
And for she thinkes me wanton, she denies
To cheare my cold heart with her sunnie eies.
How prettily she workes, oh prettie hand!
Oh happie worke! It doth me good to stand

Unseene to see her. Thus I oft have stood   15
In frostie evenings, a light burning by her,
Enduring biting cold, only to eie her.
One onely looke hath seem'd as rich to me
As a kings crowne; such is loves lunacie.
Muffeled Ile passe along, and by that trie   20
Whether she know me.
 Jane.   Sir, what ist you buy?
What ist you lacke, sir, callico, or lawne,
Fine cambricke shirts, or bands, what will you buy?
 Ham. [*aside*]. That which thou wilt not sell. Faith, yet Ile trie:
How do you sell this handkercher?   25
 Jane.   Good cheape.
 Ham. And how these ruffes?
 Jane.   Cheape too.
 Ham.   And how this band?
 Jane. Cheape too.
 Ham.   All cheape; how sell you then this hand?
 Jane. My handes are not to be solde.
 Ham.   To be given then!
Nay, faith, I come to buy.[1]
 Jane.   But none knowes when.
 Ham. Good sweete, leave worke a little while; lets play.   30
 Jane. I cannot live by keeping holliday.
 Ham. Ile pay you for the time which shall be lost.
 Jane. With me you shall not be at so much cost.
 Ham. Look, how you wound this cloth, so you wound me.
 Jane. It may be so.   35
 Ham.   Tis so.
 Jane.   What remedie?
 Ham. Nay, faith, you are too coy.
 Jane.   Let goe my hand.
 Ham. I will do any task at your command,
I would let goe this beautie, were I not
In mind to disobey you by a power
That controlles kings: I love you!   40

 [1] Qtos., 'To be given then: nay faith I come to buy'—one line.

Jane.   So, now part.
Ham. With hands I may, but never with my heart.
In faith, I love you.
Jane.   I beleeve, you doe.
Ham. Shall a true love in me breede hate in you?
Jane. I hate you not.
Ham.   Then you must love?
Jane.   I doe.
What are you better now? I love not you.[1]   45
Ham. All this, I hope, is but a womans fray
That means: come to me, when she cries: away!
In earnest, mistris,[2] I do not jest,
A true chaste love hath entred in my brest.
I love you dearely, as I love my life,   50
I love you as a husband loves a wife;
That, and no other love, my love requires.
Thy wealth, I know, is little; my desires
Thirst not for gold. Sweete, beauteous Jane, whats mine
Shall, if thou make my selfe thine, all be thine.   55
Say, judge, what is thy sentence, life or death?
Mercie or crueltie lies in thy breath..
Jane. Good Sir, I do beleeve you love me well;
For tis a seely conquest, seely pride
For one like you—I meane a gentleman—   60
To boast that by his love tricks he hath brought
Such and such women to his amorous lure;
I thinke you do not so, yet many doe,
And make it even a very trade to wooe.
I could be coy, as many women be,   65
Feede you with sunne-shine smiles and wanton lookes
But I detest witchcraft; say that I
Doe constantly beleeve you, constant have [3]—

---

[1] Qtos., 'I doe . . . not you,' one line.
[2] Pron. trisyllable. See Abbott, *Shak. Gr.*, par. 477.
[3] So punctuated in Qtos.—W.-P. put the comma after 'beleeve' and construe: 'I believe you behave yourself constant.' Not warranted by context. The adverbial use of *constant* presents no difficulty. See Maetzner, *Grammar*, III, 91 (English translation).

Ham. Why dost thou not beleeve me?
Jane.   I beleeve you;
But yet, good sir, because I will not greeve you   70
With hopes to taste fruite which will never fall,
In simple truth this is the summe of all:
My husband lives, at least, I hope he lives.
Prest was he to these bitter warres in France;
Bitter they are to me by wanting him.   75
I have but one heart, and that hearts his due.
How can I then bestow the same on you?
Whilst he lives, his I live, be it nere so poore,
And rather be his wife then a kings whore.
 Ham. Chaste and deare woman, I will not abuse thee,   80
Although it cost my life, if thou refuse me.
Thy husband, prest for France, what was his name?
 Jane. Rafe Damport.
 Ham.   Damport?—Heres a letter sent
From France to me, from a deare friend of mine,
A gentleman of place; here he doth write   85
Their names that have bin slaine in every fight.
 Jane. I hope deaths scroll containes not my loves name.
 Ham. Cannot you reade?
 Jane.   I can.
 Ham.   Peruse the same.
To my remembrance such a name I read
Amongst the rest.   See here.   90
 Jane.   Aye me, hees dead!
Hees dead! if this be true, my deare hearts slaine.
 Ham. Have patience, deare love.
 Jane.   Hence, hence!
 Ham.   Nay, sweete Jane,
Make not poore sorrow prowd with these rich teares.
I mourne thy husbands death, because thou mournst.
 Jane. That bil is forgde; 'tis signde by forgerie.   95
 Ham. Ile bring thee letters sent besides to many,
Carrying the like report: Jane, tis too true.
Come, weepe not: mourning, though it rise from love,

Helpes not the mourned, yet hurtes them that mourne.
 Jane. For Gods sake, leave me.   100
 Ham.   Whither dost thou turne?
Forget the deede,[1] love them that are alive;
His love is faded, trie how mine wil thrive.
 Jane. Tis now no time for me to think on love.
 Ham. Tis now best time for you to thinke on love,
Because your love lives not.[2]   105
 Jane.   Thogh he be dead,
My love to him shal not be buried.
For Gods sake, leave me to my selfe alone;
 Ham. Twould kil my soule, to leave thee drownd in mone.
Answere me to my sute, and I am gone;
Say to me yea or no.   110
 Jane.   No.
 Ham.   Then farewell.
One farewel wil not serve, I come again;
Come, drie these wet cheekes; tel me, faith, sweete Jane,
Yea or no, once more.
 Jane.   Once more I say: no;
Once more be gone, I pray; else wil I goe.[3]
 Ham. Nay, then I wil grow rude, by this white hand, 115
Until you change that colde no; here Ile stand
Til by your hard heart—
 Jane.   Nay, for Gods love, peace!
My sorrowes by your presence more increase.
Not that you thus are present, but al griefe
Desires to be alone; therefore in briefe 120
Thus much I say, and saying bid adew:
If ever I wed man, it shall be you.
 Ham. O blessed voyce! Deare Jane, Ile urge no more,
Thy breath hath made me rich.
 Jane.   Death makes me poore. *Exeunt.*

[1] So Q 1; other Qtos. correct to 'dead.'
[2] Qtos., 'Tis—not' as one line.
[3] Qtos., 'Then farewell . . . goe' (110–114) as prose.

[Act IV.   Scene II.   *A Street before Hodge's Shop.*]

Enter HODGE, *at his shop boord*, RAFE, FIRK, HANS, *and a* Boy
at work.

All. Hey downe a downe, downe derie.[1]

Hodge. Well said, my hearts; plie your worke to day, we loytred
yesterday; to it pell mel, that we may live to be lord maiors, or
aldermen at least.

Firke. Hey, downe a downe, derie.   5

Hodge. Well said, yfaith! How saist thou, Hauns, doth not
Firke tickle it?

Hauns. *Yaw, mester.*

Firke. Not so neither, my organe pipe squeaks this morning
for want of licoring. Hey, downe a downe, derie!   10

Hans. *Forward, Firk, tow best un jolly yongster. Hort, I, mester,
ic bid yo, cut me un pair vampres vor Mester Jeffres bootes.*[2]

Hodge. Thou shalt, Hauns.

Firke. Master!

Hodge. How now, boy?   15

Firke. Pray, now you are in the cutting vaine, cut mee out a
paire of counterfeits,[3] or else my worke will not passe currant; hey,
downe a downe!

Hodge. Tell me, sirs, are my coosin Mrs.[4] Priscillaes shooes
done?   20

---

[1] Would God that it were holiday,
   hey dery down down dery;
That with my love I might go play,
   with woe my heart is weary;
My whole delight is in her sight,
   would God I had her company,
   her company,
Hey dery down, down adown.
The first stanza of a shoemaker's song in the story of Crispine and Crispianus,
Gentle Craft, p. 20. (ed. A. F. Lange, *Palæstra*, XVIII, 32).

[2] Go on Firk, thou art . . . Hark, ay, . . . master, pray cut me, etc.

[3] A play upon *vampres* meaning (*a*) upper leathers, (*b*) any patches on old things
to give them a new appearance, (*c*) coins counterfeited(?)

[4] Qtos., 'M.'

Firke. Your coosin?   No, maister; one of your auntes, hang her; let them alone.

Rafe. I am in hand with them; she gave charge that none but I should doe them for her.

Firke. Thou do for her? then twill be a lame doing, and that she loves not.   Rafe, thou mightst have sent her to me, in faith, I would have yearkt and firkt your Priscilla.   Hey, downe a downe, derry.   This geere will not holde.   28

Hodge. How saist thou, Firke, were we not merry at Old Ford?

Firke. How, merry? why, our buttockes went jiggy joggy like a quagmyre.   Wel, Sir Roger Oatemeale, if I thought all meale of that nature, I would eate nothing but bagpuddings.   32

Rafe. Of all good fortunes my fellow Hance had the best.

Firke. Tis true, because Mistris Rose dranke to him.

Hodge. Wel, wel, worke apace.   They say, seven of the aldermen be dead, or very sicke.

Firke. I care not, Ile be none.   37

Rafe. No, nor I; but then my M. Eyre wil come quickly to be L. Mayor.[1]

Enter SIBIL.

Firke. Whoop, yonder comes Sibil.   40

Hodge. Sibil, welcome, yfaith; and how dost thou, madde wench?

Firke. Sib whoore, welcome to London.

Sibil. Godamercy, sweete Firke; good Lord, Hodge, what a delitious shop you have got!   You tickle it, yfaith.   45

Rafe. Godamercy, Sibil, for our good cheere at Old Ford.

Sibil. That you shal have, Rafe.

Firke. Nay, by the masse, we hadde tickling cheere, Sibil; and how the plague dost thou and Mistris Rose and my L. Mayor?[2] I put the women in first.   50

Sibil. Wel, Godamercy; but Gods me, I forget my self, wheres Haunce the Fleming?

Firke. Hearke, butter-boxe, nowe you must yelp out some spreken.

[1] So Qtos.   [2] So Qtos.

Hans. *Vat begaie you?* *Vat vod you, Frister?* [1] 55

Sibill. Marrie, you must come to my yong mistris, to pull on her shooes you made last.

Hans. *Vare ben your edle fro, vare ben your mistris?* [2]

Sibill. Marrie, here at our London house in Cornehill.[3]

Firke. Will no bodie serve her turne but Hans? 60

Sibill. No, sir. Come, Hans, I stand upon needles.

Hodg. Why then, Sibil, take heede of pricking.

Sibill. For that let me alone. I have a tricke in my budget. Come, Hans.

Hans. *Yaw, yaw, ic sall meete yo gane.*[4] 65

Exit HANS *and* SIBILL.

Hodge. Go, Hans, make haste againe. Come, who lacks worke?

Firke. I, maister, for I lacke my breakfast; tis munching time, and past.

Hodge. Ist so? why, then leave worke, Raph. To breakfast! Boy, looke to the tooles. Come, Raph; come, Firke. *Exeunt.* 70

[Act IV. Scene III. *The Same.*]

Enter a Servingman.

Ser. Let me see now, the signe of the Last in Towerstreet. Mas, yonders the house. What, haw! Whoes within?

Enter RAPH.

Raph. Who calles there? What want you, sir?

Serv. Marrie, I would have a paire of shooes made for a gentle-woman against to morrow morning. What, can you do them? 5

Raph. Yes, sir, you shall have them. But what lengths her foote?

Serv. Why, you must make them in all parts like this shoe;

---

[1] What do you want? Qtos., 'Vat begaie gou vat vod gou.'
[2] Where is your noble lady? Qtos., 'egle' instead of 'edle.'
[3] So Qtos. 4, 5.—Qtos. 1, 2, Cornewaile; Q 3, Cornwall.
[4] with you go.

but, at any hand, faile not to do them, for the gentlewoman is to
be married very early in the morning.   10

Raph. How? by this shoe must it be made? by this? Are you
sure, sir, by this?

Serv. How, by this? Am I sure, by this? Art thou in thy wits?
I tell thee, I must have a paire of shooes, dost thou marke me? a
paire of shooes, two shooes, made by this verie shoe, this same
shoe, against to morrow morning by foure a clock. Dost understand me? Canst thou do't?   17

Raph. Yes, sir, yes—I—I—I can do't. By this shoe, you say?
I should knowe this shoe. Yes, sir, yes, by this shoe, I can do't.
Foure a clocke, well. Whither shall I bring them?

Serv. To the signe of the Golden Ball in Watlingstreete; enquire for one Maister Hamon, a gentleman, my maister.   22

Raph. Yea, sir; by this shoe, you say?

Serv. I say, Maister Hammon at the Golden Ball; hee's the
bridegroome, and those shooes are for his bride.   25

Raph. They shal be done by this shoe; wel, well, Maister Hammon at the Golden Shoe—I would say, the Golden Ball; verie
well, verie well. But I pray you, sir, where must Maister Hammon be married?

Serv. At Saint Faiths Church, under Paules.[1] But whats that
to thee? Prethee, dispatch those shooes, and so farewel.   *Exit.*

Raph. By this shoe, said he. How am I amasde   32
At this strange accident! Upon my life,
This was the verie shoe I gave my wife,
When I was prest for France; since when, alas!   35
I never could heare of her: it is the same,
And Hammons bride no other but my Jane.

Enter FIRKE.

Firke. Snailes, Raph, thou hast lost thy part of three pots, a
countrieman of mine gave me to breakfast.

Rafe. I care not; I have found a better thing.   40

---

[1] 'At the west ende of this Jesus chapell, under the quire of Pauls, also was a
Parish church of Saint Faith, commonly called Saint Faith under Pauls, which
served for the stationers and others dwelling in Pauls churchyard, Pater Noster
Rowe, and the places neare adjoyning.' Stow, *Survey*, 266.

Firke. A thing? away! Is it a mans thing, or a womans thing?

Rafe. Firke, dost thou know this shooe?

Firke. No, by my troth; neither doth that know me! I have no acquaintance with it, tis a meere stranger to me.

Rafe. Why, then I do; this shooe, I durst be sworne,   45
Once covered the instep of my Jane.
This is her size, her breadth, thus trod my love;
These true-love knots I prickt; I hold my life,
By this old shooe I shall finde out my wife.

Firke. Ha, ha! Old shoo, that wert new! How a murren came this ague fit of foolishnes upon thee?   51

Rafe. Thus, Firke: even now here came a servingman;
By this shooe would he have a new paire made
Against to morrow morning for his mistris,
Thats to be married to a gentleman.   55
And why may not this be—my sweete Jane? [1]

Firke. And why maist not thou be—my sweete asse? Ha, ha!

Rafe. Wel, laugh and spare not! But the trueth is this:
Against to morrow morning Ile provide
A lustie crue of honest shoomakers,   60
To watch the going of the bride to church.
If she prove Jane, Ile take her in dispite
From Hammon and the divel, were he by.
If it be not my Jane, what remedy?
Hereof am I [2] sure, I shall live till I die,   65
Although I never with a woman lie.   *Exit.*

Fir. Thou lie with a woman to builde nothing but Cripplegates! [3] Well, God sends fooles fortune, and it may be, he may light upon his matrimony by such a device; for wedding and hanging goes by destiny.   *Exit.* 70

---

[1] See Abbott, *Shak. Gr.*, pars. 484, 508.

[2] So Qtos. 1, 2; others, 'I am.'

[3] 'Cripplegate, a place, saith mine author [*i. e.* John Lidgate], so called of cripples begging there; at which gate, it was said, the bodie [*i.e.* of King Edmund the Martyr] entering, miracles were wrought, as some of the lame did goe upright, praising God.' Stow, *Survey*, 28.

[Act IV. Scene IV. *London.—A Room in the Lord Mayor's House.*]

Enter HAUNS *and* ROSE, *arme in arme.*

Hans. How happie am I by embracing thee!
Oh, I did feare such crosse mishaps did raigne,
That I should never see my Rose againe.
    Rose. Sweete Lacie, since faire Oportunitie
Offers her selfe to furder our escape,   5
Let not too over-fond esteeme of me
Hinder that happie hower. Invent the meanes,
And Rose will follow thee through all the world.
    Hans. Oh, how I surfeit with excesse of joy,
Made happie by thy rich perfection!   10
But since thou paist sweete intrest to my hopes,
Redoubling love on love, let me once more
Like to a bold facde debter crave of thee,
This night to steale abroad, and at Eyres house,
Who now by death of certaine aldermen   15
Is Maior of London, and my master once,
Meete thou by Lacie, where in spite of change,
Your fathers anger, and mine uncles hate
Our happie nuptialls will we [1] consummate.
                    Enter SIBILL.
    Sib. Oh God, what will you doe, mistris? Shift for your selfe,
your father is at hand! Hees comming, hees comming! Master
Lacie, hide your selfe in my mistris! For Gods sake, shift for
your selves!
    Hans. Your father come, sweete Rose—what shall I doe?
Where shall I hide me? How shall I escape?   25
    Rose. A man, and want wit in extremitie?
Come, come, be Hauns still, play the shoomaker,
Pull on my shooe.[2]

---

[1] Qtos. 1, 2, 'me.'
[2] This dramatic device recurs in *Match mee in London*. It is used also, but with

Enter LORD MAIOR.

Hans. Mas, and thats well remembred.

Sib. Here comes your father.

Hans. Forware, metresse, tis un good skow, it sal vel dute, or ye sal neit betallen.[1]   31

Rose. Oh God, it pincheth me; what wil you do?

Hans [*aside*]. Your fathers presence pincheth, not the shoo.

L. Mai. Well done; fit my daughter well, and shee shall please thee well.   35

Hans. Yaw, yaw, ick weit dat well; for ware, tis un good skoo, tis gimait van neits leither; se ever, mine here.[2]

Enter a Prentice.

L. Mai. I do beleeve it.—Whats the newes with you?

Prent. Please you, the Earle of Lincolne at the gate
Is newly lighted, and would speake with you.[3]   40

L. Mai. The Earle of Lincolne come to [4] speake with me?
Well, well, I know his errand. Daughter Rose,
Send hence your shoomaker, dispatch, have done!
Sib, make things handsome! Sir boy, follow me.   *Exit.*

Hans. Mine uncle come! Oh, what may this portend?   45
Sweete Rose, this of our love threatens an end.

Rose. Be not dismaid at this; what ere befall,
Rose is thine owne. To witnes I speake truth,
Where thou appoints the place, Ile meete with thee.
I will not fixe a day to follow thee,   50
But presently steale hence. Do not replie:
Love which gave strength to beare my fathers hate,
Shall now adde wings to further our escape.   *Exeunt.*

far less delicacy, by Wm. Rowley in *The Shoemaker a Gentleman.* For the source
in these instances see Appendix *E* (story in *Gentle Craft*).

[1] Indeed . . . it shall give good service ('dute'='do it'), or you shall not pay.

[2] Yes, yes, I know that well, indeed, . . . 'tis made of neat's leather; only look, sir!

[3] Qtos., lines 39–40 as prose.

[4] Qtos. omit 'to.'

[Act IV.   Scene V.   *Another Room in the same House.*]

Enter L. Maior *and* Lincolne.

L. Mai. Beleeve me, on my credite, I speake truth:
Since first your nephew Lacie went to France,
I have not seene him.   It seemd strange to me,
When Dodger told me that he staide behinde,
Neglecting the hie charge the king imposed.   5
   Linc. Trust me, Sir Roger Otly, I did thinke.
Your counsell had given head to this attempt,
Drawne to it by the love he beares your child.
Here I did hope to find him in your house;
But now I see mine error, and confesse,   10
My judgment wrongd you by conceving so.
   L. Maior. Lodge in my house, say you? Trust me, my lord,
I love your nephew Lacie too too dearely,
So much to wrong his honor; and he hath done so,
That first gave him advise to stay from France.   15
To witnesse I speake truth, I let you know,
How carefull I have beene to keepe my daughter
Free from all conference or speech of him;
Not that I skorne your nephew, but in love
I beare your honour, least your noble bloud   20
Should by my meane worth be dishonoured.
   Lin. [*aside*].   How far the churles tongue wanders from his hart.
Well, well, Sir Roger Otley, I beleeve you,
With more then many thankes for the kind love,
So much you seeme to beare me.   But, my lord,   25
Let me request your helpe to seeke my nephew,
Whom if I find, Ile straight embarke for France.
So shal your Rose be free, my thoughts at rest,[1]
And much care die which now lies[2] in my brest.

----

[1] Qtos. 1, 2, 'my Rose . . . your thoughts.'
[2] So Q 2; Q 1, 'dies.'   W.–P. suggest 'lives.'

Enter SIBILL.

Sibill. Oh Lord! Help, for Gods sake! my mistris; oh, my yong
mistris!   31
   L. Ma. Where is thy mistris? Whats become of her?
   Sibill. Shees gone, shees fled!
   L. Maior. Gone! Whither is she fled?
   Sibill. I know not, forsooth; shees fled out of doores with Hauns
the shoomaker; I saw them scud, scud, scud, apace, apace!   36
   L. Maior. Which way? What, John! Where be my men?
Which way?
   Sibil. I know not, and it please your worship.
   L. Maior. Fled with a shoomaker? Can this be true?   40
   Sibil. Oh Lord, sir, as true as Gods in heaven.
   Linc. Her love turnd shoomaker? I am glad of this.
   L. Ma. A Fleming butter boxe, a shoomaker!
Will she forget her birth, requite my care
With such ingratitude? Skornd she yong Hammon   45
To love a honnikin, a needie knave?
Wel, let her flie, Ile not flie after her,
Let her starve, if she wil; shees none of mine.
   Linc. Be not so cruell, sir.

Enter FIRKE *with shooes.*

Sibil.   I am glad, shees scapt.   50
   L. Ma. Ile not account of her as of my child.
Was there no better object for her eies
But a foule drunken lubber, swill bellie,
A shoomaker? Thats brave!
   Firke. Yea, forsooth; tis a very brave shooe, and as fit as a
pudding.   56
   L. Ma. How now, what knave is this? From whence commest
thou?
   Firke. No knave, sir. I am Firke the shoomaker, lusty Rogers
cheefe lustie jorneyman, and I come hither to take up the prettie
legge of sweete Mistris Rose, and thus hoping your worshippe is
in as good health, as I was at the making hereof, I bid you farewell,
yours — — — — Firke.   63

L. Ma. Stay, stay, Sir Knave! [1]

Linc. Come hither, shoomaker!

Firke. Tis happie the knave is put before the shoomaker, or else I would not have vouchsafed to come backe to you. I am moved, for I stirre. 68

L. Ma. My lorde, this villaine calles us knaves by craft.

Firk. Then tis by the gentle craft, and to cal one knave gently, is no harme. Sit your worship merie! Sib, your yong mistris— Ile so bob them,[2] now my Maister M. Eyre is Lorde Maior of London.

L. Ma. Tell me, sirra, whoes man are you? 73

Firke. I am glad to see your worship so merrie. I have no maw to this geere, no stomacke as yet to a red peticote.

Pointing to Sibil.

Lin. He means not, sir, to wooe you to his maid,
But onely doth demand whose man you are.

Firke. I sing now to the tune of Rogero. Roger, my felow, is now my master.

Lin. Sirra, knowst thou one Hauns, a shoomaker? 80

Firk. Hauns, shoomaker? Oh yes, stay, yes, I have him. I tel you what, I speake it in secret: Mistris Rose and he are by this time—no, not so, but shortly are to come over one another with "Can you dance the shaking of the sheetes?"[3] It is that Hauns— [*Aside.*] Ile so gull these diggers! 85

L. Ma. Knowst thou, then, where he is?

Firke. Yes, forsooth; yea, marry!

Lin. Canst thou, in sadnesse—

Firke. No, forsooth; no, marrie!

L. Ma. Tell me, good honest fellow, where he is,
And thou shalt see what Ile bestow of thee. 91

Firke. Honest fellow? No, sir; not so, sir; my profession is the gentle craft; I care not for seeing, I love feeling; let me feele it here; *aurium tenus*, ten peeces of gold; *genuum tenus*, ten peeces

---

[1] Cf. *Lord Vanni.* Away Sir knave and foole. *Cargo.* Sir knave, a new word: fooles, and knaves Sir?—*Wonder of a Kingdome.*

[2] Q 1, ' then.'

[3] 'The name of an old dance. Often used with a quibble.' Bullen's note, *Insatiate Countess* II, ii, p. 165.

of silver; and then Firke is your man [*aside*] in a new paire of
strechers.[1]   96

L. Ma. Here is an Angel, part of thy reward,
Which I will give thee; tell me where he is.

Firke. No point! Shal I betray my brother? No! Shal I prove
Judas to Hans? No! Shall I crie treason to my corporation?
No, I shall be firkt and yerkt then. But give me your angell;
your angell shall tel you.   102

Lin. Doe so, good fellow; tis no hurt to thee.

Firke. Send simpering Sib away.

L. Ma. Huswife, get you in.   *Exit Sib.*   105

Firke. Pitchers have eares, and maides have wide mouthes;
but for Hauns Prauns,[2] upon my word, to morrow morning he and
yong Mistris Rose goe to this geere, they shall be married together,
by this rush, or else tourne Firke to a firkin of butter, to tanne
leather withall.   110

L. Ma. But art thou sure of this?

Firke. Am I sure that Paules steeple is a handfull higher then
London Stone,[3] or that the Pissing Conduit [4] leakes nothing but
pure Mother Bunch? Am I sure I am lustie Firke? Gods nailes,
doe you thinke I am so base to gull you.   115

Linc. Where are they married? Dost thou know the church?

Firke I never goe to church, but I know the name of it; it is
a swearing church—stay a while, tis—I, by the mas, no, no,—
tis—I, by my troth, no, nor that; tis—I, by my faith, that, that,
tis, I, by my Faithes Church under Paules Crosse. There they
shall be knit like a paire of stockings in matrimonie; there theile
be inconie.[5]   122

---

[1] Technically the same as shoe-stretchers, here: fibs, lies.   [2] Q 4, 'praunce.'

[3] An ancient stone now cased in the wall of St. Swithin's church near which it
formerly stood. It is supposed to have marked the centre from which the great
Roman military roads radiated. Stow, p. 177; *England in Shakespeare's Youth,
New Shak. Soc.* p. CVI.

[4] Known also as the conduit upon Cornhill. Cf. *Chaste Maid in Cheapside*,
III, ii. 'The sweet water,' says Jacob Rathgeb in his account of London, 1592,
'is preserved in various parts of the city in large well-built stone cisterns (conduits),
to be drawn off by corks.' *England in Shakespeare's Youth, New Shak. Soc.* p.
LXXXVI Appendix II.

[5] Qtos., 'in conie' and 'in cony.' Uncommonly fine, a rare sight. Cf. *Jew of
Malta*, IV, vi: . . . 'let music rumble Whilst I in thy *incony* lap do tumble.'

Lin. Upon my life, my nephew Lacie walkes
In the disguise of this Dutch shoomaker.
Firke. Yes, forsooth.   125
Linc. Doth he not, honest fellow?
Firke. No, forsooth; I thinke Hauns is no bodie but Hans, no
spirite.
L. Ma. My mind misgives me now, tis so, indeede.
Lin. My cosen speakes the language, knowes the trade.   130
L. Ma. Let me request your companie, my lord;
Your honourable presence may, no doubt,
Refraine their head-strong rashnesse, when my selfe
Going alone perchance may be oreborne.
Shall I request this favour?   135
Linc.   This, or what else.
Firke. Then you must rise betimes, for they meane to fal to
their hey passe and repasse, pindy pandy, which hand will you
have,[1] very earely.
L. Ma. My care shal every way equal their haste.
This night accept your lodging in my house,   140
The earlier shal we stir, and at Saint Faithes
Prevent this giddy hare-braind nuptiall.
This trafficke of hot love shal yeeld cold gaines:
They ban our loves, and weele forbid their baines.   *Exit.*[2]
Linc. At Saint Faithes Church thou saist?   145
Firke. Yes, by their troth.
Linc. Be secret, on thy life.   *Exit.*
Firke. Yes, when I kisse your wife! Ha, ha, heres no craft in
the gentle craft. I came hither of purpose with shooes to Sir
Rogers worship, whilst Rose, his daughter, be coniecatcht by
Hauns. Soft nowe; these two gulles will be at Saint Faithes
Church to morrow morning, to take Master Bridegroome and
Mistris Bride napping, and they, in the meane time, shall chop up
the matter at the Savoy. But the best sport is, Sir Roger Otly

---

[1] *hey passe, repasse,* exclamations once employed by jugglers in commanding
objects to move; *pindy pandy,* etc., variations of the terms used in playing handy-
dandy. *N. E. D.*; Alice B. Gomme, *Dict. of Brit. Folk-Lore,* Vol. I.
[2] Qtos. 1, 2, *Exeunt.*

wil find my felow lame [1] Rafes wife going to marry a gentleman, and then heele stop her in steede of his daughter. Oh brave! there wil be fine tickling sport. Soft now, what have I to doe? Oh, I know; now a messe of shoomakers meate at the Wooll Sack [2] in Ivie Lane, to cozen my gentleman of lame Rafes wife, thats true.

Alacke, alacke!   160
Girles, holde out tacke!
For nowe smockes for this jumbling
Shall goe to wracke.[3]   *Exit.*

[Act V. Scene I. *A Room in Eyre's House.*]

Enter AYRE, *his* WIFE, HAUNS, *and* ROSE.

Eyre. This is the morning, then; stay, my bully, my honest Hauns, is it not?

Hans. This is the morning that must make us two happy or miserable; therefore, if you—

Eyre. Away with these iffes and ands, Hauns, and these et caeteraes! By mine honor, Rowland Lacie, none but the king shall wrong thee. Come, feare nothing, am not I Sim Eyre? Is not Sim Eyre Lord Mayor of London? Feare nothing, Rose: let them al say what they can; dainty, come thou to me—laughest thou?   10

Wife. Good my lord, stand her friend in what thing you may.

Eyre. Why, my sweete Lady Madgy, thincke you Simon Eyre can forget his fine Dutch journeyman? No, vah! Fie, I scorne it, it shall never be cast in my teeth, that I was unthankeful. Lady Madgy, thou hadst never coverd thy Saracens head with this French flappe, nor loaden thy bumme with this farthingale, tis trash, trumpery, vanity; Simon Eyre had never walkte in a redde petticoate, nor wore a chaine of golde, but for my fine journeymans

---

[1] Qtos. 1–3, comma after 'felow.'
[2] A well known ordinary of low reputation. Cf. *Alchemist*, V, ii, 19.
[3] Qtos. print as prose.

Portigues—And shall I leave him? No! Prince am I none, yet
beare a princely minde.   20

Hans. My lorde, tis time for us to part from hence.

Eyre. Lady Madgy, Lady Madgy, take two or three of my pie-
crust eaters, my buffe-jerkin varlets, that doe walke in blacke
gownes at Simon Eyres heeles; take them, good Lady Madgy;
trippe and goe, my browne queene of perriwigs, with my delicate
Rose and my jolly Rowland to the Savoy;[1] see them linckte,
countenaunce the marriage; and when it is done, cling, cling together, you Hamborow turtle doves. Ile beare you out, come to
Simon Eyre; come, dwell with me, Hauns, thou shalt eate mincde
pies and marchpane. Rose, away, cricket; trippe and goe, my
Lady Madgy, to the Savoy; Hauns, wed, and to bed; kisse, and
away! Go, vanish!   32

Wife. Farewel, my lord.

Rose. Make haste, sweete love.

Wife.   Sheede faine the deede were done. 35

Hauns. Come, my sweete Rose; faster than deere weele runne.

                                                        They goe out.

Eyre. Goe, vanish, vanish! Avaunt, I say! By the Lorde of
Ludgate, its a madde life to be a lorde mayor; its a stirring life, a
fine life, a velvet life, a carefull life. Well, Simon Eyre, yet set a good
face on it, in the honor of Sainct Hugh. Soft, the king this day
comes to dine with me, to see my new buildings; his majesty is welcome, he shal have good cheere, delicate cheere, princely cheere.
This day, my felow prentises of London come to dine with me too,
they shall have fine cheere, gentlemanlike cheere. I promised the
mad Cappadocians,[2] when we all served at the Conduit together,[3]
that if ever I came to be Mayor of London, I would feast them al,[4]
and Ile doot, Ile doot, by the life of Pharaoh; by this beard, Sim
Eire wil be no flincher. Besides I have procurd that upon every

---

[1] Not far from the Thames. 'The chappell of this hospital serveth now as a
parish church to the tenements thereof neere adjoyning and others.' Stow, *Survey*,
p. 368.

[2] Q. I, 'Cappidosians'.

[3] As tankard-bearers, *i. e.* water-carriers. 'While London was imperfectly supplied with water, this very necessary office was performed by menial servants, or
water-bearers; and in the families of tradesmen, by their apprentices.' Nares.

[4] See Appendix *F.*

Shrovetuesday, at the sound of the pancake bell, my fine dapper
Assyrian lads shall clap up their shop windows, and away.   This
is the day, and this day they shall doot, they shall doot.   51
      Boyes, that day are you free, let masters care,
      And prentises shall pray for Simon Eyre.[1]   *Exit.*

[Act V.   Scene II.   *A Street near Saint Faith's Church.*]

Enter HODGE, FIRKE, RAFE, *and five or sixe* Shoomakers, *all
with cudgels or such weapons.*

Hodge. Come, Rafe; stand to it, Firke. My masters, as we are
the brave bloods of the shooemakers, heires apparant to Saint
Hugh, and perpetuall benefactors to all good fellowes, thou shalt
have no wrong; were Hammon a king of spades, he should not
delve in thy close without thy sufferaunce. But tell me, Rafe,
art thou sure tis thy wife?   6

Rafe. Am I sure this is Firke? This morning, when I strokte
on her shooes, I lookte upon her, and she upon me, and sighed,
askte me, if ever I knew one Rafe. Yes, sayde I. For his sake,
saide she—teares standing in her eyes—and for thou art somewhat like him, spend this peece of golde. I tooke it; my lame leg
and my travel beyond sea made me unknown. All is one for that:
I know shees mine.   13

Firke. Did she give thee this gold? O glorious glittering gold!
Shees thine owne, tis they wife, and she loves thee; for Ile stand
toot, theres no woman wil give golde to any man, but she thinkes
better of him, than she thinkes of them shee gives silver to. And
for Hamon, neither Hamon nor hangman shall wrong thee in
London. Is not our olde maister Eire Lord Mayor? Speake, my
hearts.   20

All. Yes, and Hamon shall know it to his cost.

      Enter HAMON, *his* Man, JANE *and others.*

Hodge. Peace, my bullies; yonder they come.

Rafe. Stand toot, my hearts. Firke, let me speake first.

---

[1] Qtos., as prose.

Hodge. No, Rafe, let me.—Hammon, whither away so earely?

Hamon. Unmannerly, rude slave, whats that to thee?   25

Firke. To him, sir? Yes, sir, and to me, and others. Good morow, Jane, how doost thou? Good Lord, how the world is changed with you! God be thanked!

Hamon. Villaines, handes off! Howe dare you touch my love?

All. Villaines? Downe with them! Cry clubs for prentises!

Hod. Hold, my hearts! Touch her, Hamon? Yea, and more than that: weele carry her away with us. My maisters and gentle-men, never draw your bird spittes; shooemakers are steele to the backe, men every inch of them, al spirite.[1]

All of Hamons side. Wel, and what of all this?

Hodge. Ile shew you.—Jane, dost thou know this man? Tis Rafe, I can tell thee; nay, tis he in faith, though he be lamde by the warres. Yet looke not strange, but run to him, fold him about the necke and kisse him.   39

Jane. Lives then my husband? Oh God, let me go,
Let me embrace my Rafe.

Hamon.   What meanes my Jane?

Jane. Nay, what meant you,[2] to tell me, he was slaine?

Ham. Pardon me, deare love, for being misled.[3]

[*To* RAFE] Twas rumord here in London, thou wert dead.   44

Firke. Thou seest he lives. Lasse, goe, packe home with him. Now, M. Hamon, wheres your mistris, your wife?

Serv. Swounds, master,[4] fight for her! Will you thus lose her?

All. Downe with that creature! Clubs! Downe with him!

Hodge. Hold, hold!

Ham.   Hold, foole! Sirs, he shal do no wrong.
Wil my Jane leave me thus, and breake her faith?   51

---

[1] In representing shoemakers as valiant, Dekker could say with Aristotle: 'so men say.' Deloney, too, is merely following tradition where he sings:

> For sword and shield, for bowe and shaft,
> No man can stain the Gentle Craft.
>
> *Gentle Craft*, p. 13 (Lange's ed. p. 21.)

A broadside, written about 1690, ascribes the same martial qualities to shoemakers: *Percy Soc.* I, 123. Compare also the shoemakers in *George-a Greene*, and Whittier's *Shoemakers* in *Songs of Labor.*

[2] Q 1, 'yon.'   [3] See note to III, ii, 36.   [4] Qtos., 'M.'

Firke. Yea, sir! She must, sir! She shal, sir! What then?
Mend it!

Hodge. Hearke, fellow Rafe, folowe my counsel: set the wench
in the midst, and let her chuse her man, and let her be his woman.

Jane. Whom should I choose? Whom should my thoughts affect
But him whom heaven hath made to be my love?   57
Thou art my husband, and these humble weedes
Makes thee more beautiful then all his wealth.
Therefore, I wil but put off his attire,   60
Returning it into the owners hand,
And after ever be thy constant wife.

Hodge. Not a ragge, Jane! The law's on our side; he that sowes
in another mans ground, forfets his harvest. Get thee home,
Rafe; follow him, Jane; he shall not have so much as a buske point
from thee.   66

Firke. Stand to that, Rafe; the appurtenances are thine owne.
Hammon, looke not at her!

Serv. O, swounds, no!

Firke. Blew coate, be quiet, weele give you a new liverie else;
weele make Shrove Tuesday Saint Georges Day for you.[1] Looke
not, Hammon, leare not! Ile firke you! For thy head now, one
glance, one sheepes eie, any thing at her! Touch not a ragge, least
I and my brethren beate you to clowtes.

S. Come, Master Hammon, theres no striving here.   75

Ham. Good fellowes, heare me speake; and, honest Rafe,
Whom I have injured most by loving Jane,
Marke what I offer thee: here in faire gold
Is twentie pound, Ile give it for thy Jane;
If this content thee not, thou shalt have more.   80

Hodge. Sell not thy wife, Rafe; make her not a whore.

Ham. Say, wilt thou freely cease thy claime in her,
And let her be my wife?

All.   No, do not, Rafe.

Rafe. Sirra, Hammon, Hammon, dost thou thinke, a shooe-

---

[1] 'So late as 1614, it was the custom for fashionable gentlemen to wear blue coats
on St. George's day, probably in imitation of the blue mantle worn by the Knights
of the Garter.' Chambers, *Book of Days*, April 23.

maker is so base to bee a bawde to his owne wife for commoditie?
Take thy golde, choake with it! Were I not lame, I would make
thee eate thy words.   87

    Firke. A shoomaker sell his flesh and bloud? Oh indignitie!
    Hod. Sirra, take up your pelfe, and be packing.
    Ham. I wil not touch one pennie, but in liew   90
Of that great wrong I offered thy Jane,
To Jane and thee I give that twentie pound.
Since I have faild of her, during my life,
I vow, no woman else shall be my wife.
Farewell, good fellowes of the gentle trade: 95
Your morning [1] mirth my mourning day hath made.   [*Exit.*
    Firke [*to the* Serving-man]. Touch the gold, creature, if you
dare! Y'are best be trudging. Here, Jane, take thou it. Now
lets home, my hearts.   99
    Hod. Stay! Who comes here? Jane, on againe with thy maske!

        Enter LINCOLNE, L. MAIOR *and* Servants.

    Linc. Yonders the lying varlet mockt us so.
    L. Ma. Come hither, sirra!
    Firke. I, sir? I am sirra? You meane me, do you not?
    Linc. Where is my nephew married?   104
    Firke. Is he married? God give him joy, I am glad of it. They
have a faire day, and the signe is in a good planet, Mars in
Venus.
    L. Ma. Villaine, thou toldst me that my daughter Rose
This morning should be married at Saint Faithes;
We have watcht there these three houres at the least,
Yet see we no such thing.   110
    Firke. Truly, I am sorie for't; a bride's a prettie thing.
    Hodge. Come to the purpose. Yonder's the bride and bride-
groome you looke for, I hope. Though you be lordes, you are not
to barre by your authoritie men from women; are you?
    L. Ma. See, see, my daughters maskt.   115
    Linc.   True, and my nephew,
To hide his guilt, counterfeits him lame.

        [1] Q 1, 'mornings mirth.'

Firke. Yea, truely; God helpe the poore couple, they are lame and blind.

L. Maior. Ile ease her blindnes.

Lin.   Ile his lamenes cure.   120

Firke. Lie downe, sirs, and laugh! My felow Rafe is taken for Rowland Lacy, and Jane for Mistris Damaske Rose. This is al my knavery.

L. Maior. What, have I found you, minion?

Linc.   O base wretch!
Nay, hide thy face, the horror of thy guilt.   125
Can hardly be washt off. Where are thy powers?
What battels have you made? O yes, I see,
Thou foughtst with Shame, and Shame hath conquerd thee.
This lamenesse wil not serve.

L. Ma.   Unmaske your selfe.

Lin. Leade home you daughter.   130

L. Ma.   Take your nephew hence.

Rafe. Hence! Swounds, what meane you? Are you mad?
I hope you cannot inforce my wife from me. Wheres Hamon?

L. Ma. Your wife?

Lin. What, Hammon?

Rafe. Yea, my wife; and, therfore, the prowdest of you that laies hands on her first, Ile lay my crutch crosse his pate.   136

Firke. To him, lame Rafe! Heres brave sport!

Rafe. Rose call you her? Why, her name is Jane. Looke here else; do you know her now?   [*Unmasking* JANE.]

Lin. Is this your daughter?   140

L. Ma.   No, nor this your nephew.
My Lord of Lincolne, we are both abusde
By this base, craftie varlet.

Firke. Yea, forsooth, no varlet; forsooth, no base; forsooth, I am but meane; no craftie neither, but of the gentle craft.

L. Ma. Where is my daughter Rose? Where is my child?   145

Lin. Where is my nephew Lacie married?

Firke. Why, here is good lacde mutton,[1] as I promist you.

---

[1] i. e. Lacied mutton. Merely one of Firk's characteristic pleasantries so far as Jane is concerned, but insult added to injury as regards his victims and their quest.

Lin. Villaine, Ile have thee punisht for this wrong.

Firke. Punish the jornyman villaine, but not the jorneyman shoomaker.   150

Enter DODGER.

Dodger. My lord, I come to bring unwelcome newes.
Your nephew Lacie and your daughter Rose
Earely this morning wedded at the Savoy,
None being present but the Ladie Mairesse.
Besides I learnt among the officers,
The Lord Maior vowes to stand in their defence
Gainst any that shall seeke to crosse the match.

Lin. Dares Eyre the shoomaker uphold the deede?

Firk. Yes, sir, shoomakers dare stand in a womans quarrel, I warrant you, as deepe as another, and deeper too.   155

Dod. Besides, his grace to day dines with the Maior;
Who on his knees humbly intends to fall
And beg a pardon for your nephewes fault.

Lin. But Ile prevent him! Come, Sir Roger Oteley;
The king wil doe us justice in this cause.   160
How ere their hands have made them man and wife,
I wil disjoyne the match, or loose my life.   *Exeunt.*

Firke. Adue, monsieur Dodger! Farewel, fooles! Ha, ha! Oh, if they had staide, I would have so lambde them with floutes! O heart, my codpeece point is readie to flie in peeces every time I thinke upon Mistris Rose; but let that passe, as my Ladie Mairesse saies.   167

Hodge. This matter is answerd. Come, Rafe; home with thy wife. Come, my fine shoomakers, lets to our masters, the new Lord Maior, and there swagger this Shrove Tuesday. Ile promise you wine enough, for Madge keepes the seller.

All. O rare! Madge is a good wench.

Firke. And Ile promise you meate enough, for simpring Susan keepes the larder. Ile leade you to victuals, my brave souldiers; follow your captaine. O brave! Hearke, hearke!   175

Bell ringes.

W.–P. are wrong in regarding this passage as corroborative of Schmidt's surmise (*Shak. Lex.*) that '*laced mutton* = woman's flesh, a petticoat, a smock.' [But the pun certainly implies the latter, Shakespearian, colloquialism. *Gen. Ed.*]

All. The pancake bell rings,[1] the pancake bel! Tri-lill, my hearts!

Firke. Oh brave! Oh sweete bell! O delicate pancakes! Open the doores, my hearts, and shut up the windowes! keepe in the house, let out the pancakes! Oh rare, my heartes! Lets march together for the honor of Saint Hugh to the great new hall in Gratious Streete corner, which our maister, the newe Lord Maior, hath built.

Rafe. O the crew of good fellows that wil dine at my Lord Maiors cost to day! 183

Hodge. By the Lord, my Lord Maior is a most brave man. How shal prentises be bound to pray for him and the honour of the gentlemen shoomakers! Lets feede and be fat with my lordes bountye. 187

Fir. O musical bel, stil! O Hodge, O my brethren! Theres cheere for the heavens: venson pasties[2] walke up and down piping hote, like sergeants; beefe and brewesse comes marching in drie fattes; fritters and pancakes comes trowling in in wheele barrowes; hennes and orenges hopping in porters baskets, colloppes and egges in scuttles, and tartes and custardes comes quavering in in mault shovels. 194

Enter more Prentises.

All. Whoop, looke here, looke here!

Hodge. How now, madde laddes, whither away so fast?

1 Pren. Whither? Why, to the great new hall, know you not why? The Lorde Maior hath bidden all the prentises in London to breakfast this morning. 199

---

[1] That none might forget shriving before entering on the Lenten season the great bell was rung at an early hour in every parish, but since this ringing served at the same time as a signal for beginning to fry pancakes as one of the substitutes for meat, the shriving bell came to be known as the pancake bell. According to a Catholic ecclesiastic, quoted by W. S. Walsh, *Curiosities of Popular Customs*, 385, the name belonged originally to a special bell for summoning apprentice boys and others about the house to the pancake feasts of Shrove Tide. Whatever the precise origin of the name, the function of the bell as popularly interpreted, especially after the Reformation, consisted in ushering in the feasting, merry-making, and license of Shrove Tuesday, which in Dekker's London was the great holiday of the 'prentices. Firk's exultation may be regarded as representative. See Dyer, *British Popular Customs;* Brand's *Pop. Antiquities; Notes and Queries*, 8th series, Vol. I.

[2] So Q 2. Q. 1, 'pastimes.'

All. Oh brave shoomaker, oh brave lord of incomprehensible good fellowship!   Whoo!   Hearke you!   The pancake bell rings.
                                        Cast up caps.

Firke. Nay, more, my hearts!   Every Shrovetuesday is our yeere of jubile; and when the pancake bel rings, we are as free as my Lord Maior; we may shut up our shops, and make holiday.   I'll have it calld Saint Hughes Holiday.   205

All. Agreed, agreed!   Saint Hughes Holiday.

Hodge. And this shal continue for ever.

All. Oh brave!   Come, come, my hearts!   Away, away!

Firke. O eternall credite to us of the gentle craft!   March faire, my hearts!   Oh rare!   *Exeunt.*   210

[Act V.   Scene III.   *A Street in London.*]

Enter KING *and his* Traine *over the stage.*

King. Is our Lord Maior of London such a gallant?

Nobleman. One of the merriest madcaps in your land.
Your grace wil thinke, when you behold the man,
Hees rather a wilde ruffin than a maior.
Yet thus much Ile ensure your majestie   5
In al his actions that concerne his state,
He is as serious, provident, and wise,
As full of gravitie amongst the grave,
As any maior hath beene these many yeares.

King. I am with child, til I behold this huffe cap.   10
But all my doubt is, when we come in presence,
His madnesse wil be dasht cleane out of countenance.

Nobleman. It may be so, my liege.

King.   Which to prevent,
Let some one give him notice, tis our pleasure
That he put on his woonted merriment.   15
Set forward!

All.   On afore!   *Exeunt.*

[Act V. Scene IV. *A Great Hall.*]

Enter AYRE, HODGE, FIRKE, RAFE, *and other* Shoemakers, *all with napkins* [1] *on their shoulders.*

Eyre. Come, my fine Hodge, my jolly gentlemen shooemakers; soft, where be these caniballes, these varlets, my officers? Let them al walke and waite upon my brethren; for my meaning is, that none but shoomakers, none but the livery of my company shall in their sattin hoodes[2] waite uppon the trencher of my sover-raigne.　　　　　　　　　　　　　　　　　　　　　6

Firke. O my lord, it will be rare!

Ayre. No more, Firke; come, lively! Let your fellowe prentises want no cheere; let wine be plentiful as beere, and beere as water. Hang these penny pinching fathers, that cramme wealth in innocent lamb skinnes. Rip, knaves, avaunt! Looke to my guests!

Hodge. My lord, we are at our wits end for roome; those hundred tables wil not feast the fourth part of them.　　　　　13

Ayre. Then cover me those hundred tables againe, and againe, til all my jolly prentises be feasted. Avoyde, Hodge! Runne, Rafe! Friske about, my nimble Firke! Carowse me fadome healths to the honor of the shoomakers. Do they drink lively, Hodge? Do they tickle it, Firke?　　　　　　　　　　　　　　18

Firke. Tickle it? Some of them have taken their licour standing so long that they can stand no longer; but for meate, they would eate it, and they had it.

Ayre. Want they meate? Wheres this swag-belly, this greasie kitchinstuffe cooke? Call the varlet to me! Want meat? Firke, Hodge, lame Rafe, runne, my tall men, beleager the shambles, beggar al Eastcheape, serve me whole oxen in chargers, and let sheepe whine upon the tables like pigges for want of good felowes to eate them. Want meate? Vanish, Firke! Avaunt, Hodge!　27

Hodge. Your lordship mistakes my man Firke; he means, their

---

[1] As 'sewers' or waiters. Cf. *Silent Woman*, III, iii, 57.

[2] The hood, on gala occasions something very fine in material and coloring, was an indispensable and characteristic appendage to the ancient civic liveries. Stow-Strype, Bk. V, p. 166; Herbert, *Hist. Twelve Livery Companies London*, Vol. I.

bellies want meate, not the boords; for they have drunk so much, they can eate nothing.[1]   30

Enter HANS, ROSE, *and* WIFE.

Wife. Where is my lord?

Ayre. How now, Lady Madgy?

Wife. The kings most excelent majesty is new come; hee sends me for thy honor; one of his most worshipful peeres bade me tel thou must be mery, and so forth; but let that passe.   35

Eyre. Is my soveraigne come? Vanish, my tall shoomakers, my nimble brethren; looke to my guests, the prentises. Yet stay a little! How now, Hans? How lookes my little Rose?

Hans. Let me request you to remember me.
I know, your honour easily may obtaine   40
Free pardon of the king for me and Rose,
And reconcile me to my uncles grace.

Eyre. Have done, my good Hans, my honest jorneyman; looke cheerely! Ile fall upon both my knees, till they be as hard as horne, but Ile get thy pardon.   45

Wife. Good my lord, have a care what you speake to his grace.

Eyre. Away, you Islington whitepot! hence, you hopperarse![2] you barly pudding, ful of magots! you broyld carbonado! avaunt, avaunt, avoide, Mephostophilus![3] Shall Sim Eyre learne[4] to speake of you, Ladie Madgie? Vanish, Mother Miniver cap;[5] vanish, goe, trip and goe; meddle with your partlets and your pishery pasherie, your flewes and your whirligigs; go, rub, out of mine alley! Sim Eyre knowes how to speake to a Pope, to Sultan Soliman,[6] to Tamburlaine, and he were here; and shal I melt,

---

[1] The second three-men's song was probably introduced at this point. Rhys, 79.

[2] Qtos. 1, 2, 'happerarse.'

[3] So Qtos. 1, 2. Cf. 'How now Mephostophilus!' *M. W. W.* I, i; and cobbler Juniper's exclamation in *The Case is Altered*, II, iv: 'Avoid Mephostophilus!' The comparison of Juniper and Eyre furnishes striking illustration of the characteristic differences between Jonson and Dekker in attitude and method.

[4] So Q 3. Qtos. 1, 2, 'leave.'

[5] Cf.: 'Thou shalt little Miniver, thou shalt'; Tucca in *Satiromastix*, p. 221, Pearson.

[6] Probably an allusion to Kyd's *Soliman and Perseda*, 1599. Cf. *Satiromastix*, p. 257, Pearson, and note.

shal I droope before my soveraigne? No, come, my Ladie Madgie!
Follow me, Hauns! About your businesse, my frolicke free-booters!
Firke, friske about, and about, and about, for the honour of mad
Simon Eyre, Lord Maior of London.   58
    Firke. Hey, for the honour of the shoomakers.   *Exeunt.*

[Act V. Scene V. *An Open Yard before the Hall.*]

A long flourish, or two.   Enter KING, Nobles, EYRE, *his* WIFE,
LACIE, ROSE. LACIE *and* ROSE *kneele.*

    King. Well, Lacie, though the fact was verie foule
Of your revolting from our kingly love
And your owne duetie, yet we pardon you.
Rise both, and, Mistris Lacie, thanke my Lord Maior
For your yong bridegroome here.   5
    Eyre. So, my deere liege, Sim Eyre and my brethren, the gentle-
men shoomakers, shal set your sweete majesties image cheeke by
jowle by Saint Hugh for this honour you have done poore Simon
Eyre. I beseech your grace, pardon my rude behaviour; I am a
handicrafts man, yet my heart is without craft; I would be sory
at my soule, that my boldnesse should offend my king.   11
    King. Nay, I pray thee, good Lord Maior, be even as mery
As if thou wert among thy shoomakers;
It does me good to see thee in this humour.
    Eyre. Saist thou me so, my sweete Dioclesian? Then, hump! 15
Prince am I none, yet am I princely borne. By the Lord of Ludgate, my liege, Ile be as merrie as a pie.
    King. Tel me, infaith, mad Eyre, how old thou art.
    Eyre. My liege, a verie boy, a stripling, a yonker; you see not
a white haire on my head, not a gray in this beard.[1] Everie haire,
I assure thy majestie, that stickes in this beard, Sim Eyre values
at the king of Babilons ransome, Tamar[2] Chams beard was a rub-

---

[1] Cf. Lord Vanni's discourse on old age, *Wonder of a Kingdome*, p. 222, Pearson.
[2] Q 1, 'Tama.'

bing brush toot: yet Ile shave it off, and stuffe tennis balls with it,
to please my bully king.   24
  King. But all this while I do not know your age.
  Eyre. My liege, I am sixe and fiftie yeare olde, yet I can crie
humpe! with a sound heart for the honour of Saint Hugh. Marke
this olde wench, my king: I dauncde the shaking of the sheetes
with her sixe and thirtie yeares agoe, and yet I hope to get two or
three yong lorde maiors, ere I die. I am lustie still, Sim Eyre still.
Care and colde lodging brings white haires. My sweete majestie,
let care vanish, cast it uppon thy nobles, it will make thee looke
alwayes young like Apollo, and crye humpe! Prince am I none,
yet am I princely borne.   34
  King. Ha, ha!
Say, Cornewall, didst thou ever see his like?[1]
  Nobleman. Not I, my lorde.

Enter Lincolne *and* Lord Maior.

  King.   Lincolne, what newes with you?
  Linc. My gracious lord, have care unto your selfe,
For there are traytors here.
  All. Traytors? Where? Who?   40
  Eyre. Traitors in my house? God forbid! Where be my officers?
Ile spend my soule, ere my king feele harme.
  King. Where is the traytor, Lincolne?
  Linc.   Here he stands.
  King. Cornewall, lay hold on Lacie!—Lincolne, speake,
What canst thou lay unto thy nephewes charge?   45
  Linc. This, my deere liege: your grace, to doe me honour,
Heapt on the head of this degenerous boy
Desertlesse favours; you made choise of him,
To be commander over powers in France.
But he—   50
  King. Good Lincolne, prythee, pawse a while!
Even in thine eies I reade what thou wouldst speake.
I know how Lacie did neglect our love,

---

[1] Qtos., 'Ha . . . like,' as one line.

Ranne himselfe deepely, in the highest degree,
Into vile treason—   55
    Linc.   Is he not a traytor?
    King. Lincolne, he was; now have we pardned him.
Twas not a base want of true valors fire,
That held him out of France, but loves desire.
    Linc. I wil not beare his shame upon my backe.
    King. Nor shalt thou, Lincolne; I forgive you both.   60
    Lin. Then, good my liege, forbid the boy to wed
One whose meane birth will much disgrace his bed.
    King. Are they not married?
    Linc.   No, my liege.
    Both.   We are.
    King. Shall I divorce them then? O be it farre,
That any hand on earth should dare untie   65
The sacred knot, knit by Gods majestie;
I would not for my crowne disjoyne their hands,
That are conjoynd in holy nuptiall bands.
How saist thou, Lacy, wouldst thou loose thy Rose?
    Hans. Not for all Indians wealth, my soveraigne.   70
    King. But Rose, I am sure, her Lacie would forgoe?
    Rose. If Rose were askt that question, sheed say no!
    King. You heare them, Lincolne?
    Linc.   Yea, my liege, I do.
    King. Yet canst thou find ith heart to part these two?
Who seeks, besides you, to divorce these lovers?   75
    L. Ma. I do, my gracious lord, I am her father.
    King. Sir Roger Oteley, our last maior, I thinke?
    Nobleman. The same, my liege.
    King.   Would you offend Loves lawes?
Wel, you shal have your wills, you sue to me,
To prohibite the match. Soft, let me see—   80
You both are married, Lacie, art thou not?
    Hans. I am, dread soveraigne.
    King.   Then, upon thy life,
I charge thee, not to call this woman wife.
    L. Ma. I thanke your grace.

Rose.   O my most gratious lord!

              Kneele.

 King. Naŷ, Rose, never wooe me; I tel you true,   85
Although as yet I am a batchellor,
Yet I beleeve, I shal not marry you.
 Rose. Can you divide the body from the soule,
Yet make the body live?
 King.   Yea, so profound?
I cannot, Rose, but you I must divide.   90
This faire maide, bridegroome,[1] cannot be your bride.
Are you pleasde, Lincolne? Oteley, are you pleasde?
 Both. Yes, my lord.
 King.   Then must my heart be easde;
For, credit me, my conscience lives in paine,
Til these whom I devorcde, be joynd againe.   95
Lacy, give me thy hand; Rose, lend me thine!
Be what you would be! Kisse now! So, thats fine.
At night, lovers, to bed!—Now, let me see,
Which of you all mislikes this harmony.
 L. Ma. Wil you then take from me my child perforce?   100
 King. Why, tell me, Oteley: shines not Lacies name
As bright in the worldes eye as the gay beames
Of any citizen.
 Linc.   Yea, but, my gratious lord,
I do mislike the match farre more than he;
Her bloud is too too base.   105
 King.   Lincolne, no more.
Dost thou not know that love respects no bloud,
Cares not for difference of birth or state?
The maide is yong, wel borne, faire, vertuous,
A worthy bride for any gentleman.
Besides, your nephew for her sake did stoope   110
To bare necessitie, and, as I heare,
Forgetting honors and all courtly pleasures,
To gaine her love, became a shooemaker.
As for the honor which he lost in France,

[1] In Qtos. this line begins: 'Faire maide, this bridegroome.' Corrected by Fr.

Thus I redeeme it: Lacie, kneele thee downe!— 115
Arise, Sir Rowland Lacie! Tell me now,
Tell me in earnest, Oteley, canst thou chide,
Seeing thy Rose a ladie and a bryde?
Lord Maior. I am content with what your grace hath done.
Linc. And I, my liege, since theres no remedie. 120
King. Come on, then, al shake hands: Ile have you frends;
Where there is much love, all discord ends.
What sayes my mad Lord Maior to all this love?
Eyre. O my liege, this honour you have done to my fine journey-
man here, Rowland Lacie, and all these favours which you have
showne to me this daye in my poore house, will make Simon Eyre
live longer by one dozen of warme summers more then he should.
King. Nay, my mad Lord Maior, that shall be thy name,
If any grace of mine can length thy life,
One honour more Ile doe thee: that new building, 130
Which at thy cost in Cornehill is erected,
Shall take a name from us; weele have it cald
The Leaden hall,[1] because in digging it
You found the lead that covereth the same.
Eyre. I thanke your majestie. 135
Wife. God blesse your grace!
King. Lincolne, a word with you!

Enter HODGE, FIRKE, RAFE, *and more* Shoomakers.

Eyre. How now, my mad knaves? Peace, speake softly, yonder
is the king.
King. With the olde troupe which there we keepe in pay, 140
We wil incorporate a new supply.

---

[1] It is not improbable that this name actually owes its origin to some such ar-
chitectural feature as a leaden roof, but the building first called Leadenhall ante-
dates Eyre's gift by at least a century. Early a public market—certainly by 1345
though the site at least, it seems, remained in private hands—this hall with its
premises, says Stow, was definitively confirmed to the city, through the munifi-
cence of Whittington in 1411. On the same spot Simon Eyre in 1419 erected a
public granary to which the old name was transferred. In the sixteenth century
it served also as a city armory, as the place where city pageants were prepared and
whence they started, etc. This reference to it and its founder was sure to awaken
enthusiastic response. See Stow, and Riley's *Memorials of London.*

Before one summer more passe ore my head,
France shal repent, England was injured.
What are all those?

Hans.　　　　　All shoomakers, my liege,
Sometimes my fellowes; in their companies　　　　145
I livde as merry as an emperor.[1]

King. My mad Lord Mayor, are all these shoomakers?

Eyre. All shooemakers, my liege; all gentlemen of the gentle craft, true Trojans, couragious cordwainers; they all kneele to the shrine of holy Saint Hugh.

All. God save your majesty, all shoemakers![2]

King. Mad Simon, would they anything with us?

Eyre. Mum, mad knaves! Not a word! Ile doot; I warrant you. They are all beggars, my liege; all for themselves, and I for them all, on both my knees do intreate, that for the honor of poore Simon Eyre and the good of his brethren, these mad knaves, your grace would vouchasafe some privilege to my new Leden hall, that it may be lawfull for us to buy and sell leather there two dayes a weeke.　　　　159

King. Mad Sim, I grant your suite, you shall have patent
To hold two market dayes in Leden hall,
Mondayes and Fridayes, those shal be the times.[3]
Will this content you?

All. Jesus blesse your grace!

Eyre. In the name of these my poore brethren shoomakers, I most humbly thanke your grace. But before I rise, seeing you are in the giving vaine and we in the begging, graunt Sim Eyre one boone more.　　　　168

---

[1] Q 1, 'emprov.'

[2] Qtos. 1, 2 read: '*All.* God save your maiesty, all shoemaker'; the others leave out the last two words. The shoemakers, echoing Eyre, answer the king's question in concert. W.–P. needlessly change the line to '*All shoomakers* [stage-dir.]. God save your maisty!'

[3] Leadenhall was almost certainly not used as a leather market before the fifth year of Elizabeth's reign, when Monday was appointed as a market day for workers in leather. Stow-Strype, Bk. V, 213. This allows but a short time for the tradition to arise that Simon Eyre belonged to the brotherhood of the gentle craft. Still, if the jolly and aggressive cordwainers claimed him, at first perhaps only in fun, there were few in London competent to contradict them or interested in doing so.

King. What is it, my Lord Maior?

Eyre. Vouchsafe to taste of a poore banquet that standes
sweetely waiting for your sweete presence.

King. I shall undo thee, Eyre, only with feasts;
Already have I beene too troublesome;
Say, have I not?   174

Eyre. O my deere king, Sim Eyre was taken unawares upon a
day of shroving, which I promist long ago to the prentises of
London.

   For, and't please your highnes, in time past,
   I bare the water-tankerd, and my coate
   Sits not a whit the worse upon my backe;
   And then, upon a morning, some mad boyes,   180
   It was Shrovetuesday, eevne as tis now,[1]
gave me my breakefast, and I swore then by the stopple of my
tankerd, if ever I came to be Lord Maior of London, I would feast
all the prentises. This day, my liege, I did it, and the slaves had an
hundred tables five times covered; they are gone home and vanisht;
   Yet adde more honour to the gentle trade,   186
   Taste of Eyres banquet, Simon's happie made.[1]

King. Eyre, I wil taste of thy banquet, and wil say,
I have not met more pleasure on a day.
Friends of the gentle craft, thankes to you al,   190
Thankes, my kind Ladie Mairesse, for our cheere.—
Come, lordes, a while lets revel it at home!
When all our sports and banquetings are done,
Warres must right wrongs which Frenchmen have begun.

               Exeunt.

[1] Qtos., lines 177–181, 186–187, as prose.

FINIS

APPENDIX

SOURCES IN DELONEY'S GENTLE CRAFT, 1597–8.

A. The Gentle Craft: St. Hugh's Bones.—(II, iii, 45)—Hugh, the son of a British king, on returning, destitute, to his native land is befriended by journeymen shoemakers and, for a time, becomes one of them. Cf. I, i, 25–29. During the Diocletian persecutions he is imprisoned for his faith and finally put to death. While in prison he is visited by the journeymen who minister to him in every way possible; "in requital of which kindnesse he called them Gentlemen of the Gentle Craft," a title "they engraved so deeply in their minds, that to this day it could never be razed out: like a remembrance in marble stone, which continueth time out of mind." *Gentle Craft*, chap. III, p. 13. B. M. Quarto of 1648 (page 22, A. F. Lange's ed. in *Palæstra*, XVIII).

But this is not their only reward. Passing along the place where St. Hugh's body is hanging "the flesh being picked cleane off from the bones," they recall, that, having nothing else to give, he bequeathed his bones to them. Hence "to fulfill the will of the dead" they secretly remove the skeleton from the gibbet, but in order to avoid suspicion as well as to profit by the 'virtue' of a saint's bones, they convert these bones into tools. "And never after did they travel without these tools on their backs: which ever since have been called S. Hugh's bones." Chap. IV, p. 18. (Lange's ed., *Palæstra*, XVIII, 26.)

B. A Shoemaker, a Prince born.—(III, i, 45)—Crispianus "was prest to the wars into the countray of Gaul, now called France." Here he hears the reply of Iphicrates when taunted with being the son of a shoemaker: "Indeed, my father's trade is a reproach unto me—but thou shalt understand that a shoomaker's son is a prince born; his fortune made him so and thou shalt finde no lesse." When, on returning, Crispianus, now a famous general, takes his brother's child in his arms, he says: "Now I will say and swear that a shoomaker's son is a prince born, joyning in the opinion of Iphicrates, and henceforth shoomakers shall never let their terme die." Chaps. VII–VIII, pp. 28–35. (Lange, *Palæstra*, XVIII, 44–57.)

C. The Hiring of the Journeyman.—(II, iii, 112)—Simon Eyre "could not make his ware so fast as he could have sold it, so that he stood in great need of a journeyman or two more. At the last, one of his servants spying one go along the street with a fardell at his back called to his master, saying, Sir, yonder goes Saint Hugh's bones, twenty pounds to a penney. Run presently, quoth he, and bring him hither." Hailed by the boy, "the fellow being a Frenchman that had not long been in England, turning about, said: Hea, what you sea? Will you speak wed me: Hea? What you have?" On learning that he is looking for work Eyre engages him "and to worke he went merrily, where he behaved himselfe so well, that his master made good account of him, thinking he had been a bachelor but in the end it was found otherwise." Chap. X, pp. 40-41. (Lange, 61-62.)

D. Eyre's Bargain.—(III, i)—"Now it is to be remembered, that while John Denevale (*i. e.* the French journeyman) dwelt with Simon Eyer, it chanced that a ship of the Ile of Candy was driven upon our coast, laden with all kinds of lawns and cambricks, and other linen cloth: which commodities at that time were in London very scant and exceeding dear, and by reason of a great leak the ship had got at sea,—he (*i. e.* the Greek merchant) would make what profit he could of his goods here." Ignorant of English but speaking French, the merchant chances to meet John to whom he makes known his plight. John directs him to a good lodging and promises to talk with his master, "a very honest man" who may know of some one that will deal with him for the cargo. Eyre sees his opportunity at once. With 3000 pounds ready money a profit of at least "three and three thousand pounds" may be made. Unfortunately he cannot lay down even three thousand pence. Mrs. Eyre's wit, however, solves the difficulty. Early next day Eyre is to go to the merchant as broker for one of the chief aldermen and after driving "a sound bargain" lay down a dozen angels in earnest, the balance to be paid a month after the delivery of the goods. In the afternoon, so John will tell the merchant in good faith, the alderman himself will come to receive the bill of lading and to deliver a note for the payment of the money. This alderman is to be impersonated by Eyre, but lest his household become privy to the plan the disguise is to be assumed at the house of Mrs. Eyre's cousin John Barber, who will snap off all superfluous hairs, fashion Eyre's bushy beard after the alderman's grave cut, wash him with a sweet camphire ball and besprinkle his head and face with the purest rose-water. Thereupon he is to don an alderman's dress (see note, Act III, i) and then proceed to the merchant with John Barber, "neat and fine in his apparell, as indeed all Barbers are," as his man. Finally, while the ship is coming about, Eyre is to give notice to the linen drapers of the commodities he has coming. Eyre follows his wife's counsel and suddenly finds himself wealthy. The Lord Mayor invites him to supper—this Dekker has placed after the first election—and deals with him for a part of his purchase. He becomes a merchant, "committing the government of his shop to John," and in due time is elected first sheriff and then Lord Mayor. Chaps. X, XI. (Lange, 62–72.)

E. The Shoe-fitting Scene.—(IV, iv, 28)—Owing to the enmity of Emperor Maximinus, Crispianus and Crispine, sons of the "vertuous queen of Logria, which now is called Kent," had disguised themselves and become shoemakers at Feversham. The report of their skill "in the end preferred their master to be the emperor's shooemakers; and by this means his servants went to Maximinus' court every day." On one occasion of this sort Ursula, the emperor's daughter, sees Crispine and falls in love with him. Under the pretext that the shoes he had brought last do not fit she sends for him. Crispine promises to make her a pair that will fit "for none shall set a stitch in them but mine own self." Crispine makes the shoes and appears again at court. "How now, quoth she, hast thou brought me a pair of shooes? I have, gracious madam, quoth he. Then, quoth the princesse, come thyselfe and draw them on. Therewith she sitting down, lifted up her well-proportioned legge upon his gentle knee." This time the shoes fit; Ursula rewards Crispine royally, appoints him her shoemaker, and so reveals her love *gradatim*. Chap. VI, 24. (Lange, 38.)

F. Eyre's Promise to the 'Prentices.—(V, i, 46)—"Every Sunday morning divers of these prentices did use to go to a place neer the conduit to break their fast with pudding-pies and often they would take Simon along with them; but upon a time it so fell out, that when he should draw money to pay the shot with the rest, that he had none, whereupon he merrily said unto them: My faithful friends and conduit companions, treasurers of the water tankard, and main pillers of the pudding house—if it will please you to pardon me this time and excuse me for my part of the shot, I do here vow unto you, that if ever I come to be Lord Maior of this City, I will give a breakfast unto all the prentices in London. We do take your word, quoth they and so they departed." Chap. X, p. 40. (Lange, 61.)

Middleton and Rowley

THE SPANISH GIPSY

Edited with Critical Essay and Notes by the late H. Butler Clarke, M.A., Fellow of St. John's College, Oxford

CRITICAL ESSAY [1]

Lives.—Thomas Middleton was born in London, about 1570,—the son of William Middleton, a gentleman. He may have been educated at Cambridge, and was, in all probability, a member of Gray's Inn, from 1593 or 1596. He was evidently versed in the law: more than one character in his plays is "swallowed in the quick-sands of law-quillets." He married Mary Morbeck, the daughter of a clerk in Chancery, about 1602. At that time he was already identified with the group of dramatists writing for the Admiral's men; but he soon began to write for the Paul's boys, the children of the Queen's Revels, and the Lady Elizabeth's company. Between 1604 and 1614 most of his London comedies of manners were produced. About the latter date the association with William Rowley, from which proceeded the finest work of each in romantic comedy and tragedy, was formed. In 1616–17, the Prince's acted their *Faire Quarrell*, and between June 1621 and July 10, 1623, the Elizabeth's acted their *Changeling* and *Spanish Gipsie*. In and after 1623 some of Middleton's plays are presented by the King's company. Between 1613 and 1626 he prepared many of the pageants for civic celebrations; and, from 1620 till his death, he was chronologer of the city,—a position in which Ben Jonson succeeded him. He was buried in the parish churchyard of Newington Butts, July 4, 1627. An account of his dramatic productions has been included in the introduction to this volume.

Of the life of William Rowley, joint-author with Middleton of *The Spanish Gipsie* and four other plays, hardly anything is known. *The Travailes of the three English Brothers*, in which he coöperated with Day and Wilkins, was written in 1607 for Queen Anne's men. In 1610 he was a play-actor in the Duke of York's (afterwards Prince's) company. He was with it, 1613–1615, and in 1616 appears at the head of the list of members. In 1619 he played, with members of that company, Middleton's *Inner Temple Mask*, taking the part of Plum-porridge; [and, shortly before July 4, 1620 he wrote for them, in partnership with Middleton, a

---

[1] This essay did not have the advantage of revision by its author, whose sad death occurred a few years ago. But I am sure that, as it stands, it will contribute to the literature of the subject. The sketch of Middleton's life is supplied by me.—*Gen. Ed.*

mask, *The World Tost at Tennis*. As stated in the preceding paragraph he must have been associated with the Lady Elizabeth's (Queen of Bohemia's) servants between 1621 and 1623]. The list of *Dramatis Personæ* of his play, *All's Lost by Lust* [presented by that company, probably in 1622, and printed 1633], contains the statement that the part of Jaques, "a simple, clownish gentleman," was "personated by the poet." [On Aug. 29, 1623, *The Maid in the Mill* by Fletcher and Rowley was licensed, for the King's company; and Rowley took part in the acting, as also in that of another play by the King's, Dec. 20, 1624. Because, undoubtedly, of his long association with the Prince's men, he marched with them at the funeral of James in 1625. He is not heard of later as acting; but he was listed as one of the new King's men later in that year and he is described as one of "his Majesty's servants" on the title-page of his comedy *A New Wonder*, printed 1632.] [1] Langbaine is authority for the fact that he was "beloved by those great men Shakespeare, Fletcher and Johnson." He married in 1637. The date and place of his death are, like those of his birth, unknown. Eleven plays have been preserved in connection with which Rowley's name appears as joint-author with some of the most famous dramatists of his time. Of his independent and unaided work we have a few trifling verses, a prose satire in the form of a fable entitled *A Search for Money, or the Lamentable Complaint for the Loss of the Wandering Knight Monsieur L'Argent* (1609), and four plays (see below) printed between 1632 and 1638. Of four other plays all but the names are lost. [2]

The Spanish Gipsie: Sources and Dramatic Construction.— *The Spanish Gipsie* contains two plots derived down to minute details, such as the episode of Cardochia (iv, 3) and the slaughter of the mule (iv, 1), from Cervantes' *Exemplary Novels* (*Novelas Exemplares*. 1st edit. Madrid 1613). The story which gives its name to the play is *La Gitanilla* (The little Gipsy-girl); the story of Roderigo and Clara is found, with some variation, in *La Fuerza de la Sangre* (The Power of Blood-relationship). The lifetime of Middleton and Rowley falls within the most brilliant period of Spanish literature, the age of Cervantes and Lope de Vega, of Santa Teresa and Quevedo, and of the famous rogue-stories (*novelas de pícaros*). *Don Quixote, Lazarillo de Tormes, Guzmán de*

[1] Insertions in square brackets are mine.—*Gen. Ed.*
[2] For discussion of the Middleton-Rowley plays, and of the place of the authors respectively in the history of comedy, see the Essay introductory to this volume—sections 9 and 14.—*Gen. Ed.*

Alfarache and many other Spanish stories were familiar to English readers in admirable translations. *La Celestina*, the fountain-head of Spanish novel and comedy, besides being translated had been dramatized under the title of *Calisto and Melibea* (see *Dodsley's Plays*, ed. Hazlitt). The Spanish character was well known in England owing to the close connection between the two countries in peace and in war; Spanish dress and manners were imitated, and Spanish expressions were introduced in conversation. Fletcher took three of his plots from Cervantes' Novels; Webster, Middleton and others frequently take Spain as the scene of their plays. It is, therefore, not surprising to find that their Spanish characters are not mere Englishmen tricked out with foreign names. But though both Middleton and Rowley more than once make use of Spanish themes there is nothing to show that they had any deep knowledge of things Spanish. (See note on *cocoquismo* and *germania*, II, i.) The anglicised and incorrect forms in which Spanish words are used (*e. g. grandoes, maruedi, corigidor, rialls*), though they may be partly due to printers and copyists, go to show that the authors' acquaintance with the language was, at most, a slight one. The common name Alvarez is wrongly accentuated (on the second instead of the first syllable) throughout the play. It is possible that *The Spanish Gipsie* comes to us through the excellent French translation of Cervantes' Novels by de Rosset and d'Audiguier, the first volume of which (Paris, 1615) contains *La Belle Egyptienne* and *De la Force du Sang*. They were not englished till 1640. The state of society represented is that imagined by Spanish novelists and "sword and cloak" playwrights to have existed about the beginning of the sixteenth century, which fifty years later they came to regard as their golden age. The characters also, with the bright exception of Pretiosa are the stock ones of the Spanish stage and novel, Clara, *dama;* Fernando and Alvarez, *barbas* (old men, literally "beards"); Roderigo and John, *galanes*, distinguished from the common type only by Roderigo's outrageous brutality. These are all taken directly from Cervantes; Louis, Sancho and Soto were added by the English playwrights, and lack, accordingly, the Spanish stamp. The connection between the two plots is so slight and accidental that with the help of scissors two plays could be made out of one, leaving a large part of the three middle acts disconnected and superfluous. The hero of one play (Roderigo) and the heroine of the other (Pretiosa) are brother and sister but they are unaware of the fact, and it in no wise affects the action. Louis occupies an awkward position between the two sets of characters and is throughout the butt of circumstances. He unwittingly aids in the outrage upon Clara whom he loves, but nothing comes of this dramatic situation. As a suitor, after the outrage, he is deluded with false hopes. He is cheated by his own generosity of his vengeance upon the slayer of his father. When Roderigo's treachery comes to light Louis declares himself "not so poor as put this injury up" but again he is, seemingly, fooled with a promise of "noble satisfaction." In Cervantes' story Fernando's motive for obliging Roderigo to marry his victim is "the power of blood-relationship"; he wishes to right a grandson the sight of whom has called forth in him, even before he is aware of the boy's parentage, a warm instinctive feeling of kinship. The drama suppresses the child, out of respect, perhaps for the unity of time, and with it the gentle touch that redeems the dark story. A fictitious motive is sought and Fernando sacrifices his son,—for sacrifice it would have been but for the accident of Roderigo's second outbreak of passion for Clara—to his "till now untainted blood and honour." This is a complete inversion of "honour," the external motive that makes Clara's father in Cervantes' story declare that "an ounce of public disgrace is heavier than a ton of secret shame." Clara's family are bound by the code to seek reparation, if it can be won without scandal; but Fernando is not bound to recognise their claim. Again marriage may be, on the stage, a full satisfaction for seduction, but scarcely for rape. The suppression of the child has the further unfortunate effect of leaving Clara without excuse for condoning the brutal violation she has undergone. If there is something repulsive in her cool-headed preparations for the identification of her ravisher (I, iii) still more disgusting is her dawning love for him at the end of the same scene. She knows nothing of him save his brutal passion, and his cynical haste to be rid of her as soon as it is satisfied. The instant reciprocal inclination at the second meeting

(IV, iii), if possible in nature, deserves a harsher name than that of love. Clara, if pure, could feel only horror and loathing for her aggressor; and her bridal, except for the child's sake, could be nothing but a second violation. The authors surely would not have us believe that the relation between love and the sexual act is such that the latter can, under such circumstances, give birth to the former. If the character of Clara is disagreeable, that of Roderigo is hateful. A creature of brutal impulses he insults his victim, betrays the confidence of his friend (Louis), and behaves outrageously to his father. His fit of remorse (III, i) is unconvincing, and for it he bitterly upbraids his weakness. Poetic justice would have brought down upon him punishment swift and sure, instead of a happy marriage troubled only by an instant of doubt. The climax is reached when his exultation is suddenly checked (V, i) by the words "Thy wife's a wanton;" but his momentary shame, and his admission that he ought to have married his victim, are accompanied by the selfish reflection "then had I been the happiest man alive." A great dramatic situation is wasted when we leave him basking in the smiles of the puppet, Clara. It is indeed strange that Middleton and Rowley who knew how the fiercest and most ungoverned passion can be raised to the highest tragic dignity (De Flores in *The Changeling*) by its soul-devouring earnestness should have given us the vulgar rake Roderigo. The first scene of the play has been called "horribly striking" by Sir Walter Scott, but it involves a situation in which emotion becomes merely ejaculatory and even the finest tirade is flat; from such a situation no dramatic issue is possible, the strain is too great for comedy to bear. After such a scene Roderigo's second passion, and his unexplained repentance are as colourless as Clara's unnatural and repulsive pliability. No real moral problem is involved, the dramatic one, depending entirely upon situation, finds an improbable solution in the chance that brings about the meeting of Clara and Roderigo under his father's roof.

The cruel realism of this repulsive story forms a foil to the romantic idyll of the loves of John and Pretiosa. Here we are in another world amid surroundings as graceful and pleasing as the former ones were harsh and gloomy. Here again Cervantes is closely followed, but the blood-feud between Louis and Alvarez is an addition to the Spanish story. As a high-spirited boy willing to sacrifice everything to love inspired by a worthy object, John gains all sympathies and is a bridegroom worthy of the peerless Pretiosa. Pretiosa's character had indeed been dimly foreshadowed in that of Tarsina (*Libre de Appolonio* V, 350 *seq.*); but it is improbable that Cervantes was acquainted with the book, and it would be pedantry to deny to him the glory of having created perfect in all its parts a type ever recurring and ever fresh, the original of Victor Hugo's Esmeralda and many others,—an abiding proof that ignorance is not an indispensable safeguard of innocence and a standing confirmation of the purity of all things to the pure,—a maiden free and witty, chaste and good; dancer and singer at fairs and merrymakings; companion of bawds and procuresses, clean amidst filth and turpitude; wholly illiterate, yet with native cleverness never at a loss; graceful beyond the dream of fancy; with a wild irresistible charm and a heart of gold under a mask of coquettish cynicism: worthy of a place in the world of art beside Don Quixote and Sancho themselves. The solution of the plot is, in this case, completely satisfactory to the ethical sense; and the means by which it is reached are as artistic and graceful as those employed in the other plot are violent. Intolerable insult makes John forget the assumed gipsy in the native gentleman; his bearing under threat of immediate death is simple and dignified. Pretiosa's intercession for her lover is worthy of her character; and the discovery of the real position of the lovers comes just in the nick of time. The minor characters are summarily treated: it would have been less shocking to leave the fate of the light-hearted and rollicking Diego undecided than to marry him off-hand to the prurient and lying Cardochia. It is beside the point to compare the gipsies with the more realistic vagabonds of *The Beggars' Bush* for these gipsies are really ladies and gentlemen, and as such they act and speak. No real gipsy comes upon the stage and no sympathy is shown either in the novel or the play for the hated and despised race. Cervantes indeed pronounces a half-burlesque panegyric on their mode of life but otherwise faithfully reflects public opinion in his hatred of the wanderers. Lope de Vega (*Pastores de Belen*) was one of the first to treat seriously their pretensions to soothsaying.

The chief defects of *The Spanish Gipsie* are its lack of unity, its violent contrast, and its dependence rather on situation than on character. When the persons of the two plots meet upon the stage the action is proceeding in opposite directions. Neither plot is subordinated to the other: it would be difficult to say which is the main and which the secondary one. One drama of ordinary length barely gives space for the development of two concurrent intrigues, yet here the development is curtailed in order that space may be left for loosely connected episode and somewhat aimless fooling. The play within the play in no way helps the action, it does not even spare Fernando the necessity of threatening his son with a distasteful marriage. The incident of the picture (IV, iii) serves but to raise a laugh at a serious point. The dialogue, on the other hand, even when wasted, is almost flawless in its even brilliancy. It is not, however, studded with the splendid flashes of poetry of which Middleton at times lavishes such dazzling treasures. A touch of euphuism is found here and there, *e. g.* Fernando's comments on the letter (III, iii). Pretiosa's pleading (V, i) affords a fine opportunity for effective acting. The paltry lyrics are town-bred like their writers and singers: they have none of the breezy freedom of "the merrie green woods" that marks the open air ballads of Robin Hood. Such poverty is surprising in an age that squandered gems. But sound rather than sense is aimed at, and the beat of the two marching songs is irresistible. We almost hear the tramp of feet. Sancho's burlesque parody (II, i) deserves the laugh it must have raised.

Division of Authorship.—The "always uncertain and usually profitless task of separation" (Saintsbury) offers unusual difficulties in a play to which its authors contributed only the dialogue, one scene, a minor character and certain comic excrescences. Critics are widely at variance as to the qualities which led Day, Wilkins, Middleton, Dekker, Ford, Webster and Heywood to choose Rowley as a fellow-worker. (Cf. Ward's *Dramatic Literature*, ii, 78; Swinburne's *Preface* to *Middleton*, Mermaid Series;

Saintsbury's *Elizabethan Literature*, pp. 269, 422). Rowley's verse
is often so rough that it is hardly distinguishable from prose.
His independently written plays contain no "marked element of
serious purpose" (Ward). In two of them, *A Woman never Vext*
(1632) and *A Shoomaker a Gentleman* (1638) a civic purpose is
apparent; they were seemingly written to order, the one to celebrate
a city charity, the other to glorify the craft of a city guild. *A
Match at Midnight* (1633) is a rollicking London comedy of tavern
manners and intrigue.[1] The fourth, *All's Lost by Lust* (1633)
is a rough and bloody tragedy founded on the story of King Roder-
ick of Spain, Count Julian and La Cava. A touch of pathetic
tenderness is found in the character of Robert Foster (*A Woman
never Vext*) and again in the holy virgin Winnifred and the gentle
knight Sir Hugh (*A Shoomaker*, etc.). But Rowley had seemingly
no other purpose than to amuse: a hearty guffaw was to him the
most welcome form of applause; the only two parts he is known to
have acted (see above) are comic ones; his best creation—if it be
wholly his—is the comic Welshman, Randal (*A Match at Midnight*).
It is safest, therefore, to regard him, with Mr. Saintsbury, as "a
vigorous writer of farce," and to suppose that he was primarily
an actor, whose approval and coöperation would go far to ensure
the success of a play; that his ready wit and knowledge of the stage
were sought by playwrights; that he made comic parts his specialty,
and that, in return for these services, his name appeared as joint
author, occupying, it should be noticed, always the second place.
We find his mark on Sancho and Soto, and on the play within the
play. The first and last acts of *The Spanish Gipsie*,—the acts in
fact within which the drama is contained,—are the work of one
hand, and that hand is Middleton's. How much of the somewhat
profitless chatter of Acts II, III, and IV, comes from Rowley's
pen it is impossible with certainty to determine.[2]

[1] Probably a revision of one of Middleton's.—*Gen. Ed.*

[2] From a consideration of verse-tests, invention, and style, Miss P. G. Wiggin
(*Inquiry into the Authorship of the Middleton-Rowley Plays*, Boston: 1897) assigns
the greater part of this play—all but the second act—to Middleton. Professor
Morris (Introduction to his edition) thinks that the play was written by Middleton
and revised by Rowley. I doubt the theory of revision (see Essay introductory to
this volume, § 14), but concur in the main with Morris's indication of Rowley's

Place of the Play in the History of Comedy.—*The Spanish Gipsie* lacks the fulness and freedom of the genuine Elizabethan drama and the exquisite workmanship of the comedy of manners. It is not yet immoral but its reckless indifference to the moral situation gives a foretaste of the plays and manners of the Restoration. The unreality of all but its most repulsive scene marks a step in the degeneracy or rather transformation of the drama. Nevertheless, in spite of obvious imperfections, it challenges admiration even among a race of giants. Its characters and incidents alike are the work of a greater than Middleton or Rowley. It belongs to Cervantes as much as *The Vicar of Wakefield* dramatized belongs to Goldsmith, and the freshness and distinction that mark all his handiwork come out unspoiled from the not too gentle hands of the English playwrights. Finding, as it were by chance, a perfect creation in a foreign land, and struck by its noble mould, they brought it home, animated it with somewhat of "the superb exuberance and abounding and exulting strength" (Swinburne) of the Elizabethan stage, taught it to perfection their native tongue and set it upon the stage amid the press of hurrying action. The result is a work by the greatest genius of one of the world's greatest literatures adapted, somewhat hurriedly, by first-rate craftsmen of another,—a rare combination and sufficient to explain the attraction exercised by *The Spanish Gipsie* on many great minds. Of its effect upon contemporaries we have no record, it was not printed for thirty years after its production, it was probably soon forgotten. It appeals to critics rather than to playgoers, it has no ancestry, and remained for long without descendants in England. The peculiarity that marks it among the plays of its time is its romanticism, and the romantic age was still to come. Its importance can be appreciated in the light of later development, but there is nothing to connect it causally with those developments.

Stage History. Previous Editions and the Present Text.—*The Spanish Gipsie* as appears from the office-book of Sir Henry

presence,—"By Middleton, with only here and there a slight touch by Rowley: Act I, iii, v, 1–73; II, i, 1–129, 250–293, ii, 1–119; III, i, 1–30, 114–145, ii, iii; IV, i, ii, iii, 188–238; V, i, ii, iii. Revised by Rowley, though showing here and there the original lines of Middleton: I, i, ii, iv, v, 73–123; II, i, 130–250, ii, 120–183; III, i, 31–113; IV, iii, 1–187." Lines as in Morris's edition.—*Gen. Ed.*

Herbert, then master of the revels, was played for the first time at
the Phœnix by Lady Elizabeth's servants July 9, 1623. The title-
page of the first edition states that it "was acted with great applause at the Privat House in Drury Lane and Salisbury Court."
It was revived in London after a lapse of more than two centuries and a half by the Elizabethan Stage Society (April, 1898)
with carefully studied accessories, special music and conscientious,
if not brilliant, acting. But the play was roughly handled by the
newspaper critics, one of whom styles it "a strange mixture of
romance and sheer tom-foolery, with a very elaborate and confused underplot" and declares that "except for one or two scenes
of violent melodrama, the piece has scarcely any merit."

Both the first (1653), and the second (1661), quartos of *The
Spanish Gipsie* are very carelessly printed: speeches are obviously
wrongly distributed, verses are wrongly divided, some lines make
nonsense, and the stage directions are defective. These editions
were seemingly printed from a rough acting copy. The extent
to which the text has suffered in transcription may perhaps be
judged from the incorrect forms of well-known Spanish names,
Azevida (Azevedo), Hortado de Mendonza (Hurtado de Men-
doza), Portocareco (Portocarrero). Some true readings were restored and small lacunæ filled up by Dyce from a copy of the first
edition containing manuscript emendations (Dy. MS.), derived
apparently from a better MS. than that used by the printers.
Rearranged by the skilful hands of Messrs. Dyce (Dy.) and
Bullen (B.) the text now leaves little to be desired. The title-page
of the first quarto (Q 1) runs: *The Spanish Gipsie. As it was Acted
(with great Applause) at the Privat House in Drury Lane, and Salisbury Court. Written by Thomas Middleton and William Rowley
[bracketed] Gent. Never printed before. London. Printed by I. G.
for Richard Marriot in St. Dunstan's Church-yard, Fleetstreet, 1653.*
The title-page of the second quarto (Q 2) is as prefixed to the present edition of the play. Since neither of the authors was alive in
1653, it seems unnecessary to perpetuate the imperfections of the
quartos. The present text is based upon a collation of both quartos
with the editions of Dyce and Bullen. The division into scenes
and the stage-directions (in square brackets) indicate in general

the emendations of Bullen as followed by The Mermaid. The first modern edition (Ed. 1815) appears in *Old English Plays*, published by John Martin, 1815. This is reprinted in *A Continuation of Dodsley's Old Plays*, 1816. Dyce's edition is dated 1840; Bullen's, 1885—in their respective collections of Middleton's works. The play is also edited by Ellis in his *Best Plays of Thomas Middleton* (Mermaid Series), 1887.[1] H. BUTLER CLARKE.

[1] *The Spanish Gipsie* has recently been reproduced from the quarto of 1661 with Introduction and Notes by Professor E. C. Morris (The Belles Lettres Series, Boston, 1908). For an exhaustive list of variants the scholar may be referred to this excellent edition. By its notes I have checked Butler Clarke's indications of readings.—*Gen. Ed.*

THE
SPANISH
GIPSIE.

As it was Acted (with great Applaufe)
at the Private Houfe in

DRVRY LANE,
AND
SALISBVRY COVRT.

Written by ⎧ *THOMAS MIDLETON,* ⎫ Gent.
         ⎨ AND ⎬
         ⎩ *WILLIAM ROWLEY.* ⎭

The Second Imprefsion.

LONDON,
Printed by *T.C.* and *L.P.* for *Robert Crofts*, at the Sign of the
Crown in *Chancery-lane*, under *Serjeants Inne,*
1 6 6 1.

The Persons of the Play [1]

FERNANDO DE AZEVIDA, *corigidor* [2] *of Madrill*. [3]

PEDRO DE CORTES,
FRANCISCO DE CARCOMO, } *two old Dons*.

RODERIGO, *son to Fernando*.

LOUIS DE CASTRO, *son to* DE CASTRO *slain by* ALVAREZ.

DIEGO, *Friend to* DON LOUIS.

DON JOHN, *son to* FRANCISCO DE CARCOMO, *and a lover of* CONSTANZA.

SANCHO, *a foolish gentleman and ward to* PEDRO.

SOTO, *a merry fellow, his man*.

ALVAREZ DE CASTILLA, *an old lord disguised like the father of the gipsies*.

CARLO,
ANTONIO, } *two gentlemen disguised like gipsies*.

    [Others *in like disguise*.

Servants.]

MARIA, *wife to* DON PEDRO.

CLARA, *their daughter*.

GUIAMARA, *wife to* COUNT ALVAREZ *and sister to* FERNANDO, *disguised like the mother of the gipsies, and called by the name of* EUGENIA.

CONSTANZA, *daughter to* FERNANDO, *disguised like a young Spanish gipsy, and called by the name of* PRETIOSA.

CHRISTIANA, *a gentlewoman disguised like a gipsy*.

CARDOCHIA, *a young hostess to the gipsies*.

    [*THE SCENE:* MADRID and its neighbourhood.] [4]

---

[1] Based upon the 'Drammatis Personæ' of the Qtos.
[2] Span. *corregidor*, chief magistrate.
[3] Madrid. The d in Spanish is faint (adj. Madrileño).
[4] Q I, 'The Scene Allegant' [Alicante].

The Spanish Gipsy

Act I. [Scene I. *The Neighbourhood of Madrid.*]

Enter RODERIGO, LOUIS, *and* DIEGO.

Louis. Roderigo!

Diego. Art mad?

Rod. Yes, not so much with wine: it's as rare to see a Spaniard a drunkard as a German sober, an Italian no whoremonger, an Englishman to pay his debts. I am no borachio; [1] sack, maligo,[2] nor canary breeds the calenture[3] in my brains; mine eye mads me, not my cups.

Louis. What wouldst have us do?

Rod. Do?

Diego. So far as 'tis fit for gentlemen[4] we'll venture. 10

Rod. I ask no more. I ha' seen a thing has bewitched me; a delicate body, but this in the waist [*showing the size by a sign*]; foot and leg tempting; the face I had [only] a glimpse of, but the fruit must needs be delicious, the tree being so beautiful.

Louis. Prithee, to the point. 15

Rod. Here 'tis: an old gentleman—no matter who he is—an old gentlewoman—I ha' nothing to do with her—but a young creature that follows them, daughter or servant, or whatsoever she be, her I must have: they are coming this way: shall I have her? I must have her. 20

Diego. How, how?

Louis. Thou speakest impossibilities.

Rod. Easy, easy, easy! I'll seize the young girl; stop you the old man; stay you the old woman.

---

[1] Span. *borracho*, a drunkard. [2] Malaga wine.
[3] Span. *calentura*, fever. [4] Q 1, 'a gentlemen.'

Louis. How then?   25
Rod. I'll fly off with the young bird, that's all; many of our
Spanish gallants act these merry parts every night. They are
weak and old, we young and sprightly: will you assist me?
Louis. Troth, Roderigo, anything in the way of honour.
Rod. For a wench, man, any course is honourable.   30
Louis. Nay, not any; her father, if he be[1] her father, may be
noble.
Rod. I am as noble.
Louis. Would the adventure were so!
Rod. Stand close, they come.   35

Enter PEDRO, MARIA, *and* CLARA.

Ped. 'Tis late; would we were in Madrill![2]
Mar. Go faster, my lord.
Ped. Clara, keep close.
[LOUIS *and* DIEGO *hold* PEDRO *and* MARIA; RODERIGO *seizes* CLARA.]
Cla. Help, help, help!
Rod. Are you crying out? I'll be your midwife.   40
                                        Exit with CLARA.

Ped. What mean you, gentlemen?
Mar. Villains! thieves! murderers!
Ped. Do you [not] know me? I am De Cortes, Pedro de Cortes.
Louis. De Cortes?—Diego, come away.   45
                                        Exit [*with* DIEGO].

Ped. Clara!—where is my daughter?
Mar. Clara!—these villains
Have robbed us of our comfort, and will, I fear,
Her of her honour.
Ped.[3] This had not wont to be   50
Our Spanish fashion; but now our gallants,
Our gentry, our young dons, heated with wine,—
A fire our countrymen do seldom sit at,—

---

[1] Supplied by Q 2.   [2] See Persons of the Play, *n.* 3.
[3] Q 1, Her of her honour. This had not wont
          To be our Spanish fashion.
Ped. But now our gallants, etc.

Commit these outrages.—Clara!—Maria,
Let's homeward; I will raise Madrill to find   55
These traitors to all goodness.—Clara!
   Mar. Clara!   *Exeunt.*

[Act I. Scene II. *Another Place in the Neighbourhood*
of Madrid.]

        Enter Louis *and* Diego.

  Louis. O Diego, I am lost, I am mad!
  Diego. So we are all.
  Louis. 'Tis not with wine; I'm drunk with too much horror,
Inflamed with rage, to see us two made bawds
To Roderigo's lust: did not the old man   5
Name De Cortes, Pedro de Cortes?
  Diego. Sure he did.
  Louis. O Diego, as thou lov'st me, nay, on the forfeit
Of thine own life or mine, seal up thy lips,
Let 'em not name De Cortes! stay, stay, stay!   10
Roderigo has into his father's house
A passage through a garden——
  Diego. Yes, my lord.
  Louis. Thither I must, find Roderigo out,
And check him, check him home: if he but dare—   15
No more!—Diego, along! my soul does fight
A thousand battles blacker than this night.   *Exeunt.*[1]

[Act I. Scene III. *A Bed-chamber in Fernando's House.*
Roderigo *and* Clara *discovered.*][2]

  Cla. Though the black veil of night hath overclouded
The world in darkness, yet ere many hours

---

[1] I print for the *Exit* of the Qtos., *Exeunt* where proper; and *vice versa*.
[2] Qtos., *Enter Roderigo and Clara.*

The sun will rise again, and then this act
Of my dishonour will appear before you
More black than is the canopy that shrouds it:　　　　5
What are you, pray? what are you?
　　Rod. Husht—a friend, a friend.
　　Cla. A friend? be then a gentle ravisher,
An honourable villain: as you have
Disrobed my youth of nature's goodliest portion,　　　10
My virgin purity, so with your sword
Let out that blood which is infected now
By your soul-staining lust.
　　Rod. Pish!
　　Cla. Are. you noble?　　　　　　　　　　15
I know you then will marry me; say!
　　Rod. Umh.
　　Cla. Not speak to me? are wanton devils dumb?
How are so many harmless virgins wrought
By falsehood of prevailing words to yield　　　　20
Too easy forfeits of their shames and liberty,
If every orator of folly plead
In silence, like this untongued piece of violence?
You shall not from me.
　　　　　　　　　　　　　　　　[Holding him.]
　　Rod. Phew!—no more.　　　　　　　25
　　Cla. You shall not:
Who'er you are, disease of nature's sloth,
Birth of some monstrous sin, or scourge of virtue,
Heaven's wrath and mankind's burden, I will hold you;
I will: be rough, and therein merciful,　　　　30
I will not loose my hold else.
　　Rod. There; 'tis gold.　　　　*[Offers money.]*
　　Cla. Gold? why, alas! for what? the hire of pleasure
Perhaps is payment, mine is misery;
I need no wages for a ruined name,　　　　35
More than a bleeding heart.
　　Rod. Nay, then, you're troublesome;
I'll lock you safe enough.　　　*[Shakes her off, and] exit.*

Cla. They cannot fear
Whom grief hath armed with hate and scorn of life.
Revenge, I kneel to thee! alas! 'gainst whom?   40
By what name shall I pull confusion down
From justice on his head that hath betrayed me?
I know not where I am: up, I beseech thee,
Thou lady regent of the air, the moon,
And lead me by thy light to some brave vengeance!   45
It is a chamber sure; the guilty bed,
Sad evidence against my loss of honour,
Assures so much. What's here, a window-curtain?
O Heaven, the stars appear too: ha, a chamber,   50
A goodly one? dwells rape in such a paradise?
Help me, my quickened senses! 'tis a garden
To which this window guides the covetous prospect,
A large one and a fair one; in the midst
A curious alabaster fountain stands,   55
Framed like—like what? no matter—swift, remembrance!
Rich furniture within too? and what's this?
A precious crucifix! I have enough.
                    [*Takes the crucifix, and conceals it in her bosom.*]
Assist me, O you powers that guard the innocent!

                    [*Re-*]*enter* Roderigo.

Rod. Now.   60
Cla. Welcome, if you come armèd in destruction:
I am prepared to die.
Rod. Tell me your name,
And what you are.
Cla. You urge me to a sin   65
As cruel as your lust; I dare not grant it.
Think on the violence of my defame;
And if you mean to write upon my grave
An epitaph of peace, forbear to question
Or whence or who I am. I know the heat   70
Of your desires, are [1] after the performance

---

[1] Examples of a nominative singular followed by a plural verb when a plural
genitive intervenes are common in our early writers (Dyce).

Of such a hellish act, by this time drowned
In cooler streams of penance; and for my part,
I have washed off the leprosy that cleaves
To my just shame in true and honest tears; 75
I must not leave a mention of my wrongs,
The stain of my unspotted birth, to memory;
Let it lie buried with me in the dust;
That never time hereafter may report
How such a one as you have made me live. 80
Be resolute, and do not stagger; do not,
For I am nothing.
   Rod. Sweet, let me enjoy thee
Now with a free allowance.
   Cla. Ha, enjoy me? 85
Insufferable villain!
   Rod. Peace, speak low;
I mean no second force; and since I find
Such goodness in an unknown frame of virtue,
Forgive my foul attempt, which I shall grieve for 90
So heartily, that could you be yourself
Eye-witness to my constant vowed repentance,
Trust me, you'd pity me.
   Cla. Sir, you can speak now.
   Rod. So much I am the executioner 95
Of mine own trespass, that I have no heart
Nor reason to disclose my name or quality;
You must excuse me that; but, trust me, fair one,
Were this ill deed undone, this deed of wickedness,
I would be proud to court your love like him 100
Whom my first birth presented to the world.
This for your satisfaction: what remains,
That you can challenge as a service from me,
I both expect and beg it.
   Cla. First, that you swear, 105
Neither in riot of your mirth, in passion
Of friendship, or in folly of discourse,
To speak of wrongs done to a ravished maid.

Rod. As I love truth, I swear!
Cla. Next, that you lead me   110
Near to the place you met me, and there leave me
To my last fortunes, ere the morning rise.
Rod. Say more.
Cla. Live[1] a new man: if e'er you marry—
O me, my heart's a-breaking—but if e'er   115
You marry, in a constant love to her
That shall be then your wife, redeem the fault
Of my undoing. I am lost for ever:
Pray, use no more words.
Rod. You must give me leave   120
To veil you close.
Cla. Do what you will; no time
Can ransom me from sorrows or dishonours.

                  [RODERIGO *throws a veil over her.*]
Shall we now go?
Rod. My shame may live without me,   125
But in my soul I bear my guilt about me.
Lend me your hand; now follow.   *Exeunt.*

[Act I. Scene IV. *Before Fernando's House.*]

Enter LOUIS, DIEGO, *and a* Servant.

Louis. Not yet come in, not yet?
Ser. No, I'll assure your lordship; I've seldom known him
Keep out so long; my lord usually observes
More seasonable hours.
Louis. What time of night is't?   5
Ser. On the stroke of three.
Louis. The stroke of three? 'tis wondrous strange!
Dost hear?——
Ser. My lord?
Louis. Ere six I will be here again;   10

---

[1] Qtos., 'Lay.' The emendation is from Dy. MS.

Tell thy lord so; ere six; 'a must not sleep;
Of if 'a do, I shall be bold to wake him;
Be sure thou tell'st him, do.

    Ser. My lord, I shall.   *Exit* [*into the house*].

    Louis. Diego,   15

Walk thou the street that leads about the Prado;
I'll round the west part of the city: meet me
At the Inquisition-chapel;[1] if we miss him,
We'll both back to his lodgings.   20

    Diego. At the chapel?

    Louis. Ay, there we'll meet.

    Diego. Agreed, I this way.

                  Exit LOUIS: [*as* DIEGO *is going out,*]

                  Enter DON JOHN *reading.*

    John. She is not noble, true; wise nature meant
Affection should ennoble[2] her descent,   25
For love and beauty keeps as rich a seat
Of sweetness in the mean-born as the great.
I am resolved.   *Exit.*

    Diego. 'Tis Roderigo certainly,
Yet his voice makes me doubt; but I'll o'erhear him.   *Exit.* 30

[Act I. Scene V. *A Street.*]

                  Enter LOUIS.

    Louis. That I,[3] I, only I should be the man
Made accessary and a party both
To mine own torment, at a time so near
The birth of all those comforts I have travailed with
So many, many hours of hopes and fears;   5
Now at the instant—

    [1] The topography is vague but not incorrect. The Prado bounded Madrid on E. The Inquisition was situated about the centre of the city in what is now the Calle de Isabel la Católica.

    [2] So Dy. MS; Qtos., 'enable.'

    [3] Qtos. 'That if only I.'—B. as above.

Enter RODERIGO.

                        Ha! stand! thy name,
Truly and speedily.
    Rod. Don Louis?
    Louis. The same;   10
But who art thou? speak!
    Rod. Roderigo.
    Louis. Tell me,
As you're a noble gentleman, as ever
You hope to be enrolled amongst the virtuous,   15
As you love goodness, as you wish t' inherit
The blessedness and fellowship of angels,
As you're my friend, as you are Roderigo,
As you are anything that would deserve
A worthy name, where have you been to-night?   20
O, how have you disposed of that fair creature
Whom you led captive from me? speak, O speak!
Where, how, when, in what usage have you left her?
Truth, I require all truth.
    Rod. Though I might question   25
The strangeness of your importunity,
Yet, 'cause I note distraction in the height
Of curiosity, I will be plain and brief.
    Louis. I thank you, sir.
    Rod. Instead of feeding   30
Too wantonly upon so rich a banquet,
I found, even in that beauty that invited me,
Such a commanding majesty of chaste
And humbly glorious virtue, that it did not
More check my rash attempt than draw to ebb   35
The float of those desires, which in an instant
Were cooled in their own streams of shame and folly.
    Louis. Now all increase of honours
Fall in full showers on thee, Roderigo,
The best man living!   40
    Rod. You are much transported

With this discourse, methinks.
   Louis. Yes, I am.
She told ye her name too?
   Rod. I could not urge it   45
By any importunity.
   Louis. Better still!
Where did you leave her?
   Rod. Where I found her; farther
She would by no means grant me to wait on her: 50
O, Louis, I am lost!
   Louis. This self-same lady
Was she to whom I have been long a suitor,
And shortly hope to marry.
   Rod. She your mistress, then?   Louis, since friendship   55
And noble honesty conjures our loves
To a continued league, here I unclasp
The secrets of my heart. O, I have had
A glimpse of such a creature, that deserves
A temple! If thou lov'st her—and I blame thee not,   60
For who can look on her, and not give up
His life unto her service?—if thou lov'st her,
For pity's sake conceal her; let me not
As much as know her name, there's a temption in't
Let me not know her dwelling, birth, or quality,   65
Or anything that she calls hers, but thee;
In thee, my friend, I'll see her: and t' avoid
The surfeits and those rarities that tempt me,
So much I prize the happiness of friendship,
That I will leave the city——   70
   Louis. Leave it?
   Rod. Speed me
For Salamanca; court my studies now
For physic 'gainst infection of the mind.
   Louis. You do amaze me.   75
   Rod. Here to live, and live
Without her, is impossible and wretched.
For Heaven's sake, never tell her what I was,

Or that you know me! and when I find that absence
Hath lost her to my memory, I'll dare   80
To see ye again.   Meantime, the cause that draws me
From hence shall be to all the world untold;
No friend but thou alone, for whose sake only
I undertake this voluntary exile,
Shall be partaker of my griefs: thy hand,   85
Farewell; and all the pleasures, joys, contents,
That bless a constant lover, henceforth crown thee
A happy bridegroom!
   Louis. You have conquered friendship
Beyond example.   90

Enter DIEGO.

   Diego. Ha, ha, ha! some one
That hath slept well to-night, should 'a but see me
Thus merry by myself, might justly think
I were not well in my wits.
   Louis. Diego?   95
   Diego. Yes, 'tis I, and I have had a fine fegary,[1]
The rarest wild-goose chase!
   Louis. 'T had made thee melancholy.
   Diego. Don Roderigo here? 'tis well you met him;
For though I missed him, yet I met an accident   100
Has almost made me burst with laughter.
   Louis. How so?
   Diego. I'll tell you: as we parted, I perceived
A walking thing before me, strangely tickled
With rare conceited raptures; him I dogged   105
Supposing 't had been Roderigo landed
From his new pinnace, deep in contemplation
Of the sweet voyage he stole to-night.
   Rod. You're pleasant.
   Louis. Prithee, who was't?   110
   Rod. Not I.
   Diego. You're i' the right, not you indeed;

---

[1] vagary.

For 'twas that noble gentleman Don John,
Son to the Count Francisco de Carcomo.
    Louis. In love, it seems?   115
    Diego. Yes, peppered, on my life;
Much good may't do him; I'd not be so lined[1]
For my cap full of double pistolets.
    Louis. What should his mistress be?
    Diego. That's yet a riddle   120
Beyond my resolution; but of late
I have observed him oft to frequent the sports
The gipsies newly come to th' city present.
    Louis. 'Tis said there is a creature with 'em,
Though young of years, yet of such absolute beauty,   125
Dexterity of wit, and general qualities,
That Spain reports her not without admiration.
    Diego. Have you seen her?
    Louis. Never.
    Diego. Nor you, my lord?   130
    Rod. I not remember.
    Diego. Why, then, you never saw the prettiest toy
That ever sang or danced.
    Louis. Is she a gipsy?
    Diego. In her condition, not in her complexion: 135
I tell you once more, 'tis a spark of beauty
Able to set a world at gaze; the sweetest,
The wittiest rogue! shall's see 'em? they've fine gambols,
Are mightily frequented; court and city
Flock to 'em, but the country does 'em worship: 140
This little ape gets money by the sack-full,
It trowles upon her.
    Louis. Will ye with us, friend?
    Rod. You know my other projects; sights to me
Are but vexations.   145
    Louis. O, you must be merry!—
Diego, we'll to th' gipsies.
    Diego. Best take heed

        [1] Qtos., 'lin'd': Qy. lim'd? Dy.

You be not snapped.
   Louis. How snapped?   150
   Diego. By that little fair[y];
'T has a shrewd tempting face and a notable tongue.
   Louis. I fear not either.
   Diego. Go, then.
   Louis. Will you with us?   155
   Rod. I'll come after.—   *[Exeunt* LOUIS *and* DIEGO.]
Pleasure and youth like smiling evils woo us
To taste new follies; tasted, they undo us.   *Exit.*

Act II. [Scene I. *A Room in an Inn.*]

Enter ALVAREZ, CARLO, *and* ANTONIO [*disguised as gipsies*].

   Alv. Come, my brave boys! the tailor's shears has cut us into
shapes fitting our trades.
   Car. A trade free as a mason's.
   Ant. A trade brave as a courtier's; for some of them do but
shark, and so do we.   5
   Alv. Gipsies, but no tanned ones; no red-ochre rascals umbered
with soot and bacon as the English gipsies are, that sally out upon
pullen, lie in ambuscado for a rope of onions, as if they were
Welsh freebooters; no, our stile has higher steps to climb over,
Spanish gipsies, noble gipsies.   10
   Car. I never knew nobility in baseness.
   Alv. Baseness? the arts of Cocoquismo and Germania,[1] used
by our Spanish pickeroes[2]—I mean filching, foisting,[3] nimming,
jilting[4]—we defy; none in our college shall study 'em! such gradu-
ates we degrade.   15

---

[1] *Germania* (Span.), thieves' Latin or jargon spoken by the *pickeroes* (Span.
picaros). *Cocoquismo* is obscure; it is perhaps connected with *cachuchero*, a thief
who steals gold. (Hidalgo, *Vocabulario de Germania, apud Mayans i Siscar. Origines
de la Lengua Española.* Madrid 1737.) The two words are found in conjunction
(*todo el Cocoquismo y Jermania*) in the famous rogue story *Guzman de Alfarache*
(Pt. II. Bk. ii. cap. 5), englished by James Mabbe, 1623.

[2] rogues, see note 1.

[3] He that picks the pocket is called a Foist: Dekker, *Belman of London* (Bullen).

[4] *Nimming, jilting;* obscure expressions from jargon of English thieves.

Ant. I am glad Spain has an honest company.

Alv. We'll entertain no mountebanking stroll,
No piper, fiddler, tumbler through small hoops,
No ape-carrier, baboon-bearer;
We must have nothing stale, trivial, or base:　　　　　　　20
Am I your major-domo, your teniente,[1]
Your captain, your commander?

Ant. Who but you?

Alv. So then: now being entered Madrill, the enchanted circle
of Spain, have a care to your new lessons.　　　　　　　25

Both. We listen.

Alv. Plough deep furrows, to catch deep root in th' opinion of
the best grandos,[2] dukes, marquesses, condes,[3] and other titulados;[4]
show your sports to none but them: what can you do with three
or four fools in a dish, and a blockhead cut into sippets?　　　30

Ant. Scurvy meat!

Alv. The Lacedemonians threw their beards over their shoulders,
to observe what men did behind them as well as before; you must
do['t].

Both. We shall never do't. Our muzzles are too short.　　　35

Alv. Be not English gipsies, in whose company a man's not sure
of the ears of his head, they so pilfer! no such angling; what you
pull to land catch fair: there is no iron so foul but may be gilded;
and our gipsy profession, how base soever in show, may acquire
commendations.　　　　　　　40

Car. Gipsies, and yet pick no pockets?

Alv. Infamous and roguy! so handle your webs, that they
never come to be woven in the loom of justice: take anything that's
given you, purses, knives, handkerchers, rosaries, tweezes, any toy,
any money! refuse not a maruadi, a blank:[5] feather by feather
birds build nests, grain pecked up after grain makes pullen fat.　46

Ant. The best is, we Spaniards are no great feeders.

Alv. If one city cannot maintain us, away to another! our

---

[1] lieutenant (Span.)　　　　　[2] A common form of 'grandees' (Span. *grandes*).
[3] *conde*. (Span.) a count.　　　[4] *titulado* (Span.) titled person.
[5] blank (Span. *blanca*), the smallest Spanish coin; two blanks = one maruadi.
The maruadi (Span. *maravedi*) was not a coin.

horses must have wings. Does Madrill yield no money? Sivell
shall; is Sivell closefisted? Vallidoly is open; so Cordica,[1] so Toledo.
Do not our Spanish wines please us? Italian can then, French can.
Preferment's bow is hard to draw, set all your strengths to it;
what you get, keep; all the world is a second Rochill;[2] make all
sure, for you must not look to have your dinner served in with
trumpets.   55

Car. No, no, sack-buts shall serve us.

Alv. When you have money, hide it; sell all our horses but one.

Ant. Why one?

Alv. 'Tis enough to carry our apparel and trinkets, and the less
our ambler eats, our cheer is the better. None be sluttish, none
thievish, none lazy; all bees, no drones, and our hives shall yield
us honey.   62

Enter GUIAMARA,[3] CONSTANZA,[4] CHRISTIANA, [*disguised as gipsies,
and*] CARDOCHIA.

Const. See, father, how I'm fitted; how do you like
This our new stock of clothes?

Alv. My sweet girl, excellent.—   65
See their old robes be safe.

Card. That, sir, I'll look to:
Whilst in my house you lie, what thief soever
Lays hands upon your goods, call but to me,
I'll make the[e] satisfaction.   70

Alv. Thanks, good hostess!

Card. People already throng into the inn,
And call for you into their private rooms.

Alv. No chamber-comedies: hostess, ply you your tide; flow
let 'em to a full sea, but we'll show no pastime till after dinner,
and that in a full ring of good people, the best, the noblest; no
closet-sweetmeats, pray tell 'em so.   77

Card. I shall.   *Exit.*

Alv. How old is Pretiosa?

---

[1] Qy. Côrdova?

[2] 'Rochelle was a general asylum for those persecuted Protestants who knew
not where to go.'—Ed. 1815.

[3] Qtos., always 'Eugenia.'   [4] Qtos., always 'Pretiosa.'

Gui. Twelve and upwards.   80

Const. I am in my teens, assure you, mother; as little as I am,
I have been taken for an elephant;[1] castles and lordships offered
to be set upon me, if I would bear 'em: why, your smallest clocks
are the prettiest things to carry about gentlemen.

Gui. Nay, child, thou wilt be tempted.   85

Const. Tempted? though I am no mark in respect of a huge butt,
yet I can tell you great bubbers[2] have shot at me, and shot golden
arrows, but I myself gave[3] aim, thus,—wide, four bows; short,
three and a half: they that crack me shall find me as hard as a nut
of Galisia; a parrot I am, but my teeth too tender to crack a
wanton's almond.   91

Alv. Thou art my noble girl: a many dons
Will not believe but that thou art a boy
In woman's[4] clothes; and to try that conclusion
To see if thou be'st alcumy or no,   95
They'll throw down gold in musses;[5] but, Pretiosa,
Let these proud sakers[6] and gerfalcons fly,
Do not thou move a wing; be thou[7] thyself
And not a changeling.[8]

Const. How? not a changeling;   100
Yes, father, I will play the changeling;
I'll change myself into a thousand shapes,
To court our brave spectators; I'll change my postures
Into a thousand different variations,
To draw even ladies' eyes to follow mine;   105
I'll change my voice into a thousand tones,
To chain attention: not a changeling, father?

---

[1] Morris, *Span. Gip.* 132 quotes from a letter of July 12, 1623, in *Court and Times of James I*, Vol. II, 410: 'The king of Spain hath sent hither five camels and an elephant, which going through the town this day seven night, past midnight, could not yet pass unseen;' and refers to a letter of Apr. 25, 1623, dated Madrid, from Buckingham to James, in which the same gift is mentioned. Cf. II, ii, 197; IV, i, 99.—*Gen. Ed.*

[2] drinkers.   [3] Q 2, 'give.'

[4] Q 1, 'womens'; Q 2, 'womans.'   [5] To be scrambled for.

[6] A kind of hawk. The word is Arabic derived through the Spanish, *sacre.*

[7] So Morris; Qtos. 'to.'—*Gen. Ed.*

[8] So Qtos.—Dy. Ms., repeats 'Thyself' before 'and'; unnecessarily.

None but myself shall play the changeling.[1]
Alv. Do what thou wilt, Pretiosa.   *A beating within.*
                              What noise is this?   110

                    [Re-]enter CARDOCHIA.

Card. Here's gentlemen swear all the oaths in Spain they have
seen you, must see you, and will see you.
Alv. To drown this noise let 'em enter.   [*Exit* CARD.]

                Enter SANCHO *and* SOTO.

San. Is your playhouse an inn, a gentleman cannot see you
without crumpling this taffaty cloak?   115
Soto. Nay, more than a gentleman, his man being a diminutive
don too.
San. Is this the little ape does the fine tricks?
Const. Come aloft, Jack little ape!
San. Would my jack might come aloft! please you to set the
watermill with the ivory cogs in't a-grinding my handful of purg-
ing comfits.   [*Offers comfits.*] 122
Soto. My master desires to have you loose from your company.
Const. Am I pigeon, think you, to be caught with cummin-
seeds? a fly to glue my wings to sweetmeats, and so be ta'en?
San. When do your gambols begin?
Alv. Not till we ha' dined.
San. 'Foot, then your bellies will be so full, you'll be able to
do nothing.—Soto, prithee, set a good face on't, for I cannot, and
give the little monkey that letter.   130
Soto. Walk off and hum to yourself.   [SANCHO *retires.*]
—I dedicate, sweet Destiny, into whose hand every Spaniard
desires to put a distaff, these lines of love.
                    [*Offering a paper to* CONSTANZA.]
Gui. What love? what's the matter?
Soto. Grave Mother Bumby,[2] the mark's out a' your mouth. 135
Alv. What's the paper? from whom comes it?

---

[1] From this we may infer that *The Changeling* had already been performed. See
Essay introductory to this volume, sec. 14.— *Gen. Ed.*
[2] A famous fortune-teller; she figures in one of Lyly's plays (Bullen).

Soto. The commodity wrapped up in the paper are verses; the warming-pan that puts heat into 'em, yon[1] fire-brained bastard of Helicon.

San. Hum, hum.[2]   140

Alv. What's your master's name?

Soto. His name is Don Tomazo Portacareco, nuncle to young Don Hortado de Mendonza, cousin-german to the Conde de Tindilla, and natural brother to Francisco de Bavadilla, one of the commendadors of Alcantaro, a gentleman of long standing.

Alv. And of as long a style.[3]   146

Const. Verses? I love good ones; let me see 'em.

                                                    [*Taking paper.*]

San. [*advancing*]. Good ones? if they were not good ones, they should not come from me; at the name of verses I can stand on no ground.   150

Const. Here's gold too! whose is this?

San. Whose but yours? If there be[4] any fault in the verses, I can mend it extempore; for a stitch in a man's stocking not taken up in time, ravels out all the rest.

Soto. Botcherly poetry, botcherly!   [*Aside.*] 155

Const. Verses and gold! these then are golden verses.

San. Had every verse a pearl in the eye, it should be thine.

Const. A pearl in mine eye![5] I thank you for that; do you wish me blind?

San. Ay, by this light do I, that you may look upon nobody's rhymes[6] but mine.   161

Const. I should be blind indeed then.[7]

Alv. Pray, sir, read your verses.

San. Shall I sing 'em or say 'em?

Alv. Which you can best.   165

Soto. Both scurvily.   [*Aside.*]

San. I'll set out a throat then.

---

[1] Qtos., 'you.'   [2] Restored from Dy. Ms. 'Hum, hum.'
[3] '*Alv.* . . . style.' Restored from Dy. Ms.
[4] Qtos., 'been.'   [5] Pearl in the eye: a disease.
[6] So Dy. Ms. for Qtos, 'crime.' [I prefer the latter. *Gen. Ed.*]
[7] So Dy. Ms.—Qtos, omit 'then.'

Soto. Do, master, and I'll run division behind your back.[1]
San. [*sings*]. O that I were a bee to sing
    Hum, buz, buz, hum! I first would bring 170
    Home honey to your hive, and there leave my sting.
Soto. [*sings*]. He maunders.
San. [*sings*]. O that I were a goose, to feed
    At your barn door! such corn I need,
    Nor would I bite, but goslings breed. 175
Soto. [*sings*]. And ganders.
San. [*sings*]. O that I were your needle's eye!
    How through your linen would I fly,
    And never leave one stitch awry!
Soto. [*sings*]. He'll touse ye. 180
San. [*sings*]. O would I were one of your hairs,
    That you might comb out all my cares,
    And kill the nits of my despairs!
Soto. [*sings*]. O lousy!
San. How? lousy? can rhymes be lousy? 185
Const.[2] No, no, they're excellent.
Alv. But are these all your own?
San. Mine own? would I might never see ink drop out of the
nose of any goose-quill more, if velvet cloaks have not clapped
me for 'em! Do you like 'em? 190
Const. Past all compare.
They shall be writ out: when you've as good or better,
For these and those, pray, book me down you debtor:
Your paper is long-lived, having two souls,
Verses and gold. 195
    San. Would both those were in thy[3] pretty little body, sweet
gipsy!
    Const. A pistolet and this paper? 'twould choke me.
    Soto. No more than a bribe does a constable: the verses will
easily into your head, then buy what you like with the gold, and
put it into your belly. I hope I ha' chawed a good reason for you.

---

[1] Soto's speech restored from Dy. Ms. Cf. *Match at Midnight* (act ii.) 'Here's one runs division before the fiddlers.'
[2] Qtos., *Omnes.*
[3] Qtos., 'thee.'

San. Will you chaw my jennet ready, sir?   202
Soto. And eat him down, if you say the word.   *Exit.*
San. Now the coxcomb my man is gone, because you're but a
country company of strolls, I think your stock is threadbare;
here, mend it with this cloak.   [*Giving his cloak.*] 206
    Alv. What do you mean, sir?
San. This scarf, this feather, and this hat.
                              [*Giving his scarf, &c.*]

Omnes. Dear signior!——
San. If they be never so dear:—pox o' this hot ruff! little gipsy,
wear thou that.   [*Giving his ruff.*] 211
    Alv. Your meaning, sir?
San. My meaning is, not to be an ass, to carry a burden when
I need not. If you show your gambols forty leagues hence, I'll
gallop to 'em.—Farewell, old greybeard;— adieu, mother mumble-
crust;—morrow,[1] my little wart of beauty.   *Exit.* 216

    Enter [behind] Don John, *muffled.*

    Alv. So, harvest will come in; such sunshine days
Will bring in golden sheaves, our markets raise:
Away to your task.

*Exeunt [*Alvarez, Christiana, Carlo, *and* Antonio; *and as*
    Guiamara *and* Constanza *are going out,*] Don John *pulls* [*the
    latter called*] Pretiosa *back.*

    Const. Mother! grandmother!   220
John. Two rows of kindred in one mouth?
Gui. Be not uncivil, sir; thus have you used her thrice.
John. Thrice? three thousand more: may I not use mine own?
Const. Your own! by what tenure?
John. Cupid entails this land upon me; I have wooed thee,
thou art coy: by this air, I am a bull of Tarifa, wild, mad for thee!
you told[2] I was some copper coin; I am a knight of Spain; Don
Francisco de Carcomo my father, I Don John his son; this paper
tells you more. [*Gives paper.*]—Grumble not, old granam; here's

----

[1] B. 'to-morrow.' No.   [2] Qy. 'trowed?' Dyce.

gold [*gives money*]; for I must, by this white hand, marry this
cherry-lipped, sweet-mouthed villain.　　　　　　　　　　　　231
　　Const. There's a thing called *quando.*
　　John. Instantly.
　　Gui. Art thou so willing?
　　John. Peace, threescore and five!　　　　　　　　　　　235
　　Const. Marry me? eat a chicken ere it be out o' th' shell? I'll
wear no shackles; liberty is sweet; that I have, that I'll hold. Marry
me? can gold and lead mix together? a diamond and a button of
crystal fit one ring? You are too high for me, I am too low; you too
great, I too little.　　　　　　　　　　　　　　　　　　240
　　Gui. I pray, leave her, sir, and take your gold again.
　　Const. Or if you doat, as you say, let me try you do this.
　　John. Anything; kill the great Turk, pluck out the Mogul's
eye-teeth; in earnest, Pretiosa, anything!
　　Const. Your task [1] is soon set down; turn gipsy for two years,
be one of us; if in that time you mislike not me nor I you, here's
my hand: farewell.　　　　　　　　　　　　　　[*Exit.*] 247
　　Gui. There's enough for your gold.—Witty child!
　　　　　　　　　　　　　　　　　　　　[*Aside, and*] *exit.*
　　John. Turn gipsy for two years? a capering trade;
And I in th' end may keep a dancing-school,　　　　　　　250
Having served for it; gipsy I must turn.
O beauty, the sun's fires cannot so burn!　　　　　　　*Exit.*

[Act II. Scene II.　*A Room in the House of Pedro.*]

Enter CLARA.

　　Cla. I have offended; yet, O Heaven, thou know'st
How much I have abhorred, even from my birth,
A thought that tended to immodest folly!
Yet I have fallen; thoughts with disgraces strive,
And thus I live, and thus I die alive.　　　　　　　　　　5

---

[1] Q 1, 'taste.' Q 2, 'tast'=task. [Morris justifies Q 2, by *Tw. Night*, III, 1, 87.—
Gen. Ed.]

Enter PEDRO *and* MARIA.

Ped. Fie, Clara, thou dost court calamity too much.
Mar. Yes, girl, thou dost.
Ped. Why should we fret our eyes out with our tears,
Weary [Heaven with][1] complaints? 'tis fruitless, childish
Impatience; for when mischief hath wound up   10
The full weight of the ravisher's foul life
To an equal height of ripe iniquity,
The poise will, by degrees, sink down his soul
To a much lower, much more lasting ruin
Than our joint wrongs can challenge.   15
    Mar.[2] Darkness itself
Will change night's sable brow into a sunbeam
For a discovery; and be sure,
Whenever we can learn what monster 'twas
Hath robbed thee of the jewel held so precious,   20
Our vengeance shall be noble.
    Ped. Royal, anything:
Till then let's live securely; to proclaim
Our sadness were mere vanity.
    Cla. 'A needs not;   25
I'll study to be merry.
    Ped. We are punished,
Maria, justly; covetousness to match
Our daughter to that matchless piece of ignorance,
Our foolish ward, hath drawn this curse upon us.   30
    Mar. I fear it has.
    Ped. Off with this face of grief.[3]
Here comes Don Louis.

Enter LOUIS *and* DIEGO.
Noble Sir.

    Louis. My lord,   35
I trust I have you[r] and your lady's leave

---

[1] added by ed. 1815.   [2] Qtos., *Ped.*
[3] Qtos., *Ped.* Off with this face of grief.
Die. Here comes Don Lewys, noble sir.
Lew. My lord.

T' exchange a word with your fair daughter.
  Ped. Leave
And welcome.—Hark, Maria.—Your ear too.
  Diego. Mine, my lord?   40
  Louis. Dear Clara, I have often sued for love,
And now desire you would at last be pleased
To style me yours.
  Cla. Mine eyes ne'er saw that gentleman
Whom I more nobly in my heart respected   45
Than I have you, yet you must, sir, excuse me,
If I resolve to use awhile that freedom
My younger days allow.
  Louis. But shall I hope?
  Cla. You will do injury to better fortunes.   50
To your own merit, greatness, and advancement,
Which I beseech you not to slack.
  Louis. Then hear me:
If ever I embrace another choice,
Until I know you elsewhere matched, may all   55
The chief of my desires find scorn and ruin!
  Cla. O me!
  Louis. Why sigh you, lady?
  Cla. 'Deed, my lord, I am not well.
  Louis. Then all discourse is tedious;   60
I'll choose some fitter time; till when, fair Clara——
  Cla. You shall not be unwelcome hither, sir;
That's all that I dare promise.
  Louis. Diego.
  Diego. My lord?   65
  Louis. What says Don Pedro?
  Diego. He'll go with you.
  Louis. Leave us.—   [*Exit* DIEGO.]
Shall I, my lord, entreat your privacy?
  Ped. Withdraw, Maria; we'll follow presently.   70
                     Exeunt [MARIA *and* CLARA].
  Louis. The great corigidor,[1] whose politic stream

[1] See Persons of the Play, *n.* 2.

Of popularity glides on the shore
Of every vulgar praise, hath often urged me
To be a suitor to his Catholic Majesty
For a repeal from banishment for him   75
Who slew my father; compliments in vows
And strange well-studied promises of friendship;
But what is new to me, still as he courts
Assistance for Alvarez, my grand enemy,
Still he protests how ignorant he is   80
Whether Alvarez be alive or dead.
To-morrow is the day we have appointed
For meeting, at the Lord Francisco's house,
The Earl of Carcomo; now, my good lord,
The sum of my request is, you will please   85
To lend your presence there, and witness wherein
Our joint accord consists.
    Ped. You shall command it.
    Louis. But first, as you are noble, I beseech you
Help me with your advice what you conceive   90
Of great Fernando's importunity,
Or whether you imagine that Alvarez
Survive or not?
    Ped. It is a question, sir,
Beyond my resolution: I remember   95
The difference betwixt your noble father
And Conde de Alvarez; how it sprung
From a mere trifle first, a cast of hawks,
Whose made the swifter flight, whose could mount highest,
Lie longest on the wing: from change of words   100
Their controversy grew to blows, from blows
To parties, thence to faction; and, in short,
I well remember how our streets were frighted
With brawls, whose end was blood; till, when no friends
Could mediate their discords, by the king   105
A reconciliation was enforced,
Death threatened [to] the first occasioner
Of breach, besides the confiscation

Of lands and honours: yet at last they met
Again; again they drew to sides, renewed   110
Their ancient quarrel; in which dismal uproar
Your father hand to hand fell by Alvarez:
Alvarez fled; and after him the doom
Of exile was se[n]t out: he, as report
Was bold to voice, retired himself to Rhodes;   115
His lands and honours by the king bestowed
On you, but then an infant.
    Louis. Ha, an infant?
    Ped. His wife, the sister to the corigidor,
With a young daughter, and some few that followed her,   120
By stealth were shipped for Rhodes, and by a storm
Shipwrecked at sea: but for the banished Conde,
'Twas never yet known what became of him:
Here's all I can inform you.
    Louis. A repeal?   125
Yes, I will sue for't, beg for't, buy it, anything
That may by possibility of friends
Or money, I'll attempt.
    Ped. 'Tis a brave charity.
    Louis. Alas! poor lady, I could mourn for her!   130
Her loss was usury more than I covet;
But for the man, I'd sell my patrimony
For his repeal, and run about the world
To find him out; there is no peace can dwell
About my father's tomb, till I have sacrificed   135
Some portion of revenge to his wronged ashes.
You will along with me?
    Ped. You need not question it.
    Louis. I have strange thoughts about me: two such furies
Revel amidst my joys as well may move   140
Distraction in a saint, vengeance and love.
I'll follow, sir.
    Ped. Pray, lead the way, you know it.—   *Exit* [LOUIS].

Enter SANCHO [*without his cloak, hat, &c.,*] *and* SOTO.

How, now? from whence come you, sir?[1]

San. From flaying myself, sir.   145

Soto. From playing with fencers, sir; and they have beat him out of his clothes, sir.

Ped. Cloak, band, rapier, all lost at dice?

San. Nor cards neither.

Soto. This was one of my master's dog-days, and he would not sweat too much.   151

San. It was mine own goose, and I laid the giblets upon another coxcomb's trencher: you are my guardian, best beg me for a fool[2] now.

Soto. He that begs one begs t'other.   155

Ped. Does any gentleman give away his things thus?

San. Yes, and gentlewomen give away their things, too.

Soto. To gulls sometimes, and are cony-catched for their labour.

Ped. Wilt thou ever play the coxcomb?

San. If no other parts be given me, what would you have me do?

Ped. Thy father was as brave a Spaniard   161
As ever spake the haut Castilian tongue.

San. Put me in clothes, I'll be as brave as he.

Ped. This is the ninth time thou hast played the ass,   165
Flinging away thy trappings and thy cloth
To cover others, and go naked thyself.

San. I'll make 'em up ten, because I'll be even with you.

Ped. Once more your broken walls shall have new hangings.

Soto. To be well hung is all our desire.   170

Ped. And what course take you next?

San. What course? why, my man Soto and I will go make some maps.

Ped. What maps?

Soto. Not such maps[3] as you wash houses with, but maps of countries.   176

---

[1] This line is given by Qtos. to Soto.
[2] To beg a person for a fool is to apply to have him legally declared a lunatic.
[3] mops.

San. I have an uncle in Sivell, I'll go see him; an aunt in Siena
in Italy, I go see her.

Soto. A cousin of mine in Rome, I go to him with a mortar.[1]

San. There's a courtesan in Venice, I'll go tickle her.   180

Soto. Another in England, I'll go tackle her.

Ped. So, so! and where's the money to do all this?

San. If my woods,[2] being cut down, cannot fill this pocket,
cut 'em into trapsticks.

Soto. And if his acres, being sold for a maruedi a turf for larks[3]
in cages, cannot fill this pocket, give 'em to gold-finders.[4]   186

Ped. You'll gallop both to the gallows; so fare you well. *Exit.*

San. And be hanged you! new clothes, you'd best.

Soto. Four cloaks, that you may give away three, and keep one.

San. We'll live as merrily as beggars; let's both turn gipsies.

Soto. By any means; if they cog,[5] we'll lie; if they toss, we'll
tumble.   192

San. Both in a belly, rather than fail.

Soto. Come, then, we'll be gipsified.

San. And tipsified too.   195

Soto. And we will show such tricks and such rare gambols,
As shall put down the elephant and camels.[6]   *Exeunt.*

Act III. [Scene I. *A Street.*]

Enter Roderigo *disguised like an Italian.*

Rod. A thousand stings are in me: O, what vile[7] prisons
Make we our bodies to our immortal souls!
Brave tenants to bad houses; 'tis a dear rent
They pay for naughty lodging: the soul, the mistress;
The body, the caroch that carries her;   5
Sins, the swift wheels that hurry her away;
Our will, the coachman rashly driving on,

---

[1] Fr. *mortier*, a peculiarly shaped cap worn by lawyers. To go to Rome with a
mortar was a proverbial expression meaning to go on a fool's errand.

[2] Qtos., 'wookes.'   [3] Qtos., 'markes.'

[4] A person who cleaned jakes was jocularly styled a gold finder (Bullen).

[5] Thieves' Latin, 'cheat.'   [6] Cf. II, i, 82.   [7] Qtos., 'vild.'

Till coach and carriage both are quite o'erthrown.
My body yet 'scapes bruises; that known thief
Is not yet called to th' bar: there's no true sense   10
Of pain but what the law of conscience
Condemns us to; I feel that. Who would lose
A kingdom for a cottage? an estate
Of perpetuity for a man's life
For annuity of that life?—Pleasure!—a spark   15
To those celestial fires that burn about us;
A painted star to that bright firmament
Of constellations which each night are set
Lighting our way; yet thither how few get! [1]
How many thousand in Madrill drink off   20
The cup of lust, and laughing, in one month,
Not whining as I do! Should this sad lady
Now meet me, do I know her? should this temple,
By me profaned, lie in the ruins here,
The pieces would scarce show her me: would they did!   25
She's mistress to Don Louis; by his steps,
And this disguise, I'll find her. To Salamanca
Thy father thinks thou'rt gone; no, close here stay;
Where'er thou travell'st, scorpions stop thy way.
Who are these? [2]   30

Enter SANCHO *and* SOTO [*disguised*] *as Gipsies.*

San. Soto, how do I show?

Soto. Like a rusty armour new scoured; but, master, how
show I?

San. Like an ass with a new piebald saddle on his back.

Soto. If the devil were a tailor, he would scarce know us in these
gaberdines.   36

San. If a tailor were the devil, I'd not give a louse for him, if he
should bring up this fashion amongst gentlemen, and make it
common.

Rod. The freshness of the morning be upon you both!   40

San. The saltness of the evening be upon you single!

---

[1] Lines 12-19, variously punctuated by Qtos, and editors.
[2] Q 1 reads 'stop thy way: these'. Corrected from Dy. Ms.

Rod. Be not displeased, that I abruptly thus
Break in upon your favours; your strange habits
Invite me with desire to understand
Both what you are and whence, because no country—   45
And I have measured some—shows [1] me your like.

Soto. Our like? no, we should be sorry we or our clothes should
be like fish, new, stale, and stinking in three days.

San. If you ask whence we are, we are Egyptian Spaniards;
if what we are, *ut, re, mi, fa, sol,* jugglers, tumblers, anything, anywhere, everywhere.   51

Rod. A good fate hither leads me by the hand.—   [*Aside.*]
Your quality I love; the scenical school
Has been my tutor long in Italy,
For that's my country; there have I put on   55
Sometimes the shape of a comedian,
And now and then some other.

San. A player! a brother of the tiring house! [2]

Soto. A bird of the same feather!

San. Welcome! wu't turn gipsy?   60

Rod. I can nor dance nor sing; but if my pen
From my invention can strike music-tunes,
My head and brains are yours.

Soto. A calf's head and brains were better for my stomach.

San. A rib of poetry!   65

Soto. A modicum of the Muses! a horse-shoe of Helicon!

San. A magpie of Parnassus! welcome again! I am a firebrand
of Phœbus myself; we'll invoke together, so you will not steal my
plot.

Rod. 'Tis not my fashion.   70

San. But now-a-days 'tis all the fashion.

Soto. What was the last thing you writ? a comedy?

Rod. No! 'twas a sad, too sad a tragedy.
Under these eaves I'll shelter me.   [*See gipsies approaching.*]

San. See, here comes our company.   75
Do our tops spin as you would have 'em?

Soto. If not, whip us round.

---

[1] So B.—Qtos., 'shew.'   [2] theatrical dressing-room.

Enter ALVAREZ, [GUIAMARA, CONSTANZA, CHRISTIANA, CARLO,
     ANTONIO, *and others, disguised as before.*] [1]

San. I sent you a letter to tell you we were upon a march.

Alv. And you are welcome.—Yet these fools will trouble us!
                                                    [*Aside.*]

Gui. Rich fools shall buy our trouble.   80

San. Hang lands! it's nothing but trees, stones, and dirt. Old
father, I have gold to keep up our stock. Precious Pretiosa, for
whose sake I have thus transformed myself out of a gentleman into
a gipsy, thou shalt not want sweet rhymes, my little musk-cat;
for besides myself, here's an Italian poet, on whom I pray throw
your welcomes.   86

Omnes. He's welcome!

Const. Sir, you're most welcome; I love a poet,
So he writes chastely; if your pen can sell me
Any smooth quaint romances, which I may sing,   90
You shall have bays and silver.

Rod.   Pretty heart, no selling;
What comes from me is free.

San. And me too.

Alv. We shall be glad to use you, sir: our sports   95
Must be an orchard, bearing several trees,
And fruits of several taste; one pleasure dulls.
A time may come when we, besides these pastimes,
May from the grandoes and the dons of Spain
Have leave to try our skill even on the stage,   100
And then your wits may help us.

San. And mine too.

Rod. They are your servants.

Const. Trip softly through the streets till we arrive
You know at whose house, father.   105

San. [*sings*].
             Trip it, gipsies, trip it fine,
                 Show tricks and lofty capers;
             At threading needles we repine,
                 And leaping over rapiers:

[1] Q 2, *Enter Alvarez, Eugenia, Pretiosa, and all the Gipsies.* Hereafter I print

Pindy-pandy rascal toys!   110
   We scorn cutting purses;
Though we live by making noise,
   For cheating none can curse us.

Over high ways, over low,
   And over stones and gravel,   115
Though we trip it on the toe,
   And thus for silver travel;
Though our dances waste our backs,
   At night fat capons mend them;
Eggs well brewed in buttered sack,   120
   Our wenches say befriend them.

O that all the world were mad!
   Then should we have fine dancing;
Hobby-horses would be had,
   And brave girls keep a-prancing;   125
Beggars would on cock-horse ride,
   And boobies fall a-roaring,
And cuckolds, though no horns be spied,
   Be one another goring.

Welcome, poet, to our ging! [1]   130
   Make rhymes, we'll give thee reason;
Canary bees thy brains shall sting,
   Mull-sack did ne'er speak treason;
Peter-see-me [2] shall wash thy noul [3]
   And maligo glasses fox [4] thee;   135
If, poet, thou toss not bowl for bowl,
   Thou shalt not kiss a doxy.   *Exeunt.*

without comment the real names in stage-directions, for the assumed of the
Qtos.
[1] gang.   [2] *i. e. Pedro Ximenes*, a sweet Spanish wine.
[3] noddle.   [4] intoxicate.

[Act III. Scene II. *A Garden belonging to Francisco's House.*]

Enter FERNANDO, FRANCISCO DE CARCOMO, DON JOHN, PEDRO, MARIA, LOUIS *and* DIEGO.

Fer. Louis de Castro, since you circled are
In such a golden ring of worthy friends,
Pray, let me question you about that business
You and I last conferred on.
    Louis. My lord, I wish it.   5
    Fer. Then, gentlemen, though you all know this man,
Yet now look on him well, and you shall find
Such mines of Spanish honour in his bosom
As but in few are treasured.
    Louis. O, my good lord——   10
    Fer. He's son to that De Castro o'er whose tomb
Fame stands writing a book, which will take up
The age of time to fill it with the stories
Of his great acts; and that his honoured father
Fell in the quarrel of those families,   15
His own and Don Alvarez de Castilla.
    Fran. The volume of those quarrels [1] is too large
And too wide printed in our memory.
    Louis. Would it had ne'er come forth!
    Omnes. So wish we all.   20
    Fer. But here's a son as matchless as the father,
For his mind's [2] bravery; he lets blood his spleen,
Tears out the leaf in which the picture stands
Of slain De Castro, casts a hill of sand
On all revenge, and stifles it.   25
    Omnes. 'Tis done nobly!
    Fer. For I by him am courted to solicit
The king for the repeal of poor Alvarez,

---

[1] Qtos., 'families.' Corrected by Ed. 1815.
[2] Q 1, 'For he mindes bravery.'

Who lives a banished man, some say, in Naples.
   Ped. Some say in Aragon.
   Louis. No matter where;   30
That paper folds in it my hand and heart,
Petitioning the royalty of Spain
To free the good old man, and call him home:
But what hope hath your lordship that these beams   35
Of grace shall shine upon me?
   Fer. The word royal.
   Omnes. And that's enough.
   Louis. Then since this sluice is drawn up to increase
The stream, with pardon of these honoured friends   40
Let me set ope another, and that's this;
That you, my lord Don Pedro, and this lady
Your noble wife, would in this fair assembly,
If still you hold me tenant to your favour,
Repeat [1] the promise you so oft have made me,   45
Touching the beauteous Clara for my wife.
   Ped. What I possess in her, before these lords
I freely once more give you.
   Mar. [2] And what's mine,
To you, as right heir to it, I resign.   50
   Omnes. What would you more?
   Louis. What would I more? the tree bows down his head
Gently to have me touch it, but when I offer
To pluck the fruit, the top branch grows so high
To mock my reaching hand, up it does fly;   55
I have the mother's smile, the daughter's frown.
   Omnes. O, you must woo hard!
   Fer. Woo her well; she's thine own.
   John. That law holds not 'mongst gipsies; I shoot hard,
And am wide off from the mark.   [*Aside.*] 60
                        Flourish [*within*].

   Fer. Is this, my lord, your music?
   Fran. None of mine.

[1] Q 1, 'Repeale.'—Ed. 1815, as above.
[2] Qtos., *Al.*

Enter Soto [*disguised as before,*] *with a cornet in his hand.*

Soto. A crew of gipsies with desire
To show their sports are at your gates a-fire.
   Fran. How, how, my gates a-fire, knave?   65
   John. Art panting? I am a-fire I'm sure!   [*Aside.*]
   Fer. What are the things they do?
   Soto. They frisk, they caper, dance and sing,
Tell fortunes too, which is a very fine thing;
They tumble—how? not up and down,   70
As tumblers do, but from town to town:
Antics they have and gipsy-masquing,
And toys which you may have for asking:
They come to devour nor wine nor good cheer,
But to earn money, if any be here;   75
But being asked, as I suppose,
Your answer will be, in your t'other hose, [1]
For there's not a gipsy amongst 'em that begs,
But gets his living by his tongue and legs.
If therefore you please, dons, they shall come in: 80
Now I have ended, let them begin.
   Omnes. Ay, ay, by any means.
   Fran. But, fellow, bring you music along with you too?
   Soto. Yes, my lord, both loud music and still music; the loud
is that which you have heard, and the still is that which no man
can hear.   *Exit.* 86
   Fer. A fine knave!
   Fran. There's report of a fair gipsy,
A pretty little toy, whom all our gallants
In Madrill flock to look on: this she, trow?   90
   John.[2] Yes, sure 'tis she—I should be sorry else. [*Aside.*]

---

[1] I left my money in my other trousers' pocket. See Morris, 132.—*Gen. Ed.*
[2] This line is printed as a continuation of Francisco's speech by Qtos.—*John,*
restored from Dy. Ms.

Enter ALVAREZ, GUIAMARA, CONSTANZA, [CHRISTIANA, CARLO, ANTONIO,] RODERIGO, SANCHO, SOTO, *and all the Gipsies [disguised, as before, with the following Song].*

> *Come, follow your leader, follow;*
> *Our convoy be Mars and Apollo!*
> *The van comes brave up here;*
> *(Answer.)—As hotly comes the rear:*　　95
> 　　*(Omnes). Our knackers are the fifes and drums,*
> 　　*Sa, sa, the gipsies' army comes!*
>
> *Horsemen we need not fear,*
> *There's none but footmen here;*
> *The horse sure charge without;*　　100
> *Or if they wheel about,*
> 　　*(Omnes.) Our knackers are the shot that fly,*
> 　　*Pit-a-pat rattling in the sky.*
>
> *If once the great ordnance play,*
> *That's laughing, yet run not away,*　　105
> *But stand the push of pike,*
> *Scorn can but basely strike;*
> 　　*(Omnes.) Then let our armies join and sing,*
> 　　*And pit-a-pat make our knackers ring.*
>
> *Arm, arm! what bands are those?*　　110
> *They cannot be sure our foes;*
> *We'll not draw up our force,*
> *Nor muster any horse;*
> 　　*(Omnes.) For since they pleased to view our sight,*
> 　　*Let's this way, this way give delight.*　　115
>
> *A council of war let's call,*
> *Look either to stand or fall;*
> *If our weak army stands,*
> *Thank all these noble hands;*
> 　　*(Omnes.) Whose gates of love being open thrown,* 120
> 　　*We enter, and then the town's our own.*

Fer. A very dainty thing!

Fran. A handsome creature!

Ped. ¹ Look what a pretty pit there's in her chin!

John. Pit? 'tis a grave to bury lovers in.²   125

Rod. My father? ³ disguise guard me!   [*Aside.*]

San. Soto, there's De Cortes my guardian, but he smells not us.

Soto. Peace, brother gipsy.—Would any one here know his fortune?

Omnes. Good fortunes all of us!   130

Ped. 'Tis I, sir, needs a good one: come, sir, what's mine?

Mar. Mine and my husband's fortunes keep together;
Who is't tells mine?

San. I, I; hold up, madam; fear not your pocket, for I ha' but two hands.   [*Examining her hands.*] 135

> *You are sad, or mad, or glad,*
> *For a couple of cocks that cannot be had;*
> *Yet when abroad they have picked store of grain,*
> *Doodle-doo they will cry on your dunghills again.*

Mar. Indeed I miss an idle gentleman,   140
And a thing of his a fool, but neither sad
Nor mad for them: would that were all the lead
Lying at my heart!

Ped. [*while* SOTO *examines his hand*]. What look'st thou on so long?   145

Soto. So long! do you think good fortunes are fresh herrings, to come in shoals? bad fortunes are like mackerel at midsummer: you have had a sore loss of late.

Ped. I have indeed; what is't?

Soto. I wonder it makes you not mad, for—   150

> *Through a gap in your ground thence late hath been stole*
> *A very fine ass and a very fine foal;*

---

¹ Qtos., *Ro.*

² So Cervantes '*ese no es hoyo, sino sepultura de deseos vivos.*'

³ Qtos., 'fathers.'

> *Take heed, for I speak not by habs and by nabs* [1]
> *Ere long you'll be horribly troubled with scabs.*

Ped. I am now so; go, silly fool.   155
Soto. I ha' gi'n't him.   [*Aside.*]
San. O Soto, that ass and foal fattens me!
Fer. The mother of the gipsies, what can she do?
I'll have a bout with her.
John. I with the gipsy daughter.   160
Fran. To her, boy.
Gui. [*examining* FERNANDO's *hand*].

> *From you went a dove away,*
> *Which ere this had been more white*
> *Than the silver robe of day;*   165
> *Her eyes, the moon has none so bright.*
> *Sate she now upon your hand,*
> *Not the crown of Spain could buy it;*
> *But 'tis flown to such a land,*
> *Never more shall you come nigh it:*   170
> *Ha! yes, if palmistry tell true,*
> *This dove again may fly to you.*

Fer. Thou art a lying witch; I'll hear no more.
San. If you be so hot, sir, we can cool you with a song.
Soto. And when that song's done, we'll heat you again with a
dance.   176
Louis. Stay, dear sir; send for Clara, let her know her fortune.
Mar. 'Tis too well known.
Louis. 'Twill make her merry to be in this brave company.
Ped. Good Diego, fetch her.   *Exit* DIEGO. 180
Fran. What's that old man? has he cunning too?
Omnes. More than all we!
Louis. Has he? I'll try his spectacles. [1]
Fer. Ha! Roderigo there? the scholar
That went to Salamanca, takes he degrees   185

---

[1] *Hab or nab* = 'at random.'
[2] knowledge of the future by glasses perspective. Morris 132.—*Gen. Ed.*

I' th' school of gipsies? let the fish alone,
Give him line: this is the dove—the dove?—the raven
That beldam [1] mocked me with.   [*Aside.*]

 Louis [*while* ALVAREZ *examines his hand*]. What worms pick
you out there now?   190
 Alv. This:

> *When this line the other crosses,*
> *Art tells me 'tis a book of losses:—*
> *Bend your hand thus:—O, here I find*
> *You have lost a ship in a great wind.*   195

 Louis. Lying rogue, I ne'er had any.
 Alv. Hark, as I gather,
That great ship was De Castro called, your father.
 Louis. And I must hew that rock that split him.
 Alv. Nay, an you threaten——   [*Retires.*] 200
 Fran. And what's, Don John, thy fortune?
Thou'rt long fumbling at it.
 John. She tells me tales of the moon, sir.
 Const. And now 'tis come to the sun, sir.

[*To* FRAN.] *Your son would ride, the youth would run,*   205
  The youth would sail, the youth would fly;
He's tying a knot will ne'er be done,
He shoots, and yet has ne'er an eye:
You have two, 'twere good you lent him one,
And a heart too, for he has none.   210

 Fran. Hoyday! lend one of mine eyes?
 San. They give us nothing; we'd [2] best put on a bold face and
ask it.

  [*Sings.*] *Now that from the hive*
   You gathered have the honey,   215
  Our bees but poorly thrive
   Unless the banks be sunny;

---

[1] Q 2, 'bedlam.'
[2] Q 1, 'hee'd.'—Dy. as above.

> *Then let your sun and moon,*
> *Your gold and silver shine,*
> *My thanks shall humming fly to you,*　　　220
> *(Omnes.) And mine, and mine, and mine.*
> 　　　[FRAN., FER., &c., give money.]

ALV. [*sings*]. *See, see, you* [1] *gipsy-toys,*
> *You mad girls, you merry boys,*
> *A boon voyage we have made,*
> *Loud peals must then be had;*　　　225
> *If I a gipsy be,*
> *A crack-rope I'm for thee:*
> *O, here's a golden ring!*
> *Such clappers please a king,*
> 　　　*(Omnes). Such clappers please a king.*　　　230

ALV. [*sings*]. *You pleased may pass away;*
> *Then let your bell-ropes stay;*
> *Now chime, 'tis holyday,*
> 　　　*(Omnes.) Now chime, 'tis holyday.*

Const. No more of this, pray, father; fall to your dancing.
　　　[CONST., CAR., &c.,] dance.

Louis. Clara will come too late now.　　　236

Fer. 'Tis great pity.——
Besides your songs, dances, and other pastimes,
You do not, as our Spanish actors do, make trial of a stage? [2]

Alv. We are, sir, about it;　·　　　240
So please your high authority to sign us
Some warrant to confirm us.

Fer. My hand shall do't,
And bring the best in Spain to see your sports.

Alv. Which to set off, this gentleman, a scholar——　　　245

Rod. Pox on you!　　　　　[*Aside.*]

Alv. Will write for us.

---

[1] Q 1, 'your.'—B. as above.
[2] ''Tis . . . stage?' Morris's punctuation. Preferable to preceding editions: 'pity, . . . stage.'—*Gen. Ed.*

Fer. A Spaniard, sir?

Rod. No, my lord, an Italian.

Fer. Denies his country too? my son sings gipsy-ballads!   250
[Aside.]

Keep as you are, we'll see your poet's vein,
And yours for playing: time is not ill spent
That's thus laid out in harmless merriment.

Exeunt Gipsies [ALVAREZ, GUIAMARA, CONSTANZA, CHRISTIANA,
CARLO, ANTONIO, RODERIGO, SANCHO, SOTO, *and others*] *dancing.*

Ped. My lord of Carcomo, for this entertainment
You shall command our loves.   255

Fran. You're nobly welcome.

Ped. The evening grows upon us: lords, to all
A happy time of day.

Fer. The like to you, Don Pedro.

Louis. To my heart's sole lady   260
Pray let my service humbly be remembered;
We only missed her presence.

Mar. I shall truly
Report your worthy love.   *Exeunt* PEDRO *and* MARIA.
[taking leave.] 265

Fer. You shall no further;
Indeed, my lords, you shall not.

Fran. With your favour,
We will attend you home.

[Re-]enter DIEGO.

Diego. Where's Don Pedro?——
O sir!   270

Louis. Why, what's the matter?

Diego. The Lady Clara,
Passing near to my lord corigidor's house,
Met with a strange mischance.

Fer. How? what mischance?   275

Diego. The jester that so late arrived at court,
And there was welcome for his country's sake,
By importunity of some friends, it seems,
Had borrowed from the gentleman of your horse

The backing of your mettled Barbary;   280
On which being mounted, whilst a number gazed
To hear what jests he could perform on horseback,
The headstrong beast, unused to such a rider,
Bears the press of people on [1] before him;
With which throng the Lady Clara meeting,   285
Fainted, and there fell down, not bruised, I hope,
But frighted and entranced.
    Louis. Ill-destined mischief!
    Fer. Where have you left her?
    Diego. At your house, my lord;   290
A servant coming forth, and knowing who
The lady was, conveyed her to a chamber;
A surgeon, too, is sent for.
    Fer. Had she been my daughter,
My care could not be greater than it shall be   295
For her recure.
    Louis. But if she miscarry,
I am the most unhappy man that lives.   *Exit.*
    Fer. Diego, coast about the fields,
And overtake Don Pedro and his wife;   300
They newly parted from us.
    Diego. I'll run speedily.   *Exit.*
    Fer. A strange mischance: but what I have, my lord
Francisco, this day noted, I may tell you;
An accident of merriment and wonder.   305
    Fran. Indeed, my lord!
    Fer. I have not thoughts enough
About me to imagine what th' event
Can come to; 'tis indeed about my son;
Hereafter you may counsel me.   310
    Fran. Most gladly.—

            [Re-]enter LOUIS.

How fares the lady?
    Louis. Called back to life,

               [1] 'on' supplied by Dy.

But full of sadness.

   Fer. Talks she nothing?   315

   Louis. Nothing;

For when the women that attend on her
Demanded how she did, she turned about,
And answered with a sigh: when I came near,
And by the love I bore her begged a word   320
Of hope to comfort me in her well-doing,
Before she would reply, from her fair eyes
She greets me with a bracelet of her tears,
Then wished me not to doubt; she was too well;
Entreats that she may sleep without disturbance   325
Or company until her father came:
And thus I left her.

   Fran. Sir,[1] she's past the worst;
Young maids are oft so troubled.

   Fer. Here come they   330
You talk of.—

        [Re-]enter PEDRO *and* MARIA.

           Sir, your daughter, for your comfort,
Is now upon amendment.

   Mar. O, my lord,
You speak an angel's voice!   335

   Fer. Pray, in and visit her,[2]
I'll follow instantly.   *[Exeunt* PEDRO *and* MARIA.]—
      You shall not part
Without a cup of wine, my lord.

   Fra. 'Tis now   340
Too troublesome a time.—Which way take you,
Don Louis?

   Louis. No matter which; for till I hear

---

[1] Qtos., 'For.'—Dy. Ms., 'Sir.'

[2] We are to suppose a change of scene: the company has arrived at the entrance to Fernando's house. Dy., B. [Morris discards the suggestion as violent and reads 'Fer. Pray on . . .' 'Fra. to Fer. You shall . . . lord.' 'Fer. 'Tis now . . . Louis.' 'Louis to Fer. No matter . . . corigidor.' 'Louis to Fra. I am . . . entertainment.' 'Fra. You have . . . courtesy.'—Gen. Ed.]

My Clara be recovered, I am nothing.—
My lord corigidor, I am your servant						345
For this free entertainment.
    Fer. You have conquered me
In noble courtesy.
    Louis. O, that no art
But love itself can cure a love-sick heart!			*Exeunt.* 350

[Act III.   Scene III.   *A Room in Fernando's House.*]

CLARA [*discovered seated*] in a chair, PEDRO *and* MARIA [*standing*]
by her.

    Mar. Clara, hope of mine age!
    Ped. Soul of my comfort! .
Kill us not both at once: why dost thou speed
Thine eye in such a progress 'bout these walls?
    Cla. Yon large window						5
Yields some fair prospect; good my lord, look out
And tell me what you see there.
    Ped. Easy suit:
Clara, it overviews a spacious garden,
Amidst which stands an alablaster fountain,					10
A goodly one.
    Cla. Indeed, my lord!
    Mar. Thy griefs grow wild,[1]
And will mislead thy judgment through thy weakness
If thou obey thy weakness.						15
    Cla. Who owns these glorious buildings?
    Ped. Don Fernando
De Azevida, the corigidor
Of Madrill, a true noble gentleman.
    Cla. May I not see him?						20
    Mar. See him, Clara? why?

---

[1] Qtos., 'wide.' Corrected by Ed. 1815.

Cla. A truly noble gentleman, you said, sir?
Ped. I did: lo, here he comes in person.[1]—

Enter FERNANDO.

                           We are,
My lord, your servants,   25
   Fer. Good, no compliment.—
Young lady, there attends below a surgeon
Of worthy fame and practice; is't your pleasure
To be his patient?
   Cla. With your favour, sir,   30
May I impart some few but needful words
Of secrecy to you, to you yourself,
None but yourself?
   Fer. You may.
   Ped. Must I not hear 'em?   35
   Mar. Nor I?
   Cla. O yes.—Pray, sit, my lord.
   Fer. Say on.
   Cla. You have been married?
   Fer. To a wife,[2] young lady.   40
Who, while the Heavens did lend her me, was fruitful
In all those virtues which styles woman good.
   Cla. And you had children by her?
   Fer. Had, 'tis true;
Now have but one, a son, and he yet lives;   45
The daughter (as if in her birth the mother
Had perfected the errand she was sent for
Into the world) from that hour took her life
In which the other that gave it her lost hers;
Yet shortly she unhappily, but fatally,   50
Perished at sea.
   Cla. Sad story!
   Fer. Roderigo,

---

[1] Qtos., *Ped.* I did: loe here he comes in person.
We are, my lord, your servants.
[2] Q 2, 'wise young lady.'

My son——
    Cla. How is he called, sir?   55
    Fer. Roderigo;
He lives at Salamanca; and I fear
That neither time, persuasions, nor his fortunes,
Can draw him thence.
    Cla. My lord, d'ye know this crucifix?   60
                            [*Showing the crucifix.*]
    Fer. You drive me to amazement! 'twas my son's,
A legacy bequeathed him from his mother
Upon her deathbed, dear to him as life;
On earth there cannot be another treasure
He values at like rate as he does this.   65
    Cla. O, then I am a cast-away!
    Mar. How's that?
    Ped. Alas! she will grow frantic!
    Cla. In my bosom,
Next to my heart, my lord, I have laid up,   70
In bloody character[s], a tale of horror.
Pray, read the paper; and if there you find

                         [*Giving a paper.*]

Aught that concerns a maid undone and miserable,
Made so by one[1] of yours, call back the piety
Of nature to the goodness of a judge,[2]   75
An upright judge, not of a partial father;
For do not wonder that I live to suffer
Such a full weight of wrongs, but wonder rather
That I have lived to speak them: thou, great man,
Yet read, read on, and as thou readst consider   80
What I have suffered, what thou ought'st to do,
Thine own name, fatherhood, and my dishonour.
Be just as Heaven and fate are, that by miracle
Have in my weakness wrought a strange discovery.
Truth copied from my heart is texted there: 85

---

[1] Qy. 'son'?—Dy.
[2] Subordinate the promptings of paternal feeling ('the piety of nature') to the duty of an upright judge.—*Gen. Ed.*

Let now my shame be th'roughly understood;
Sins are heard farthest when they cry in blood.
    Fer. True, true, they do not cry but holla here;
This is the trumpet of a soul drowned deep
In the unfathomed seas of matchless sorrows.   90
I must lock fast the door.   *Exit.*
    Mar. I have no words
To call for vengeance.
    Ped. I am lost in marvel.

> *[Re-]enter* FERNANDO.

    Fer. Sir,[1] pray sit as you sat before. White paper,   95
This should be innocence; these letters gules
Should be the honest oracles of revenge:
What's beauty but a perfect white and red?
Both here well mixed limn truth so beautiful,
That to distrust it, as I am a father,   100
Speaks me as foul as rape hath spoken my son;
'Tis true?
    Cla. 'Tis true.
    Fer. Then mark me how I kneel
Before the high tribunal of your injuries.   [*Kneels.*] 105
Thou too, too-much-wronged maid, scorn not my tears,
For these are tears of rage, not tears of love,—
Thou father of this too, too-much-wronged maid,—
Thou mother of her counsels and her cares,
I do not plead for pity to a villain;   110
O, let him die as he hath lived, dishonourably,
Basely and cursedly!   I plead for pity
To my till now untainted blood and honour:
Teach me how I may now be just and cruel,
For henceforth I am childless.   115
    Cla. Pray, sir, rise;
You wrong your place and age.
    Fer. [*rising*]. Point me my grave
In some obscure by-path, where never memory
                    [1] So Qtos. B., 'Sit.'

Nor mention of my name may be found out.   120
   Cla. My lord, I can weep with you, nay, weep for ye,
As you for me; your passions are instructions,
And prompt my faltering tongue to beg at least
A noble satisfaction, though not revenge.
   Fer. Speak that again.   125
   Cla. Can you procure no balm
To heal a wounded name?
   Fer. O, thou'rt as fair
In mercy as in beauty! wilt thou live,
And I'll be thy physician?   130
   Cla. I'll be yours.
   Fer. Don Pedro, we'll to counsel;
This daughter shall be ours.—Sleep, sleep, young angel,
My care shall wake about thee.
   Cla. Heaven is gracious,   135
And I am eased!
   Fer. We will be yet more private;
Night [1] curtains o'er the world; soft dreams rest with thee!
The best revenge is to reform our crimes,
Then time crowns sorrows, sorrows sweeten times.   140
          Exeunt [all except CLARA, *on whom the scene shuts].*

Act IV. [Scene I. *A Court before an Inn.*]

Enter ALVAREZ, SANCHO, SOTO, ANTONIO, CARLO, GUIAMARA, CONSTANZA, CHRISTIANA, *and* DON JOHN [*and others disguised, as before*]. *A shout within.*

   Omnes. Welcome, welcome, welcome!
   Soto. More sacks to the mill.
   San. More thieves to the sacks.
   Alv. Peace!
   Const. I give you now my welcome without noise.   5
   John. 'Tis music to me.   *[He offers to kiss her.]*
   Omnes. O sir!

               [1] Qtos., 'Might.'

San. You must not be in your mutton before we are out of our veal.

Soto. Stay for vinegar to your oysters; no opening till then.

Gui. No kissing till you're sworn.   11

John. Swear me then quickly,
I have brought gold for my admission.

Alv. What you bring leave, and what you leave count lost.

San. I brought all my teeth, two are struck out; them I count lost, so must you.   16

Soto. I brought all my wits; half I count lost, so must you.

John. To be as you are, I lose father, friends,
Birth, fortunes, all the world: what will you do
With the beast I rode on hither?   20

San. A beast? is't a mule? send him to Muly Crag-a-whee [1] in Barbary.

Soto. Is't an ass? give it to a lawyer, for in Spain they ride upon none else. [2]

John. Kill him by any means, lest, being pursued,   25
The beast betray me.

Soto. He's a beast betrays any man.

San. Except a bailiff to be pumped.

John. Pray, bury [3] the carcass and the furniture.

San. Do, do; bury the ass's household stuff, and in his skin 30
sew any man that's mad for a woman.

Alv Do so then, bury it: now to your oath.

Gui. All things are ready.

Alv. Thy best [4] hand lay on this turf of grass,
  There thy heart lies, vow not to pass   35
  From us two years for sun nor snow,
  For [5] hill nor dale, howe'er winds blow;

---

[1] The sultans of Barbary all took the title of Muly; but 'Crag-a-whee' does not resemble or suggest the name of anyone. Q 1 prints Muly Crag a whee.   Cf. enigmatical phrase in *A Shoemaker a Gentleman*, Act II, p. D. 2 (edit. 1638) 'Due gat a whee.' 'Mully Mumen, king of the Moors', is mentioned in *All's Lost by Lust*, Act II.

[2] The lawyer's *mule* was proverbial in Spain.

[3] Q 1, 'buy.'   [4] Qy. 'left.'? Dy.

[5] Bullen suggests, 'O'er hill, o'er dale, howe'er winds blow.'

    Vow the hard earth to be thy bed,
    With her green cushions under thy head;
    Flower-banks or moss to be thy board,   40
    Water thy wine——
San. And drink like a lord.
Omnes. Kings can have but coronations;
    We are as proud of gipsy-fashions:
    Dance, sing, and in a well-mixed border   45
    Close this new brother of our order.
Alv. What we get with us come share,
    You to get must vow to care;
    Nor strike gipsy, nor stand by
    When strangers strike, but fight, or die;   50
    Our gipsy-wenches are not common,
    You must not kiss a fellow's leman;
    Nor to your own, for one you must,
    In songs send errands of base lust.
Omnes. Dance, sing, and in a well-mixed border   55
    Close this new brother of your order.
John. On this turf of grass I vow
    Your laws to keep, your laws allow.

Omnes. A gipsy! a gipsy! a gipsy!
Gui. Now choose what maid has yet no mate,   60
She's yours.
John. Here then fix I my fate.
    [*Takes* Constanza *by the hand and*] *offers to kiss* [*her.*]
San. Again fall to before you ha' washed?
Soto. Your nose in the manger before the oats are measured,
jade, so hungry?   65

Alv. Set foot to foot; those garlands hold;
    ¹ *Now mark* [*well*] *what more is told.*
    By cross arms, the lover's sign,
    Vow, as these flowers themselves entwine,

---

¹ Qtos., '*Teach him how, now mark what more is told.*' The first three words are
a stage direction.

   Of April's wealth building a throne   70
   [1] *Round, so your love to one or none;*
   By those touches of your feet,
   You must each night embracing meet,
   Chaste, howe'er disjoined by day;
   You the sun with her must play,   75
   She to you the marigold,
   To none but you her leaves unfold;
   Wake she or sleep, your eyes so charm,
   Want, woe, nor weather do her harm.

Car. [2] *This is your market now of kisses,*   80
   Buy and sell free each other blisses.
John. Most willingly.
Omnes. *Holydays, high-days, gipsy-fairs,*
   When kisses are fairings, and hearts meet in pairs.

Alv. All ceremonies end here: welcome, brother gipsy! 85
San. And the better to instruct thee, mark what a brave life
'tis all the year long.
[*Sings.*] *Brave Don, cast your eyes*
   On our gipsy fashions:
   In our antic hey-de-guize[3]   90
   We go beyond all nations;
   Plump Dutch
   At us grutch,
   So do English, so do French,
   He that lopes   95
   On the ropes,
   Show me such another wench.[4]

   We no camels have to show,
   Nor elephant [5] *with growt head;*
   We can dance, he cannot go,   100
   Because the beast is corn-fed;

---

[1] Bullen suggests ' . . . a throne, to bound your love.' [2] Q 1, *Cla.*
[3] a rustic dance.
[4] Dyce suggests 'wrench' = caper.   [5] See II, i, 82, *n.*

> No blind bears
>   Shedding tears,
> For a collier's whipping;
>   Apes nor dogs,
>   Quick as frogs,
> Over cudgels skipping.
>
> Jack-in-boxes,[1] nor decoys,
>   Puppets, nor such poor things,
> Nor are we those roaring boys
>   That cozen fools with gilt rings;[1]
>   For an ocean,
>   Not such a motion[2]
> As the city Nineveh;
>   Dancing, singing,
>   And fine ringing,
> You these sports shall hear and see.

Come now, what shall his name be?
  Const. His name shall now be Andrew.—Friend Andrew, mark
    me:
Two years I am to try you: prove fine gold,
The uncracked diamond of my faith shall hold.
  John. My vows are rocks of adamant.
  Const. Two years you are to try me: black when I turn
May I meet youth and want, old age and scorn!
  John. King's diadems shall not buy thee.
  Car. Do you think
You can endure the life, and love it?
  John. As usurers doat upon their treasure.
  Soto. But when your face shall be tanned
Like a sailor's worky-day hand——
  San. When your feet shall be galled,
And your noddle be malled——
  Soto. When the woods you must forage,

105

110

115

120

125

130

---

[1] Bullen refers to Grosart's Dekker (iii, 286–289, and iii, 148) for these forms of swindling.

[2] puppet-show.

And not meet with poor pease-porridge—— 135
　　San. Be all to-be-dabbled, yet lie in no sheet——
　　Soto. With winter's frost, hail, snow, and sleet;
What life will you say it is then?
　　John. As now, the sweetest.
　　Diego—within.—Away! away! the corigidor has sent for you. 140
　　San. [*sings*]. *Hence merrily! fine to get money!* [1]
　　　　Dry are the fields, the banks are sunny,
　　　　Silver is sweeter far than honey;
　　　　　　Fly like swallows,
　　　　We for our conies must get mallows; 145
　　　　Who loves not his dill,[2] *let him die at the gallows.*
　　　　Hence, bonny girls, foot it trimly,
　　　　Smug up your beetle-brows, none look grimly;
　　　　To show a pretty foot, O 'tis seemly!　　[*Exeunt all.*]

　　　Enter CARDOCHIA, *and stays* SOTO [*as he is going out*].

　　Card. Do you hear, you gipsy? gipsy! 150
　　Soto. Me?
　　Card. There's a young gipsy newly entertained;
Sweet gipsy, call him back for one two words,
And here's a jewel for thee.
　　Soto. I'll send him. 155
　　Card. What's his name?
　　Soto. Andrew.　　　　　　　　　　　　　　[*Exit.*]
　　Card. A very handsome fellow; I ha' seen courtiers
Jet up and down in their full bravery,
Yet here's a gipsy worth a drove of 'em. 160

　　　　　[*Re-*]*enter* DON JOHN.

　　John. With me, sweetheart?
　　Card. Your name is Andrew?
　　John. Yes.
　　Card. You can tell fortunes, Andrew?
　　John. I could once. 165

---

[1] I insert the exclamation point before 'fine.'—*Gen. Ed.*
[2] For 'dill,' or 'dell,' girl, Bullen refers to Grosart's Dekker, iii, 106.

But now I ha' lost that knowledge; I'm in haste,
And cannot stay to tell you yours.
    Card. I cannot tell yours then;
And 'cause you're in haste, I'm quick; I am a maid——
    John. So, so, a maid quick?   170
    Card. Juanna Cardochia,
That's mine own name; I am my mother's heir
Here to this house, and two more.
    John. I buy no lands.
    Card. They shall be given you, with some plate and money,   175
And free possession during life of me,
So the match like you; for so well I love you,
That I, in pity of this trade of gipsying,
Being base, idle, and slavish, offer you
A state to settle you, my youth and beauty,   180
Desired by some brave Spaniards, so I may call you
My husband: shall I, Andrew?
    John. 'Las! pretty soul,
Better stars guide you! may that hand of Cupid
Ache, ever shot this arrow at your heart!   185
Sticks there one such indeed?
    Card. I would there did not,
Since you'll not pluck it out.
    John. Good sweet, I cannot;
For marriage, 'tis a law amongst us gipsies   190
We match in our own tribes; for me to wear you,
I should but wear you out.
    Card. I do not care;
Wear what you can out, all my life, my wealth,
Ruin me, so you lend me but your love,   195
A little of your love!
    John. Would I could give it,
For you are worth a world of better men,
For your free noble mind! all my best wishes
Stay with you; I must hence.   200
    Card. Wear for my sake
This jewel.

John. I'll not rob you, I'll take nothing.

Card. Wear it about your neck but one poor moon;   205
If in that time your eye be as 'tis now,
Send my jewel home again, and I protest
I'll never more think on you; deny not this,
Put it about your neck.

    John. Well then, 'tis done.   *[Putting on jewel.]*

    Card. And vow to keep it there.   210

    John. By all the goodness
I wish attend your fortunes, I do vow it!   *Exit.*

    Card. Scorned! thou hast tempered poison to kill me
Thyself shall drink; since I cannot enjoy thee,
My revenge shall.   215

Enter DIEGO.

Diego. Where are the gipsies?

Card. Gone. Diego, do you love me?

Diego. Love thee, Juanna?
Is my life mine? it is but mine so long
As it shall do thee service.   220

    Card. There's a young [1] gipsy newly entertained.

    Diego. A handsome rascal; what of him?

    Card. That slave in obscene language courted me,
Drew rialls [2] out, and would have bought my body,
Diego, from thee.

    Diego. Is he so itchy? I'll cure him.   225

    Card. Thou shalt not touch the villain, I'll spin his fate;
Woman strike[s] sure, fall the blow ne'er so late.

    Diego. Strike on, since [3] thou wilt be a striker. [4]

    Exeunt.

---

[1] Qtos., 'younger.' Dy. Ms., as above.
[2] (Span. *reales*) small silver coins.
[3] Q 1, 'sinne.'   [4] A cant term for a dissolute person (Bullen).

[Act IV.   Scene II.   *A Room in Fernando's House.*]

Enter FERNANDO, FRANCISCO, PEDRO, *and* LOUIS.

Fer. See, Don Louis; an arm,[1]
The strongest arm [1] in Spain, to the full length
Is stretched to pluck old Count Alvarez home
From his sad banishment.
    Louis. With longing eyes,   5
My lord, I expect the man: your lordship's pardon,
Some business calls me from you.
    Fer. Prithee, Don Louis,
Unless th' occasion be too violent,
Stay and be merry with us; all the gipsies   10
Will be here presently.
    Louis. I'll attend your lordship
Before their sports be done.
    Fer. Be your own carver.   *Exit* [LOUIS].
[*To* FRAN.] Not yet shake off these fetters?   I see a son   15
Is heavy when a father carries him
On his old heart.
    Fran. Could I set up my rest [2]
That he were lost, or taken prisoner,
I could hold truce with sorrow; but to have him   20
Vanish I know not how, gone none knows whither,
'Tis that mads me.
    Ped. You said he sent a letter.
    Fran. A letter? a mere riddle; he's gone to see[k]
His fortune in the wars; what wars have we?   25
Suppose we had, goes any man to th' field
Naked, unfurnished both [of] arms and money?
    Fer. Come, come, he's gone a-wenching; we in our youth
Ran the self-same bias.

---

[1] Qtos., 'army.' Dy. Ms., as above.
[2] 'Set up my rest' = be assured; an expression borrowed from the game of primero (Bullen).

Enter DIEGO.

Diego. The gipsies, my lord, are come.   30
Fer. Are they? let them enter.   *Exit* DIEGO.
My lord De Cortes, send for your wife and daughter;
Good company is good physic: take the pains
To seat yourselves in my great chamber. See,
They are here.—   *Exeunt* [FRANCISCO *and* PEDRO].   35

Enter ALVAREZ, DON JOHN, RODERIGO, ANTONIO, CARLO, GUIA-
   MARA, CONSTANZA, CHRISTIANA, SANCHO, *and* SOTO [*disguised
   as before*].

What's your number?[1]
San. The figure of nine casts us all up, my lord.
Fer. Nine? let me see—you are ten, sure.
Soto. That's our poet, he stands for a cipher.
Fer. Ciphers make numbers:—what plays have you?—   40
Alv. Five or six, my lord.
Fer. It's well so many already.
Soto. We are promised a very merry tragedy, if all hit right,
of Cobby Nobby.
Fer. So, so; a merry tragedy! There is a way   45
Which the Italians and the Frenchmen use,
That is, on a word given, or some slight plot,
The actors will extempore fashion out
Scenes neat and witty.
Alv. We can do that, my lord;   50
Please you bestow the subject.
Fer. Can you?—Come hither,
You master poet: to save you a labour,
Look you, against your coming I projected
This comic passage [*producing a paper*]; your drama, that's the
scene——   56
Rod. Ay, ay, my lord.
Fer. I lay in our own country, Spain.
Rod. 'Tis best so.
Fer. Here's a brave part for this old gipsy; look you,   60

---
[1] Q 1, '*Al.* See they are here. What's your number?'

The father: read the plot; this young she-gipsy,
This lady: now the son, play him yourself.

    Rod. My lord, I am no player.

    Fer. Pray, at this time,
The plot being full, to please my noble friends,   65
Because your brains must into theirs put language,
Act thou the son's part; I'll reward your pains.

    Rod. Protest, my lord——

    Fer. Nay, nay, shake off protesting;
When I was young, sir, I have played myself.   70

    San. Yourself, my lord? you were but a poor company then.

    Fer. Yes, full enough, honest fellow.—Will you do it?

    Rod. I'll venture.

    Fer. I thank you: let this father be a Don
Of a brave spirit.—Old gipsy, observe me——   75

    Alv. Yes, my lord.

    Fer. Play him up high; not like a pantaloon,
But hotly, nobly, checking this his son,
Whom make a very rake-hell, a deboshed fellow.
This point, I think, will show well.   80

    Rod. This of the picture?
It will indeed, my lord.

    San. My lord, what part play I?

    Fer. What parts dost use to play?

    San. If your lordship has ever a coxcomb, I think I could fit
you.   86

    Fer. I thank your coxcombship.

    Soto. Put a coxcomb upon a lord!

    Fer. There are parts to serve you all; go, go, make ready,
And call for what you want.   *Exit.* 90

    Alv. Give me the plot; our wits are put to trial.
What's the son's name? Lorenzo: that's your part.

                                 [*To* RODERIGO.]

Look only you to that; these I'll dispose:
Old Don Avero, mine; Hialdo, Lollio,
Two servants,—you for them.   [*To* SANCHO *and* SOTO.] 95

    San. One of the foolish knaves give me; I'll be Hialdo.

Soto. And I, Lollio.

San. Is there a banquet in the play? we may call for what we will.

Rod. Yes, here is a banquet.   100

San. I'll go, then, and bespeak an ocean of sweetmeats, marmalade, and custards.

Alv. Make haste to know what you must do.

San. Do? call for enough; and when my belly is full, fill my pockets.   105

Soto. To a banquet there must be wine; fortune's a scurvy whore, if she makes not my head sound like a rattle, and my heels dance the canaries.[1]

Alv. So, so; despatch whilst we employ our brains
To set things off to th' life.   110

Rod. I'll be straight with you.—

Exeunt [all except RODERIGO].

Why does my father put this trick on me;
Spies he me through my vizard? if he does,
He's not the King of Spain, and 'tis no treason;
If his invention jet upon a stage,   115
Why should not I use action?   A deboshed fellow!
A very rake-hell! this reflects on me,
And I'll retort it: grown a poet, father?
No matter in what strain your play must run,
But I shall fit you for a roaring son.   *Exit.* 120

[Act IV. Scene III. *A large Apartment in Fernando's House.*]

Enter FRANCISCO, PEDRO, FERNANDO, DIEGO, MARIA, *and* CLARA, [*and* Servants].

Fer. Come, ladies, take your places   *Flourish within.*
          This their music?
'Tis very handsome: O, I wish this room

[1] a lively dance.   Cf. Shaks. *All's Well*, II, i, 'make you dance canari.'

Were freighted but with [pleasures,] [1] noble friends,
As are to you my welcomes!—Begin there, masters.   5
  San. [*within*]. Presently, my lord; we want but a cold capon
for a property.
  Fer. Call, call for one.

Enter SANCHO [*as*] the Prologue.

Now they begin.

  San. *Both short and sweet some say is best;*   10
We will not only be sweet, but short:
Take you pepper in the nose,[2] *your mar our sport.*
  Fer. By no means pepper.
  San. *Of your love measure us forth but one span;*
We do though not the best, the best we can.   *Exit.* 15
  Fer. A good honest gipsy!

Enter ALVAREZ [*as* AVERO], *and* SOTO [*as* LOLLIO].

  Alv. *Slave, where's my son, Lorenzo?*
  Soto. *I have sought him, my lord, in all four elements: in earth,*
my shoes are full of gravel; in water, I drop at nose with sweating;
in air, wheresoever I heard noise of fiddlers, or the wide mouths of
gallon pots roaring; and in fire, what chimney soever I saw smoking
with good cheer, for my master's dinner, as I was in hope.
  Alv. *Not yet come home? before on this old tree*
Shall grow a branch so blasted, I'll hew it off,
And bury it at my foot!   Didst thou inquire   25
At my brother's?
  Soto. *At your sister's.*
  Alv. *At my wife's father's?*
  Soto. *At your uncle's mother's: no such sheep has broke through their*
hedge; no such calf as your son sucks or bleats in their ground.   30
  Alv. *I am unblessed to have but one son only,*
One staff to bear my age up,[3] *one taper left*
To light me to my grave, and that burns dimly;

---

[1] The bracketed word was inserted by Dyce; also 'freighted' for Qtos., 'frighted.'
[2] *i. e.* If you are angry, take offence (Bullen).
[3] Cf. *Roaring Girl*, I, i, This son . . .
The crutch unto my age.

That leaves me darkling hid in clouds of woe:
He that should prop me is mine overthrow.   35
 Fer. Well done, old fellow! is't not?
 Omnes. Yes, yes, my lord.
 Soto. Here comes his man Hialdo.

Enter SANCHO [as HIALDO].

 Alv. Where's the prodigal your master, sirrah?   39
 San. Eating acorns amongst swine, draff amongst hogs, and
gnawing bones amongst dogs: has lost all his money at dice, his wits
with his money, and his honesty with both; for he bum-fiddles[1] me,
makes the drawers curvet, pitches the plate over the bar, scores up the
vintner's name in the Ramhead, flirts his wife under the nose, and
bids you with a pox send him more money.   45
 Alv. Art thou one of his curs to bite me too?
To nail thee to the earth were to do justice.
 San. Here comes Bucephalus my prancing master; nail me now who
dares.

Enter RODERIGO [as LORENZO].

 Rod. I sit like an owl in the ivy-bush of a tavern; Hialdo, I have
drawn red wine from the vintner's own hogshead.   51
 San. Here's two more, pierce them too.
 Rod. Old Don, whom I call father, am I thy son? if I be, flesh
me with gold, fat me with silver; had I Spain in this hand, and Portu-
gal in this, puff it should fly: where's the money I sent for? I'll tickle
you for a rake-hell!   [*Aside.*] 56
 San. Not a marvedi.[2]
 Alv. Thou shalt have none of me.
 Soto. Hold his nose to the grin'stone, my lord.
 Rod. I shall have none?   60
 Alv. Charge me a case of pistols;
What I have built I'll ruin: shall I suffer
A slave to set his foot upon my heart?
A son? a barbarous villain? or if heaven save thee
Now from my justice, yet my curse pursues thee.   65

---

[1] See. *N. E. D. sub. voce.*   [2] See note II, i, 45.

Rod. Hialdo, carbonado [1] thou the old rogue my father.

San. Whilst you slice into collops the rusty gammon his man there.

Rod. No money?   Can taverns stand without Anon,[2] anon? fiddlers
live without scraping? taffaty[3] girls look plump without pampering?
If you will not lard me with money, give me a ship, furnish me to sea.

Alv. To have thee hanged for piracy?   71

San. Trim, tram, hang master, hang man!

Rod. Then send me to the West Indies, buy me some office there.

Alv. To have thy throat cut for thy quarrelling?

Rod. Else send me and my ningle,[4] Hialdo, to the wars.   75

San. A match; we'll fight dog, fight bear.

Enter ANTONIO [as HERNANDO].

Alv.[5] O dear Hernando, welcome!—Clap wings to your heels,
[To SOTO.]

And pray my worthy friends bestow upon me
Their present visitation.—   [*Exit* SOTO.]
[6] Lorenzo, see the anger of a father;   80
Although it be as loud and quick as thunder,
Yet 'tis done instantly: cast off thy wildness,
Be mine, be mine, for I to call thee home
Have, with my honoured friend here, Don Hernando,
Provided thee a wife.   85

Rod. A wife! is she handsome? is she rich? is she fair? is she witty?
is she honest? hang honesty! has she a sweet face, cherry-cheek, straw-
berry-lip, white skin, dainty eye, pretty foot, delicate legs, as there's a
girl now?

Ant. It is a creature both for birth and fortunes,   90
And for most excellent graces of the mind,
Few like her are in Spain.

Rod. When shall I see her?—
Now, father, pray take your curse off.

Alv. I do: the lady   95

---

[1] i. e., cut into rashers for broiling (Bullen).

[2] Cf. *Match at Midnight*, Act II.   'The *More wine, boy*, the nimble Anon, anon,
Sir.'

[3] prostitutes.   [4] favourite (Bullen).   [5] Qtos., *An.*

[6] Qtos. give rest of speech to *Ant.*   Ed. 1815 corrects.

Lives from Madrill very near fourteen leagues,
But thou shalt see her picture.
   Rod. That! that! most ladies in these days are but very fine pictures.

Enter CARLO,[1] DON JOHN, GUIAMARA, CONSTANZA, [*and*] CHRIS-
      TIANA [*as friends of* AVERO].

   Alv. Ladies, to you first welcome; my lords, Alonzo,
And you worthy marquis, thanks for these honours.—   100
Away you!   [*Exit* SANCHO.]
To th' cause now of this meeting.   My son Lorenzo,
Whose wildness you all know, comes now to th' lure,
Sits gently; has called home his wandering thoughts,
And now will marry.   105
   Const. A good wife fate send him!
   Gui. One staid may settle him.
   Rod. Fly to the mark, sir; show me the wench, or her face, or any-
thing I may know 'tis a woman fit for me.
   Alv. She is not here herself, but here's her picture.   110
                                          [*Shows*] a picture.
   Fer. My Lord De Carcomo, pray, observe this.
   Fran. I do, attentively.—Don Pedro, mark it.

               [*Re-*]*enter* SOTO.

   Soto [*to* JOHN]. If you ha' done your part, yonder's a wench
would ha' a bout with you.   *Exit.*
   John. Me?   *Exit.* 115
   Diego. A wench!   *Exit.*
   Alv. Why stand you staring at it? how do you like her?
   Rod. Are you in earnest?
   Alv. Yes, sir, in earnest.
   Rod. I am not so hungry after flesh to make the devil a cuckold. 120
   Ant. Look not upon the face, but on the goodness
That dwells within her.
   Rod. Set fire on the tenement!
   Alv. She's rich; nobly descended.
   Rod. Did ever nobility look so scurvily?   125

                ¹Q 1 misprints *Claro.*

Alv. I'm sunk in fortunes, she may raise us both.

Rod. Sink, let her to her granam! marry a witch? have you fetched a wife for me out of Lapland?[1] an old midwife in a velvet hat were a goddess to this: that a red lip?

Const. There's a red nose.   130

Rod. That a yellow hair?

Gui. Why, her teeth may be yellow.

Rod. Where's the full eye?

Chris. She has full blabber-cheeks.

Alv. Set up thy rest, her marriest thou or none.   135

Rod. None then: were all the water in the world one sea, all kingdoms one mountain, I would climb on all fours up to the top of that hill, and headlong hurl myself into that abyss of waves, ere I would touch the skin of such rough haberdine,[2] for the breath of her picture stinks hither.   140

A noise within. [*Re-*]*enter* DON JOHN, DIEGO, CARDOCHIA, SANCHO, *and* SOTO, *in a hurry.*

Fer. What tumult's this?

{ *San.* Murder, murder, murder!

{ *Soto.* One of our gipsies is in danger of hanging, hanging![3]

Ped. Who is hurt?

Diego. 'Tis I, my lord, stabbed by this gipsy.   145

John. He struck me first, and I'll not take a blow From any Spaniard breathing.

Ped. Are you so brave?

Fer. Break up your play; lock all the doors.

Diego. I faint, my lord.   150

Fran. Have him to a surgeon.—

[*Servants* remove DIEGO.]
How fell they out?

Card. O, my good lord, these gipsies when they lodged At my house, I had a jewel from my pocket Stolen by this villain.   155

John. 'Tis most false, my lords;

---

[1] The Lapps were supposed to be witches.
[2] Inferior salt-cod (Bullen).   [3] Qtos., *San. Soto,* 'Murder . . . hanging.'

Her own hands gave it me.
   Const. She that calls him villain,
Or says he stole——
   Fer. Hoyday! we hear your scolding. 160
   Card. And the hurt gentleman finding it in his bosom,
For that he stabbed him.
   Fer. Hence with all the gipsies!
   Ped. Ruffians and thieves; to prison with 'em all!
   Alv. My lord, we'll leave engagements in plate and money
For all our safe forthcomings; punish not all 166
For one's offence; we'll prove ourselves no thieves.
   San. O Soto, I make buttons![1]
   Soto. Would I could make some, and leave this trade!
   Fer. Iron him then, let the rest go free; but stir not 170
One foot out of Madrill. Bring you in your witness.
[*Exeunt* JOHN *in custody of* Servants, ALVAREZ, GUIAMARA, CON-
   STANZA, CHRISTIANA, ANTONIO, CARLO, *and* CARDOCHIA.]
   Soto. Prick him with a pin, or pinch him by the elbow; anything.
   San. My lord Don Pedro, I am your ward; we have spent a little
money to get a horrible deal of wit, and now I am weary of it.
   Ped. My runaways turned jugglers, fortune-tellers? 175
   Soto. No great fortunes.
   Fer. To prison with 'em both: a gentleman play the ass!
   San. If all gentlemen that play the ass should to prison, you
must widen your jails.—Come, Soto, I scorn to beg; set thy foot
to mine, and kick at shackles. 180
   Fer. So so; away with 'em!
   Soto. Send all our company after, and we'll play there, and be as
merry as you here.
                Exeunt [SANCHO *and* SOTO *with* Servants].
   Fer. Our comedy turned tragical! Please you, lords, walk:
This actor here and I must change a word, 185
And I come to you.
   Omnes. Well, my lord, your pleasure.
              Exeunt [*all except* FERNANDO *and* RODERIGO].
   Fer. Why, couldst thou think in any base disguise

---

[1] See *N. E. D. sub voce.*

To blind my sight? fathers have eagles' eyes.
But pray, sir, why was this done? why, when I thought you   190
Fast locked in Salamanca at your study,
Leaped you into a gipsy?
    Rod. Sir, with your pardon,
I shall at fit time to you show cause for all.
    Fer. Meantime, sir, you have got a trade to live by: 195
Best to turn player; an excellent ruffian, ha!
But know, sir, when I had found you out, I gave you
This project of set purpose; 'tis all myself;
What the old gipsy spake must be my language;
Nothing are left me but my offices   200
And thin-faced honours; and this very creature,
By you so scorned, must raise me by your marrying her.
    Rod. You would not build your glory on my ruins?
    Fer. The rascal has belied the lady,
She is not half so bad; all's one, she's rich.   205
    Rod. O, will you sell [1] the joys of my full youth
To dunghill muck? seek out some wretch's daughter,
Whose soul is lost for gold then: you're more noble
Than t' have your son, the top-branch of your house,
Grow in a heap of rubbish: I must marry a thing   210
I shall be ashamed to own, ashamed to bring her
Before a sunbeam.
    Fer. I cannot help it, sir;
Resolve upon't, and do't.
    Rod. And do't, and die!   215
Is there no face in Spain for you to pick out
But one to fright me? when you sat the play here,
There was a beauty, to be lord of which
I would against an army throw defiance.
    Fer. She? alas!   220
    Rod. How? she! [2] at every hair of hers
There hangs a very angel; this! I'm ready
To drop down looking at it: sir, I beseech you

[1] Qtos., 'see.'—Dy. Ms., as above.
[2] Qtos., 'How! how!—Dy. Ms., as above.

Bury me in this earth [*kneels*], on which I'm humbled
To beg your blessing on me, for a gipsy, 225
Rather than—O, I know not what to term it!
Pray, what is that young pensive piece of beauty?
Your voice for her; I eyed her all the scene.
  Fer. I saw you did.
  Rod. Methought 'twas a sweet creature. 230
  Fer. Well, though my present state stands now on ice,
I'll let it crack and fall rather than bar thee
Of thy content; this lady shall go by then.
  Rod. Hang let her there, or anywhere!
  Fer. That young lannard, 235
Whom you have such a mind to, if you can whistle her
To come to fist, make trial; play the young falconer;
I will not mar your marriage nor yet make;
Beauty, no wealth,—wealth, ugliness,—which you will, take.
  Rod. I thank you, sir. [*Exit* FERNANDO.]—Put on your mask,
    good madam. [*To the picture.*] 241
The sun will spoil your face else. *Exit.*

Act V. [Scene I. *A Room in Fernando's House.*]

Enter FERNANDO, FRANCISCO, PEDRO, RODERIGO, CLARA, MARIA,
as from church over the stage. [*As the others exeunt,*] FERNANDO
stays RODERIGO.

  Fer. Thou hast now the wife of thy desires.
  Rod. Sir, I have,
And in her every blessing that makes life
Loth to be parted with.
  Fer. Noble she is, 5
And fair; has to enrich her blood and beauty,
Plenty of wit, discourse, behaviour, carriage.
  Rod. I owe you duty for a double birth,
Being in this happiness begot again,
Without which I had been a man of wretchedness. 10

Fer. Then henceforth, boy, learn to obey thy fate;
Tis fallen upon thee; know it, and embrace it;
Thy wife's a wanton.
    Rod. A wanton?
    Fer. Examine through the progress of thy youth   15
What capital [1] sin, what great one 'tis, for 'tis
A great one thou'st committed.
    Rod. I, a great one?
    Fer. Else Heaven is not so wrathful to pour on thee
A misery so full of bitterness: 20
I am thy father; think on't, and be just;
Come, do not dally.
    Rod. Pray, my lord,—
    Fer. Fool, 'twere
Impossible that justice should rain down   25
In such a frightful horror without cause.
Sir, I will know it; rather blush thou didst
An act thou dar'st not name, than that it has
A name to be known by.
    Rod. Turn from me then,   30
And as my guilt sighs out this monster,—rape,
O, do not lend an ear!
    Fer. Rape? fearful!
    Rod. Hence,
Hence springs my due reward.   35
    Fer. Thou'rt none of mine,
Or if thou be'st, thou dost belie the stamp
Of thy nativity.
    Rod. Forgive me!
    Fer. Had she,   40
Poor wrongèd soul, whoe'er she was, no friend,
Nor father, to revenge? had she no tongue
To roar her injuries?
    Rod. Alas! I know her not!
    Fer. Peace! thou wilt blaze a sin beyond all precedent: 45
Young man, thou shouldst have married her; the devil

[1] So Ed. 1815. Qtos., 'sins.'

Of lust that riots in thy eye should there
Have let fall love and pity, not on this stranger
Whom thou hast doted on.

    Rod. O, had I married her,   50
I had been then the happiest man alive!

    [*Re-*]*enter* CLARA, MARIA, *and* PEDRO, *from behind the arras.*

    Cla. As I the happiest woman, being married:
Look on me, sir.

    Ped. You shall not find a change
So full of fears as your most noble father,   55
In his wise trial, urged.

    Mar. Indeed you shall not,
The forfeit of her shame shall be her pawn.

    Rod. Why pray, d'ye mock my sorrows? now, O, now,
My horrors flow [1] about me!   60

    Fer. No, thy comforts,
Thy blessings, Roderigo.

    Cla. By this crucifix   [*Showing crucifix.*]
You may remember me.

    Rod. Ha! art thou   65
That lady wrongèd?

    Cla. I was, but now am
Righted in noble satisfaction.

    Rod. How can I turn mine eyes, and not behold
On every side my shame?   70

    Fer. No more: hereafter
We shall have time to talk at large of all:
Love her that's now thine own; do, Roderigo;
She's far from what I charactered.

    Cla. My care   75
Shall live about me to deserve your love.

    Rod. Excellent Clara!—Fathers both, and mother,
I will redeem my fault.

    Fer., Ped., Mar. Our blessings dwell on ye!

            [1] Qtos., 'flew.'

[*Re-*]*enter* LOUIS *and* FRANCISCO.

Louis. Married to Roderigo?   80
Fran. Judge yourself:
See where they are.   *Exit.*
  Louis. Is this your husband, lady?
  Cla. He is, sir: Heaven's great hand, that on record
Fore-points the equal union of all hearts,   85
Long since decreed what this day hath been perfected.
  Louis. 'Tis well then; I am free, it seems.
  Cla. Make smooth,
My lord, those clouds, which on your brow deliver
Emblems of storm; I will, as far as honour   90
May privilege, deserve a noble friendship
As you from me deserve a worthy memory.
  Louis. Your husband has proved himself a friend [to me] [1]
Trusty and tried; he's welcome, I may say,
From the university.   95
  Rod. To a new school
Of happy knowledge, Louis.
  Louis. Sir, I am not so poor to put this injury up:
The best blood flows within you is the price.
  Rod. Louis, for this time calm your anger; and if   100
I do not give you noble satisfaction,
Call me to what account you please.
  Louis. So, so.—I come for justice t'ye,
And you shall grant it.
  Fer. Shall and will.   105
  Louis. With speed too;
My poor friend bleeds the whiles.
  Fer. You shall yourself,
Before we part, receive the satisfaction
You come for.—Who attends?   110
  Servant within. My lord?
  Fer. The prisoner!
  Servant [*within*]. He attends your lordship's pleasure.

[1] The words in brackets are not in Qtos. Dy. inserts.

Enter CONSTANZA, GUIAMARA, *and* ALVAREZ.

Louis. What would this girl?
Foh, no tricks; get you to your cabin, huswife;   115
We have no ear for ballads.
    Fer. Take her away.
    Cla. A wondrous lovely ¹ creature!
    Const. Noble gentlemen,
If a poor maid's, a gipsy-virgin's tears   120
May soften the hard edge of angry justice,
Then grant me gracious hearing; as you're merciful
I beg my husband's life!
    Fer. Thy husband's, little one?
    Const. Gentle sir, our plighted troths are chronicled   125
In that white book above which notes the secrets
Of every thought and heart; he is my husband,
I am his wife.
    Louis. Rather his whore.
    Const. Now, trust me,   130
You're no good man to say so; I am honest,
'Deed, la, I am; a poor soul, that deserves not
Such a bad word: were you a better man
Than you are, you do me wrong.
    Louis. The toy grows angry!   135
    Cla. And it becomes her sweetly; troth, my lord,
I pity her.
    Rod. I thank you, sweet.²
    Louis. Your husband,
You'll say, is no thief.   140
    Const. Upon my conscience, he is not.
    Louis. Dares not strike a man.
    Const. Unworthily
He dares not; but if trod upon, a worm
Will turn again.   145
    Louis. That turning turns your worm

---

¹ So Dy. Ms.—Qtos., 'lively.'
² Qtos, 'sir.'—Dy. Ms. as above.

Off from the ladder, minion.
   Const. Sir, I hope
You're not his judge; you are too young, too choleric,
Too passionate; the price of life or death   150
Requires a much more grave consideration
Than your years warrant: here [1] sit they, like gods,
Upon whose head[s] the reverend badge of time
Hath sealed the proof of wisdom; to these oracles
Of riper judgment, lower in my heart   *[Kneels.]* 155
Than on my knees, I offer up my suit,
My lawful suit, which begs they would be gentle
To their own fames, their own immortal stories.
O, do not think, my lords, compassion thrown
On a base low estate, on humble people,   160
Less meritorious than if you had favoured
The faults of great men! and indeed great men
Have oftentimes great faults: he whom I plead for
Is free; the soul of innocence itself
Is not more white: will you pity him?   165
I see it in your eyes, 'tis a sweet sunbeam,
Let it shine out; and to adorn your praise,
The prayers of the poor shall crown your days,
And theirs are sometimes heard. [2]
   Fer. Beshrew the girl,   170
She has almost melted me to tears!
   Louis. Hence, trifler!—Call in my friends!

     Enter DON JOHN, DIEGO, CARDOCHIA, [*and* Servants].

What hope of ease?
   Diego. Good hope, but still I smart;
The worst is in my pain.   175
   Louis. The price is high
Shall buy thy vengeance: to receive a wound
By a base villain's hand, it maddens [3] me.
   John. Men subject to th' extremity of law

---

[1] Q 1, 'he sit;' Q 2 'they sit like gods.'—Dy. Ms. as above.
[2] Qtos., 'something hard.'—Dy Ms., as above.
[3] So. Dy.—Q 1, 'madds'; Q 2, 'mads.'

Should carry peace about 'em to their graves;   180
Else, were you nobler than the blood you boast of,
Could any way, my lord, derive you, know
I would return sharp answer to your slanders;
But it suffices, I am none of aught
Your rage misterms me.   185
    Louis. None of 'em? no rascal?
    John. No rascal.
    Louis. Nor no thief?
    John. Ask her that's my accuser: could your eyes
Pierce through the secrets of her foul desires,   190
You might without a partial judgment look into
A woman's lust and malice.
    Card. My good lords,
What I have articled against this fellow,
I justify for truth.   195
    John. On then, no more:
This being true she says, I have deserved
To die.
    Fer. We sit not here to bandy words,
But minister [the]¹ law, and that condemns thee   200
For theft unto the gallows.
    Const. O my misery!
Are you all ² marble-breasted? are your bosoms
Hooped round with steel? to cast away a man,
More worthy life and honours than a thousand   205
Of such as only pray unto the shadow
Of abused greatness!
    John. 'Tis in vain to storm;
My fate is here determinèd.
    Const. Lost creature,   210
Art thou grown dull too? is my love so cheap
That thou court'st thy destruction 'cause I love thee?—
My lords, my lords!—Speak, Andrew, prithee, now,
Be not so cruel to thyself and me;
One word of thine will do't.   215

    ¹ Qtos., omit 'the.'   ² So Q 1.— Q 2, 'so.'

Fer. Away with him!
To-morrow is his day of execution.
   John. Even when you will.
   Const. Stay, man; thou shalt not go,
Here are more women yet.—Sweet madam, speak!   220
You, lady, you methinks should have some feeling
Of tenderness; you may be touched as I am:
Troth, were't your cause, I'd weep with you, and join
In earnest suit for one you held so dear.
   Cla. My lord, pray speak in his behalf.   225
   Rod. I would,
But dare not; 'tis a fault so clear and manifest.
   Louis. Back with him to his dungeon!
   John. Heaven can tell
I sorrow not to die, but to leave her   230
Who whiles I live is my life's comforter.   [*Exit with* Servants.]
   Card. Now shall I be revenged!
                    [*Aside, and*] *exit* [*with* Diego].
   Const. O me unhappy!   [*Swoons.*]
   Fer. See, the girl falls!
Some one look to her.   235
   Cla. 'Las, poor maid!
   Gui. Pretiosa!
She does recover: mine honourable lord——
   Fer. In vain: what is't?
   Gui. Be pleased to give me private audience;   240
I will discover something shall advantage
The noblest of this land.
   Fer. Well, I will hear thee;
Bring in the girl.

[*Exeunt* Fernando, Maria, Pedro, Clara, Roderigo, Guiamara,
    and Constanza: Alvarez *stays* Louis.][1]

   Louis. Aught with me; what is't?   245
I care not for thy company, old ruffian;
Rascal, art impudent?
            [1] Q 2, *Exit.   Manet Lewys, Alvarez.*

Alv. To beg your service.

Louis. Hang yourself!

Alv. By your father's soul, sir, hear me!　　　　　250

Louis. Despatch!

Alv. First promise me you'll get reprieve
For the condemnèd man, and by my art
I'll make you master of what your heart on earth
Can wish for or desire.　　　　　255

Louis. Thou liest; thou canst not!

Alv. Try me.

Louis. Do that, and then, as I am noble,
I will not only give thy friend his life,
But royally reward thee, love thee ever.　　　　　260

Alv. I take your word; what would you?

Louis. If thou mock'st me,
'Twere better thou wert damned!

Alv. Sir, I am resolute.

Louis. Resolve me, then, whether the Count Alvarez,　　　　　265
Who slew my father, be alive or dead?

Alv. Is this the mighty matter? the count lives.

Louis. How?

Alv. The count lives.

Louis. O fate! Now tell me where,　　　　　270
And be my better genius.

Alv. I can do't:
In Spain 'a lives; more, not far from Madrill,
But in disguise, much altered.

Louis. Wonderful scholar!　　　　　275
Miracle of artists! Alvarez living?
And near Madrill too? now, for Heaven's sake, where?
That's all, and I am thine.

Alv. Walk off, my lord,
To the next field, you shall know all.　　　　　280

Louis. Apace, then! I listen to thee with a greedy ear:
The miserable and the fortunate
Are alike in this, they cannot change their fate.　　　　*Exeunt.*[1]

[1] Qtos., *Ex. at one dore. Enter presently at the other.*

[Act V. Scene II. *A Field*.

Enter Alvarez *and* Louis.]

Alv. Good, good: you would fain kill him, and revenge
Your father's death?
Louis. I would.
Alv. Bravely, or securely? [1]
Louis. Not basely, for the world!   5
Alv. We are secure.   [*Produces*] two swords.
Young Louis, two more trusty blades than these
Spain has not in her arm[our]y: [2] with this
Alvarez slew thy father; and this other
Was that the King of France wore when great Charles   10
In a set battle took him prisoner;
Both I resign to thee.
Louis. This is a new mystery.
Alv. Now see this naked bosom; turn the points
Of either on this bulwark, if thou covet'st,   15
Out of a sprightly youth and manly thirst
Of vengeance, blood; if blood be thy ambition,
Then call to mind the fatal blow that struck
De Castro, thy brave father, to his grave;
Remember who it was that gave that blow,   20
His enemy Alvarez: hear, and be sudden,
Behold Alvarez!
Louis. Death, I am deluded!
Alv. Thou art incredulous; as fate is certain,
I am the man.   25
Louis. Thou that butcher?
Alv. Tremble not, young man, trust me, I have wept
Religiously to wash off from my conscience
The stain of my offence: twelve years and more,
Like to a restless pilgrim I have run   30

---

[1] So Qtos., meaning 'sneakishly.'   Dy. Ms. has 'scurvily.'
[2] Qtos., 'army.'

From foreign lands to lands to find out death.
I'm weary of my life; give me a sword:
That thou mayst know with what a perfect zeal
I honour old De Castro's memory,
I'll fight with thee; I would not have thy hand   35
Dipped in a wilful murder; I could wish
For one hour's space I could pluck back from time
But thirty of my years, that in my fall
Thou might'st deserve report: now if thou conquer'st,
Thou canst not triumph; I'm half dead already,   40
Yet I'll not start a foot.
 Louis. Breathes there a spirit
In such a heap of age? [1]
 Alv. O, that I had
A son of equal growth with thee, to tug   45
For reputation! by thy father's ashes,
I would not kill thee for another Spain,
Yet now I'll do my best. Thou art amazed;
Come on.
 Louis. Twelve tedious winters' banishment?   50
'Twas a long time.
 Alv. Could they redeem thy father,
Would every age had been twelve ages, Louis,
And I for penance every age a-dying!
But 'tis too late to wish.   55
 Louis. I am o'ercome;
Your nobleness hath conquered me: here ends
All strife between our families, and henceforth
Acknowledge me for yours.
 Alv. O, thou reviv'st   60
Fresh horrors to my fact! for in thy gentleness
I see my sin anew.
 Louis. Our peace is made;
Your life shall be my care: 'twill be glad news
To all our noble friends.   65
 Alv. Since Heaven will have it so,

   [1] Qtos., 'rage'; Ed. 1815, 'rags'; Dy. Ms., as above.

I thank thee, glorious majesty! My son,
For I will call thee [so,] [1] ere the next morrow
Salute the world, thou shalt know stranger mysteries.

    Louis. I have enough to feed on: sir, I'll follow ye.   70

                                                  Exeunt.

[Act V.   Scene III.   *A Room in Fernando's House.*]

Enter GUIAMARA, FERNANDO *and* CONSTANZA.

    Fer. Don John, son to the Count of Carcomo?
Woman, take heed thou trifle not.
    Gui. Is this,
My lord, so strange?
    Fer. Beauty in youth, and wit   5
To set it forth, I see, transforms the best
Into what shape love fancies.
    Const. Will you yet
Give me my husband's life?
    Fer. Why, little one,   10
He is not married to thee.
    Const. In his faith
He is; and faith and troth I hope bind faster
Than any other ceremonies can;
Do they not, pray, my lord?   15
    Fer. Yes, where the parties
Pledged are not too unequal in degree,
As he and thou art.
    Const. This is new divinity.
    Gui. My lord, behold this child well: in her face   20
You may observe, by curious insight, something
More than belongs to every common birth.
    Fer. True, 'tis a pretty child.
    Gui. The glass of misery
Is, after many a change of desperate fortune,   25

                  [1] Qtos., omit 'so.'

At length run out: you had a daughter called
Constanza?
 Fer. Ha!
 Gui. A sister, Guiamara,
Wife to the Count Alvarez?   30
 Fer. Peace, O, peace!
 Gui. And to that sister's charge you did commit
Your infant daughter, in whose birth your wife,
Her mother, died?
 Fer. Woman thou art too cruel!   35
 Const. What d'ye mean, granam? 'las, the nobleman
Grows angry!
 Fer. Not I, indeed I do not:—
But why d'ye use me thus?
 Gui. Your child and sister,   40
As you supposed, were drowned?
 Fer. Drowned? talking creature!
Supposed?
 Gui. They live; Fernando, from my hand,
Thy sister's hand, receive thine own Constanza, 45
The sweetest, best child living.
 Const. Do you mock me?
 Fer. Torment me on; yet more, more yet, and spare not;
My heart is now a-breaking; now!
 Gui. O brother!   50
Am I so far removed off from your memory,
As that you will not know me? I expected
Another welcome home: look on this casket,

        [Showing] a casket.

The legacy your lady left her daughter,
When to her son she gave her crucifix.   55
 Fer. Right, right; I know ye now.
 Gui. In all my sorrows,
My comfort has been here, she should be [yours,] [1]
Be yours [at last.] [1]—Constanza, kneel, sweet child,
To thy old father.   60

    [1] Not in Qtos. Supplied by Dy.

Const. How? my father?　　　　　　　　　　[*Kneels.*]
　Fer. Let not
Extremity of joys ravish life from me
Too soon, Heaven, I beseech thee! Thou art my sister,
My sister Guiamara![1] How have mine eyes　　　65
Been darkened all this while! 'tis she!
　Gui. 'Tis, brother;
And this Constanza, now no more a stranger,
No Pretiosa henceforth.
　Fer. My soul's treasure,　　　　70
Live to an age of goodness; and so thrive
In all thy ways, that thou mayst die to live!
　Const. But must I call you father?
　Fer. Thou wilt rob me else
Of that felicity, for whose sake only　　　75
I am ambitious of being young again:
Rise, rise, mine own Constanza!
　Const. [*rising*]. 'Tis a new name,
But 'tis a pretty one; I may be bold
To make a suit t'ye?　　　　80
　Fer. Anything.
　Const. O father,
And if you be my father, think upon
Don John my husband! without him, alas,
I can be nothing!　　　　85
　Fer. As I without thee;
Let me alone, Constanza.—Tell me, tell me,
Lives yet Alvarez?
　Gui. In your house.
　Fer. Enough:　　　　90
Cloy me not; let me by degrees disgest
My joys.—Within, my Lords Francisco, Pedro!
Come all at once! I have a world within me;
I am not mortal sure, I am not mortal:
　　　　[1] Q 1, 'Guyamare.'

Enter FRANCISCO, PEDRO, MARIA, RODERIGO, [*and*] CLARA.

My honourable lord[s],[1] partake my blessings;   95
[The] [1] Count Alvarez lives here in my house;
Your son, my Lord Francisco, Don John, is
The condemned man falsely accused of theft;
This, my Lord Pedro, is my sister Guiamara;
Madam, this [is] [1] Constanza, mine own child,   100
And I am a wondrous merry man.—Without!
The prisoner!

Enter ALVAREZ, LOUIS, DON JOHN, DIEGO, SANCHO, SOTO, *and*
CARDOCHIA.

   Louis. Here, free and acquitted,
By her whose folly drew her to this error;
And she for satisfaction is assured [2]   105
To my wronged friend.
   Card. I crave your pardons;
He whose I am speaks for me.
   Diego. We both beg it!
   Fer. Excellent! admirable! my dear brother!   110
   Alv. Never a happy man till now; young Louis
And I are reconciled.
   Louis. For ever, faithfully, religiously.
   Omnes. My noble lord, most welcome!
   Alv. To all my heart pays what it owes, due thanks: 115
Most, most, brave youth, to thee!
   John. I all this while
Stand but a looker-on; and though my father
May justly tax the violence of my passions,
Yet if this lady, lady of my life,   120
Must be denied, let me be as I was,
And die betimes.
   Const. You promised me——
   Fer. I did.—
My lord of Carcomo, you see their hearts   125

       [1] Supplied by Dy.   [2] affianced.

Are joined already, so let our consents
To this wished marriage.
   Fran. I forgive thine errors;
Give me thy hand.
   Fer. [*to Constanza*].   Me thine.—But wilt thou love   130
My daughter, my Constanza?
   John. As my bliss.
   Const. I thee as life, youth, beauty, anything
That makes life comfortable.
   Fer. Live together one, ever one!   135
   Omnes. And Heaven crown your happiness!
   Ped. Now, sir, how like you a prison?
   San. As gallants do a tavern, being stopped for a reckoning,
scurvily.
   Soto. Though you caged us up never so close, we sung like
cuckoos.   141
   Fer. Well, well, you be yourself now.
   San. Myself?—am I out of my wits, Soto?
   Fer. Here now are none but honourable friends:
Will you, to give a farewell to the life   145
You ha' led as gipsies, these being now found none,
But noble in their births, altered in fortunes,
Give it a merry shaking by the hand,
And cry adieu to folly?
   San. We'll shake our hands, and our heels, if you'll give us
leave.   [*A*] *dance.* 151
   Fer. On, brides and bridegrooms! to your Spanish feasts
Invite with bent knees all these noble guests.
                                [*Exeunt omnes.*]

John Fletcher

RULE A WIFE AND HAVE A WIFE

Edited with Critical Essay and Notes by George Saintsbury, M. A., LL. D., Professor in the University of Edinburgh

CRITICAL ESSAY[1]

Literary Estimate: Sources of the Play.—Of the voluminous collection of "Beaumont & Fletcher's" work, perhaps—certainly of those plays which so far as dates go (for it was not licensed till 1624, eight years after Beaumont's death, nor printed till nearly twice as long after his coadjutor's) may be attributed to Fletcher unassisted—*Rule a Wife and Have a Wife* has been the most kindly treated by its editors and commentators. Centos of foregone opinions are easy but not specially edifying exercises of criticism. It is sufficient to say that the very moderate depreciation of the poet-critic Darley, who pronounces the piece "not so much a comedy as an olla podrida of comicalities," is about the unkindest thing that any one of importance, so far as I remember, has said of it. The author of that wonderful burst of exquisite incoherence, *Nepenthe,* —I do not use the periphrasis without intention,—half points and half explains away this judgment elsewhere by calling the play a drama "which will keep a careless temper in a state of perpetual exhilaration, and a fastidious one in a state of as perpetual regret that so much *vis comica* has been frittered away instead of rendered more effective by compactness." Fletcher would not have been at a loss for a *tu quoque* in respect of *Sylvia* and *Nepenthe,* of *Becket* and *Ethelstan;* but *tu quoque* is not argument, any more than blank verse is.

Darley has, however, touched in the remark last cited the undoubted cause of the popularity of our play, which it must be remembered continued to be an acted play till well within the present century. Not a few things which have not been generally, may be justly and shall be, said against *Rule a Wife and Have a Wife.* Much, though not all, that has been said in its favour is just. But one thing is indisputable, it never *drags.* I really do not

---

[1] For dates and the detailed discussion of the comedies of Fletcher and of Beaumont, see the Essay introductory to this volume, sections 11, 12, 15, 16. For particulars concerning lives, Gayley's *Beaumont, the Dramatist* (N. Y. 1914).—*Gen Ed.*

think it excessive to say that no better instance can be produced of the special virtue of the mixed and compound, as opposed to the simple, plot. The imposture *v.* impudence of Leon and Margarita, the paste-cut-paste of Estifania and Perez, and the more isolated action of the brute Cacafogo, catch each other up with such unfailing alertness that the spectator, I suppose,—that the reader, I know—never feels a moment's dulness. Now this is a great thing in any kind of literature: in dramatic literature there is hardly a sin that it will not cover.

At the same time there are sins in *Rule a Wife and Have a Wife*, and some which are not quite venial. No great stress need be laid on the extreme prominence of Fletcherian redundancy, which we should expect in a play dating apparently from the close of the poet's career, but which goes so far that nearly half the play must be hendecasyllabic. That was the way the world went then, and Fletcher himself was still master enough to avoid the shambling stuff, half verse, half prose, into which that way sometimes led even his younger collaborator Shirley, and in which almost all Shirley's contemporaries stumbled and staggered. The bold indulgence in trisyllabic values within the line, though it has frightened some editors who did not understand it, is even less reprehensible. Fletcher seems to allow his beast dangerous vagaries, but he knows perfectly well how to ride him.

More serious objections may be taken to the character-mongering. The personages are not excessively real; their morality, though not specially naughty, is sometimes very particularly disagreeable; and their probability is sometimes remarkably small. This especially applies to Leon and Margarita, and it applies more to Margarita than to Leon. The latter is a bold and ready-witted fellow enough; but he is as little of a gentleman when he hires himself out as wittol expectant and warranted fool as when he breaks the express conditions of the hiring. As for Margarita, one may have an almost sinful tenderness for feminine frailty from Helen of Troy to her own contemporary and namesake of Valois, and further still, and yet have none for her. At first she is merely impudent—impudent without passion, without loveableness, without grace, without any quality more engaging than that which makes a hungry dog growl and whine for bones. Even what Johnson said to Boswell, "This lady of yours, sir, is very fit for a brothel," is too good for her: even in the seventeenth century playwrights from Dekker to Chamberlayne could at any rate people such establishments with denizens not merely bestial. Secondly, Margarita's reformation is an altogether excessive instance of those improbabilities, not to say impossibilities, in this kind, the absence of which in Shakespeare has been justly held to differentiate him, almost more than anything else, from his fellows. Yet she has been treated with remarkable leniency. Even Dyce— a critic of rather ferocious morality sometimes, who is shocked not merely by the abnormalities of Lelia in *The Captain*, but by the passionate and charming Celia of *The Humorous Lieutenant*—has not a word to say against Margarita, though he gently shakes his head at the whole fable as "rather unpleasing." To me the most unpleasing thing in it is this businesslike and cold-blooded baggage, the description of whose beauty and girlishness makes her unendeared impudence all the more distasteful. The only redeeming touch in her is not her improbable and uninteresting reformation, but her tears of rage when Leon shows himself in his true colours.

Still we must remember that hardly anybody ever thinks of any character in connection with *Rule a Wife and Have a Wife* save Perez and Estifania; and fortunately Perez and Estifania are more than enough to save the play. Fletcher required, and he has used, none of his poetry in drawing them; he has not even vouchsafed many (or perhaps any) of those individually and yet universally vivifying touches which he could give. But of stage life each has abundance, of stage individuality more than a sufficiency: and the way in which they play up to each other is very nearly perfection. Perez, both rook and pigeon as he is, appears to be a good soldier, and not by any means a wholly bad fellow; Estifania, adventuress and thief, is *bonne diablesse* in her way, and we are not expected to accept the old woman's account of her literally. It is a complete case of Gascon and sesqui-Gascon; nor is the Copper Captain so completely overmatched in the play as his original was in Cervantes' novel.

For there is no reasonable doubt that the subject, in so far as the

Captain and his Dalilah are concerned, is taken from the "Exemplary" collection of that great person. Indeed, so far as the mere outlines of the plot or sub-plot are concerned, there is very little innovation upon *El Casamiento Engañoso*. Perez is Campuzano—a name actually occurring in the play—Margarita is Donna Clementa, and so forth. But the story is the same, the very details—not merely of the gold chain which is not gold at the end, but of the "white hand" of the veiled Estifania at the beginning—are retained with the usual carelessness and self-reliance of the Elizabethans in this respect. As usual also, Fletcher has made what he borrows his own; and if an original could be found for the title-plot, or for the part of Cacafogo, there is no doubt that this would apply equally.

It is perhaps to this part of Cacafogo that the kindness of commentators, above referred to, may seem most excessive. Campbell, not a gushing critic, is quite enthusiastic over it; and others hardly less so, there being even a tradition that Fletcher intended here to rival Falstaff. Let us hope that the misdeeds of the father at Fotheringay were not visited upon the son in the shape of any such preposterous idea. There are some letters alike in Falstaff and in Cacafogo; they are both baffled by women; and there the parallel ends. But it is fair to note more fully what has been glanced at already, the way in which the farcical part contributes to that peculiarly exhilarating and interesting bustle which has been said to be the great charm of the play. The interests of the main and secondary plots are kept so nearly level that there might have been some danger of their refusing to blend—of their presenting that appearance of two separate things, merely strapped together, which is so common in the minor and not so uncommon in the major Elizabethans. Now this part of Cacafogo, in a curiously happy manner, prevents any appearance of division by the introduction of a third between the two. Also it dispenses the author from those "waits," those passages of interval and padding, which are so common, so almost inevitable, in the comedy of intrigue. Where, in ordinary cases, such a passage would occur, Cacafogo puts in an appearance and shades off the acute comedy of Perez and Estifania into farce, just as that comedy itself lightens the serious—the, at last, possibly tragic—comedy of Leon and Margarita. It is in part at least, thanks to him, that as Swinburne puts it concisely, the play is "in pure comedy, the acknowledged and consummate master-piece" of its author—a judgment to which I can take no exception save that, as will have been seen already, I should myself substitute "cunningly blended" for "pure."

As far as the Perez and Estifania part goes, it is no doubt pure enough. I have said that Fletcher, closely as he has stuck to what Cervantes gave him, has yet made it his own, and he has done so among other things by a cunning exercise of improving his original. In the Cervantic anecdote, which is very likely historical, Campuzano is a much completer cully than Perez, and Estifania is almost what the Old Woman here paints her as being. Fletcher, attending to that wise necessity of making his characters not disgusting, which some foolish critics nowadays deny, and which he himself not too wisely neglects in Margarita, has touched both up, not in the least with rose pink, but out of mere sordid drab. Perez, as I have said, for all his touch of roguery, is by no means a bad fellow, and has, somewhere "behind the faggots," a sense of honour which makes his worst punishment when he finds himself duped badly, and thinks he is duped worse than he is. Estifania, too, is more mischievous and intriguing than positively bad-blooded, and though she has no objection to cheating, and still less to tormenting her husband, does not seem devoid of a certain affection for him, as he is also not devoid of a good deal for her. And no wonder, for not only "the rogue is witty," but she has a sort of naughty charm as well as good looks. In fact, Fletcher here sketches (with few, if any, models) that notion of an extremely human couple—far from moral or blameless, but humanly and humanely immoral and blamable—the development of which in the latter half of the century is one of the best, and one of the least commonly recognized, dramatic achievements of his scholar Dryden. The Copper Captain and his slightly brazen lady are not oppressively virtuous or fulsomely fond, but they are not repulsively vicious or disgustingly heartless. The very scheme of the play deprives it of the adventitious charms of some of its author's pieces, though it must be admitted that some of Fletcher's exquisite lyrics appear in plays apparently as little suited to them. But "Beauty, clear and fair," or "Tell me, dearest," would be no doubt out of keeping with the brisk and shrewd but extremely prosaic tone of the whole piece. It is a comedy of intrigue pure and simple; nor are there many better of the kind in any language.

Previous Editions and the Present Text.—As for the text, what follows will not be found exactly identical with any previously printed. The play first appeared in quarto (Q) in 1640, and so was not included in the first folio of 1647, wherein the players gathered up, and at last issued, the carefully treasured manuscript pieces which, to the number of just two-thirds of the whole, had not been issued separately either during or after the lifetime of the authors. F_2 therefore (the edition of 1679 in which Herringman and two other publishers gathered up the entire works) is here (F). This is the edition known from a famous passage of Charles Lamb, and certainly a handsome and desirable possession, though, alas! not to be now obtained for "fifteen, or was it sixteen," shillings. The boast of the publishers, that by aid of some private information they had carefully corrected it, is said by some editors not to be justified in reference to the first folio; but this, since that first folio does not contain the play, does not concern us. I should say that, so far as our own subject is concerned, there are unusual marks of careful and rather intelligent editing, side by side of course with others of that forgetfulness of the true style and language of the giant race before the flood which came upon their not exactly puny but less gigantic successors after it. The original quarto was printed at Oxford, not in London, and Weber (of whose own work, by the way, I think, after careful examination, rather more highly than I once did) compliments the University on its being much better than the usual London versions. When Theobald took the play in hand (see notes, *infra*) he was not in the vein; and his successors of 1750, Seward and Sympson, luxuriated as usual (though not to their fullest degree) in gratuitous emendation, and particularly in that fatal cutting and trimming of the metre to the rigid decasyllable which was the natural consequence of eighteenth-century delusions on that subject. At the same time they deserve all thanks for getting over the drudgery of supplying reasonable scene divisions and stage directions, etc., and for arranging the verse, not always on erroneous principles. I have not thought it necessary to examine minutely the edition of 1778 (nominally Colman's), the chief merit of which has been generally recognized to be a negative one, to wit, its rejection of the meddlings of the father of the Swan of Lichfield. But Weber, partly, no doubt, under the influence of Scott, partly also from his own studies in Middle English, had a much juster notion of metre than had been possible earlier, and this is perhaps his strongest point. Darley, who, when Southey's mental affliction made it impossible for him to contribute an introduction to Moxon's edition, undertook the work, was either not expected or not allowed to do anything to the text. His introduction itself, with some mannerisms and eccentricities, is a very valuable piece of criticism. The worst thing in all these editions is the substitution of the ugly abbreviations "I've," "I'd," "I'm," etc., for the full forms which are almost invariable in the originals. Dyce it is superfluous to praise. A critic in *Churton's Literary Register* for 1845 observed, it seems, that "Mr. Dyce's note" on something "is an admirable specimen of his fitness for editing Beaumont and Fletcher." This, "wrote sarcastic," in *Churton's Literary Register* after the well-known manner of certain critics, may be written sincerely of almost every note of his. But he was sometimes a very little given to the besetting sin of scholars—the itch to amend; and I have sometimes gone back from him to the old texts, with careful comparison of both of which that now presented has been prepared.[1]

GEORGE SAINTSBURY.

[1] This seems wiser than to reprint here Q, printed fifteen years after Fletcher's death, or F, printed thirty-nine years still later. There is no certainty that either followed the author's original manuscript. The student, moreover, may find F, with variants from Q, in Glover and Waller's *B. and F.*, Vol. III (*Camb. Engl. Classics*). Collating Professor Saintsbury's text with one of Q prepared for me by Mr. George England from the B. M. copy, I have in what follows bracketed insertions, frequently insignificant, and added those footnotes which without comment indicate some other divergences from Q. I have also put together an Appendix in which the reader will find the quarto arrangement of such lines and stage-directions as have been altered in the present edition. It is noteworthy that Q abounds in 'um's for 'em's, in Fletcher's 'yee's for 'you's (object as well as subject), and in his 'y'are's; and, also, that the modern 'I'll,' 'I'd,' 'you'll,' 'we're,' 'we've,' etc., are with some uniformity, respectively, 'Ile,' 'I wood' (or 'I had'), 'you will,' 'we are,' 'we have,' etc., in the quarto.—*Gen. Ed.*

RVLE A WIFE
And have a Wife.

A COMOEDY.

ACTED BY HIS
Majesties Servants.

Written by

J OHN F LETCHER

Gent.

VIGNETTE

OXFORD,
Printed by L EONARD L ICHFIELD
Printer to the Univerſity.
A NNO 1 6 4 0.

[The Persons of the Play [1]

DUKE OF MEDINA.
JUAN DE CASTRO, *a Colonel.*
SANCHIO, }
ALONZO, } *Officers in the Army.*
MICHAEL PEREZ, *the Copper Captain.*
LEON, *Brother to* ALTEA.
CACAFOGO, *a rich Usurer.*
MARGARITA.
ALTEA, *her Servant.*
CLARA.
ESTIFANIA.
Three Old Ladies.
An Old Woman, *and* Maid.

THE SCENE: VALLADOLID, and a COUNTRY-HOUSE near it.]

[1] Q and F none. Ed. 1750, *Men:* 'Juan de Castro, a *Spanish* Colonel.' 'Leon, brother to Altea, *and by her contrivance marry'd to Margarita.*' *Women:* 'Margarita, *a wanton Lady marry'd to Leon, by whom she is reclaim'd.*' 'Clara, *a Spanish Lady.*' 'Estifania, *a Woman of Intrigue marry'd to Perez.*' Scene: *Spain.* Dyce brackets Sanchio, Alonzo, and Michael Perez as simply 'captains'; omits 'rich' before 'usurer'; adds 'ladies, coachman, boy, and menservants'; describes Margarita as 'a rich heiress'; and brackets Altea and Estifania and ladies as 'her attendants.' The enumeration inserted above is Darley's after Weber and Ed. 1778.

Rule a Wife and Have a Wife [1]

Prologue [2]

Pleasure attend ye! and about ye sit
The springs of mirth, fancy, delight, and wit,
To stir you up! Do not your looks let fall,
Nor to remembrance our late errors call,
Because this day we are Spaniards all again,   5
The story of our play, and our scene Spain:
The errors too, do not for this cause hate;
Now we present their wit, and not their state.
Nor, ladies, be not angry, if you see
A young fresh beauty, wanton, and too free,   10
Seek to abuse her [3] husband; still 'tis Spain;
No such gross errors in your kingdom reign: [4]
We're vestals all, and though we blow the fire,
We seldom make it flame up to desire;
Take no example neither to begin,   15
For some by precedent delight to sin;
Nor blame the poet if he slipt aside
Sometimes lasciviously, if not too wide.
But hold your fans close, and then smile at ease;

[1] After line 25 in Q.

[2] PROLOGUE.—Ed. 1750 puts before the *Dramatis Personæ*, and reads 'you' for 'ye' in l. 3. All editors, even Dyce, have strangely accepted Sympson's alteration of 'You're vestals all' for 'We're,' the reading of Q and F. I can see no reason whatever for this. It makes nonsense of the rest of the sentence, for as Heath (quoted from Ms. by Dyce) justly says, it was the vestals who attended to the fire; and Dyce's argument that it is ridiculous to suppose that the poet would make players call themselves vestals is of no value. It might be ironic; as it certainly would be to apply the word to an Elizabethan audience.

[3] Q, 'your.'   [4] Q, 'raignes.'

A cruel scene did never lady please.   20
Nor, gentlemen, pray be not you displeas'd,
Though we present some men fool'd, some diseas'd,
Some drunk, some mad: We mean not you, you're free: ⎫
We tax no further than our comedy;   ⎬
You are our friends; sit noble then, and see!   ⎭ 25

Act I. Scene I. [*Valladolid. The Lodgings of Juan de Castro.*]

Enter Juan de Castro *and* Michael Perez.

Perez. [1] Are your companies full, colonel?
Juan. No, not yet, sir;
    Nor will not be this month yet, as I reckon.
    How rises your command?
Perez. We pick up still,   5
    And, as our monies hold out, we have men come:
    About that time I think we shall be full too.
    Many young gallants go.
Juan. And unexperienced:
    The wars are dainty dreams to young hot spirits;   10
    Time and experience will allay those visions.
    We have strange things to fill our numbers: [2]
    There's one Don Leon, a strange [3] goodly fellow,
    Recommended to me from some noble friends,
    For my alferez; [4] had you but seen his person,   15
    And what a giant's promise it protesteth!
Perez. I have heard of him, and that he hath serv'd before too.
Juan. But no harm done, nor never meant, Don Michael,

---

[1] In this scene Q abbreviates the speech-name of Michael Perez as *Mich.* or *Mi;* elsewhere, as *Per.* I have systematized speech-names.
[2] Ed. 1750 'fills the numbers up' by adding 'up' itself to the line.
[3] Theobald, with less than his usual acumen, suggested 'strong,' and below, with singular perversity, 'strange.' If we distort the text at all the same word should be in both places.
[4] ensign.

That came to my ears yet. Ask him a question,
He blushes like a girl, and answers little, 20
To the point less; he wears a sword, a good one,
And good clothes too; he's whole-skin'd, has no hurt yet;
Good promising hopes; I never yet heard certainly
Of any gentleman that saw him angry.

Perez. Preserve him; he'll conclude a peace if need be. 25
Many as strong as he will go along with us,
That swear as valiantly as heart can wish,
Their mouths charged with six oaths at once, and whole ones,
That make the drunken Dutch creep into mole-hills.

Juan. 'Tis true, such we must look for. But, Michael Perez, 30
When heard you of Donna Margarita, the great heiress?

Perez. I hear every hour of her, though I never saw her;
She is the main discourse. Noble Don Juan de Castro,
How happy were that man could catch this wench up,
And live at ease! She's fair and young, and wealthy, 35
Infinite wealthy, and as gracious too
In all her entertainments, as men report.

Juan. But she is proud, sir, that I know for certain,
And that comes seldom without wantonness:
He that shall marry her, must have a rare hand. 40

Perez. 'Would I were married! I would find that wisdom
With a light rein to rule my wife. If ever woman
Of the most subtlest [1] mould went beyond me,
I'd give the boys leave to hoot me out o' th' parish.

Enter a Servant.

Serv. Sir,
There be two gentlewomen attend to speak with you. 45

Juan. Wait on 'em in.

Perez. Are they two handsome women?

Serv. They seem so, very handsome; but they're veil'd, sir.

Perez. Thou put'st sugar in my mouth; how it melts with me! 50
I love a sweet young wench.

Juan. Wait on them in, I say. *Exit* Serv.

---

[1] So Q; F, 'subtile'—not so well, but followed in the eighteenth century eds.

Perez. Don Juan!

Juan. How you itch, Michael! how you burnish?
 Will not this soldier's heat out of your bones yet?   55
 Do your eyes glow now?

Perez. There be two.

Juan. Say honest;
 What shame [1] have you then?

Perez. I would fain see that: 60
 I have been i' th' Indies twice, and have seen strange things;
 But, two honest women!—One I read of once.

Juan. Pr'ythee, be modest.

Perez. I'll be anything!

  Enter Servant, ESTIFANIA *and* DONNA CLARA *veiled.*

Juan. You're welcome, ladies.   65

Perez. Both hooded! I like 'em well tho'
 They come not for advice in law sure hither!
 May be they'd learn to raise the pike; I am for 'em.
 They are very modest; 'tis a fine preludium. [*Aside.*]

Juan. With me, or with this gentleman, would you speak, lady? 70

Clara. With you, sir, as I guess; Juan de Castro. [*Unveils.*]

Perez. Her curtain opens; she's a pretty gentlewoman.

Juan. I am the man, and shall be bound to fortune,
 I may do any service to your beauties.

Clara. Captain, I hear you're marching down to Flanders, 75
 To serve the Catholic king.

Juan. I am, sweet lady.

Clara. I have a kinsman, and a noble friend,
 Employ'd in those wars; may be, sir, you know him;
 Don Campusano, captain of carbines,   80
 To whom I would request your nobleness
 To give this poor remembrance. [*Gives*] *a letter.*

Juan. I shall do it;
 I know the gentleman, a most worthy captain.

Clara. Something in private.   85

---

[1] Theob. 'what *share*'—again a very bad emendation and worthier of the hero of the *Dunciad* than of the author of certain suggestions on Shakespeare.

Juan. Step aside: I'll serve thee. *Ex[eunt]* JUAN *and* CLARA.
Perez. Pr'ythee, let me see thy face.
Estif. Sir, you must pardon me:
 Women of our sort, that maintain fair memories,
 And keep suspect off from their chastities,
 Had need wear thicker veils.   90
Perez. I am no blaster of a lady's beauty,
 Nor bold intruder on her special favours;
 I know how tender reputation is,
 And with what guards it ought to be preserv'd, lady; 95
 You may to me.
Estif. You must excuse me, signior;
 I come not here to sell myself.
Perez. As I am a gentleman!
 By th' honour of a soldier!   100
Estif. I believe you;
 I pray you be civil; I believe you'd see me,
 And, when you've seen me, I believe you'll like me;
 But in a strange place, to a stranger too,
 As if I came on purpose to betray you!   105
 Indeed, I will not.
Perez. I shall love you dearly;
 And 'tis a sin to fling away affection:
 I have no mistress, no desire to honour
 Any but you.—Will not this oyster open? [*Aside.*] 110
 I know not, you have struck me with your modesty—
 She will draw sure—[*Aside.*]—so deep, and taken from me
 All the desire I might bestow on others—
 Quickly, before they come!
Estif. Indeed, I dare not: 115
 But, since I see you're so desirous, sir,
 To view a poor face that can merit nothing
 But your repentance—
Perez. It must needs be excellent.
Estif. And with what honesty you ask it of me; 120
 When I am gone let your man follow me,
 And view what house I enter; thither come;

For there I dare be bold to appear open,
And, as I like your virtuous carriage, then
I shall be able to give welcome to you—   125

            Enter JUAN, CLA[RA *and*] *a* Servant.

She hath done her business; I must take my leave, sir.
Perez. I'll kiss your fair white hand, and thank you, lady:
    My man shall wait, and I shall be your servant.—
    Sirrah, come near; hark!   [*Whispers.*]
Serv. I shall do it faithfully.   *Exit.* 130
Juan. You will command me no more services?
Clara. To be careful of your noble health, dear sir,
    That I may ever honour you.
Juan. I thank you,
    And kiss your hands.—Wait on the ladies down there! 135
                        Exeunt Ladies *and* Servant.
Perez. You had the honour to see the face that came to you?
Juan. And 'twas a fair one; what was yours, Don Michael?
Perez. Mine was i' th' eclipse, and had a cloud drawn over it;
    But, I believe, well, and I hope 'tis handsome;
    She had a hand would stir a holy hermit.   140
Juan. You know none of 'em?
Perez. No.
Juan. Then I do, captain;
    But I'll say nothing till I see the proof on't.—
    Sit close, Don Perez, or your worship's caught: 145
    I fear a fly.[1]   [*Aside.*]
Perez. Were those she brought love-letters?
Juan. A packet to a kinsman now in Flanders.
    Yours was very modest, methought.
Perez. Some young unmanaged thing: 150
    But I may live to see—
Juan. 'Tis worth experience.
    Let's walk abroad, and view our companies.   *Exeunt.*[2]

---

[1] In the angling sense—a gay bait with a barb in it.
[2] Q, *Exit.*

[Act I.   Scene II.   *The Street*.]

Enter SANCHIO *and* ALONZO.

Sanc. What, are you for the wars, Alonzo?
Alon. It may be ay,
    It may be no; e'en as the humour takes me.
    If I find peace among the female creatures,
    And easy entertainment, I'll stay at home;   5
    I'm not so far oblig'd yet to long marches
    And mouldy biscuits, to run mad for honour.
    When you are all gone, I have my choice before me.
Sanc. Of which hospital thou'lt sweat in. Wilt thou never
    Leave whoring?   10
Alon. There is less danger in't than gunning, Sanchio:
    Though we be shot sometimes, the shot's not mortal;
    Besides, it breaks no limbs.
Sanc. But it disables 'em; dost thou see how thou pull'st
    Thy legs after thee, as they hung by points?   15
Alon. Better to pull 'em thus, than walk on wooden ones;
    Serve bravely for a billet to support me.
Sanc. Fie, fie! 'tis base.
Alon. Dost thou count it base to suffer?
    Suffer abundantly? 'tis the crown of honour.   20
    You think it nothing to lie twenty days
    Under a surgeon's hands, that has no mercy.
Sanc. As thou hast done, I am sure. But I perceive now
    Why you desire to stay; the Orient [1] heiress,
    The Margarita, sir!   25
Alon. I would I had her.
Sanc. They say she will marry.
Alon. Yes, I think she will.
Sanc. And marry suddenly, as report goes, too!
    She fears her youth will not hold out, Alonzo.   30
Alon. I would I had the sheathing on't.

---

[1] 'Orient,'—of course merely a play on the 'pearl'-meaning of *Margarita*.

Sanc. They say too
    She has a greedy eye, that must be fed
    With more than one man's meat.
Alon. 'Would she were mine!   35
    I would cater for her well enough. But, Sanchio,
    There be too many great men that adore her;
    Princes, and princes' fellows, that claim privilege.
Sanc. Yet those stand off i' th' way of marriage,
    To be tied to a man's pleasure is a second labour.[1]   40
Alon. She has bought a brave house here in town.
Sanc. I've heard so.
Alon. If she convert it now to pious uses,
    And bid poor gentlemen welcome!
Sanc. When comes she to it?   45
Alon. Within these two days; she's i' th' country yet,
    And keeps the noblest house!
Sanc. Then there's some hope of her.
    Wilt thou go my way?
Alon. No, no, I must leave you,   50
    And repair to an old gentlewoman
    That has credit with her, that can speak a good word.
Sanc. Send thee good fortune! but make thy body sound first.
Alon. I am a soldier, and too sound a body
    Becomes me not. Farewell, Sanchio!   *Exeunt.*[2]

[1] Monck Mason rather stupidly suggested, and Dyce very strangely adopts, as a gloss on this 'To obtain a man's pleasure is the first labour: to be tied to it a second.' Fletcher never said anything so insipid. 'Labour' and 'pleasure' are *opposed;* and the suggestion is that to be tied to a pleasure makes it cease to be *pleasure* at all and become another kind of ('a second') *labour.*

[2] Q, *Exit.*

[Act I. Scene III. *The Same.*]

Enter a Servant *of* MICHAEL PEREZ.

Serv. 'Tis this or that house, or I've lost my aim;
    They are both fair buildings. She walked plaguy fast;

              Ent[er] ESTIF[ANIA].

    And hereabouts I lost her.—Stay! that's she,
    'Tis very she. She makes me a low court'sy.
    Let me note the place; the street I will [1] remember.   5

           Exit [ESTIFANIA *into a house*].

    She's in again. Certain some noble lady:
    How happy should I be if she love my master!
    A wondrous goodly house; here are brave lodgings,
    And I shall sleep now like an emperor,
    And eat abundantly. I thank my fortune!   10
    I'll back with speed, and bring him happy tidings.   *Exit.*

[Act I. Scene IV. *The Country. An Apartment in the Villa of Margarita.*]

Enter three old Ladies.

1 Lady. [2] What should it mean, that in such haste we're sent for?
2 Lady. Belike the lady Margaret has some business
    She'd break to us in private.
3 Lady. It should seem so.
    'Tis a good lady, and a wise young lady.   5
2 Lady. And virtuous enough too, I warrant ye,
    For a young woman of her years: 'Tis pity
    To load her tender age with too much virtue.
3 Lady. 'Tis more sometimes than we can well away with. [3]

---

[1] Q, 'well.'   [2] Q, omitting *Lady*, has 1, 2, 3, throughout.
[3] The ignorance of modern critics has been known to object to this excellent idiom, which occurs in the Bible (Isaiah i. 13) and elsewhere. It probably conveys the sense of 'swallowing,' not, as Richardson thought, of 'moving in unison with.'

Enter ALTEA.

Altea. Good morrow, ladies!   10
All. Morrow, my good madam!
1 Lady. How does the sweet young beauty, Lady Margaret?
2 Lady. Has she slept well after her walk last night?
1 Lady. Are her dreams gentle to her mind?
Altea. All's well;   15
    She's very well; she sent for you thus suddenly,
    To give her counsel in a business
    That much concerns her.
2 Lady. She does well and wisely,
    To ask the counsel of the ancient'st, madam;   20
    Our years have run through many things she knows not.
Altea. She would fain marry.
1 Lady. 'Tis a proper calling,
    And well beseems her years. Who would she yoke with?
Altea. That's left to argue on. I pray come in,   25
    And break your fast; drink a good cup or two,
    To strengthen your understandings; then she'll tell ye.
2 Lady. And good wine breeds good counsel; we'll yield to ye.
                                     Exeunt.

[Act I. Scene V. *Valladolid. The Street.*]

Enter JUAN DE CASTRO *and* LEON.

Juan. Have you seen any service?
Leon. Yes.
Juan. Where?
Leon. Everywhere.
Juan. What office bore you?   5
Leon. None; I was not worthy.
Juan. What captains know you?
Leon. None; they were above me.
Juan. Were you never hurt?
Leon. Not that I well remember,   10

But once I stole a hen, and then they beat me.
Pray ask me no long questions; I have an ill memory.
Juan. This is an ass.—Did you never draw your sword yet?
Leon. Not to do any harm, I thank Heaven for't.
Juan. Nor ne'er ta'en prisoner?   15
Leon. No, I ran away,
For I had ne'er no money to redeem me.
Juan. Can you endure a drum?
Leon. It makes my head ache.
Juan. Are you not valiant when you're drunk?   20
Leon. I think not;
But I am loving, sir.
Juan. What a lump is this man!—
Was your father wise?
Leon. Too wise for me, I'm sure;   25
For he gave all he had to my younger brother.
Juan. That was no foolish part, I'll bear you witness.
Canst thou lie with a woman?
Leon. I think I could make shift, sir;
But I am bashful.   30
Juan. In the night?
Leon. I know not;
Darkness indeed may do some good upon me.
Juan. Why art thou sent to me to be my officer,
Ay, and commended too, when thou dar'st not fight?   35
Leon. There be more officers of my opinion,
Or I am cozen'd, sir; men that talk more too.
Juan. How wilt thou 'scape a bullet?
Leon. Why, by chance;
They aim at honourable men; alas, I am none, sir.   40
Juan. This fellow has some doubts in's talk, that strike me;
He cannot be all fool.—

Ent[er] ALONZO.[1]

Welcome, Alonzo!
Alon. What have you got there?   Temperance into

---

[1] Q, *Ent. Alonzo*, before 'He cannot be all foole.' On stage-directions see Appendix *B.—Gen. Ed.*

Your company? the spirit of peace? we shall have wars   45
By the ounce then.—

Ent[er] CACA[FOGO].

Oh, here's another pumpion;
Let him loose for luck sake, the cramm'd son
Of a starv'd usurer, Cacafogo,
Both their brains butter'd cannot make two spoonfuls.   50
Cac. My father's dead; I am a man of war too.
Monies, demesnes; I have ships at sea too, captains.
Juan. Take heed o' th' Hollanders; your ships may leak else.
Cac. I scorn the Hollanders; they are my drunkards.
Alon. Put up your gold, sir; I will borrow it else.   55
Cac. I'm satisfied, you shall not.—Come out; I know thee;
Meet mine anger instantly!
Leon. I never wronged ye.
Cac. Thou hast wrong'd mine honour;
Thou look'dst [1] upon my mistress thrice lasciviously;   60
I'll make it good.
Juan. Do not heat yourself; you will surfeit.
Cac. Thou wan'st [2] my money too, with a pair of base bones,
In whom there was no truth; for which I beat thee,
I beat thee much; now I will hurt thee dangerously;   65
This shall provoke thee.   *He strikes* [*him*].
Alon. You struck too low by a foot, sir.
Juan. You must get a ladder when you'd beat this fellow.
Leon. I cannot chuse but kick again; pray pardon me! [*Kicks him.*]
Cac. Had'st thou not ask'd my pardon, I had kill'd thee.   70
I leave thee as a thing despis'd! *Beso las manos a vuestra
señoria!* [3]   *Exit* CACA.

---

[1] Q, 'look'st.'

[2] So Q. Editors variously 'want'st' 'wann'st,' etc. The required meaning is undoubted.

[3] Theobald first put this into something like Spanish, and Dyce into Spanish itself. Q and F have a good example of the wonderful gibberish which usually does duty for foreign languages in seventeenth-century printing. *Assoles manus a vostra siniare a Maistre.* 'A very acute Spaniard to whom I [Dyce] submitted the Spanish was unable to conjecture what the last two words meant.' But surely it requires no extraordinary acuteness in an Englishman to see that '*a Maistre*' is a clumsy *French* gloss on '*a siniare,*' *i. e.* 'señoria.'

Alon. You have 'scap'd by miracle, there is not, in all Spain,
    A spirit of more fury than this fire-drake.
Leon. I see he's hasty; and I would give him leave
    To beat me soundly, if he would take my bond.   75
Juan. What shall I do with this fellow?
Alon. Turn him off:
    He will infect the camp with cowardice,
    If he go with thee.
Juan. About some week hence, sir,   80
    If I can hit upon no abler officer,
    You shall hear from me.
Leon. I desire no better.   *Exeunt.*[1]

[Act I. Scene VI. *A Splendid Apartment in Margarita's Town House.*]

Enter ESTIFANIA *and* PEREZ.

Perez. You have made me now too bountiful amends, lady,
    For your strict carriage when you saw me first.
    These beauties were not meant to be conceal'd;
    It was a wrong to hide so sweet an object;
    I could now chide you, but it shall be thus.   [*Kisses her.*] 5
    No other anger ever touch your sweetness!
Estif. You appear to me so honest and so civil,
    Without a blush, sir, I dare bid you welcome.
Perez. Now let me ask your name.
Estif. 'Tis Estifania: 10
    The heir of this poor place.
Perez. Poor, do you call it?
    There's nothing that I cast mine eyes upon,
    But shews both rich and admirable; all the rooms
    Are hung as if a princess were to dwell here;   15
    The gardens, orchards, every thing so curious!
    Is all that plate your own, too?
Estif. 'Tis but little,

[1] Q, *Exit.*

Only for present use; I have more and richer,
When need shall call, or friends compel me use it.   20
The suits you see of all the upper chambers
Are those that commonly adorn the house:
I think I have, besides, as fair as Sevil,[1]
Or any town in Spain can parallel.

Perez [*aside*]. Now if she be not married, I have some hopes.—25
    Are you a maid?

Estif. You make me blush to answer;
    I ever was accounted so to this hour,
    And that's the reason that I live retir'd, sir.

Perez. Then would I counsel you to marry presently,   30
    —If I get can her, I am made for ever—   [*Aside.*]
    For every year you lose, you lose a beauty;
    A husband now, an honest careful husband,
    Were such a comfort! Will you walk above stairs?

Estif. This place will fit our talk; 'tis fitter far, sir;   35
    Above there are day-beds, and such temptations
    I dare not trust, sir.—

Perez. She is excellent wise withal too.—   [*Aside.*]

Estif. You nam'd a husband; I am not so strict, sir,
    Nor tied unto a virgin's solitariness,   40
    But if an honest, and a noble one,
    Rich, and a soldier (for so I have vow'd he shall be)
    Were offer'd me, I think I should accept him;
    But, above all, he must love.

Perez. He were base else.—   45
    There's comfort minister'd in the word soldier.
    How sweetly should I live!   [*Aside.*]

Estif. I am not so ignorant,
    But that I know well how to be commanded,
    And how again to make myself obey'd, sir.   50
    I waste but little, I have gather'd much;
    My rial not the less worth, when 'tis spent,
    If spent by my direction; to please my husband,

---

[1] Q, 'civill,' an obvious phonetic misprint, which puzzled some one concerned with F, and made him read, 'as fair, as civil, *as* any town.'

I hold it as indifferent in my duty,
To be his maid i' th' kitchen, or his cook,   55
As in the hall to know myself the mistress.
Perez. Sweet, rich, and provident! now fortune stick to me!—
                                                     [*Aside.*]
    I am a soldier, and a bachelor, lady;
And such a wife as you I could love infinitely;
They that use many words, some are deceitful: 60
I long to be a husband, and a good one;
For 'tis most certain I shall make a precedent
For all that follow me to love their ladies.
I'm young, you see, able I'd have you think too;
If't please you know, try me, before you take me.   65
'Tis true, I shall not meet in equal wealth with you;
But jewels, chains, such as the war has given me,
A thousand ducats [1] I dare presume on
In ready gold (now as your care may handle it)
As rich clothes too as any he bears arms, lady!   70
Estif. You are a true gentleman, and fair, I see by ye:
   And such a man I'd rather take—
Perez.   'Pray do so!
   I'll have a priest o' th' sudden.
Estif.   And as suddenly   75
   You will repent too.
Perez.   I'll be hang'd or drown'd first,
   By this, and this, and this kiss!   [*Kisses her.*]
Estif.   You are a flatterer;
   But I must say there was something when I saw you first,   80
   In that most noble face that stirr'd my fancy.
Perez. I'll stir it better ere you sleep, sweet lady.
   I'll send for all my trunks, and give up all to ye,
   Into your own dispose, before I bed ye;
   And then, sweet wench—   85
Estif. You have the art to cozen me.   *Exeunt.*

---

[1] This passage greatly disturbed the eighteenth-century believers in rigid deca-
syllables. First in 1754 Seward inserted 'too,' and later editors, including Darley,
rearranged the whole context at their discretion. The text is good enough for the
beginning of the decadence. [For the line-scheme of Q, see Appendix *A*. *Gen. Ed.*]

Act II. Scene I. [*The Country.—An Apartment in the Villa of Margarita.*]

Enter MARGARITA, *two* Ladies, *and* ALTEA.[1]

Marg. Sit down, and give me your opinions seriously.
1 Lady. You say you have a mind to marry, lady?
Marg. 'Tis true, I have, for to preserve my credit;
    Yet not so much for that as for my state, ladies;
    Conceive me right, there lies the main o' th' question: 5
    Credit I can redeem, money will imp it;
    But when my money's gone, when the law shall
    Seize that, and for incontinency strip me of all?
1 Lady. D'ye find your body so malicious that way?
Marg. I find it as all bodies are that are young and lusty,   10
    Lazy, and high fed; I desire my pleasure,
    And pleasure I must have.
2 Lady. 'Tis fit you should have;
    Your years require it, and 'tis necessary,
    As necessary as meat to a young lady;   15
    Sleep cannot nourish more.
1 Lady. But might not all this be, and keep you single?
    You take away variety in marriage,
    The abundance of the pleasure you are barr'd then;
    Is't not abundance that you aim at?   20
Marg. Yes;
    Why was I made a woman?
2 Lady. And every day a new?
Marg. Why fair and young, but to use it?
1 Lady. You are still i' th' right; why would [2] you marry then? 25
Altea. Because a husband stops all doubts in this point,
    And clears all passages.
2 Lady. What husband mean ye?

    [1] In Q Altea is given in the speeches as '4,' which puzzled editors before Weber, but, as he and all since have seen, there is no real difficulty. In the order of speech Marg. is 1, the Ladies 2 and 3, and Altea 4. Q omits *Lady*.
    [2] Wrongly altered to 'should' by 1778, Weber and Darley.

Altea. A husband of an easy faith, a fool,
 Made by her wealth, and moulded to her pleasure; 30
 One, though he see himself become a monster,
 Shall hold the door, and entertain the maker.

2 Lady. You grant there may be such a man.

1 Lady. Yes, marry;
 But how to bring 'em to this rare perfection? 35

2 Lady. They must be chosen so; things of no honour,
 Nor outward honesty.

Marg. No, 'tis no matter;
 I care not what they are, so they be lusty.

2 Lady. Methinks now, a rich lawyer; some such fellow, 40
 That carries credit and a face of awe,
 But lies with nothing but his clients' business.

Marg. No, there's no trusting them: they are too subtle;
 The law has moulded 'em of natural mischief.

1 Lady. Then, some grave governor, 45
 Some man of honour, yet an easy man.

Marg. If he have honour I'm undone; I'll none such:
 I'll have a lusty man; honour will cloy me.

Altea. 'Tis fit you should, lady;
 And to that end, with search, and wit, and labour, 50
 I have found one out, a right one and a perfect;
 He is made as strong as brass, is of brave years too,
 And doughty of complexion.

Marg. Is he a gentleman?

Altea. Yes, and a soldier; as gentle as you would wish him; 55
 A good fellow, wears good clothes.

Marg. Those I'll allow him;
 They are for my credit.   Does he understand
 But little?

Altea. Very little. 60

Marg. 'Tis the better.
 Have not the wars bred him up to anger?

Altea. No;
 He will not quarrel with a dog that bites him;
 Let him be drunk or sober, he's one silence. 65

Marg. [He] has no capacity what honour is?
　For that's the soldier's god.
Altea. Honour's a thing too subtile for his wisdom;
　If honour lie in eating, he's right honourable.
Marg. Is he so goodly a man, d'ye say?　　　　　　70
Altea. As you shall see, lady;
　But, to all this, he's but a trunk.
Marg. I would have him so,
　I shall add branches to him to adorn him.
　Go, find me out this man, and let me see him;　75
　If he be that motion that you tell me of,
　And make no more noise, I shall entertain him.
　Let him be here.
Altea. He shall attend your ladyship.　　　　　*Exeunt.*

[Act II. Scene II. *Valladolid.—The Lodgings of Don
Juan.*]

Enter JUAN, ALONZO, *and* PEREZ.

Juan. Why, thou art not married indeed?
Perez. No, no; pray think so.
　Alas, I am a fellow of no reckoning,
　Not worth a lady's eye!
Alon. Wouldst thou steal a fortune,　　　　　5
　And make none of all thy friends acquainted with it,
　Nor bid us to thy wedding?
Perez. No, indeed!
　There was no wisdom in't, to bid an artist,
　An old seducer, to a female banquet!　　　　　10
　I can cut up my pye without your instructions.
Juan. Was it the wench i' th' veil?
Perez. Basta! 'twas she;
　The prettiest rogue that e'er you looked upon,
　The loving'st thief!　　　　　　　　　　　15

Juan. And is she rich withal too?
Perez. A mine, a mine! there is no end of wealth, colonel.
  I am an ass, a bashful fool! Pr'ythee, colonel,
  How do thy companies fill now?
Juan. You are merry, sir;   20
  You intend a safer war at home, belike now?
Perez. I do not think I shall fight much this year, colonel;
  I find myself given to my ease a little.
  I care not if I sell my foolish company;
  They are things of hazard.   25
Alon. How it angers me,   [*Aside.*]
  This fellow at first sight should win a lady,
  A rich young wench; and I, that have consum'd
  My time and art in searching out their subtleties,
  Like a fool'd alchemist, blow up my hopes still!—   30
  When shall we come to thy house and be freely merry?
Perez. When I have manag'd her a little more;
  I have a house to entertain an army.
Alon. If thy wife be fair, thou'lt have few less come to thee.
Perez. But where they'll get entertainment is the point, signior; 35
  I beat no drum.
Alon. You need none but her tabor.
*Perez.*¹ May be I'll march, after a month or two
  To get me a fresh stomach. I find, colonel,
  A wantonness in wealth, methinks I agree not with;   40
  'Tis such a trouble to be married too,
  And have a thousand things of great importance,
  Jewels, and plates ² and fooleries, molest me;
  To have a man's brains whimsied with his wealth!
  Before, I walk'd contentedly.   45

---

¹ By the omission of Perez's name in Q and F the whole speech was assigned to Alonzo, making sheer nonsense.

² Dyce altered this to 'plate,' disagreeing with Nares, who cites the passage with others, as illustrating the use of the plural for 'silver coins.' But though 'plate' suits the sense rather better, and certainly occurs elsewhere in the play, it seems a very strong measure to make the alteration in the text not merely of Q and F, but of the passages in Shakespeare (*A. and C.*), and Marlowe (*Jew of Malta*), which give 'plates' for coins.

Enter Servant.

Serv. My Mistress, sir, is sick, because you are absent;
    She mourns, and will not eat.
Perez. Alas, my jewel!
    Come, I'll go with thee.—Gentlemen, your fair leaves!
    You see I am tied a little to my yoke;   50
    Pray pardon me! 'would ye had both such loving wives!
Juan. I thank you   *Ex[eunt]* PEREZ [*and*] Serv[ant].
    For your old boots!—Never be blank, Alonzo,
    Because this fellow has outstript thy fortune!
    Tell me ten days hence what he is, and how   55
    The gracious state of matrimony stands with him.
    Come, let's to dinner. When Margarita comes,
    We'll visit both; it may be then your fortune.   *Exeunt.*

[Act II. Scene III. *The Country.—An Apartment in
Margarita's Villa.*]

Ent[er] MARGARITA, ALTEA, [*and*] *the* Ladies.[1]

Marg. Is he come?
Altea. Yes, madam; [he] has been here this half hour.
    I have question'd him of all that you can ask him,
    And find him as fit as you had made the man:
    He'll make the goodliest shadow for iniquity!   5
Marg. Have ye search'd him, ladies?
Omnes.[2] He's a man at all points, a likely man!
Marg. Call him in, Altea.

    [*Exit* ALTEA, *and re-enters with* LEON.][3]

    A man of a good presence!—Pray you come this way,—
    Of a lusty body: Is his mind so tame?   10
Altea. Pray ye question him; and if you find him not

---

    [1] The numerical muddle referred to above, Sc. i., has again caused difficulties
in the heading and speech-numbering of this scene. As before there are *two* 'ladies,'
and Altea as the fourth personage, is indicated by 4.
    [2] Q, 'Omnes. Is a man.'
    [3] Q has '*Exit Lady*,' l. 8; margin; and underneath—'*Ent. Leon, Altea.*'

Fit for your purpose, shake him off; there's no harm done.

Marg. Can you love a young lady?—How he blushes!

Altea. Leave twirling of your hat, [and] hold you head up,
 And speak to th' lady.   15

Leon. Yes, I think I can;
 I must be taught; I know not what it means, madam.

Marg. You shall be taught. And can you, when she pleases,
 Go ride abroad, and stay a week or two?
 You shall have men and horses to attend ye,   20
 And money in your purse.

Leon. Yes, I love riding;
 And when I am from home I am so merry!

Marg. Be as merry as you will. Can you as handsomely,
 When you are sent for back, come with obedience,   25
 And do your duty to the lady loves you?

Leon. Yes, sure, I shall.

Marg. And when you see her friends here,
 Or noble kinsmen, can you entertain
 Their servants in the cellar, and be busied,   30
 And hold your peace, whate'er you see or hear of?

Leon. 'Twere fit I were hang'd else.

Marg. Let me try your kisses.   [*Kisses him.*]
 How the fool shakes!—I will not eat you, sir.—
 Beshrew my heart, he kisses wondrous manly!—   35
 Can you do anything else?

Leon. Indeed, I know not;
 But if your ladyship will please to instruct me,
 Sure I shall learn.

Marg. You shall then be instructed.   40
 If I should be this lady that affects you,
 Nay, say I marry you—

Altea. Hark to the lady.

Marg. What money have you?

Leon. None, madam, nor friends.   45
 I would do anything to serve your ladyship.

Marg. You must not look to be my master,[1] sir,

¹ Q, 'Mr.'

Nor talk i' th' house as though you wore the breeches;
No, nor command in anything.

Leon. I will not;   50
    Alas, I am not able; I have no wit, madam.

Marg. Nor do not labour to arrive at any;
    'Twill spoil your head. I take ye upon charity,
    And like a servant you must be unto me;
    As I behold your duty I shall love ye,   55
    And, as you observe me, I may chance lie with ye,
    Can you mark these?

Leon. Yes, indeed, forsooth.

Marg. There is one thing,
    That if I take you in I put ye from me,   60
    Utterly from me; you must not be saucy,
    No, nor at any time familiar with me;
    Scarce know me, when I call ye not.

Leon. I will not.
    Alas, I never knew myself sufficiently.   65

Marg. Nor must not now.

Leon. I'll be a dog to please ye.

Marg. Indeed, you must fetch and carry as I appoint ye.

Leon. I were to blame else.

Marg. Kiss me again.—A strong fellow!   70
    There is a vigour in his lips:—If you see me
    Kiss any other, twenty in an hour, sir,
    You must not start, nor be offended.

Leon. No,
    If you kiss a thousand I shall be contented;   75
    It will the better teach me how to please ye!

Altea. I told ye, madam!

Marg. 'Tis the man I wished for.—
    The less you speak—

Leon. I'll never speak again, madam,   80
    But when you charge me; then I'll speak softly too.

Marg. Get me a priest; I'll wed him instantly.—
    But when you are married, sir, you must wait upon me,
    And see you observe my laws.

Leon. Else you shall hang me.   85
Marg. I'll give ye better clothes when you deserve 'em.—
  Come in, and serve for witnesses.
Omnes. We shall, madam.
Marg. And then away to th' city presently;
  I'll to my new house and new company. [*Exit with* Ladies.] 90
Leon. A thousand crowns are thine; and [1] I am a made man.
Altea. Do not break out too soon!
Leon. I know my time, wench.
                                                                  Exeunt.

[Act **II.** Scene **IV.** *Valladolid.—A Room in Margarita's House.*]

Enter CLARA *and* ESTIFANIA, *with a paper.*

Clara. What, have you caught him?
Estif. Yes.
Clara. And do you find him
  A man of those hopes that you aim'd at?
Estif. Yes, too;   5
  And the most kind man, and the ablest also
  To give a wife content! He's sound as old wine,
  And to his soundness rises on the palate;
  And there's the man! I find him rich too, Clara.
Clara. Hast thou married him?   10
Estif. What, dost thou think I fish without a bait, wench?
  I bob for fools? He is mine own, I have him.
  I told thee what would tickle him like a trout;
  And, as I cast it, so I caught him daintily,
  And all he has I have stow'd at my devotion.   15
Clara. Does thy lady know this? She's coming now to town,
  Now to live here in this house.
Estif. Let her come;

---

[1] Dyce, taking the '&' of Q and the 'and' of F as ='an'='if,' prints 'an'. I am not so sure of this. Altea's answer seems to show that she thought the 'making' complete, and was only afraid of Leon's showing his hand prematurely.

She shall be welcome, I am prepared for her;
She is mad sure if she be angry at my fortune,   20
For what I have made bold.
Clara. Dost thou not love him?
Estif. Yes, entirely well,
  As long as there he stays, and looks no further
  Into my ends; but when he doubts, I hate him,   25
  And that wise hate will teach me how to cozen him.
  [A lady-tamer he, and reads men warnings,] [1]
  How to decline their wives and curb their manners,
  To put a stern and strong rein to their natures;
  And holds he is an ass not worth acquaintance,   30
  That cannot mould a devil to obedience.
  I owe him a good turn for these opinions,
  And, as I find his temper, I may pay him.

Enter PEREZ.

  Oh, here he is; now you shall see a kind man.
Perez. My Estifania! shall we to dinner, lamb?   35
  I know thou stay'st for me.
Estif. I cannot eat else.
Perez. I never enter, but methinks a paradise
  Appears about me.
Estif. You are welcome to it, sir.   40
Perez. I think I have the sweetest seat in Spain, wench;
  Methinks the richest too. We'll eat i' the garden,
  In one o' th' arbours, (there 'tis cool and pleasant,)
  And have our wine cool'd [2] in the running fountain.
  Who's that?   45
Estif. A friend of mine, sir.
Perez. Of what breeding?
Estif. A gentlewoman, sir.
Perez. What business has she?
  Is she a learned woman i' th' mathematics?   50

---

[1] There is no authority for this line, which was inserted by Seward; but as something of the kind had clearly dropped out, it has been accepted ever since.
[2] Q has 'cold.'

Can she tell fortunes?

Estif. More than I know, sir.

Perez. Or has she e'er a letter from a kinswoman,
That must be deliver'd in my absence, wife?
Or comes she from the doctor to salute you,   55
And learn your health?   She looks not like a confessor.

Estif. What need all this? why are you troubled, sir?
What do you suspect? she cannot cuckold you;
She is a woman, sir, a very woman.

Perez. Your very woman may do very well, sir,   60
Toward the matter; for, though she cannot perform it
In her own person, she may do it by proxy:
Your rarest jugglers work still by conspiracy.

Estif. Cry ye mercy, husband! you are jealous then,
And happily suspect me?   65

Perez. No, indeed, wife.

Estif. Methinks you should not till you have more cause,
And clearer too.   I am sure you have heard say, husband,
A woman forc'd will free herself through iron;
A happy, calm, and good wife, discontented,   70
May be taught tricks.

Perez. No, no, I do but jest with you.

Estif. To-morrow, friend, I'll see you.

Clara. I shall leave you
Till then, and pray all may go sweetly with you.   75
                    Exit. Knock[*ing within*].

Estif. Why, where's this girl?   Who's at the door?

Perez. Who knocks there?
Is't for the king you come, you knock so boist'rously?
Look to the door.

Enter Maid.

Maid [*apart to* Estif.] My lady! as I live, mistress, my lady's   80
    come!
She's at the door; I peeped through, and I saw her,
And a stately company of ladies with her.

Estif. This was a week too soon; but I must meet with her,

And set a new wheel going, and a subtile one,   85
Must blind this mighty Mars, or I am ruin'd.

Perez. What are they at door?

Estif. Such, my Michael,
As you may bless the day they enter'd here;
Such for our good!   90

Perez. 'Tis well.

Estif. Nay, 'twill be better
If you will let me but dispose the business,
And be a stranger to't, and not disturb me:
What have I now to do but to advance your fortune?   95

Perez. Do; I dare trust thee. I am ashamed I am [1] angry;
I find thee a wise young wife.

Estif. [*apart*]. I'll wise your worship
Before I leave you!—'Pray you walk by, and say nothing,
Only salute them,[2] and leave the rest to me, sir: 100
I was born to make you a man.   [*Exit.*]

Perez. The rogue speaks heartily;
Her good will colours in her cheeks; I am born to love her.
I must be gentler to these tender natures;
A soldier's rude harsh words befit not ladies,   105
Nor must we talk to them as we talk to our officers.
I'll give her way, for 'tis for me she works now;
I am husband, heir, and all she has.

Enter MARG[ARITA,] ESTIF[ANIA,] LEON, ALTEA, *and* Ladies.

Who are these? what flanting things?   A woman
Of rare presence! excellent fair! This is too big   110
For a bawdy-house, too open-seated too.

Estif. My husband, lady!

Marg. You have gain'd a proper man.

Perez. Whate'er I am, I am your servant, lady.   *Kisses her*[3].

Estif. [*apart to* PEREZ]. Sir, be rul'd now, and I shall make ye
rich: 116
This is my cousin; that gentleman dotes on her,

---

[1] Seward altered 'am' to 'was' which Dyce accepts, I think, unnecessarily.
[2] Q, 'him.'   [3] Q, '*Kisses Estif.*'

Even to death; see how he observes her.
Perez. She is a goodly woman.
Estif. She's a mirror, 120
    But she is poor; she were for a prince's side else.
    This house she has brought him to, as to her own,
    And presuming upon me, and upon my courtesy,—
    (Conceive me short),—he knows not but she's wealthy:
    Or, if he did know otherwise, 'twere all one, 125
    He's so far gone
Perez. Forward. She has a rare face.
Estif. This we must carry with discretion, husband,
    And yield unto her for four days.
Perez. Yield our house up, 130
    Our goods, and wealth?
Estif. All this is but in seeming,
    To milk the lover on. D'you see this writing?
    Two hundred pound a-year, when they are married,
    Has she seal'd to [1] for our good: The time's unfit now; 135
    I'll shew it you to-morrow.
Perez. All the house?
Estif. All, all, and we'll remove too, to confirm him;
    They'll into th' country suddenly again
    After they are match'd, and then she'll open to him. 140
Perez. The whole possession, wife? Look what you do.
    A part o' th' house—
Estif. No, no, they shall have all,
    And take their pleasure too; 'tis for our 'vantage.
    Why, what's four days? Had you a sister, sir, 145
    A niece or mistress, that requir'd this courtesy,
    And should I make a scruple to do you good?
Perez. If easily it would come back—
Estif. I swear, sir,
    As easily as it came on. Is it not pity 150
    To let such a gentlewoman for a little help?
    You give away no house.
Perez. Clear but that question.

                 [1] Q, 'too.'

Estif. I'll put the writings into your hand.
Perez. Well then.　　　　　　　　　　　　　　　　　　　155
Estif. And you shall keep them safe.
Perez. I'm satisfied.
　　　'Would I had the wench so too.
Estif. When she has married him,
　　　So infinite his love is link'd unto her,　　　　　160
　　　You, I, or any one that helps at this pinch,
　　　May have Heaven knows what.
Perez. I'll remove the goods straight,
　　　And take some poor house by; 'tis but for four days.
Estif. I have a poor old friend; there we'll be.　　　165
Perez. 'Tis well then.
Estif. Go handsome off, and leave the house clear.
Perez. Well.
Estif. That little stuff we'll use shall follow after,
　　　And a boy to guide ye.　Peace, and we are made both!　170
　　　　　　　　　　　　　　　　　　Exit PER[EZ].
Marg. Come, let's go in.　Are all the rooms kept sweet, wench?
Estif. They're sweet and neat.
Marg. Why, where's your husband?
Estif. Gone, madam.
　　　When you come to your own, he must give place, lady.　175
Marg. Well, send you joy!　You would not let me know't,
　　　Yet I shall not forget ye.
Estif. Thank your ladyship!　　　　　　　　　　　*Exeunt.*

Act III.　Scene I.　[*An Apartment in Margarita's House.*]

　　　　Enter MARGARITA, ALTEA, *and* Boy.

Altea.[1] Are you at ease now? is your heart at rest,
　　　Now you have got a shadow, an umbrella,
　　　To keep the scorching world's opinion

　　　[1] Q indicates *Altea* by 4, in all speech-headings but the first.

From your fair credit?

Marg. I'm at peace, Altea: 5
    If he continue but the same he shews,
    And be a master of that ignorance
    He outwardly professes, I am happy.
    The pleasure I shall live in, and the freedom,
    Without the squint-eye of the law upon me,   10
    Or prating liberty of tongues, that envy!

Altea. You are a made woman.

Marg. But if he should prove now
    A crafty and dissembling kind of husband,
    One read in knavery, and brought up in the art   15
    Of villainy conceal'd?

Altea. 'My life, an innocent.

Marg. That's it I aim at,
    That's it I hope too; then I'm sure I rule him;
    For innocents are like obedient children   20
    Brought up under a hard mother-in-law, a cruel,
    Who being not us'd to breakfasts and collations,
    When they have coarse [1] bread offer'd 'em, are thankful,
    And take it for a favour too. Are the rooms
    Made ready to entertain my friends?   25
    I long to dance now, and to be wanton;
    Let me have a song. Is the great couch up
    The Duke of Medina sent?

Altea. 'Tis up and ready.

Marg. And day-beds in all chambers?   30

Altea. In all, lady;
    Your house is nothing now but various pleasures;
    The gallants begin to gaze too.

Marg. Let 'em gaze on;
    I was brought up a courtier, high and happy,   35
    And company is my delight, and courtship,
    And handsome servants at my will. Where's my good hus-
        band?
    Where does he wait?

                 [1] Q, 'course.'

Altea. He knows his distance, madam;   40
  I warrant you he's busy in the cellar,
  Amongst his fellow-servants, or asleep,
  'Till your command awake him.
Marg. 'Tis well, Altea;
  It should be so; my ward I must preserve him.—   45

Enter LEON [*and* Servant].

Who sent for him? how dare he come uncall'd for?
His bonnet on too!
Altea. Sure he sees you not.
Marg. How scornfully he looks!
Leon. Are all the chambers   50
  Deck'd and adorn'd thus for my lady's pleasure?
  New hangings every hour for entertainment,
  And new plate bought, new jewels, to give lustre?
Serv. They are, and yet there must be more and richer;
  It is her will.   55
Leon. Hum. Is it so? 'tis excellent.
  It is her will, too, to have feasts and banquets,
  Revels, and masques?
Serv. She ever lov'd 'em dearly,
  And we shall have the bravest house kept now, sir!   60
  I must not call ye master (she has warn'd me)
  Nor must not put my hat off to ye.
Leon. 'Tis no fashion;
  What though I be her husband, I am your fellow.
  I may cut first?   65
Serv. That's as you shall deserve, sir.
Leon. And when I lie with her—
Serv. May be I'll light ye;
  On the same point you may do me that service.

Enter a Lady.[1]

1 Lady. Madam, the Duke Medina, with some captains,   70
  Will come to dinner, and have sent rare wine,
  And their best services.

[1] Q, *1 Lady.*

Marg. They shall be welcome.
 See all be ready in the noblest fashion,
 The house perfum'd. Now I shall take my pleasure, 75
 And not my neighbour Justice maunder at me.—
 Go, get your best clothes on; but, till I call ye,
 Be sure you be not seen. Dine with the gentlewomen,
 And behave yourself cleanly, sir; 'tis for my credit.

    Enter a second Lady.[1]

2 Lady. Madam, the lady Julia—   80
Leon. That's a bawd,   [*Apart.*]
 A three-pil'd bawd, bawd-major to the army.
2 Lady. Has brought her coach to wait upon your ladyship,
 And to be inform'd if you will take the air this morning.
Leon. The neat air of her nunnery.   85
Marg. Tell her, no;
 I' th' afternoon I'll call on her.
2 Lady. I will, madam.   *Exit.*
Marg. Why are not you gone to prepare yourself?
 May be you shall be sewer to the first course.— 90
 A portly presence!—Altea, he looks lean;
 'Tis a wash knave, he will not keep his flesh well.
Altea. A willing, madam, one that needs no spurring.
Leon. 'Faith, madam, in my little understanding,
 You had better entertain your honest neighbours, 95
 Your friends about ye, that may speak well of ye,
 And give a worthy mention of your bounty.
Marg. How now? what's this?
Leon. 'Tis only to persuade ye:
 Courtiers are but tickle things to deal withal, 100
 A kind of marchpane men, that will not last, madam;
 An egg and pepper goes further than their potions,
 And in a well-built body, a poor parsnip
 Will play his prize above their strong potabiles.
Marg. The fellow's mad!   105
Leon. He that shall counsel ladies,

     [1] Q, *2 Lady.*

That have both liquorish and ambitious eyes,
Is either mad or drunk, let him speak gospel.
Altea. He breaks out modestly.   [*Apart.*]
Leon. Pray you be not angry;   110
My indiscretion has made bold to tell ye
What you'll find true.
Marg. Thou dar'st not talk?
Leon. Not much, madam:
You have a tie upon your servant's tongue;   115
He dares not be so bold as reason bids him;
'Twere fit there were a stronger on your temper.
Ne'er look so stern upon me; I am your husband,
But what are husbands? Read the new world's wonders,
Such husbands as this monstrous world produces,   120
And you will scarce find such deformities; [1]
They are shadows to conceal your venial virtues,
Sails to your mills, that grind with all occasions,
Balls that lie by you, to wash out your stains,
And bills nail'd up with horns [2] before your stories, 125
To rent out lust. [3]
Marg. Do you hear him talk?
Leon. I have done, madam;
An ox once spoke, as learned men deliver;
Shortly I shall be such; then I'll speak wonders?   130
'Till when, I tie myself to my obedience.   *Exit.*
Marg. First, I'll untie myself! Did you mark the gentleman,
How boldly and how saucily he talk'd,
And how unlike the lump I took him for,
The piece of ignorant dough? He stood up to me,   135
And mated my commands! this was your providence,
Your wisdom, to elect this gentleman,
Your excellent forecast in the man, your knowledge!
What think you now?
Altea. I think him an ass still;   140

---

[1] Monck Mason transposed these lines, and Dyce approves the transposition. Again it seems to me superfluous, though not impossible.
[2] Q and F, singular.   [3] Q and F, 'last,' a clear misprint.

This boldness some of your people have blown into him,
This wisdom too, with strong wine; 'tis a tyrant,
And a philosopher also, and finds out reasons.

Marg. I'll have my cellar lock'd, no school kept there,
Nor no discovery. I'll turn my drunkards,   145
Such as are understanding in their draughts,
And dispute learnedly the *whys* and *wherefores*,
To grass immediately; I'll keep all fools,
Sober or drunk, still fools, that shall know nothing,
Nothing belongs to mankind, but obedience;   150
And such a hand I'll keep over this husband!

Altea. He will fall again; my life, he cries by this time;
Keep him from drink; he has a high constitution.

Ent[er] LEON.

Leon. Shall I wear my new suit, madam?

Marg. No, your old clothes,   155
And get you into the country presently,
And see my hawks well train'd; you shall have victuals,
Such as are fit for saucy palates, sir,
And lodgings with the hinds; it is too good too.

Altea. Good madam, be not so rough with repentance: [1]   160
You see now he's come round again.

Marg. I see not what I expect to see.

Leon. You shall see, madam, if it shall please your ladyship—

Altea. He's humbled;
Forgive, good lady.   165

Marg. Well, go get you handsome,
And let me hear no more.

Leon [*aside*]. Have you yet no feeling?
I'll pinch you to the bones then, my proud lady!   *Exit.*

Marg. See you preserve him thus, upon my favour;   170
You know his temper, tie him to the grindstone;
The next rebellion I'll be rid of him.
I'll have no needy rascals I tie to me,

---

[1] Seward assigned the first line of this speech to Leon, superfluously no doubt.

Dispute my life. Come in, and see all handsome.
Altea [*aside*]. I hope to see you so too; I've wrought ill else.   175
                                                             Exeunt.[1]

[Act III. Scene II.   *A Room in a mean Hovel.*]

Enter PEREZ.

Perez. Shall I never return to mine own house again?
    We are lodg'd here in the miserablest dog-hole,
    A conjuror's circle gives content above it;
    A hawk's mew is a princely palace to it:
    We have a bed no bigger than a basket,   5
    And there we lie like butter clapt together,
    And sweat ourselves to sauce immediately.
    The fumes are infinite inhabit here too,
    And to that so thick, they cut like marmalet;
    So various too, they'll pose a gold-finder!   10
    Never return to mine own paradise?—
    Why, wife, I say! why, Estifania!
*Estif.—within.—*I am going presently.
Perez. Make haste, good jewel!
    I'm like the people that live in the sweet [2] islands: 15
    I die, I die, if I stay but one day more here;
    My lungs are rotten with the damps that rise,
    And I cough nothing now but stinks of all sorts.
    The inhabitants we have are two starved rats
    (For they are not able to maintain a cat here),   20
    And those appear as fearful as two devils;
    They have eat a map of the whole world up already,
    And if we stay a night, we are gone for company.
    There's an old woman that's now grown to marble,

___
[1] Q, *Exit.*
[2] Theobald, who seems to have had very poor and unhappy brains in reference
to this play, wanted to read '*sweat* islands'! Of course the phrase refers to the un-
healthiness of the West Indies, which produce sugar.

Dried in this brick-kiln,[1] and she sits i' the chimney,   25
(Which is but three tiles, rais'd like a house of cards),
The true proportion of an old smok'd sibyl;
There is a young thing too, that nature meant
For a maid-servant, but 'tis now a monster;
She has a husk about her like a chestnut   30
With laziness [2] and living under the line here;
And these two make a hollow sound together,
Like frogs, or winds between two doors that murmur.

Ent[er] Estifania.

Mercy, deliver me!—Oh, are you come, wife?
Shall we be free again?   35
Estif. I am now going,
And you shall presently to your own house, sir:
The remembrance of this small vexation
Will be [3] argument of mirth for ever.
By that time you have said your orisons,   40
And broke your fast, I shall be back, and ready
To usher you to your old content, your freedom.
Perez. Break my neck rather! Is there any thing here to eat
But one another, like a race of cannibals?
A piece of butter'd wall you think is excellent!   45
Let's have our house again immediately;
And pray you take heed unto the furniture,
None be embezzled!
Estif. Not a pin, I warrant you.
Perez. And let 'em instantly depart.   50
Estif. They shall both,
(There's reason in all courtesies) they must both,
For by this time I know she has acquainted him,
And has provided too; she sent me word, sir,
And will give over gratefully unto you.   55
Perez. I'll walk i' th' church-yard;

---

[1] Q and F, 'hill.'
[2] Q, 'basinesse'; F, 'basiness', the editor of the last having probably made the right correction, but fallen a victim to the original printer's blunder of 'b' for 'l.'
[3] Seward inserted 'an' here.

The dead cannot offend more than these living,
An hour hence I'll expect ye.
Estif. I'll not fail, sir.
Perez. And do you hear, let's have a handsome dinner,   60
And see all things be decent as they have been,
And let me have a strong bath to restore me!
I stink like a stall-fish, shambles, or an oil-shop.[1]
Estif. You shall have all—[*Aside.*] (which some interpret noth-
ing.)—   65
I'll send ye people for the trunks afore-hand,
And for the stuff.
Perez. Let 'em be known and honest;
And do my service to your niece.
Estif. I shall, sir;   70
But if I come not at my hour, come thither,
That they may give you thanks for your fair courtesy.
And pray ye be brave, for my sake!
Perez. I observe ye.   *Exeunt.*

[Act III. Scene III. *The Street.*]

Enter JUAN DE CASTRO, SANCHO, *and* CACAFOGO.

Sanc. Thou art very brave.
Cac. I have reason; I have money.
Sanc. Is money reason?
Cac. Yes, and rhyme [2] too, captain.
If ye have no money, ye're an ass.   5
Sanc. I thank you.
Cac. Ye have manners; [3] ever thank him that has money.
Sanc. Wilt thou lend me any?
Cac. Not a farthing, captain;
Captains are casual things.   10

---

[1] This is the reading of Q and F, with a comma added (in 1778) at 'stall-fish.'
Seward substituted 'stale,' which Dyce adopts, shifting, however, the hyphen to
'fish-shambles'. The original may well be kept.
  [2] Q, 'ruine.'   [3] Q, 'meaner.'

Sanc. Why, so are all men;
    Thou shalt have my bond.
Cac. Nor bonds nor fetters, captain:
    My money is mine own; I make no doubt on't.
Juan. What dost thou do with it?   15
Cac. Put it to pious uses,
    Buy wine and wenches, and undo young coxcombs
    That would undo me.
Juan. Are those hospitals?
Cac. I first provide to fill my hospitals   20
    With creatures of mine own, that I know wretched,
    And then I build; those are more bound to pray for me:
    Besides, I keep the inheritance in my name still.
Juan. A provident charity! Are you for the wars, sir?
Cac. I am not poor enough to be a soldier,   25
    Nor have I faith enough to ward a bullet:
    This is no lining for a trench, I take it.
Juan. Ye have said wisely.
Cac. Had you but my money,
    You would swear it, colonel; I'd rather drill at home 30
    A hundred thousand crowns, and with more honour,
    Than exercise ten thousand fools with nothing:
    A wise man safely feeds, fools cut their fingers.
Sanc. A right state usurer; why dost thou not marry,
    And live a reverend justice?   35
Cac. Is't not nobler
    To command a reverend justice, than to be one?
    And for a wife, what need I marry, captain,
    When every courteous fool that owes me money,
    Owes me his wife too, to appease my fury?   40
Juan. Wilt thou go to dinner with us?
Cac. I will go,
    And view the pearl of Spain, the orient fair one,
    The rich one too, and I will be respected;
    I bear my patent here: I will talk to her;   45
    And when your captainships shall stand aloof,
    And pick your noses, I will pick the purse

Of her affection.

Juan. The duke dines there to-day, too,
  The Duke of Medina.   50

Cac. Let the king dine there,
  He owes me money, and so far's my creature;
  And certainly I may make bold with mine own, captain.

Sanc. Thou wilt eat monstrously.

Cac. Like a true-born Spaniard;   55
  Eat as I were in England, where the beef grows!
  And I will drink abundantly, and then
  Talk you as wantonly as Ovid did,
  To stir the intellectuals of the ladies;
  I learnt it of my father's amorous scrivener.   60

Juan. If we should play now, you must supply me.

Cac. You must pawn a horse-troop
  And then have at ye, colonel!

Sanc. Come, let's go.
  This rascal will make rare sport! how the ladies   65
  Will laugh [at] him! [leave anger! ¹]

Juan. If I light on him,
  I'll make his purse sweat too.

Cac. Will you lead, gentlemen?   *Exeunt.*

[Act III. Scene IV. *The Street before the mean Hovel.*]

Enter PEREZ, *an* Old Woman, *and* Maid.

Perez. Nay, pray ye come out, and let me understand ye,
  And tune your pipe a little higher, lady;
  I'll hold ye fast.   Rub! how came my trunks open?
  And my goods gone? what picklock spirit—

Old Wom. Ha! what would you have?   5

Perez. My goods again; how came my trunks all open?

---

¹ Q omits 'at,' and has 'Leave ager,' which F leaves out altogether. And perhaps with reason, for what has 'anger' to do here? 'Leave ager' was probably a simple 'irreption' of the kind so frequent.

Old Wom. Are your trunks open?
Perez. Yes, and clothes gone,
 And chains and jewels!—How she smells like hung beef!—
 The palsy and picklocks!—Fie, how she belches   10
 The spirit of garlic!
Old Wom. Where's your gentlewoman?
 The young fair woman?
Perez. What's that to my question!
 She is my wife, and gone about my business.   15
Maid. Is she your wife, sir?
Perez. Yes, sir: is that wonder?
 Is the name of wife unknown here?
Old Wom. Is she truly,
 Truly your wife?   20
Perez. I think so, for I married her,
 It was no vision, sure!
Maid. She has the keys, sir.
Perez. I know she has; but who has all my goods, spirit?
Old Wom. If you be married to that gentlewoman,   25
 You are a wretched man; she has twenty husbands.
Maid. She tells you true.
Old Wom. And she has cozen'd all, sir.
Perez. The devil she has!—I had a fair house with her,
 That stands hard by, and furnish'd royally.   30
Old Wom. You are cozen'd too; 'tis none of hers, good gentleman![1]
 It is a lady's.—What's the lady's name, wench?
Maid. The lady Margarita; she was her servant,
 And kept the house, but going from her, sir,
 For some lewd tricks she play'd—   35
Perez. Plague o' the devil!
 Am I, i' th' full meridian of my wisdom,
 Cheated by a stale quean?—What kind of lady
 Is that that owes the house?
Old Wom. A young sweet lady.   40

---

[1] Seward, relying on the Old Woman's phrase below, read 'good gentlewoman,' and Dyce thinks him 'probably right.' But the correction, though not certainly wrong, is unnecessary.

Perez. Of a low stature?
Old Wom. She's indeed but little,
  But she is wondrous fair.
Perez. I feel I'm cozen'd;
  Now I am sensible I am undone!   45
  This is the very woman sure, that cousin,
  She told me would entreat but for four days,
  To make the house hers: I am entreated sweetly!
Maid. When she went out this morning, (that I saw, sir,)
  She had two women at the door attending,   50
  And there she gave 'em things, and loaded 'em;
  But what they were—I heard your trunks to open,
  If they be yours.
Perez. They were mine while they were [1] laden,
  But now they've cast their calves, they're not worth owning. 55
  Was she her mistress, say you?
Old Wom. Her own mistress,
  Her very mistress, sir, and all you saw
  About and in that house was hers.
Perez. No plate,   60
  No jewels, nor no hangings?
Maid. Not a farthing;
  She's poor, sir, a poor shifting thing!
Perez. No money?
Old Wom. Abominable poor, as poor as we are,   65
  Money as rare to her, unless she steal it.
  But for one civil gown her lady gave her,
  She may go bare, good gentlewoman!
Perez. I am mad now!
  I think I am as poor as she; I'm wide else.   70
  One civil suit I have left too, and that's all,
  And if she steal that, she must flay [2] me for it.—
  Where does she use?
Old Wom. You may find truth as soon:
  Alas, a thousand conceal'd corners, sir, she lurks in;   75
  And here she gets a fleece, and there another,

[1] Q, 'are.'   [2] Q, 'flea.'

And lives in mists and smokes where none can find her.

Perez. Is she a whore too?

Old Wom. Little better, gentleman:

    I dare not say she is so, sir, because she is yours, sir;   80

    But these five years she has firk'd a pretty living,

    Until she came to serve.—I fear he will knock

    My brains out for lying.[1]   [*Apart.*]

Perez. She has served me faithfully;

    A whore and thief? two excellent moral learnings,   85

    In one she-saint! I hope to see her legend.

    Have I been fear'd for my discoveries,

    And courted by all women to conceal 'em?

    Have I so long studied the art of this sex,

    And read the warnings to young gentlemen?   90

    Have I profess'd to tame the pride of ladies,

    And make 'em bear all tests, and am I trick'd now?

    Caught in mine own noose?—Here's a royal left yet;

    There's for your lodging and your meat for this week!

    A silk-worm lives at a more plentiful ordinary,   95

    And sleeps in a sweeter box. Farewell, great-grandmother!

    If I do find you were an accessary,

    ('Tis but the cutting off two smoky minutes)

    I'll hang ye presently.

Old Wom. And I[2] deserve it.   100

    I tell but truth.

Perez. Nor I, I am an ass, mother!   *Exeunt.*

[1] Seward cut out the words 'for lying' which (as Coleridge pleasantly observed) shows that his own brains were out. The O. W. *was* lying, that is to say exaggerating Estifania's naughtiness at Estifania's own bidding.

[2] Dyce again doubtfully 'an' for 'and': others quite gratuitously 'I'd' for 'I.' But I do not quite understand 'nor' (for which F has 'not') in the line 102. 'And' would be clear enough. [I think it should run '*O. W.* An I deserve it, I tell not truth. *Per.* Nor I,'—which is jocosely true.—*Gen. Ed.*]

[Act III. Scene V. *A Hall in the Town-house of Margarita.*]

Enter the Duke MEDINA, JUAN DE CASTRO, ALONZO, SANCHIO, CACAFOGO, [*and*] Attendants.

Duke. A goodly house!
Juan. And richly furnish'd too, sir.
Alon. Hung wantonly!—I like that preparation;
  It stirs the blood unto a hopeful banquet,
  And intimates the mistress free and jovial.   5
  I love a house where pleasure prepares welcome.
Duke. Now, Cacafogo, how like you this mansion?
  'Twere a brave pawn.
Cac. I shall be master of it;
  'Twas built for my bulk, the rooms are wide and spacious,   10
  Airy and full of ease, and that I love well.
  I'll tell you when I taste the wine, my lord,
  And take the height of her table with my stomach,
  How my affections stand to the young lady.

Enter MARGARITA, ALTEA, Ladies, *and* Servants.

Marg. All welcome to your grace, and to these soldiers!   15
  You honour my poor house with your fair presence,
  Those few slight pleasures that inhabit here, sir,
  I do beseech your grace command; they are yours;
  Your servant but preserves 'em to delight you.
Duke. I thank you, lady! I am bold to visit you,   20
  Once more to bless mine eyes with your sweet beauty.
  'T has been a long night since you left the court,
  For till I saw you now, no day broke to me.
Marg. Bring in the duke's meat!
Sanc. She's most excellent.   25
Juan. Most admirable fair as e'er I look'd on;
  I had rather command her than my regiment.
Cac. I'll have a fling; 'tis but a thousand ducats,

Which I can cozen up again in ten days,
And some few jewels, to justify my knavery. 30
Say, I should marry her? she'll get more money
Than all my usury, put my knavery to it.
She appears the most infallible way of purchase.
I could wish her a size or two stronger for the encounter,
For I am like a lion where I lay hold; 35
But these lambs will endure a plaguy load,
And never bleat neither; that, sir,[1] Time has taught us.—
I am so virtuous now, I cannot speak to her;
The arrant'st shamefac'd ass!—I broil away too.

Enter LEON.

Marg. Why, where's this dinner? 40
Leon. 'Tis not ready, madam,
　　Nor shall not be until I know the guests too;
　　Nor are they fairly welcome till I bid 'em.
Juan. Is not this my alferez? He looks another thing?
　　Are miracles afoot again? 45
Marg. Why, sirrah!
　　Why, sirrah, you!
Leon. I hear you, saucy woman;
　　And as you are my wife, command your absence!
　　And know your duty; 'tis the crown of modesty. 50
Duke. Your wife!
Leon. Yes, good my lord, I am her husband;
　　And 'pray take notice that I claim that honour,
　　And will maintain it.
Cac. If thou be'st her husband, 55
　　I am determin'd thou shalt be my cuckold;
　　I'll be thy faithful friend.
Leon. Peace, dirt and dunghill!
　　I will not lose mine anger on a rascal;
　　Provoke me more, I will beat thy blown body 60

---

[1] 1778, Weber and Darley 'Sir Time' which Dyce very properly rejects. 'Sir' in soliloquy addressed to an imaginary interlocutor is neither uncommon nor in the least surprising.

Till thou rebound'st again like a tennis-ball.
Alon. This is miraculous!
Sanc. Is this the fellow
　That had the patience to become a fool,
　A flirted fool, and on a sudden break　　　　　　　65
　(As if he would shew a wonder to the world)
　Both into bravery, and fortune too?
　I much admire the man; I am astonish'd!
Marg. I'll be divorc'd immediately.
Leon. You shall not;　　　　　　　　　　　　　　70
　You shall not have so much will to be wicked.
　I am more tender of your honour, lady,
　And of your age. You took me for a shadow,
　You took me to gloss over your discredit,
　To be your fool; you had thought you had found a coxcomb: 75
　I am innocent of any foul dishonour I mean to ye;
　Only I will be known to be your lord now,
　And be a fair one too, or I will fall for't.
Marg. I do command ye from me, thou poor fellow,
　Thou cozen'd fool!　　　　　　　　　　　　　　80
Leon. Thou cozen'd fool? 'Tis not so,
　I will not be commanded: I am above ye!
　You may divorce me from your favour, lady,
　But from your state you never shall; I'll hold that,
　And hold it to my use; the law allows it!　　　　85
　And then maintain your wantonness; I'll wink at it.
Marg. Am I brav'd thus in mine own house?
Leon. 'Tis mine, madam;
　You are deceiv'd, I am lord of it; I rule it,
　And all that's in't. You have nothing to do here, madam, 90
　But as a servant to sweep clean the lodgings,
　And at my further will to do me service;
　And so I'll keep it.
Marg. As you love me, give way!
Leon. It shall be better[1] I will give none, madam:　95

---

[1] Seward transferred 'It shall be better' to Marg. and has not wanted approvers. But it is needless. [Q makes one line of 'As . . . better.'—*Gen. Ed.*]

I stand upon the ground of mine own honour,
And will maintain it. You shall know me now
To be an understanding feeling man,
And sensible of what a woman aims at,
A young proud woman, that has will to sail with;   100
An itching woman, that her blood provokes too.
I cast my cloud off, and appear myself,
The master of this little piece of mischief!
And I will put a spell about your feet, lady;
They shall not wander but where I give way now.   105
Duke. Is this the fellow that the people pointed at,
For the mere sign of man, the walking image?
He speaks wondrous highly.
Leon. As a husband ought, sir,
In his own house; and it becomes me well too.   110
I think your grace would grieve, if you were put to it,
To have a wife or servant of your own,
(For wives are reckon'd in the rank of servants)
Under your own roof to command you.
Juan. Brave!   115
A strange conversion! Thou shalt lead in chief now.
Duke. Is there no difference betwixt her and you, sir?
Leon. Not now, [my] lord; my fortune makes me even;
And, as I am an honest man, I'm nobler.
Marg. Get me my coach!   120
Leon. Let me see who dares get it
Till I command; I'll make him draw your coach too,[1]
And eat your coach (which will be hard diet)
That executes your will.—Or, take your coach, lady;
I give you liberty; and take your people,   125
Which I turn off, and take your will abroad with you;
Take all these freely, but take me no more;
And so farewell!
Duke. Nay, sir, you shall not carry it   [*Draws.*]
So bravely off; you shall not wrong a lady   130

---

[1] Also needless is another change of his, though approved by Dyce, the shifting of 'too' to the middle of the next line after the second 'coach.'

In a high huffing strain, and think to bear it:
We stand not by as bawds to your brave fury,
To see a lady weep.

Leon. They are tears of anger,
  (I beseech ye note 'em) not worth pity;   135
  Wrung from her rage, because her will prevails not;
  (She would swound ¹ now, if she could not cry)
  Else they were excellent, and I should grieve too;
  But falling thus, they shew nor sweet, nor orient.
  Put up, my lord; this is oppression,   140
  And calls the sword of justice to relieve me,
  The law to lend her hand, the king to right me;
  All which shall understand how you provoke me.
  In mine own house to brave me! is this princely?
  Then to my guard; and if I spare your grace,   [*Draws.*] 145
  And do not make this place your monument,
  Too rich a tomb for such a rude behaviour,—
  (I have a cause will kill a thousand of ye)—
  Mercy, forsake me!

Juan. Hold, fair sir, I beseech you!   150
  The gentleman but pleads his own right nobly.

Leon. He that dares strike against the husband's freedom,
  The husband's curse stick to him, a tam'd cuckold!
  His wife be fair and young, but most dishonest,
  Most impudent, and have no feeling of it,   155
  No conscience to reclaim her from a monster!
  Let her lie by him like a flattering ruin,
  And at one instant kill both name and honour!
  Let him be lost, no eye to weep his end,
  Nor find no earth that's base enough to bury him!   160
  Now, sir, fall on! I am ready to oppose you.

Duke. I have better thought. I pray, sir, use your wife well.

Leon. Mine own humanity will teach me that, sir.—
  And now you are all welcome, all, and we'll to dinner:
  This is my wedding-day.   165

---

² Quite wantonly altered by the last century editors, Weber, and Darley, to 'swoon.'

Duke. I'll cross your joy yet.   [*Aside.*]

Juan. I have seen a miracle! hold thine own, soldier!
Sure they dare fight in fire that conquer women.

Sanc. [He] has beaten all my loose thoughts out of me,
As if he had thresh'd 'em out o' the husk.   170

Enter PEREZ.

Perez. 'Save ye!
Which is the lady of the house?

Leon. That's she, sir;
That pretty lady, if you'd speak with her.

Juan. Don Michael, Leon; another darer come.[1]   175

Perez. Pray do not know me; I am full of business:
When I have more time I'll be merry with ye.—
It is the woman.—Good madam, tell me truly,
Had you a maid call'd Estifania?

Marg. Yes, truly, had I.   180

Perez. Was she a maid, do you think?

Marg. I dare not swear for her;
For she had but a scant fame.

Perez. Was she your kinswoman?

Marg. Not that I ever knew. Now I look better,   185
I think you married her: Give you much joy, sir.
You may reclaim her; 'twas a wild young girl.

Perez. Give me a halter!—Is not this house mine, madam?
Was not she owner of it? 'Pray speak truly!

Marg. No, certainly; I'm sure my money paid for it;   190
And I ne'er remember yet I gave it you, sir.

Perez. The hangings and the plate too?

Marg. All are mine, sir,
And everything you see about the building:
She only kept my house when I was absent,   195
And so ill kept it, I was weary of her.

Sanc. What a devil ails he?

Juan. He's [2] possessed, I'll assure you.

---

[1] Dyce adopted the Ms. suggestion of Heath to make 'Leon' a speech-heading, and transfer 'another darer come' to him. This is ingenious, but I doubt it very much. Q has 'come?'

[2] Q, 'Is' (omitting 'He').

Perez. Where is your maid?

Marg. Do not you know that have her?   200
    She is yours now; why should I look after her?
    Since that first hour I came, I never saw her.

Perez. I saw her later; 'would the devil had had her!
    It is all true, I find; a wild-fire take her!

Juan. Is thy wife with child, Don Michael? thy excellent wife? 205
    Art thou a man yet?

Alon. When shall we come and visit thee?

Sanc. And eat some rare fruit? thou hast admirable orchards.
    You are so jealous now! pox o' your jealousy,
    How scurvily you look!   210

Perez. Prithee leave fooling;
    I'm in no humour now to fool and prattle.—
    Did she ne'er play the wag with you?

Marg. Yes, many times,
    So often that I was asham'd to keep her;   215
    But I forgave her, sir, in hope she would mend still,
    And had not you o' th' instant married her,
    I had put her off.

Perez. I thank ye; I am blest still!
    Which way soe'er I turn, I am a made man;   220
    Miserably gull'd beyond recovery.

Juan. You'll stay and dine?

Perez. Certain I cannot, captain.
    Hark in thine ear; I am the arrant'st puppy,
    The miserablest ass! But I must leave ye;   225
    I am in haste, in haste!—Bless you, good madam
    And you prove as good as my wife!   *Exit.*

Leon. Will you
    Come near, sir? will your grace but honour me,
    And taste our dinner? you are nobly welcome.   230
    All anger's past, I hope, and I shall serve ye.

Juan. Thou art the stock of men, and I admire thee.   *Exeunt.*

Act IV.   Scene I.   [*The Street.*]

Enter PEREZ.

Perez. I'll go to a conjuror but I'll find this polecat,
This pilfering whore!   A plague of veils, I cry,
And covers for the impudence of women!
Their sanctity in show will deceive devils.—

Enter ESTIFANIA, *with a Casket.*

It is my evil angel; let me bless me!   5

Estif. 'Tis he; I'm caught; I must stand to it stoutly,
And shew no shake of fear; I see he's angry,
Vex'd at the uttermost!

Perez. My worthy wife,
I have been looking of your modesty   10
All the town over.

Estif. My most noble husband,
I am glad I have found ye; for in truth I'm weary,
Weary and lame, with looking out your lordship.

Perez. I've been in bawdy-houses.   15

Estif. I believe you,
And very lately too.

Perez. 'Pray ye pardon me;—
To seek your ladyship.   I have been in cellars,
In private cellars, where the thirsty bawds   20
Hear your confessions: I have been at plays,
To look you out amongst the youthful actors:
At puppet-shows (you are mistress of the motions!):
At gossipings I hearken'd after you,
But amongst those confusions of lewd tongues   25
There's no distinguishing beyond a Babel:
I was amongst the nuns, because you sing well;
But they say yours are bawdy songs, they mourn for ye:
And last I went to church to seek you out;
'Tis so long since you were there, they have forgot you.   30

Estif. You have had a pretty progress; I'll tell mine now.

To look you out, I went to twenty taverns—
Perez. And are you sober?
Estif. Yes, I reel not yet, sir.—
 Where I saw twenty drunk, most of 'em soldiers; 35
 There I had great hope to find you disguis'd too:
 From hence to th' dicing-house; there I found quarrels
 Needless and senseless, swords, and pots, and candlesticks,
 Tables and stools, and all in one confusion,
 And no man knew his friend: I left this chaos, 40
 And to the chirurgeon's went; he will'd me stay,
 "For," says he learnedly, "if he be tippled,
 Twenty to one he whores, and then I hear of him;
 If he be mad he quarrels, then he comes too."
 I sought you where no safe thing would have ventur'd, 45
 Amongst diseases base and vile, vile[1] women,
 For I remember'd your old Roman axiom,
 The more the danger, still the more the honour!
 Last, to your confessor I came, who told me,
 You were too proud to pray: And here I've found you. 50
Perez. She bears up bravely, and the rogue is witty;
 But I shall dash it instantly to nothing.— [*Aside.*]
 Here leave we off our wanton languages,
 And now conclude we in a sharper tongue.
 Why am I cozen'd?[2] 55
Estif. Why am I abused?
Perez. Thou most vile, base, abominable—
Estif. Captain!
Perez. Thou stinking, over-stew'd, poor, pocky—
Estif. Captain! 60
Perez. D'ye echo me?
Estif. Yes, sir, and go before ye,
 And around about ye! Why do you rail at me
 For that that was your own sin, your own knavery?

---

[1] Q, 'vild' as commonly, which Dyce retains. But this, which is already 'vile' in F, seems unnecessary unless in a facsimile.

[2] Q and F give both this and the following question to Estifania, and so does 1750. The editors of 1778, not eager innovators, gave the first to Perez, and there can be little doubt that they were right.

Perez. And brave me too?   65
Estif. You had best now draw your sword, captain!
    Draw it upon a woman, do, brave captain!,
    Upon your wife, oh, most renowned captain!
Perez. A plague upon thee! answer me directly?
    Why didst thou marry me?   70
Estif. To be my husband;
    I had thought you had had infinite, but I'm cozen'd.
Perez. Why didst thou flatter me, and shew me wonders?
    A house and riches, when they are but shadows,
    Shadows to me?   75
Estif. Why did you work on me
    (It was but my part to requite you, sir!)
    With your strong soldier's wit, and swore you would bring me
    So much in chains, so much in jewels, husband,
    So much in right rich clothes?   80
Perez. Thou hast 'em, rascal;
    I gave 'em to thy hands, my trunks and all,
    And thou hast open'd 'em, and sold my treasure.
Estif. Sir, there's your treasure; sell it to a tinker
    To mend old kettles: Is this noble usage?   85
    Let all the world view here the captain's treasure!
    A man would think now, these were worthy matters.
                              [*Opens the casket.*]
    Here's a shoeing-horn-chain gilt over,—how it scenteth!
    Worse than the mouldy dirty heel it serv'd for:
    And here's another of a lesser value,   90
    So little I would shame to tie my dog in't!
    These are my jointure!   Blush, and save a labour,
    Or these else will blush for you.
Perez. A fire subtle ye!
    Are ye so crafty?   95
Estif. Here's a goodly jewel;
    Did you not win this at Goletta, captain?
    Or took it in the field from some brave bashaw?
    How it sparkles—like an old lady's eyes!
    And fills each room with light—like a close lanthorn!   100

This would do rarely in an abbey window,
To cozen pilgrims.
Perez. Pr'ythee leave prating.
Estif. And here's a chain of whitings' eyes for pearls;
A mussel-monger would have made a better.   105
Perez. Nay, pr'ythee, wife, my clothes, my clothes!
Estif. I'll tell you;
Your clothes are parallels to these, all counterfeit.
Put these and them on, you're a man of copper,
A kind of candlestick; these you thought, my husband,   110
To have cozen'd me withal, but I am quit with you.
Perez. Is there no house then, nor no grounds about it?
No plate, nor hangings?
Estif. There are none, sweet husband;
Shadow for shadow is an equal justice.   115
Can you rail now? 'Pray put your fury up, sir,
And speak great words; you are a soldier; thunder!
Perez. I will speak little; I have play'd the fool,
And so I am rewarded.
Estif. You have spoke well, sir;   120
And now I see you are so conformable,
I'll heighten you again: Go to your house,
They are packing to be gone; you must sup there;
I'll meet you, and bring clothes, and clean shirts after,
And all things shall be well.—I'll colt you once more,   125
                                                   [*Aside.*]
And teach you to bring copper!
Perez. Tell me one thing,
I do beseech thee, tell me, tell me truth, wife;
(However, I forgive thee) art thou honest?
The beldame swore—   130
Estif. I bid her tell you so, sir;
It was my plot. Alas, my credulous husband!
The lady told you too—
Perez. Most strange things of thee.
Estif. Still 'twas my way, and all to try your sufferance: 135
And she denied the house?

Perez. She knew me not,
  No, nor no title that I had.
Estif. 'Twas well carried.
  No more; I'm right and straight.   140
Perez. I would believe thee,
  But Heav'n knows how my heart is. Will you follow me?
Estif. I'll be there straight.
Perez. I am fool'd, yet dare not find it.   *Exit* PEREZ.
Estif. Go, silly fool! thou may'st be a good soldier   145
  In open field, but for our private service
  Thou art an ass; I'll make thee so, or miss else.—

Ent[er] CAC [AFOGO].

  Here comes another trout that I must tickle,
  And tickle daintily, I have lost my end else.—
  May [1] I crave your leave, sir?   150
Cac. Pr'ythee be answer'd, thou shalt crave no leave;
  I am in my meditations; do not vex me;
  A beaten thing, but this hour a most bruis'd thing,
  That people had compassion on, it look'd so;
  The next, Sir Palmerin: Here's fine proportion!   155
  An ass, and then an elephant; sweet justice!
  There's no way left to come at her now; no craving;
  If money could come near, yet I would pay him;
  I have a mind to make him a huge cuckold,
  And money may do much! a thousand ducats?   160
  'Tis but the letting blood of a rank heir.
Estif. 'Pray you hear me.
Cac. I know thou hast some wedding ring to pawn now,
  Of silver, and gilt, with a blind posy in't,
  "Love and a mill-horse should go round together,"   165
  Or thy child's whistle, or thy squirrel's chain:
  I'll none of 'em.—I would she did but know me,
  Or 'would this fellow had but use of money,
  That I might come in any way!
Estif. I am gone, sir;   170

[1] Q unnecessarily repeats *Estif.* before 'May.'

And I shall tell the beauty sent me to ye,
The Lady Margarita—
Cac. Stay, I prithee;
 What is thy will? I turn me wholly to ye,
 And talk now till thy tongue ache; I will hear ye. 175
Estif. She would entreat you, sir!
Cac. She shall command, sir!
 Let it be so, I beseech thee, my sweet gentlewoman;
 Do not forget thyself.
Estif. She does command then 180
 This courtesy, because she knows you are noble—
Cac. Your mistress, by the way?
Estif. My natural mistress—
 Upon these jewels, sir—they're fair and rich,
 And, view 'em right— 185
Cac. To doubt 'em is an heresy.
Estif. A thousand ducats; 'tis upon necessity
 Of present use; her husband, sir, is stubborn.
Cac. Long may he be so!
Estif. She desires withal 190
 A better knowledge of your parts and person;
 And, when you please to do her so much honour—
Cac. Come, let's despatch.
Estif. In troth I've heard her say, sir,
 Of a fat man, she has not seen a sweeter. 195
 But in this business, sir—
Cac. Let's do it first,
 And then dispute; the lady's use may long for't.
Estif. All secrecy she would desire; she told me
 How wise you are. 200
Cac. We are not wise to talk thus!
 Carry her the gold; I'll look her out a jewel
 Shall sparkle like her eyes, and thee another.
 Come, pr'ythee come, I long to serve thy lady,
 Long monstrously!—Now, valour, I shall meet ye, 205
 You that dare dukes!
Estif. [*aside*]. Green goose, you are now in sippets. *Exeunt.*

[Act IV. Scene II. *Another Street.*]

Enter the DUKE, SANCHIO, JUAN, [*and*] ALONZO.

Duke. He shall not have his will, I shall prevent him;
   I have a toy here that will turn the tide,
   And suddenly, and strangely. Here, Don Juan,
   Do you present it to him.   [*Gives him a paper.*]
Juan. I am commanded.   *Exit.*   5
Duke. A fellow founded out of charity,
   And moulded to the height, contemn his maker,
   Curb the free hand that fram'd him? This must not be.
Sanc. That such an oyster-shell should hold a pearl,
   And of so rare a price, in prison! Was she made   10
   To be the matter of her own undoing,
   To let a slovenly unwieldy fellow,
   Unruly and self-will'd, dispose her beauties?
   We suffer all, sir, in this sad eclipse;
   She should shine where she might shew like herself,   15
   An absolute sweetness, to comfort those admire her,
   And shed her beams upon her friends.[1] We are gull'd all,
   And all the world will grumble at your patience,
   If she be ravish'd thus.
Duke. Ne'er fear it, Sanchio,   20
   We'll have her free again, and move at court
   In her clear orb. But one sweet handsomeness
   To bless this part of Spain, and have that slubber'd!
Alon. 'Tis every good man's cause, and we must stir in it.
Duke. I'll warrant he shall be glad to please us,   25
   And glad to share too: We shall hear anon
   A new song from him; let's attend a little.   *Exeunt.*

[1] Here Q unnecessarily repeats speech-name *Sanc.*, and opens new line.

[Act IV.   Scene III.   *An Apartment in Margarita's House.*]

Ent[er] LEON, *and* JUAN *with a Commission.*

Leon. Colonel,[1] I am bound to you for this nobleness.
    I should have been your officer, 'tis true, sir;
    (And a proud man I should have been to have serv'd you)
    It has pleas'd the king, out of his boundless favours,
    To make me your companion; this commission   5
    Gives me a troop of horse.
Juan. I rejoice at it,
    And am a glad man we shall gain your company;
    I am sure the king knows you are newly married,
    And out of that respect gives you more time, sir.   10
Leon. Within four days I am gone, so he commands me,
    And 'tis not mannerly for me to argue it;
    The time grows shorter still.   Are your goods ready?
Juan. They are aboard.
Leon. Who waits there?   15

        Enter Servant.

Serv. Sir.
Leon. D'ye hear, ho!
    Go, carry this unto your mistress, sir,
    And let her see how much the king has honour'd me;
    Bid her be lusty, she must make a soldier.   *Exit* [Servant]. 20
    [Lorenzo!]

        Enter LORENZO.

Lor. Sir.
[*Leon.*] Go, take down all the hangings,
    And pack up all my clothes, my plate and jewels,
    And all the furniture that's portable.—   25
    Sir, when we lie in garrison, 'tis necessary
    We keep a handsome port, for the king's honour.—

---

[1] It is perhaps barely desirable to say that here and elsewhere the originals have 'Coronel.'

And, do you hear, let all your lady's wardrobe
Be safely plac'd in trunks; they must go along too.
Lor. Whither must they go, sir?   30
Leon. To the wars, Lorenzo,
And you and all; I will not leave a turn-spit,
That has one dram of spleen against a Dutchman.
Lor. Why then, St. Jaques, hey! you've made us all, sir; [1]
And, if we leave ye—Does my lady go too?   35
Leon. The stuff must go to-morrow towards the sea, sir;
All, all must go.
Lor. Why, Pedro, Vasco, Diego!
Come, help me; come, come, boys; soldadoes, comrades!
We'll flay these beer-bellied rogues; come away quickly!   40
                                                        Exit.
Juan. He has taken a brave way to save his honour, [*Apart.*]
And cross the duke; now I shall love him dearly.
By the life of credit, thou art a noble gentleman!

Enter MARGARITA, *led by two* Ladies.

Leon. Why, how now, wife? what, sick at my preferment?
This is not kindly done.   45
Marg. No sooner love ye,
Love ye entirely, sir, brought to consider
The goodness of your mind and mine own duty,
But lose you instantly, be divorc'd from you?
This is a cruelty: I'll to the king,   50
And tell him 'tis unjust to part two souls,
Two minds so nearly mix'd.
Leon. By no means, sweetheart!
Marg. If he were married but four days, as I am—
Leon. He would hang himself the fifth, or fly his country. [*Aside.*]55
Marg. He would make it treason for that tongue that durst
But talk of war, or anything to vex him.
You shall not go.
Leon. Indeed I must, sweet wife.
What, shall I lose the king for a few kisses?   60
                    [1] Q, 'sit.'

We'll have enough.
Marg. I'll to the duke my cousin,
    He shall to th' king.
Leon. He did me this great office,
    I thank his grace for't; should I pray him now   65
    To undo't again? Fie, 'twere a base discredit.
Marg. 'Would I were able, sir, to bear you company;
    How willing should I be then, and how merry!
    I will not live alone.
Leon. Be in peace; you shall not.   *Knock[ing] within.* 70
Marg. What knocking's this? Oh, Heaven, my head! why rascals!
    I think the war's begun i' th' house already.
Leon. The preparation is; they're taking down
    And packing up the hangings, plate and jewels,
    And all those furnitures that shall befit me   75
    When I lie in garrison.

                Enter Coachman.

Coachman. Must the coach go too, sir?
Leon. How will your lady pass to th' sea else easily?
    We shall find shipping for't there to transport it.
Marg. I go? alas!   80
Leon. I'll have a main care of ye;
    I know ye are sickly; he shall drive the easier,
    And all accommodation shall attend ye.
Marg. 'Would I were able!
Leon. Come, I warrant ye;   85
    Am not I with ye, sweet?—Are her clothes pack'd up,
    And all her linens?—Give your maids direction;
    You know my time's but short, and I am commanded.
Marg. Let me have a nurse,
    And all such necessary people with me,   90
    And an easy bark!
Leon. It shall not trot, I warrant you;
    Curvet it may sometimes.
Marg. I am with child, sir.
Leon. At four days' warning? this is something speedy. 95

Do you conceive, as our jennets do, with a west wind?
My heir will be an arrant fleet one, lady;
I'll swear you were a maid when I first lay with you.
Marg. Pray, do not swear; I thought I was a maid too;
    But we may both be cozen'd in that point, sir. 100
Leon. In such a strait point, sure I could not err, madam.
Juan. This is another tenderness to try him; [*Apart.*]
    Fetch her up now.
Marg. You must provide a cradle,
    And what a trouble's that! 105
Leon. The sea shall rock it,
    'Tis the best nurse; 'twill roar and rock together;
    A swinging storm will sing you such a lullaby!
Marg. 'Faith, let me stay, I shall but shame you, sir.
Leon. An you were a thousand shames, you shall along with me;
    At home I'm sure you'll prove a million: 111
    Every man carries the bundle of his sins
    Upon his own back; you are mine, I'll sweat for ye.

Enter DUKE, ALONZO, [*and*] SANCHIO.

Duke. What, sir, preparing for your noble journey?
    'Tis well, and full of care: 115
    I saw your mind was wedded to the war,
    And knew you would prove some good man for your
        country;—
    Therefore, fair cousin, with your gentle pardon,
    I got this place. What, mourn at his advancement? 120
    You are to blame; he'll come again, sweet cousin;
    Meantime, like sad Penelope and sage,
    Among your maids at home, and huswifely—
Leon. No, sir, I dare not leave her to that solitariness;
    She's young, and grief or ill news from those quarters 125
    May daily cross her; she shall go along, sir.
Duke. By no means, captain!
Leon. By all means, an't please ye.
Duke. What, take a young and tender-bodied lady,
    And expose her to those dangers, and those tumults; 130

A sickly lady too!
Leon. 'Twill make her well, sir;
    There's no such friend to health as wholesome travel.
Sanc. Away, it must not be.
Alon. It ought not, sir;   135
    Go hurry her! It is not humane, captain.
Duke. I cannot blame her tears; fright her with tempests,
    With thunder of the war!
    I dare swear, if she were able—
Leon. She's most able;   140
    And 'pray ye swear not; she must go, there's no remedy;
    Nor greatness, nor the trick you had to part us,
    Which I smell too rank, too open, too evident,—
    And, I must tell you, sir, 'tis most unnoble,—
    Shall hinder me: Had she but ten hours' life,   145
    Nay less, but two hours, I would have her with me;
    I would not leave her fame to so much ruin,
    To such a desolation and discredit,
    As her weakness and your hot will would work her to.—

Enter PEREZ.

What masque is this now?   150
More tropes and figures to abuse my sufferance?
What cousin's this?
Juan. Michael van Owl, how dost thou?
    In what dark barn, or tod of aged ivy,
    Hast thou lain hid?   155
Perez. Things must both ebb and flow, colonel,
    And people must conceal, and shine again.—
    You are welcome hither, as your friend may say, gentlemen;[1]
    A pretty house you see, handsomely seated,
    Sweet and convenient walks, the waters crystal.   160
Alon. He's certain mad.
Juan. As mad as a French tailor,
    That has nothing in his head but ends of fustians.

[1] Q and F, 'gentleman'; but the alteration made silently in 1750, and followed since, seems imperative.

Perez. I see you are packing now, my gentle cousin,
And my wife told me I should find it so; 165
'Tis true I do. You were merry when I was last here,
But 'twas your will to try my patience, madam.
I am sorry that my swift occasions
Can let you take your pleasure here no longer;
Yet I would have you think, my honour'd cousin, 170
This house and all I have are all your servants.
Leon. What house, what pleasure, sir? what do you mean?
Perez. You hold the jest so stiff, 'twill prove discourteous
This house I mean, the pleasures of this place.
Leon. And what of them? 175
Perez. They are mine, sir, and you know it;
My wife's I mean, and so conferr'd upon me;
The hangings, sir, I must entreat your servants,
That are so busy in their offices,
Again to minister to their right uses; 180
I shall take view o' th' plate anon, and furnitures
That are of under place. You're merry still, cousin,
And of a pleasant constitution;
Men of great fortunes make their mirths *ad placitum*.
Leon. Pr'ythee, good stubborn wife, tell me directly, 185
Good evil wife, leave fooling, and tell me honestly,
Is this my kinsman?
Marg. I can tell ye nothing.
Leon. I've many kinsman, but so mad a one,
And so fantastic—All the house? 190
Perez. All mine,
And all within it. I will not bate you an ace on't.
Can you not receive a noble courtesy,
And quietly and handsomely as ye ought, coz,
But you must ride o' th' top on't. 195
Leon. Canst thou fight?
Perez. I'll tell you presently; I could have done, sir.
Leon. For you must law and claw before you get it.
Juan. Away; no quarrels!
Leon. Now I am more temperate, 200

I'll have it prov'd, if you were never yet in Bedlam,
Never in love, (for that's a lunacy)
No great state left you that you never look'd for,
Nor cannot manage, (that's a rank distemper)
That you were christen'd, and who answer'd for you;　　205
And then I['ll] yield.

Perez. [He] has half persuaded me I was bred i' th' moon:
I have ne'er a bush at my breech? Are not we both mad?
And is not this a fantastic house we're in,
And all a dream we do? Will you walk out, sir?　　210
And if I do not beat thee presently
Into a sound belief as sense can give thee,
Brick me into that wall there for a chimney-piece,
And say I was one o' th' Cæsars, done by a seal cutter.

Leon. I'll talk no more; come, we'll away immediately.　　215

Marg. Why then, the house is his, and all that's in it;—
I'll give away my skin, but I'll undo you!　　[*Aside.*]
I gave it to his wife: You must restore, sir,
And make a new provision.

Perez. Am I mad now,　　220
Or am I christen'd? You, my pagan cousin,
My mighty Mahound kinsman, what quirk now?—
You shall be welcome all; I hope to see, sir,
Your grace here, and my coz; we are all soldiers,
And must do naturally for one another.　　225

Duke. Are ye blank at this? then I must tell ye, sir,
Ye have no command! Now ye may go at pleasure,
And ride your ass-troop: 'Twas a trick I use[d]
To try your jealousy, upon entreaty,
And saving[1] of your wife.　　230

Leon. All this not moves me,
Nor stirs my gall, nor alters my affections.—
You have more furniture, more houses, lady,
And rich ones too, I will make bold with those;
And you have land i' th' Indies, as I take it;　　235

---

[1] It has been proposed to read 'craving' for this. Dyce does not approve this; but he has accepted other things less acceptable.

Thither we'll go, and view a while those climates,
Visit your factors there, that may betray you:
'Tis done; we must go.
Marg. Now thou art a brave gentleman,
    And, by this sacred light, I love thee dearly.—   240
    The house is none of yours, I did but jest, sir; [*To* Perez.]
    Nor you are no coz of mine; I beseech you vanish;
    I tell you plain, you have no more right than he has;
    That senseless thing, your wife, has once more ¹ fool'd ye;
    Go you, and consider!   245
Leon. Good morrow, my sweet cousin!
    I should be glad, sir—
Perez. By this hand she dies for't,
    Or any man that speaks for her!   *Exit* Perez.
Juan. These are fine toys.   250
Marg. Let me request you stay but one poor month,
    You shall have a commission, and I'll go too;
    Give me but will so far.
Leon. Well, I will try you.—
    Good morrow to your grace; we have private business.   255
Duke. If I miss thee again, I am an arrant bungler. [*Aside.*]
Juan. Thou shalt have my command, and I'll march under thee;
    Nay, be thy boy, before thou shalt be baffled,
    Thou art so brave a fellow.
Alon. I have seen visions!   *Exeunt.* 260

---

¹ This passage has been made a great crux. It reads in Q, and F follows:

    I tell you plaine you have no more right then he
    Has, that senselesse thing, your wife has once more fool'd ye.

This is not unintelligible, provided we do not bother ourselves about the identification of the 'senseless thing' with any particular member of the company. Seward, giving himself this trouble, and finding nobody suitable but Cacafogo, who is not present, proposed dropping 'he,' and making the 'senseless thing' a chair, etc. 1775 keeps all the words, and alters the punctuation to 'he has; that, senseless thing,' etc., and Weber follows, though with some approval of Mason's conjecture '*thou* senseless thing.' This Dyce adopts. The Moxon text drops the comma at 'that,' so as to make the senseless thing not Perez, but Estifania. If I cared for conjectural emendations, I think I should read:

    you have no more right than has
  That senseless thing, your wife: *she* has once more fooled you.

Act V. Scene I. [*The same.*]

Enter LEON *with a letter, and* MARGARITA.

Leon. Come hither, wife; do you know this hand?
Marg. I do, sir;
　　'Tis Estifania's, that was once my woman.
Leon. She writes to me here, that one Cacafogo,
　　An usuring jeweller's son (I know the rascal)　　　5
　　Is mortally fallen in love with ye—
Marg. Is a monster:　Deliver me from mountains!
Leon. Do you go a-birding for all sorts of people?—
　　And this evening will come to ye and shew ye jewels,
　　And offers anything to get access to ye:　　　　10
　　If I can make or sport or profit on him,
　　(For he is fit for both) she bids me use him;
　　And so I will, be you conformable,
　　And follow but my will.
Marg. I shall not fail, sir.　　　　　　　　　　15
Leon. Will the duke come again, do you think?
Marg. No, sure, sir.
　　[He] has now no policy to bring him hither.
Leon. Nor bring you to him, if my wit hold,[1] fair wife!
　　Let's in to dinner.　　　　　　　*Exeunt.*　20

[Act V. Scene II.　*The Street.*]

Enter PEREZ.

Perez. Had I but lungs enough to bawl sufficiently,
　　That all the queans in Christendom might hear me,
　　That men might run away from contagion,
　　I had my wish: 'Would it were most high treason,
　　Most infinite high, for any man to marry!　　　5

[1] There is a quarrel over this comma, which does not appear in Q and F.　Most put it at 'hold': Dyce, thinking this 'very absurd,' at 'fair.'

I mean for any man that would live handsomely,
And like a gentleman, in his wits and credit.
What torments shall I put her to? Phalaris' bull now—
'Pox, they love bulling too well, though they smoke for't—
Cut her a-pieces? every piece will live still,   10
And every morsel of her will do mischief;
They have so many lives, there's no hanging of 'em;
They are too light to drown, they're cork and feathers;
To burn too cold, they live like salamanders.
Under huge heaps of stones to bury her,   15
And so depress her as they did the giants?
She will move under more than built old Babel.
I must destroy her.

Enter Cacafogo, *with a casket.*

Cac. Be cozen'd by a thing of clouts, a she-moth,
That ev'ry silk-man's shop breeds! to be cheated,   20
And of a thousand ducats, by a whim-wham!
Perez. Who's that is cheated? speak again, thou vision!
But art thou cheated? minister some comfort!
Tell me directly, art thou cheated bravely?
Come, pr'ythee come; art thou so pure a coxcomb   25
To be undone? do not dissemble with me;
Tell me, I conjure thee.
Cac.   Then keep thy circle,
For I am a spirit wild that flies about thee,
And, whoe'er thou art, if thou be'st human,   30
I'll let thee plainly know, I'm cheated damnably.
Perez. Ha, ha, ha!
Cac. Dost thou laugh! Damnably, I say, most damnably.
Perez. By whom, good spirit! speak, speak! ha, ha, ha!
Cac. I'll utter—laugh 'till thy lungs crack—by a rascal woman, 35
A lewd, abominable, and plain woman.
Dost thou laugh still?
Perez. I must laugh; pr'ythee pardon me;
I shall laugh terribly.
Cac.   I shall be angry,   40

Terrible angry; I have cause.

Perez. That's it,
And 'tis no reason but thou shouldst be angry,
Angry at heart; yet I must laugh still at thee.
By a woman cheated? art sure it was a woman? 45

Cac. I shall break thy head; my valour itches at thee.

Perez. It is no matter. By a woman cozen'd?
A real woman?

Cac. A real devil;
Plague of her jewels, and her copper chains, 50
How rank they smell!

Perez. Sweet cozen'd sir, let me see them;
I have been cheated too, (I would have you note that)
And lewdly cheated, by a woman also,
A scurvy woman; I am undone, sweet sir, 55
Therefore I must have leave to laugh.

Cac. Pray ye take it. [*Gives him the casket.*]
You are the merriest undone man in Europe;
What need we fiddles, bawdy songs, and sack,
When our own miseries can make us merry? 60

Perez. Ha, ha, ha!
I have seen these jewels; what a notable pennyworth
Have you had next your heart! You will not take, sir,
Some twenty ducats—

Cac. Thou art deceiv'd; I will take— 65

Perez. To clear your bargain now?

Cac. I'll take some ten,
Some anything, some half ten, half a ducat.

Perez. An excellent lapidary set those stones sure;
Do you mark their waters? 70

Cac. Quicksand choak their waters,
And hers that brought [1] 'em too! But I shall find her.

Perez. And so shall I, I hope; but do not hurt her;
You cannot find in all this kingdom,
If you had need of cozening, (as you may have, 75
For such gross natures will desire it often,

------

[1] Q and F, 'bought.'

It is at some time too a fine variety)
A woman that can cozen you so neatly.—
She has taken half mine anger off with this trick. *Exit.*
Cac. If I were valiant now, I would kill this fellow; 80
I have money enough lies by me, at a pinch,
To pay for twenty rascals' lives that vex me.
I'll to this lady; there I shall be satisfied. *Exit.*

[Act V. Scene III. *An Apartment in Margarita's House.*]

Enter LEON *and* MARGARITA.

Leon. Come, we'll away unto your country-house,
And there we'll learn to live contentedly [1] :
This place is full of charge, and full of hurry;
No part of sweetness dwells about these cities.
Marg. Whither you will, I wait upon your pleasure; 5
Live in a hollow tree, sir, I'll live with you.
Leon. Ay, now you strike a harmony, a true one,
When your obedience waits upon your husband,
And your sick will aims at the care [2] of honour.
Why, now I dote upon ye, love ye dearly, 10
And my rough nature falls like roaring streams,
Clearly and sweetly into your embraces.
Oh, what a jewel is a woman excellent,
A wise, a virtuous, and a noble woman!
When we meet such, we bear our stamps on both sides, 15
And through the world we hold our current virtues;
Alone, we are single medals, only faces,
And wear our fortunes out in useless shadows.
Command you now, and ease me of that trouble;
I'll be as humble to you as a servant: 20
Bid whom you please, invite your noble friends,

[1] Q and F, 'contently,' which Dyce keeps, and which is perhaps right.
[2] Seward, quite unnecessarily, 'cure.'

They shall be welcome all; visit acquaintance,
Go at your pleasure, now experience
Has link'd you fast unto the chain of goodness!   24
—*Clashing swords. A cry within:* "Down with their swords!"—
What noise is this? what dismal cry?

Marg. 'Tis loud too:
Sure there's some mischief done i' th' street; look out there.

Leon. Look out, and help!

Enter a Servant.

Serv. Oh, sir, the Duke Medina—   30

Leon. What of the Duke Medina?

Serv. Oh, sweet gentleman,
Is almost slain.

Marg. Away, away, and help him!
All the house help!   *Ex[eunt* MARG. *and*] Servant.   35

Leon. How slain?—Why, Margarita! why, wife!—
Sure, some new device they have afoot again,
Some trick upon my credit; I shall meet it.
I'd rather guide a ship imperial
Alone, and in a storm, than rule one woman.   40

Enter DUKE, MARGARITA, SANCHIO, ALONZO, [*and*] Servant.

Marg. How came you hurt, sir?

Duke. I fell out with my friend, the noble colonel;
My cause was naught, for 'twas about your honour,
And he that wrongs the innocent ne'er prospers;
And he has left me thus. For charity,[1]   45
Lend me a bed to ease my tortur'd body,
That ere I perish, I may shew my penitence!
I fear I am slain.

Leon. Help, gentlemen, to carry him.
There shall be nothing in this house, my lord,   50
But as your own.

Duke. I thank you, noble sir.

Leon. To bed with him; and, wife, give your attendance.

[1] Q, 'thus for charity.'

Enter JUAN.

Juan. Doctors and surgeons—
Duke. Do not disquiet me,
    But let me take my leave in peace. 55
      Exeunt [1] DUKE, SANCH., ALON., MARG. [*and*] Servants.
Leon. Afore me,
    'Tis rarely counterfeited!
Juan. True, it is so, sir;
    And take you heed this last blow do not spoil ye. 60
    He is not hurt, only we made a scuffle,
    As though we purpos'd anger; that same scratch
    On's hand he took, to colour all, and draw compassion,
    That he might get into your house more cunningly.
    I must not stay. Stand now, and ye're a brave fellow. 65
Leon. I thank you, noble colonel, and I honour you.—
    Never be quiet? *Exit* JUAN.

Enter MARGARITA.

Marg. He's most desperate ill, sir;
    I do not think these ten months will recover him.
Leon. Does he hire my house to play the fool in? 70
    Or does it stand on fairy ground? We're haunted! [2]
    Are all men and their wives troubled with dreams thus?
Marg. What ail you, sir?
Leon. Nay, what ail you, sweet wife,
    To put these daily pastimes on my patience? 75
    What dost thou see in me, that I should suffer thus?
    Have not I done my part like a true husband,
    And paid some desperate debts you never look'd for?
Marg. You have done handsomely, I must confess, sir.
Leon. Have I not kept thee waking like a hawk? 80
    And watch'd thee with delights to satisfy thee,
    The very tithes of which had won a widow?
Marg. Alas, I pity you.

[1] Q, *Exit.*
[2] Q and F, comma after 'haunted' and after 'ground.' Editors have punctuated variously.

Leon. Thou wilt make me angry;
 Thou never saw'st me mad yet.   85
Marg. You are always,
 You carry a kind of Bedlam still about you.
Leon. If thou pursuest me further, I run stark mad;
 If you have more hurt dukes or gentlemen,
 To lie here on your cure, I shall be desperate!   90
 I know the trick, and you shall feel I know it.
 Are ye so hot that no hedge can contain ye?
 I'll have thee let blood in all the veins about thee,
 I'll have thy thoughts found too, and have them open'd,
 Thy spirits purg'd, for those are they that fire ye.   95
 Thy maid shall be thy mistress, thou the maid
 To all those servile labours that she reach [1] at,
 And go though cheerfully, or else sleep empty;
 That maid shall lie by me, to teach you duty,
 You in a pallet by, to humble ye,   100
 And grieve for what you loose.
Marg.   I have lost myself, sir,
 And all that was my base self, disobedience;   *Kneels.*
 My wantonness, my stubbornness, I have lost too:
 And now, by that pure faith good wives are crown'd with, 105
 By your own nobleness—
Leon.   I take ye up,
 And wear ye next my heart; see you be worth it.

       Enter ALTEA.

 Now, what with you?
Altea.   I come to tell my lady,   110
 There is a fulsome fellow would fain speak with her.
Leon. 'Tis Cacafogo; go, and entertain him,
 And draw him on with hopes.
Marg.   I shall observe you.
Leon. I have a rare design upon that gentleman;   115

 [1] This is an obviously corrupt passage, which various editors have mended variously, Dyce supposing a dropped line. But 'reach,' as Sympson saw, comes in awkardly anyhow. One might guess '*aches* at,' if guessing were *tanti*. Q and F have 'And all.'

And you must work too.

Altea. I shall, sir, most willingly.

Leon. Away then both, and keep him close in some place,
From the duke's sight; and keep the duke in too;
Make 'em believe both: I'll find time to cure 'em. 120

Exeunt.

[Act V. Scene IV. *The Street.*]

Enter PEREZ *and* ESTIFANIA, *with a pistol and a dagge*[r].

Perez. Why, how dar'st thou meet me again, thou rebel, [*Draws.*]
And know'st how thou hast us'd me thrice, thou rascal?
Were there not ways enough to fly my vengeance,
No holes nor vaults to hide thee from my fury,
But thou must meet me face to face to kill thee? 5
I would not seek thee to destroy thee willingly,
But now thou com'st to invite me, and com'st upon me:
How like a sheep-biting rogue, taken i' th' manner,
And ready for the halter, dost thou look now!
Thou hast a hanging look, thou scurvy thing! 10
Hast ne'er a knife,
Nor never a string, to lead thee to Elysium?
Be there no pitiful 'pothecaries in this town,
That have compassion upon wretched women,
And dare administer a dram of rats-bane, 15
But thou must fall to me?

Estif. I know you have mercy. [*Kneels.*]

Perez. If I had tons of mercy, thou deserv'st none.
What new trick's now afoot, and what new houses
Have you i' th' air? what orchards in apparition? 20
What canst thou say for thy life?

Estif. Little or nothing;
I know you'll kill me, and I know 'tis useless
To beg for mercy. Pray, let me draw my book out,
And pray a little! 25

Perez. Do; a very little,

    For I have further business than thy killing;
    I have money yet to borrow. Speak when you are ready.
Estif. Now, now, sir, now!—*Shews a pistol.*—Come on! do you start
    off from me?   30
    Do you sweat,[1] great captain?—have you seen a spirit?
Perez. Do you wear guns?
Estif. I am a soldier's wife, sir,
    And by that privilege I may be arm'd.
    Now, what's the news? and let's discourse more friendly,   35
    And talk of our affairs in peace.
Perez. Let me see,
    Pr'ythee, let me see thy gun; 'tis a very pretty one.
Estif. No, no, sir; you shall feel.
Perez. Hold, [hold,] you villain!   40
    What, thine own husband?
Estif. Let mine own husband then
    Be in's own wits.—There, there's a thousand ducats!—
                                        [Shows a purse.]
    Who must provide for you?—And yet you'll kill me.
Perez. I will not hurt thee for ten thousand millions.   45
Estif. When will you redeem your jewels? I have pawn'd 'em,
    You see for what;—we must keep touch.
Perez. I'll kiss thee,
    And, get as many more, I'll make thee famous.—
    Had we the house now!   50
Estif. Come along with me;
    If that be vanish'd, there be more to hire, sir.
Perez. I see I am an ass, when thou art near me.   *Exeunt.*

[Act V. Scene V. *A Chamber in Margarita's House.*]

Enter LEON, MARGARITA, *and* ALTEA, *with a taper.*

Leon. Is the fool come?
Altea. Yes, and i' th' cellar fast,
    And there he stays his good hour till I call him;

                    [1] Q, 'swear.'

He will make dainty music 'mong the sack-butts.
I have put him just, sir, under the duke's chamber.   5
Leon. It is the better.
Altea. [He] has giv'n me royally,
And to my lady a whole load of portigues.
Leon. Better and better still.—Go, Margarita,
Now play your prize:—You say you dare be honest;   10
I'll put you to your best.[1]
Marg. Secure yourself, sir;
Give me the candle; pass away in silence.
> *Exeunt* LEON *and* ALTEA. [MARG.] *knocks.*[2]
*Duke.—Within.—*Who's there? Oh, oh!
Marg. My lord!   15
*Duke.—Within—*Have you brought me comfort?
Marg. I have, my lord:
Come forth; 'tis I. Come gently out; I'll help you;—

> *Enter* DUKE, *in a gown.*

Come softly too. How do you?
Duke. Are there none here?   *Noise below.* 20
Let me look round; we cannot be too wary.
Oh, let me bless this hour! Are you alone, sweet friend?
Marg. Alone, to comfort you.
> CACAFOGO *makes a noise below.*
Duke. What's that you tumble?
I've heard a noise this half hour under me,   25
A fearful noise.
Marg. The fat thing's mad i' th' cellar,   [*Aside.*]
And stumbles from one hogshead to another;
Two cups more and he ne'er shall find the way out.—
What do you fear? Come, sit down by me cheerfully;   30
My husband's safe.—How do your wounds?
Duke. I've none, lady;
My wounds I counterfeited cunningly,
And feign'd the quarrel too, to enjoy you, sweet:
Let's lose no time.—*Noise below.*—Hark, the same noise again!

---

[1] Some alter to 'test,' needlessly.   [2] Q, *Exit,* etc. 'She' for 'Marg.'

Marg. What noise? why look you pale?   I hear no stirring.—   36
 (This goblin in the vault will be so tippled!)   [*Aside.*]
 You are not well, I know by your flying fancy;
 Your body's ill at ease; your wounds—
Duke. I've none;   40
 I am as lusty, and as full of health,
 High in my blood—
Marg. Weak in your blood, you would say.
 How wretched is my case, willing to please you,
 And find you so disable!   45
Duke. Believe me, lady—
Marg. I know, you'll venture all you have to satisfy me,
 Your life I know; but is it fit I spoil you?
 Is it, my love, do you think?
Cac.—Below.—Here's to the duke!   50
Duke. It nam'd me certainly;
 I heard it plainly sound.
Marg. You are hurt mortally,
 And fitter for your prayers, sir, than pleasure.
 What starts you make!   I would not kiss you wantonly,   55
 For the world's wealth.—Have I secur'd my husband,
 And put all doubts aside, to be deluded?
Cac.—Below.—I come, I come.
Duke. Heav'n bless me!
Marg. And bless us both, for sure this is the devil!   60
 I plainly heard it now; he'll come to fetch you!
 A very spirit, for he spoke under ground,
 And spoke to you just as you would have snatch'd me.
 You are a wicked man, and sure this haunts you:
 'Would you were out o' th' house!   65
Duke. I would I were,
 O' that condition I had leap'd a window.
Marg. And that's the least leap, if you mean to 'scape, sir.
 Why, what a frantic man you were to come here,
 What a weak man to counterfeit deep wounds,   70
 To wound another deeper!
Duke. Are you honest then?

Marg. Yes, then, and now, and ever; and excellent honest,
And exercise this pastime but to shew you,
Great men are fools sometimes as well as wretches: 75
'Would you were well hurt, with any hope of life,
Cut to the brains, or run clean through the body,
To get out quietly as you got in, sir!
I wish it like a friend that loves ye dearly;
For if my husband take ye, and take you thus 80
A counterfeit, one that would clip his credit,
Out of his honour he must kill you presently;
There is no mercy, nor an hour of pity:
And for me to entreat in such an agony,
Would shew me little better than one guilty. 85
Have you any mind to a lady now?
Duke. 'Would I were off fair!
If ever lady caught me in a trap more—
Marg. If you be well and lusty—fie, fie; shake not!
You say you love me; come, come bravely now; 90
Despise all danger; I am ready for ye.
Duke. She mocks my misery: Thou cruel lady!
Marg. Thou cruel lord! wouldst thou betray my honesty,
Betray it in mine own house, wrong my husband,
Like a night thief, thou dar'st not name by daylight? 95
Duke. I am most miserable.
Marg. You are indeed;
And, like a foolish thing, you have made yourself so.
Could not your own discretion tell ye, sir,
When I was married I was none of yours? 100
Your eyes were then commanded to look off me,
And I now stand in a circle and secure;
Your spells nor power can never reach my body.
Mark me but this, and then, sir, be most miserable;
'Tis sacrilege to violate a wedlock, 105
You rob two temples, make yourself twice guilty,
You ruin hers, and spot her noble husband's.
Duke. Let me be gone. I'll never more attempt ye.
Marg. You cannot go; 'tis not in me to save ye:

Dare you do ill, and poorly then shrink under it?   110
Were I the Duke Medina I would fight now,
For you must fight, and bravely, it concerns you;
You do me double wrong if you sneak off, sir,
And all the world would say I lov'd a coward;
And you must die too, for you will be kill'd,   115
And leave your youth, your honour, and your state,
And all those dear delights you worshipp'd here.

Duke. The noise again!   *Noise below.*

*Cac.—Below.—*Some small beer, if you love me.

Marg. The devil haunts you sure; your sins are mighty;   120
    A drunken devil too, to plague your villainy.

Duke. Preserve me but this once!

Marg. There's a deep well
    In the next yard, if you dare venture drowning:
    It is but death.   125

Duke. I would not die so wretchedly.

Marg. Out of a garret-window I will let you down then;
    But say the rope be rotten? 'tis huge high too.

Duke. Have you no mercy?

Marg. Now you are frighted thoroughly,   130
    And find what 'tis to play the fool in vice,
    And see with clear eyes your detested folly,[1]
    I'll be your guard.

Duke. And I'll be your true servant,
    Ever from this hour virtuously to love ye,   135
    Chastely and modestly to look upon ye,
    And here I seal it.   [*Kisses her.*]

Marg. I may kiss a stranger,
    For you must now be so.

    Ent[er] LEON, JUAN, ALONZO, [*and*] SANCHIO.

Leon. How do you, my lord?   140
    Methinks you look but poorly on this matter.

---

[1] In Q and F 'folly' ends *both* lines, 131, 132,—of course by one of those echo-slips so common in manuscript and not quite unknown in print. Much guessing has taken place as to which to discard and what to put in its place. The text, which is that of Dyce, following Ed. 1778, is good enough.

Has my wife wounded ye? you were well before.
'Pray, sir, be comforted; I have forgot all,
Truly forgiven too.—Wife, you are a right one,
And now with unknown nations I dare trust you. 145
Juan. No more feign'd fights, my lord; they never prosper.

[*Enter* ALTEA, *and* CACAFOGO *drunk.*]

Leon. Who's this? the devil in the vault?
Altea. 'Tis he, sir,
And as lovingly drunk, as though he had studied it.
Cac. Give me a cup of sack, and kiss me, lady! 150
Kiss my sweet face, and make thy husband cuckold!—
An ocean of sweet sack!—Shall we speak treason?
Leon. He's devilish drunk.
Duke. I had thought he had been a devil;
He made as many noises, and as horrible. 155
Leon. Oh, a true lover, sir, will lament loudly.—
Which of the butts is your mistress?
Cac. Butt in thy belly!
Leon. There's two in thine I'm sure, 'tis grown so monstrous.
Cac. Butt in thy face! 160
Leon. Go, carry him to sleep.
A fool's love should be drunk; he has paid well for't too.
When he is sober, let him out to rail,
Or hang himself; there will be no loss of him.

Exeunt [1] CACAFOGO *and* Serv[ant].

Enter PEREZ *and* ESTIFANIA.

Who's this? my Mahound cousin? 165
Perez. Good, sir; 'tis very good! 'Would I had a house, too!
(For there's no talking in the open air)
My Termagant coz, I would be bold to tell you,
I durst be merry too; I tell you plainly,
You have a pretty seat, you have the luck on't, 170
A pretty lady too; I have miss'd both:
My carpenter built in a mist, I thank him!
Do me the courtesy to let me see it,

[1] Q, *Exit.*

See it but once more. But I shall cry for anger!
I'll hire a chandler's shop close under you,   175
And, for my foolery, sell soap and whip-cord.
Nay, if you do not laugh now, and laugh heartily,
You are a fool, coz.
Leon.   I must laugh a little,
And now I have done.—Coz, thou shalt live with me,   180
My merry coz; the world shall not divorce us.
Thou art a valiant man, and thou shalt never want.
Will this content thee?
Perez.   I'll cry, and then I'll be thankful,
Indeed I will, and I'll be honest to you: 185
I would live a swallow here, I must confess.—
Wife, I forgive thee all, if thou be honest;
At thy [1] peril, I believe thee excellent.
Estif.   If I prove otherwise, let me beg first.
Leon. [2]   Hold, this is yours; some recompense for service: 190
                                    [*Gives money to* ESTIF.]
Use it to nobler ends than he that gave it.
Duke.   And this is yours, your true commission, sir.   [*To* LEON.]
Now you are a captain.
Leon.   You are a noble prince, sir;
And now a soldier, gentlemen. [3]   195
Omnes.   We all rejoice in't.
Juan.   Sir, I shall wait upon you through all fortunes.
Alon.   And I.
Altea.   And I must needs attend my mistress.
Leon.   Will you go, sister?   200
Altea.   Yes, indeed, good brother;
I have two ties, my own blood, and my mistress.
Marg.   Is she your sister?
Leon.   Yes, indeed, good wife,
And my best sister; for she prov'd so, wench,   205
When she deceiv'd you with a loving husband.

---

[1] Some, quite needlessly, 'my.'
[2] *Leon* is omitted in Q and F, but it is evidently required.
[3] Q and F, 'Gentleman, we all rejoice in't'; closing line 195, and without *Omnes.*

Altea. I would not deal so truly for a stranger.
Marg. Well, I could chide you;
But it must be lovingly, and like a sister.—
I'll bring you on your way, and feast you nobly,   210
(For now I have an honest heart to love you)
And then deliver you to the blue Neptune.
Juan. Your colours you [1] must wear, and wear 'em proudly,
Wear 'em before the bullet, and in blood too:
And all the world shall know we are Virtue's servants.   215
Duke. And all the world shall know, a noble mind
Makes women beautiful, and envy blind.   *Exeunt.*

[1] Monck Mason conjectured 'we,' which Dyce rather surprisingly adopts.

The Epilogue

Good night, our worthy friends! and may you part
Each with as merry and as free a heart
As you came hither! To those noble eyes,
That deign to smile on our poor faculties,
And give a blessing to our labouring ends,
As we hope many, to such Fortune sends [1]
Their own desires, wives fair as light, as chaste!
To those that live by spite, wives made in haste!

[1] The text is that of Q and F. Dyce cuts off both *s*'s; others, valiantly sacrificing the rhyme, only that of 'sends.' No correction is *absolutely* necessary. The singular 'end' is very awkward, and 'sends' requires only a moderate ellipse = 'As we hope many (blessings) *to those to whom* Fortune sends,' etc. As much as this is often packed into the much enduring 'rules.'

APPENDIX

A. The Division of Lines in the Quarto. Act I, i, 5 of the present text
ends in the Quarto with the word *out;* line 6 ends in Q with *thinke;* l. 7
with *goe;* l. 45 with *speak;* l. 46 with *yee;* l. 58 with *then;* l. 68 with *picke;*
l. 69 with *preludium;* l. 70 with *gentleman;* next line with *lady;* l. 97 with
come; l. 99 with *souldier.*

Act I, ii, 9 ends in Q with *thou;* l. 14 with *um;* l. 15 with *they;* next line
with *points;* l. 54 with *souldier;* l. 55 with *not;* next line with *Sanchio.*

Act I, iv, 1 ends in Q with *hast;* l. 28 with *counsell;* next line with *ye.*

Act I, v, 21 ends in Q with *sir;* l. 42 with *Welcome, Alonzo;* l. 44 with
company; l. 46 with *pumpion;* l. 49 with *buttered;* l. 52 with *too;* next line
with *Captains;* l. 56 with *not;* next line with *instantly;* l. 68 with *beat;*
next line with *fellow.*

Act I, vi, 10 ends in Q with *place;* l. 48 with *well;* l. 57 with *stick;* next
line with *lady;* l. 66 with *wealth;* l. 67 with *warre;* l. 68 with *dare;* l. 69 with
your; l. 70 with *as;* next line with *lady;* l. 73 with *sudden;* l. 75 with *too;*
l. 80 with *you;* next line with *fancy.*

Act II, i, 8 of the present text ends in Q with *me,* next line with *all;*
l. 21 with *woman;* l. 34 with *rare;* next line with *perfection;* l. 63 with *him.*

Act II, ii, 34 ends in Q with *lesse;* next line with *thee.*

Act II, iii, 64 ends in Q with *sufficiently;* l. 74 with *contented;* l. 78 with
speake; l. 83 with *wait.*

Act II, iv, 105 ends in Q with *to;* l. 106 with *she;* next line with *has;* l. 114
with *now;* l. 115 with *cozen;* next line with *observes her;* l. 128 with *wealth;*
l. 155 with *too.*

Act III, i, 25 ends in Q with *now;* next line with *up;* l. 85 with *her;* l. 140
with *blowne;* l. 141 with *wine;* l. 142 with *finds;* next line with *reasons.*

Act III, iii, 11 ends in Q with *bond;* l. 36 with *one;* l. 43 with *orient;*
next line with *respected;* l. 49 with *Medina;* l. 67 with *too.*

Act III, iv, 19 ends in Q with *wife;* l. 42 with *faire;* l. 55 with *worth;* next
line with *you;* l. 57 with *saw;* l. 60 with *hangings;* next line with *thing;*
l. 79 with *because;* l. 80 with *firkt;* next line with *living;* l. 82 with *my;*
next line with *lying;* l. 100 with *truth.*

Act III, v, 46 ends in Q with *you;* l. 89 with *in't;* l. 90 with *madam;* l. 94

with *better;* l. 95 with *madame;* l. 115 with *lead;* next line with *now;* l. 134 with *pitty;* l. 148 with *me;* l. 171 with *house;* next line with *lady;* and the next with *her;* l. 214 with *her;* l. 228 with *me.*

Act IV, i, 16 ends in Q with *too;* l. 37 with *found;* next line with *candle-sticks;* l. 94 with *crafty.*

Act IV, ii, 10 ends in Q with *prison;* next line with *undoing;* l. 17 with *friends;* next line with *all.*

Act IV, iii, 17 ends in Q with *sir;* l. 62 with *king;* l. 104 with *that;* l. 219 with *cozen;* l. 243 with *he;* l. 246 with *sir.*

Act V, i, 2 ends in Q with *Estifanias;* next line with *woman;* l. 13 with *will.*

Act V, ii, 40 ends in Q with *cause;* next line with *shouldst be angry;* l. 67 with *halfe ten;* next line with *ducket.*

Act V, iii, 32 ends in Q with *slain;* next line with *house help;* the next with *Margarita,* and the next with *againe;* l. 107 with *heart;* next line with *with you.*

Act V, iv, 7 ends in Q with *me;* next line with *upon me;* l. 10 with *knife;* l. 29 with *now, shews a pistol;* next line with *me;* l. 39 with *husband.*

Act V, v, 12 ends in Q with *candle;* the next with *silence;* l. 40 with *health;* l. 80 with *counterfeit;* l. 81 with *honour;* l. 82 with *presently;* l. 138 with *so;* l. 148 with *it;* l. 195 with *int;* l. 202 with *bloud;* next line with *mistris;* l. 204 with *sister;* next line with *wench;* l. 215 with *know;* next line with *servants.*

Epilogue l. 8 ends with *spight;* next line with *hast.*

B. The Position of Stage Directions in the Quarto.—The stage directions of Q are given *without brackets* in the present text; but in the following cases a change of position has been made.

In Act I, v, Q places *Ent. Alonzo* above l. 42;

In Act I, v, Q places *Ent. Caca.,* at the end of l. 45;

In Act II, iv, Q places *Exit Per* at end of l. 170;

In Act III, i, Q places *Enter Leon* at the end of l. 43;

In Act IV, i, Q places *Enter Estif.,* etc., below l. 5;

In Act V, iii, Q places *Enter Altea* at the end of l. 107;

In Act V, v, Q places *Enter Duke,* etc., at the end of l. 17;

In Act V, v, Q places *Noise below* at the end of l. 21; second *noise below* at end of l. 33.

The Quarto has only Actus i, Scena i; Actus ii, Scena i, and so on through the play: no further subdivision into scenes, and no indication of localities.

Gen. Ed.

Philip Massinger

A NEW WAY TO PAY OLD DEBTS

*Edited with Critical Essay
and Notes by Brander Mat-
thews, Litt. D., Professor in
Columbia University.*

CRITICAL ESSAY

Life.—Philip Massinger was a member of an old Salisbury family. His father, Arthur Massinger, was an Oxford man, who had been Fellow of Merton (1572), and who had been member of parliament for Weymouth and Melcombe Regis (1588–9 and 1593) and for Shaftesbury (1601). Arthur Massinger was "confidential servant or house-steward at Wilton to Henry Herbert, second Earl of Pembroke, and retained the post under his first master's son, William, third earl, the patron and friend of Shakespere." When his son dedicated *The Bondman* to Philip Herbert he declared that Arthur Massinger had spent many years happily "in the service of your honorable house, and died a servant to it,"—the death occurring apparently in 1606.

Baptized on November 24th, 1583, Philip Massinger was perhaps named after the brother of the wife of the second Earl of Pembroke, Sir Philip Sidney. In his youth he may have been a page at Wilton; and it is likely that he owed to the liberality of the second earl the opportunity of going to Oxford, being entered at St. Alban Hall May 14th, 1602, and leaving the university in 1606, the year of his father's death, and without taking a degree—perhaps because he had, as Wood informs us, "applied his mind more to poetry and romances . . . than to logic or philosophy." Thrown on his own resources, although still clinging to the Herbert family, he went up to London at the age of twenty-three; and for a third of a century he supported himself meagrely by his pen. The only form of literature by which a poet might then hope to make a living was the drama; and like so many others he turned to the stage, for which, as it chanced, he had a richer native gift than the most of those who were his rivals.

With many of these rivals he seems to have been on terms not only of friendship but of intimacy, forming partnerships with them for the revising of old plays and for the writing of new ones. The habit of collaboration has always obtained in periods of high dramatic productivity; and Massinger allied himself at one time or another with Nathaniel Field, Robert Daborne, Cyril Tourneur, Dekker, and more especially Fletcher, with whom his association was long-continued and prolific. In 1616 he was writing for the King's men, going over to the Queen's men in 1623 and returning to the King's men after Fletcher's death in 1625. Although he wrote one play, *The Great Duke of Florence*, for the Queen's servants in 1627, the most of his work for the last score years of his life was done for the one company, the King's men. His death took place in his house on the Bankside, Southwark, near the Globe Theater, in the middle of March 1639–1640; and he was buried in the yard of St. Saviour's church. Some writers have seen pathos in the entry of burial in the parish-register,— "Philip Massinger, a stranger"—but this qualification meant merely that he was not a member of the parish.

It is possible that Massinger had been converted to Roman Catholicism; but this is little more than a supposition based on the frail support of the tone of certain passages in two of his plays, *The Renegade* and *The Virgin Martyr*. Whatever his religious tenets his political opinions are clear enough, at least in the later years of his life. He was an adherent of the popular party, loyally taking sides with the Herberts against Buckingham. Gardiner has pointed out "that in many of Massinger's plays we have a treatment of the politics of the day so plain and transparent, that any one who possesses only a slight acquaintance with the history of the reigns of the first two Stuarts can read it at a glance." In this he was perhaps unconsciously following the example set by John Lyly two score years earlier. There are four plays in which Massinger managed to insert allusions to contemporary politics and sought to move the minds of playgoers to sympathize with the party headed by the Herberts;—*The Bondman, Believe as You List, The Emperor of the East,* and *The Maid of Honour*. Massinger was in receipt of a pension from the Earl of Pembroke; and after his death this seems to have been continued to his widow.

Plays written by Massinger alone.—There is no satisfactory edition of Massinger prepared in accordance with the critical demands of modern scholarship. Gifford's edition is now a century old, and it did not include *Believe as You List*, the Ms. of which was discovered only in 1844. Perhaps it is fortunate that the work has not been undertaken until the labours of many British, American and German investigators have put us in a position to make out the list of Massinger's plays with a clearer approach to certainty than would have been possible even in the later years of the nineteenth century. Just as the more scientific study of the paintings of the old masters, and a more rigorous comparison of their extant drawings, has resulted in many startling changes of attribution, pictures hitherto accepted as the work of one now being assigned confidently to another, an application of metrical tests, a more minute investigation into the vocabulary and into the tricks of style, and a more careful analysis of the specific qualities—both rhetorical and dramaturgic—of each of the playwrights, as revealed in his undisputed plays, has seemed to justify a reassignment of the authorship of many a drama hitherto ascribed to the wrong writer. For example, it has been made to appear very probable that Massinger was a part-author of not a few of the plays ordinarily accredited to Beaumont and Fletcher. Indeed his work seems to be so clearly commingled with theirs that the best way out of a doubtful situation would be to edit the works of Beaumont, of Fletcher, and of Massinger all together.

But if it is not easy to keep track of Massinger's many collaborations or to trace out his chance revision of other men's work, the list of the plays for which he is solely—or at least chiefly—responsible is not difficult to draw up. There are fifteen of these, and they have been arranged in approximate chronological order by Mr. Robert Boyle, as follows:—

1. *The Duke of Milan*, acted by the King's men at Blackfriars, probably written about 1618; and published in 1623.

2. *The Unnatural Combat*, acted by the King's men at the Globe, probably written about 1619; and published in 1639.

3. *The Bondman*, acted at the Cockpit, licensed in 1623; and published in 1624.

4. *The Renegado*, acted by the Queen's men, licensed in 1624; and published in 1630.

5. *The Parliament of Love*, licensed for the Cockpit in 1624; and printed only in 1805 from an imperfect Ms.

6. *A New Way to Pay Old Debts*, acted by the Queen's men at the Phœnix, probably written in 1625–6; and published in 1632.

7. *The Roman Actor*, acted by the Queen's men at Blackfriars; licensed in 1626; and published in 1629.

8. *The Maid of Honour*, acted by the Queen's men at the Phœnix; and published in 1632.

9. *The Picture*, licensed in 1629; and published in 1630.

10. *The Great Duke of Florence*, licensed in 1627 for the Queen's servants; and published in 1635.

11. *The Emperor of the East*, licensed for the King's men in 1631; published 1635.

12. *Believe as You List*, sent back by Henry Herbert in 1631 because it contained dangerous matter; printed only in 1848.

13. *The City Madam*, licensed in 1632; published in 1658.

14. *The Guardian*, licensed for the King's men in 1633, published in 1655.

15. *The Bashful Lover*, licensed in 1636; published in 1655.

Plays written by Massinger in Collaboration.—In drawing up another list of more than a score of plays in the writing of which Massinger may or may not have collaborated, Mr. Boyle admits that "Massinger's hand can only be detected by internal evidence of style, characterizations and metre." Here we leave the safe ground of fact for the shifting sands of conjecture; and the personal equation instantly obtrudes itself. Mr. Boyle, for example, expresses his belief that *Henry VIII* is "doubtless by Massinger and Fletcher," and he is convinced that *The Two Noble Kinsmen* is "entirely by Massinger and Fletcher"; whereas Swinburne, with characteristic emphasis declares that in the last scene of the latter play "the reader stands convicted of eyeless and earless incompetence who cannot see at once and say for certain where Shakspere breaks off, where Fletcher strikes in, and again where Shakspere resumes and winds up the broken thread of tragic harmony."

Mr. Boyle may be right in ascribing to Massinger a share of the authorship both of *Henry VIII* and of *The Two Noble Kinsmen;* but he has not as yet won over to his opinion a majority of those most competent to judge. He is more likely to be right when he credits Massinger with having had a hand in certain plays hitherto loosely assigned to Beaumont and Fletcher, including *The Bloody Brother, The Custom of the Country, The Little French Lawyer*, and *The Spanish Curate*. He believes that Field aided Massinger in *The Fatal Dowry*, probably written before 1619 and published in 1632. He thinks that Dekker was Massinger's partner in *The Virgin Martyr*, licensed in 1620 and published in 1621. There is no doubt that Massinger's manner is more obviously present in *The Fatal Dowry* and in *The Virgin Martyr* than it is in the little group of plays above cited as generally ascribed to Beaumont and Fletcher. As for *The Old Law* published in 1656 as the joint work of Massinger, Middleton and Rowley, the convincing analysis of Professor Edgar Coit Morris makes it probable that this play was originally written by Middleton, and was afterwards touched up by Rowley, to receive a final revision by Massinger,—possibly for the coronation ceremonies in 1625.

Mr. Morris has not contented himself with tests merely metrical and rhetorical; he has gone deeper and sought to analyze the specific dramaturgic peculiarities of the several playwrights whose handiwork he is seeking to distinguish. He is not only more thorough than most of the others who have been tempted into this fascinating form of the higher criticism, he is far more cautious, warning his readers that it certainly is a delicate matter to assert "that the work of one man ends at a given line, and that the work of another follows, with no other evidence than the general dramatic characteristics of the two men to support the assertion." And the most of those who have rashly adventured themselves in these delicate matters have done so without knowledge or inquiry as to the usual methods of collaborators. They have assumed that if they think they recognize the general style of a certain writer in a given scene or act then this writer is necessarily to be greeted as the author of that part of the play and to be credited with its invention.

But if the collaboration has been a true collaboration, if the two partners have combined to invent, to elaborate, to construct a plot, and to fit it with characters proper to its complete conduct, then there has been a chemical union of their several qualities, and not a merely mechanical mixture, thereafter separable into its constituent elements. Every scene and every act of *Froufrou*, for example, is the joint work of Meilhac and Halévy. When there is a true collaboration of this sort, it is really of no great importance which of the two held the pen in the writing of any given scene. The one who did so was scarcely more than the amanuensis, he was no more the author even of what he penned than was his partner. Augier tells us, that when he and Labiche had devised a play together, they worked out a very detailed scenario, and that then Labiche asked to be allowed to do the actual writing, a favour which Augier kindly granted, making only a few slight modifications in the completed. Ms. which Labiche in time brought him. The application of the ordinary tests of the higher criticism to the result of this collaboration would surely prove that it was the work of Labiche alone and that Augier had nothing whatever to do with it; and yet we know that this result of internal evidence is absolutely contradicted by external evidence,—by the testimony of the two authors themselves.

On the other hand, it is probable that the method of the collaborators was sometimes not that of a conjoint effort, but that of a division of labour, each doing the share of the work for which he was best fitted, one handling the serious plot, for example, and the other taking the comic scenes for his portion. It is possible also that after the play had been plotted by both together, each wrote two of the five acts, dividing the fifth between them. This we know to have been the practice of the fertile and ingenious Spanish playwrights who were contemporary with these Englishmen. Montalvan records for our enlightenment that when he and Lope de Vega once collaborated in a three-act play, the two authors wrote an act apiece and divided the third act between them. But in the Lope de Vega-Montalvan play, as in the Augier-Labiche play, the invention and the construction was done by the two authors working together; and each was entitled to credit for the whole drama, even though the half of it was not put on paper by him.

Perhaps it is the present writer's own experience as a collaborator in fiction and in the drama which makes him rather doubtful of the finality of most of these attempted distributions of scenes and acts between two or three different authors. He remembers his own constant difficulty, after the work was completed, in recognizing what had been his own share of it; and he recalls the absolute impossibility of an attempt to disentangle specific passages as clearly his own or his collaborator's. Professor Morris has shown his wisdom in the cautiousness of his comment on one passage, when he declares that there can be little doubt that the most of a certain scene in *The Old Law* was "phrased" by Massinger. This much metrical and rhetorical tests may help us to;—which of two collaborators *phrased* a given scene. But it cannot have been uncommon for one of them to devise a striking situation which chanced afterward to be phrased not by the inventor but by the other partner to the collaboration.

Massinger as a Poet.—Swinburne has dwelt on the fact that Massinger was the old dramatist who most tardily won recognition from modern critics, and he intimates also that even now Massinger is not so highly esteemed as a dramatic poet as he deserves to be. If this is admitted, two reasons may be suggested to account for it. The first of these is that Massinger is not Elizabethan but Jacobean and Caroline; and that he is a true representative of the silver age of the English dramatic poetry rather than of the golden. When he wrote the spirit of the nation was changing,—and changing for the worse: there was lessened vitality in the people; there was increasing corruption in the upper classes; there were weaker figures upon the throne. The mighty effort, which had made Shakspere possible, had spent itself at last. As Mr. Arthur Symons has picturesquely declared, "Massinger is the late twilight of the long and splendid day of which Marlowe was the dawn."

The second reason is more personal to Massinger himself. A dramatic poet he is beyond question, but he is far greater as dramatist than he is as poet. His inferiority to Marlowe, for example, as a poet is as obvious as his superiority over Marlowe as a playwright. His merit is in the structure and conduct of each of his plays as a whole; and this is not detachable and portable like the unforgettable phrases of Marlowe. There is an even eloquence in Massinger's writing, but scarcely a single sentence wherein he has packed "infinite riches in a little room." As Mr. Symons says, it is not hard to find in plenty, lines that are easy, flowing, vigorous, persuasive, "but nowhere a line in which colour and music make a magical delight of golden concords." Not only Marlowe but Webster and Ford far more often than Massinger yield us passages that sing themselves into the memory. Lowell doubted if there were so many "striking images or pregnant sayings to be found in his works as may be found in those of very inferior men." Of course, this test of the familiar quotation is unfair to all but the witty poets, to the phrase-makers; and it is doubly unfair when applied to a dramatist whose noblest speeches,—like that of Sforza to Charles in *The Duke of Milan*, for instance, often derive much of their nobility from the situation which evokes them. Yet the absence of these readily cited sentences from Massinger's pages is surely one reason why he failed to receive due meed of praise as early as other poets whose merits lay more on the surface.

Not only does Massinger lack instinctive felicity of phrase, he is also without the lyric grace of the earlier Elizabethans or the imaginative fervour of the later dramatic poets. His chariot-wheels never catch fire by their own motion; nor is his Pegasus a winged courser. Wisely enough he attempts few high flights; and his muse is pedestrian. The power of his most forcible passages is not so much poetical as rhetorical, not to call it oratorical; and at times he is frankly argumentative. Coleridge asserted that Massinger's style was "differenced in the smallest degree possible from animated conversation by the vein of poetry." Swinburne declares that "it is radically and essentially unlike the style of his rivals: it is more serviceable, more business-like, more eloquently practical and more rhetorically effusive—but never effusive beyond the bounds of effective rhetoric—than the style of any Shaksperian or of any Jonsonian dramatist."

But if Massinger rarely rises into the loftier levels of pure poetry he rarely falls into flatness and flaccidity. Swinburne, filing a plea of confession and avoidance, asserts that in Massinger "if the irrepressible barrister too often intrudes on the ground of the dramatic poet, it must be allowed that his pleading, if sometimes prosaic in expression and conventional in rhetoric, is seldom or never ineffective either through flatulence of style or through tenuity of matter." And Charles Lamb thought Massinger's style "the purest and most free from violent metaphors and harsh constructions of any of the dramatists who were his contemporaries." His blank verse, vigorous, varied and flexible, was an admirable instrument for a dramatist, who was after all not a master of tragedy plumbing the dark abysses of the soul, but a playwright who told on the stage strange and interesting stories. But his style, whatever its merits and its demerits, is not really conversational as Coleridge and Lamb seem to suggest: at least the world would be stranger than it is if men and women held converse in the parenthetical and elliptical manner affected by the characters in Massinger's plays.

Massinger as a Playwright.—It is only when he is considered as a playwright, pure and simple, that Massinger shows to best advantage and that he takes rank over his contemporary rivals. As a playwright, pure and simple, Massinger demands a place immediately after Shakspere; and it is upon Shakspere that he has plainly enough modelled himself. *The Duke of Milan*, for instance, is an obvious imitation of *Othello*, inferior as it is in logic, in plausibility, in power and in beauty. Massinger's subject-matter is abundantly romantic, not to call it frankly fantastic. He deals in disguises and discoveries; he builds up plots and counterplots, ingeniously planned, even if rarely plausible in our modern eyes now that we are accustomed to a more realistic treatment of motive and to a less summary and less arbitrary psychology. There is in his plays little pretence of the reality and the complexity of life; and it would be unkind to apply to them the standard of commonsense. But this is a test only a few of the pieces of the old dramatists could withstand, and some of Shakspere's most delightful plays, *The Merchant of Venice* for one, and *Much Ado about Nothing* for another, are charming to us now only because we are quite willing to make believe with the poet and to venture with him for a little while into a realm where anybody may do anything for any motive at any moment.

To us again who have seen how far the mere technic of playmaking has been carried by Scribe, and who can appreciate the solidity of dramaturgic craftsmanship exhibited by Ibsen, there seems to be something not unfairly to be called childish in the primitive devices that Massinger is willing to employ now and again, and in the wilful artifices by which he gets his characters into striking situations. Yet in this he is of his time, no more and no less; and his machinations are on the whole rather less puerile than those of most of his contemporaries—and he does less violence than they to the plain facts of human nature as we know it. His plots were contrived to hold the interest of his contemporaries, and he could not foresee that we might try them by a severer standard. They are built to bring about situations in which the actors could display themselves;—and it is well always to remember that those plays in which the actors have the most to do interest us most in the theatre.

It is true that these plots are not the inevitable result of the characters, but are rather obviously the work of the playwright himself, thrusting his personages into the situations he has elaborated. The situations, however, are effective on the stage and the characters lend themselves to the efforts of the actors. Moreover Massinger reveals the instinct of the born playwright in that he puts at the core of his piece a struggle,—a clash of contending desires, a stark assertion of the human will,—which is essential to the drama and which differentiates the drama from every other form of literature. This struggle he sets before the spectators clearly and carefully; and herein again he reveals himself as a pupil of Shakspere's. His expositions are generally excellent, taking us at once into the heart of the subject, arousing lively expectancy, and creating the wish to see how the conflict of forces is to finish. He has also the knack of ending his acts with an interrogation-mark, to carry attention across the intermission.

The proof of the play is in the performance: and Massinger's dramas lingered longer in the theatre than those of any of his contemporaries—excepting only Shakspere. Certain comedies of Beaumont and Fletcher and of Ben Jonson were acted now and again in the eighteenth century, although they all dropped out of the list of acting plays early in the nineteenth. Merely noting that Rowe's *Fair Penitent*, long popular in the play houses, was a plagiarism from Massinger's *Fatal Dowry*, we may record that eight other of the dramas of which Massinger is undoubtedly the author were altered and revived in the final years of the eighteenth century. The version of *The City Madam* known as *Riches*, served to display the histrionic genius of Edmund Kean, who found also in *A New Way to Pay Old Debts* one of his best parts. Indeed *A New Way to Pay Old Debts*, continued to be acted in America until the final quarter of the nineteenth century. (See, below, under Stage-

History.) No better evidence could there be of Massinger's
superiority as a playwright, as a writer of dramas to be performed
by actors in a theatre.

Massinger as a Comic Dramatist.—No two critics have ever
agreed on a definition of comedy, just as no two critics have ever
accepted exactly the same definition of humour, which must ever
be a chief ingredient of comedy. Massinger's comedies do not
belong in the same class with the comedies of Aristophanes, with
the comedies of Molière, with the comedies of Sheridan. One of
them, *The Guardian* entitles itself "a comical history"; and this
is not absolutely satisfactory even as a description of that particular
piece. Many of the plays of the Jacobean and Caroline dramatists
are hybrids: they are not tragic in tone and in termination; nor
are they richly humorous in situation or in character. The playwright has aimed to set on the stage a pleasing tale, with a medley
of serious scenes and of incidents intended to call forth laughter.
Coleridge found that a play of Massinger's when read in the study
was as interesting as a novel; and we may be certain it was still
more entertaining when acted in the theatre.

Massinger's comedy is more clearly akin to the dramatic-romance
as we find it in Beaumont and Fletcher than it is to the romantic-
comedy which Shakspere brought to perfection from the hesitating
attempts of Peele and Greene. It has little or no relation to the
comedy-of-humours of Jonson, although certain of the more strongly
marked comic characters, like Justice Greedy, are echoes of the
Jonsonian formula. Its closest analogue is not to be found among
its contemporaries but among certain dramas popular in the nineteenth century, like Augier's *Maitre Guérin* and Mirbeau's *Les
Affaires sont les Affaires*, in which there is a vigorously picturesque
treatment of contemporary character. If space permitted here it
would not be difficult to draw up a list of points of resemblance between *A New Way to Pay Old Debts*, and Ibsen's *Pillars of
Society*.

And this brings us to the frank admission that although Massinger wrote successful plays which we are forced to call comedies,
for lack of a better term, his humour is generally rather grim, not to
designate it saturnine, and his wit is often forced. He had but

little *vis comica*, the power of compelling laughter, the sheer sense of fun, the spontaneous gaiety, the enjoyment of a joke for its own sake,—the *vis comica* which is so delightful in Molière, in Regnard, in Labiche. Although it would not be quite fair to insist that Massinger jokes with difficulty, it is not unfair to remark that he often labours at his jesting. He is guilty again and again of the most inexpensive of jibes,—the would-be comic comment on the name of a character so called on purpose that the comment might be made. Although there is little breadth in his humour and little sparkle in his wit, he can at times get real fun out of an absurd character or out of a grotesque situation.

In *Believe as You List* there is genuine gaiety in the talk of the fat man who is more than a mere echo of Falstaff; and in *The Guardian* there is a robust playfulness in Durazzo, which is laughter-provoking, although his attitude toward the other sex is not now acceptable. In *A New Way to Pay Old Debts* Marrall's astonishment at Wellborn's reception in Lady Allworth's house is good acting humour—that is, it affords ample opportunity to a comic actor. In *The Maid of Honour* Camiola's attitude toward Sylli is exceptional in its gentle appreciation of absurdity. These instances are perhaps sufficient to make us feel that Professor Morris is unduly severe when he dismisses Massinger's humour as "elephantine"; and yet they are not enough to justify a denial of Mr. Symons's assertion that although a play of Massinger's "is styled a comedy, it is certainly not for laughter that we turn to it." Yet in considering Massinger's humour as in considering his poetry we must ever bear in mind that he wrote to be acted, not to be read; and that even if we do not turn to *A New Way to Pay Old Debts* for laughter, we might find ourselves tempted to it in the theatre by what might leave us quite unmoved in the library. A merely literary criticism may perhaps consider Marrall and Greedy as unsuccessful attempts to provide "comic relief" for the more sombre episodes of the play; but the dramatic criticism of Lamb and Hazlitt survives to inform us that these parts were both of them broadly effective in the hands of competent comedians. Greedy is but a mask of caricature, an insatiable stomach substituted for the whole man: he is not unlike certain of the least convincing figures of Dickens created by a similar simplification of humanity; and it is well for us to remember that many of these caricatures of Dickens's have been highly effective on the stage when his novels were dramatized.

A New Way to Pay Old Debts: The Plot.—With the striking exception of Ben Jonson, the old dramatists cared little for a simple symmetry of plot; and they rarely sought to deal with a single action having a beginning, a middle and an end, as we find it in Sophocles, in Racine and in Ibsen. Even Shakspere seems to achieve this directness only when the weight of his theme impels him to it; and in his comedies, for example, in *Much Ado about Nothing*, we are sometimes in doubt whether the serious plot or the comic plot is really the centre of the action. Massinger seems to have taken as his model those plays of Shakspere in which the story is least straggling; and he far excels Beaumont and Fletcher in the unity he is able to impart to his plots, in their directness, and therefore in their increased effectiveness. In *A New Way to Pay Old Debts*, as in the companion comedy of the *City Madam*, he deals with but a single story. The scheme is artificial and the conduct of the plot is at some moments arbitrary; but he tells his tale with all his customary dexterity.

Taine once asserted that the art of playmaking was as capable of improvement as the art of watchmaking; and there is no doubt that our modern playwrights have learnt many a trick of the trade unknown to Massinger. But the main principles of the dramaturgic art Massinger possessed and could put to good service. He begins with an exposition of Wellborn's plight. He sets up distinctly the appalling character of Sir Giles Overreach and he explains early and clearly what it is that his domineering personality wishes to accomplish. He brings out sharply the opposing forces; and he arouses the interest of expectancy by Wellborn's whisper to Lady Allworth. He ends every act by some phrase which suggests without revealing the future complications of the plot;—at the end of the fourth act, for example, there is an excellent use of dramatic irony. He never digresses; he keeps Sir Giles constantly in the centre of the play; he works up steadily to the irresistible catastrophe which the spectators are artfully allowed to guess at but which overturns Sir Giles with the overwhelming unexpectedness of a tornado.

Massinger may have found a hint for his plot and his chief figure in Middleton's *A Trick to Catch the Old One;* or he may have taken both from real life, from the career of a certain Sir Giles Mompesson. Gardiner declared unhesitatingly that "Massinger treated of the events of the day under a disguise hardly less thin than that which shows off the figures in the caricatures of Aristophanes or the cartoons of *Punch*"; and no doubt the learned historian had warrant for his assertion. Granting that Massinger did have Mompesson in mind when he invented this play, the Sir Giles of fiction far transcends the Sir Giles of fact,—just as Trissotin is not a mere photograph of the Abbé Cotin but a largely limned portrait of the type to which the model belonged. The identification of characters in literature with persons in life is a little too facile to be altogether satisfactory. So also the allegation of an indebtedness to an earlier play by another author is always easy to bring and always difficult to deny, since there is ever an initial similarity between Monmouth and Macedon; yet it is not at all unlikely that Massinger may have owed nothing to Middleton's play.

The Characters.—Standing out powerfully is the sinister figure of Sir Giles Overreach, one of the most vigorous creations to be found in any play of that period,—or indeed of any period. To my mind he is not to be classed with the Harpagon or the Tartuffe of Molière, as one critic has suggested, but rather with the Consul Berwick of Ibsen, the Montjoye of Feuillet, the Lechat of M. Mirbeau's more recent *Les Affaires sont les Affaires.* He belongs to the type of the "strong man," as the French dramatists have projected it, *l'homme fort.* He has his analogues in the business world of to-day,—in the unscrupulous speculator, the railroad wrecker, joying in his own evil deeds, and playing the game of fraud and crime for its own sake, and not as he supposes for the stakes alone. Despite his title he is an upstart, a self-made man, with a contemptuous envy toward the improvident caste from which his birth excludes him. His final impenitence and his impotent rage, bring the play to a fit conclusion. There is an obvious lack of plausibility, of characteristic cunning and caution in his proffer to Lord Lovel of Lady

Allworth's house or of any other in the neighbourhood. It is unlikely that such a man should thus "give himself away," as the phrase is. And his frank admission of his villainy to his own daughter is also out of keeping; and perhaps even his disclosure of his plans so plainly to Marrall is not in accord with his wily methods. But his boldness is equal to his courage; and repeated success had tended to make him reckless. The cynical frankness of Marrall also is extreme, and out of nature; and yet Marrall is just the foil needful to set off the powerful personality of Sir Giles. Wellborn again is artfully contrasted with Sir Giles; he has a cousinly kinship with Charles Surface, a type which has ever been a favourite with playwrights and with the playgoing public,—perhaps because our wholesome distrust of the hypocrite and the pharisee leads us to a preference for the prodigal son over his elder brother. Wellborn's final reformation is at the bidding of the author and not from the natural promptings of the character. Lord Lovel is a lightly sketched portrait of a gentleman, pairing off appropriately enough with Lady Allworth.

For a wonder the women in this play are not unpleasant and not unladylike, as are so many of the female characters in the author's other plays. Massinger, who followed Shakspere in many ways, did not or could not copy the purity, the grace, the pervasive charm, the feminine subtlety, which characterize the women of Shakspere. Massinger had little or no real insight into the female heart; the hidden springs of action are hidden from him. His women are all painted from the outside only. They are not convincing; they lack essential womanliness. In many of his plays, the heroines are coarse-grained, vulgar-minded and foul-mouthed. In *A New Way* they are pleasant enough, and although mere outline sketches, both of them, they are not falsely coloured. Margaret indeed has the minor attractiveness of an effaced personality. The repugnant plainness of speech with which Sir Giles addresses his daughter and with which she retorts, is due partly no doubt to the manners of the time, partly perhaps to the fact that the female characters were all impersonated by boys, and partly also to Massinger's own defects of taste and to his relish for the coarse word.

Massinger as a Moralist.—Massinger has the liking of his age for stories of lust and gore set on the stage with no shrinking from details which we would feel to be offensive and repellent; and he is often foul both in phrase and in thought. Yet he is justly held to be a moralist, conscious of a purpose in the picture of life that he is presenting. To a certain extent he suggests Hogarth, a moralist also with an obvious enjoyment in his own portrayal of degrading vice and its appalling consequences. He is anxious to scourge evil; but he does not shrink from the contemplation of it; he even dwells on it with an apparent complacency. He is heavy-handed and coarse-fibred ethically as well as æsthetically. Morally he has no taste; but none the less does he insist upon preaching, in season and out. His plays abound in hortatory didacticism, often most inartistically applied.

As a result of this desire to point his moral so that not the most careless spectator could fail to find it, he again and again forces his wicked folk not only to admit their own wickedness but to comment on it. This practice is so frequent in his plays that it is now counted as one of the characteristic mannerisms by which Massinger's share in a collaboration can be identified. In *A New Way* Tap speaking of himself says that

> "Unthankful knaves are ever so rewarded."

Marrall kicked out in the final act and threatened, says that

> "This is the haven
> False servants still arrive at" (act V., sc. 1).

And Sir Giles unmasked and at bay tries in vain to draw his sword, saying

> "Ha! I am feeble:
> Some undone widow sits upon mine arm
> And takes away the use of 't; and my sword,
> Glued to my scabbard with wronged orphans tears,
> Will not be drawn" (act V., sc. 1).

For Sir Leslie Stephen Massinger's plays are spoilt by this gross lapse from dramatic veracity. A speech like that just quoted from Sir Giles "is a description of a wicked man from outside; and wickedness from outside is generally unreasonable and preposterous. When it is converted by simple alteration of pronouns, into the villain's own account of himself, the internal logic which serves as a pretext disappears, and he becomes a mere monster." Swinburne, who has praised Massinger more amply than any other modern critic, admitted that there is so much truth in this charge of Sir Leslie's that he was "not disposed to enquire whether there may not be something to be said in deprecation or extenuation of the charge." But even if a defense is impossible, an explanation may perhaps be attempted. Massinger was unwilling to trust to the attention of the turbulent and illiterate groundlings before whom his plays were presented, and still less to their intelligence,— just as Plautus was afraid of the stupidity of the Roman rabble. Massinger prefers to drive his moral home however inartistically, rather than risk the danger of its not being perceived at all. As the playwright has not the novelist's privilege of commenting on his action, he puts the comment in the mouth of the characters. Schiller was guilty of a blunder much the same in *Fiesco* (Act I, viii and again in Act II, xv). Molière when he published *Tartuffe* felt forced to put a footnote to a dangerous speech of his chief character reminding the reader that it was a villain who was speaking; and Thackeray did the same thing in *Barry Lyndon*.

A New Way: Stage-History.—As I have already said, the dramaturgic merit of *A New Way to Pay Old Debts* is made evident by the fact that it was the only drama by an Elizabethan or Jacobean playwright—excepting only Shakspere's—which held the stage until the final quarter of the nineteenth century. At the end of the eighteenth a comedy or two of Ben Jonson's might still be seen in the theatre now and again; and also a comedy or two of Beaumont and Fletcher's. But Massinger's masterpiece continued to be performed for at least fifty years after those plays by his contemporaries had been laid on the shelf finally. It had been revived at Drury Lane in 1748 by David Garrick, who did not appear in it himself however, assigning *Sir Giles* to Bridges, an actor otherwise undistinguished; and eleven years later the part passed to a performer named Burden. In 1781 Henderson acted *Overreach* at Covent Garden; and in 1783 Kemble appeared in it at Drury Lane. Both Pope and Cooke took up the part in rivalry with Kemble; and then in 1816 Edmund Kean made it his own. A little later Vandenhoff and Junius Brutus Booth risked the dangerous comparison with Kean. Here in the United States

Cooke and Kean and Booth presented themselves in the character of *Sir Giles;* and they were followed in time by Edwin Booth and by E. L. Davenport. The domineering and unscrupulous personality of Massinger's *Overreach* affords a splendid histrionic opportunity to an actor who can compose a character largely and who can command the power needed for the final scene.

The persistent popularity of *A New Way to Pay Old Debts* on the stage is shown by its inclusion in all the collections of acting plays,—in Mrs. Inchbald's, in "The London Stage," in Dibdin's "London Theater," in Oxberry's "New English Drama," and in the later series of Lea, of Lacy, and of French, printed especially for the use of the actors themselves. The stage version prepared by John Kemble was published in 1816; and another adaptation published in 1818 vaunted itself as the "only edition containing the stage-business."

The Present Text.—*A New Way to Pay Old Debts* was first published in quarto in 1633. It was included in the more or less complete editions of Massinger's works edited by Coxeter, (1759) by J. Monck Mason (1779) and by William Gifford (1805, 1813); it is to be found also among the selections from Massinger which appeared in the Mermaid Series with an introduction by Arthur Symons, (1887–9); among the Temple Dramatists, edited by G. Stronach, 1904, and in W. A. Neilson's *Chief Elizabethan Dramatists*, 1911. For the loan of the quarto of 1633 (Q) here reproduced, I was indebted to the late Beverly Chew, Esq., of New York, whose kindness to students of English literature is to be acknowledged not now for the first time. From Mr. Chew's copy the text has been transcribed by Lewis Lewisohn, A. M., a graduate student in Columbia University, who has collated it carefully with the reprints.[1] The emendations and suggestions of Coxeter, Mason and Gifford are indicated by C., M. and G. respectively.

BRANDER MATTHEWS.

[1] In conforming the punctuation to something like modern usage, the General Editor has made as few changes as possible, and has altogether refrained from alteration when the sense might be altered. The style of capitals and of letters, such as *i, j, u, v,* has in accordance with the rule of this series been modernized. Indications of scene and, in general, the directions in square brackets are from Gifford.

A New Way to Pay

OLD DEBTS

A COMOEDIE

As it hath beene often acted at the Phoenix in Drury-Lane, by the Queenes
Maiesties servants.

THE AUTHOR.
PHILIP MASSINGER.

LONDON,

Printed by E. P. for Henry Seyle, dwelling in S.
Pauls Church-yard, at the signe of the
Tygers head. Anno. M.DC.
XXXIII

To The
RIGHT HONORABLE
ROBERT
EARLE OF CARNARVAN,
Master Falconer of England.

My Good Lord.
Pardon, I beseech you, my boldnesse in presuming to shelter this Comoedie under the wings of your Lordships favour and protection, I am not ignorant (having never yet deserv'd you in my service) that it cannot but meete with a severe construction, if, in the clemencie of your noble disposition, you fashion not a better defence for mee than I can fancie for myselfe. All I can alleage is, that divers *Italian* Princes, and Lords of eminent rancke in *England*, have not disdain'd to receave Poems of this nature; nor am I wholly lost in my hopes, but that your Honor (who have ever exprest your selfe a favourer, and friend to the Muses) may vouchsafe, in your gratious acceptance of this trifle, to give me encouragement to present you with some labourd worke, and of a higher straine hereafter. I was borne a devoted servant to the thrice noble Family of your incomparable Lady, and am most ambitious, but with a becoming distance, to be knowne to your Lordship; which, if you please to admit, I shall embrace it as a bounty that, while I live, shall oblige me to acknowledge you for my noble Patron, and professe my selfe to be

Your Honours true servant,

PHILIP MASSINGER.

To The Ingenious
AUTHOR MASTER
PHILIP MASSINGER.

ON HIS COMEDIE
Called, A new way to pay
old Debts.

This is rare charity, and thou couldst not
So proper to the time have found a plot:
The whilst you teach to pay, you lend, the age
We wretches live in; that to come, the stage,
The thronged audience that was thither brought   5
Invited by your fame, and to be taught
This lesson. All are growne indebted more,
And when they looke for freedome ran in score.
It was a cruell courtesie to call,
In hope of liberty, and then, enthrall   10
The nobles of your bond-men gentry, and
All besides, those that did not understand.
They were no men of credit, banckroupts borne
Fit to be trusted with no stocke, but scorne.
You have more wisely credited to such,   15
That though they cannot pay, can value much.
I am your debtor too, but to my shame
Repay you nothing backe, but your own fame.
HENRY MOODY. Miles.

To his friend the author.

You may remember how you chid me when
I ranckt you equall with those glorious men,
Beaumont and Fletcher: if you love not praise
You must forbeare the publishing of playes.
The craftie mazes of the cunning plot;   5
The polish'd phrase, the sweet expressions, got
Neither by theft, nor violence, the conceipt
Fresh and unsullied: all is of weight,
Able to make the captive reader know
I did but justice when I plac't you so.   10
A shamefast blushing would become the brow
Of some weake virgin writer, We allow
To you a kind of pride; and there, where most
Should blush at commendations, you should boast.
If any thinke I flatter, let him looke   15
Of[f] from my idle trifles on thy booke.
                              THOMAS JAY. *Miles.*

Dramatis Personæ.

LOVELL. *An English Lord.*[1]
SIR GILES OVERREACH. *A cruell extortioner.*
WELBORNE. *A prodigall.*[2]
ALWORTH.[3] *A young gentleman, page to* LORD LOVELL.
GREEDY. *A hungry justice of peace.*
MARRALL. *A Tearme-driver. A creature of* SIR GILES OVERREACH.
ORDER. ⎫
AMBLE. ⎬ *Servants to the* LADY ALWORTH.[4]
FURNACE. ⎪
WATCHALL. ⎭
WILL-DOE. *A parson.*
TAPWELL. *An alehouse keeper.*
THREE CREDITORS.
THE LADIE ALWORTH. *A rich widdowe.*
MARGARET. OVERREACH *his daughter.*
WAITING WOMAN.
CHAMBERMAIDE.
FROTH. TAPWELL'S *wife.*

[*THE SCENE:* The Country near NOTTINGHAM: [5]]

[1] G. has 'Lord Lovell,' and omits '*An English Lord.*'
[2] G., 'Frank Wellborne.'   [3] G., 'Tom Allworth.'
[4] G. changes the order of the *Dramatis personæ*, placing the servants of Lady Alworth after 'Willdo' and 'Tapwell.' Then 'Creditors, Servants,' etc., and 'Froth' before 'Waiting woman' etc.
[5] G. supplies.

A New Way to Pay Old Debts:

A COMEDIE.

Actus Primus, Scena Prima.

[Before Tapwell's House]

WELBORNE, TAPWELL, FROTH.[1]

Welborne. No bouze? nor no tobacco?
Tapwell. Not a sucke, sir,
Nor the remainder of a single canne
Left by a drunken porter, all night palde [2] too.
   Froth. Not the dropping of the tappe for your mornings draught,
     sir.   6
'Tis veritie I assure you.
   Welborne. Verity, you brach! [3]
The divell turn'd precision? [4]   Rogue, what am I?
   Tapwell. Troth, durst I trust you with a looking glasse,   10
To let you see your trimme shape, you would quit me,
And take the name your selfe.
   Welborne. How! dogge?
   Tapwell. Even so, sir.
And I must tell you if you but advance,   15
Your Plimworth [5] cloke, you shall be soone instructed
There dwells, and within call, if it please your worship,
   A potent monarch, call'd the [6] constable,

---

[1] G., *Enter Wellborn in tattered apparel, Tapwell and Froth.*
[2] grown flat.   [3] bitch.   [4] puritan.
[5] G., 'Plymouth.' C. and M., 'pile-worn.' ' Plymouth cloak '=cudgel. Cf., ' Welsh
rabbit' and 'Cape Cod turkey'=codfish.   [6] G., 'A.'

That does command a citadell call'd the stockes;
Whose guards are certain files of trusty [1] billmen,   20
Such as with great dexterity will hale [2]
Your tatter'd, louzie—
    Welborne. Rascall! slave!
    Froth. No rage, sir.
    Tapwell. At his own perill.   Doe not put your selfe   25
In too much heate, there being no water neare
To quench your thirst, and sure for other liquor,
As mighty ale or beere, they are things I take it
You must no more remember; not in a dreame, sir.
    Wellborne. Why, thou unthankfull villaine, dar'st thou talke
        thus?   31
Is not thy house, and all thou hast, my gift?
    Tapwell. I find it not in chalke, and Timothie Tapwell
Does keepe no other register.
    Welborne. Am I not hee   35
Whose riots fed, and cloth'd thee? wert thou not
Borne on my fathers land, and proud to bee
A drudge in his house?
    Tapwell. What I was, sir, it skills not;
What you are is apparent.   Now, for a farewell;   40
Since you talke of father, in my hope it will torment you,
I'le briefly tell your story.   Your dead father,
My quondam master, was a man of worship,
Old Sir John Wellborne, justice of the [3] peace, and *quorum*,
And stood faire to bee *custos rotulorum;*   45
Bare the whole sway of the shire; kep't a great house;
Reliev'd the poore, and so forth; but hee dying,
And the twelve hundred a yeare comming to you,
Late Master Francis, but now forlorne Welborne—
    Welborne. Slave, stoppe, or I shall lose my selfe.   50
    Froth. Very hardly;
You cannot out of your way.
    Tapwell. But to my story.
You were then a lord of akers; the prime gallant;

---

    [1] G., 'rusty'; C. and M., 'lusty.'   [2] G., 'haul.'   [3] G. omits 'the.'

And I your under-butler; note the change now.   55
You had a merry time of't: hawkes, and hounds,
With choice of running horses; mistresses
Of all sorts, and all sizes, yet so hot
As their embraces made your lordships melt;
Which your uncle, Sir Giles Overreach observing,   60
Resolving not to lose a droppe of 'em,[1]
On foolish mortgages, statutes, and bonds,
For a while suppli'd your loosenesse, and then left you.
 Welborne. Some curate hath penn'd this invictive, mongrell,
And you have studied it.   65
 Tapwell. I have not done yet:
Your land gone, and your credit not worth a token,
You grew the common borrower, no man scap'd
Your paper-pelletts, from the gentleman
To the beggers on high wayes, that sold you switches   70
In your gallantry.
 Welborne. I shall switch your braines out.
 Tapwell. Where poore Tim Tapwell with a little stocke
Some forty pounds or so, bought a small cottage,
Humbled my selfe to marriage with my Froth here;   75
Gave entertainment—
 Welborne. Yes, to whores, and canters,
Clubbers by night.
 Tapwell. True, but they brought in profit;
And had a gift to pay for what they call'd for;   80
And stucke not like your mastership. The poore income
I glean'd from them, hath made mee in my parish,
Thought worthy to bee scavinger, and in time
May rise to be overseer of the poore;
Which if I doe, on your petition, Welborne,   85
I may allow you thirteene pence a quarter,
And you shall thanke my worship.
 Welborne. Thus, you doggebolt,
And thus.   *Beates and kicks him.*
 Tapwell. [*To his wife*] Cry out for helpe!   90
<hr>
[1] G. incloses this line in parentheses.

Welborne. Stirre and thou diest:
Your potent prince, the constable, shall not save you.
Heare me, ungrateful hell-hound; did not I
Make purses for you? then you lick'd my bootes,
And thought your holy day cloke too coarse to cleane 'em.   95
'Twas I that, when I heard thee sweare if ever
Thou could'st arrive at forty pounds thou would'st
Live like an emperour; 'twas I that gave it,
In ready gold.   Denie this, wretch.
     Tapwell. I must, sir,   100
For from the taverne to the taphouse, all,
On forfeiture of their licenses, stand bound
Never to remember who their best guests were,
If they grew poore like you.
     Welborne. They are well rewarded   105
That beggers themselves to make such cuckolds rich.
Thou viper, thankelesse viper; impudent bawde!
But since you are grow'n [1] forgetful, I will helpe
Your memory, and tread thee into mortar:
Not leave one bone unbroken. [2]   110
     Tapwell. Oh!
     Froth. Aske mercie.
     Well. 'Twill not be granted.

Enter ALLWORTH.

Alworth. Hold, for my sake hold.
Deny me, Franke? they are not worth your anger.   115
     Welborne. For once thou hast redeem'd them from this scepter:
                                             His Cudgell. [3]
But let 'em vanish, creeping on their knees,
And if they grumble, I revoke my pardon.
     Froth. This comes of your prating, husband, you presum'd
On your ambling wit, and must use your glib tongue   120
Though you are beaten lame for't.
     Tapwell. Patience, Froth.
There's law to cure our bruizes.

---

[1] G. omits 'grow'n.'   [2] G. adds stage-direction, [*Beats him again.*
[3] As explanatory of 'scepter.'

They goe off on their hands and knees.

Welborne. Sent to your mother?
Alworth. My lady, Franke, my patronesse! my all!   125
Shee's such a mourner for my father's death,
And in her love to him, so favours mee,
That I cannot pay too much observance to her.
There are few such stepdames.
Welborne. 'Tis a noble widdow,   130
And keepes her reputation pure, and cleere
From the least taint of infamie; her life
With the splendour of her actions leaves no tongue
To envy, or detraction. Prethee tell mee,
Has shee no suitors?   135
Alworth. Even the best of the shire, Franke,
My lord excepted. Such as sue and send,
And send, and sue againe, but to no purpose.
Their frequent visits have not gain'd her presence;
Yet shee's so far from sullennesse, and pride,   140
That I dare undertake you shall meete from her
A liberall entertainment. I can give you
A catalogue of her suitors names.
Welborne. Forbeare it,
While I give you good counnsail. I am bound to it: 145
Thy father was my friend, and that affection
I bore to him, in right descends to thee;
Thou art a handsome, and a hopeful youth,
Nor will I have the least affront sticke on thee,
If I with any danger can prevent it.   150
Alworth. I thanke your noble care; but, pray you, in what
Doe I run the hazard?
Welborne. Art thou not in love? Put it not off with wonder.
Alworth. In love at my yeares?
Welborne. You thinke you walke in clouds, but are transparant;
I have heard all, and the choice that you have made;   156
And with my finger can point out the north starre,
By which the loadstone of your follie's guided.

And to confirme this true, what thinke you of
Faire Margaret, the only child, and heyre　　　　　160
Of cormorant Overreach? does it blush? and start,
To heare her only nam'd? blush at your want
Of wit and reason.

 Alworth. You are too bitter, sir.

 Welborne. Wounds of this nature are not to be cur'd　　165
With balmes, but corrosives, I must bee plaine:
Art thou scarce manumiz'd from the porters lodge,[1]
And yet sworne servand to the pantophle,
And dar'st thou dreame of marriage?　I feare
'Twill bee concluded for impossible,　　　　　170
That there is now, nor ere shall bee hereafter,
A handsome page, or players boy of fourteene,
But either loves a wench, or drabs love him;
Court-waiters not exempted.

 Alworth. This is madnesse.　　　　　175
How ere you have discover'd my intents,
You know my aims are lawfull, and if ever
The queene of flowers, the glory of the spring,
The sweetest comfort to our smell, the rose
Sprang from an envious brier, I may inferre　　180
There's such disparitie in their conditions,
Betweene the godess of my soule, the doughter,
And the base churle her father.

 Welborne. Grant this true,
As I beleeve it; canst thou ever hope　　　　　185
To enjoy a quiet bed with her, whose father
Ruin'd thy state?

 Alworth. And yours too.

 Welborne. I confesse it.
True; I must tell you as a friend, and freely,　　190
That where impossibilities are apparant,
'Tis indiscretion to nourish hopes.
Canst thou imagine, (let not selfe-love blind thee,)
That Sir Giles Overreach,—that, to make her great

  [1] G. explains that this is 'The first degree of servitude.'

In swelling titles, without touch of conscience,   195
Will cut his neighbours throate, and I hope his owne too,—
Will ere consent to make her thine?   Give or'e,
And thinke of some course sutable to thy rancke,
And prosper in it.
   Alworth. You have well advised me.   200
But in the meane time, you, that are so studious
Of my affaires, wholly neglect your owne.
Remember your selfe, and in what plight you are.
   Welborne. No matter, no matter.
   Alworth. Yes, 'tis much materiall: 205
You know my fortune, and my meanes; yet something
I can spare from my selfe, to helpe your wants.
   Welborne. How's this?
   Alworth. Nay bee not angry.   There's eight peeces
To put you in better fashion.   210
   Welborne. Money from thee?
From a boy? a stipendary? [1] one that lives
At the devotion of a stepmother,
And the uncertaine favour of a lord?
Ile eate my armes first.   Howsoe're blind fortune   215
Hath spent the utmost of her malice on mee;
Though I am vomited out of an alehouse,
And thus accoutred; know not where to eate,
Or drinke, or sleepe, but underneath this canopie;
Although I thanke thee, I despise thy offer.   220
And as I, in my madnesse broke my state
Without the assistance of anothers braine,
In my right wits Ile peece it; at the worst
Dye thus, and bee forgotten.
   Alworth. A strange humor.   *Exeunt.* 225

        [1] G., 'stipendiary.'

Actus Primi, Scena Secunda. [*A Room in Lady Allworth's House.*]

ORDER, AMBLE, FURNACE, WATCHALL.

Order. Set all things right, or, as my name is Order,
And by this staffe of office that commands you,
This chaine, and dubble ruffe, symboles of power,
Who ever misses in his function,
For one whole weeke makes forfeiture of his breakefast,   5
And privilege in the wine-seller.
 Amble. You are merrie.
Good Master Steward.
 Furnace. Let him; Ile bee angry.
 Amble. Why, fellow Furnace, 'tis not twelve a clocke yet,   10
Nor dinnertaking up; then, 'tis allowed,
Cookes by their places may bee cholericke.
 Furnace. You thinke you have spoke wisely, goodman Amble,
My ladie's goe-before.
 Order. Nay, nay; no wrangling.   15
 Furnace. Twit me with the authority of the kitchin?
At all houres, and all places Ile be angrie;
And thus provok'd, when I am at my prayers
I will bee angry.
 Amble. There was no hurt meant.   20
 Furnace. I am friends with thee, and yet I will be angry.
 Order. With whom?
 Furnace. No matter whom: yet now I thinke on't
I am angrie with my lady.
 Watchall. Heaven forbid, man.   25
 Order. What cause has she given thee?
 Furnace. Cause enough, Master Steward.
I was entertain'd by her to please her palat,
And till she foreswore eating I perform'd it.
Now since our master, noble Alworth died,   30
Though I cracke my braines to find out tempting sauces,

And raise fortifications in the pastrie,
Such as might serve for modells in the Low-Countries,
Which if they had beene practis'd at Breda,
Spinola might have throwne his cap at it, and ne're tooke it—[1] 35
  Amble. But you had wanted matter there to worke on.
  Furnace. Matter? with six egges and a strike of rie-meale
I had kep't the towne till doomesday, perhaps longer.
  Order. But, what's this to your pet against my lady?
  Furnace. What's this? Marrie, this: when I am three parts
    rosted,
                                      41
And the fourth part parboyld, to prepare her viands,
Shee keepes her chamber, dines with a panada,[2]
Or water cruell,[3] my sweat never thought on.
  Order. But your art is seene in the dining-roome.   45
  Furnace. By whom?
By such as pretend love to her, but come
To feed upon her. Yet, of all the harpies,
That doe devoure her, I am out of charity
With none so much as the thinne-gutted squire   50
That's stolne into commission.
  Order. Justice Greedy:
  Furnace. The same, the same. Meate's cast away upon him;
It never thrives. He holds this paradoxe,
Who eates not well, can ner'e doe justice well: 55
His stomacke's as insatiate as the grave,
Or strumpetts ravenous appetites.[4]
  Watchall. One knockes.[5] ALWORTH *knockes, and enters.*[6]
  Order. Our late young master!
  Amble. Welcome, sir.   60
  Furnace. Your hand,
If you have a stomake, a cold bake-meate's ready.

---

[1] G. notes 'Spinola sat down before Breda on the 26th August 1624 and the town did not surrender till the 1st of July in the following year'; and he also points out that the raising of fortifications in pastry was a fashionable practice frequently mentioned among the details of great entertainments.
[2] *Panada*, candle with slices of bread in it.
[3] G., 'gruell.'
[4] G., [*knocking within.*
[5] G., [*Exit.*
[6] G., *Re-enter Watchall with Allworth.*

Order. His fathers picture in little.
Furnace. We are all your servants.
Amble. In you he lives.   65
Alworth. At once, my thankes to all.
This is yet some comfort. Is my lady stirring?

Enter *the* LADY ALWORTH, Wayting woman, Chambermaid.

Order. Her presence answer for us.
Lady.[1] Sort those silkes well?
Ile take the ayre alone.   70
                    Exeunt Waiting woman, *and* Chambermaide.
Furnace. You aire and aire,
But will you ever tast but spoone-meate more?
To what use serve I?
Lady. Prethee, be not angry;
I shall er'e long. I' the meane time, there is gold   75
To buy thee aprons, and a sommer suite.
Furnace. I am appeas'd, and Furnace now grows Cooke.[2]
Lady. And as I gave directions, if this morning
I am visited by any, entertaine 'em
As heretofore: but say in my excuse   80
I am indispos'd.
Order. I shall, Madam.
Lady. Doe, and leave me.
Nay, stay you, Alworth.
                    Exeunt ORDER, AMBLE, FURNACE, WATCHALL.
Alworth. I shall gladly grow here,   85
To waite on your commands.
Lady. So soone turn'd courtier?
Alworth. Stile not that courtship, madam, which is duty,
Purchas'd on your part.
Lady. Well, you shall o'ercome,[3]   90
Ile not contend in words. How is it with
Your noble master?

---

[1] G. always has *L. All.*   [2] C. emended 'cool'; followed by M. and G.
[3] Q, 'or'e come.'

Alworth. Ever like himselfe;
No scruple lessend in the full weight of honour,
He did command me (pardon my presumption)   95
As his unworthy deputy to kisse
Your ladyships faire hands.
    Lady. I am honour'd in
His favour to mee.   Does he hold his purpose
For the Low-Countreyes?   100
    Alworth. Constantly, good madam,
But he will in person first present his service.
    Lady. And how approve you of his course? you are yet
Like virgin parchement capable of any
Inscription vitious, or honorable.   105
I will not force your will, but leave you free
To your owne election.
    Alworth. Any forme you please,
I will put on: but might I make my choice
With humble emulation I would follow   110
The path my lord markes to me.
    Lady. 'Tis well answer'd,
And I commend your spirit: you had a father
(Bless'd be his memory) that, some few houres
Before the will of heaven tooke him from me,   115
Who ¹ did commend you, by the dearest tyes
Of perfect love betweene us, to my charge:
And, therefor, what I speake you are bound to heare
With such respect as if he liv'd in me.
He was my husband, and how ere you are not   120
Sonne of my wombe, you may be of my love,
Provided you deserve it.
    Alworth. I have found you
(Most honor'd madam) the best mother to me,
And with my utmost strengths of care, and service,   125
Will labour that you never may repent
Your bounties showr'd upon me.
    Lady. I much hope it.

---

¹ Retained by editors.   It should be omitted.—*Gen. Ed.*

These were your fathers words: [1] If ere my sonne
Follow the warre, tell him it is a schoole   130
Where all the principles tending to honour,
Are taught if truly followed: but for such
As repaire thither, as a place in which
They doe presume they may with licence practice
Their lusts, and riots, they shall never merit   135
The noble name of souldiers. To dare boldly
In a faire cause, and for the countries safety
To runne upon the cannons mouth undaunted;
To obey their leaders, and shunne mutenies;
To beare with patience, the winters cold,   140
And sommers scorching heate, and not to faint
When plenty of provision failes, with hunger,
Are the essentiall parts make up a souldier,
Not swearing, dice, or drinking.

    Alworth. There's no syllable   145
You speake, but is to me an oracle,
Which but to doubt, were impious.

    Lady. To conclude:
Beware ill company, for often men
Are like to those with whom they do converse;   150
And from one man I warn'd [2] you, and that's Welborne:
Not cause hee's poore, that rather claimes your pitty,
But that hee's in his manners so debauch'd,
And hath to vitious courses sold himselfe.
'Tis true your father lov'd him, while he was   155
Worthy the loving, but if he had liv'd
To have seene him as he is, he had cast him off
As you must doe.

    Alworth. I shall obey in all things.

    Lady. You [3] follow me to my chamber, you shall have gold 160
To furnish you like my sonne, and still supplied,
As I heare from you.

    Alworth. I am still your creature.   *Exeunt.*

---

[1] From ' If ' to ' drinking ',—G., italics.   [2] G., 'warn.'
[3] G. omits ' you '.

Actus Primi, Scena Tertia. [*A Hall in the Same.*]

OVERREACH, GREEDIE ORDER, AMBLE, FURNACE, WATCHALL, MARALL.

Greedie. Not to be seene?

Overreach. Still cloistered up? Her reason.
I hope, assures her, though she make her selfe
Close prisoner ever for her husbands losse,
'Twill not recover him.   5

Order. Sir, it is her will,
Which we that are her servants ought to serve it.[1]
And not dispute. How ere, you are nobly welcome;
And if you please to stay, that you may thinke so,
There came, not six dayes since from Hull, a pipe   10
Of rich Canarie, which shall spend it selfe
For my ladies honour.

Greedie. Is it of the right race?

Order. Yes, Master Greedie.

Amble. How his mouth runs or'e!   15

Furnace. Ile make it run, and run. Save your good worship!

Greedie. Honest Master Cooke, thy hand, againe. How I love
thee:
Are the good dishes still in being? speake, boy.

Furnace. If you have a mind to feed, there is a chine   20
Of beefe well seasoned.

Greedie. Good!

Furnace. A pheasant larded.

Greedie. That I might now give thanks for't!

Furnace. Other kukushawes.[2]   25
Besides there came last night from the forrest of Sherwood
The fattest stagge I ever cooked.

Greedie. A stagge, man?

Furnace. A stagge, sir, part of it prepar'd for dinner,
And bak'd in puffpast.   30

---

[1] G. omits 'it.'   [2] G., 'kickshaws.'

Greedie. Puffpast too, Sir Giles!
A ponderous chine of beefe! a pheasant larded!
And red deere too, Sir Giles, and bak'd in puffpast!
All businesse set aside, let us give thankes here.
    Furnace. How the leane sceleton's rap'd!   35
    Overreach. You know wee cannot.
    Marrall. Your worships are to sit on a commission,
And if you faile to come, you lose the cause.
    Greedie. Cause me no causes. I'le prove't, for such a dinner
We may put off a commission: you shall find it   40
Henrici decimo quarto.
    Overreach. Fie, Master Greedie.
Will you loose me a thousand pounds for a dinner?
No more for shame. We must forget the belly,
When we thinke of profit.   45
    Greedy. Well, you shall o'errule [1] me;
I could en'e crie now. Doe you heare, Master Cooke.
Send but a corner of that immortall pastie,
And I, in thankefulnesse, will by your boy •
Send you a brace of three-pences.   50
    Furn. Will you be so prodigall?

        Enter WELBORNE.

    Over. Remember me to your lady. Who have wee here?
    Welb. You know me:
    Over. I did once, but now I will not,
Thou art no blood of mine. Avaunt, thou begger,   55
If ever thou presume to owne me more;
Ile have thee cag'd, and whipp'd.
    Greed. Ile grant the warrant.
Thinke of Piecorner, Furnace.
        Exeunt OVERREACH, GREEDIE, MARRALL.
    Watch. Will you out, sir?   60
I wonder how you durst creep [2] in.
    Ord. This is rudenesse
And sawcie impudence.

       [1] Q, 'oe'erule.'   [2] Q, 'creeps.'—G. corrects.

Amb. Cannot you stay
To be serv'd among your fellowes from the basket,[1]   65
But you must presse [2] into the hall?
   Furn. Prethee, vanish
Into some outhouse, though it be the piggestie,
My skullion shall come to thee.

Enter ALWORTH.

Welb. This is rare: 70
Oh, here's Tom Alworth.   Tom!
   Alw. We must be strangers,
Nor would I have you seene here for a million.   *Exit* ALWORTH.
   Welb. Better, and better.   He contemnes mee too?

Enter [3] Woman *and* Chambermaide.

Wom. Foh, what a smell's here! what thing's this?   75
   Chamb. A creature
Made out of the privie.   Let us hence for loves sake,
Or I shall sowne.[4]
   Wom. I beginne to faint already.

Exeunt Woman, & Chamber maide.

Watch. Will you know your way?   80
   Amb. Or shall wee teach it you,
By the head and shoulders?
   Welb. No: I will not stirre.
Doe you marke, I will not.   Let me see the wretch
That dares attempt to force me.   Why, you slaves,   85
Created only to make legges and cringe;
To carrie in a dish, and shift a trencher;
That have not soules only to hope a blessing
Beyond blacke [5] jackes, or flagons; you that were borne
Only to consume meate, and drinke, and batten   90
Upon reversions: Who advances?   Who
Showes me the way?
   Ord. My lady.

---

[1] From the basket = from the broken meats given to beggars.
[2] Q, 'preste.'—G. corrects.   [3] G., 'Waiting Woman.'
[4] G., 'swoon.'   [5] Q, 'blaske.'

Enter LADY [ALLWORTH] Woman, Chambermaide.

Chamb. Here's the monster.
Wom. Sweet madam, keepe your glove to your nose.   95
Chamb. Or let me
Fetch some perfumes may be predominant,
You wrong your selfe else.
Welb. Madam, my designes
Beare me to you.   100
Lad. To me?
Welb. And though I have met with
But ragged entertainement from your groomes here,
I hope from you to receive that noble usage
As may become the true friend of your husband,   105
And then I shall forget these.
Lady. I am amaz'd,
To see and heare this rudenesse. Dar'st thou thinke,
Though sworne, that it can ever find beleefe,
That I, who to the best men of this countrey,   110
Deni'd my presence since my husbands death,
Can fall so low, as to change words with thee?
Thou sonne of infamie, forbeare my house,
And know, and keepe the distance that's betweene us,
Or, though it be against my gentler temper,   115
I shall take order you no more shall be
An eye-sore for [1] me.
Welb. Scorne me not, good lady:
But as in forme you are angelicall
Imitate the heavenly natures, and vouchsafe   120
At the least a while to heare me. You will grant
The blood that runs in this arme is as noble
As that which fills your veines; those costly jewells,
And those rich clothes you weare; your mens observance,
And womens flatterie, are in you no vertues;   125
Nor these ragges, with my poverty, in me vices.
You have a faire fame, and, I know, deserve it;

————
[1] G., 'to.'

Yet, lady, must I say in nothing more
Than in the pious sorrow you have show'n
For your late noble husband.   130
  Ord. How she starts!
  Furn. And hardly can keepe finger from the eye
To heare him named.
  Lady. Have you ought else to say?
  Welb. That husband, madam, was once ın his fortun   135
Almost as low as I.   Want, debts, and quarrells
Lay heavy on him: let it not be thought
A boast in me, though I say I releev'd him.
'Twas I that gave him fashion; mine the sword
That did on all occasions second his;   140
I brought him on and off with honour, lady:
And when in all mens judgements he was sunke,
And in his owne hopes not to be bung'd up.[1]
I step'd unto him, tooke him by the hand,
And set him upright.   145
  Furn. Are not wee base rogues
That could forget this?
  Welb. I confesse you made him
Master of your estate; nor could your friends,
Though he brought no wealth with him, blame you for't;   150
For he had a shape, and to that shape a minde
Made up of all parts, either great, or noble,
So winning a behaviour, not to be
Resisted, madam.
  Lady. 'Tis most true.   He had.   155
  Welb. For his sake then, in that I was his friend,
Doe not contemne me.
  Lad. For what's past, excuse me,
I will redeeme it.   Order, give the gentleman
A hundred pounds.   160
  Welb. No, madam, on no termes:
I will nor begge, nor borrow six pence of you,
But be suppli'd elsewhere, or want thus ever.

     [1] G., 'buoy'd.'

Only one suite I make, which you deny not
To strangers: and 'tis this.   *Whispers to her.* 165
  Lad. Fie, nothing else?
  Welb. Nothing; unlesse you please to charge your servants
To throw away a little respect upon mee.
  Lad. What you demand is yours.
  Welb. I thanke you, lady.   170
Now what can be wrought out of such a suite,
Is yet in supposition; I have said all,
When you please you may retire. [*Exit* LADY ALLWORTH] Nay,
  all's forgotten;
And, for a luckie omen to my project,
Shake hands, and end all quarrells in the cellar.   175
  Ord. Agreed, agreed.
  Furn. Still merry Master Welborne.   *Exeunt.*

Actus Secundi, Scena Prima.

[*A Room in Overreach's House.*]

OVERREACH, MARRALL.

  Overreach. Hee's gone, I warrant thee; this commission crush'd
him.
  Marrall. Your worship have the way on't, and ne're misse[1]
To squeeze these unthrifts into ayre: and yet
The chapp-falne justice did his part, returning   5
For your advantage the certificate
Against his conscience and his knowledge too,
(With your good favour) to the utter ruine
Of the poore farmer.
  Over. 'Twas for these good ends   10
I made him a justice. He that bribes his bellie,
Is certaine to command his soule.
  Mar. I wonder

    [1] G., 'Your worships have the way on't,' *etc.*

(Still with your licence) why, your worship having
The power to put this thinne-gut in commission,   15
You are not in't your selfe?
   Over. Thou art a foole;
In being out of office I am out of danger
Where if I were a justice, besides the trouble,
I might, or out of wilfulnesse or error,   20
Run my selfe finely into a *praemunire*,
And so become a prey to the informer.
No, I'le have non of 't; 'tis enough I keepe
Greedie at my devotion: so he serve
My purposes, let him hang or damne, I care not.   25
Friendship is but a word.
   Mar. You are all wisdome.
   Over. I would be worldly wise; for the other wisdome
That does prescribe us a well-govern'd life,
And to doe right to others, as our selves,   30
I value not an atome.
   Mar. What course take you,
With your good patience, to hedge in the mannour
Of your neighbor, Master Frugall? as 'tis sayd
He will not sell, nor borrow, nor exchange,   35
And his land lying in the midst of your many lordshipps,
Is a foule blemish.
   Over. I have thought on't, Marrall,
And it shall take.   I must have all men sellers,
And I the only purchaser.   40
   Mar. 'Tis most fit, sir.
   Over. I'le therefore buy some cottage neare his mannour,[1]
Which done, I'le make my men break ope his fences,
Ride o're his standing corne, and in the night
Set fire on his barnes or breake his cattells legges.   45
These trespasses draw on suites, and suites expences,
Which I can spare, but will soone begger him.
When I have harried him thus two or three yeare,

---

[1] G. likens the proposed device of *Sir Giles* to Ahab's and to evil practices scored
by Seneca and by Juvenal.

Though he sue *in forma pauperis*, in spite
Of all his thrift and care, he'le grow behind-hand.   50
 Mar. The best I ever heard; I could adore you.
 Over. Then, with the favour of my man of law,
I will pretend some title: want will force him
To put it to arbitrement; then if he sell
For halfe the value, he shall have ready money,   55
And I possesse his land.
 Mar. 'Tis above wonder!
Welborne was apt to sell, and needed not
These fine arts, sir, to hooke him in.
 Over. Well thought on.   60
This varlet, Marrall, lives too long, to upbraide me
With my close cheate put upon him. Will nor cold,
Nor hunger kill him?
 Mar. I know not what to thinke on't.
I have us'd all meanes; and the last night I caus'd   65
His host, the tapster, to turne him out of doores;
And have beene since with all your friends and tenants,
And, on the forfeit of your favour, charg'd them,
Though a crust of moldie bread would keepe him frō starving,
Yet they should not relieve him. This is done, sir.   70
 Over. That was something, Marrall; but thou must goe further,
And suddainly, Marrall.
 Mar. Where, and when you please, sir.
 Over. I would have thee seeke him out, and, if thou canst,
Perswade him that 'tis better steale than begge.   75
Then, if I prove he has but rob'd a hen-roost,
Not all the world shall save him from the gallowes.
Doe anything to worke him to despaire,
And 'tis thy masterpeece.
 Mar. I will doe my best, sir.   80
 Over. I am now on my maine work with the Lord Lovell,
The gallant minded, popular Lord Lovell,
The minion of the peoples love.   I heare
Hee's come into the country, and my aimes are
To insinuate my selfe into his knowledge,   85

And then invite him to my house.

    Mar. I have you:

This points at my young mistres.

    Over. She must part with

That humble title, and write honourable,   90

Right honorable, Marrall, my right honorable daughter,

If all I have, or e're shall get, will doe it.

I will have her well attended; there are ladies

Of errant knights decay'd, and brought so low,

That for cast clothes and meate will gladly serve her.   95

And 'tis my glory, though I come from the cittie,

To have their issue, whom I have undone,

To kneele to mine as bond-slaves.

    Mar. 'Tis fit state, sir.

    Over. And therefore, Ile not have a cambermaide   100

That tyes her shooes, or any meaner office,

But such whose fathers were right worshipfull.

'Tis a rich mans pride; there having ever beene

More than a fewde, a strange antipathie

Betweene us and true gentry.   105

Enter WELBORNE.

    Mar. See, who's here, sir.

    Over. Hence monster! prodigie!

    Welb. Sir, your wifes nephew;

Shee and my father tumbled in one belly.

    Over. Avoid my sight! thy breath's infectious, rogue.   110

I shun thee as the leprosie or the plague.

Come hither, Marrall—this is the time to worke him.

    Mar. I warrant you, sir.   *Exit* OVER.

    Welb. By this light, I thinke hee's mad.

    Mar. Mad! had you tooke compassion on your selfe,   115

You long since had beene mad.

    Welb. You have tooke [1] a course

Betweene you and my venerable uncle,

To make me so.

<hr />

           [1] G., 'ta'en.'

Mar. The more pale spirited, you,   120
That would not be instructed, I sweare deepely—
　Welb. By what?
　Mar. By my religion.
　Welb. Thy religion!
The divells creed,—but what would you have done?   125
　Mar. Had there beene but one tree in all the shire,
Nor any hope to compasse [1] penny halter,
Before, like you, I had outliv'd my fortunes,
A with [2] had serv'd my turne to hang my selfe.
I am zealous in your cause: pray you hang your selfe, 130
And presently, as you love your credit.[3]
　Welb. I thanke you.
　Mar. Will you stay till you dye in a ditch? or lice devoure
　　you?—
Or, if you dare not doe the feate your selfe,   135
But that you'le put the state to charge and trouble,
Is there no purse to bee cut? house to be broken?
Or market women with egges that you may murther,
And so dispatch the businesse?
　Welb. Heer's varietie,   140
I must confesse; but I'le accept of none
Of all your gentle offers, I assure you.
　Mar. Why, have you hope ever to eat againe?
Or drinke?　Or be the master of three farthings?
If you like not hanging, drowne your selfe; take some course 145
For your reputation.
　Welb. 'Twill not do, deare tempter,
With all the rhetorike the fiend hath taught you.
I am as farre as thou art from despaire;
Nay, I have confidence, which is more than hope,   150
To live, and suddainely better than ever.
　Mar. Ha! ha! these castles you build in the aire
Will not perswade me or to give or lend
A token to you.

---

[1] G., 'a penny halter.'   [2] G., 'withe.'
[3] C. and M. omit this line.   G. restores it.

Welb. Ile be more kind to thee.   155
Come thou shalt dine with me.
　Mar. With you.
　Welb. Nay more, dine gratis.
　Mar. Under what hedge, I pray you?　Or at whose cost?
Are they padders? [1] or abram-men, [2] that are your consorts?　160
　Welb. Thou art incredulous; but thou shalt dine
Not alone at her house, but with a gallant lady;
With mee, and with a lady.
　Mar. Lady! what lady?
With the Lady of the Lake, or Queene of Fairies?   165
For I know, it must be an inchanted dinner.
　Welb. With the Lady Alworth, knave.
　Mar. Nay, now there's hope
Thy braine is crack'd.
　Welb. Marke there, with what respect   170
I am entertain'd.
　Mar. With choice, no doubt, of dogge-whippes,
Why, doest thou ever hope to passe her porter?
　Welb. 'Tis not far off, go with mee: trust thine owne eyes.
　Mar. Troth, in my hope, or my assurance rather,   175
To see thee curvet and mounte like a dogge in a blanket
If ever thou presume to passe her theshold,
I will endure thy company.
　Welb. Come along then.   *Exeunt.*

[1] footpads.
[2] Tramps pretending to insanity the better to intimidate.

Actus Secundi, Scena Secunda. [*A Room in Lady*
Allworth's House.]

ALWORTH, WAITING–WOMAN, CHAMBER–MAIDE, ORDER, AMBLE, FURNACE, WATCHALL.

Woman. Could you not command your leasure one houre longer?
Chamberm. Or halfe an houre?
Alw. I have told you what my hast is:
Besides being now anothers, not mine owne,
How e're I much desire to enjoy you longer,   5
My duty suffers, if to please my selfe
I should neglect my lord.
 Wom. Pray you, doe me the favour
To put these few quince-cakes into your pocket;
They are of mine owne preserving.   10
 Chamb. And this marmulade;
'Tis comfortable for your stomacke.
 Wom. And at parting
Excuse me if I begge a farewell from you.
 Chamb. You are still before me, I move the same suite, sir 15
        [ALWORTH] [1] *kisses 'em severally.*
Furn. How greedie these chamberers are of a beardlesse chinne!
I thinke [2] the titts will ravish him.
 Alw. My service
To both.
 Wom. Ours waites on you.   20
 Chamb. And shall doe ever.
 Ord. You are my ladyes charge, be therefore carefull
That you sustaine your parts.
 Wom. We can beare I warrant you.
       Exeunt Woman *and* Chambermaide.
 Furn. Here; drinke it off, the ingredients are a [3] cordiall, 25
And this the true elixir; it hath boild

---

[1] G. inserts.   [2] Q, 'thinne,'—G. corrects.   [3] G. omits 'a.'

Since midnight for you.   'Tis the quintessence
Of five cockes of the game, ten dozen of sparrowes,
Knuckells of veale, potato rootes, and marrow;
Currall,[1] and ambergreece: were you two years elder,   30
And I had a wife, or gamesome misstresse
I durst trust you with neither.   You neede not baite
After this, I warrant you; though your journey's long,
You may ride on the strength of this till tomorrow morning.
     Alw. Your courtesies overwhelme me: I much grieve   35
To part from such true friends, and yet find comfort;
My attendance on my honorable Lord.
(Whose resolution holds to visit my lady)
Will speedily bringe me backe.
               Knocking at the gate[2]*;* MARALL *and* WELBORNE *within*.
     Mar. [3]Dar'st thou venture further?   40
     Welb. [3]Yes, yes, and knocke againe.
     Ord. 'Tis he; disperse.
     Amb. Performe it bravely.
     Furn. I know my cue, nere doubt me.
                    [4]*They go off severall wayes*.
     Watch. Beast that I was to make you stay: most welcome,   45
You were long since expected.
     Welb. Say so much
To my friend, I pray you.
     Watch. For your sake I will, sir.
     Mar. For his sake!   50
     Welb. Mum; this is nothing.
     Mar. More than ever
I would have beleev'd though I had found it in my primer.
     Alw. When I have giv'n you reasons for my late harshnesse,
You'le pardon and excuse me; for, beleeve me   55
Though now I part abruptly, in my service
I will deserve it.

---

[1] Coral.   [2] G., [*knocking within.   Exit Watchall.*
[3] G., [*within*.]
[4] G., [*Exeunt all but Allworth.   Re-enter Watchall, introducing Wellborne and Marrall.*

Mar. Service! with a vengeance!

Welb. I am satisfied: farewell, Tom.

Alw. All joy stay with you.　　　*Exit* ALW.　*Enter* AMBLE. 60

Amb. You are happily encounter'd; I yet never
Presented one so welcome, as I know
You will be to my lady.

Mar. This is some vision;
Or, sure, these men are mad, to worship a dunghill;　　65
It cannot be a truth.

Welb. Be still a pagan
An unbeleeving infidell, be so, miscreant,
And meditate on blanketts and on dogge-whippes.

[Re-]enter FURNACE.

Furn. I am glad you are come; untill I know your pleasure, 70
I knew not how to serve up my ladies dinner.

Mar. His pleasure! is it possible?

Welb. What's thy will?

Furn. Marry, sir, I have some growse, and turkie chicken,
Some rayles,[1] and quailes, and my lady will'd me aske you　75
What kind of sawces best affect your palat,
That I may use my utmost skill to please it.

Mar. The divell's enter'd this cooke; sawce for his palat!
That on my knowledge, for almost this twelve month,
Durst wish but cheeseparings, and browne bread on Sundayes. 80

Welb. That way I like 'em best.

Furn. It shall be done, sir.　　　　　*Exit* FURNACE.

Welb. What thinke you of the hedge we shall dine under?
Shall we feed gratis?

Mar. I know not what to thinke;　　　85
Pray you, make me not mad.

[Re-]enter ORDER.

Ord. This place becomes you not;
Pray you walke, sir, to the dining roome.

Welb. I am well here

---

[1] reed-birds.

'Till her ladiship quitts her chamber.   90
    Mar. Well here, say you?
'Tis a rare change! but yesterday you thought
Your selfe well in a barne, wrapp'd up in pease-straw.

        [Re-]enter Woman *and* Chamber-maide.

    Wom. O sir, you are wish'd for.
    Chamb. My lady dream't, sir, of you.   95
    Wom. And the first command she gave, after she rose
Was (her devotions donne) to give her notice
When you approch'd here.
    Chamb. Which is done on my vertue.
    Mar. I shall be converted, I begin to grow   100
Into a new beleefe, which saints, nor angells
Could have woone me to have faith in.
    Wom. Sir, my lady.

        Enter Lady [Allworth].

    Lady. I come to meete you, and languish'd till I saw you
This first kisse is for forme; I allow a second   105
To such a friend.[1]
    Mar. To such a friend!   Heav'n blesse me!
    Welb. I am whoole [2] yours, yet, madam, if you please
To grace this gentleman with a salute—
    Mar. Salute me at his bidding!   110
    Welb. I shall receave it
As a most high favour.
    Lady. Sir, you may command me.[3]
    Welb. Run backward from a lady? and such a lady?
    Mar. To kisse her foote is to poore me a favour   115
I am unworthy of—   *Offers to kisse her foote.*
    Lady. Nay, pray you, rise,
And since you are so humble, I'le exalt you:
You shall dine with me to day, at mine owne table.
    Mar. Your ladiships table?   I am not good enough   120

[1] G., [*Kisses Wellborn.*   [2] G., 'wholly.'
[3] G., [*Advances to salute Marrall.*

To sit at your stewards boord.
    Lady. You are too modest:
I will not be deni'd.

[*Re-*]*enter* FURNACE.

    Furn. Will you still be babling
Till your meate freeze on the table? The old tricke still: 125
My art ne're thought on!
    Lady. Your arme, Master Welborne:
Nay, keep us company.[1]
    Mar. I was never so grac'd.
           Exeunt WELBORNE, Lady, AMBLE, MARRALL, Woman.[2]
    Order. So! we have play'd our parts, and are come off well. 130
But if I know the mistery, why my lady
Consented to it, or why Master Welborne
Desir'd it, may I perish!
    Furn. Would I had
The roasting of his heart, that cheated him,   135
And forces the poore gentleman to these shiftes!
By fire! (for cookes are Persians, and sweare by it)
Of all the griping, and extorting tyrants
I ever heard or read of, I ne're met
A match to Sir Giles Overreach.   140
    Watch. What will you take
To tell him so, fellow Furnace?
    Furn. Just as much
As my throate is worth, for that would be the price on't.
To have a usurer that starves him selfe,   145
And weares a cloke of one and twenty yeares
On [3] a sute of fourteene groates, bought of the Hangman,
To grow rich, and then purchase, is too common:
But this Sir Giles feedes high, keepes many servants,
Who must at his command doe any outrage;   150
Rich in his habit; vast in his expences;
Yet he to admiration still increases

[1] G., [*To Marrall.*   [2] G., *and Chambermaid.*
[3] C. and M., 'or.'

In wealth, and lordships.
    Ord. He frights men out of their estates,
And breakes through all law-netts, made to curbe ill men,   155
As they were cobwebbs. No man dares reprove him.
Such a spirit to dare and power to doe were never
Lodg'd so unluckily.

[*Re-*]*enter* AMBLE.

    Amble. Ha! ha! I shall burst.
    Ord. Containe thy selfe, man.   160
    Furn. Or make us partakers
Of your suddaine mirth.
    Amb. Ha! ha! my lady has got
Such a guest at her table, this terme-driver Marrall,
This snippe of an attourney.   165
    Furn. What of him, man?
    Amb. The knave thinkes still hee's at the cookes shop in Ramme-
        alley,[1]
Where the clarkes divide, and the elder is to choose;
And feedes so slovenly.   170
    Furn. Is this all?
    Amb. My lady
Dranke to him for fashion sake, or to please Master Welborne.
As I live he rises, and takes up a dish
In which there were some remnants of a boild capon,   175
And pledges her in white broth.
    Furn. Nay, 'tis like
The rest of his tribe.
    Amb. And when I brought him wine,
He leaves his stoole, and after a legge or two   180
Most humbly thankes my worship.
    Ord. Rose [2] already.
    Amb. I shall be chid.

---

    [1] Ram-Alley leads from the Temple into Fleet street. It was known for the
number of its cook-shops.
    [2] G., 'Risen.'

[*Re-*]*enter* Lady [ALLWORTH], WELBORNE, MARRALL.

Furn. My lady frownes.
 Lady. You waite well.   185
Let me have no more of this, I observ'd your jeering.
Sirra, I'le have you know, whom I thinke worthy
To sit at my table, be he ne're so meane,
When I am present is not your companion.
 Ord. Nay, shee'le preserve what's due to her.   190
 Furn. This refreshing
Followes your flux of laughter.
 Lady.[1] You are master,
Of your owne wille.   I know so much of manners
As not to enquire your purposes; in a word,   195
To me you are ever welcome, as to a house
That is your owne.
 Welb. Marke that.
 Mar. With reverence, sir,
An it like your worship.   200
 Welb. Trouble your selfe no farther,[2]
Deare madam; my heart's full of zeale and service,
How ever in my language I am sparing.
Come Master Marrall.
 Mar. I attend your Worship.   *Exeunt* WELB. MAR. 205
 Lad. I see in your lookes you are sorry, and you know me
An easy mistris: bee merry; I have forgot all.
Order, and Furnace come with me; I must give you
Further directions.
 Ord. What you please.   210
 Furn. We are ready.   [*Exeunt.*]

[1] G., [*To Wellborn.*]   [2] G., 'further.'

Actus Secundi, Scena Tertia. [*The Country near Lady Allworth's House.*]

WELBORNE, MARRALL.

Welborne. I thinke I am in a good way.
Marrall. Good sir; the best way,
The certaine best way.
    Welb. There are casualities
That men are subject to.[1]   5
    Mar. You are above 'em,
And as you are already worshipfull,
I hope e're long you will increase in worship,
And be right worshipfull.
    Welb. Prethee doe not flowt mee.   10
What I shall be, I shall be. Is't for your ease,
You keepe your hat off?
    Mar. Ease, and [2] it like your worship.
I hope Jacke Marrall shall not live so long,
To prove himselfe such an unmannerly beast,   15
Though it haile hazell nutts, as to be cover'd
When your worshipp's present.
    Welb. Is not this a true rogue,   *Aside.*
That out of meere hope of a future cosnage
Can turne thus suddainely? 'tis ranke already.   20
    Mar. I know your worshipp's wise, and needs no counsell:
Yet if, in my desire to doe you service,
I humbly offer my advice (but still
Under correction) I hope I shall not
Incurre your high displeasure.   25
    Welb. No; speake freely.
    Mar. Then in my judgement, sir, my simple judgement,
(Still with your worshipps favour) could wish you

---

[1] Q, 'too.'   [2] G., 'an.'

A better habit, for this cannot be
But much distastfull to the noble lady,   30
(I say no more) that loves you; for, this morning,
To me (and I am but a swine to her)
Before the assurance of her wealth perfum'd you,
You savour'd not of amber.
    Welb. I doe now, then?   *Kisses the end of his cudgell.* [1] 35
    Mar. This your battoone hath got a touch of it.
Yet, if you please, for change I have twenty pounds here
Which, out of my true love, I [2] presently
Lay downe at your worshipps feet: 'twill serve to buy you
A riding suite.   40
    Welb. But where's the horse?
    Mar. My gelding
Is at your service: nay, you shall ride me
Before your worship shall be put to the trouble
To walke a foote. Alas, when you are lord   45
Of this ladies mannour (as I know you will be)
You may with the lease of glebe land, call'd Knaves-acre,
A place I would manure, requite your vassal.
    Welb. I thanke thy love; but must make no use of it;
What's twenty pounds?   50
    Mar. 'Tis all that I can make, sir.
    Welb. Doest thou thinke that [3] though I want clothes I could
    not have 'em,
For one word to my lady?
    Mar. As I know not that.   55
    Welb. Come I'le tell thee a secret, and so leave thee.
I'le not give her the advantage, though she be
A gallant minded lady, after we are married
(There being no woman, but is sometimes froward)
To hit me in the teeth, and say she was forc'd   60
To buy me[4] wedding clothes, and tooke me on
With a plaine riding-suite, and an ambling nagge.
No, I'le be furnish'd something like my selfe.

---

[1] G. places this stage direction after next line.   [2] G., 'I'll.'
[3] G. omits 'that.'   [4] G., 'my.'

And so farewell; for thy suite touching Knaves-acre,
When it is mine, 'tis thine.   65
  Mar. I thanke your worship.   *Exit* Welb.
How was I coozen'd in the calculation
Of this mans fortune; my master coozen'd too,
Whose pupil I am in the art of undoing men,
For that is our profession! Well, well, Master Welborne,   70
You are of a sweet nature, and fit againe to be cheated:
Which, if the fates please, when you are possess'd
Of the land and lady; you *sans question* shall be.
I'le presently thinke of the meanes.   *Walke*[1] *by musing.*

Enter Overreach.[2]

  Over. Sirrha, take my horse.   75
I'le walke to get me an appetite; 'tis but a mile,
And exercise will keep me from being pursie.
Ha! Marrall! is he conjuring? perhaps
The knave has wrought the prodigall to doe
Some outrage on himselfe, and now he feeles   80
Compunction in his conscience for't: no matter
So it be done, Marrall!
  Marrall. Sir.
  Over. How succeed we
In our plan with Welborne?   85
  Mar. Never better, sir.
  Over. Has he hang'd or drown'd himselfe?
  Mar. No sir, he lives.
Lives once more to be made a prey to you,
A greater prey than ever.   90
  Over. Art thou in thy witts?
If thou art, reveale this miracle, and briefely.
  Mar. A lady, sir, is falne in love with him.
  Over. With him? what lady?
  Mar. The rich Lady Alworth.   95
  Over. Thou dolt; how dar'st thou speake this?
  Mar. I speake truth.

[1] G., *Walks.*   [2] G., *Speaking to a Servant within.*

And I doe so but once a yeare, unlesse
It be to you, sir.   We din'd with her ladyship,
I thanke his worship.   100
 Over. His worship!
 Mar. As I live, sir,
I din'd with him at the great ladyes table,
Simple as I stand here, and saw when she kiss'd him,
And would, at his request, have kiss'd me too;   105
But I was not so audacious, as some youths are,
And ¹ dare do any thing be it ne're so absurd,
And sad after performance.
 Over. Why, thou rascall!
To tell me these impossibilities: 110
Dine at her table? and kisse him? or thee?
Impudent varlet, have not I my selfe,
To whom great countesses dores have oft flew open,
Ten times attempted, since her husbands death
In vaine to see her, though I came,—a suitor?   115
And yet your good sollicitor-ship, and rogue—Welborne,
Were brought into her presence, feasted with her!
But that I know thee a dogge that cannot blush,
This most incredible lye would call up one
On thy buttermilke cheekes.   120
 Mar. Shall I not trust my eyes, sir?
Or tast? I feele her good cheere in my belly.
 Over. You shall feele me, if you give not over, sirra.
Recover your braines agen, and be no more gull'd
With a beggers plot assisted by the aides   125
Of serving men and chambermaides; for beyond these
Thou never saw'st a woman, or I'le quit you
From my imployments.
 Mar. Will you credit this yet?
On my confidence of their marriage I offere'd Welborne   130
(I would give a crowne now, I durst say his worship)—   *Aside.*
My nagge, and twenty pounds.
 Over. Did you so I doe? ¹   *Strikes him downe.*

  ¹ G., 'That.'   ² G., 'Did you so, idiot?'

Was this the way to worke him to despaire,
Or rather to crosse me?   135
  Mar. Will your worship kill me?
  Over. No, no; but drive the lying spirit out of you.
  Mar. Hee's gone.
  Over. I have done then: now, forgetting
Your late imaginerie feast and lady,   140
Know, my Lord Lovell dines with me to morrow.
Be careful nought be wanting to receave him,
And bid my daughters women trimme her up.
Though they paint her, so she catch the lord, I'le thanke 'em,
There's a peece for my late blowes.   145
  Mar. I must yet suffer:
But there may be a time—   *Aside.*
  Over. Doe you grumble?
  Mar. No, sir.   [*Exeunt.*]

Actus Tertii, Scena Prima.

[*The Country near Overreach's House.*]

LOVELL, ALWORTH, SERVANTS.

  Lovell. Walke the horses downe the hill: something in private,
I must impart to Alworth.   *Exeunt servi.*
  Alw. O, my lord,
What sacrifice of reverence, dutie, watching,
Although I could put off the use of sleepe,   5
And ever waite on your commands to serve 'em;
What dangers, though in ne're so horri'd shapes,
Nay, death it selfe, though I should run to meet it,
Can I, and with a thankfull willingnesse suffer!
But still the retribution will fall short   10
Of your bounties showr'd upon me.
  Lov. Loving youth,
Till what I purpose be put into act,

Doe not o're-prize it; since you have trusted me
With your soules nearest, nay, her dearest secret,   15
Rest confident 'tis in a cabinet lock'd,
Treachery shall never open.   I have found you
(For so much to your face I must professe,
How e're you guard you[r] modesty with a blush for't)
More zealous in your love and service to me   20
Than I have beene in my rewards.
   Alw. Still great ones
Above my merit.
   Lov. Such your gratitude calls 'em:
Nor am I of that harsh and rugg'd [1] temper   25
As some great men are tax'd with, who imagine
They part from the respect due to their honours
If they use not all such as follow 'em,
Without distinction of their births, like slaves.
I am not so condition'd: I can make   30
A fitting difference betweene my foot-boy
And a gentleman by want compell'd to serve me.
   Alw. 'Tis thankefully acknowledg'd: you have beene
More like a father to me than a master.
Pray you pardon the comparison.   35
   Lov. I allow it;
And to give you assurance I am pleas'd in't,
My carriage and demeanor to your mistrisse,
Faire Margaret, shall truely witness for me
I can command my passions.   40
   Alw. 'Tis a conquest
Few lords can boast of when they are tempted.   Oh!
   Lov. Why do you sigh? can you be doubtfull of mee?
By that faire name I in the warres have purchas'd,
And all my actions hitherto untainted,   45
I will not be more true to mine owne honour,
Than to my Alworth.
   Alw. As you are the brave Lord Lovell,
Your bare word only given is an assurance

---

[1] G., 'rugged.'

Of more validity and weight to me   50
Than all the othes bound up with imprecations,
Which, when they would deceive, most courtiers practize:
Yet being a man (for sure to stile you more
Would relish of grosse flatterie) I am forc'd
Against my confidence of your worth and vertues,   55
To doubt, nay more, to feare.
    Lov. So young, and jealous?
    Alw. Were you to encounter with a single foe,
The victorie were certaine; but to stand
The charge of two such potent enemies,   60
At once assaulting you, as wealth and beauty,
And those two seconded with power, is oddes
Too great for Hercules.
    Lov. Speake your doubts and feares,
Since you will nourish 'em, in plainer language,   65
That I may understand 'em.
    Alw. What's your will,
Though I lend armes against my selfe (provided
They may advantage you), must be obeyed.
My much lov'd lord, were Margaret only faire,   70
The cannon of her more than earthly forme,
Though mounted high, commanding all beneath it,
And ramm'd with bullets of her sparkeling eyes,
Of all the bulwarkes that defend your senses
Could batter none,[1] but that which guards your sight.   75
But when the well tun'd accents of her tongue
Make musicke to you, and with numerous sounds
Assault your hearing (such as if Ulysses [2]
Now liv'd againe, how ere he stood the Sirens,
Could not resist) the combat must grow doubtfull   80
Betweene your reason and rebellious passions.
Add this too; when you feele her touch, and breath
Like a soft westerne wind when it glides o're
Arabia, creating gummes and spices;
And, in the van, the nectar of her lippes,   85

[1] So G.—Q, 'more.'   [2] G., 'Such as Ulysses, if [he],' etc.

Which you must tast, bring the battalia on,
Well arm'd, and strongly lin'd with her discourse
And knowing manners, to give entertainment,—
Hyppolitus himselfe would leave Diana,
To follow such a Venus.   90
   Lov. Love hath made you
Poeticall, Alworth.
   Alw. Grant all these beat off,
Which if it be in man to doe, you'le doe it,
Mammon in Sir Giles Overreach stepps in   95
With heapes of ill got gold, and so much land,
To make her more remarkable, as would tire
A falcons winges in one day to fly over.
O my good lord, these powerfull aydes, which would
Make a mishapen negro beautifull,   100
(Yet are but ornaments to give her lustre,
That in her selfe is all perfection) must
Prevaile for her. I here release your trust.
'Tis happinesse, enough, for me to serve you,
And sometimes with chast eyes to looke upon her.   105
   Lov. Why, shall I sweare?
   Alw. O, by no meanes, my lord;
And wrong not so your judgement to the world
As from your fond indulgence to a boy,
Your page, your servant, to refuse a blessing   110
Divers great men are rivalls for.
   Lov. Suspend
Your judgement 'till the triall. How far is it
'T Overreach house?
   Alw. At the most, some halfe houres riding;   115
You'le soone be there.
   Lov. And you the sooner freed
From your jealous feares.
   Alw. O that I durst but hope it!   *Exeunt.*

Actus Tertii, Scena Secunda. [*A Room in Overreach's House.*]

OVERREACH, GREEDIE, MARRALL.

Overreach. Spare for no cost, let my dressers cracke with the weight
Of curious viands.
Greedie. Store indeed's no sore, sir.
Over. That proverb fitts your stomacke, Master Greedie.   5
And let no plate be seene but what's pure gold,
Or such whose workmanship exceeds the matter
That it is made of; let my choicest linnen
Perfume the roome, and, when we wash, the water
With pretious powders mix'd so please my lord [1]   10
That he may with envie wish to bath so ever.
Mar. 'Twill be very chargeable.
Over. Avant you, drudge!
Now all my labour'd ends are at the stake,
I'st time to thinke of thrift?   Call in my daughter.   15
And, Master Justice, since you love choice dishes,
And plenty of 'em—
Greed. As I doe indeed, Sir,
Almost as much as to give thankes for 'em.
Over. I doe conferre that providence,[2] with my power   20
Of absolute command to have abundance,
To your best care.
Greed. I'le punctually discharge it
And give the best directions.   Now I am
In mine owne conceite a monarch, at the least   25
Arch-president of the boyl'd, the roast, the bak'd;
For which I will eate often, and give thankes

---

[1] C. and M., 'with precious powders mix, to please my Lord.'
[2] C., 'province.' G., 'providence.' The parallel passage adduced by G. is not convincing.

When my bellies brac'd up like a drumme; and that's pure justice.
  Over. It must bee so: should the foolish girle prove modest,
Exit GREEDIE.

Shee may spoile all; she had it not from me,   30
But from her mother; I was ever forward,
As she must bee, and therefore I'le prepare her.

[*Enter*] MARGARET.

Alone—and let your women waite without.
  Marg. Your pleasure, sir?
  Over. Ha, this is neate dressing!   35
These orient pearles, and diamonds well plac'd too!
The gowne affects me not, it should have beene
Embroider'd o're and o're with flowers of gold;
But these rich jewells and quaint fashion helpe it.
And how below? since oft the wanton eye   40
The face observ'd, descends unto the foot;
Which being well proportion'd, as yours is,
Invites as much as perfect white and red,
Though without art. How like you your new woman
The Lady Downfalne?   45
  Marg. Well, for a companion;
Not as a servant.
  Over. Is she humble, Meg?
And carefull too, her ladiship forgotten?
  Marg. I pitty her fortune.   50
  Over. Pitty her? Trample on her.
I tooke her up in an old tamin [1] gowne,
(Even starv'd [2] for want of two penny chopps) to serve thee:
And if I understand shee but repines
To doe thee any duty, though ne're so servile,   55
I'le packe her to her knight, where I have lodg'd him,
Into the Counter,[3] and there let 'em howle together.
  Marg. You know your owne wayes, but for me I blush
When I command her that was once attended
With persons not inferior to my selfe   60

---

[1] a coarse linsey woolsey stuff.   [2] Q, 'strau'd.'   [3] prison.

In birth.
    Over. In birth? Why art thou not my daughter?
The blest child of my industrie and wealth?
Why foolish girle, was't not to make thee great,
That I have ran,[1] and still pursue those wayes   65
That hale downe curses on mee, which I minde not?
Part with these humble thoughts, and apt thy selfe
To the noble state I labour to advance thee;
Or, by my hopes to see thee honorable,
I will adopt a stranger to my heyre,   70
And throw thee from my care; doe not provoke mee.
    Marg. I will not, sir; mould mee which way you please.
    Over. How! interrupted?   [*Re-*]*enter* GREEDIE.
    Greed. 'Tis matter of importance.
The cooke, sir, is selfe-will'd and will not learne   75
From my experience: there's a fawne brought in, sir,
And, for my life, I cannot make him rost it
With a Norfolke dumpling in the belly of it,
And, sir, we wisemen [2] know without the dumpling
'Tis not worth three pence.   80
    Over. Would it were whole in thy belly
To stuffe it out.   Cooke it any way; prethee leave me
    Greed. Without order for the dumpling?
    Over. Let it be dumpl'd
Which way thou willt, or tell him I will scalld him   85
In his owne caldron.
    Greed. I had lost my stomake,
Had I lost my mistrisse dumpling. I'le give thanks for['t].
    Over. But to our businesse, Megge; you have heard who dines
here?   *Exit* GREEDIE.
    Marg. I have sir.   91
    Over. 'Tis an honourable man,
A lord, Megge, and commands a regiment
Of souldiers, and, what's rare, is one him selfe;
A bold and understanding one; and to be   95
A lord and a good leader, in one volume,

    [1] G., 'run'.   [2] G., 'wise men.'

Is granted unto few but such as rise up
The Kingdomes glory.

[*Re-*]*enter* GREEDIE.

 Greed. I'le resigne my office
If I be not better obey'd.   100
 Over. Slight, art thou franticke?
 Greed. Franticke! twould make me a franticke and stark-mad,
Were I not a justice of peace and coram [1] too,
Which this rebellious cooke cares not a straw for.
There are a dozen of woodcockes—   105
 Over. Make thy selfe
Thirteene, the bakers dozen.
 Greed. I am contented,
So they may be dress'd to my minde; he has found out
A new device for sawce, and will not dish 'em 110
With tosts and butter. My father was a taylor,
And my name, though a justice, Greedie Woodcocke;
And, 'ere I'le see my linage so abus'd,
I'le give up my commission.
 Over. Cooke! rogue, obey him!   115
I have given the word, pray you, now remove your selfe
To a coller of brawne, and trouble me no farther. [2]
 Greed. I will, and meditate what to eate at dinner.
             Exit GREEDIE.

 Over. And as I said, Meg, when this gull disturb'd us,
This honourable lord, the collonell,   120
I would have thy husband.
 Mar. There's too much disparity
Betweene his quality and mine to hope it.
 Over. I more than hope, and doubt not to effect it.
Be thou no enemy to thy selfe, my wealth 125
Shall weigh his titles downe, and make you equalls.
Now for the meanes to assure him thine; observe me:
Remember hee's a courtier and a soldier,
And not to be trifl'd with; and, therefore, when

 [1] G., 'quorum.'   [2] G., 'further.'

He comes to woo you, see you doe not coye it.   130
This mincing modesty has spoyl'd many a match
By a first refusall, in vaine after hop'd for.
   Mar. You'le have mee, sir, preserve the distance that
Confines a virgin?
   Over. Virgin me no virgins.   135
I must have you lose that name, or you lose me.
I will have you private—start not—I say private:
If thou art my true daughter, not a bastard,
Thou wilt venture alone with one man, though he came
Like Jupiter to Semele, and come off, too.   140
And, therefore, when he kisses you, kisse close.
   Marg. I have heard this is the strumpetts fashion, sir,
Which I must never learne.
   Over. Learne any thing,
And from any creature that may make thee great;   145
From the divell him selfe.
   Marg. This is but divelish doctrine.
   Over. Or, if his blood grow hot, suppose he offer
Beyond this, doe not you stay 'till it coole,
But meete his ardor; if a couch be neare,   150
Sit downe on't, and invite him.
   Marg. In your house?
Your owne house, sir! For heav'ns sake, what are you then?
Or what shall I be, sir?
   Over. Stand not on forme;   155
Words are no substances.
   Marg. Though you could dispense
With your owne honour; cast aside religion,
The hopes of heaven or feare of hell, excuse mee.
In worldly policie this is not the way   160
To make me his wife; his whore I grant it may doe.
My maiden honour so soone yeelded up,
Nay prostituted, cannot but assure him
I, that am light to him, will not hold weight.
When he is [1] tempted by others: so, in judgement,   165

-----
[1] C. and M. omit 'he is.' G., 'Whene'er tempted' *etc.*

When to his lust I have given up my honour,
He must, and will forsake me.
    Over. How? forsake thee?
Doe I weare a sword for fashion? or is this arme
Shrunke up? or wither'd? does there live a man   170
Of that large list I have encountered with,
Can truly say I e're gave inch of ground,
Not purchas'd with his blood that did oppose me?
Forsake thee when the thing is done? he dares not.
Give me but proofe he has enjoy'd thy person,—   175
Though all his captaines, ecchos to his will,
Stood arm'd by his side to justify the wrong,
And he himselfe in the head of his bold troope,—
Spite of his lordship and his collonelship,
Or the judges favour, I will make him render   180
A bloody and a strict accompt, and force him,
By marrying thee, to cure thy wounded honour!
I have said it.

            Enter MARRALL.

    Mar. Sir, the man of honor[']s come,
Newly alighted.   185
    Over. In, without reply;
And doe as I command, or thou art lost.   *Exit* MARG.
Is the lowd musicke I gave order for
Readie to receive him?
    Mar. 'Tis, sir.   190
    Over. Let 'em sound
A princely welcome. Roughnesse a while leave mee;
For fawning now, a stranger to my nature,
Must make way for mee.

    Loud musicke. Enter LOVELL, GREED., ALW., MAR.

    Lov. Sir, you meete your trouble.   195
    Over. What you are pleas'd to stile so, is an honour
Above my worth and fortunes.
    Alw. Strange, so humble.   [*Aside.*]

Over. A justice of peace, my lord.[1]

Lov. Your hand, good sir.	200

Greed. This is a lord; and some thinke this a favour;
But I had rather have my hand in my dumpling.

Over. Roome for my lord.

Lov. I misse, sir, your faire daughter,
To crowne my welcome.	205

Over. May it please my lord
To taste a glasse of Greeke wine first, and suddainely
She shall attend my lord.

Lov. You'le be obey'd, sir.	*Exeunt omnes preter* OVER.

Over. 'Tis to my wish; as soone as come, aske for her!	210
Why, Megge! Megge Overreach! [*Re-enter* MARGARET.] How!
    teares in your eies!
Ha! drie 'em quickely, or I'le digge 'em out.
Is this a time to whimper? Meete that greatnesse
That flies into thy bosome; thinke what 'tis	215
For me to say, "My honorable daughter."
And thou, when I stand bare, to say "Put on,"
Or "Father you forget yourselfe." No more,
But be instructed, or expect—He comes.

Enter LOVELL, GREEDIE, ALWORTH, MARRALL.	*They salute.*

A blacke-brow'd girle, my lord.[2]	220

Lov. As I live a rare one.

Alw. Hee's tooke already: I am lost.

Over. That kisse
Came twanging off; I like it. Quit the roome.	*The rest off.*
A little bashfull, my good lord, but you	225
I hope will teach her boldnesse.

Lov. I am happy
In such a scholler: but—

Over. I am past learning,
And therefore leave you to your selves. Remember—*to his
daughter.*	*Exit* OVERREACH. 231

Lov. You see, faire lady, your father is sollicitous

---

[1] G., [*Presents Greedy to him.*	[2] G., [*Lord Lovell salutes Margaret.*

To have you change the barren name of virgin
Into a hopefull wife.

    Marg. His [1] hast, my lord,   235
Holds no power o're my will.

    Lov. But o're your duty.

    Marg. Which, forc'd too much, may breake.

    Lov. Bend rather, sweetest:
Thinke of your yeares.   240

    Marg. Too few to match with yours:
And choicest fruites too soone pluck'd, rot and wither.

    Lov. Doe you thinke I am old?

    Marg. I am sure I am too young.

    Lov. I can advance you.   245

    Marg. To a hill of sorrow,
Where every houre I may expect to fall,
But never hope firme footing. You are noble,
I of a low descent, how ever rich;
And tissues match'd with skarlet suite but ill.   250
O my good lord, I could say more, but that
I dare not trust these walls.

    Lov. Pray you trust my eare then.

            [Re-]enter OVER. *listning.*

    Over. Close at it! whispering! this is excellent!
And, by their postures, a consent on both parts.   255

            [Re-]enter GREED. *[also behind.]*

    Greed. Sir Giles, Sir Giles!

    Over. The great fiend stop that clapper!

    Greed. It must ring out, sir, when my belly rings noone:
The back'd meates are run out, the rost turn'd powder.

    Over. I shall powder you.   260

    Greed. Beate me to dust, I care not.
In such a cause as this, I'le dye a martyr.

    Over. Marry and shall: you barathrum of the shambells. [2]
                      Strikes him.

---

[1] Q, 'He.'—G. corrects.

[2] G. notes the borrowing of this word from Horace: *Pernicies et tempestas, barathrumque macelli.* By the Jacobean dramatists barathrum was used as= an abyss.

Greed. How! strike a justice of peace? 'tis pettie treason,
Edwardi quinto. But that you are my friend   265
I could commit you without bayle, or main-prise.

Over. Leave your balling, sir, or I shall commit you
Where you shall not dine to-day. Disturbe my lord,
When he is in discourse!

Greed. I'st a time to talke   270
When we should be munching?

Lov. Ha! I heard some noise.

Over. Mum, villaine! vanish! shall we breake a bargaine
Almost made up.   *Thrust* GREEDIE *off*.

Lov. Lady, I understand you;   275
And rest most happy in your choice, beleeve it,
I'le be a carefull pilot to direct
Your yet uncertaine barke to a port of safety.

Marg. So shall your honour save two lives, and bind us
Your slaves for ever.   280

Lov. I am in the act rewarded,
Since it is good; how e're you must put on
An amorous carriage towards me, to delude
Your subtle father.

Marg. I am prone to that.   285

Lov. Now breake wee off our conference. Sir Giles!
Where is Sir Giles?

Enter OVERREACH, *and the rest*.[1]

Over. My noble lord; and how
Does your lordship find her?

Lov. Apt, Sir Giles, and comming;   290
And I like her the better.

Over. So doe I too.

Lov. Yet should we take forts at the first assault
'Twere poore in the defendant; I must cofirme her
With a love letter or two, which I must have   295
Deliver'd by my page, and you give way too't.

[1] G., [*Overreach comes forward*.
Re-enter Allworth, Marrall, and Greedy.

Over. With all my soule, a towardly gentleman.
Your hand, good Master Alworth; know my house
Is ever open to you.
  Alw. 'Twas shut 'till now.   *Aside.* 300
  Over. Well done, well done, my honorable daughter:
Th'art so already: know this gentle youth,
And cherish him my honorable daughter.
  Mar. I shall with my best care. *Noise within as of a coch.*
  Over. A coch.   305
  Greed. More stops
Before we goe to dinner! O my gutts!

   Enter LADIE [ALLWORTH] *and* WELBORNE.

  Lad. If I find welcome
You share in it; if not I'le backe againe,
Now I know your ends; for I am [1] come arm'd for all 310
Can be objected.
  Lov. How! the Lady Alworth!
  Over. And thus attended!
  Mar. No, I am a dolt;
    LOVELL *salutes the* LADY, *the* LADIE *salutes* MARGARET.
The spirit of lyes had enter'd me.   315
  Over. Peace, Patch,[2]
'Tis more than wonder! an astonishment
That does possesse me wholly!
  Lov. Noble lady,
This is a favour to prevent [3] my visit,   320
The service of my life can never equall.
  Lad. My lord, I lay'd waite for you, and much hop'd
You would have made my poore house your first inne:
And therefore doubting that you might forget me,
Or too long dwell here having such ample cause 325
In this unequall'd beauty for your stay;
And, fearing to trust any but my selfe

---

[1] G. omits 'am.'
[2] Patch was the name of a fool kept by Cardinal Wolsey.
[3] anticipate.

With the relation of my service to you,
I borrow'd so much from my long restraint,
And tooke the ayre in person to invite you. 330
   Lov. Your bounties are so great they robbe me, madam,
Of words to give you thankes.
   Lad. Good Sir Giles Overreach. *Salutes him.*
How doest thou, Marrall? lik'd you my meate so ill,
You'le dine no more with me? 335
   Greed. I will when you please,
And ¹ it like your ladyship.
   Lad. When you please, Master Greedie
If meat can doe it, you shall be satisfied,
And now, my lord, pray take into your knowledge 340
This gentleman, howe're his outsids course,² *Presents* WELBORN.
His inward linings are as fine, and faire,
As any mans: wonder not I speake at large:
And, howsoe'er his humour carries him
To be thus accoutred, or what taint soever 345
For his wild life hath stucke upon his fame,
He may e're long, with boldnesse, rancke himselfe
With some that have contemned him. Sir Giles Overreach,
If I am welcome, bid him so.
   Over. My nephew. 350
He has beene too long a stranger: faith, you have;
Pray, let it bee mended. LOVELL *conferring with* WELBORNE.
   Mar. Why, sir, what doe you meane?
This is rogue Welborne, monster, prodigie,
That should hang, or drowne himselfe, no man of worship, 355
Much lesse your nephew.
   Over. Well, sirra, we shall reckon
For this hereafter.
   Mar. I'le not lose my jeere
Though I be beaten dead for it. 360
   Welb. Let my silence plead
In my excuse, my lord, till better leasure
Offer it selfe to heare a full relation

¹ G., 'An.' ² coarse.

Of my poore fortunes.
    Lov. I would heare, and helpe 'em.   365
    Over. Your dinner waites you.
    Lov. Pray you, lead, we follow.
    Lad. Nay, you are my ghest; come, deere Master Welborne.
                    Exeunt; manet GREEDIE.
    Greed. Deare Master Welborne! So shee said; Heav'n! heav'n!
If my belly would give me leave I could ruminate   370
All day on this: I have granted twenty warrants
To have him committed, from all prisons in the shire,
To Nottingham jayle; and now, *deare Master Welborne!*
And *my good nephew!* But I play the foole
To stand here prating, and forget my dinner.   375
Are they set, Marrall?   [*Re-*]*enter* MARRALL.
    Mar. Long since; pray you a word, sir.
    Greed. No wording now.
    Mar. In troth, I must; my master,
Knowing you are his good friend, makes bold with you,   380
And does intreat you, more ghests being come in
Then he expected, especially his nephew,
The table being full too, you would excuse him,
And suppe with him on the cold meate.
    Greed. How! no dinner   385
After all my care?
    Mar. 'Tis but a pennance for
A meale; besides, you broke your fast.
    Greed. That was
But a bit to stay my stomacke: a man in commission   390
Give place to a tatterdemallion?
    Mar. No bugge [1] words, sir;
Should his worship heare you?
    Greed. Lose my dumpling too?
And butter'd tosts and woodcocks?   395
    Mar. Come, have patience.
If you will dispense a little with your worship,

---

[1] Frightening, terrific. Cf., in *Winters Tale*, 'The bug which you would fright me with.'

And sit with the waiting woemen, you ¹ have dumpling,
Woodcocke, and butter'd tosts too.
    Greed. This revivies me   400
I will gorge there sufficiently.
    Mar. This is the way, sir.   *Exeunt.*

Actus Tertii, Scena Tertia.   [*Another Room in Overreach's House.*]

OVERREACH *as from dinner.*

    Overreach. Shee's caught! O woemen! she neglects my lord,
And all her complements appli'd to Welborne!
The garments of her widdowhood lay'd by,
She now appeares as glorious as the spring.
Her eyes fix'd on him; in the wine shee drinkes,   5
He being her pledge, she sends him burning kisses,
And sitts on thornes, till she be private with him.
She leaves my meate, to feed upon his lookes;
And if in our discourse he be but nam'd,
From her a deepe sigh followes. But why grieve I   10
At this? it makes for me; if she prove his,
All that is hers is mine, as I will worke him.

Enter MARRALL.

    Mar. Sir, the whole boord is troubled at your rising
    Over. No matter, I'le excuse it. Prethee, Marrall,
Watch an occasion to invite my nephew   15
To speake with me in private.
    Mar. Who? the rogue
The lady scorn'd to looke on?
    Over. You are a wagge.

Enter LADY, *and* WELBORNE.

    Mar. See, sir, shee's come, and cannot be without him.   20
    Lad. With your favour, sir, after a plenteous dinner,
             ¹ G., 'you'll.'

I shall make bold to walke a turne or two
In your rare garden.
  Over. There's an arbor too
If your ladieship please to use it.   25
    Lad. Come, Master Welborne.   *Exeunt* LADY *and* WELBORNE.
  Over. Grosser, and grosser! now I beleeve the Poet
Fain'd not but was historicall, when he wrot
Pasiphae was enamour'd of a bull:
This ladies lust's more monstrous. My good lord,   30

       Enter LOVELL, MARGARET *and the rest.*

Excuse my manners.
  Lov. There needes none, Sir Giles,
I may e're long say Father, when it pleases
My dearest mistrisse to give warrant to it.
  Over. She shall seale to it, my lord, and make me happy.   35
  Marg. My lady is return'd.

       [*Re-*]*enter* WELB. *and the* LAD[Y].

  Lad. Provide my coach,
I'le instantly away: my thanks, Sir Giles,
For my entertainment.
  Over. 'Tis your noblenesse   40
To thinke it such.
  Lad. I must doe you a further wrong
In taking away your honorable ghest.
  Lov. I waite on you, madam.   Farewell, good Sir Giles.
  Lad. Good Mistresse Margaret: nay come Master Welborne, 45
I must not leave you behind, in sooth I must not.
  Over. Robbe me not Madam, of all joyes at once
Let my nephew stay behind: he shall have my coach,
(And after some small conference betweene us)
Soone overtake your ladyship.   50
  Lad. Stay not long, sir.
  Lov. This parting kisse:[1] you shall every day heare from me
By my faithfull page.   *Exeunt* LOVELL, LADY, ALWORTH, MAR-
                           GARET, MARRALL.

     [1] G., [*Kisses Margaret.*]

Over. Daughter, to your chamber.[1]   You may wonder, nephew,
After so long an enmity betweene us   55
I should desire your friendship?
Well: so I doe, sir.
   Welb. 'Tis strange to me.[2]
   Over. But I'le make it no wonder,
And, what is more, unfold my nature to you.   60
We worldly men, when wee see friends and kinsmen
Past hope suncke in their fortunes, lend no hand
To lift 'em up, but rather set our feet
Upon their heads, to presse 'em to the bottome;
As I must yeeld, with you I practis'd it.   65
But now I see you in a way to rise,
I can and will assist you. This rich lady
(And I am glad of it) is enamour'd of you;
'Tis too apparent, nephew.
   Welb. No such thing: 70
Compassion rather, sir.
   Over. Well, in a word,
Because your stay is short: I'le have you seene
No more in this base shape; nor shall shee say
She married you like a begger, or in debt.   75
   Welb. Hee'le run in to the noose, and save my labor.   *Aside.*
   Over. You have a trunke of rich clothes, not far hence,
In pawne. I will redeeme 'em, and that no clamor
May taint your credit for your petty debts,
You shall have a thousand pounds to cut 'em off,   80
And goe a freeman to the wealthy lady.
   Welb. This done, sir, out of love, and no ends else—
   Over. As it is, nephew.
   Welb. Bindes me still your servant.
   Over. No complements; you are stay'd for. E're y'ave supp'd 85
You shall heare from me. My coach, knaves, for my nephew:
To morrow I will visit you.

---

[1] G., [*Exit Margaret.*]
[2] G., '*Welb.* So I do, Sir;
        'Tis strange to me.'

Welb. Heer's an uncle
In a mans extreames! how much they doe belye you
That say you are hard-harted.   90
    Over. My deeds, nephew,
Shall speake my love, what men report, I weigh not.   *Exeunt.*
                    Finis Actus Tertii.

Actus Quarti, Scena Prima.

[*A Room in Lady Allworth's House.*]

LOVELL, ALWORTH.

Lovell. 'Tis well: give me my cloke; I now discharge you
From further service. Minde your owne affaires,
I hope they will prove successefull.
    Alw. What is blest
With your good wish, my lord, cannot but prosper.   5
Let after times report, and to your honor
How much I stand engag'd, for I want language
To speake my debt: yet if a teare or two
Of joy for your much goodnesse can supply
My tongues defects, I could—   10
    Lov. Nay, doe not melt:
This ceremoniall thankes to mee's superfluous.
    Overreach within. Is my Lord stirring?
    Lov. 'Tis he! oh, here's your letter: let him in.
                    Enter OVER. GRED. MAR.
    Over. A good day to my lord.   15
    Lov. You are an early riser, Sir Giles.
    Over. And reason to attend your lordship.
    Lov. And you too Master Greedie, up so soone?
    Greed. In troth, my lord after the sun is up
I cannot sleep, for I have a foolish stomacke   20
That croakes for breakefast. With your lordships favour,
I have a serious question to demand

Of my worthy friend Sir Giles.
   Lov. Pray you use your pleasure.
   Greed. How far, Sir Giles, and pray you answer me   25
Upon your credit, hold you it to be
From your manor house, to this of my Lady Alworths.
   Over. Why, some four mile.
   Greed. How! four mile?   Good Sir Giles,
Upon your reputation thinke better,   30
For if you doe abate but one halfe quarter
Of five you doe yourselfe the greatest wrong
That can be in the world: for foure miles riding
Could not have rais'd so huge an appetite
As I feele gnawing on me.   35
   Mar. Whither [1] you ride,
Or goe a foote, you are that way still provided
And it please your worship.
   Over. How now, sirra? prating
Before my lord: no difference?   Go to my nephew;   40
See all his debts discharg'd, and help his worship
To fit on his rich suite.
   Mar. I may fit you too;
Toss'd like a dogge still.   *Exit* MARRALL.
   Lov. I have writt this morning   45
A few lines to my mistresse, your faire daughter.
   Over. 'Twill fire her, for shee is wholly yours already:
Sweet master Alworth, take my ring: 'twill carry you
To her presence I dare warrant you; and there pleade
For my good Lord, if you shall find occasion.   50
That done, pray ride to Nottingham, get a licence,
Still by this token.   I'le have it dispatch'd,
And suddainely my lord, that I may say
My honorable, nay, right honorable daughter.   54
   Greed. Take my advice, young gentleman: get your breakefast.
'Tis unwholsome to ride fasting.   I'le eate with you
And eate to purpose.
   Over. Some Furies in that gut:

[1] G., 'Whether.'

Hungry againe! did you not devoure this morning,
A shield of brawne, and a barrell of Colchester oysters?   60
  Greed. Why that was, sir, only to scoure my stomacke,
A kind of preparative. Come, gentleman
I will not have you feed like the hangman of Vlushing.[1]
Alone, while I am here.
    Lov. Hast your returne.   65
    Alw. I will not faile, my lord.
    Greed. Nor I, to line
My Christmas coffer.   *Exeunt* GREEDIE *and* ALWORTH.
    Over. To my wish, we are private.
I come not to make offer with my daughter   70
A certaine portion,—that were poore, and triviall:
In one word I pronounce all that is mine,
In lands, or leases, ready coine, or goods,
With her, my lord, comes to you; nor shall you have
One motive to induce you to beleeve,   75
I live too long, since every yeare I'le add
Something unto the heape, which shall be yours too.
    Lov. You are a right kind father.
    Over. You shall have reason
To thinke me such. How doe you like this seate?   80
It is well wooded, and well water'd, the acres
Fertile, and rich; would it not serve for change
To entertaine your friends in a sommer progresse?
What thinkes my noble lord?
    Lov. 'Tis a wholsome aire,   85
And well built pile, and she that's mistresse of it
Worthy the large revennue.
    Over. Shee, the mistresse?
It may be so for a time: but let my lord
Say only that he likes it, and would have it,   90
I say e're long 'tis his.
    Lov. Impossible.
    Over. You doe conclude too fast, not knowing me,
Nor the engines that I worke by. 'Tis not alone
                    [1] G., 'Flushing.'

The Lady Alworths lands, for those once Welbornes   95
(As by her dotage on him, I know they will be,)
Shall soone be mine, but point out any mans
In all the shire, and say they lie convenient,
And usefull to your lordship, and once more
I say aloud, they are yours.   100
  Lov. I dare not owne
What's by unjust and cruell meanes extorted.
My fame and credit are more deare to me,
Than so to expose 'em to be censur'd by
The publike voice.   105
  Over. You run, my lord, no hazard.
Your reputation shall stand as faire
In all good mens opinions as now:
Nor can my actions, though condemn'd for ill,
Cast any foule aspersion upon yours;   110
For though I doe contemne report my selfe,
As a meere sound, I still will be so tender
Of what concerns you in all points of honour,
That the immaculate whitenesse of your fame,
Nor your unquestion'd integrity   115
Shall e're be sullied with one taint or spot
That may take from your innocence and candor.
All my ambition is to have my daughter
Right honorable which my lord can make her;
And might I live to dance upon my knee   120
A young Lord Lovell, borne by her unto you,
I write *nil ultra* to my proudest hopes.
As for possessions, and annuall rents
Equivalent to maintaine you in the port,[1]
Your noble birth, and present state requires,   125
I doe remove that burthen from your shoulders,
And take it on mine owne: for though I ruine
The country to supply your riotous wast,
The scourge of prodigalls want shall never find you.
  Lov. Are you not frighted with the imprecations   130

    [1] condition, carriage.

And curses of whole families made wretched
By your sinister practices?
 Over. Yes, as rocks are
When foamie billowes split themselves against
Their flinty ribbes; or as the moone is moved   135
When wolves, with hunger pin'd, howle at her brightnesse.
I am of a solid temper, and like these
Steere on a constant course: with mine owne sword
If call'd into the field, I can make that right,
Which fearefull enemies murmur'd as a wrong.[1]   140
Now, for these other pidling complaints
Breath'd out in bitterness, as when they call me
Extortioner, tyrant, cormorant, or intruder
On my poore neighbors right, or grand incloser
Of what was common, to my private use;   145
Nay, when my eares are pierc'd with widdowes cries,
And undon orphants wash with teares my theshold,
I only thinke what 'tis to have my daughter
Right honorable; and 'tis a powerfull charme
Makes me insensible of remorse, or pitty.   150
Or the least sting of conscience.
 Lov. I admire [2]
The toughnesse of your nature.
 Over. 'Tis for you
My lord, and for my daughter, I am marble;   155
Nay, more, if you will have my character
In little, I enjoy more true delight
In my arivall to my wealth these darke
And crooked wayes, than you shall e're take pleasure
In spending what my industry hath compass'd.   160
My hast commands me hence; in one word, therefore,
Is it a match?
 Lov. I hope that is past doubt now.
 Over. Then rest secure: not the hate of all mankind here,
Nor feare of what can fall on me here after,   165
Shall make me studie ought but your advancement

   [1] G., 'murmurd at as wrong.'   [2] wonder at.

One story higher. An earle if gold can do it.
Dispute not my religion, nor my faith;
Though I am borne thus headlong by my will,
You may make choice of what beleefe you please,   170
To me they are equall; so my lord good morrow.   *Exit.*
  Lov. Hee's gone—I wonder how the earth can beare
Such a portent! I, that have liv'd a souldier,
And stood the enemies violent charge undaunted,
To heare this blasphemous beast am bath'd all over   175
In a cold sweat: yet like a mountaine he,
Confirm'd in atheisticall assertions,
Is no more shaken than Olimpus [1] is
When angry Boreas loades his double head
With suddaine drifts of snow.   180

            Enter AMBLE, LADY [ALLWORTH], Woman.

  Lad. Save you, my lord.
Disturbe I not your privacie?
  Lov. No, good madam;
For your owne sake I am glad you came no sooner,
Since this bold, bad man, Sir Giles Overreach   185
Made such a plaine discoverie of him selfe,
And read this morning such a divellish matins,
That I should thinke it a sinne next to his
But to repeat it.
  Lad. I ne're press'd, my lord,   190
On others privacies; yet, against my will,
Walking, for health sake, in the gallerie
Adjoyning to your lodgings, I was made
(So vehement and loud he was) partaker
Of his tempting offers.   195
  Lov. Please you to command
Your servants hence and I shall gladly hear
Your wiser counsail.
  Lad. 'Tis, my lord, a wommans,
But true and hearty; wait in the next roome,   200
    [1] G. notes that Massinger has here mistaken Olympus for Parnassus.

But be within call: yet not so neere to force me
To whisper my intents.
    Amb. We are taught better
By you, good madam.
    Wom. And well know our distance.   205
    Lad. Doe so, and talke not; twill become   *Exeunt* AMBLE
    your breeding.   *and* Woman.
Now, my good lord; if I may use my freedome,
As to an honour'd friend?
    Lov. You lessen else   210
Your favour to me.
    Lad. I dare then say thus;
As you are noble (how e're common men
Make sordid wealth the object, and sole end
Of their industrious aimes) 'twill not agree   215
With those of eminent blood (who are ingag'd
More to prefer their honours, than to increase
The state left to 'em, by their ancestours)
To study large additions to their fortunes
And quite neglect their births: though I must grant   220
Riches well got to be a usefull servant,
But a bad master.
    Lov. Madam, 'tis confessed;
But what infer you from it?
    Lad. This, my Lord;   225
That as all wrongs, though thrust into one scale
Slide of themselves off, when right fills the other,
And cannot bide the triall: so all wealth
(I meane if ill acquir'd) cemented to honor
By vertuous wayes atchiev'd, and bravely purchas'd,   230
Is but as rubbage powr'd into a rivier
(Howe're intended to make good the banke)
Rendring the water that was pure before,
Polluted, and unwholsome. I allow
The heire of Sir Giles Overrech, Margaret,   235
A maide well qualified, and the richest match
Our north part can make boast of; yet she cannot

With all that she brings with her fill their mouthes,
That never will forget who was her father;
Or that my husband Alworths lands, and Welbornes　　240
(How wrunge from both needs now no repitition)
Were reall motive that more work'd your lordship
To joyn your families than her forme and vertues.
You may conceave the rest.
　　Lov. I doe, sweet madam;　　245
And long since have consider'd it.　I know
The summe of all that makes a just man happy
Consists in the well choosing of his wife:
And there, well to discharge it, does require
Equality of yeares, of birth, of fortune,　　250
For beauty being poore, and not cried up
By birth or wealth, can truely mixe with neither.
And wealth, where there's such difference in yeares,
And faire descent, must make the yoke uneasie:
But I come neerer.　　255
　　Lad. Pray you, doe, my lord.
　　Lov. Were Overreach' states [1] thrice centuple'd; his daughter
Millions of degrees much fairer than she is,
(How e're I might urge presidents [2] to excuse me)
I would not so adulterate my blood　　260
By marrying Margaret, and so leave my issue
Made up of several peeces, one part skarlet
And the other London-blew.　In my owne tombe
I will interre my name first.
　　Lad. I am glad to heare this.　　*Aside.* 265
Why then, my lord, pretend you marriage to her?
Dissimulation but tyes false knots
On that straite line, by which you hitherto
Have measur'd all your actions?
　　Lov. I make answer,　　270
And aptly, with a question.　Wherefore have you,
That, since your husbands death, have liv'd a strict
And chaste nuns life, on the suddaine giv'n your selfe

---

[1] Q, 'Were Overreach, that's.'—G. corrects.　　[2] precedents.

To visits and entertainments? thinke you, madam,
'Tis not growne publike conference? or that favours   275
Which you too prodigally have throwne on Welborne,
Being too reserv'd before, incurre not censure?
   Lad. I am innocent heere, and on my life I sweare
My ends are good.
   Lov. On my soule, so are mine   280
To Margaret: but leave both to the event;
And since this friendly privacie does serve
But as an offer'd meanes unto our selves
To search each other farther; you having showne
Your care of mee, I, my respect to you;   285
Denie me not, but still in chaste words, madam,
An after-noones discourse.
   Lad. So; I shall heare you.   [*Exeunt.*]

Actus Quarti, Scena Secunda.   [*Before Tapwell's
        House.*]

TAPWELL, FROTH.

   Tapwell. Undone, undone! this was your counsaile, Froth.
   Froth. Mine! I defie thee. Did not Master Marrall
(He has marr'd all I am sure) strictly command us
(On paine of Sir Giles Overreach displeasure)
To turne the gentleman out of dores?   5
   Tapw. 'Tis true
But now hee's his uncles darling, and has got
Master Justice Greedie (since he filled his belly)
At his commandement, to doe anything;
Woe, woe to us!   10
   Froth. He may prove mercifull.
   Tap. Troth, we do not deserve it at his hands.
Though he knew all the passages of our house,
As the receiving of stolne goods, and bawdrie,
When he was rogue Welborne, no man would beleeve him,   15
And then his information could not hurt us.

But now he is Right Worshipfull againe,
Who dares but doubt his testimonie? me thinkes
I see thee, Froth, already in a cart
For a close bawde, thine eyes ev'n pelted out   20
With durt, and rotten egges, and my hand hissing
(If I scape the halter) with the letter *R*.,
Printed upon it.
    Froth. Would that were the worst:
That were but nine dayes wonder, as for credit   25
We have none to lose; but we shall lose the money
He owes us and his custome, there's the hell on't.
    Tap. He has summon'd all his creditours by the drum;
And they swarme about him like so many souldiers
On the pay day, and has found out such *a new way*   30
To pay his old debts, as 'tis very likely
He shall be chronicl'd for it.
    Froth. He deserves it
More than ten pageants. But are you sure his worship
Comes this way to my ladie[']s?   35

        A cry within, Brave Master Welborne.

    Tapw. Yes I heare him.
    Froth. Be ready with your petition and present it
To his good grace.

Enter WELB. *in a rich habit*,[1] GREED., ORD., FURN., *three* Creditors:
    TAPW. *kneeling delivers his bill of debt*.[2]

    Welb. How's this! petition'd too?
But note what miracles the payment of   40
A little trash, and a rich suite of clothes,
Can worke upon these rascalls. I shall be,
I thinke, Prince Welborne.
    Mar. When your worship[']s married
You may be, I know what I hope to see you.   45
    Welb. Then looke thou for advancement.
    Mar. To be knowne

    [1] G., *followed by Marrall, Greedy etc.*   [2] G., *delivers his petition.*

Your worships bayliffe is the marke I shoot at.
 Welb. And thou shalt hit it.
 Mar. Pray you, sir, dispatch   50
These needie followers, and for my admittance,[1]
Provided you'll defend *This interim,* TAPWELL *and* FROTH
 me from Sir Giles, *flattering and bribing Justice* GREEDY.[2]
Whose service I am weary of, I'le say something
You shall give thankes for.   55
 Welb. Feare me not Sir Giles.
 Greed. Who? Tapwell? remember[3] thy wife brought me
Last new yeares tide, a couple of fat turkies.
 Tapw. And shall doe every christmas, let your worship
But stand my friend now.   60
 Greed. How? with Master Welborne?
I can doe anything with him, on such termes.
See you this honest couple: they are good soules
As ever drew out fosset;[4] have they not
A payre of honest faces?   65
 Welb. I o'reheard you,
And the bribe he promis'd, you are cousend in 'em,
For of all the scumme that grew rich by my riots
This for a most unthankefull knave, and this
For a base bawde and whore, have worst deserv'd me, 70
And therefore speake not for 'em. By your place
You are rather to do me justice: lend me your eare,
Forget his turkies, and call in his licence,
And at the next faire, I'le give you a yoke of oxen
Worth all his poultry.   75
 Greed. I am chang'd on the suddaine
In my opinion! come neere; neerer, rascall!
And, now I view him better, did you e're see
One looke so like an arch-knave? his very countenance,
Should an understanding judge but looke upon him, 80
Would hang him, though he were innocent.
 Tap. Froth. Worshipfull sir.

---

[1] his advancement.   [2] G. omits this stage direction entirely.
[3] G., 'I remember.'   [4] faucit.

Greed. No, though the great Turke came, insteed of turkies,
To begge my favour, I am inexorable:
Thou hast an ill name: besides thy musty ale,   85
That hath destroy'd many of the Kings leige people,
Thou never hadst in thy house, to stay mens stomackes,
A piece of Suffolke cheese, or gammon of bacon,
Or any esculent, as the learned call it,
For their emolument, but sheere drinke only.   90
For which grosse fault I heere doe damne thy license,
Forbidding thee ever to tap or draw;
For instantly, I will in mine owne person
Command the constable to pull downe thy signe;
And doe it before I eate.   95
 Froth. No mercie?
 Greed. Vanish!
If I shew any, may my promis'd oxen gore me.
 Tapw. Unthankefull knaves are ever so rewarded.
     Exeunt GREEDIE, TAPWELL, FROTH.
 Welb. Speake; what are you?   100
 1. Creditor. A decay'd vintner, sir,
That might have thrived, but that your worship broke me
With trusting you with muskadine [1] and egges,
And five pound suppers, with your after drinkings,
When you lodg'd upon the Banckside.   105
 Welb. Remember.[2]
 1. Cred. I have not beene hasty, nor e're layd to arrest you,
And therefore, sir—
 Welb. Thou art an honest fellow:
I'le set thee up againe. See his bill pay'd,   110
What are you?
 2. Cred. A taylor once, but now meere botcher.
I gave you credit for a suite of clothes,
Which was all my stocke; but you failing in payment,
I was remov'd from the shop-boord, and confin'd   115
Under a stall.
 Welb. See him pay'd—And botch no more.

---

[1] a sweet wine made from Muscat grapes.   [2] G., 'I remember.'

2. *Cred.* I aske no interest, sir.

Welb. Such taylors need not;
If their bills are pay'd in one and twenty yeare   120
They are seldomn losers. O, I know thy face—
Thou wert my surgeon: you must tell no tales,
Those dayes are done. I will pay you in private.

· *Ord.* A royall gentleman!

Furn. Royall as an emperour!   125
He'le prove a brave master; my good lady knew
To choose a man.

Welb. See all men else discharg'd;
And since *Old debts are clear'd by a new Way*,
A little bountie, will not misbecome mee;   130
There's something, honest cooke, for thy good breakefasts;
And this for your respect, take't, 'tis good gold
And I able to spare it.

Ord. You are too munificent.

Furn. Hee was ever so.   135

Welb. Pray you, on before.

3. *Cred.* Heaven blesse you!

Mar. At foure a clocke the rest know where to meet me.

                    Exeunt Ord. Furn. Credit.

Welb. Now, Master Marrall, what's the weightie secret
You promis'd to impart?   140

Mar. Sir, time nor place
Allow me to relate each circumstance;
This only in a word: I know Sir Giles
Will come upon you for security
For his thousand pounds, which you must not consent to.   145
As he growes in heat, as I am sure hee will,
Be you but rough, and say hee's in your debt
Ten times the summe, upon sale of your land.
I had a hand in't—(I speake it to my shame)
When you were defeated of it.   150

Welb. That's forgiven.

Mar. I shall deserve't then; urge him to produce [1]

[1] G., 'I shall deserve it: then urge him to produce.'

The deed in which you pass'd it over to him,
Which I know hee'le have about him to deliver
To the Lord Lovell, with many other writings,   155
And present moneys. I'le instruct you further,
As I waite on your worship. If I play not my price
To your full content, and your uncles much vexation,
Hang up *Jacke Marrall.*
   Welb. I relie upon thee.   *Exeunt.* 160

Actus Quarti, Scena Ultima.   [*A Room in Overreach's
House.*]

ALWORTH, MARGARET.

   Alworth. Whither [1] to yeeld the first praise to my lords
Unequall'd temperance, or your constant sweetnesse,
That I yet live, my weake hands fasten'd on
Hopes anchor, spite of all stormes of despaire
I yet rest doubtfull.   5
   Marg. Give it to Lord Lovell.
For what in him was bounty, in mee's duty.
I make but payment of a debt, to which
My vowes in that high office register'd,
Are faithfull witnesses.   .   10
   Alw. 'Tis true, my dearest,
Yet when I call to mind how many faire ones
Make wilfull shipwracke of their faiths, and oathes
To God and man, to fill the armes of greatnesse,
And you rise up [no] [2] lesse than a glorious starre   15
To the amazement of the world, that hold out
Against the sterne authority of a father,
And spurne at honour when it comes to court you,
I am so tender of your good, that faintly
With your wrong I can wish my selfe that right   20
You yet are pleas'd to do mee.
    [1] G., 'whether.'   [2] So G., first inserted by Dodsley.

Marg. Yet, and ever.
To me what's title, when content is wanting?
Or wealth rak'd up together with much care,
And to be kept with more, when the heart pines, 25
In being dispossest of what it longs for,
Beyond the Indian mines? or the smooth brow
Of a pleas'd sire, that slaves me to his will,
And, so his ravenous humour may bee feasted
By my obedience, and he see me great, 30
Leaves to my soule nor faculties nor power
To make her owne election?
    Alw. But the dangers
That follow the repulse—
    Marg. To me they are nothing: 35
Let Alworth love, I cannot be unhappy.
Suppose the worst, that in his rage he kill me,
A teare or two, by you dropt on my hearse
In sorrow for my fate, will call backe life
So far, as but to say that I die yours; 40
I then shall rest in peace. Or should he prove
So cruell, as one death would not suffize
His thirst of vengeance, but with lingring torments
In mind and body I must waste to ayre,
In poverty joyn'd with banishment,—so you share 45
In my afflictions (which I dare not wish you,
So high I prize you), I could undergoe 'em,
With such a patience as should looke downe
With scorne on his worst malice.
    Alw. Heaven avert 50
Such trialls of your true affection to me!
Nor will it unto you that are all mercie
Shew so much rigour: but since wee must run
Such desperate hazards, let us doe our best
To steere betweene 'em. 55
    Marg. Your lord's ours, and sure,
And though but a young actor second me
In doing to the life, what he has plotted.

Enter OVERREACH [*behind*].

The end may yet prove happy: now, my Alworth—[*Seeing her*
   Alw. To your letter, and put on seeming anger.   *father.*] 60
   Marg. I'le pay my lord all debts due to his title,
And when with termes, not taking from his honour,
He does sollicite me, I shall gladly heare him.
But in this peremptory, nay, commanding way,
'Tappoint a meeting, and without my knowledge, 65
A Priest to tye the knot can ne're be undone
'Till death unlose it, is [1] a confidence
In his lordship will deceive him.
   Alw. I hope better,
Good lady. 70
   Marg. Hope, sir, what you please: for me
I must take a safe and secure course; I have
A father, and without his full consent,
Though all the lords of the land kneel'd for my favour,
I can grant nothing. 75
   Over. I like this obedience. [2]
But whatsoever my lord writes, must, and shall bee
Accepted and embrac'd. Sweet Master Alworth,
You shew your selfe a true and faithfull servant
To your good lord, he has a jewell of you. 80
How? frowning, Meg? are these lookes to receive
A messenger from my lord? what's this? give me it.
   Marg. A peece of arrogant paper like th'inscriptions.
   Over. Faire mistresse from your servant learne all joyes
               OVERREACH *read the letter.*
That we can hope for, if deferr'd, prove toyes; 85
Therefore this instant, and in private, meete
A husband, that will gladly at your feet
Lay downe his honours, tendring them to you
With all content, the church being payd her due. [3]
Is this the arrogant peece of paper? Foole, 90
Will you still be one? in the name of madnesse, what

---

[1] Q, 'as'.   [2] G., [*Comes forward.*   [3] Q, roman; G., italics.

Could his good honour write more to content you?
Is there ought else to be wisht after these two,
That are already offer'd?   Marriage first,
And lawfull pleasure after: what would you more?   95

   Marg. Why, sir, I would be married like your daughter;
Not hurried away i' the night I know not whither,
Without all ceremonie: no friends invited
To honour the solemnity.

   Alw. An't please your honour,   100
For so before tomorrow I must stile you:
My lord desires this privacie in respect
His honourable kinsmen are far off,
And his desires to have it done brooke not
So long delay as to expect their comming;   105
And yet he stands resolv'd, with all due pompe—
As running at the ring, playes, masques, and tilting—
To have his marriage at court celebrated
When he has brought your honour up to London.

   Over. He tells you true; 'tis the fashion on my knowledge: 110
Yet the good lord to please your peevishnes
Must put it off forsooth, and lose a night
In which perhaps he might get two boyes on thee.
Tempt me no farther,[1] if you do, this good [2]   [*Points to his sword.*
Shall pricke thee to him.

   Marg. I could be contented,   116
Were you but by to do a fathers part,
And give me in the church.

   Over. So my lord have you
What do I care who gives you?   Since my lord   120
Does purpose to be private, I'le not crosse him.
I know not, Master Alworth, how my lord
May be provided, and there fore there's a purse
Of gold: 'twill serve this nights expence, to morrow
I'le furnish him with any summes.   In the meane time   125
Use my ring to my chaplaine; he is benefic'd
At my manor of Gotam, [3] and call'd Parson Will-doe.

   [1] G., 'further.'   [2] G., 'goad'; also stage-direction.   [3] G., 'Got 'em.'

'Tis no matter for a licence, I'le beare him out in't.
   Marg. With your favour, sir, what warrant is your ring?
He may suppose I got that twenty wayes   130
Without your knowledge, and then to be refus'd,
Were such a staine upon me, if you pleas'd, sir,
Your presence would do better.
   Over. Still perverse?
I say againe I will not crosse my lord,   135
Yet I'le prevent [1] you too.   Paper and incke there?
   Alw. I can furnish you.
   Over. I thanke you, I can write then.   *Writes on his booke.*
   Alw. You may, if you please, put out the name of my lord,
In respect he comes disguis'd, and only write   140
Marry her to this gentleman. [2]
   Over. Well advis'd.   Margaret *kneeles.*
'Tis done, away; my blessing, girle? thou hast it.
Nay, no reply, begone; and, good Master Alworth,
This shall be the best nights worke, you ever made.   145
   Alw. I hope so, sir.   *Exeunt* Alworth, *and* Margaret.
   Over. Farewell, now all's cocke-sure:
Methinkes I heare already knights, and ladies
Say "Sir Giles Overreach, how is it with
Your honourable daughter? has her honour   150
Slept well to-night? or will her honour please
To accept this monkey? dog? or paraquit? [3]
(This is state in ladies), or my eldest sonne
To be her page, and wait upon her trencher?"
My ends! my ends are compass'd! then for Welborne   155
And the lands; were he once married to the widdow,
I have him here.   I can scarce containe my selfe,
I am so full of joy; nay joy all over.
              Exit; the end of the fourth Act.

---

[1] anticipate.   [2] Q, roman.   [3] G., 'paroqueto'.

Actus Quinti, Scena Prima.
[A Room in Lady Allworth's House.]

LOVELL, LADY [ALLWORTH], AMBLE.

Lady. By this you know, how strong the motives were
That did, my lord, induce me to dispence
A little with my gravity, to advance
(In personating some few favours to him)
The plots and projects of the downe-trod Welborne.   5
Nor shall I e're repent (although I suffer
In some few mens opinions for't) the action.
For he, that ventur'd all for my deare husband,
Might justly claime an obligation from me
To pay him such a courtesie: which had I   10
Coiley, or over-curiously denied,
It might have argu'd me of little love
To the deceas'd.
     Lov. What you intended, madam,
For the poore gentleman, hath found good successe,   15
For as I understand his debts are pay'd,
And he once more furnish'd for faire imployment;
But all the arts that I have us'd to raise
The fortunes of your joy, and mine, young Alworth,
Stand yet in supposition, though I hope well;   20
For the young lovers are in wit more pregnant,
Than their yeares can promise; and for their desires,
On my knowledge they are equall.
     Lady. As my wishes
Are with yours, my lord; yet give me leave to feare   25
The building though well grounded: to deceive
Sir Giles, that's both a lyon and a fox
In his proceedings, were a worke beyond
The strongest undertakers, not the triall
Of two weake innocents.   30
     Lov. Despaire not, madam:

Hard thinges are compass'd oft by easie meanes;
And judgment, being a gift derived from heaven,
Though sometimes lodg'd i' the hearts of worldly men
(That ne're consider from whom they receive it)　　　　35
Forsakes such as abuse the giver of it.
Which is the reason, that the politicke
And cunning statesman, that beleeves he fathomes
The counsels of all kingdomes on the earth,
Is by simplicity oft overreached.[1]　　　　40
　　Lady. May he be so! yet, in his name to expresse it—
Is it a good omen?
　　Lov. May it to my selfe
Prove so good, lady, in my suite to you:
What thinke you of the motion?　　　　45
　　Lady. Troth, my lord,
My owne unworthinesse may answer for me;
For had you, when that I was in my prime,
My virgin-flower uncropp'd, presented me
With this great favour; looking on my lownesse　　　　50
Not in a glasse of selfe-love, but of truth,
I could not but have thought it as a blessing
Far, far beyond my merit.
　　Lov. You are too modest,
And undervalue that which is above　　　　55
My title, or whatever I call mine.
I grant, were I a Spaniard, to marry
A widow might disparage me; but being
A true-borne Englishman, I cannot find
How it can taint my honour; nay what's more,　　　　60
That which you thinke a blemish is to me
The fairest lustre.　You alreadie, madam,
Have given sure proofes how dearely you can cherish
A husband that deserves you: which confirmes me,
That if I am not wanting in my care　　　　65
To doe you service, you'le be still the same
That you were to your Alworth: in a word

　　　　　　　　[1] Q, 'overreach.'—G., as above.

Our yeares, our states, our births are not unequall,
You being descended nobly and alli'd so;
If then you may be wonne to make me happy,   70
But joyne your lipps to mine, and that shall be
A solemne contract.
 Lady. I were blind to my owne good
Should I refuse it, yet, my lord, receive me
As such a one, the studie of whose whole life   75
Shall know no other object but to please you.
 Lov. If I returne not, with all tendernesse,
Equall respect to you, may I die wretched.
 Lady. There needs no protestation, my lord,
To her that can not doubt, [1] you are welcome, sir.   80
Now you looke like your selfe. *Enter* WELBORNE.
 Welb. And will continue.
Such is my free acknowledgement that I am
Your creature, madam, and will never hold
My life mine owne, when you please to command it.   85
 Lov. It is a thankefullnesse that well becomes you;
You could not make choice of a better shape
To dresse your mind in.
 Lady. For me I am happy
That my endevours prosper'd. Saw you of late   90
Sir Giles, your uncle?
 Welb. I heard of him, madam,
By his minister Marrall; he's growne into strange passions
About his daughter. This last night he look'd for
Your lordship at his house, but missing you,   95
And she not yet appearing, his wise-head
Is much perplex'd and troubled.
 Lov. It may be,
Sweetheart, my project tooke.
Enter OVER. *with distracted lookes, driving* MARRALL *before him.* [2]
 Lad. I strongly hope.   100
 Over. [3] Ha! find her, boobie; thou huge lumpe of nothing,

---

[1] G. inserts here *Enter Welborn.*
[2] G. omits this direction here.   [3] G., [*within*].

I'le bore thine eyes out else.

Welb. May it please your lordship,
For some ends of mine owne, but to withdraw
A little out of sight, though not of hearing.   105
You may perhaps have sport.

   Lov. You shall direct me.[1]   *Stepps aside.*

   Over. I shall *sol fa* you, rogue.

   Mar. Sir, for what cause
Doe you use me thus?   110

   Over. Cause, slave? Why, I am angrie,
And thou a subject only fit for beating,
And so to coole my choler. Looke to the writing;
Let but the seale be broke upon the box,
That has stepp'd[2] in my cabinet these three yeares,   115
I'le racke thy soule for't.

   Mar. I may yet crie quittance,
Though now I suffer, and dare not resist.   *Aside.*

   Over. Lady, by your leave, did you see my daughter, lady?
And the lord her husband? Are they in your house?   120
If they are, discover, that I may bid 'em joy;
And, as an entrance to her place of honour,
See your ladyship on her left hand, and make courtsies
When she nodds on you; which you must receive
As a speciall favour.   125

   Lady. When I know, Sir Giles,
Her state requires such ceremony, I shall pay it
But in the mean time, as I am myselfe,
I give you to understand, I neither know,
Nor care where her honour is.   130

   Over. When you once see her
Supported, and led by the lord her husband
You'le be taught better. Nephew!

   Welb. Sir.

   Over. No more?   135

   Welb. 'Tis all I owe you.

---

[1] G. here inserts the stage direction *Enter Overreach, with distracted looks, etc.*
[2] G., 'slept.'

Over. Have your redeem'd ragges
Made you thus insolent?
    Welb. Insolent to you?   *In scorne.*
Why what are you, sir, unlesse in your yeares,   140
At the best, more than my selfe?
    Over. His fortune swells him:
'Tis rancke [1] he's married.
    Lady. This is excellent!
    Over. Sir, in calme language (though I seldome use it)   145
I am familiar with the cause, that makes you
Beare up thus bravely; there's a certaine buz
Of a stolne marriage, do you heare? of a stolne marriage,
In which, 'tis said, there's somebody hath beene coozin'd.
I name no parties.   150
    Welb. Well, sir, and what followes?
    Over. Marry, this; since you are peremptory. Remember,
Upon meere hope of your great match, I lent you
A thousand pounds: put me in good security,
And suddainely, by mortgage or by statute,   155
Of some your new possessions, or I'le have you
Dragg'd in your lavender robes [2] to the gaole. You know me,
And therefore do not trifle.
    Welb. Can you be
So cruell to your nephew now hee's in   160
The way to rise? was this the courtesie
You did me in pure love, and no ends else?
    Over. End me no ends: ingage the whole estate,
And force your spouse to signe it, you shall have
Three or foure thousand more, to rore and swagger,   165
And revell in bawdy tavernes.
    Welb. And begge after:
Meane you not so?
    Over. My thought are mine, and free.
Shall I have security?   170
    Welb. No: indeed you shall not:

[1] evident.
[2] apparel freshly taken out of pawn. 'To lay up in lavender'=to **pawn**.

Nor bond, nor bill, nor bare acknowledgement;
Your great lookes fright not me.
    Over. But my deeds shall:
Outbrav'd?   *They both draw; the servants enter.* 175
    Lady. Helpe! murther, murther!
    Welb. Let him come on,
With all his wrongs, and injuries about him,
Arm'd with his cut-throate practices to guard him;
The right that I bring with me will defend me, 180
And punish his extortion.
    Over. That I had thee
But single in the field!
    Lady. You may; but make not
My house your quarrelling scene 185
    Over. Were't in a church
By heaven, and hell, I'le do't.
    Mar. Now put him to
The shewing of the deed.   *[Aside to* WELLBORN.]
    Welb. This rage is vaine, sir; 190
For fighting, feare not you shall have your hands full,
Upon the least incitement; and whereas
You charge me with a debt of a thousand pounds,
If there be law, (how e're you have no conscience)
Either restore my land, or I'le recover 195
A debt, that's truely due to me from you,
In value ten times more than what you challenge.
    Over. I, in thy debt! O impudence! did I not purchase
The land left by thy father? that rich land,
That had continued in Welbornes name 200
Twenty descents; which, like a riotous foole,
Thou didst make sale of? is not here inclos'd
The deed that does confirme it mine?
    Mar. Now, now!
    Welb. I doe acknowledge none; I ne're pass'd o're 205
Any such land. I grant, for a yeare or two
You had it in trust; which if you doe discharge,
Surrendring the possession, you shall ease

Your selfe and me of chargeable suits in law,
Which, if you prove not honest, (as I doubt it)   210
Must of necessity follow.
    Lady. In my judgement
He does advise you well.
    Over. Good! Good! conspire
With your new husband, lady; second him   215
In his dishonest practices; but when
The mannor is extended to my use,[1]
You'le speake in a humble[2] key, and sue for favour.
    Lady. Never: do not hope it.
    Welb. Let despaire first sease me.   220
    Over. Yet, to shut up thy mouth, and make thee give
Thy selfe the lye, the [3] lowd lye, I draw out
The precious evidence; if thou canst forsweare
Thy hand, and seale, and make a forfeit of   *Opens the box.*[4]
Thy eares to the pillory: see, here's that will make   225
My interrest cleare. Ha!
    Lady. A faire skinne of parchment.
    Welb. Indented, I confesse; and labells too;
But neither wax nor words. How! thunder-strooke?
Not a syllable to insult with? my wise uncle,   230
Is this your precious evidence? is this that makes
Your interest cleare?
    Over. I am o'rewhelm'd with wonder!
What prodigie is this? what subtle divell
Hath raz'd out the inscription? The wax   235
Turn'd into dust! The rest of my deede's whole,
As when they were deliver'd! and this onely
Made nothing! doe you deale with witches, raskall?
There is a statute [5] for you, which will bring
Your necke in a hempen circle. Yes, there is;   240
And now 'tis better thought; for, cheater, know

---

[1] When I am seized with the manor.   [2] G., 'an humbler.'
[3] G., 'and loud lie.'
[4] G., [*Opens the box, and displays the bond.*
[5] G. notes that this statute had been passed in the first year of James.

This juggling shall not save you.
   Welb. To save thee
Would begger the stocke of mercy.
   Over. Marrall!   245
   Mar. Sir.
   Over. Though the witnesses are dead,—   *Flattering him.*[1]
     your testimony
Helpe with an oath or two; and for thy master,
Thy liberall master, my good honest servant,[2]   250
I know, you will sweare anything to dash
This cunning slight: besides, I know thou art
A publicke notarie, and such stand in law
For a dozen witnesses; the deede being drawne too
By thee, my carefull Marrall, and deliver'd   255
When thou wert present, will make good my title.
Wilt thou not sweare this?
   Mar. I? no, I assure you.
I have a conscience, not seer'd up like yours;
I know no deeds.   260
   Over. Wilt thou betray me?
   Mar. Keepe him
From using of his hands; I'le use my tongue
To his no little torment.
   Over. Mine owne varlet   265
Rebell against me?
   Mar. Yes, and uncase [3] you too.
The *ideot;* the *Patch;* the *slave!* the *boobie;*
The propertie fit only to be beaten
For your morning exercise; your *footeball,* or   270
Th' unprofitable lumpe of flesh; your *drudge* [4]
Can now anatomize you, and lay open
All your blacke plotts; and levell with the earth
Your hill of pride; and with these gabions [5] guarded,
Unloade my great artillerie, and shake,   275

---

[1] G. omits.
[2] Q has comma after 'two,' and period after 'servant.'
[3] take the skin off, flay.   [4] Italics: G.   [5] earth-filled, wicker cylinders.

Nay pulverize the walls you thinke defend you.
 Lady. How he foames at the mouth with rage!
 Welb. To him againe.
 Over. O that I had thee in my gripe, I would teare thee
Joint after joint.   280
 Mar. I know you are a tearer;
But I'le have first your fangs par'd off, and then
Come nearer to you, when I have discover'd,
And made it good before the judge, what wayes
And divelish practices you us'd to coozen   285
With an armie of whole families, who yet live,[1]
And, but enrol'd for souldiers, were able
To take in Dunkerke.
 Welb. All will come out.
 Lady. The better.   290
 Over. But that I will live, rogue, to torture thee,
And make thee wish, and kneele in vaine to dye,
These swords that keepe thee from me should fix here,
Although they made my body but one wound,
But I would reach thee.   295
 Lov. Heav'ns hand is in this,
One ban-dogge [2] worrie the other.   *Aside.*
 Over. I play the foole,
And make my anger but ridiculous.
There will be a time, and place, there will be cowards, 300
When you shall feel what I dare do.
 Welb. I thinke so:
You dare do any ill, yet want true valour
To be honest, and repent.
 Over. They are words I know not,   305
Nor e're will learne. Patience, the beggers vertue,

   Enter GREEDIE *and* PERSON WILL-DOE.

Shall find no harbour here; after these stormes
At length a calme appeares. Welcome, most welcome:

---

[1] G., 'And devilish practices, you used to cozen with
  An army of whole families who yet alive,' etc.
[2] dog so fierce that it had to be kept bound up.

There's comfort in thy lookes, is the deed done?
Is my daughter married? Say but so, my chaplaine,   310
And I am tame.
   Will-doe. Married? yes, I assure you.
   Over. Then vanish all sad thoughts; there's more gold for thee.
My doubts and feares are in the titles drown'd
Of my right honorable, my right honorable daughter.   315
   Greede. Here will I [1] be feasting; at least for a month
I am provided: emptie gutts, croke no more,
You shall be stuff'd like baggepipes, not with wind
But bearing [2] dishes.
   Over. Instantly be here?   *Whispering to* WILL-DOE. 320
To my wish, to my wish! Now you that plot against me
And hop'd to trippe my heeles up, that contemn'd me,
                                             Loud musicke.
Thinke on't and tremble,—they come; I heare the musicke.
A lane there for my lord!
   Welb. This sodaine heate   325
May yet be cool'd, sir.
   Over. Make way there for my lord!

Enter ALWORTH *and* MARGARET.

   Marg. Sir, first your pardon, then your blessing, with
Your full allowance of the choice I have made
As ever you could make use of your reason: [3]   *Kneeling.* 330
Grow not in passion: since you may as well
Call backe the day that's past, as untie the knot
Which is too strongly fasten'd.   Not to dwell
Too long on words, this's my husband.
   Over. How!   335
   Alw. So I assure you: all the titles [4] of marriage
With every circumstance are past. Alas, sir,
Although I am no lord, but a lords page,
Your daughter, and my lov'd wife mournes not for it.

---

[1] G. omits 'I.'   [2] heavy, parturient.—*Gen. Ed.*
   [3] G. has period after 'made'; comma, after 'reason.'   But the sentence has meaning as it stands in Q, above.—*Gen. Ed.*   [4] G., 'rites.'

And, for right honourable sonne in law, you may say,   340
Your dutifull daughter.
 Over. Divell: are they married?
 Will-doe. Doe a fathers part, and say, heav'n give 'em joy.
 Over. Confusion and ruine! speake, and speake quickly,
Or thou art dead.
 Will-doe. They are married.   345
 Over. Thou had'st better
Have made a contract with the king of fiends
Than these. My braine turnes!
 Will-doe. Why this rage to me?   350
Is not this your letter, sir? and these the words?
Marry her to this gentleman.
 Over. It cannot:
Nor will I e're beleeve it, 'sdeath! [1] I will not;
That I, that in all passages I touch'd   355
At worldly profit, have not left a print
Where I have trod for the most curious search
To trace my footstepps, should be gull'd by children,
Baffull'd, and fool'd, and all my hopes and labours
Defeated and made void!   360
 Welb. As it appeares,
You are so, my grave uncle.
 Over. Village nurses
Revenge their wrongs with curses; I'le not wast
A syllable, but thus [2] take the life   365
Which wretched I gave to thee.   *Offers to kill* MARGARET.
 Lov. Hold, for your owne sake!
Though charity to your daughter has quite left you,
Will you do an act, though in your hopes lost here,
Can leave no hope for peace or rest hereafter?   370
Consider; at the best you are but a man,
And cannot so create your aimes, but that
They may be crooss'd.

---

[1] So G.—Q, 'beleeve it's death I will not," [which might be punctuated 'believe.
It's death! I will not that I . . . should be gulled,' *etc.*—*Gen. Ed.*]
[2] G., 'I take the life.'

Over. Lord, thus I spit at thee,
And at thy counsaille; and againe desire thee   375
And as thou art a souldier, if thy valour
Dares shew it selfe, where multitude and example
Lead not the way, lets quit the house, and change
Six words in private.
    Lov. I am ready.   380
    Lad. Stay, sir,
Contest with one distracted?
    Welb. You'le grow like him
Should you answer his vaine challenge.
    Over. Are you pale?   385
Borrow his help, though Hercules call it oddes
I'le stand against both, as I am hem'd in thus.
Since, like the Libian-Lyon in the toyle,
My fury cannot reach the coward hunters
And only spends it selfe, I'le quit the place.   390
Alone I can do nothing: but I have servants
And friends to second me; and if I make not
This house a heape of ashes (by my wrongs,
What I have spoke I will make good!) or leave [1]
One throat uncut,—if it be possible   395
Hell add to my afflictions.   *Exit* OVERREACH.
    Mar. Is't not brave sport?
    Greed. Brave sport? I am sure it has tane away my stomacke;
I do not like the sawce.
    Alw. Nay, weep not, dearest: 400
Though it expresse your pittie, what's decreed
Above, wee cannot alter.
    Lady. His threats move mee
No scruple, madam.
    Mar. Was it not a rare tricke   405
(And it please your worship) to make the deed nothing?
I can do twenty neater, if you please
To purchase and grow rich; for I will be
Such a sollicitor and steward for you,

---

[1] Q, 'leau'd'; G. corrects.

As ever [1] worshipfull had.   410
   Welb. I do beleeve thee.
But first discover the quaint means you us'd
To raze out the conveyance?
   Mar. They are mysteries
Not to be spoke in publicke: certaine mineralls   415
Incorporated in the incke, and wax?
Besides, he gave me nothing, but still fed me
With hopes and blowes; and that was the inducement
To this Conumbrum. [2] If it please your worship
To call to memorie, this mad beast once caus'd me   420
To urge you, or to drowne or hang your selfe;
I'le doe the like to him if you command me.
   Welb. You are a raskall! He that dares be false
To a master, though unjust, will ne're be true
To any other: looke for no reward,   425
Or favour from me, I will shun thy sight
As I would doe a basiliskes. Thanke my pittie
If thou keep thy eares; howe're, I will take order
Your practice shall be silenc'd.
   Greed. I'le commit him.   430
   Welb. That were to little purpose;
His conscience be his prison. Not a word,
But instantly begone.
   Ord. Take this kicke with you.
   Amb. And this.   435
   Furn. If that I had my cle[a]ver here,
I would divide your knaves head.
   Mar. This is the haven,
False servants still arrive at.   *Exit* MAR. [*Re-*]*enter* OVER.
   Lad. Come agen!   440
   Lov. Feare not, I am your guard.
   Welb. His lookes are ghastly.
   Will-doe. Some little time I have spent, under your favours,
In physicall studies, and if my judgement erre not
Hee's mad beyond recovery: but observe him,   445

<hr />

  [1] G., 'never.'   [2] G., 'conundrum.'

And looke to your selves.
  Over. Why, is not the whole world
Included in my selfe? to what use then
Are friends, and servants? Say there were a squadron
Of pikes, lined through with shot, when I am mounted   450
Upon my injuries, shall I feare to charge 'em?
No: I'le through the battalia, and that routed,

Flourishing his sword unsheathed.[1]

I'le fall to execution. Ha! I am feeble:
Some undone widdow sits upon mine arme,
And takes away the use of't; and my sword,   455
Glew'd to my scabberd with wrong'd orphans teares,
Will not be drawne. Ha! what are these? Sure, hangmen,
That come to bind my hands, and then to dragge me
Before the judgement seate: now they are new shapes,
And do appeare like furies,—with steele whippes   460
To scourge my ulcerous soule? shall I then fall
Ingloriously, and yeeld? No!—Spite of fate
I will be forc'd to hell like to my selfe.
Though you were legions of accursed spirites,
Thus would I flie among you.[2]   465
  Welb. There's no helpe
Disarme him first, then bind him.
  Greed. Take a *mittimus*,
And carry him to Bedlam.
  Lov. How he fomes!   470
  Welb. And bites the earth.
  Will-doe. Carry him to some darke roome,
There try what art can do for his recovery.
  Marg. O my deare father!   *They force* OVERREACH *off.*
  Alw. You must be patient, mistresse.   475
  Lov. Here is a president [3] to teach wicked men,
That when they leave religion, and turne atheists,
Their owne abilities leave 'em. Pray you, take comfort;
I will endeavour you shall be his guardians

---

[1] G. corrects, *sheathed.*   [2] G., [*Rushes forward.*   [3] precedent.

In his distractions: and for your land, Master Welborne, 480
Be it good or ill in law, I'le be an umpire
Betweene you, and this, th' undoubted heire
Of Sir Giles Overreach; for me, here's the anchor
That I must fix on.
    Alw. What you shall determine, 485
My lord, I will allow of.
    Welb. 'Tis the language
That I speake too; but there is something else
Beside the repossession of my land,
And payment of my debts, that I must practise. 490
I had a reputation, but 'twas lost
In my loose course; and till [1] I redeeme it
Some noble way I am but halfe made up.
It is a time of action; if your lordship
Will please to conferre a company upon mee 495
In your command, I doubt not in my service
To my king, and country, but I shall do something
That may make me right agen.
    Lov. Your suite is granted,
And you lov'd for the motion. 500
    Welb. Nothing wants then
But your allowance.[2]

---

[1] G., 'until.'   [2] G., [*To the Spectators.*

The Epilogue.

But your allowance, and in that, our all
Is comprehended; it being knowne, nor we,
Nor he that wrot the comedie, can be free   505
Without your mannumission; which if you
Grant willingly, as a faire favour due
To the Poets, and our labours, (as you may,
For we despaire not, gentlemen, of the play)
We jointly shall professe your grace hath might   510
To teach us action, and him how to write.

FINIS.

Richard Brome

THE ANTIPODES

Edited with Critical Essay and
Notes by George Pierce Baker,
Professor in Harvard University

CRITICAL ESSAY

Life.—The stage-keeper, speaking the Induction to Ben Jonson's *Bartholomew Fayre*, introduces Richard Brome to posterity. "But for the whole play," he says, "will you have the truth on't?—I am looking, lest the poet hear me, or his man, Master Brome, behind the arras—it is like to be a very conceited scurvy one, in plain English." That was said at the new Hope Theater, Oct. 31, 1614. Probably Jonson's "man" was at least twenty at the time, which would carry his birth back to 1595; but if some words of Brome's in the "Dedication" of his *Joviall Crew*, in 1652, may be taken literally, he was then nearer seventy than sixty, and the date of his birth would be forced back to *circa* 1585. He wrote the play as the "issue of my old age" and later added: "You know, Sir, I am old, and cannot cringe, nor court with the powder'd and ribbanded Wits of our daies." The portrait, in strict Puritan dress, which makes the frontispiece of the *Five New Playes* published in 1653, shows a well preserved but grizzled face. The poor reproduction in the Pearson reprint takes some thirty years from the portrait. Certainly Brome was dead by 1653, for in "To the Reader" of the *Five New Playes*, Alexander Brome writes: "The Author bid me tell you, that, now he is dead, he is of Falstaff's mind, and cares not for Honour."

That Brome was once Jonson's servant we learn from some lines of the latter—"magisterial enough"—prefixed, in 1632, to *The Northern Lasse*, but they hardly warrant Sir A. W. Ward's statement that Brome apparently remained so till his master's death in 1637:[1]

To my old Faithful Servant, and (by his continu'd Vertue) my loving Friend, the Author of this Work, Mr. Richard Brome.

> I had you for a Servant, once, Dick Brome;
> And you perform'd a Servants faithful parts,
> Now, you are got into a nearer room,
>   Of Fellowship, professing my old Arts.
> And you do doe them well, with good applause,
>   Which you have justly gainèd from the Stage,
> By observation of those Comick Lawes
> Which I, your Master, first did teach the Age, *etc.*

[1] *English Dramatic Literature*, III, 126.

417

Brome's presence behind the arras during the first production of *Bartholo-mew Fayre* suggests that "servant" was used in its broader Elizabethan sense and meant, in this case, private secretary or amanuensis, but the following from "To the Reader" in the *Five New Playes* of 1659 favours the stricter use of the word. "And yet there are a sort (one would wonder there should be) who think they lessen this Author's worth when they speak of the relation he had to Ben. Johnson. We very thankfully embrace the Objection, and desire they would name any other Master that could better teach a man to write a good Play. . . . And were not already the Antients too much trod on, we could name famous wits who served far meaner Masters than *Ben. Johnson*. For, none vers'd in Letters but know the wise Aesop was born and bred a wretched slave; *Lucian* a Stone-cutter, *Virgil* himself begotten by a Basket-maker, born in a ditch, and then preferred to an under Groom in the stable; nay, (to instance in our *Authors* own order) *Naevius* the Comedian a Captains mans man; *Plautus* servant to a poor Baker, *Terence* a slave as well as *Aesop;* and (which for our purpose is most of all) our *Authors* own *Master* handled the *Trowel* before he grew acquainted with *Seianus* or *Cataline*."

Two interpretations are possible also of the lines continuing the gratu-latory verses of Ben Jonson already quoted:—

> You learn'd it well, and for it serv'd your Time,
> A Prentiship, which few do now adayes:
> Now each Court-Hobby-Horse, will wince in Rhime,
> Both learnèd and unlearnèd, all write Playes.

It is usually said that this means Brome, as an apprentice in play-writing, practised for seven years before he really established a reputation, but it may mean that, while a servant of Jonson for seven years he was also his student and disciple. On the one hand, when we first hear of Brome as a dramatist, in 1623,—some nine years after the production of *Bartholo-mew Fayre*,—he was collaborating with Jonson's son, in a lost play, *A Fault in Friendship*. On the other hand, it is true that about seven years later, Brome seems first to have established himself in public favour.

Of his antecedents and family we know only that a brother Stephen prefixes some flattering verses to the 1632 edition of *The Northern Lasse*. Alexander Brome, who placed on the market the ten plays contained in the 1653 and 1659 editions, disclaims any relationship. Henry Brome, the publisher of several of the plays, seems from his impersonality and his ignorance as to Richard Brome shown in his "Note to the Readers" before *The Queenes Exchange* (1657), not to have been a relative. In laudatory verses prefacing the 1659 *New Playes*, Alexander Brome wrote:

his Estate
He has secur'd against the common Fate
Of leaving to young *heirs*, whose high desires
Are to spend all, and be accounted *Squires*.
He was his own *Executor*, and made
Ev'n with the world, and that small *All* he had
He without *Law* or *Scribe* put out of doubt;
Poor he came into th' world, and *poor* went out.
His *soul* and *body* higher powers claim,
There's nothing left to play with but his name.

The preliminary verses of the *Northern Lasse* show that by 1632 he had won both the professional regard and the personal liking of widely different members of the older school of dramatists—Ford and Dekker as well as Jonson. Among other men who wrote similar verse in his honour are Shirley, Tatham, John Hall, Sir Aston Cokaine, and probably T(homas) S(tanley). Though his feeling toward the courtly dramatists was hostile and his attitude toward life was consistently that of the middle-class Englishman of his day, his work or his personality gained him patrons of rank. This his lines to the Earl of Newcastle on the latter's play, *The Variety*,[1] his dedication to him of the *Sparagus Garden*, and his dedication to the Earl of Hertford of *The Antipodes* demonstrate.

Apparently four of the companies of Brome's day produced his plays: the King's men at the Globe and the Blackfriars; the King's Revels'[2] company and the Queen's men, successively, at Salisbury Court; and Beeston's boys (The King's and Queen's company), newly formed in 1637, at the Cockpit, in Drury Lane. Excepting *The Antipodes*, there is no published evidence that he was connected with more than one company at a time.[3] It is probable that from *circa* 1629 to *circa* 1634 he wrote for the King's men; from *circa* 1634 to the closing of the theatres by the plague in May, 1636, for the King's Revels' company; for the Queen's men from the permanent reopening of the theatres in October, 1637, till some date in 1638, for certainly the note at the end of *The Antipodes* shows that in 1638 he was writing for Beeston's boys, for whom he worked till the final closing of the theatres. In his dedication of *A Joviall Crew*, he says: "It had the luck to tumble last of all in the Epidemicall ruine of the Scene"; and we learn from the title-page that it was acted in 1641. *A Fault in Friendship* was licensed Oct. 2, 1623 for the Prince's men (Red Bull), and

[1] Pearson, II; printed just before 'The Actors Names' preceding *The Weeding of Covent Garden.*
[2] Professor Wallace has found a 1635 contract of Brome with the King's Revels' Co. calling for three plays a year. *R. Brome*, C. E. Andrews, 14.
[3] Professor Wallace connects Brome with the Red Bull and King's men in 1634. *Idem.*

The Lovesick Maid, or The Honour of Young Ladies in Feb. 1629.[1] It was acted by the King's men in that year. Brome's extant plays are: surely or probably for the King's men—*The City Witt, or the Woman Wears the Breeches*, probably early, and revised for Beeston's boys after Jonson's death in 1637;[2] *The Northern Lasse*, published in 1632;[3] *The Weeding of Covent Garden, or the Middlesex Justice of Peace*, originally written just after the building of the piazza, in 1631–32, and revised ten years later for the boy actors,[4] *The Queenes Exchange*, "Acted at the Black-Friers, by His Majesties Servants"[5]; *The Novella*, "Acted at the Black-Friers, by His Majesties Servants, Anno, 1632[6]; *The Court Begger*, 1632[7], revised *circa* 1640 for the Boys; and *The Late Lancashire Witches*, published in 1634 as a play by T. Heywood and Brome "lately acted at the Globe,"[8] probably an old play of Heywood's made over by Brome or Heywood and Brome together; surely or probably for the King's Revels—*The Sparagus Garden*, "Acted in the yeare 1635, by the then Company of the Revels, at Salisbury Court";[9] *Queen and Concubine*,[10] *The New Academy*, or *The New Exchange*[11]; surely or probably for the Queen's

---

[1] *Chron. Eng. Drama*, Fleay, I, 36.

[2] Fleay, *idem*, points out that a ballad, 'A Woman would wear the Breeches' was entered Nov. 26, 1629; the Prologue, evidently written for a revival, says:—

> It bore just Judgement, and the seal of Ben.
> Some in this round may have both seen't, and heard,
> Ere I, that beare its title, wore a Beard.

[3] Title-page.

[4] The Prologue of Nabbes's *Covent Garden*, acted in 1632 as the title-page states, refers to Brome's play. 'Another Prologue,' Pearson, II, says:—

> Take the same survaigh
> Into your fancie, as our Poet took
> Of Covent Garden, when he wrote the book,
> Some ten years since.

[5] Title-page. In I, 2, are the words: 'We have prayed for the King this seven years.' If *seven* does not here mean merely an indefinite number, it dates the play, as Fleay notes, in 1632.   [6] Title-page.

[7] The title-page reads: 'Acted at the *Cockpit*, by His Majesties Servants, Anno 1632,' a manifest absurdity, for that company was never at the Cockpit and in 1632 was acting at the Globe. Mr. Fleay guesses, rightly probably, that the reading should be: 'Acted at the Cockpit [by Beeston's boys, after 1637], and by His Majesties Servants, Anno 1632.' *Chron.* I, 41.   [8] Title-page.

[9] Title-page.

[10] Fleay assigns this play to the King's Revels' Co. because of the last line of Sc. 7, Act V.

[11] There is probably a double entendre, not heretofore remarked, in the dialogue on p. 99, Pearson, II:

> *Hannah.* Can you reade?
> *Valentine.* I had done ill to venter (as I ha' done)

men—*A Mad Couple Well Match'd* [1]; *The English Moor,* or *The Mock-Marriage,* [2] *The Damoiselle,* [3] or *The New Ordinary; The Antipodes,* 1638, acted by this company but written for the Beeston boys at the Cockpit: for the Boys—*A Joviall Crew,* 1641; revivals of *The City Witt, The Weeding of Covent Garden,* and *The Court Begger.* [4] There is no evidence which satisfactorily places *The Love-sick Court, or the Ambitious Politique.* Three lost plays were entered under Brome's name, *Wit in a Madness,* March 19, 1640, *Christianetta,* and *The Jewish Gentleman,* Aug. 4, 1640. *The Apprentice's Prize* and *The Life and Death of Sir Martin Skink* (both lost) were entered Apr. 8, 1664 as by Heywood and Brome. They probably belonged to the period of *The Late Lancashire Witches, circa* 1634. *Tom Hoyden o' Tanton Deane,* mentioned in the epilogue to *The Court Begger* as Brome's, was probably *The Sparagus Garden,* in which there is a character of the name. The Epilogue says:
"Hee'l bring him (Hoyden) hither shortly in a new Motion, and in a new paire o' Slops and new nether stocks." Possibly the first edition, 1640, of *The Sparagus Garden* represents a revision of that play for the Beeston boys in which a former sub-title, *Or Tom Hoyden of Taunton Deane* was dropped.

Brome's Reputation as a Dramatist.—Evidently Richard Brome was very successful in his own day. Before 1642, three of his plays, *The Northern Lasse, The Antipodes,* and *The Sparagus Garden* were printed, the first going through two editions before 1640 and through four between 1632 and the end of the century. Of seven plays entered in 1640, three are lost, but four, *The Weeding of*

On Salisbury Plain else.
This probably means not only that he who would play the highwayman must be able to con his neck verse, but also that the man unable to read could not attempt acting on the stage of Salisbury Court theatre.
[1] Fleay, *Hist. of Stage,* 357, gives this in a list of plays acquired by Beeston's boys, in 1639, from the Queen's men.
[2] The Prologue apparently refers to some recent serious outbreak of the plague and so suggests Oct. 1637 as the date; but the play may go back to 1631–2 and the King's men.
[3] The Prologue refers to the struggle for the laureateship, after Jonson's death in Aug. 1637, between D'Avenant and May, settled by the election of the former, Dec. 13, 1638. The lines (p. 454, Pearson, 1) 'See how you carry de hands like de *Comedien* dat act de shangling,' though this has not before been remarked, point to a recent revival of *The Changeling* by the company acting *The Damoiselle.* As the former play is listed (*Hist. of Stage,* 357) among the plays of the Queen's men handed over to Beeston in 1639, *The Damoiselle* is clearly a Queen's men's play.
[4] For a slightly different ordering of Brome's plays, see *Chron.* I, 36–41.

Covent Garden, A New Academy, The Love-sick Court, and *The English Moor,* with the addition of *The Queen and the Concubine,* were printed in 1659 as the second set of *Five New Playes.* The prefatory material of this edition implies that the *Five New Playes* of 1653 [1] and the edition of *The Queenes Exchange* in 1657 had been so successful as to warrant a new venture with Brome's work. His success certainly aroused the jealousy of that precocious son of Ben, Thomas Randolph, who wrote in a reply to Jonson's wrathful lines on quitting the stage after the failure of his *New Inn:*

> And let those things in plush
> Till they be taught to blush,
> Like what they will, and more contented be
> With what Broome swept from thee.

In the 1640 edition of Jonson, the original line in his ode was changed to read "Brome's sweepings." Posterity, too, liked Brome's work, for the *Northern Lasse* was given often between 1660 and 1760, and *A Joviall Crew,* both as play and revamped as an operetta, long held the stage. Mrs. Behn based her *Debauchee,* printed in 1677, on the *Mad Couple Well Match'd.* The publication of Brome's works in 1873, in the Pearson reprints, practically introduced him to students. Since that time judgments of his writings have differed widely, from the grudging commendation of J. A. Symonds in his review of the Pearson edition, [2] in which he declared that in *A Joviall Crew* the English "love of a life of adventure and nearness to nature is perfectly adjusted to the valet's point of view" to Mr. Swinburne's admiration for much of Brome's work and unstinted praise of *The Antipodes.*[3]

It is easy to see why Randolph's phrase, "what Broome swept from thee" amused the public and stuck to Brome, for it is undeniable that his plays often suggest the work of men who preceded him

---

[1] There seem to have been two editions of the *Five New Playes* of 1653 and 1659. At least Greg, *List of Eng. Plays,* 14, names a second of the 1659 edition; and the editor of this text owns a copy of the 1653 edition not heretofore noted. It was issued not by Moseley, Marriott and Dring, but "Printed for J. F. and are to be sold by J. Sweeting at his shop at the Angel in Popeshead Alley, 1654." This copy lacks at the end the list of books published by Moseley. Apparently it is the 1653 edition with a new title-page.

[2] *The Academy,* March 21, 1874.   [3] *The Fortnightly,* LVII, 500.

as dramatists. But whose work among the men of his group, even Massinger's and Shirley's, does not? Roughly his plays divide into two sets, the comedies of manners and the romantic plays— *The Love-sick Court, The Queen and Concubine,* and *The Queenes Exchange.* The model for the romantic plays, whether consciously chosen or not, is evident enough,—Fletcher, or possibly Fletcher deteriorating in Massinger. Indeed, if one wish to descry the inherent faults of the Fletcherian method in plays such as *Valentinian* or *Bonduca,* one can best trace them in such plays as these of a follower of Fletcher. In Brome's romantic plays there is Fletcher's crowding of incident on incident, his swift alternation of grave and gay, and even in greater measure his subordination or sacrifice of consistent or sustained characterization to momentary effect; but the lack in Brome of rich imaginativeness, of clear visualization of the characters, the emphasis on the vulgar or the coarsely trite, as compared with the real wit of Fletcher, the complete absence of beautiful poetry, reveal how theatric and even melodramatic essentially much of Fletcher's work was. It is hard to read patiently these romantic plays of Brome, so devoid are they of idealism, large imaginativeness, and any delicately poetic conception. Instead, they are crowded, as is modern melodrama, which they much resemble, with whatever the past experience of the dramatist has taught him his public likes. In these romantic plays Brome is unintelligently imitative.

Especially in Comedy: his Method.—It is not, however, on these that his reputation should rest, but on his comedies. Of course, he is a son of Ben, perhaps more thoroughly than any of the men so called. He uses freely, especially in his earlier work, "humour" characterization, but even in this he more resembles Jonson in his best period, that of *The Alchemist, Epicoene* and *Bartholomew Fayre,* than his earlier and more exaggerated humour characterization. Brome introduces his figures carefully, as did Jonson, letting some other character describe them before they enter; he has special Jonsonian situations in mind at times,—for instance, the temptation of Diana by Letoy (*Antipodes,* V, iv) is reminiscent of Volpone's temptation of Celia; plays and characters of his master are even referred to;and there are little tricks of phrase, vocabulary, and even elision, which, perhaps unconsciously, he imitates. Yet no one can read carefully the best of Brome's plays without recognizing that strong as was the impress of Jonson's genius on Brome, its effect was in externals rather than essentials,—he is no servile copyist. Feeling this unlikeness even in likeness, some critics have said that Brome copied Middleton, but surely this dodges the situation rather than analyzes and states it. It is not only because his figures are less slab-sided characterizations than those in the earliest comedies of Jonson that Brome's work resembles Jonson's in his comedies *The Alchemist* and *Epicoene*, but because, as in those plays, there is a complicated plot. Like Middleton, he works in a combination of the comedy of manners and the comedy of intrigue, developing a complicated story of varied incident through numerous figures carefully studied from types of current London life. Each man realized that comedy of manners combined with an interesting plot always has a stronger hold on the public than what Jonson favoured, character studies. Each worked among the same group of people, the tradesman class and those of rank who preyed upon them or were themselves gulled. Each has moments, even characters that are Jonsonese, as one or the other uses humour characterization. But there is no evidence of direct imitation of Middleton by Brome; and it is to be remembered, not only that in the days of Brome's success Middleton was busied with his romantic rather than his realistic work, but that the plays which Brome's work most resembles belong to the first decade of the century, years before Brome's first known play. Brome is wholly without the rich if cynical humour of Middleton, just as he never shows the moral sniff with which Jonson thrusts some of his characters before us. Indeed, the three possible approaches, morally, to dramatic material are well illustrated in the three dramatists: the moral, even the didactic, in Jonson; the unmoral, the impersonal so favoured by Zola, in Middleton; and the callous or even the immoral enjoyment of the vulgar and the vicious in Brome.

In the first place, then, Brome increasingly places his emphasis where Jonson did not, on plot; secondly, his approach to his material differs from that of either Middleton or Jonson; and thirdly, he worked slowly toward plays individual, if not unique. It is much easier to be unjust than just to Brome, for till 1638 he was little more than the successful "practical dramatist" of to-day. He, too, studied his public closely, caring mainly to give it what he thought it wanted, and writing each play according to a well-considered and well-tried formula to which he held himself with a certain dogged conscientiousness. This is really true of all the plays except *A Joviall Crew* and *The Antipodes*. The audiences were sated: every possible kind of source had been ransacked for plots; characterization had been carried to the highest possible point; technique had been mastered; surpassing poetic expression attained. After all, such technique, such perfection of poetry, even the highest order of characterization are caviare to the general public. Then, as always from the birth of the drama to the present day, situation, story, plot, were the prime attractions for the public. But as novel situations were exceedingly difficult or impossible to find, the dramatists told the old stories anew, hoping by crowding the stage with new, or at least slightly different characters, by piling incident on incident, by working in anything for which the public had shown a predilection, to make their plays succeed. Hence, for instance, the brief masques which Brome introduces into almost every one of his plays. Hence, too, the songs which persist in his work, though he only once shows any marked lyric skill. [1] In fact, Brome is an admirable specimen of decadent art and morals, or of morals in art. Artistically speaking, what especially characterizes him in the bulk of his plays is a certain hard facility, combined with a strong theatric sense, a probable swiftness in turning out comedies of manners fuller of plot than was usual with Jonson, not throughout characterized so much by humours, but without moral impulse or artistic import. In him we reach the other extreme from John Lyly, whose plays for children were clean, dainty, fantastic, written with the thought constantly in mind that boys were to act them. What is most charming in Lyly is that childhood is reverently used for artistic ends. In

[1] The first song preceding *The Queen and Concubine*, beginning: 'What if a Day, or a Moneth or a Year.' It is so fine that one suspects it belongs to one of the earlier dramatists. Pearson, II.

Brome's earlier plays revamped for Beeston's boys, they are set the task, not of course new for the companies of children since 1600, of portraying types of humanity of which they should have had no knowledge, and which they could not depict without injury to themselves. But Brome goes further than his predecessors in desecrating childhood, as the part of Crack in the *Court Beggar* shows. It reveals the callousness, the brutality of the audiences which could find amusement in the precocious worldly knowledge and rottenness of a child's mind. Brome paints his world in such sympathy with it that his plays are valuable documents toward a social history of his day, but his is a very brutal world.

A Joviall Crew and The Antipodes.—Yet, the two plays excluded from what has just been said, *A Joviall Crew* and *The Antipodes*, written between 1637–8 and 1641, show that he was capable of much better things. Usually he fell into the fallacy of all these "practical dramatists." They are always so sure the playwright must give an audience what he thinks it wants that they are blind to the fact that their own greatest successes give that public something more than what they ordinarily premise are the demands. Doubtless in *A Joviall Crew* Brome is indebted to Fletcher's *Beggers Bush* for the idea of writing a play about the customs of the beggars, but in the play romanticism really comes home to English common life. There is psychological truth, too, in the use of the spring *wanderlust* of the hero as the motive force of the play. Moreover, Brome does not allow his plot to be lost sight of in his mass of detail, a fault too common with his greater master, Jonson. In this romantic story set in a realistic study of the beggars, and filled with songs, Brome, no doubt unconsciously, carries the comedy of manners a stage nearer the ballad opera of the eighteenth century typified in the *Beggars' Opera*.

It is, however, above all in *The Antipodes* that Brome excels.[1] How little farce there is in the drama of 1590–1642—not particular scenes, but whole plays! Here is a farce Gilbertian in its whimsicality, well planned, well sustained. In farce the crowding of in-

[1] Brome may have got his first suggestion for Peregrine's mania for exploration from the satire of his time (see Hall's *Satires*, IV, 6, ll. 58–70; or Rowland's *Letting of Humour's Blood*, Sat. I) but the skilful development of the suggestion is his.

cident on incident beloved of Brome is a merit, the selective emphasizing of the most striking characteristic of a person, or of that most useful to the dramatist, is right. At last, the Jonsonese method, always in humour-characterization verging upon the selective exaggeration of farce, has emerged into it. The play deserves Swinburne's high praise: "The logic of the burlesque, its topsy-turvy coherence, its preposterous harmony, its incongruous congruity of contradictions is as perfect as its exuberance of spontaneous and various fertility in fancy and fun is inexhaustible and superb." Moreover, in this case one has a hint that the real Brome, though willing ordinarily to look at life as he thought his public wished, really took it more seriously, for the conditions he selects in London life for burlesquing often imply a thoughtful judgment, and at times his audience must first have laughed, then cringed a little as the thrust came home to them. One can but question, after reading these two plays, whether just as the theatres closed Brome was not entering upon a period of dramatic writing which would have given him much higher rank than what now survives can win for him. On the one hand, he was moving toward the ballad opera of the eighteenth century, just as D'Avenant was moving toward the Heroic Drama of the Restoration; on the other, he could hardly have failed to try to repeat his success with *The Antipodes*, and thus farce, which does not get its full development till the nineteenth century, might have developed much earlier.

His Place in the History of Comedy.—A student of the drama could not, however, neglect Brome even had he not written the two plays just commented upon; indeed, in tracing the relations of period to period, the other comedies are even more important. Nothing among the many long-accepted misjudgments which fill the pages of the earlier accounts of the English drama is more absurd than the treatment of the period of 1642–1660 as an actual closing of one part of the history of our drama and birth of a second part. The theatres were closed; but the Drolls, the vulgarized condensations of plays formerly popular, were given; there were surreptitious performances; plays were issued and avidly read. The old traditions of the stage—about the hardest traditions of all not only to kill, but even markedly to change—could not die in eighteen years, especially when men like D'Avenant lived on into the new period, working in both the new and the old conditions. What had been a steady sequence of dramatic performances became intermittent and rare, that is all; the old traditions among the dramatists, the old likings in the public survived. The Court, returning from France, could affect the finish given the new plays, the placing of the emphasis on one group rather than another in society,—the Restoration dramatists treat not so much the tradesman class of Brome as the courtly or at least the fashionable set,—but the men and women of Etheredge, Wycherley, and above all Vanbrugh, have the same ideals, or rather lack of them, the same absorption in mere pleasure, the same underlying brutality which were characteristic of the people in Shirley's and in Brome's comedies of manners. How an audience could derive pleasure from a character like Sir John Brute (*The Provoked Wife*) no longer causes amazement if one knows Brome's plays. Brome, Shadwell, Wycherley, Vanbrugh: Shirley, Etheredge, Congreve; the lines of descent are easy enough to see for him who is not wilfully blinding himself with some theory. What is Gallic in all this is grafted upon a sturdy, persistent English stock—coarse in fibre, bitter to our taste, but dear to more than one generation of its buyers.

For all these reasons, then, Brome deserves a place in such a collection as is this volume. He is a genuine and very successful "Son of Ben," who develops farce before 1642 farther than anyone else; who carries one kind of Fletcherian work a stage nearer the ballad opera of the eighteenth century; who supplies us with information as to the middle-class ideals, habits, interests of 1625–42 which make it possible to understand a later public's appreciation of the Restoration comedy; and above all, he is the author of the ingenious and diverting *Antipodes*, a veritable document as to English social history in 1638.

Previous Editions and the Present Text.—Though all the quartos seen of *The Antipodes* are dated 1640, there were at least two versions of the edition, as the note to Act III, iii, 35, shows. Apparently the press was stopped to correct the omission of *res* after *yea* of *yeares*, and in the correcting a half line, seven lines below, dropped out. The imperatives of some of the stage directions and the length of time before the articles called for are used suggest that the MS. used by the printer was a prompt copy. The confusion in marking the scenes shows that the MS. was hastily prepared for the press, and this may possibly account for the pieces of prose in which a rough rhythm is discernible. Except in the Pearson edition of 1873 (Vol. III, No. 3), *The Antipodes* has not been reprinted. To the few articles treating Brome already mentioned should be added the dissertation of Dr. E. K. R. Faust, Halle, 1887. This text is based on a collation of the two versions, which seem to differ only in the correction named. They are indicated in my footnotes as A. The version reading *yea* for *yeares* is from a copy formerly in the library of Mr. Robert Hoe of New York; that correcting this error, but dropping the half-line, is in the library of Harvard College.

GEO. P. BAKER.

Since this essay was written and the accompanying edition of *The Antipodes* prepared, there have appeared the following articles and dissertations bearing upon the subject: Emil Koeppel, *Studien über Shakespeare's Wirkung auf Zeitgenössische Dramatiker* (*Mat. zur Kunde d. ält. engl. Dram.*, No. 9) 1905, and *Ben Jonson's Wirkung, u. s. w.* (*Angl. Forschungen*, No. 20) 1906; F. E. Schelling in *Elizab. Drama*, 2 vols., 1908; Ronald Bayne, *Lesser Jacobean and Caroline Dramatists* (*Camb. Hist. Lit.*, Vol. VI) 1910; H. F. Allen, *A Study of the Comedies of Richard Brome, especially as Representative of Dramatic Decadence*, 1912; and C. E. Andrews, *Richard Brome, a Study of his Life and Works* (*Yale Studies in English*) 1913. The last of these is an especially detailed and fruitful dissertation, and with C. W. Wallace's article on *Shakespere and the Blackfriars* (*Century Maga.*, Sept. 1910) adds somewhat to our knowledge of Brome's theatrical affiliations. On this matter Professor Baker has inserted a few words in what precedes; but otherwise his presentation stands as originally prepared.—*Gen. Ed.*

THE
ANTIPODES:

A COMEDIE.

Acted in the yeare 1638. by the Queenes
Majesties Servants, at *Salisbury*
Court in Fleet-street.

The Author *Richard Brome.*

Hic totus volo rideat Libellus. Mart.

LONDON:

Printed by *J. Okes*, for *Francis Constable*, and
are to be sold at his shops in Kings-
street at the signe of the Goat,
and in Westminster-Hall. 1640.

To

THE RIGHT

Honourable

WILLIAM

Earle of *Hertford*,[1] &c.

My Lord: The long experience I have had of your Honours favourable intentions towards me hath compell'd me to this presumption; but I hope your goodnesse will be pleased to pardon what your benignity was the cause of, viz., the errour of my dedication. Had your candor not encourag'd me, in this I had beene innocent; yet (I beseech you) thinke not I intend it any other then your recreation at your retirement from your weighty employments, and to be the declaration of your gracious encouragements towards me, and the testimony of my gratitude. If the publicke view of the world entertayn it with no lesse welcome then that private one of the stage already has given it, I shall be glad the world owes you the thankes; if it meet with too severe construction, I hope your protection. What hazards soever it shall justle with, my desires are it may pleasure your Lordship in the perusall, which is the only ambition he is conscious of who is,

My Lord,

Your Honour's

humbly devoted

Richard Brome.

[1] William Seymour (1588-1660), second Earl of Hertford, created Marquis of Hertford, 1640. He was Lord Lieutenant for Bath and Wells, Governor of Prince Charles, Privy Councillor, and Lord Chancellor of Oxford. 'He loved his book above all exercises,' Clarendon.

To censuring Criticks, on the approved Comedy, *The Antipodes.*

Ionson's alive! The world admiring stands,
And to declare his welcome there, shake hands.
Apollo's pensioners may wipe their eyes,
And stifile their abortive elegies;[1]
Taylor his goose-quill may abjure againe,
And, to make paper deare, scribling refraine;[2]
For sure there's cause of neither: Ionson's ghost
Is not a tenant i'the Elizian coast,
But, vext with too much scorne at your dispraise,[3]
Silently stole unto a grove of bayes.
Therefore, bewaile your errours, and entreat
He will returne unto the former seat,
Whence he was often pleas'd to feed your eare
With the choice dainties of his theatre.
But I much feare he'le not be easily wonne
To leave his bower, where griefe and he alone
Do spend their time, to see how vainly wee
Accept old toyes for a new Comedie.
Therefore, repaire to him, and praise each line
Of his *Vulpone*,[4] *Sejanus, Cateline,*—
But stay, and let me tell you where he is;
He sojournes in his Brome's *Antipodes.*

C. G.[5]

[1] *Jonsonius Virbius,* the huge collection of commemorative verse by friends of Jonson, appeared in 1638.

[2] The publications of John Taylor, the water-poet, number upwards of 120.

[3] *The New Inn* failed, 1629; *The Magnetic Lady* made no real success, 1632; *The Tale of a Tub* failed, 1633. For Jonson's consequent anger, see *Ode to Himself,* 1629.   [4] Volpone is never a dissyllable in Jonson's play.

[5] Christopher Goad, member of Queen's company, 1631; of King's Revels' company, 1632–36. (Fleay, *Hist. Stage,* 321, 330.) When the theatres reopened after the plague (Oct. 1637), the Queen's company took Salisbury Court, previously the home of the King's Revels' company, incorporating some of its old members. Probably Goad was one of these. There are lines by C. G. before Brome's *Sparagus Garden; The Unfortunate Mother,* Nabbes; and *The Rebellion,* Rawlins, all published, 1640. W. C. Hazlitt guesses for C. G., Charles Gerbier.

The PROLOGUE.

Opinion, which our author cannot court,
  (For the deare daintinesse of it) has of late
From the old way of playes possest a sort [1]
  Only to run to those that carry state
In scene magnificent and language high,
  And cloathes worth all the rest, except the action. [2]
And such are only good those leaders cry—
  And into that beleefe draw on a faction,—
    That must despise all sportive, merry wit
    Because some such great play had none in it.

But it is knowne (peace to their memories)
  The Poets late sublimèd from our age, [3]
Who best could understand and best devise
  Workes that must ever live upon the stage,
Did well approve and lead this humble way
  Which we are bound to travaile in to-night;
And, though it be not trac'd so well as they
  Discover'd it by true Phœbean light,
    Pardon our just ambition yet, that strive
    To keep the weakest branch o'th' stage alive.

I meane the weakest in their great esteeme
  That count all slight that's under us, or nigh,
And only those for worthy subjects deeme—
  Fetch'd or reach'd at (at least) from farre or high;

[1] Flock, crowd.

[2] Brome refers to plays like Killigrew's *Pallantus and Eudora*, published 1638; Cartwright's *Royal Slave*, acted 1636; T. Heywood's masque, *Love's Mistress*, published 1636. The first had scenes fitted to it throughout, the third had scenes designed by Inigo Jones.

[3] Dekker died *circa* 1632; Chapman in 1634; Jonson in 1637.

When low and home-bred subjects have their use
As well as those fetch'd from on high, or farre,
And 'tis as hard a labour for the Muse
    To moove the earth as to dislodge a starre.
        See, yet, those glorious playes; and let their sight
        Your admiration moove, these your delight.

To the Author on his Comedy,

The Antipodes.

Steer'd by the hand of Fate ore swelling seas,
Me thought I landed on th' Antipodes;
Where I was straight a stranger; for tis thus:
Their feet do tread against the tread of us.
My scull mistooke: thy book, being in my hand,
Hurried my soule to th' Antipodian strand,
Where I did feast my fancy and mine eyes
With such variety of rarities
That I perceive thy muse frequents some shade
Might be a grove for a Pierian maide.
Let ideots prate; it boots not what they say:
Th' Antipodes to wit and learning may
Have ample priv'ledge; for among that crew
I know there's not a man can judge of you.

                            Rob. Chamberlain.[1]

[1] Flourished 1640–1660. Sent by Peter Ball, solicitor-general to the Queen, whose clerk he was, to Exeter College, Oxford. Never took degree. Popular with University wits. His literary work consists of original apothegms; *The Swaggering Damsell*, comedy, 1640; some short poems; and collections of ancient jokes. *D. N. B.*

The Persons in the Play.[1]

BLAZE, *an Herauld Painter.*
JOYLESSE, *an old Country Gentleman.*
HUGHBALL, *a Doctor of Physicke.*
BARBARA, *Wife to* BLAZE.
MARTHA, *Wife to* PERIGRINE.
LETOY, *a Phantasticke Lord.*
QUAYLPIPE, *his Curate.*
PERIGRINE, *sonne to* JOYLESSE.
DIANA, *wife to* JOYLESSE.
BY-PLAY, *a conceited servant to* LETOY.
TRULOCKE, *a close friend to* LETOY.
Followers of the Lord LETOYES, *who are actors in the By-play.*

[*SCENE:* LONDON.]

[1] Her Majesty's Servants were formed at the accession of Charles I (1625). Till 1637 they acted at the Cockpit or Phœnix, in Drury Lane; from Oct. 1637 to 1642 at Salisbury Court. This theatre, built in 1629, was originally the barn or granary at the lower end of the great back-yard or court of Salisbury House. It resembled the Globe, but was inferior to it and the Cockpit. *Old Shaks. Soc. Pub.* IV, 91. Fleay, *Hist. Stage,* 332.

The Antipodes.

Act I. Scene I.   [*A Room in the House of Blaze*] [1]

[*Enter*] BLAZE [*and*] JOYLESSE. [2]

Bla. To me, and to the city, sir, you are welcome,
And so are all about you. We have long
Suffer'd in want of such faire company,
But now that times calamity has given way
(Thankes to high Providence) to your kinder visits,   5
We are—like halfe-pin'd wretches that have lain
Long on the plankes of sorrow, strictly tyed
To a forc'd abstinence from the sight of friends—
The sweetlier fild with joy. [3]

Joy. Alas, I bring   10
Sorrow too much with me to fill one house,
In the sad number of my family!

Bla. Be comforted, good sir: my house, which now
You may be pleas'd to call your owne, is large
Enough to hold you all; and for your sorrowes,   15
You came to lose 'hem; and I hope the meanes
Is readily at hand. The doctor's comming,
Who, as by letters I advertis'd you,
Is the most promising man to cure your sonne

---

[1] Scenes I–4 are in this room.

[2] Throughout the quarto, entrances at the beginning of an act are in a line below the act division. In the other scenes of an act, the entrance is on the same line as the act division.

[3] Lines changed, or added, to refer to the plague, which closed the theatres, except for the week of Feb. 24–Mch. I, from May 12, 1636, to Oct. 2, 1637. Fleay, *Hist. Stage*, 340.

The kingdome yields. It will astonish you   20
To heare the mervailes he hath done in cures
Of such distracted ones as is your sonne,
And not so much by bodily physicke (no,
He sends few recipes to th' apothecaries)
As medicine of the minde, which he infuses   25
So skilfully, yet by familiar wayes,
That it begets both wonder and delight
In his observers, while the stupid patient
Finds health at unawares.
    Joy. You speak well of him;   30
Yet I may feare my sonnes long-growne disease
Is such he hath not met with.
    Bla. Then Ile tell you, sir,
He cur'd a country gentleman that fell mad
For spending of his land before he sold it;   35
That is, 'twas sold to pay his debts. All went
That way for a dead horse, as one would say:
He had not money left to buy his dinner
Upon that wholesale day. This was a cause
Might make a gentleman mad, you'll say; and him   40
It did, as mad as landlesse squire could bee.
This doctor by his art remov'd his madnesse,
And mingled so much wit among his braines,
That, by the overflowing of it meerely,
He gets and spends five hundred pound a-yeare now   45
As merrily as any gentleman
In Darbyshire. I name no man; but this
Was pretty well, you'll say.
    Joy. My sonne's disease
Growes not that way.   50
    Bla. There was a lady mad,—
I name no lady, but starke mad she was
As any in the country, city, or almost
In court could be,—
    Joy. How fell she mad?   55
    Bla. With study,

Tedious and painfull study; and for what
Now, can you thinke?
   Joy. For painting, or new fashions;
I cannot thinke for the philosophers stone.[1]   60
   Bla. No, 'twas to finde a way to love her husband,
Because she did not and her friends rebuk'd her.
   Joy. Was that so hard to find, if she desir'd it?
   Bla. She was seven years in search of it, and could not,
Though she consum'd his whole estate by it.   65
   Joy. Twas he was mad, then.
   Bla. No, he was not borne
With wit enough to loose; but mad was she
Untill this doctor tooke her into cure;
And now she lies as lovingly on a flockebed [2]   70
With her owne knight as she had done on downe
With many others,—but *I* name no parties.
Yet this was well, you'l say.
   Joy. Would all were well!
   Bla. Then, sir, of officers and men of place,   75
Whose sences were so numm'd they understood not
Bribes from dew fees, and fell on premunires,[3]
He has cur'd diverse, that can now distinguish,
And know both when and how to take of both,
And grow most safely rich by't. Tother day   80
He set the braines of an attorney right
That were quite topsie turvy overturn'd
In a pitch ore the barre,[4] so that (poore man)
For many moones he knew not whether he
Went on his heels or's head, till he was brought   85
To this rare doctor.   Now he walkest again
As upright in his calling as the boldest
Amongst 'hem. This was well, you'l say.

---

[1] According to the alchemists a soluble solid believed to have the property of
transmuting baser metals into silver or gold, and of prolonging life. *Cent. Dict.*
[2] A bed filled with locks of wool or cloth cut fine.
[3] Colloquial for 'Were in a predicament'; see Congreve's *Double Dealer*, IV, iii.
Originally *præmunire* was a writ for the execution of statutes against certain acts
of submission to papal authority.   [4] Punning for 'disbarred'?

Joy. Tis much.

Bla. And, then, for horne mad citizens, my neighbours,　　90
He cures them by the dozens, and we live
As gently with our wives as rammes with ewes.

Joy. "We," doe you say? Were you one of his patients?

Bla. [*aside*]. 'Slid, he has almost catch'd me! No, sir, no;
I name no parties, *I*, but wish you merry.　　95
I straine to make you so, and could tell forty
Notable cures of his to passe the time
Untill he comes.

Joy. But, pray, has he the art
To cure a husbands jealousie?　　100

Bla. Mine, sir, he did. [*Aside.*] 'Sfoot, I am catcht againe.

Joy. But still you name no party. Pray how long,
Good Master Blaze, has this so famous doctor,
Whom you so well set out, beene a professor?

Bla. Never in publike; nor indures the name　　105
Of doctor,—though I call him so,—but lives
With an odde lorde in towne that lookes like no lord,—
My doctor goes more like a lord than he.

　　　　　　　　　　　　　　　　　　[*Enter*] Doctor.[1]

O welcome, sir. I sent mine owne wife for you:
Ha you brought her home againe?　　110

Act 1. Scen[e] 2.

BLAZE, DOCTOR, JOYLESSE.

Doct. She's in your house
With gentlewomen who seeme to lodge here.

Bla. Yes, sir, this gentlemans wife and his sonnes wife.
[*Aside to* DOCTOR.] They all ayle something, but his sonne, tis
　　thought,
Is falling into madnesse, and is brought　　5
Up by his carefull father to the towne here,

　　　　　　　[1] A, *Ex. Doctor.*

To be your patient: speake with him about it.
   Doct. How doe you finde him, sir? Do's his disease
Take him by fits, or is it constantly
And at all times the same?   10
   Joy. For the most part
It is onely inclining still to worse
As he growes more in dayes; by all the best
Conjectures we have met with in the countrey
Tis found a most deepe melancholy.   15
   Doct. Of what yeares is he?
   Joy. Of five and twenty, sir.
   Doct. Was it borne with him? Is it naturall
Or accidentall? Have you or his mother
Beene so at any time affected?   20
   Joy. Never.
Not shee unto her grave—nor I till then—
Knew what a sadnesse meant; though, since, I have
In my sonnes sad condition and some crosses
In my late marriage, which at further time   25
I may acquaint you with.
   Bla. [*aside*]. The old man's jealous
Of his young wife! I finde him by the question
He put me to ere while.
   Doct. Is your sonne married?   30
   Joy. Diverse yeares since, for we had hope a wife
Might have restrain'd his travelling thoughts, and so
Have beene a meanes to cure him; but it fail'd us.
   Doct. What has he in his younger yeares been most
Addicted to,—what study, or what practise?   35
   Joy. You have now, sir, found the question which, I thinke,
Will lead you to the ground of his distemper.
   Doct. That's the next way to the cure. Come, quickely, quickly.
   Joy. In tender yeares he always lov'd to read
Reports of travailes and of voyages,   40
And when young boyes like him would tire themselves
With sports and pastimes, and restore their spirits
Againe by meate and sleepe, he would whole dayes

And nights—sometimes by stealth—be on such bookes
As might convey his fancy round the world.   45
  Doct. Very good; on.
  Joy. When he grew up towards twenty,
His minde was all on fire to be abroad;
Nothing but travaile still was all his aime:
There was no voyage or forraine expedition   50
Be said to be in hand but he made sute
To be made one in it. His mother and
My selfe oppos'd him still in all and, strongly
Against his will, still held him in; and wonne
Him into marriage, hoping that would call   55
In his extravagant thoughts; but all prevail'd not,
Nor stayd him (though at home) from travailing
So farre beyond himselfe that now, too late,
I wish he had gone abroad to meet his fate.
  Doct. Well, sir, upon good termes Ile undertake   60
Your sonne.   Let's see him.
  Joy. Yet there's more,—his wife, sir.
  Doct. Ile undertake her too.   Is she mad too?
  Bla. They'll ha' mad children, then.
  Doct. Hold you your peece.   65
  Joy. Alas, the danger is they will have none.
He takes no joy in her, and she no comfort
In him; for, though they have bin three yeeres wed,
They are yet ignorant of the marriage-bed.
  Doct. I shall finde her the madder of the two, then.   70
  Joy. Indeed, she's full of passion, which she utters,
By the effects, as diversly as severall [1]
Objects reflect upon her wand'ring fancy,—
Sometimes in extream weepings, and anon
In vehement laughter; now in sullen silence,   75
And presently in loudest exclamations.
  Doct. Come, let me see 'hem, sir; Ile undertake
Her too.   Ha' you any more?   How does your wife?
  Joy. Some other time for her.

            [1] different.

Doct. Ile undertake   80
Her, too:—and you your selfe, sir (by your favour,
And some few yellow [1] spots which I perceive
About your temples) may require some councell.

Act i.   Scene 3.

Enter Barbara.

Bla. [*aside*]. So he has found him.
Joy. But my sonne, my sonne, sir?
Bla. Now Bab, what newes?
Bar. There's newes too much within
For any home-bred, christian understanding.   5
Joy. How does my sonne?
Bar. He is in travaile, sir.
Joy. His fits upon him?
Bar. Yes.   Pray, Doctor Hughball,
Play the man-midwife and deliver him   10
Of his huge timpany of newes,—of Monsters,
Pigmies, and gyants,[2] apes, and elephants,
Griffons, and crocadiles, men upon women,
And women upon men, the strangest doings,—
As farre beyond all christendome as 'tis to't.[3]   15
Doct. How, how?
Bar. Beyond the moone and starres I think,
Or mount in Cornwall [4] either.
Bla. How prettily like a foole she talkes!
And she were not mine owne wife, I could be   20
So taken with her.
Doct. 'Tis most wondrous strange!
Bar. He talks much of the kingdome of Cathaya,[5]

[1] In the seventeenth century yellow was the colour of jealousy.
[2] *The Voiage and Travayle of Sir John Maundeville, Knight.* J. Ashton. 1887.
Pigmies, ch. lxiii; giants, ch. xcii.
[3] 'As far beyond ordinary ways as it is to these distant lands.'
[4] St. Michael's Mount, near Penzance, Cornwall.
[5] Northern China. Ashton, ch. lxvi.

Of one great Caan,[1] and goodman Prester John,[2]
(What e're they be,) and sayes that Caan's a clowne   25
Unto the John he speaks of; and that John
Dwels up almost at Paradice. But sure his mind
Is in a wildernesse,[3] for there he sayes
Are geese that have two heads a peece, and hens [4]
That beare more wooll upon their backs than sheep,—   30
    Doct. O, Mandevile! Lets to him. Lead the way, sir.
    Bar. And men with heads like hounds!
    Doct. Enough, enough.
    Bar. You'll finde enough within, I warrant yee.
       [*Exeunt at one side* JOYLESS, DOCTOR *and* BLAZE.][5]

[Act I. Scene 4.]

Ent[er at the other side] MAR[THA].

And here comes the poore mad, gentlemans wife,
Almost as mad as he. She haunts me all
About the house to impart something to me.
Poore heart, I gesse her griefe, and pitty her;—
To keepe a maiden-head three yeares after marriage   5
Under wed-locke and key! Insufferable, monstrous!—
It turnes into a wolfe [6] within the flesh

---

[1] Caane in Mandeville. The Khan was Emperor of Cathay. Ashton, ch. lxviii.

[2] Old French *prestre*, modern *prêtre*. 'In the 12th and 13th centuries there was a firm belief that ruling over a vast population in the Far East was a most wealthy and powerful monarch of that name, who claimed to be descended from one of the three Kings who adored the infant Christ.' Ashton, note, p. 173, also chs. lxxxvii, xcvii–c, and Intro. M. D'Arezac's *History of the Tartars*, 1838, pp. 165–68. Peregrine not only brings together countries widely separated geographically, but in ll. 25–26 contradicts Mandeville, ch. lxxv.

[3] Brome is thinking of Mandeville's words as to 'Paradise terrestre' and Prester John's 'lordeship of Wildernesse,' chs. cii, ciii, Ashton.

[4] Geese, hounds, id. ch. lxi; hens, ch. lxiii.

[5] A, *Ex.* 3. *Ent. Martha* beside ll. 32–33.—Though A fails to mark a new scene, it calls the entrance of Letoy and Blaze, l. 91, 'Scene 5.'

[6] Lupus, cancer. In Brome's day raw flesh was placed upon the affected places. See Sampson's *Webster*, 1904.

Not to be fed with chickens and tame pigeons.
I could wish maids be warn'd by't not to marry
Before they have wit to lose their maidenheads,   10
For feare they match with men whose wits are past it.
What a sad looke! And what a sigh was there!
Sweet Mistris Joylesse, how is't with you now?
   Mar. When I shall knowe, Ile tell. Pray tell me first,
How long have you beene married?   15
   Bar. [*aside*]. Now she is on it. Three yeares, forsooth.
   Mar. And, truely, so have I; we shall agree, I see.
   Bar. If you'll be merry.
   Mar. No woman merrier, now I have met with one
Of my condition. Three yeares married, say you? Ha, ha, ha! 20
   Bar. What ayles she, trow? [1]
   Mar. Three yeares married! Ha, ha, ha!
   Bar. Is that a laughing matter?
   Mar. Tis just my story. And you have had no child.
That's still my story. Ha, ha, ha!   25
   Bar. Nay, I have had two children.
   Mar. Are you sure on't,
Or does your husband onely tell you so?
Take heed o'that, for husbands are deceitfull.
   Bar. But I am o'the surer side. I am sure   30
I groan'd for mine and bore 'hem, when at best
He but beleeves he got 'hem.
   Mar. Yet both he
And you may be deceiv'd, for now Ile tell you
My husband told me, fac'd me downe, and stood on't   35
We had three sonnes, and all great travellers;—
That one had shooke the great Turke by the beard.
I never saw 'hem, nor am I such a foole
To thinke that children can be got and borne,
Train'd up to men, and then sent out to travell,   40
And the poore mother never know nor feele
Any such matter. There's a dreame indeed!
   Bar. Now you speake reason, and tis nothing but

----

[1] think you.

Your husbands madnesse that would put that dreame
Into you.   45
    Mar. He may put dreames into me, but
He nere put child, nor anything towards it yet,
To me to making. Something, sure, belongs   *Weepe*[s].
To such a worke; for I am past a child,
My selfe, to thinke they are found in parsley beds,   50
Strawberry banks, or rosemary bushes, though
I must confesse I have sought and search'd such places,
Because I would faine have had one.
    Bar. [*aside*]. Lasse, poore foole!
    Mar. Pray tell me, for I thinke no body heares us,   55
How came you by your babes? I cannot thinke
Your husband got them you.
    Bar. [*aside*]. Foole, did I say?
She is a witch, I thinke. Why not my husband?
Pray, can you charge me with another man?   60
    Mar. Nor with him neither. Be not angry, pray now;
For were I now to dye, I cannot guesse
What a man do's in child-getting. I remember
A wanton mayd once lay with me, and kiss'd
And clip't, and clap't me strangely, and then wish'd   65
That I had beene a man to have got her with childe.
What must I then ha' done, or (good now, tell me)
What has your husband done to you?
    Bar. [*aside*]. Was ever
Such a poore peece of innocence three yeeres married!   70
Does not your husband use to lye with you?
    Mar. Yes, he do's use to lye with me, but he do's not
Lye with me to use me as he [1] should, I feare;
Nor doe I know to teach him. Will you tell me?
Ile lye with you and practise, if you please.   75
Pray take me for a night or two, or take
My husband and instruct him but one night:—
Our countrey folkes will say you London wives
Doe not lye every night with your owne husbands.

                [1] A, 'she'.

Bar. Your countrey folkes should have done well to ha' sent   80
Some newes by you! But I trust none told you there,
We use to leave our fooles to lye with mad-men.
  Mar. Nay, now againe y'are angry.
  Bar. No, not I,
But rather pitty your simplicity.   85
Come Ile take charge and care of you,—
  Mar. I thanke you.
  Bar. And wage[1] my skill against my doctors art.
Sooner to ease you of these dangerous fits
Then he shall rectifie your husbands wits.[2]   90
  Mar. Indeed, indeed, I thanke you.

                          [*Exeunt* BARBARA & MARTHA.]

Act 1. Scene 5. [*A Room in Letoy's House.*]

[*Enter*] Letoy [*and*] Blaze.

  Let. Why, broughtst thou not mine armes and pedegree
Home with thee, Blaze, mine honest heralds painter?
  Bla. I have not yet, my lord, but all's in readinesse
According to the heralds[3] full directions.
  Let. But has he gone to the root; has he deriv'd me   5
Ex origine, ab antiquo? Has he fetch'd me
Farre enough, Blaze?
  Bla. Full foure descents beyond
The Conquest, my good lord, and findes that one
Of your French ancestry came in with the Conqueror.   10
  Let. Jefrey Letoy; twas he from whom the English
Letoys[4] have our descent, and here have tooke
Such footing that we'll never out while France
Is France and England England,

---

[1] wager, set.   [2] A, *Ex*, after *wits*.
[3] The Heralds' College, instituted in the fifteenth century, consisted of the earl marshal, three kings-at-arms, six heralds, and three pursuivants. Its chief business is granting armorial bearings or coats of arms, and tracing and preserving genealogies.   [4] A, *Letoy's.*

And the sea passable to transport a fashion: [1]   15
My ancestors and I have been beginners
Of all new fashions in the Court of England
From before *Primo Ricardi Secundi* [2]
Untill this day.
  Bla. I cannot thinke, my lord,   20
They'll follow you in this,[3] though.
  Let. Marke the end.
I am without a precedent for my humour,[4]—
But is it spread, and talk'd of in the towne?
  Bla. It is, my lord, and laught at by a many.   25
  Let.[5] I am more beholding to them then all the rest;
Their laughter makes me merry; others mirth,
And not mine owne it is, that feeds me, that
Battens [6] me as poore mens cost do's usurers.
But tell me, Blaze, what say they of me, ha?   30
  Bla. They say, my lord, you look more like a pedlar
Then like a lord, and live more like an emperor.
  Let. Why, there they ha' me right; let others shine
Abroad in cloth o'bodkin; [7] my broad cloath
Pleases mine eye as well, my body better.   35
Besides, I'm sure tis paid for (to their envy),—
I buy with ready money; and at home here
With as good meat, as much magnificence,
As costly pleasures, and as rare delights,
Can satisfie my appetite and senses   40
As they with all their publique shewes and braveries.
They runne at ring, and tilt 'gainst one another;
I and my men can play a match at football,
Wrastle a hansome fall, and pitch the barre, [8]

---

[1] Letoy is punning on the *toy* in his name, meaning conceit, fashion.
[2] 1377.   [3] this conceit.
[4] In the Jonsonian sense.   [5] A gives this speech to Blaze.
[6] fattens.
[7] Baudekin, a rich embroidered or brocaded silk fabric, woven originally with a warp of gold thread; in time applied to any rich brocade, even shot-silk.
[8] This sport—like throwing the hammer—was a favourite with nobility till the seventeenth century, when it interested only soldiers and the common people. Strutt's *Sports and Pastimes*, 1801, p. 245.

And crack the cudgells,—and a pate sometimes,—   45
Twould doe you good to see't.
    Bla. More then to feel't.
    Let. They hunt the deere, the hare, the fox, the otter,
Polcates, or harlots,—what they please; whilst I
And my mad grigs, my men, can runne at base,[1]   50
And breathe our selves at barly-breake [2] and dancing.
    Bla. Yes, my lord, i'the countrey, when you are there.
    Let. And now I am here i'th city, sir, I hope
I please my selfe with more choyse home delights
Then most men of my ranke.   55
    Bla. I know, my lord,
Your house in substance is an amphitheater
Of exercise and pleasure.
    Let. Sir, I have
For exercises,—fencing, dancing, vaulting;   60
And for delight, musique of all best kindes;
Stage-playes and masques are nightly my pastimes;
And all within myselfe: my owne men are
My musique and my actors; I keepe not
A man or boy but is of quality,—[3]   65
The worst can sing or play his part o'th' violls,
And act his part, too, in a comedy;
For which I lay my bravery [4] on their backs;
And where another lord undoes his followers
I maintaine mine like lords. And there's my bravery!   70
    *Hoboyes.[5] A service as for dinner passe over the stage, borne by many
servitors, richly apparreld, doing honour to* LETOY *as they passe.*
Now tell me, Blaze, looke these like pedler's men?
    Bla. Rather an emperors, my lord.
    Let. I tell thee,
These lads can act the emperors lives all over,

---

[1] prisoner's base.
[2] Played by six people, three of each sex, coupled by lot. A piece of ground was divided into three compartments, the middle called Hell. The couple in this were to catch the others, and must not separate before they succeeded. The others might break hands whenever they were hard pressed. Halliwell-Phillips, *Dict.*, p. 143.
[3] of the actor's profession.   [4] fine livery.   [5] oboes.

And Shakespeares chronicled histories to boot,   75
And were that *Cæsar*, or that English Earle [1]
That lov'd a play and player so well, now living,
I would not be out-vyed in my delights.
   Bla. My lord, tis well.
   Let. I love the quality of playing; I, I love a play with all   80
My heart,—a good one,—and a player that is
A good one, too, with all my heart. As for the poets,
No men love them, I thinke, and, therefore,
I write all my playes my selfe, and make no doubt
Some of the court will follow   85
Me in that too. [2] Let my fine lords
Talke o' their horse-tricks, and their jockies that
Can out-talke them; let the gallants boast
Their May-games, play-games, and their mistresses;
I love a play in my plaine cloaths, I,   90
And laugh upon the actors in their brave ones.
                          Enter QAILP[IPE.]

   Quail. [3] My lord, your dinner stayes prepar'd.
   Let. Well, well,
Be you as ready with your grace as I
Am for my meate, and all is well. *Ex*[*it*] QUAIL[PIPE.] [4] Blaze, we
   have rambled   95
From the maine poynt this while. It seems by his letter,
My doctor's busie at thy house. I know who's there .
Beside. Give him this ring; tell him it wants
A finger. Farewell, good Blaze.   [*Exit* LETOY.]
   Bla. "Tell him it wants a finger!" my small wit   100
Already finds what finger it must fit.   [*Exit* BLAZE.]

[1] Nero; the Earl of Leicester. Through the latter, actors first gained, in 1576,
a permanent home in London, at the Theatre. For years before a company had
travelled under protection of the Earl's name.
  [2] Brome was jealous of the courtier dramatists. In the epilogue to his *Court
Begger* he accused them of buying their plays of University scholars. Pearson, II,
271.
  [3] A, *Re* for Retainer. Quailpipe is a device to take quails by imitating their call.
The leading part Quailpipe takes in the tricks played on Peregrine makes his name
fitting.   [4] In A this stands after 'as I.'

Act i.   Scene 6.   [*A Room in the House of Blaze.*] [1]

Enter DOCTOR, PEREGRINE, *a booke* [2] *in his hand;* JOYLESSE, DIANA.

Doct. Sir, I applaud your noble disposition,
And even adore the spirit of travaile in you,
And purpose to waite on it through the world:
In which I shall but tread againe the steps
I heretofore have gone.   5
    Per. All the world o're ha' you bin already?
    Doct. Over and under too.
    Per. In the Antipodes?
    Doct. Yes, through and through;
No isle nor angle in that neather world   10
But I have made discovery of. Pray, sir, sit.
[*To* JOYLESS]. And, sir, be you attentive; I will warrant
His speedy cure without the helpe of Gallen, [3]
Hippocrates, [4] Avicen, [5] or Dioscorides. [6]
    Dia. A rare man!   Husband, truely I like his person   15
As well as his rare skill.
    Joy. Into your chamber!
I do not like your liking of mens persons.
    Doct. Nay, lady, you may stay. Heare and admire,
If you so please, but make no interruptions.   20
    Joy. [*aside to* DIANA]. And let no looser words, or wandring
        looke,
Bewray an intimation of the slight
Regard you beare your husband, lest I send you
Upon a further pilgrimage than he
Feignes to convay my sonne.   25

---

[1] So also Scene 7.   [2] Mandeville. See l. 28.
[3] Born about 130 A. D.   Long the supreme authority on medical science.
[4] Called the 'Father of Medicine.' *Circa* 460 B. C.–*circa* 377 B. C.
[5] Corrupt for Ibn Sina. 980–1037 A. D. The most celebrated Arabian physician and philosopher.
[6] Dioscorides Pedacius, or Pedianus, who lived in the first or second century A. D., was author of a treatise on materia medica.

Dia. O jealousie!

Doct. Doe you thinke, sir, to th' Antipodes such a journey?

Per. I thinke there's none beyond it; and that Mandevile,
Whose excellent worke this is, was th' onely man
That e're came neare it.   30

Doct. Mandevile went farre.

Per. Beyond all English legges that I can read of.

Doct. What thinke you, sir, of Drake, our famous countriman?

Per. Drake was a dy'dapper [1] to Mandevile.
Candish, and Hawkins, Furbisher, [2] all our voyagers   35
Went short of Mandevile.   But had he reach'd
To this place here, [*He turns the pages of the book.*]—yes, here,—
   this wildernesse,
And seene the trees of the sunne and moone, that spoke [3]
And told King Alexander of his death, he then
Had left a passage ope for travailers   40
That now is kept and guarded by wild beasts,—
Dragons, and serpents, elephants white and blue,
Unicornes, and lyons of many colours,
And monsters more, as numberlesse as namelesse.

Doct. Stay there!   45

Per. Read here else. [4]   Can you read?
Is it not true?

Doct. No truer than I ha' seen't.

Dia. Ha' you bin there, sir; ha' you seene those trees?

Doct. And talk'd with 'hem, and tasted of their fruit.   50

Per. Read here againe, then: it is written here
That you may live foure or five hundred yeere. [5]

---

[1] nobody.

[2] Peregrine selects the first and the second Englishman to circumnavigate the globe, Drake and Cavendish; a third, Richard Hawkins, who started to go round the world, but died off Porto Rico; and the first English Arctic explorer, Martin Frobisher.

[3] A, 'speake.' Possibly Brome intentionally mixed the tenses, but in the passage from ch. xcix of Mandeville which Peregrine accurately summarizes the words are: '*spoke to Kyng Alexander*' (Ashton.)   [4] 'if you do not believe it.'

[5] 'Men saye that folks that kepe these trees [which spoke to King Alexander] and eate the fruit of them, they live foure or five hundred yeare through vertue of the fruite.' Ch. xcix, Ashton.

Dia. Brought you none of that fruit home with you, sir?

Joy. You would have some of't, would you, to have hope
T'out-live your husband by't?   55

Dia. I'd [1] ha't for you,
In hope you might out-live your jealousie.

Doct. Your patience both, I pray; I know the griefe
You both doe labour with, and how to cure it.

Joy. Would I had given you halfe my land, 'twere done.   60

Dia. Would I had given him halfe my love, to settle
The tother halfe free from incumbrances
Upon my husband.

Doct. [*to* PEREGRINE.] Doe not thinke it strange, sir:
Ile make your eyes witnesses of more   65
Than I relate, if you'll but travaile with me.
You heare me not deny that all is true
That Mandevile delivers of his travailes,
Yet I my selfe may be as well beleev'd.

Per. Since you speake reverently of him, say on.   70

Doct. Of Europe Ile not speake; tis too neare home:
Who's not familiar with the Spanish garbe,[2]
Th' Italian shrug, French cringe, and German hugge?
Nor will I trouble you with my observations
Fetcht from Arabia, Paphlagonia,   75
Mesopotamia, Mauritania,
Syria, Thessalia, Persia, India;
All still is too neare home.   Though I have touch'd
The clouds upon the Pyrenæan mountaines,
And bin on Paphos isle, where I have kist   80
The image of bright Venus, all is still
Too neare home to be boasted.

Dia. That I like well
In him, too; he will not boast of kissing [3]
A woman too neare home.

Doct. These things in me
Are poore; they sound in a farre travellers eare [4]   85

---

[1] A, 'Y'd.'   [2] manner.   [3] 'That . . . kissing,' in A one line.
[4] 'These . . . eare.'   In A the two lines break after *sound*.

Like the reports of those that beggingly
Have put out,[1] on returnes from Edenburgh,
Paris, or Venice, or perhaps Madrid,
Whither a millaner [2] may with halfe a nose
Smell out his way, and is not neare so difficult   90
As for some man in debt and unprotected
To walke from Charing-crosse to th' old Exchange.[3]
No, I will pitch no nearer than th' Antipodes,
That which is farthest distant, foot to foote
Against our region.   95
    Dia. What, with their heeles upwards?
Blesse us! how scape they breaking o' their necks?
    Doct. They walke upon firm earth, as we doe here,
And have the firmament over their heads,
As we have here.   100
    Dia. And yet just under us!
Where is Hell then? If they whose feet are towards us,
At the lower part of the world, have Heaven, too,
Beyond their heads, where's Hell?
    Joy. You may find that   105
Without inquiry. Cease your idle questions.
    Dia. Sure Hell's above ground, then, in jealous husbands.
    Per. What people, sir,—I pray proceed,—what people
Are they of the Antipodes? Are they not such
As Mandevile writes of, without heads or necks,   110
Having their eyes plac'd on their shoulders and
Their mouths amidst their breasts? [4]
    Dia. I so, indeed,
Though heeles goe upwards, and their feet should slip,
They have no necks to breake!   115
    Doct. Silence, sweete lady;

---

   [1] published.
   [2] Note S. Johnson's derivation of the word from Milan. Perhaps the following shows the reference in Brome's mind: 'For you know we Milaners love to strut upon Spanish leather.' *Honest Whore,* Dekker.
   [3] That is, across the London of Brome's day. The Old Exchange stood in Cornhill where the Royal Exchange now is.
   [4] Ashton, ch. lxii.

Pray give the gentleman leave to understand me.
The people through the whole world of Antipodes,
In outward feature, language, and religion,
Resemble those to whom they are supposite: 120
They under Spaine appeare like Spaniards,
Under France, French-men, under England, English,
To the exterior shew; but in their manners,
Their carriage, and condition of life
Extreamly contrary.   To come close to you,   125
What part o'th' world's Antipodes shall I now
Decipher to you, or would you travaile to?
   Per. The furthest off.
   Doct. That is th' Antipodes of England.[1]
The people there are contrary to us.   130
As thus: here (Heaven be prais'd) the magistrates
Governe the people; there the people rule
The magistrates.
   Dia. There's pretious bribing, then!
   Joy. You'l hold your peace.   135
   Doct. Nay, lady, tis by nature.
Here generally men governe the women,—
   Joy. I would they could else.[2]
   Dia. You will hold your peace!
   Doct. But there the women over-rule the men.   140
If some men faile here in their power, some women
Slip their holds there.   As parents, here, and masters
Command, there they obey the childe and servant.
   Dia. But pray, sir, is't by nature or by art
That wives oresway their husbands there?   145
   Doct. By nature.
   Dia. Then art's above nature, as they are under us.
   Doct. In briefe, sir, all
Degrees of people, both in sex and quality,
Deport themselves in life and conversation   150
Quite contrary to us.

   [1] Prester John's land 'lyeth foote against foote to Englande.'   Mandeville, ch.
ciii.   [2] elsewhere.

Dia. Why then, the women
Doe get the men with child; and put the poore fooles
To grievous paine, I warrant you, in bearing.
 Joy. Into your chamber; get you in, I charge you. 155
 Doct. [*to* JOYLESS.] By no meanes, as you tender your sonnes
  good.
[*To* DIANA.] No, lady, no; that were to make men women,
And women men. But there the maids doe woe
The batchelors, and tis most probable
The wives lie uppermost. 160
 Dia. That is a trim,
Upside-downe, Antipodian tricke indeed!
 Doct. And then at christenings and gossips feasts,
A woman is not seene; the men doe all
The tittle-tattle duties, while the women 165
Hunt, hawke, and take their pleasure.
 Per. Ha' they good game, I pray, sir?
 Doct. Excellent;
But by the contraries to ours, for where
We hawke at pheasant, partrich, mallard, heron, 170
With goshawke,[1] tarfell,[2] falcon, laneret,[3]
Our hawks become their game, our game their hawks;
And so the like in hunting: there the deere
Pursue the hounds, and (which you make thinke strange)
I ha' seene one sheepe worry a dozen foxes, 175
By moone-shine, in a morning before day.
They hunt trayne-sents with oxen, and plow with dogges.
 Per. [*laughing*]. Hugh, hugh, hugh!
 Dia. Are not their swannes all blacke, and ravens white?
 Doct. Yes, indeed are they; and their parrets teach 180
Their mistresses to talke.
 Dia. That's very strange.
 Doct. They keepe their cats in cages,

---

[1] So called because flown at geese. Richardson, *Dict.*
[2] The male of the goshawk; also sometimes applied to male eagle. Halliwell-Phillips, *Dict.*
[3] A kind of falcon; the diminutive title because the male, lanneret, is smaller than the female, lanner. *Cent. Dict.*

From mice that would devour them else; and birds
Teach 'hem to whistle, and cry "Beware the rats, Pusse."   185
But these are frivolous nothings.   I have knowne
Great ladyes ride great horses, run at tilt,
At ring, races, and hunting matches, while
Their lords at home have painted, pawned their plate
And jewels to feast their honourable servants;   190
And there the merchants wives doe deale abroad,
Beyond seas, while their husbands cuckold them
At home.
    Dia. Then there are cuckolds, too, it seemes,
As well as here.   195
    Joy. Then you conclude here are.
    Dia. By hearesay, sir; I am not wife enough
To speake it on my knowledge yet.
    Joy. Not yet.
    Doct. Patience, good sir!   200
    Per. Hugh, hugh, hugh!
    Doct. What, do you laugh? that there is cuckold-making
In the Antipodes?   I tell you, sir,
It is not so abhorr'd here as tis held
In reputation there; all your old men   205
Doe mary girles, and old women boyes,
As generation were to be maintain'd
Onely by cuckold-making.
    Joy. Monstrous!
    Doct. Pray, your patience.   210
There's no such honest men there in their world
As are their lawyers: they give away
Their practice, and t'enable 'hem to doe so,
Being all handy-crafts, or labouring men,
They work, poore hearts, full hard in the vacations,   215
To give their law for nothing in the terme times.
No fees are taken; which makes their divines,
Being generally covetous, the greatest wranglers,
In law sutes, of a kingdome. You have not there
A gentleman in debt, though citizens   220

Haunt them with cap in hand to take their wares
On credit.
    Dia. What fine sport would that be here now!
    Doct. All wit, and mirth, and good society
Is there among the hirelings, clownes, and tradesmen;   225
And all their poets are puritanes.
    Dia. Ha' they poets?
    Doct. And players, too; but they are all the sobrest,
Precisest people pickt out of a nation.
    Dia. I never saw a play.   230
    Doct. Lady, you shall.
    Joy. She shall not.
    Doct. She must, if you can hope for any cure.
Be govern'd, sir; your jealousie will grow
A worse disease than your sonnes madnesse else.   235
You are content I take the course I told you of
To cure the gentleman?
    Joy. I must be, sir.
    Doct. Say, Master Perigrine, will you travaile now
With mee to the Antipodes, or has not   240
The journey wearied you in the description?
    Per. No, I could heare you a whole [1] fortnight, but
Let's loose no time; pray talke on as we passe.
    Doct. [*taking up*] *a bowle on the table.* First, sir, a health to
        auspicate our travailes,
And wee'll away.   245

Act I.   Scene 7.

Ent[er] BLA[ZE].

    Per. Gi' mee't. What's he? One sent,
I feare, from my dead mother to make stop
Of our intended voyage.
    Doct. No, sir; drink.

        [1] In A *whole* ends a line, and *A Bowle on the table* stands by it.

Bla. [*aside to* Doctor]. My lord, sir, understands the course
    y'are in   5
By your letters, he tells mee; and bad me gi' you
This ring, which wants a finger here, he sayes.
    Per. Wee'll not be stayd.
    Doct. No, sir, he brings me word
The marriner calls away; the winde and tyde   10
Are faire, and they are ready to weigh anchor,
Hoyst sayles, and onely stay for us. Pray drinke, sir.
    Per. A health then to the willing winds and seas,
And all that steere towards th' Antipodes.
    Joy. He has not drunke so deepe a draught this twelvmonth. 15
    Doct. Tis a deepe draught indeed; and now tis downe,
And carries him downe to the Antipodes,—
I meane but in a dreame.
    Joy. Alasse, I feare!
See, he beginnes to sink.   20
    Doct. Trust to my skill.
    [*To* Joyless.] Pray take an arme, and see him in his cabbin.
    [*To* Diana.] Good lady, save my ring that's fallen there.
    Dia. In sooth, a mervailous neate and costly one!
    Bla. [*aside*]. So, so, the ring has found a finger.   25
    Doct. Come, sir, aboord, aboord, aboord, aboord!
                     [*Exeunt all except* Blaze.]
    Bla. To bed, to bed, to bed; I know your voyage,
And my deare lords deare plot. I understand
Whose ring hath past here by your slight of hand.
                           [*Exit* Blaze.]

Act 2.   Scene 1.   [*A Room in Letoy's House.*] [1]

[*Enter*] Letoy [*and*] Doctor.

To night saiest thou, my Hughball?
    Doct. By all meanes;
And if your play takes to my expectation,—

    [1] The same for scenes 2 and 3.

As I not doubt [1] my potion workes to yours,—
Your fancy and my cure shall be cry'd up   5
Miraculous. O y'are the lord of fancy!
    Let. I'm not ambitious of that title, sir.
No, the Letoys are of antiquity,
Ages before the fancyes [2] were begot,
And shall beget still new to the worlds ends.   10
But are you confident o'your potion, Doctor?
Sleeps the young man?
    Doct. Yes, and has slept these twelve houres,
After [3] a thousand mile an houre out-right,
By sea and land; and shall awake anone   15
In the Antipodes.
    Let. Well sir, my actors
Are all in readinesse, and, I thinke, all perfect
But one that never will be perfect in a thing
He studies; yet he makes such shifts extempore   20
(Knowing the purpose what he is to speake to)
That he moves mirth in me 'bove all the rest;
For I am none of those poeticke furies
That threats the actors life, in a whole play
That addes a syllable, or takes away: [4]   25
If he can frible [5] through, and move delight
In others, I am pleas'd.
    Doct. It is that mimick fellow which your lordship
But lately entertain'd? [6]
    Let. The same.   30
    Doct. He will be wondrous apt in my affaire,
For I must take occasion to interchange
Discourse with him sometimes amidst their scenes,
T'informe my patient, my mad young travellor,
In diverse matters.   35
    Let. Doe; put him to't: I use't myselfe sometimes.
    Doct. I know it is your way.

---

[1] A common transposition with Jonson and Brome.
[2] That is, *toy* is the old word for whim, *fancy* the modern.   [3] At the rate of.
[4] Is Brome thinking of Jonson?
[5] trifle.   [6] took into service.

Let. Well, to the businesse.
Hast wrought the jealous gentleman, old Joylesse,
To suffer his wife to see our comedy?   40
Doct. She brings your ring, my lord, upon her finger,
And he brings her in's hand.   I have instructed her
To spurre his jealousie of o'the legges.
Let. And I will helpe her in't.
Doct. The young distracted   45
Gentlewoman, too, that's sicke of her virginity,
Yet knowes not what it is, and Blaze and's wife,
Shall all be your guests to night; and not alone
Spectators, but (as we will carry it) actor[s] [1]
To fill your comicke scenes with double mirth.   50
Let. Go fetch 'hem then, while I prepare my actors.
                                          Ex[it] Doc[tor.]

Within there, hoe!
            ⎰ 1. This is my beard and haire.
            ⎪ 2. My lord appointed it for my part.
[*Actors*] ⎨ 3. No, this is for you; and this is yours, this grey one. 55
Within.   ⎪ 4. Where be the foyles and targets [2] for the women?
            ⎱ 1. Here, can't you see?
Let. What a rude coyle is there?   But yet it pleases me.
[*Actors*] ⎰ 1. You must not weare that cloak and hat.
Within.   ⎱ 2. Who told you so?   I must   60
In my first scene; and you must weare that robe.
Let. What a noyse make those knaves!   Come in, one of you.

             Enter Quaile-pipe, 3 Actors, *and* Byplay.

Are you the first that answers to that name?

Act 2.   Scene 2. [3]

Qua. My lord?
Let. Why are not you ready yet?
Qua. I am not to put on my shape before
I have spoke the Prologue; and for that, my lord,

---

[1] A, 'actor.'   [2] shields.
[3] A appends the entrance just marked to this line.

I yet want something. 5
   Let. What, I pray, with your grave formality?
   Qua. I want my beaver-shooes and leather-cap
To speake the Prologue in; which were appoynted
By your lordships owne direction.
   Let. Well, sir, well; 10
There they be for you; I must looke to all.
   Qua. Certes, my lord, it is a most apt conceit,
(The comedy being the world turn'd upside-downe)
That the presenter weare the capitall beaver
Upon his feet, and on his head shooe-leather. 15
   Let. Trouble not you your head with my conceite,
But minde your part. Let me not see you act now [1]
In your scholasticke way you brought to towne wi'yee,
With see saw sacke a downe like a sawyer;
Nor in a comicke scene play Hercules Furens,[2] 20
Tearing your throat to split the audients eares.
And you, sir, you had got a tricke of late
Of holding out your bum in a set speech;
Your fingers fibulating [3] on your breast,
As if your buttons or your band[4]-strings were 25
Helpes to your memory: let me see you in't
No more, I charge you. No, nor you, sir, in
That over-action of the legges I told you of,
Your singles and your doubles,[5] looke you,—thus,—
Like one o'th' dancing masters o'the Beare-garden; 30
And when you have spoke, at end of every speech,
Not minding the reply, you turne you round
As tumblers doe, when, betwixt every feat,
They gather wind by firking up their breeches.

   [1] Brome has in mind *Hamlet*, III, ii. In *The Return from Parnassus*, Kempe, referring to University players, says: 'The slaves are somewhat proud, and, besides it is good sport, in a part, to see them never speake in their walke but at the end of the stage, just as though in walking with a fellow we should never speake but at a stile, a gate, or a ditch, when a man can go no further.' Macray, 1887.
   [2] Tragedy of Seneca, translated into English, 1561. In 1595 Henslowe's *Diary* mentions *Hercules* in two parts by Martin Slaughter, or Slater. Here the phrase probably only means to rant.   [3] fiddling.
   [4] neckband.   [5] small and large steps.

Ile none of these absurdities in my house,   35
But words and action married so together
That shall strike harmony in the eares and eyes
Of the severest, if judicious criticks.
  Qua. My Lord, we are corrected.
  Let. Goe, be ready.   [*Exeunt* QUAILPIPE *and three Actors.*]
[*To* BY-PLAY.] But you, sir, are incorrigible, and   41
Take licence to your selfe to adde unto
Your parts your owne free fancy, and sometimes
To alter, or diminish, what the writer
With care and skill compos'd; and when you are   45
To speake to your coactors in the scene,
You hold interloquutions with the audients.
  By. That is a way, my lord, has bin allow'd
On elder stages, to move mirth and laughter.
  Let. Yes, in the dayes of Tarlton [1] and Kempe,[2]   50
Before the stage was purg'd from barbarisme
And brought to the perfection it now shines with.
Then fooles and jesters spent their wits, because
The poets were wise enough to save their owne
For profitabler uses. Let that passe.   55
To night Ile give thee leave to try thy wit
In answering my doctor, and his patient
He brings along with him to our Antipodes.
  By. I heard of him, my lord. Blaze gave me light
Of the mad patient; and that he never saw   60
A play in's life: it will be possible
For him to thinke he is in the Antipodes
Indeed, when he is on the stage among us,
When't has beene thought by some that have their wits
That all the players i' th'towne were sunke past rising.[2]   65

---

[1] A clown celebrated for extemporal rhyming and jigs—ludicrous songs, often accompanied by a dance. Died 1588. Ward, *Dram. Lit.* I, 454, ed. 1899.
[2] Successor of Tarleton. 'Greatly applauded for his buffoonery, his extemporal wit, and his performance of the jig.' Probably played Peter and Dogberry in *Romeo and Juliet* and *Much Ado*. Died, probably, 1603.
[3] Another reference to the closing of the theatres by the plague between May, 1636 and Oct. 1637.

Let. Leave that, sir, to th' event. See all be ready,
Your musicke, properties, and———
    By. All, my lord;
Onely we want a person for a mute.
    Let. Blaze when he come shall serve. Goe in.   70
                               Ex[it] Byp[lay].

My guests I heare are comming.

Act 2. Scene 3.

Enter Blaze, Joylesse, Diana, Martha, Barb[ara].

Bla. My lord, I am become your honours usher,
To these your guests,—the worthy Mr. Joylesse,
With his faire wife and daughter-in-law.
    Let. They're welcome:
And you in the first place, sweet Mistris Joylesse,   5
You weare my ring, I see; you grace me in it.
    Joy. His ring! What ring? How came she by 't?
    Blaz. [*aside*]. Twill worke.
    Let. [*aside*]. I sent it as a pledge of my affection to you,
For I before have seene you, and doe languish   10
Untill I shall enjoy your love.
    Joy. He courts her!
    Let. Next, lady,—you—I have a toy for you too.
    Mar. My child shall thanke you for it when I have one:
I take no joy in toyes since I was married.   15
    Let. Prettily answer'd! I make you no stranger,
Kind Mistris Blaze.
    Bar. Time was, your honour us'd
Me strangely, too, as you'll doe these, I doubt not.
    Let. Honest Blaze,   20
Prethee goe in; there is an actor wanting.
    Bla. Is there a part for me? How shall I study't?
    Let. Thou shalt say nothing.
    Bla. Then, if I doe not act
Nothing as well as the best of 'em, let me be hist.   *Exit.* 25

Joy. I say restore the ring, and backe with me!
Dia. To whom shall I restore it?
Joy. To the lord that sent it.
   Dia. Is he a lord? I alwayes thought and heard   [*Aside.*]
Ith' country lords were gallant creatures. He   30
Looks like a thing not worth it; tis not his:
The doctor gave it me, and I will keepe it.
   Let. I use small verball courtesie, Mr. Joylesse,
You see, but what I can, in deed Ile doe.
You know the purpose of your comming, and   35
I can but give you welcome. If your sonne
Shall receive ease in't, be the comfort yours,
The credit of't my doctors. You are sad.
   Joy. My lord, I would entreat we may returne;
I feare my wife's not well.   40
   Let. Returne! Pray slight not so my courtesie.
   Dia. Besides, sir, I am well; and have a minde
(A thankfull one) to taste my lords free bounty.
I never saw a play, and would be loath
To lose my longing now.   45
   Joy. [*aside*]. The aire of London
Hath tainted her obedience already;
And should the play but touch the vices of it,[1]
She'd learne and practise 'hem. Let me beseech
Your lordships reacceptance of   50
The unmerited favour that she weares here,
And your leave for our departure.[2]
   Let. I will not
Be so dishonoured, nor become so ill
A master of my house, to let a lady   55
Leave it against her will and from her longing.
I will be plaine wi'yee, therefore. If your haste
Must needs post you away, you may depart:
She shall not[3] till the morning, for mine honour.
   Joy. Indeed tis a high poynt of honour in   60

[1] London.   [2] In A the ll. 50–52 end in *the un, and, departure.*
[3] A, 'not not.'

A lord, to keepe a private gentlemans wife
From him.
   Dia. I love this plaine lord better than
All the brave, gallant ones that ere I dream't on.
   Let. Tis time we take our seats: so, if you'll stay,   65
Come sit with us; if not, you know your way.
   Joy. Here are we fallen through the doctors fingers
Into the lords hands. Fate deliver us!
          Ex[eunt] omnes.

Act 2.   Scene 4.   [*A Hall in Letoy's House.*] [1]

Enter, in sea-gownes and caps, DOCTOR, *and* PERIGRINE *brought in a
chaire by 2* Sailers. *Cloaks and hats brought in.*

   Doct. Now the last minute of his sleeping fit
Determines.[2]   Raise him on his feete. So, so:
Rest him upon mine arme. Remove that chaire.
Welcome a shore, sir, in th' Antipodes.
   Per. Are we arriv'd so farre?   5
   Doct. And on firme land.
Sailers, you may returne now to your ship.   *Ex[eunt]* Sail[ors].
   Per. What worlds of lands and seas have I past over,
Neglecting to set downe my observations!
A thousand thousand things remarkable   10
Have slipt my memory, as if all had beene
Meere shadowy phantasmes or phantasticke dreames.
   Doct. We'll write as we returne, sir: and tis true,
You slept most part o' th' journey hitherward,
The aire was so somniferous. And twas well;   15
You scap'd the calenture [3] by't.
   Per. But how long doe you thinke I slept?
   Doct. Eight moneths and some odde days,

---

   [1] The same for the rest of the act.   [2] ends.
   [3] A delirium sometimes caused, particularly on shipboard within the tropics, by
excessive heat.

Which was but as so many houres and minutes
Of ones owne naturall countrey sleepe.   20
   Per. Eight moneths————
   Doct. Twas nothing for so young a braine.
How thinke you, one of the seven Christian Champions,[1]
David by name, slept seven yeares in a leek-bed?
   Per. I thinke I have read it in their famous History.   25
   Doct. But what chiefe thing of note now in our travells
Can you call presently to mind? Speake like a traveller.
   Per. I doe remember, as we past the verge
O' th' upper world, comming downe, down-hill,
The setting sunne, then bidding them good night,   30
Came gliding easily downe by us, and strucke
New day before us, lighting us our way,
But with such heate that, till he was got farre
Before us, we even melted.
   Doct. [*aside*]. Well wrought, potion!—Very well observ'd, sir. 35
But now we are come into a temperate clime,
Of equall composition of elements
With that of London, and as well agreeable
Unto our nature as you have found that aire.
   Per. I never was at London.   40
   Doct. Cry you mercy. [2]
This, sir, is Anti-London. That's the Antipodes
To the grand city of our nation;
Just the same people, language, and religion,
But contrary in manners, as I ha' told you.   45
   Per. I doe remember that relation,
As if you had but given it me this morning.[3]

---

[1] An old ballad runs:—
'St. George, he was for England, St. Dennis was for France; St. James for Spain,
whose valiant hand Did Christian Fame advance: St. Anthony for Italy; Andrew
for Scots ne'er fails; Patrick, too, for Ireland; St. David was for Wales.'—*The
Seven Champions of Christendom*, John Kirke, acted at the Cockpit and the Bull,
was printed, 1638.
[2] Seeing that Peregrine has forgotten his recent coming to London, the Doctor
instantly resolves to humour him.
[3] See. Act 1, sc. 6, ll. 116–33.

Doct. Now cast your sea-weeds off, and don [1] fresh garments.
Hearke, sir, their musicke.

[*They*] *shift* [*their sea-gowns and caps for the cloaks and hats*].

Act 2. Scene 5. [2]

Hoboyes. Enter LETOY, JOYLESSE, DIANA, MARTHA, BARBARA, *in
masques. They sit at the other end of the stage.*

Let. Here we may sit, and he not see us.
Doct. Now see one of the natives of this country;
Note his attire, his language, and behaviour.

Enter QUAILPIPE [*as*] Prologue.

Qua. Our farre fetch'd title over lands and seas
Offers unto your view th'Antipodes.   5
But what Antipodes now shall you see?
Even those that foot to foot 'gainst London be,
Because no traveller that knowes that state
Shall say we personate or imitate
Them in our actions; for nothing can,   10
Almost, be spoke, but some or other man
Takes it unto himselfe, and sayes the stuffe,
If it be vicious, or absurd enough,
Was woven upon his backe.   Farre, farre be all
That bring such prejudice mixt with their gall.   15
This play shall no satyrick timist [3] be,
To taxe or touch at either him, or thee,
That art notorious.   Tis so farre below
Things in our orbe, that doe among us flow,
That no degree, from Keyser to the clowne,   20
Shall say "This vice or folly was mine owne."
Let. This had bin well now, if you had not dreamt
Too long upon your sillables.   *Ex*[*it* QUAILPIPE.[4]]

___

[1] A, 'do'n.'   [2] A places this line between *musicke* and *shift*.
[3] satirist.   [4] A, *Ex. Prol.*

Dia. The Prologue call you this, my lord?

    Bar. Tis my lords reader, [1] and as good a lad   25
Out of his function as I would desire
To mixe withall in civill conversation.

    Let. Yes, lady, this was prologue to the play,
As this is to our sweet ensuing pleasures.   *Kisses* [DIANA].

    Joy. Kissing indeed is prologue to a play   30
Compos'd by th' Divell, and acted by the Children
Of his Blacke Revelles,[2] may hell take yee for't!

    Mar. Indeed I am weary, and would faine goe home.

    Bar. Indeed, but you must stay and see the play.

    Mar. The play? What play? It is no childrens play,   35
Nor no child-getting play, pray, is it?

    Bar. You'll see anon. O, now the actors enter.   *Flourish.*

Act 2.   Scene 6.

Enter two Sergeants,[3] *with swords drawne, running before a*
Gentleman.

    Gent. Why doe you not your office, courteous friends?
Let me entreat you stay and take me with you;
Lay but your hands on mee; I shall not rest
Untill I be arrested. A sore shoulder ache
Paines and torments me, till your vertuous hands   5
Doe clap or stroake it.

    1 Ser. You shall pardon us.

    2 Ser. And I beseech you pardon our intent,
Which was, indeed, to have arrested you;

---

[1] A youth of eighteen could become a reader in churches and chapels lacking a clergyman.

[2] Brome plays upon the title of the Children of the Chapel Royal as a dramatic company after 1603, Queen's Revels' children, and possibly on Blackfriars, the name of their theatre for some years after 1599.

[3] Under-officers appointed to serve writs and to make arrests; also called catch-poles from the instruments (shaped something like a pitchfork, with barbed springs at the sides to hold firmly a prisoner's neck) with which they caught criminals. See Shaw, *Dresses and Decorations*, II.

But sooner shall the charter of the city   10
Be forfeited then varlets like our selves
Shall wrong a gentlemans peace.   So fare you well, sir.
   Gent. O y'are unkinde.   *Ex[eunt* Sergeants].
   Per. Pray what are those?
   Doct. Two catchpoles   15
Runne from a gentleman, it seemes, that would
Have bin arrested.

Act 2. Scene 7.[1]

Enter Old Lady, *and* BYPLAY *like a Servingman.*[2]

   La. Yonder's your master:
Goe take him you in hand, while I fetch breath.
   Byp. O, are you here?   My lady and my selfe
Have fought you sweetly,—[3]
   Let. You and your lady, you   5
Should ha' said, puppy.
   Byp. For we heard you were
To be arrested.   Pray, sir, who has bail'd you?
I wonder who of all your bold acquaintance
That knowes my lady durst baile off her husband.   10
   Gent. Indeed I was not touch'd.
   Byp. Have you not made
An end by composition, and disburs'd
Some of my ladies money for a peace
That shall beget an open warre upon you?[4]   15
Confesse it, if you have; for 'twill come out.
She'll ha' you up,[5] you know.   I speak it for your good.
   Gent. I know't, and Ile entreate my lady wife
To mend thy wages tother forty shillings
A yeare for thy true care of me.   20
   La. 'Tis well, sir.

[1] In A this follows l. 16 of sc. 6.
[2] A places this line beside ll. 1–3.   [3] Ironical.
[4] From his wife's anger.   [5] make you give an account of yourself.

But now (if thou hast impudence so much
As face to face to speak unto a lady
That is thy wife, and supreame head) tell me
At whose sute was it, or upon what action?   25
Debts I presume you have none; for who dares trust
A ladyes husband who is but a squire,
And under covert barne?[1] It is some trespasse—
Answer me not till I finde out the truth.
   Gent. The truth is——   30
   La. Peace!
How darst thou speake the truth
Before thy wife? Ile finde it out my selfe.
   Dia. In truth she handles him handsomely.
   Joy. Doe you like it?
   Dia. Yes, and such wives are worthy to be lik'd   35
For giving good example.
   Let. Good! Hold up
That humour by all meanes.
   La. I thinke I ha' found it.   40
There was a certaine mercer sent you silkes
And cloth of gold, to get his wife with child;
You slighted her, and answered not his hopes;
And now he layes [2] to arrest you: is't not so?
   Gent. Indeed, my lady wife, tis so.   45
   La. For shame!
Be not ingratefull to that honest man,
To take his wares and scorne to lye with his wife,
Do't, I command you. What did I marry you for?
The portion that you brought me was not so   50
Aboundant, though it were five thousand pounds,
(Considering, too, the joincture that I made you,)
That you should disobey me.
   Dia. It seemes the husbands

---

[1] Corruption of *baron*. This term is used of a wife because by the laws of the realm
she is *in potestate viri*, and therefore disabled to contract with any to the prejudice
of herself or her husband without his allowance and confirmation. Cowell's *Inter-
preter*.
[2] has men lie in wait.

In the Antipodes bring portions, and　　　　　55
The wives make joinctures.

　　Joy. Very well observ'd.

　　Dia. And wives, when they are old and past child-bearing,
Allow their youthfull husbands other women.

　　Let. Right.　And old men give their young wives like licence.　60

　　Dia. That I like well.　Why should not our old men
Love their young wives as well?

　　Joy. Would you have it so?

　　Let. Peace, master Joylesse, you are too lowd.
Good, still.　　　　　65

　　Byp. Doe as my lady bids; you got her woman
With child at halfe these words.

　　Gent. O, but anothers
Wife is another thing.　Farre be it from
A gentlemans thought to doe so, having a wife　　　　　70
And hand-mayd of his owne that he lovs [1] better.

　　Byp. There said you well; but take heed, I advise you,
How you love your owne wench, or your owne wife,
Better then other mens.

　　Dia. Good antipodian counsell!　　　　　75

　　La. Goe to that woman; if she prove with childe,
I'll take it as mine owne.

　　Gent. Her husband would
Doe so.　But from my house I may not stray.

　　Mar. If it be me your wife commends you to,　　　　　80
You shall not need to stray from your owne house:
I'll goe home with you.

　　Bar. Precious! what doe you meane?
Pray keepe your seat; you'll put the players out.

　　Joy. Here's goodly stuffe! Shee's in the Antipodes too.　　　85

　　Per. [*seeing* LETOY *and his guests*]. And what are those?

　　Doct. All Antipodeans.
Attend, good sir.

　　La. You know your charge; obey it.

　　　　　[1] Pearson, 'likes.'

Act 2. Scene 8.

Enter Wayting Woman, *great bellyed.*

Wom. What is his charge, or whom must he obey,
Good madam, with your wilde authority?
You are his wife, tis true, and therein may,
According to our law, rule and controwle him;
But you must know, withall, I am your servant,   5
And bound by the same law to governe you,
And be a stay to you in declining age,
To curbe and qualifie your head-strong will,
Which otherwise would ruine you. Moreover,
Though y'are his wife, I am a breeding mother   10
Of a deare childe of his; and therein claime
More honor from him then you ought to challenge.
  La. In sooth,[1] she speakes but reason.
  Gent. Pray, let's home, then.
  Wom. You have something there to looke to, one would thinke,
If you had any care. How well you saw   16
Your father at schoole to-day, and knowing how apt
He is to play the trewant.
  Gent. But is he not
Yet gone to schoole?   20
  Wom. Stand by, and you shall see.

Act 2. Scene 9.

Enter three Old Men *with sachells, &c.*

All. 3. "Domine, domine duster.
Three knaves in a cluster," &c.[2]
  Gent. O, this is gallant pastime! Nay, come on!
Is this your schoole? Was that your lesson, ha?

---

[1] One word in A.   [2] A prints these two lines as one.

   1 Old. Pray now, good son, indeed, indeed—　　　5
   Gent. Indeed
You shall to schoole.　Away with him; and take
Their wagships with him,—the whole cluster of 'hem!
   2 Old. You shant send us now, so you shant.
   3 Old. We be none of your father, so we beant.　　　10
   Gent. Away with 'hem, I say; and tell their schoole-mistris
What trewants they are, and bid her pay 'hem soundly.
   All 3. O, O, O.
   Byp. Come, come, ye gallows-clappers! ¹
   Dia. Alasse, will no body beg pardon for　　　15
The poore old boyes?
   Doct. Sir, gentle sir, a word with you.
   Byp. To strangers, sir, I can be gentle.
   Let. Good.
Now marke that fellow; he speakes extempore.　　　20
   Dia. Extempore call you him?　He's a dogged fellow
To the three poore old things there.　Fie upon him!
   Per. Do men of such faire years here go to schoole?
   Byp. They would dye dunces else.
   Per. Have you no young men schollers, sir, I pray,　　　25
When we have beardlesse doctors?
   Doct. [*aside*]. He has wip'd my lips.²—You question very wisely,
   sir.
   Byp. So, sir, have wee,—and many reverend teachers,
Grave counsellors at law, perfect statesmen,
That never knew use of rasor; which may live,　　　30
For want of wit, to loose their offices.
These were great schollers in their youth, but when
Age growes upon men here their learning wasts,
And so decayes, that if they live untill
Threescore, their sons send them to schoole againe:　　　35
They'd dye as speechlesse else as new born children.
   Per. Tis a wise nation, and the piety
Of the young men most rare and commendable;
Yet give me, as a stranger, leave to beg

---

¹ gallows-birds.　　　　² Scored on me,—as we say today.

Their liberty this day; and what they loose by't,   40
My father, when he goes to schoole, shall answer.
 Joy. I am abus'd on that side too.
 Byp. Tis granted.
Hold up your heads, and thanke the gentleman,
Like schollers, with your heeles now.   45
 All 3. Gratias, Gratias, Gratias.   *Ex[eunt].*[1]
 Dia. Well done, sonne Peregrine; he's in's wits, I hope.
 Joy. If you lose yours the while, where's my advantage?
 Dia. And, trust me, twas well done, too, of Extempore
To let the poore old children loose. And now   50
I looke well on him, he's a proper man.
 Joy. She'll fall in love with the actor and undoe me.
 Dia. Do's not his lady love him, sweet my lord?
 Let. Love? Yes, and lye with him, as her husband do's
With's mayd. It is their law in the Antipodes.   55
 Dia. But we have no such lawes with us.
 Joy. Doe you approve of such a law?
 Dia. No, not so much
In this case, where the man and wife doe lye
With their inferiour servants; but in the other,   60
Where the old citizen would arrest the gallant
That tooke his wares and would not lye with's wife,
There it seemes reasonable, very reasonable.
 Joy. Do's it?
 Dia. Mak't your owne case: you are an old man;   65
I love a gentleman; you give him rich presents
To get me a child (because you cannot); must not
We looke to have our bargaine?
 Joy. Give me leave,
Now, to be gone, my lord, though I leave her   70
Behinde me; shee is mad, and not my wife,
And I may leave her.
 Let. Come, you are mov'd, I see.
I'll settle all; but first, prevaile with you
To taste my wine and sweet meats. The comedians   75

    [1] A, *Exit.*

Shall pause the while. This you must not deny me.
                    Exit [LETOY *with* MARTHA, DIANA, *and* BARBARA].
Joy. I must not live here alwaies; that's my comfort.
                                        Exit [JOYLESS].

 Per. I thanke you, sir, for the poore mens release:
It was the first request that I have made
Since I came in these confines.   80
 Byp. Tis our custome
To deny strangers nothing; yea, to offer
Of any thing we have that may be usefull,
In curtesie to strangers. Will you, therefore,
Be pleas'd to enter, sir, this habitation,   85
And take such vyands, beverage, and repose,
As may refresh you after tedious travailes?
 Doct. Thou tak'st him right, for I am sure he's hungry.
 Per. All I have seene since my arrivall are
Wonders, but your humanity excells.   90
 Byp. Vertue in the Antipodes onely dwells.
      [*Exeunt* PEREGRINE, DOCTOR, *and* BYPLAY.]

Act 3.   Scene 1.   [*A Hall in Letoy's House.*] [1]

[*Enter*] LETOY, JOYLESSE, DIANA, MARTHA, [*and*] BARBARA.

 Let. Yet, Mr. Joylesse, are you pleas'd? You see
Here's nothing but faire play, and all above boord.
 Joy. But it is late, and these long intermissions,
By banqueting and courtship twixt the acts,
Will keep backe the catastrophe of your play   5
Untill the morning light.
 Let. All shall be short.
 Joy. And then, in midst of scenes,
You interrupt your actors, and tye them
To lengthen time in silence while you hold   10
Discourse by th'by. [2]

 [1] The whole act is in this hall.   [2] talk aside.

Let. Poxe o' thy jealousie
Because I give thy wife a looke or word
Sometimes! What if I kisse,—thus; Ile not eate her.
　Joy. Soe, so, his banquet workes with him!　　　　15
　Let. And for my actors, they shall speake, or not speake,
As much, or more, or lesse, and when I please;
It is my way of pleasure, and Ile use it.
So sit: they enter.　　　　　　　　　　　*Flourish.*

Act 3.　Scene 2.

Enter Lawyer, *and* Poet.

　Law. Your case is cleare; I understand it fully,
And need no more instructions. This shall serve
To firke [1] your adversary from court to court.
If he stand out upon rebellious legges
But till Octavus [2] Michaelis next,　　　　　　5
Ile bring him on submissive knees.
　Dia. What's he?
　Let. A lawyer: and his clyent there, a poet.
　Dia. Goes law so torne, and poetry so brave?
　Joy. Will you but give the actors leave to speake,　　　10
They may have done the sooner.
　Law. Let me see;
This is your bill of parcells.
　Poet. Yes, of all
My several wares, according to the rates　　　　　15
Delivered unto my debitor.
　Dia. Wares, does he say?
　Let. Yes, poetry is good ware
In the Antipodes, though there be some ill payers,
As well as here; but law there rights the poets.　　　20
　Law. Delivered, too; and for the use of the Right Worshipfull

---

[1] drag.
[2] A, 'Octabis'. Michaelmas Day is Sept. 29. The eighth day from a feast day—
the octave—was one of the times for returning writs. The date here is Oct. 7.

Mr. Alderman Humblebee, as followeth: [*Reads.*][1] "Imprimis"—
Umh, I cannot read your hand; your character[2]
Is bad, and your orthography much worse.
Read it your selfe, pray.   25
    Dia. Doe aldermen
Love poetry in Antipodea[n] London?
    Let. Better than ours doe custards;[3] but the worst
Pay-masters living, there,—worse than our gallants,—
Partly for want of money, partly wit.   30
    Dia. Can aldermen want wit and money too?
That's wonderfull.
    Poet. Imprimis, sir, here is
For three religious madrigalls to be sung
By th' holy vestalls in Bridewell[4] for the   35
Conversion of our city wives and daughters,
Ten groats[5] a peece: it was his owne agreement.
    Law. Tis very reasonable.
    Poet. Item: twelve hymnes
For the twelve sessions during his shrievalty,   40
Sung by the quire of New-gate[6] in the praise
Of city clemency, (for in that yeare
No guiltlesse person suffer'd by their judgement)
Ten groats a peece also.
    Law. So; now it rises.   45
    Dia. Why speaks your poet so demurely?
    Let. Oh,
Tis a precise tone he has got among
The sober sister-hood.
    Dia. Oh, I remember   50
The doctor said poets were all puritans

---

[1] After *Imprimis* in A.   [2] Punning: handwriting, personal character.
[3] An immense custard was a conspicuous part of a City feast in Brome's time. When the City kept a fool, it was customary for him, at public entertainments, to leap into a bowl of custard set for the purpose. Gifford's *Jonson*.
[4] A prison—especially for street-walkers—just off Fleet St. between Whitefriars St. and Ludgate Circus.
[5] Fourpence; but often used for any small sum.
[6] A prison in the gate of this name.

In the Antipodes. But where's the doctor?
And where's your sonne, my Joylesse?
    Let. Doe not minde him.
    Poet. Item: 55
A disticke, graven in his thumb-ring,[1]
Of all the wise speeches and sayings of all
His alder [2] predecessors, and his brethren
In two kings reignes.
    Law. There was a curious peece!   60
    Poet. Two peeces [3] he promised to me for it.
Item: inscriptions in his hall, and parlour,
His gallery,[4] and garden,—round the walls,—
Of his owne publicke acts betweene the time
He was a common councell man and shriefe,   65
One thousand lines put into wholsome verse.
    Law. Here's a summe towards indeed! a thousand verses!
    Poet.. They come to,[5] at the knowne rate of the city,
(That is to say, at forty pence the score,)
Eight pounds, six shillings, eight pence.   70
    Law. Well, sir, on.
    Poet. Item: an elegy for Mistris Alderwoman
Upon the death of one of her coach-mares
She priz'd above her daughter, being crooked [6]——
    Dia. The more beast she!   75
    Mar. Ha, ha, ha!
    Bar. Enough, enough, sweet-heart!
    Mar. Tis true, for I should weep for that poore daughter;
Tis like she'll have no children. Pray, now, looke;
Am not I crooked too?   80
    Bar. No, no; sit downe.

---

[1] In Brome's day thumb rings, set with jewels of enormous size, were affected by magistrates and grave citizens. Gifford's *Jonson.*

[2] Both elder and aldermen. 'Thou wilt do well, if thou wilt be ruled by thy betters, that is myselfe, and such grave Aldermen of the play-house as I am.' Kempe, Act IV, sc. V. *Return from Parnassus*, Macray.

[3] A Spanish coin equal to a dollar.

[4] 'Hang no pictures in the hall, nor in the dining-chamber, in any case, but in the gallery only, for 'tis not courtly else.' Albius, in *The Poetaster*, 1601.

[5] A, 'too.'   [6] Modifies 'daughter.'

Poet. Item: a love epistle for the Aldermanikin, his sonne,
And a booke of the godly life and death
Of Mistris Katherine Stubs,[1] which I have turn'd
Into sweet meetre, for the vertuous youth   85
To woe an ancient lady widow with.
   Law. Heres a large summe in all, for which Ile try
His strength in law till he *peccavi* cry;
When I shall sing, for all his present bignesse,
   Jamq: opus exegi quod nec Jovis ira, nec ignis.[2]   90
   Dia. The lawyer speaks the poets part.
   Let. He thinkes
The more; the poets in th' Antipodes
Are slow of tongue, but nimble with the pen.
   Poet. The counsaile and the comfort you have given   95
Me requires a double fee.   *Offers mony.*
   Law. Will you abuse me, therefore?
I take no fees, double nor single,[3] I.
Retaine your money; you retaine not me else:
Away, away; you'll hinder other clyents.   100
   Poet. Pray give me leave to send, then, to your wife?
   Law. Not so much as a poesie for her thimble,
For feare I spoyle your cause.
   Poet. Y'ave warned me, sir.   *Exit.*
   Dia. What a poore [4] honest lawyer's this!   105
   Let. They are all so
In th' Antipodes.

Act 3.   Scene 3.

Enter a spruce yong Captaine.

   Law. Y'are welcome, captaine.
In your two causes I have done my best.
   Cap. And whats the issue, pray, sir?

[1] Mentioned in Cartwright's *The Ordinary.* Bishop Corbet says:
      And in some barn hear cited many an author,
      Kate Stubbs, Anne Ascue, or the Ladies Daughter. *Iter Boreale.*
                              Ancient Brit. Drama, III, 164, note.

[2] Ovid, *Meta.* XV, 871.   [3] large and small.   [4] humble?

Law. Truely, sir,
Our best course is not to proceed to triall.   5
   Cap. Your reason?   I shall then recover nothing.
   Law. Yes, more by composition than the Court
Can lawfully adjudge you, as I have labour'd:
And, sir, my course is, where I can compound
A difference, Ile not tosse nor bandy it   10
Into the hazzard of a judgement.
   Dia. Still
An honest lawyer, and tho ¹ poore; no marvaile!
   Let. A kisse for thy conceite!
   Joy. A sweet occasion!   15
   Cap. How have you done, sir?
   Law. First, you understand
Your severall actions, and your adversaries:
The first a battery against a coach-man
That beate you sorely.   20
   Dia. What hard-hearted fellow
Could beat so spruce a gentleman, and a captaine?
   Cap. By this faire hilt he did, sir, and so bruis'd
My armes, so crush'd my ribs, and stitch'd my sides,
That I have had no heart to draw my sword since.   25
And shall I put it up,² and not his purse
Be made to pay for't?
   Law. It is up already, sir,
If you can be advis'd. Observe, I pray,
Your other actions, 'gainst your feathermaker,   30
And that of trespasse for th'incessant trouble
He puts you to by importunate requests
To pay him no money, but take longer day.
   Cap. Against all humane reason, for although
I have bought feathers of him these four yeares ³   35

---

¹ then; still so used in Somersetshire.   Halliwell-Phillips *Dict.*
² endure it.
³ The copy of A in Mr. Robert Hoe's library has 'yea' here, and below, in l. 42, has a colon after ' day ', beginning the next line with ' More than at first.' The Harvard Library copy reads as does this text. Evidently, in correcting the omission of the final letters of 'yeares', the half line dropped out unnoticed.

And never paid him a penny, yet he duns me
So desperately to keepe my money still
As if I ought him nothing; he haunts and breaks my sleepes.
I sweare, sir, by the motion of this I weare now,   *Shakes it.*[1]
I have had twenty better feathers of him, and as ill paid for,   40
Yet still he duns me to forbeare my payment
And to take longer day.
I ha' not said my prayers in
Mine owne lodging, sir, this twelvemoneths day,
For sight or thought of him; and how can you   45
Compound this action, or the other of
That ruffian coachman that durst lift a hand
'Gainst a commander?
    Law. Very easily thus:
The coachman's poore, and scarce his twelvemoneths wages,   50
Tho't be five markes [2] a yeare, will satisfie.[3]
    Cap. Pray name no summe in markes; I have had too many
Of's markes already.
    Law. So you owe the other
A debt of twenty pound, the coachman now   55
Shall for your satisfaction beat you out
Of debt.
    Cap. Beate me againe?
    Law. No, sir, he shall beate
For you your feather man till he take his money.   60
    Cap. So Ile be satisfied; and helpe him to
More customers of my ranke.
    Law. Leave it to me, then.
It shall be by posterity repeaten
That souldiers ought not to be dund or beaten.   65
Away and keepe your money!
    Capt. Thanke you, sir.   [*Exit* Captain.]
    Dia. An honest lawyer still! How he considers
The weake estate of a young gentleman
At armes——But who comes here, a woman?   70

[1] the feather in his cap.   [2] thirteen shillings fourpence.
[3] satisfy your claim.

Act 3.   Scene 4.

Enter Buffe Woman. [1]

Let. Yes, that has taken up the newest fashion
Of the towne-militasters.
    Dia. Is it buffe,[2]
Or calfe skin, troe [3]?   She lookes as she cold beate
Out a whole taverne garrison before her   5
Of mill tasters call you 'em?   If her husband
Be an old, jealous man now, and can please her   Lawyer
                                             reads on papers.
No better then most ancient husbands can,
I warrant she makes her selfe good upon him.
    Joy. Tis very good; the play begins to please me.   10
    Buff. [*to* Lawyer].   I wayt to speake w'yee, sir, but must I stand
Your constring and piercing of your scriblings.
    Law. Cry mercy, lady.
    Dia. " Lady," does he call her?
    Law. Thus farre I have proceeded in your cause   15
Ith' Marshalls [4] court.
    Buff. But shall I have the combate?
    Law. Pray observe
The passages of my proceedings, and
The pro's and contras in the windings, workings   20
And carriage of the cause.
    Buff. Fah on your passages,
Your windy workings, and your fislings at
The barre: come me toth' poynt.   Is it decreed

---

[1] A places this and the scene division beside ll. 68–70. The type of the last letter
of 'Buffe' is worn, but the entrance, Act 4, sc. 4, shows that the word is 'Buffe' not
'Buffo' as Pearson prints it.   *Buffe-woman*, from the old verb buff, to strike, is
prize-fighter.
  [2] Strictly buffalo hide, but usually ox hide.   Diana quibbles on the toughness of
the latter as compared with calf-skin.   [3] trow, think you.
  [4] A court which had jurisdiction of causes to which domestic servants were
parties; held by the steward of the king's household.   Bouvier, *Law Dict.*

A combate? 25
   Law. Well, it is; and heer's your order.
   Buff. Now thou hast spoken like a lawyer;
And heer's thy fee.
   Law. By no meanes, gentle lady.
   Buff. Take it, or I will beat thy carcasse thinner 30
Then thou hast worne thy gowne here.
   Law. Pardon me.
   Buff. Must I then take you in hand?
   Law. Hold, hold; I take it.
   Dia. Alas, poore man! He will take money yet 35
Rather then blowes; and so farre he agrees
With our rich lawyers, that sometimes give blowes,
And shrewd ones, for their money.
   Buff. Now victory
Affoord me, Fate, or bravely let me dye. 40
           Exit [Buffe-woman; *the* Lawyer *draws aside*].
   Let. Very well acted that.
   Dia. Goes she to fight now?
   Let. You shall see that anon.

Act 3. Scene 5.

Enter a Beggar, *and a* Gallant.

   Dia. What's here, what's here?
A courtier, or some gallant, practising
The beggars trade,—who teaches him, I thinke.
   Let. Y'are something neare the subject.
   Beg. Sir, excuse me; I have 5
From time to time supplyed you without hope
Or purpose to receive least retribution
From you; no, not so much as thankes, or bare
Acknowledgement of the free benefits
I have confer'd upon you. 10

Gal. Yet, good unkle——

Beg. Yet doe you now, when that my present store
Responds not my occasions, seeke to oppresse me
With vaine petitionary breath for what I may not
Give without feare of dangerous detriment?			15

Dia. In what a phrase the ragged orator
Displayes himselfe!

Let. The beggars are the
Most absolute courtiers in th' Antipodes.

Gal. If not a peece, yet spare me halfe a peece [1]			20
For goodnesse sake, good sir; did you but know
My instant want, and to what vertuous use
I would distribute it, I know you would not
Hold backe your charity.

Dia. And how feelingly			25
He begges! Then, as the beggers are the best
Courtiers, it seemes the courtiers are best beggers
In the Antipodes; how contrary in all
Are they to us!

Beg. Pray to what vertuous uses			30
Would you put money to now, if you had it?

Gal. I would bestow a crowne in ballads,
Love-pamphlets, and such poeticall rarities,
To send downe to my lady grandmother.
She's very old, you know, and given much			35
To contemplation. I know she'l send me for 'em,
In puddings, bacon, sowse and pot-butter,
Enough to keepe [2] my chamber all this winter:
So shall I save my fathers whole allowance
To lay upon my backe, and not be forc'd			40
To shift out from my study for my victualls.

Dia. Belike he is some student.

Beg. There's a crowne.[3]

Gal. I would bestow another crowne in
Hobby-horses and rattles for my grand-father,			45
Whose legges and hearing faile him very much;

[1] dollar.			[2] supply.			[3] five shillings.

Then, to preserve his sight, a Jack-a-lent [1]
In a greene sarsnet [2] suite;—he'l make my father
To send me one of scarlet, or hee'l cry
His eyes out for't.   50
   Dia. Oh politique young student!
   Beg. I have but just a fee left for my lawyer;
If he exact not that, Ile give it thee.
   Dia. He'l take no fee (that's sure enough, young man,)
Of beggars, I know that.   55
   Let. You are deceiv'd.
   Dia. Ile speake to him my selfe, else, to remit it.
   Joy. You will not sure. Will you turne actor too?
Pray doe be put in for a share amongst em [3]!
   Dia. How must I be put in?   60
   Joy. The players will quickly
Shew you, if you performe your part; perhaps
They may want one to act the whore amongest 'em.
   Let. Fye Master Joylesse, y'are too fowle.
   Joy. My lord,   65
She is too faire, it seemes, in your opinion
For me; therefore, if you can finde it lawfull,
Keepe her; I will be gone.
   Let. Now I protest
Sit, and sit civilly, till the play be done;   70
Ile lock thee up else, as I am true Letoy!
   Joy. Nay, I ha' done———   *Whistles "Fortune, my foe."* [4]
   Law. Give me my fee, I cannot heare you else.
   Beg. Sir, I am poore, and all I get is at
The hands of charitable givers; pray, sir,—   75
   Law. You understand me, sir: your cause is to be
Pleaded to-day, or you are quite orethrowne in't;

---

[1] A stuffed puppet, dressed in rags, which was thrown at throughout Lent.
Nares, *Dict.*
  [2] A fine, thin silk stuff, plain or twilled, especially valued for its softness.
  [3] The principal actors in a company were usually shareholders.
  [4] The first stanza of this ballad runs:—'Fortune, my foe, why dost thou frown
on me? And will my fortune never better be? Wilt thou, I say, forever, breed my
pain? And wilt thou not restore my joys again?' Nares, *Dict.*

The Judge by this tyme is about to sit;
Keepe fast your money, and forgoe your wit.   *Exit.*
 Beg. Then I must follow and entreate him to it;   80
Poore men in law must not disdaine to doe it.   *Exit.*
 Gal. Doe it then. Ile follow you and heare the cause.   *Exit.*
 Dia. True Antipodians still, for, as with us
The gallants follow lawyers, and the beggers them,
The lawyer here is follow'd by the begger,   85
While the gentleman followes him.
 Let. The morall is, the lawyers here prove beggers,
And beggers only thrive by going to law.
 Dia. How take [1] the lawyers, then, the beggers money,
And none else by their wills?   90
 Let. They send it all
Up to our lawyers, to stop their mouths
That curse poore clyents that are put upon 'em
In forma pauperis. [2]
 Dia. In truth most charitable;   95
But sure that money's lost by th' way sometimes.
Yet, sweet my lord, whom do these beggers beg of
That they can get aforehand so for law?
Who are their benefactors?
 Let. Usurers, usurers.   100
 Dia. Then they have usurers in th' Antipodes too?
 Let. Yes, usury goes round the world, and will doe [3]
Till the generall conversion of the Jewes.
 Dia. But ours are not so charitable, I feare.
Who be their usurers?   105
 Let. Souldiers and courtiers chiefly;
And some that passe for grave and pious churchmen.
 Dia. How finely contrary th'are still to ours!

---

[1] A, 'takes.'
[2] 'That charitable law, for the admission of poor suitors *in forma pauperis,* without fee to counsellor, attorney or clerk, whereby poor men became rather able to vex than unable to sue.' Bacon, *Hist. of Henry VII.* p. 135.
[3] Query: 'do't'?

Act 3. Scene 6.[1]

Let. [*aside*]. Why doe you not enter? What, are you asleepe?

Enter BYPLAY.

Byp. My lord, the madde young gentleman—
Joy. What of him?
Byp. He has got into our tyring-house,[2] amongst us,
And tane a strict survey of all our properties: 5
Our statues and our images of gods; our planets and our constella-
      tions;
Our giants, monsters, furies, beasts, and bug-beares,
Our helmets, shields, and vizors,[3] haires, and beards;
Our pastbord March-paines,[4] and our wooden pies.
      Let. Sirrah, be briefe; be not you, now, as long   10
In[5] telling what he saw as he surveying.
      Byp. Whether he thought twas some inchanted castle,
Or temple, hung and pild with monuments[6]
Of uncouth and of various aspects,
I dive not to his thoughts. Wonder he did   15
A while, it seem'd, but yet undanted stood;
When on the suddaine, with thrice knightly force
And thrice, thrice puissant arme he snatcheth downe
The sword and shield that I played Bevis[7] with,
Rusheth amongst the foresaid properties,   20
Kils monster after monster; takes the puppets
Prisoners; knocks downe the Cyclops; tumbles all
Our jigambobs and trinckets to the wall.
Spying at last the crowne and royall robes

---

[1] A misnumbers the scene, 5. In A, *Enter Byplay* makes one line with the marking of the scene.
[2] dressing-room.   [3] vizards.
[4] Ornamental devices, usually made with sugar and white of egg from powdered
pistachio nuts or almonds.
[5] In A this word ends the preceding line.   [6] memorials.
[7] A, 'Bovis.' For Sir Bevis of Hampton see Ashton's *Romances of Chivalry.*

Ith upper wardrobe, next to which by chance　　　　　25
The divells vizors hung, and their flame-painted
Skin coates, those he remov'd with greater fury,
And (having cut the infernall, ugly faces
All into mamocks ¹) with a reverend hand
He takes the imperiall diadem, and crownes　　　　　30
Himselfe King of the Antipodes; and beleeves
He has justly gaind the kingdome by his conquest.
　　Let. Let him injoy his fancy.
　　Byp. Doctor Hughball
Hath sooth'd him in't, so that nothing can　　　　　35
Be said against it.　He begins to governe,
With purpose to reduce the manners
Of this country to his owne: h'has constituted
The doctor his chiefe officer; whose secretary
I am to be.　You'l see a court well orderd.　　　　40
　　Let. I see th'event already by the ayme

　　　　　　　　　　　　　Letoy *w[h]ispers*
　　　　　　　　　　　　　with Barbara.

The doctor takes.　Proceed you with your play,
And let him see it in what state he pleases.
　　Byp. I goe, my lord.　　　　　*Exit* [Byplay].
　　Dia. Trust me, this same Extempore　　　　45
(I know not's tother name) pleases me better
For absolute action then all the rest.
　　Joy. You were best beg him of his lord.
　　Dia. Say you so?
He's busie or Ide move him.　　　[*They talk aside.*]　50
　　Let. Prithee doe so,
Good Mistres Blaze.—*To* Marth[a].²—Goe with her, gentle lady:
Doe as she bids you; you shall get a child by't.
　　Mar. Ile doe as any body bids me for a childe.
　　　　　　　　　[Letoy, Barbara *and* Martha *talk aside.*]
　　Joy. Diana, yet be wife; beare not the name　　55
Of sober chastity to play the beast in.
　　Dia. Thinke not your selfe, nor make your selfe a beast
　　¹ fragments.　　　　　　　　² After 'Lady' in A.

Before you are one; and when you appeare so,
Then thanke your selfe. Your jealousie durst not trust me
Behinde you in the country, and since Ime here,   60
Ile see, and know, and follow th'fashion.   If
It be to cuckold you, I cannot helpe it.
   Joy. I now could wish my sonne had beene as farre
In the Antipodes as he thinkes himselfe,
Ere I had runne this hazzard.   65
   Let. [*to* BARBARA]. Y'are instructed.
   Bar. And Ile perform't, I warrant you, my lord.
                     Ex[*eunt*] BA[RBARA *and*] MAR[THA].
   Dia. [*to* JOYLESS]. Why should you wish so? Had you rather
    loose
Your son then please your wife?   You shew your love both waies.
   Let. Now whats the matter?   70
   Joy. Nothing, nothing,——
   Let. Sit; the actors enter.   *Flourish.*

Act 3.   Scene 7.

Enter BYPLAY [*as*] *the* Governour; Mace-bearer, Sword-bearer,
   Officer. *The mace and sword* [*are*] *laid on the table.* *The* Gov-
   ernour *sits.*[1]
   Dia. What's he, a king?
   Let. No, tis the city Governor,
And the chiefe Judge within their Corporation.
   Joy. Here's a city

          Enter PEREGRINE *and* DOCTOR.

Like to be well govern'd then——   5
   Let. Yonder's a king; doe you know him?
   Dia. Tis your sonne,
My Joylesse; now y'are pleas'd.
   Joy. Would you were pleas'd

---

  [1] A runs act, scene, and stage direction together. Through the rest of the act
the scenes are numbered one less than they should be.

To cease your huswifry in spinning out   10
The play at length thus.
 Doct. Heere, sir, you shall see
A poynt of justice handled.
 Byp. Officer.
 Off. My lord.   15
 Byp. Call the defendant and the plaintiffe in.
 Sword. Their counsell and their witnesses.
 Byp. How now!
How long ha you beene free oth poyntmakers,[1]
Good Master Hilt and scaberd carrier,—   20
Which [2] is in my hands now. Do you give order
For counsell and for witnesses in a cause
Fit for my hearing or for me to judge, haw?
I must be rul'd and circumscrib'd by lawyers, must I,
And witnesses, haw? No, you shall know   25
I can give judgement, be it right or wrong,
Without their needlesse proving and defending:
So bid the lawyers goe and shake their eares,
If they have any, and the witnesses
Preserve their breath to prophesie of dry summers.   30
Bring me the plaintiffe and defendant only,—
But the defendant first; I will not heare
Any complaint before I understand
What the defendant can say for himselfe.[3]   [*Exit* Officer.]
 Per. I have not known such down right equity.   35
If he proceeds as he begins, Ile grace him.

---

 [1] Punning: those who make points for lacings, and those who correct with dis-
tinctions.
 [2] The sword of office and scabbard, which Byplay takes up as he speaks.
 [3] This speech was probably given in the manner of some noted judge. Was Brome
satirizing the hated Star Chamber?

Act 3. Sce[ne] 8.

Enter Gentleman, *and* Officer.

By. Now, sir, are you the plaintiffe or defendant, haw?

Gent. Both, as the case requires, my lord.

Byp. I cannot
Heare two at once; speake first, as y'are defendant.

Gent. Mine adversary doth complaine— 5

Byp. I will heare no
Complaint. I say speake your defence.[1]

Gent. For silkes and
Stuffes receiv'd by me—

Byp. A mercer is he, haw? 10

Gent. Yes, my good lord, he doth not now complain—

Byp. That I like well.

Gent. For money nor for wares
Againe; but he complaines——

By. "Complaines" againe? Do you double with me, haw? 15

Gent. In his wives cause.

Byp. Of his wife, does he, haw? That I must confesse
Is many a good mans case. You may proceed.

Gent. In money I tender him double satisfaction,
With his own wares again, unblemished, undishonor'd. 20

Byp. That is, unworne, unpawned.

Dia. What an odde
Jeering judge is this!

Gent. But unto me
They were delivered upon this condition, 25
That I should satisfie his wife.

Byp. Heel have
Your body for her then, unlesse I empt
My brest of mercy to appease her for you.
Call in the plaintiffe.—*Exit* Officer.— [2] Sir, stand you aside. 30

[1] A has a comma after 'Complaint.' Perhaps the better punctuation is:
I will heare no
Complaint, I say: speake your defence.
[2] After 'aside' in A.

Dia. Oh, tis the flinching gentleman that broake
With the kind citizens wife. I hope the judge
Will make him an example.

Act 3.   Scene 9.

Enter Citizen *and* Officer.

Byp. Come you forwards.
Yet nerer, man. I know my face is terrible,
And that a citizen had rather lose
His debt then that a Judge should truely know
His dealings with a gentleman; yet speake: 5
Repeat without thy shop booke now, and without
Feare it may rise in judgement here against thee,
What is thy full demand, what satisfaction
Requirest thou of this gentleman?
   Cit. And please you, sir——   10
   Sword. Sir! you forget your selfe.
   By. Twas well said, Sword-bearer;
Thou knowst thy place, which is to shew correction.
   Cit. My lord, an't please you, if it like your honour,—
   By. La! an intelligent citizen, and may grow   15
In time himselfe to sit in place of worship.
   Cit. I aske no satisfaction of the gentleman
But to content my wife. What her demand is,
Tis best knowne to her selfe; please her, please me,
An't please you, sir—my lord, an't like your honour.   20
But before he has given her satisfaction,
I may not fall my suit, [1] nor draw my action.
   By. You may not?
   Cit. No, alacke a day, I may not;
Nor find content nor peace at home, and't please you,—   25
My lord, an't like your honour, I would say.
An't please you, what's a tradesman that

           [1] let the suit drop.

Has a faire wife without his wife, an't please you?
And she without content is no wife. Considering
We trades-men live by gentlemen, an't please you,   30
And our wives drive a halfe trade with us, if the gentlemen
Breake with our wives, our wives are no wives to us,
And we but broken trades-men, an't please you,
And't like your honour, my good lord, and't please you.

   By. You argue honestly.   35

   Cit. Yet, gentlemen—
A lacke a day, and please you, and like your honour,—
Will not consider our necessities,
And our desire in general through the city
To have our sonnes all gentlemen like them.   40

   By. Nor, though [1] a gentleman consume
His whole estate among ye, yet his sonne
May live t'inherit it?

   Cit. Right, right, and't please you,—
Your honour, my good lord, and't please you.   45

   By. Well,
This has so little to be said against it,
That you say nothing. Gentleman,[2] it seems
Y'are obstinate, and will stand out——

   Gent. My lord,   50
Rather then not to stand out with all mens wives
Except mine owne, Ile yield me into prison.

   Cit. Alacke a day!

   Dia. If our young gentlemen
Were like those of th' Antipodes, what decay   55
Of trade would here bee, and how full the prisons!

   Gent. I offer him any other satisfaction,—
His wares againe, or money twice the value.

   By. That's from the poynt.

   Cit. I, I, alacke a day!   60
Nor doe I sue to have him up in prison.
Alacke a day, what good (good gentleman)
Can I get by his body?

   [1] Nor consider that, though—   [2] A, 'Gentlemen.'

By. Peace, I should
Now give my sentence, and for your contempt,—   65
Which is a great one, such as if let passe
Unpunished may spread forth a dangerous
Example to the breach of city custome,
By gentlemens neglect of tradesmens wives,
I should say—[1] for this contempt commit you   70
Prisoner from sight of any other woman
Untill you give this mans wife satisfaction,
And she release you; justice so would have it.
But as I am a citizen by nature,
(For education made it so,) Ile use   75
Urbanity in your behalfe towards you;
And as I am a gentleman by calling,
(For so my place must have it,) Ile performe
For you the office of a gentleman
Towards his wife. I, therefore, order thus: 80
That you bring me the wares here into court,
(I have a chest shall hold 'hem, as mine owne);
And you send me your wife; Ile satisfie her
My selfe. Ile do't, and set all streight and right:
Justice is blinde, but Judges have their sight.   85
   Dia. And feeling, too, in the Antipodes.
Han't they, my lord?
   Joy. What's that to you, my lady?
   Within. Dismisse the court.
   Let. Dismisse the court. Cannot you heare the prompter?   90
Ha' you lost your eares, Judge?
   By. No. [*To* Officer.] Dismisse the court.
Embrace you, friends; and to shun further strife,
See you send me your stuffe, and you your wife.
                    [BYPLAY *moves toward* PEREGRINE.]
   Per. Most admirable justice!   95
   Dia. Protest,[2] Extempore plaid the Judge, and I

---

[1] The parenthesis in A begins with 'which,' l. 66, and ends with 'wives,' l. 69.
[2] This word seems, at least early in the 16th century, to have been an affectation.
A character in *Sir Gyles Goosecap* (1606) says:—'There is not a duke's son in France

Knew him not all this while.

   Joy. What over-sight
Was there!

   Dia. He is a properer man methinks   100
Now than he was before: sure I shall love him.

   Joy. Sure, sure, you shall not, shall you?

   Dia. And I warrant
By his judgement speech ee'n now he loves a woman well;
For he said, if you noted him, that he   105
Would satisfie the citizens wife himselfe.
Methinks a gentlewoman might-please him better.

                           Byplay *kneeles and kisses*

   Joy. How dare you talke so?   Peregrines *hand.*

   Dia. What's he a doing now, troe?

   Per. Kneele downe   110
Againe. Give me a sword, some body.

   Let. The king's about to knight him.

   By. Let me pray
Your Majesty be pleased yet to with-hold
That undeserved honour [1] till you first   115
Vouchsafe to grace the city with your presence,
Accept one of our Hall [2]-feasts, and a freedome, [3]
And freely use our purse for what great summes
Your Majesty will please.

   Dia. What subjects there are   120
In the Antipodes!

   Let. None in the world so loving.

   Per. Give me a sword, I say. Must I call thrice?

   Let. No, no, take mine, my liege.

   Per. Yours! What are you?   125

   Doct. A loyall lord; one of your subjects too.

---

dare say, "I protest," till he be one and thirty years old at least; for the inheritance
of that word is not to be possessed before.' Gifford's *Jonson*.

  [1] James was much criticized for creating 2323 knights, selling knighthood as cheap
as £30, and in 1629 the right of the Crown to force knighthood on the landed
gentry was revived by Charles in order to make the gentry compound for the
refusal of it. Green, *Short Hist.* III, 1071.

  [2] Guildhall.   [3] freedom of the City.

Per. He may be loyall; he's a wondrous plaine one.

Joy. Prithee, Diana, yet lets slip away
Now while he's busie.

Dia. But where's your daughter-in-law?   130

Joy. Gone home, I warrant you, with Mistris Blaze.
Let them be our example.

Dia. You are cosen'd.

Joy. Y'are an impudent whore!

Dia. I know not what I may be   135
Made by your jealousie.

Per. Ile none o' this.   [*Seeing sword of the* Sword-bearer.]
Give me that princely weapon.

Let. Give it him.

Sword. It is a property you know, my lord,   140
No blade, but a rich scabbard with a lath in't.

Let. So is the sword of Justice for ought he knows.

Per. It is inchanted![1]

By. Yet on me let it fall,
Since tis Your Highnesse will, scabbard and all.   145

Per. Rise up, our trusty, well-beloved knight.

By. Let me finde favour in your gracious sight
To taste a banquet now, which is prepar'd,
And shall be by your followers quickly shar'd.

Per. My followers?   Where are they?   150

Let. [*aside*]. Come, sirs, quickly.

Ent[er] 5. or 6. Courtiers.

Per. Tis well; lead on the way.
          [*Exeunt* PEREGRINE *and* DOCTOR *with the* actors.]

Dia. And must not we
Goe to the banquet too?

Let. He must not see   155
You yet.   I have provided otherwise
For both you in my chamber; and from thence
Wee'll at a window see the rest oth' Play,—

---

[1] Because it will not come from its scabbard.

Or if you needs, sir, will stay here, you may.

Joy. Was ever man betray'd thus into torment?   160

Ex[eunt.]

Act 4. Scene 1. [*The Same Hall.*][1]

Enter DOCTOR *and* PEREGRINE.

Doct. Now, sir, be pleas'd to cloud your princely raiment
With this disguise.   Great kings have done the like,
To make discovery of passages
Among the people: thus you shall perceive
What to approve and what correct among 'hem.   5

Per. And so Ile cherish, or severely punish.

Puts on a cloake and hat.[2]

Enter an Old Woman *reading:*[3] *to her, a young* Maid [*with a book*].

Doct. Stand close, sir, and observe.

Old [Wom.] "Royall pastime, in a great match betweene the tanners and the butchers, sixe dogges of a side, to play single at the game, Bear, for fifty pound, and a tenne pound supper for their dogs and themselves.   Also you shall see two ten dogge-courses at the Great Beare."[4]   12

Maid. Fie, granny, fie, can no perswasions,
Threatenings, nor blowes prevaile, but you'll persist
In these prophane and diabolicall courses,   15
To follow bear baitings when you can scarce
Spell out their bills with spectacles?

Old [Wo.] What though

---

[1] So throughout the act.   [2] In A this direction stands beside ll. 3–4.
[3] reading a hand-bill.
[4] 'The bears and bulls were fastened behind, and then worried by great English bull-dogs.   To this entertainment there often followed that of whipping a blinded bear, performed by five or six men standing circularly with their whips, which they exercised upon him without mercy, as he could not escape because of his chain. He defended himself, throwing down all who were not active enough to get out of his reach, and tearing their whips out of their hands, and breaking them.' Hentzner, *Itinerary*, Orford translator, p. 42.   See also Laneham's *Pageants at Kenilworth,* Phila. 1822, p. 25.

My sight be gone beyond the reach of spectacles
In any print but this, and though I cannot—*Strikes downe her book.*[1]
No, no, I cannot read your meditations,   21
Yet I can see the royall [2] game plaid over and over,
And tell which dogge does best, without my spectacles.
And though I could not, yet I love the noyse;
The noyse revives me, and the Bear-Garden scent   25
Refresheth much my smelling.
   Maid. Let me entreat you
Forbeare such beastly pastimes; th'are sathanicall.
   Old [*Wo.*] Take heed, child, what you say; tis the kings game.
   Per. What is my game?   30
   Doct. Bear-baiting, sir, she meanes.
   Old. [*Wo.*] "A beare's a princely beast, and one side venison,"
Writ a good author once. You yet want yeares,
And are with bawbles pleas'd: Ile see the beares.   *Exit.*
   Maid. And I must beare with it: she's full of wine,   35
And for the present wilfull, but in due
Season Ile humble her,—but we are all
Too subject to infirmity.

Act 4.   Scene 2.

Enter a yong Gentleman, *and an old* Serving-man. [*The* Maid *stands
aside watching them.*]

   Gent. Boy—boy.
   Ser. Sir.
   Gent. Here, take my cloake.
   Per. Boy, did he say?
   Doct. Yes, sir, old servants are   5
But boyes to masters, be they nere so young.
   Gent. Tis heavy, and I sweat.
   Ser. Take mine and keepe you warme then;

[1] A places this beside ll. 19–22.
[2] For the great popularity of bear-baiting with Queen Elizabeth see Strutt, 1801,
pp. 192–93.

Ile weare yours.

   Gent. Out, you varlet,   10
Dost thou obscure it as thou meantst to pawne it?
Is this a cloake unworthy of the light?
Publish it, sirrah!—Oh, presumptuous slave,
Display it on one arme——Oh, ignorance!

   Ser. Pray load your asse your selfe as you would have it.   15

   Gent. Nay, prethee be not angry: thus; and now
Be sure you bear't at no such distance, but
As't may be knowne appendix to this booke.[1]

   Per. This custome I have seene with us.

   Doct. Yes, but   20
It was deriv'd from the Antipodes.

   Maid. It is a dainty creature, and my blood
Rebells against the spirit: I must speake to him.

   Ser. Sir, here's a gentlewoman makes towards you.

   Gent. Me? She's deceiv'd; I am not for her mowing.   25

   Maid. Faire sir, may you vouchsafe my company?

   Gent. No truly, I am none of those you look for.
The way is broad enough; unhand me, pray you.

   Maid. Pray, sir, be kinder to a lasse that loves you.

   Gent. Some such there are, but I am none of those.   30

   Maid. Come, this is but a coppy [2] of your countenance.
I ha knowne you better than you thinke I doe.

   Gent. What ha you knowne me for?

   Maid. I knew you once.
For halfe a peece I take it.   35

   Gent. You are deceiv'd
The whole breadth of your nose.[3] I scorne it.

   Maid. Come, be not coy, but send away your servant,
And let me gi' you a pint of wine.

   Gent. Pray keepe   40
Your courtesie. I can bestow the wine
Upon my selfe, if I were so dispos'd
To drinke in tavernes; fah!

   Maid. Let me bestow't

---

[1] himself.   [2] pretence.   [3] completely.

Upon you at your lodging then; and there   45
Be civilly merry.
    Gent. Which if you doe,
My wife shall thanke you for it; but your better
Course is to seeke one fitter for your turne;
You'll lose your aime in me; and I befriend you   50
To tell you so.
    Maid. Gip gaffer shotten, fagh![1]   *[She] kicks [him].*
Take that for your coy counsell.
    Gent. Helpe! Oh, helpe!
    Ser. What meane you, gentlewoman?   55
    Maid. That to you, sir.   *Kicks [Servant].*
    Gent. O murther, murther!
    Ser. Peace, good master,
And come away. Some cowardly jade I warrant
That durst not strike a woman.   60

Act 4. Scene 3.

Enter Constable, *and* Watch.

    Con. What's the matter?
    Ser. But and we were your match——
    Watch. What would you doe?
Come, come, afore the constable: now, if
You were her match, what would you doe, sir?   5
    Maid. Doe?
They have done too much already, sir: a virgin   *[She] weeps.*
Shall not passe shortly for these street-walkers,
If some judicious order be not taken.
    Gent. Heare me the truth.   10
    Con. Sir, speake to your companions:
I have a wife and daughters, and am bound
By hourely precepts to heare women first,
Be't truth or no truth; therefore, virgin, speake,

[1] Get out, you withered old grandfather.

And feare no bug beares; I will doe thee justice.   15

   Mayd. Sir, they assayld me, and with violent hands,
When words could not prevaile, they would have drawne mee
Aside unto their lust, till I cryed murder.

   Gent. Protest, sir, as I am a gentleman,
And as my man's a man, she beat us both,   20
Till I cryd murder.

   Ser. That's the woefull truth on't.

   Con. You are a party, and no witness, sir;
Besides y'are two, and one is easier
To be beleev'd. Moreover as you have the oddes   25
In number, what were justice if it should not support
The weaker side? Away with them to the Counter! [1]

   Per. Call you this justice?

   Doct. In th' Antipodes.   29

   Per. Here's much to be reform'd. Young man, thy vertue
Hath wonne my favour; goe, thou art at large.

                                    [*The* Gentleman *hesitates.*]

   Doct. [*aside*]. Be gone.

   Gent. [*aside*]. He puts me out; my part is now
To bribe the constable.

   Doct. [*aside*]. No matter; goe.   35

                         Ex[*eunt*] [2] Gent[leman] *and* Servant.

   Per. And you, sir, take that sober-seeming wanton.
And clap her up, till I heare better of her;
Ile strip you of your office and your eares else.

   Doct. At first shew mercy.

   Per. They are an ignorant nation,   40
And have my pitty mingled with correction:
And, therefore, damsell, for you are the first
Offender I have noted here, and this
Your first offence for ought I know—

   Maid. Yes, truely.   45

   Doct. [*aside to* Maid]. That was well said.

   Per. Goe, and transgresse no more;

---

[1] There were three Counter, or Compter, prisons in London: in Wood St., Cheapside; in the Poultry; and in Southwark.   [2] A, *Exit.*

And as you finde my mercy sweet, see that
You be not cruell to your grandmother
When she returnes from beare-baiting.   50
   Doct. [*aside*]. So, all be gone.
          Ex[eunt all except PEREGRINE *and* DOCTOR].

[Act 4.   Scene 4.] [1]

Enter Buffe woman, *her head and face bleeding, and many* Women,
as from a prize. [2]

   Per. And what are these?
   Doct. A woman fencer, that has plaid a prize,
It seemes, with losse of blood.
   Per. It doth amaze me.   *They passe over.*
What can her husband be, when shee's a fencer?   5
   Doct. He keepes a schoole, and teacheth needle-worke,
Or some such arts which we call womanish.
   Per. Tis most miraculous and wonderfull.
   Man scould within. Rogues, varlets, harlots, ha you done
Your worst, or would you drowne me? Would you take my life? 10
   Women within. Ducke him againe, ducke him againe.
   Per. What noise is this?
   Doct. Some man, it seemes, that's duckt for scolding.
   Per. A man for scolding?
   Doct. You shall see.   15

Act 4.   Scene 5. [3]

Enter Women *and* Man-scold.

   [1] *Wom.* So, so,
Enough, enough; he will be quiet now.
   Mansc. How know you that, you divell-ridden witch you?
How, quiet; why quiet? Has not the law past on me,

---

[1] No scene division is marked in A.   [2] contest.
[3] A, calling this scene 4, misnumbers the remaining scenes of the act.

Over and over me, and must I be quiet?   5
   1 *Wom.* Will you incurre the law the second time?
   Mansc. The lawes the river, ist?   Yes, tis a river
Through which great men, and cunning, wade or swimme;
But meane and ignorant must drowne in't.   No,
You hagges and hel-hounds, witches, bitches, all,   10
That were the law, the judge, and executioners,
To my vexation, I hope to see
More flames about your eares then all the water
You cast me in can quench.
   3 *Wom.* In with him againe; he calls us names.   15
   2 *Wom.* No, no; I charge yee no.
   Mansc. Was ever harmelesse creature so abus'd?
To be drench'd under water, to learne dumbnesse
Amongst the fishes, as I were forbidden
To use the naturall members I was borne with,   20
And of them all the chiefe that man takes pleasure in,
The tongue! Oh me, accursed wretch!   [*He*] *weepes.*
   Per. Is this a man?
I aske, not by his beard, but by his teares.
   2 *Wom.* This showre will spende the fury of his tongue,   25
And so the tempest's over.
   3 *Wom.* I am sorry for't;
I would have had him duck'd once more.
But some body will shortly raise the storme
In him againe, I hope, for us, to make   30
More holiday-sport of him.
                    Ex[*eunt* Women *and* Man-scold *severally*].
   Per. Sure these are dreames,
Nothing but dreames.
   Doct. No, doubtlesse we are awake, sir.
   Per. Can men and women be so contrary   35
In all that we hold proper to each sex?
   Doct. [*aside*]. I'me glad he takes a taste of sence in that yet.
   Per. 'Twill aske long time and study to reduce
Their manners to our government.
   Doct. These are   40

Low things and easie to be qualified ¹——
But see, sir, here come courtiers; note their manners.

Act 4.   Scene 6.

Enter a Courtier [*counting his money; at a distance another follows*].

  1 Cour. This was three shillings yesterday. How now!
All gone but this? Six pence for leather soles
To my new greene silke stockings, and a groate ²
My ordinary ³ in pompions ⁴ bak'd with onions.
  Per. Doe such eate pompions?   5
  Doct. Yes, and clownes musk-mellons.
  1 Cour. Three pence I lost at nyne-pines; but I got
Six tokens ⁵ towards that at pigeon holes ⁶——
'S nayles wheres the rest; is my poake ⁷ bottome broake?

    [Second Courtier *coming up behind the* First].

  2 Cour. What, Jacke! A pox oretake thee not; how dost?   10
           [*He*] *kicke*[*s the* first Courtier].
  1 Cour. What with a vengeance aylst? Dost thinke my breech
Is made of bell-mettall? Take that!
        [*He gives the* Second Courtier *a*] *box o'th eare.*
  2 Cour. In earnest?
  1 Cour. Yes, till more comes.⁸ [*Seizing hair of* Second Courtier.]
  2 Cour. Pox rot your hold; let goe my locke. Dee thinke   15
Y'are currying of your fathers horse againe?
  1 Cour. Ile teach you to abuse a man behind
Was troubled too much afore.   *They buffet.* ⁹

---

  ¹ regulated.   ² fourpence.
  ³ Usually a place where a table d'hôte could be had, but here merely dinner.
  ⁴ pumpkins.
  ⁵ A small piece of brass, copper, or lead, issued by tradesmen, generally worth
1d, ½d or ¼d.
  ⁶ Like the modern bagatelle: the arches for the balls resembled the entrances to
a dove-cote.   ⁷ pocket.
  ⁸ Punning: seriously; money given as guarantee of full payment.
  ⁹ In A after 'behind.' The next scene division and the entrance stand beside
l. 18.

Act 4. Sc[ene] 7.

Ent[er] 3. Court[ier.]

3 *Cour.* Hay, there boyes, there;
Good boyes are good boyes still. There, Will; there, Jack;—
          [*The* Second Courtier *knocks down the* First].
Not a blow, now he's downe.

2 *Cour.* 'Twere base, I scorn't.

1 *Cour.* There's as proud fall as stand, in court or city.   5

3 *Cour.* That's well said, Will. Troth I commend you both.
How fell you out? I hope in no great anger.

2 *Cour.* For mine owne part, I vow I was in jest.

1 *Cour.* But I have told you twice and once,[1] Will, jest not
With me behind; I never could endure   10
(Not of a boy) to put up things behinde:
And that my tutor knew; I had bin a schollar else.
Besides, you know my sword was nock'd [2] i'th 'fashion,
Just here behinde, for my backe-guard and all;
And yet you would do't,   15
I had as liefe you would take a knife——

3 *Cour.* Come, come,
Y'are friends. Shake hands; Ile give you halfe a dozen [3]
At the next ale-house, to set all right and streight,—
And a new song, a dainty one; here tis.   [*Shows*] *a ballad.*

1 *Cour.* O, thou art happy that canst reade;   21
I would buy ballads, too, had I thy learning.

3 *Cour.* Come, we burn day-light, and the ale may sowre.
                              Ex[eunt Courtiers].

Per. Call you these courtiers? They are rude silken [4] clowns,
As course within as water-men or car-men.   25

Doct. Then look on these; here are of those conditions.

---

[1] once for all.
[2] Breeched, from *nock*, breech. He wore his sword straight across behind.
'Why dost wear a sword only to hurt men's feet that kick thee?' *Court Begger,*
ed. Pearson, II, 230.   [3] mugs of ale?   [4] dressed in silk.

Act 4.　Scen[e] 8.

Ent[er] Carman & Waterman.[1]

Wat. Sir, I am your servant.

Car. I am much oblig'd,
Sir, by the plenteous favours your humanity
And noble vertue have conferr'd upon me,
To answer with my service your deservings.　　5

Wat. You speake what I should say.　Be, therefore, pleas'd
T'unload, and lay the wait of your commands
Upon my care to serve you.

Car. Still your courtesies,
Like waves of a spring-tide, ore-flow the bankes　　10
Of your abundant store; and from your channell,
Or streame of faire affections, you cast forth
Those sweet refreshings on me (that were else
But sterile earth) which cause a gratitude
To grow upon me, humble, yet ambitious　　15
In my devoire, to doe you best of service.

Wat. I shall no more extend my utmost labour
With oare and saile to gaine the lively-hood
Of wife and children then to set a shore
You and your faithfull honourers at the haven　　20
Of your best wishes.

Car. Sir, I am no lesse
Ambitious, to be made the happy meanes,
With whip and whistle, to draw up or drive
All your detractors to the gallowes.　　25

---

[1] A puts the entrance beside ll. 26 and 1.

Act 4. Scene 9.

Enter Sedan-man.[1]

Wat. See,
Our noble friend.
   Sed. Right happily encountred——
I am the just admirer of your vertues.
   [*Car. and Wat.*][2] We are, in all, your servants.   5
   Sed. I was in quest
Of such elect society to spend
A dinner-time withall.
   [*Car. and Wat.*] Sir, we are for you.
   Sed. Three are the golden number in a taverne;   10
And at the next of best,[3] with the best meate
And wine the house affoords (if you so please)
We will be competently merry. I
Have receiv'd, lately, letters from beyond seas,
Importing much of the occurrences   15
And passages of forraigne States. The knowledge
Of all I shall impart to you.
   Wat. And I
Have all the new advertisements from both
Our universities of what has past   20
The most remarkably of late.
   Car. And from
The Court I have the newes at full,
Of all that was observable this progresse.[4]
   Per. From Court?   25
   Doct. Yes, sir: they know not there they have
A new King here at home.
   Sed. Tis excellent!

---

[1] A prints the entrance beside l. 1.   [2] A puts 2 here and at the beginning of l. 9.
[3] the nearest tavern of the best kind.
[4] royal journey.

We want but, now, the newes-collecting gallant
To fetch his dinner, and materialls
For his this weeks dispatches.   30
   Wat. I dare thinke,
The meat and newes being hot upon the table,
He'll smell his way to't.
   Sed. Please you to know yours, sir?
   Car. Sir, after you.   35
   Sed. Excuse me.
   Wat. By no meanes, sir.
   Car. Sweet sir, lead on.
   Sed. It shall be as your servant
Then, to prepare your dinner.   [*He leads the way.*]   40
   Wat. Pardon me.
   Car. Insooth, Ile follow you.
   Wat. Yet tis my obedience.
          Ex[eunt, the Waterman *before the* Carman].
   Per. Are these but labouring men, and tother courtiers? 45
   Doct. Tis common here, sir, for your watermen
To write most learnedly, when your courtier
Has scarce ability to read.
   Per. Before I reigne
A moneth among them they shall change their notes,   50
Or Ile ordaine a course to change their coats.
I shall have much to doe in reformation.
   Doct. Patience and counsell will goe through it, sir.
   Per. What if I crav'd a counsell from New England?
The old will spare me none.[1]   55
   Doct. [*aside*]. Is this man mad?
My cure goes fairely on.—Doe you marvaile that
Poore men out-shine the courtiers? Looke you, sir,
A sicke-man giving counsell to a physitian;
And there's a puritan trades-man teaching a   60
Great traveller to lye; that ballad-woman

---

[1] There was no parliament between 1629 and 1640. Men were forbidden to speak of its reassembling.

Gives light to the most learned antiquary
In all the kingdome.
    Bal. Buy new ballads, come.
    Doct. A naturall foole, there, giving grave
      instructions.
T'a lord embassador; that's a schismatick
Teaching a scrivener [2] to keep his eares;
A parish clearke, there, gives the rudiments
Of military discipline to a generall;
And there's a basket-maker confuting Bellarmine.[3]   70
    Per. Will you make me mad?
    Doct. We are saild, I hope,
Beyond the line of madnesse. Now, sir, see
A states-man, studious for the common-wealth,
Solicited by projectors of the country.

These persōs
passe over
the stage in
couples, ac- 65
cording as he
describes them.[1]

Act 4. Sc[ene] 10.

Ent[er] Byplay *like a* Statesman, [*and*] 3. *or* 4. Projectors [4] *with*
bundles of papers.[5]

    Byp. Your projects are all good; I like them wel,
Especially these two: this for th' increase of wooll;
And this for the destroying of mice. They'r good,
And grounded on great reason. As for yours,

---

  [1] A puts this beside ll. 62–68.
  [2] Wm. Prynne, barrister, (1600–1669). In his *Histrio-mastix*, 1633, a general attack on the stage, he was held to glance at the king and queen. He was sentenced, Feb. 7, 1634, to imprisonment, a fine of £5000, expulsion from Lincoln's Inn, was rendered incapable of returning to his profession, degraded from his University degree, and set in the pillory, where he was to lose his ears. Yet in 1637 he was again in the Star Chamber for attacking the Declaration of Sports and the bishops. The stumps of his ears were shorn off, June 30, in the pillory. On July 27 he was sent to what was intended to be perpetual banishment. *Ency. Brit.*
  [3] Robert Francis Romulus Bellarmine, Cardinal, (1542–1621) Catholic theologian and controversialist. His controversy with James I, who after the Gunpowder Plot passed severe laws against Roman Catholics, gave him prominence.
  [4] Promoters.   [5] A, running together the marking of the scene and the entrance, places all this beside lines 70–75 of the preceding scene and the first line of Scene 10.

For putting downe the infinite use of jacks,[1]   5
(Whereby the education of young children,
In turning spits, is greatly hindred)
It may be look'd into.   And yours against
The multiplicity of pocket-watches,
(Whereby much neighbourly familiarity,   10
By asking, "What de'yee gesse it is a clocke?"
Is lost when every puny clerke can carry
The time oth' day in's breeches,) this, and these,
Hereafter may be lookt into.   For present,
This for the increase of wool,—that is to say,   15
By fleying of live horses and new covering them
With sheeps-skins,—I doe like exceedingly.
And this for keeping of tame owles in cities,
To kill up rats and mice, whereby all cats
May be destroyed, as an especiall meanes   20
To prevent witch-craft and contagion.
   Per. Here's a wise businesse!
   Pro. Will your honour now
Be pleas'd to take into consideration
The poore mens suits for briefes, to get reliefe.   25
By common charity throughout the kingdome,
Towards recovery of their lost estates?
   Byp. What are they?   Let me heare.
   Pro. First, here's a gamster, that sold house and land
To the knowne value of five thousand pounds,   30
And by misfortune of the dice lost all,
To his extreame undoing,—having neither
A wife or child to succour him.
   Byp. A batchelour!
   Pro. Yes, my good lord.   35
   Byp. And young, and healthfull?
   Pro. Yes.
   Byp. Alas, tis lamentable; he deserves much pitty.

---

[1] When instruments for pulling off boots and turning spits were introduced, they were given the name Jack—formerly applied to the foot-boys who performed these tasks. Nares, *Dict.*

Per. How's this?

Doct. Observe him further, pray, sir. 40

Pro. Then, here's a bawd, of sixty odde yeares standing.

Byp. How old was she when she set up?

Pro. But foure
And twenty, my good lord. She was both ware
And merchant, flesh and butcher, (as they say,) 45
For the first twelve yeares of her house-keeping:
She's now upon fourescore, and has made markets
Of twice foure thousand choyse virginities,
And twice their number of indifferent geare,[1]—
No riffe raffe was she ever knowne to cope for. 50
Her life is certifi'd here by the justices
Adjacent to her dwelling——

Byp. She is decai'd?

Pro. Quite trade-fallen, my good lord, now in her dotage;
And desperately undone by ryot. 55

Byp. 'Lasse good woman.

Pro. She has consum'd in prodigall feasts and fidlers,
And lavish lendings to debauch'd comrades,
That suckt her purse, in jewels, plate, and money,
To the full value of sixe thousand pounds. 60

Byp. She shall have a collection, and deserves it.

Per. Tis monstrous, this!

Pro. Then here are divers more,
Of pandars, cheaters, house and high-way robbers,
That have got great estates in youth and strength, 65
And wasted all as fast in wine and harlots
Till age o'retooke 'hem, and disabled them
For getting more.

Byp. For such the law provides
Reliefe within those counties where they practis'd. 70

Per. Ha! what, for thieves?

Doct. Yes, their law punisheth
The rob'd, and not the thiefe, for surer warning
And the more safe prevention. I have seene

[1] kind, sort.

Folkes whipt for losing of their goods and money,   75
And the picke-pockets cherish'd.
    Byp. The weale publicke.
As it severely punisheth their neglect,
Undone by fire ruines,[1] shipwracke, and the like,
With whips, with brands, and losse of carelesse eares,[2]   80
Imprisonment, banishment, and sometimes death;
And carefully maintaineth houses of correction
For decay'd schollars and maim'd souldiers;
So doth it finde reliefe and almes-houses
For such as liv'd by rapine and by cosenage.   85
    Per. Still worse and worse! Abhominable, horrid!
    Pro. Yet here is one, my lord, 'bove all the rest,
Whose services have generally bin knowne,
Though now he be a spectacle of pitty.
    Byp. Who's that?   90
    Pro. The captaine of the cut-purses, my lord;
That was the best at's art that ever was,
Is fallen to great decay by the dead palsie
In both his hands, and craves a large collection.
    Byp. Ile get it him.   95
    Per. You shall not get it him.
Doe you provide whips, brands, and ordaine death,
For men that suffer under fire or shipwracke
The losse of all their honest gotten wealth,
And finde reliefe for cheaters, bawdes, and thieves?   100
Ile hang yee all.
    Byp. Mercy, great king!
    Omnes. O mercy!
    Byp. Let not our ignorance suffer in your wrath
Before we understand Your Highnesse lawes.   105
We went by custome, and the warrant which
We had in your late predecessors raigne;
But let us know your pleasure, you shall finde
The state and common-wealth in all obedient
To alter custome, law, religion, all,   110

---

[1] Who are ruined by fire. See l. 98.   [2] ears of the careless.

To be conformable to your commands.[1]
Per. Tis a faire protestation; and my mercy
Meets your submission. See you merit it
In your conformity.
Byp. Great sir, we shall. 115
In signe whereof we lacerate these papers,
And lay our necks beneath your kingly feet.

LETOY, DIANA, JOYLESSE, *appeare above.*[2]

Per. Stand up, you have our favour.
Dia. And mine too!
Never was such an actor as Extempore! 120
Joy. You were best to flye out of the window to him.
Dia. Me thinkes I am even light [3] enough to doe it.
Joy. I could finde in my heart to quoit thee at him.
Dia. So he would catch me in his armes I car'd not.
Let. Peace both of you, or you'l spoyle all. 125
Byp. Your Grace
Abounds—abounds. Your Grace—I say, abounds—
Let. Pox o' your mumbling chops! Is your braine dry?
Doe you pump?
Dia. He has done much, my lord, and may 130
Hold out a little.
Let. Would you could hold your peace
So long.
Dia. Doe you sneap [4] me, too, my lord.
Joy. Ha, ha, ha! 135
Let. Blockehead!
Joy. I hope his hotter zeale to's actors
Will drive out my wives love-heat.
Dia. I had
No need to come hither to be sneapt. 140
Let. Hoyday! The rest will all be lost. We now give over

---

[1] Glancing at the revolutionary changes of Charles and his ministers?
[2] A places this beside ll. 116–18. These actors are on the upper stage, here supposed to represent a window in a gallery. See ll. 121, 149, 151.
[3] Punning: not heavy, wanton.   [4] rebuke.

The play, and doe all by Extempore,
[*To* Joyless.] For your sonnes good, to sooth him into's wits.
If you'l marre all, you may. [*Aside to* Byplay.] Come nearer,
    cockscombe;
Ha you forgotten, puppy, my instructions   145
Touching his subjects and his marriage?
   Byp. [*aside*]. I have all now, my lord.
   Per. What voyce was that? [1]
   Byp. A voyce out of the clouds, that doth applaud
Your highnesse welcome to your subjects loves,—   150
   Let. So, now he's in. [2] Sit still, I must goe downe
And set out things in order.   *Ex*[*it*].
   Byp. A voyce that doth informe me of the tydings
Spread through your kingdome of your great arrivall,
And of the generall joy your people bring   155
To celebrate the welcome of their king.   *Showts within.*
Hearke how the countrey shouts with joyfull votes,
Rending the ayre with musick of their throats.
                              Drum & trumpets.
Hearke how the souldier with his martiall noise
Threatens your foes, to fill your crowne with joyes.   160
                              Haughboyes. [3]
Hearke how the city, with loud harmony,
Chaunts a free welcome to your majesty.   *Soft musick.*
Heark how the Court prepares your grace to meet
With solemne musick, state, and beauty sweet.

[1] Peregrine has his back turned to the upper stage.   [2] in his part.
[3] A puts *Haughboyes* beside l. 161 and *Soft musick* beside l. 163.

Act 4.　Sce[ne] 11.[1]

The soft musicke playing, ent[er] by two and two divers Courtiers;
MARTHA *after them, like a* Queene, *between two* boyes, *in
robes,—her train borne up by* BARBARA. *All the* Lords *kneele
and kisse* PERIGRINES *hand.* MARTHA *approaching, he starts
backe, but is drawne on by* BYPLAY *and the* DOCTOR. LETOY
enters and mingles with the rest, and seemes to instruct them all.

　　Dia. O here's a stately show!　Looke, Master Joylesse,
Your daughter-in-law presented like a queene
Unto your sonne; I warrant now he'l love her.
　　Joy. A queene?
　　Dia. Yes, yes, and Mistris Blaze is made　　　　　　　5
The mother of her maides,[2]—if she have any;
Perhaps the Antipodian Court has none.
See, see, with what a majesty he receives 'hem.

SONG.

Health, wealth, and joy our wishes bring,
All in a welcome to our king:　　　　　　　　　10
May no delight be found,
Wherewith he be not crown'd.
Apollo with the Muses,
Who arts divine infuses,
With their choyce chyrlonds [3] decke his head　　　15
Love and the Graces make his bed;
And to crowne all, let Hymen to his side
Plant a delicious, chast, and fruitfull bride.

　　Byp. Now, sir, be happy in a marriage choyce
That shall secure your title of a king.　　　　　　20
See, sir, your state presents to you the daughter,
The onely childe and heire apparant of

---

[1] Beside l. 164 in A.　　　　[2] The chief of the Court maids of honour.
[3] garlands.

Our late deposed and deceased soveraigne,
Who with his dying breath bequeath'd her to you.

    Per. A crowne secures not an unlawfull marriage: 25
I have a wife already.

    Doct. No, you had, sir;
But she's deceast.

    Per. How know you that?

    Doct. By sure advertisment; and that her fleeting spirit   30
Is flowne into and animates this princesse.

    Per. Indeed, she's wondrous like her.

    Doct. Be not slacke
T'embrace and kisse her, Sir.   *He kisses her and retires.*

    Mar. He kisses sweetly;   35
And that is more than ere my husband did.
But more belongs then kissing to child-getting;
And he's so like my husband, if you note him,
That I shall but lose time and wishes by him;
No, no, Ile none of him.   40

    Bar. Ile warrant you he shall fulfill your wishes.

    Mar. O but try him you first; and then tell me.

    Bar. There's a new way, indeed, to choose a husband!
Yet twere a good one to barre foole-getting.

    Doct. Why doe you stand aloofe, sir?   45

    Per. Mandivell writes
Of people neare the Antipodes, called Gadlibriens,[1]
Where on the wedding-night the husband hires
Another man to couple with his bride,
To cleare the dangerous passage of a maidenhead.   50

    Doct. 'Slid, he falls backe againe to Mandevile madnesse!

    Per. She may be of that serpentine generation
That stings oft times to death, as Mandevile writes.

    Doct. She's no Gadlibrien, sir, upon my knowledge.
You may as safely lodge with her as with   55
A mayd of our owne nation.   Besides,
You shall have ample counsell; for the present,

---

[1] For the original of this and of ll. 52–53, see Halliwell's *Maundeville,* 1839,
pp. 285–86.

Receive her, and intreat her to your chappell.

    Byp. For safety of your kingdome, you must do it.

Haughtboies. Ex[eunt] in state as LETOY *directs [all on lower stage].*

                             Manet LETOY.[1]

    Let. So, so, so, so, this yet may prove a cure,—   60

    Dia. [*to* JOYLESS]. See, my lord now is acting by himselfe.

    Let. And Letoy's wit cryd up triumphant hoe.

Come, Master Joylesse and your wife, come downe

Quickly; your parts are next.

                 [*Exeunt above* JOYLESS *and* DIANA.]

             I had almost

Forgot to send my chaplaine after them.   65

You, Domine, where are you?

Act 4. Sce[ne] 12.

Enter QUAILPIPE *in a fantasticall shape.*[2]

    Qua. Here, my lord.

    Let. What, in that shape? [3]

    Quail.[4] Tis for my part, my lord,

Which is not all perform'd.

    Let. It is, sir, and the play for this time. We   5

Have other worke in hand.

    Quai. Then have you lost

Action (I dare be bold to speake it) that

Most of my coat [5] could hardly imitate.

    Let. Goe shift your coat, sir, or for expedition   10

Cover it with your owne, due to your function.

Follyes, as well as vices, may be hid so.

Your vertue is the same.[6] Dispatch, and doe

As Doctor Hughball shall direct you. Go.   *Exit* QUAIL[PIPE].

---

[1] In A beside ll. 59–63, with *Exit* for *Exeunt.*

[2] A puts scene division and entrance beside ll. 64–66 of the preceding scene.

[3] dress.   [4] A, *Chap.* for Chaplain.

[5] As we say, 'Gentlemen of the cloth' for the clergy.

[6] As if you had played your part.

Act 4. Sce[ne] 13.

Enter JOYLESS, [*and*] DIANA.[1]

Now, Master Joylesse, doe you note the progresse,
And the faire issue likely to insue,
In your sons cure?   Observe the doctors art:
First, he has shifted your sonnes knowne disease
Of madnesse into folly, and has wrought him   5
As farre short of a competent reason as
He was of late beyond it.   As a man
Infected by some fowle disease is drawne
By physicke into an anatomy [2]
Before flesh fit for health can grow to reare him,   10
So is a mad-man made a foole before
Art can take hold of him to wind him up
Into his proper center,[3] or the medium
From which he flew beyond himselfe.   The doctor
Assures me now, by what he has collected   15
As well from learned authors as his practise,
That his much troubled and confused braine
Will by the reall knowledge of a woman,
Now opportunely tane, be by degrees
Setled and rectified,—with the helpes beside   20
Of rest and dyet, which he'le administer.
    Dia. But tis the reall knowledge of the woman
(Carnall, I think you meane) that carries it.
    Let. Right, right.
    Dia. Nay, right or wrong, I could even with   25
If he were not my husbands son, the doctor
Had made my selfe his recipe, to be the meanes
Of such a cure.
    Joy. How, how?

---

[1] A places scene division and entrance beside line 14 of Scene 12. and ll. 1–2.
[2] skeleton.
[3] As we say of a man unwell that he is 'off his centre.' 'Medium', centre of
gravity, is in apposition with 'centre.'

   Dia. Perhaps that course might cure your madness, too,   30
Of jealousy, and set all right on all sides.
[*Aside.*] Sure, if I could but make him such a foole,
He would forgo his madnes and be brought
To christian sence againe.
   Joy. Heaven grant me patience,   35
And send us to my country home againe!
   Dia. Besides, the yong mans wife's as mad as he;
What wise worke will they make!
   Let. The better, fear't not.
Bab Blaze shall give her counsel; and the youth   40
Will give her royall satisfaction,
Now, in this kingly humour. [*Aside to* DIANA.] I have a way
To cure your husbands jealousy my selfe.
   Dia. [*aside*]. Then I am friends again: even now I was not,
When you sneapt me, my lord.   45
   Let. [*aside*]. That you must pardon.
Come, Mr. Joylesse. The new married paire
Are towards bed by this time; we'le not trouble them,
But keep a house-side to our selfes. Your lodging
Is decently appointed.   50
   Joy. Sure your lordship
Meanes not to make your house our prison?
   Let. By
My lordship but I will for this one night!
See, sir, the keyes are in my hand. Y'are up,[1]   55
As I am true Letoy. Consider, sir,
The strict necessity that tyes you to't,
As you expect a cure upon your sonne.
Come, lady, see your chamber.
   Dia. I doe waite   60
Upon your lordship.
   Joy. I both wait and watch;
Never was man so master'd by his match.[2]   *Ex[eunt] omn[es].*

---

[1] You're trapped.   [2] wife.

Act 5. Scene 1. [*A Chamber in Letoy's House.*] [1]

JOYLESSE [*discovered*], *with a light in his hand.*

Joy. Diana! ho! where are you? She is lost.
Here is no further passage. All's made fast.
This was the bawdy way by which she scap'd
My narrow watching. Have you privy posternes .
Behind the hangings in your strangers chambers?   5
She's lost from me for ever. Why, then, seek I?
O my dull eyes, to let her slip so from yee,
To let her have her lustfull will upon me!
Is this the hospitality of lords?
Why, rather, if he did intend my shame   10
And her dishonour, did he not betray me
From her, out of his house, to travaile in
The bare suspition of their filthinesse?
But hold me a nose-witnesse to its ranknesse!—
No, this is sure the lordlier way, and makes   15
The act more glorious in my sufferings. O——
[*Kneeling*] May my hot curses on their melting pleasures
Cement them so together in their lust
That they may never part, but grow one monster!

Act 5. Scene 2.

Enter BARBARA.

Bar. [*aside*]. Good gentleman! he is at his prayers now
For his mad sonnes good night-worke with his bride.
Well fare your heart, sir; you have pray'd to purpose;
But not all night, I hope. Yet sure he has,
He looks so wild for lacke of sleepe. Y'are happy, sir.   5
Your prayers are heard, no doubt, for I'm perswaded
You have a childe got you to-night.

[1] Scenes 1–4 are in this room.

Joy. Is't gone
So farre, doe you thinke?
    Bar. I cannot say how farre: 10
Not fathome deepe, I thinke, but to the scantling [1]
Of a child-getting, I dare well imagine.
For which, as you have pray'd, forget not, sir,
To thanke the lord oth' house.
    Joy. For getting me   15
A child? Why I am none of his great lordships tenants,
Nor of his followers, to keepe his bastards.
                  [BARBARA *starts to go out.*]
Pray stay a little.
    Bar. I should goe tell my lord
The newes: he longs to know how things doe passe.   20
    Joy. Tell him I take it well, and thanke him.
I did before despaire of children, I.
But Ile goe wi'yee and thanke him.
    Bar. Sure his joy
Has madded him: here's more worke for the doctor.   25
    Joy. But tell me first: [*drawing his dagger*] were you their bawd
that speak this?
    Bar. What meane you with that dagger?
    Joy. Nothing; I
But play with't. Did you see the passages
Of things? I aske, were you their bawd?   30
    Bar. Their bawd?
I trust she is no bawd that sees, and helpes
(If need require) an ignorant lawfull paire
To doe their best.
    Joy. Lords actions all are lawfull.   35
And how? and how?
    Bar. These old folkes love to heare.
Ile tell you,[2] sir—and yet I will not neither.
    Joy. Nay, pray thee, out with't.
    Bar. Sir, they went to bed.   40
    Joy. To bed! Well, on.

---

[1] sample, rough draft.   [2] Pearson, 'you you.'

Bar. On?   They were off, sir, yet;
And yet a good while after.   They were both
So simple that they knew not what, nor how,
For she's, sir, a pure maid.   45
    Joy. Who dost thou speake of?
    Bar. Ile speake no more, lesse you can looke more tamely.
    Joy. Goe, bring me to 'hem then.   Bawd, will you goe?
                [*He threatens her with his dagger.*]
    Bar. Ah——

Act 5.   Scene 3.

Enter BYPLAY *and holds* JOYLESSE.

Byp. What aile you, sir?   Why bawd? whose bawd is she?
    Joy. Your lords bawd, and my wives.
    Byp. You are jealous mad.
Suppose your wife be missing at your chamber,
And my lord, too, at his; they may be honest: 5
If not, what's that to her, or you, I pray,
Here in my lords owne house?
    Joy. Brave, brave, and monstrous!
    Byp. Shee has not seene them.   I heard all your talke.
The child she intimated is your grandchild   10
In *posse*, sir, and of your sonnes begetting,
    Bar. I,[1] Ile be sworne I meant, and said so too!
    Joy. Where is my wife?
    Byp. I can give no account.
If she be with my lord I dare not trouble 'hem;   15
Nor must you offer at it; no, nor stab your selfe,   BYP[LAY] *takes*
But come with me.   Ile counsell, or at least   *away his dagger.*
Governe you better.   Shee may be, perhaps,
About the bride-chamber, to heare some sport;
For you can make her none, 'lasse, good old man,—   20
    Joy. I'me most insufferably abus'd!

[1] Ay.

Byp. Unlesse
The killing of your selfe may do't; and that
I would forbeare, because perhaps 'twould please her.
    Joy. If fire, or water, poyson, cord, or steele,   25
Or any meanes be found to do it, Ile doe it;
Not to please her, but rid me of my torment. [JOYLESS *rushes out.*][1]
    Byp. I have more care and charge of you than so.
                           [*Exit* BYPLAY.]
    Bar. What an old desperate man is this, to make
Away your selfe for feare of being a cuckold!   30
If every man that is, or that but knowes
Himselfe to be oth' order, should doe so,
How many desolate widowes would here be.
They are not all of that minde. Here's my husband.

Act 5. Scene 4.

Ent[er] BLAZE *with a habit in his hand.*

    Bla. Bab! Art thou here?
    Bar. Looke well. How thinkst thou, Tony?
Hast not thou, neither, slept to-night?
    Bla. Yes, yes.
I lay with the butler. Who was thy bed-fellow?   5
    Bar. You know I was appoynted to sit up.
    Bla. Yes, with the doctor in the bride-chamber.
But had you two no waggery? Ha!
    Bar. Why, how now, Tony?
    Bla. Nay, facks,[2] I am not jealous.   10
Thou knowst I was cur'd long since, and how.
I jealous! I an asse! A man sha'n't aske
His wife shortly how such a gentleman does,
Or how such a gentleman did, or which did best,
But she must thinke him jealous.   15
    Bar. You need not: for
If I were now to dye on't, nor the doctor

---

[1] A puts *Ex. Joy. and Byp.* after ll. 27–28.   [2] by my faith.

Nor I came in a bed to night,—I meane
Within a bed.
　　Bla. Within, or without, or over, or under,　　　20
I have no time to thinke o' such poore things.
　　Bar. What's that thou carriest, Tony?
　　Bla. O ho, Bab.
This is a shape.[1]
　　Bar. A shape? what shape, I prethee, Tony?　　　25
　　Bla. Thou'lt see me in't anon; but shalt not know me
From the starkst foole ith' towne.　And I must dance
Naked in't, Bab.
　　Bar. Will here be dancing, Tony?
　　Bla. Yes, Bab.　My lord gave order for't last night.　　　30
It should ha'bin ith' play; but because that
Was broke off, he will ha't to-day.
　　Bar. O Tony,
I did not see thee act ith' Play.
　　Bla. O, but　　　35
I did though, Bab,—two mutes.[2]
　　Bar. What, in those breeches?
　　Bla. Fie! foole, thou understandst not what a mute is.
A mute is a dumbe speaker in the play.
　　Bar. Dumbe speaker! That's a bull.　Thou wert the bull　　　40
Then, in the Play.　Would I had seene thee rore.
　　Bla. That's a bull, too, as wise as you are, Bab.
A mute is one that acteth speakingly,
And yet sayes nothing.　I did two of them:
The sage man-midwife, and the basket-maker.　　　45
　　Bar. Well, Tony, I will see thee in this thing.
And tis a pretty thing.
　　Bla. Prethee, good Bab,
Come in and help me on with't in our tyring-house;
And helpe the gentlemen, my fellow dancers;　　　50
And thou shalt, then, see all our things, and all
Our properties, and practice to the musicke.
　　Bar. O Tony, come; I long to be at that.　　　*Exeunt.*

---

[1] costume.　　　[2] Noun, a silent actor; verb, to void.

Act 5. Scene 5.   [*Another Chamber in Letoy's House.*] [1]

LETOY, *and* DIANA.

Dia. My lord, your strength and violence prevaile not:
There is a Providence above my vertue,
That guards me from the fury of your lust.
   Let. Yet, yet, I prethee yield. Is it my person
That thou despisest? See, here's wealthy treasure,   *A table set 5*
Jewells that Cleopatra would have left   *forth, covered*
Her Marcus [2] for.   *with treasure.*
   Dia. My lord, tis possible
That she who leaves a husband may be bought
Out of a second friendship.   10
   Let. Had stout Tarquin
Made such an offer, he had done no rape,
For Lucrece had consented, sav'd her owne,
And all those lives that followed in her cause.
   Dia. Yet then she had beene a loser.   15
   Let. Wouldst have gold?
Mammon, nor Plutus' [3] selfe, should over-bid me,
For Il'd give all. First, let me raine a showre
To out-vie that which overwhelmed Danaë;
And after that another; a full river   20
Shall from my chests perpetually flow
Into thy store.
   Dia. I have not much lov'd wealth,
But have not loath'd the sight of it till now
That you have soyld it with that foule opinion   25
Of being the price of vertue. Though the metall
Be pure and innocent in it selfe, such use
Of it is odious, indeed damnable,
Both to the seller and the purchaser:

---

[1] A misprints the scene as 2, Pearson as IV. The remaining scenes are in this room.   [2] Marc Antony.
[3] A, *Pluto's.* Note the resemblance of this scene to the temptation of Celia, *Volpone,* III, 6.

Pitty it should be so abus'd.   It beares   30
A stampe upon't which but to clip is treason.
Tis ill us'd there, where law the life controules;
Worse, where tis made a salary for soules.
  Let. Deny'st thou wealth?   Wilt thou have pleasure, then,
Given and ta'ne freely, without all condition?   35
Ile give thee such as shall, if not exceed,
Be at the least comparative with those
Which Jupiter got the demy-gods [1] with, and
Juno was mad she mist.
  Dia. My lord, you may   40
Glose o're and gild the vice which you call pleasure
With god-like attributes, when it is, at best,
A sensuality so farre below
Dishonourable that it is meere beastly;
Which reason ought to abhorre; and I detest it   45
More than your former hated offers.
  Let. Lastly,
Wilt thou have honour?   Ile come closer to thee,
For now the flames of love grow higher in me,
And I must perish in them, or enjoy thee;   50
Suppose I finde by power, or law, or both,
A meanes to make thee mine, by freeing
Thee from thy present husband?
  Dia. Hold, stay there.
Now should you [2] utter volumes of perswasions;   55
Lay the whole world of riches, pleasures, honours,
Before me in full grant, that one last word,
Husband, and from your owne mouth spoke, confutes
And vilifies even all.   The very name
Of husband, rightly weigh'd and well remembred,   60
Without more law or discipline, is enough
To governe woman-kinde in due obedience,
Master all loose affections, and remove
Those idolls which, too much, too many love;
And you have set before me, to beguile   65

---

[1] The children of gods and mortals.   [2] A has 'I.'

Me of the faith I owe him. But, remember
You grant I have a husband; urge no more.
I seek his love; tis fit he loves no whore.
　　Let. [*aside*]. This is not yet the way.—You have seene, lady,
My ardent love, which you doe seeme to slight,　　　70
Though to my death, pretending zeale to your husband.
My person, nor my proffers are so despicable
But that they might (had I not vow'd affection
Intirely to your selfe) have met with th' embraces
Of greater persons, no lesse faire, that can,　　　75
Too, if they please, put on formality,
And talke in as divine a straine as you.
This is not earnest. Make my word but good,
Now, with a smile, Ile give thee a thousand pound.
Looke o' my face—come—prithee looke, and laugh not—　　　80
Yes, laugh, and dar'st—Dimple this cheek a little;
Ile nip it else.
　　Dia. I pray forbeare, my lord:
I'me past a childe, and will be made no wanton.
　　Let. How can this be? So young, so vigorous,　　　85
And so devoted to an old mans bed!
　　Dia. That is already answerd. He's my husband.
You are old, too, my lord.
　　Let. Yes, but of better metall;—
A jealous old man, too, whose disposition　　　90
Of injury to beauty and young blood
Cannot but kindle fire of just revenge
In you, if you be woman, to requite
With your owne pleasure his unnaturall spight.
You cannot be worse to him than he thinkes you,　　　95
Considering all the open scornes and jeeres
You cast upon him, to a flat defiance;
Then the affronts I gave, to choake his anger;
And lastly your stolne absence from his chamber;
All which confirmes—we have as good as told him—　　　100
That he's a cuckold. Yet you trifle time,
As 'twere not worth the doing.

Dia. Are you a lord?
Dare you boast honor and be so ignoble?
Did not you warrant me upon that pawne,—   105
Which can take up no mony,—your blanck honour,
That you would cure his jealousie, which affects him
Like a sharpe sore, if I to ripen it
Would set that counterfeit face of scorne upon him
Onely in shew of disobedience? Which   110
You wonne me to upon your protestation
To render me unstain'd to his opinion,
And quit me of his jealousie for ever.
    Let. No, not unstain'd, by your leave, if you call
Unchastity a staine. But for his yellows,[1]   115
Let me but lye with you and let him know it,
His jealousie is gone, all doubts are clear'd,
And for his love and good opinion,
He shall not dare deny't. Come, be wise,
And this is all. All is as good as done   120
To him already; let't be so with us;
And trust to me, my power, and your owne,
To make all good with him. If not,—now marke,—
To be reveng'd for my lost hopes (which yet
I pray thee save) Ile put thee in his hands   125
Now in his heat of fury; and not spare
To boast thou art my prostitute; and thrust yee
Out of my gates, to try't out [2] by your selves.
    Dia. This you may doe, and yet be still a lord?
This can I beare and still be the same woman!   130
I am not troubled now; your wooing oratory,
Your violent hands, (made stronger by your lust,)
Your tempting gifts, and larger promises
Of honor and advancements, were all frivolous;
But this last way of threats, ridiculous   135
To a safe minde that beares no guilty grudge.
My peace dwells here, while yonder sits my judge:
And in that faith Ile dye.

   [1] jealousy.   [2] settle the matter.

Act 5. Scene 6.[1]

Let. [*aside*]. She is invincible!—
Come. Ile relate you to your husband.

En[ter] JOYLESSE *and* BYPLAY.

Joy. No,
Ile meet her with more joy then I receiv'd [2]
Upon our marriage-day. My better soule,   5
Let me againe embrace thee.
    Byp. Take your dudgeon,[3] sir;
I ha done you simple service.
    Joy. O my lord,
My lord, you have cur'd my jealousie. I thanke you,   10
And more, your man, for the discovery;
But most the constant meanes, my vertuous wife,
Your medicine, my sweet lord.
    Let. She has tane all
I meane to give her, sir. [*Aside to* BYPLAY.] Now sirrah, speake. 15
    Byp. I brought you to the stand [4] from whence you saw
How the game went;—
    Joy. Oh my deare, deare Diana.
    Byp. I seem'd to doe it against my will, by which I gain'd
Your bribe of twenty peeces.[5]   20
    Joy. Much good doe thee.[6]
    Byp. But I assure you, my lord gave [7] me order
To place you there after, it seemes, he had
Well put her to't within.
    Joy. Stay, stay, stay, stay;   25
Why may not this be then a counterfeit action,

---

[1] A omits the scene number, placing scene division and entrance beside ll. 138 and 1.
[2] Received her with. Brome is fond of ellipsis.
[3] So called because the handle was of wood with a grain (*dudgeon*), or was carved with lines.
[4] Not marked in text. Supposedly behind the arras.
[5] dollars.　　　　　　[6] do't?　　　　[7] A, 'give.'

Or a false mist to blinde me with more error?
The ill I fear'd may have beene done before,
And all this but deceit to dawbe it ore.
    Dia. Doe you fall backe againe?   30
    Joy. Shugh, give me leave.   *[Drawing dagger.]*
    Byp. I must take charge, I see, o'th' dagger againe.
            [He takes the dagger from JOYLESS.]
    Let. Come, Joylesse, I have pitty on thee; heare me.
I swear upon mine honor she is chast.
    Joy. Honor! an oath of glasse!   35
    Let. I prithee heare me.
I try'd and tempted her for mine owne ends
More then for thine.
    Joy. That's easily beleev'd.
    Let. And had she yielded, I not onely had   40
Rejected her, for it was ne're my purpose
(Heaven, I call thee to witnesse) to commit
A sinne with her, but layd a punishment
Upon her greater then thou couldst inflict.
    Joy. But how can this appeare?   45
    Let. Doe you know your father, lady?
    Dia. I hope I am so wise a childe.[1]
    Let. [*to* BYPLAY.] Goe call
In my friend Truelocke.
    Byp. Take your dagger, sir,   50
Now I dare trust you.
    Let. Sirrah, dare you foole
When I am serious? Send in Master Truelocke.   *Exit* BYP[LAY].
    Dia. That is my fathers name.
    Joy. Can he be here?   55
    Let. Sir, I am neither conjurer nor witch,
But a great fortune-teller, that [2] you'l finde,
You are happy in a wife, sir, happier——yes,
Happier by a hundred thousand pound
Then you were yesterday——   60

---

[1] Referring to the saying: 'It's a wise child that knows its own father.'
[2] who says that.

Joy. So, so; now he's mad.

Let. I meane in possibilities,—provided that
You use her well, and never more be jealous.

Joy. Must it come that way?   [*He walks away restlessly.*]

Let. Looke you this way, sir,   65
When I speake to you; Ile crosse your fortune else,
As I am true Letoy.

Joy. Mad, mad, he's mad!
Would we were quickly out on's fingers yet.

Let. When saw you your wives father?   Answer me!   70

Joy. He came for London foure dayes before us.

Let. Tis possible he's here then.   Doe you know him?
                    [*To* DIANA *as*] TRUELOCKE [1] *enter[s].*

Act 5. Sc[ene] 7.

Dia. O, I am happy in his sight.   Deare sir.   *She kneeles.*

Let. Tis but so much knee-labour lost; stand up,
Stand up, and minde me.

True. You are well met, sonne Joylesse.

Joy. How, have you beene conceald, and [in] this house? [2]   5
Here's mystery in this.

Tru. My good lords pleasure.

Let. Know, sir, that I sent for him, and for you,
Instructing your friend Blaze, my instrument,
To draw you to my doctor with your sonne: 10
Your wife I knew must follow. What my end
Was in't shall quickely be discover'd to you
In a few words of your supposed father.

Dia. "Supposed father"!

Let. Yes; come, Master Truelocke,   15
My constant friend of thirty yeares acquaintance,
Freely declare with your best knowledge now

---

[1] A, calling this scene 6, places the stage directions after ll. 1–2, and mis-numbers the remaining scenes. A, *Enter Truelocke.*

[2] A, 'How have you beene conceald, and this house?'

Whose childe this is.

Tru. Your honor do's as freely

Release me of my vow, then, in the secret   20

I lock'd up in this brest, these seaventeene yeares,

Since she was three dayes old?

Let. True, Master Truelocke,

I doe release you of your vow. Now speake.

Tru. Now she is yours, my lord, your onely daughter;   25

And know you, Master Joylesse, for some reason

Knowne to my lord, and large reward to me,

Shee has beene from the third day of her life

Reputed mine; and that so covertly

That not her lady mother, nor my wife,   30

Knew to their deaths the change of my dead infant,—

Nor this sweet lady. Tis most true we had

A trusty nurses help and secresie,

Well paid for, in the carriage of our plot.

Let. Now shall you know what mov'd me, sir.

I was   35

A thing beyond a mad-man, like your selfe

Jealous; and had that strong distrust, and fancied

Such proofes unto my selfe against my wife,

That I conceiv'd the childe was not mine owne,

And scorn'd to father it; yet I gave to breed her   40

And marry her as the daughter of this gentleman,

Two thousand pound I guesse you had with her.

But since your match, my wife upon her death-bed

So clear'd her selfe of all my foule suspitions

(Blest be her memory!) that I then resolv'd   45

By some quaint way, for I am still Letoy,

To see and try her throughly, and so much

To make her mine as I should find her worthy.

And now thou art my daughter and mine heire;—

Provided still, for I am still Letoy,   50

You honourably love her, and defie

The cuckold-making fiend, foule jealousie.

Joy. My lord, tis not her birth and fortune, which

Do joyntly claime a priviledge to live
Above my reach of jealousie, shall restraine   55
That passion in me, but her well-tried vertue:
In the true faith of which I am confirmd,
And throughly cur'd.
    Let. As I am true Letoy,
Well said. I hope thy son is cur'd by this too.   60

Act 5. Sce[ne] 8.

Enter BARBARA.[1]

Now, Mistris Blaze! Here is a woman now!
I cur'd her husbands jealousie, and twenty [2] more
Ith' towne, by meanes I and my doctor wrought.
    Bar. Truly, my lord, my husband has tane bread
And drunke upon't [3] that under Heaven he thinkes   5
You were the meanes to make me an honest woman,
Or, at the least, him a contented man.
    Let. Ha done, ha done.
    Bar. Yes, I beleeve you have done;
And if your husband, lady, be cur'd, as he should be,   10
And as all foolish, jealous husbands ought to be,
I know what was done first, if my lord tooke
That course with you as me——
    Let. Prithee what camst thou for?
    Bar. My lord, to tell you, as the doctor tels me,   15
The bride and bridegroome, both, are comming on
The sweetliest to their wits againe.
    Let. I told you.
    Bar. Now you are a happy man, sir; and I hope
A quiet man.   20
    Joy. Full of content and joy.

---

[1] A places scene division and entrance by ll. 60 and 1.
[2] This number, four, and forty were used for indefinite amounts.
[3] 'He confessed most solemnly—for he has taken the sacrament.'

Bar. Content! So was my husband when he knew
The worst he could by his wife. Now youle live quiet, lady.
    Let. Why flyest thou off thus, woman, from the subject
Thou wert upon?   25
    Bar. I beg your honours pardon:
And now Ile tell you. Be it by skill or chance,
Or both, was never such a cure as is
Upon that couple: now they strive which most
Shall love the other.   30
    Let. Are they up, and ready? [1]
    Bar. Up! Up, and ready to lye downe againe;
There is no ho [2] with them.
They have bin in th' Antipodes to some purpose,
And now are risen, and return'd themselves.   35
He's her dear Per, and she is his sweet Mat;
His kingship and her queenship are forgotten;
And all their melancholly and his travailes past,
And but suppos'd their dreams.
    Let. Tis excellent.   40
    Bar. Now, sir, the doctor—for he is become
An utter stranger to your sonne, and so
Are all about em—craves your preference,
And such as he's acquainted with.
    Let. Go, sir,   45
And go you,[3] daughter.
    Bar. [*aside*]. Daughter! that's the true trick
Of all old whore-masters, to call their wenches
Daughters.
    Let. Has he knowne you, friend Trulock, too?   50
    True. Yes, from his child-hood.
    Let. Go, then, and possess him,
Now he is sensible, how things have gone;
What arte, what meanes, what friends have bin imploy'd
In his rare cure; and win him by degrees   55
To sense of where he is. Bring him to me;
And I have yet an entertainment for him

---

[1] dressed.   [2] whoa.   [3] Pearson, 'your.'

Of better settle-braine then drunkards porridge,
To set him right.   As I am true Letoy,
I have one toy left.   Go, and go you; why stayst thou?   60
                 Ex[eunt] JOY[LESS, TRULOCK *and* DIANA].
   Bar. If I had beene a gentle-woman borne,
I should have bin your daughter, too, my lord.
   Let. But never as she is.
You'le know anon.
   Bar. Neat city-wives flesh yet may be as good   65
As your course countrey gentlewomans blood.   *Exit* BAR[BARA].
   Let. Goe with thy flesh to Turn-bull shambles.   Hoe!
Within there!

Act 5.   Sce[ne] 9.

Ent[er] Quailpipe.[1]

   Qua. Here, my lord.
   Let. The musicke, songs,
And dance, I gave command for—are they ready?
   Qua. All, my good lord: and, in good sooth, I cannot
Enough applaude your honours quaint conceit   5
In the designe,—so apt, so regular, so pregnant, so acute,
And so withall poetice legitimate,
As I may say justly, with Plautus.————[2]
   Let. Prithee say no more,
But see upon my signall given they act   10
As well as I design'd.
   Qua. Nay not so well,
My exact lord, but as they may, they shall.   *Exit* [QUAILPIPE].
   Let. I know no flatterer in my house but this;
But for his custome [3] I must beare with him.   15
'Sprecious, they come already!   [*To musicians without.*]   Now
   beginne.

   [1] A puts scene division and entrance by l. 68.
   [2] A has no punctuation between 'As I' and the dash, setting this and the next
two speeches as prose.   [3] 'Because it is his way.'

Act 5. Sce[ne] 10.[1]

A solemne lesson [2] *upon the recorders.* [3]   *Ent[er]* TRUELOCKE, JOY-
LESSE *and* DIANA, PEREGRINE *and* MARTHA, DOCTOR, *and*
BARBARA. LETOY *meets them.* TRUELOCKE *presents* PEREGRINE
and MARTHA *to him. He salutes them. They seeme to make
some short discourse. Then* LETOY *appoints them to sit.* PERE-
GRINE *seemes somthing amazed. The musicke ceases.*

Let. Againe you are welcome, sir; and welcome all.

Per. I am what you are pleas'd to make me;
But withall so ignorant of mine owne condition,—
Whether I sleepe, or wake, or talke, or dreame;
Whether I be, or be not; or if I am,   5
Whether I doe, or doe not any thing;
For I have had, if I now wake, such dreames,
And been so far transported in a long
And tedious voyage of sleep that I may fear
My manners can acquire no welcome,   10
Where men understand themselves.

Let. [*aside*]. This is musick.
Sir, you are welcome; and I give full power
Unto your father, and my daughter here, your mother,
To make you welcome.   JOYLESSE *whispers* PEREGRINE.   15

Per. How, your daughter, sir?

Doct. [*aside*]. My lord, you'l put him backe againe if you trouble
his braine with new discoveries.

Let. [*aside*]. Fetch him you on againe, then: pray, are you Letoy,
or I?   20

Joy. Indeed it is so, sonne.

Doct. [*aside*]. I feare your show will but perplex him too.

Let. [*aside*]. I care not, sir; Ile have it to delay
Your cure a while, that he recover soundly.
Come, sit again; again you are most welcome.   25

---

[1] A places the scene division beside l. 15 of the preceding scene.
[2] strain.   [3] A kind of flageolet, usually with seven holes and a mouthpiece.

Act 5. Sce[ne] 11.

A most untunable florish.   Ent[er] Discord *attended by* Folly,
Jealousie, Melancholy, *and* Madnesse.

[*Let.*] [1] There's an unwelcome guest,—uncivill Discord, that
traines into my house her followers, Folly, and Jealousie, Melancholy, and Madnesse.

Bar. My husband presents Jealousie in the black and yellow
jaundied [2] sute there, halfe like man, and tother halfe like woman,
with one horne and asse-eare[s] upon his head.   6

Let. Peace, woman. [*To* Peregrine.] Marke what they doe. But,
by the way, conceive me this but shew, sir, and devise. [3]

Per. I thinke so.

Let. How goes he backe againe now, doctor? [4] sheugh!   10

Discord. Song in untunable notes.

Come forth, my darlings, you that breed
The common strifes that discord feed.
Come in the first place, my deare Folly;
Jealousie next, then Melancholy;
And last come Madnesse; thou art hee   15
That bearst th' effects of all those three.
Lend me your aydes; so Discord shall you crowne,
And make this place a kingdome of our owne.

[1] A and Pearson omit the name.   [2] jaundiced.
[3] A, 'Peace woman, marke what they doe:—but but by the way, conceive me
this, but shew sir, and devise.'
[4] Said mockingly with reference to the similar exclamation of the Doctor, ll.
17–18 of the preceding scene.

Act 5.   Scene 12.

They dance.[1]

After a while they are broke off by a flourish, and the approach of
Harmony *followed by* Mercury, Cupid, Bacchus *and* Apollo.
Discord *and her faction fall downe.*

Let. See Harmony approaches, leading on
Gainst Discords factions foure [2] great deities,
Mercury, Cupid, Bacchus, and Apollo,—
Wit against Folly, Love against Jealousie,
Wine against Melancholly, and 'gainst Madnesse, Health.   5
Observe the matter and the method,—
   Per. Yes.
   Let. And how upon the approach of Harmony,
Discord and her disorders are confounded.[3]

Harmony. Song.

Come Wit, come Love, come Wine, come Health,   10
Mayntainers of my common-wealth,
Tis you make Harmony compleate;
And from the spheares, her proper seate,
You give her power to raigne on earth,
Where Discord claimes a right by birth.   15
Then let us revell it while we are here,
And keepe possession of this hemisphere.

After a straine or two, Discord *cheares up her faction. They all
rise, and mingle in the dance with* Harmony *and the rest.*
                                        Daunce.
   Let. Note there how Discord cheares up her disorders
To mingle in defiance with the vertues.   *Ex[eunt]* Discord [*and*
But soone they vanish; and the mansion quit   *her followers*]. 20
Unto the gods of health, love, wine, and wit,

---

[1] A puts this beside the scene division.   [2] A and Pearson, 'feare'.
[3] struck down.

Who triumph in their habitation new
Which they have taken, and assigne to you;
In which they now salute you, bid [1] you bee
　　　[Harmony *and her followers*] *salute* [PEREGRINE *and*] *exe*[*unt*]. [2]
Of cheare; and for it, lay [3] the charge on me.　　　　　25
And unto me y'are welcome; welcome all.
Meat, wine, and mirth shall flow, and what I see
Yet wanting in your cure, supplied shall be.
　　　Per. Indeed I finde me well.
　　　Mar. And so shall I　　　　　30
After a few such nights more.
　　　Bar. Are you there?
Good Madam, pardon errors of my tongue.
　　　Dia. I am too happy made to thinke of wrong.
　　　Let. We will want nothing for you that may please,　　　　　35
Though we dive for it toth' Antipodes.

　　[1] A 'bids.'　　　　[2] A, *Salute Exe.* beside l. 24.　　　　[3] A, 'layes'.

The Epilogue.[1]

Doct. Whether my cure be perfect yet or no,
It lies not in my doctor-ship to know.
Your approbation may more raise the man
Then all the Colledge of Physitians [2] can;
And more health from your faire hands may be wonne   5
Then by the stroakings of the seaventh sonne.[3]
Per. And from our travailes in th' Antipodes
We are not yet arriv'd from off the seas,
But on the waves of desprate feares we roame
Untill your gentler hands doe waft us home.   10

Courteous Reader: You shal find in this booke more then was
presented upon the stage, and left out of the presentation for
superfluous length, as some of the players pretended. I thought
good al should be inserted according to the allowed [4] original,
and as it was at first intended for the Cock-pit stage in the right
of my most deserving friend Mr. William Beeston,[5] unto whom
it properly appertained. And so I leave it to thy perusal, as it
was generally applauded and well acted at Salisbury Court.

Farewell, RI. BROME.

[1] A puts these words beside l. 36.
[2] It met first in 1518 at the house of Linacre, the founder. Lectures were founded
in 1583. After the accession of Charles I the college met in a house at the bottom
of Amen Corner. Thornbury, *Old and New London*, I, 393.
[3] The seventh son in a family was supposed to be endowed with special powers.
[4] By the Master of the Revels, whose consent was necessary before a play could
be given.
[5] Beeston connected with the Cockpit 1637–1642. In 1637 he helped to form a
company of boys to act there, for whom *The Antipodes* was apparently intended.

FINIS.

James Shirley

THE ROYAL MASTER

Edited with Critical Essay and Notes by Sir Adolphus William Ward, Litt.D., F.B.A., Master of Peterhouse, Cambridge.

CRITICAL ESSAY

Life.—James Shirley was born, 18 September, 1596, in or near the parish of St. Mary Woolchurch in the City of London, and educated in Merchant Taylors' School and at St. John's College, Oxford, whence he migrated to Catharine Hall, Cambridge. Here he graduated in or before 1618, in which year he printed his first poem *Eccho, or The Unfortunate Lovers*, supposed to be identical with *Narcissus, or The Self-Lover*, an imitation of *Venus and Adonis*, published by him in 1646. After taking orders and proceeding M. A., he from 1623–5 held the mastership of the grammar school at St. Albans in Hertfordshire, having previously (according to Wood) joined the Church of Rome, of which he ever afterwards remained a steadfast adherent. In 1625 (or perhaps rather earlier) he abandoned his scholastic life, and moved to London, where he lived in Gray's Inn and 'set up for a play-writer.' This vocation he without intermisson pursued till 1642, meeting with favour from King Charles I and Queen Henrietta Maria and many personages of their court, and so far as is known enjoying the goodwill of all his fellow-playwrights with whom he was brought into contact. In 1633 he came forward to attack Prynne, then awaiting his sentence for having published *Histriomastix;* and in the following year he furnished the text of a masque presented by the Inns of Court as an anti-puritan demonstration. But he neither received, nor seems to have desired any personal preferment. In 1636, or thereabouts, he paid a visit to Dublin, where his friend Ogilby at this time opened a new theatre; and here and at the Castle, before the lord deputy (Wentworth), he produced some plays. He seems to have permanently returned to London in 1640, and there continued his activity as a dramatist till the suppression of the play-houses in 1642. Up to this date he is known to have written for performance as many as 30 tragedies or comedies of his own, besides 'correcting' one or two by certain writers. To these have to be added a few masques and entertainments, composed by him both before and during the downfall of the regular drama. After the outbreak of the Civil War he appears for a short time to have followed the military fortunes of his patron, the Earl of Newcastle. He then returned to London, where he was encouraged in divers publishing ventures by the liberality of Thomas Stanley and other friends; but before long he fell back on 'his old trade of teaching school' and tried his hand at educational literature. In 1653 he published *Six New Plays*, of which, however, five had been published before the outbreak of the troubles; and a few others followed. But when the theatres reopened, and the revival of his own among other pre-Restoration plays met with considerable favour, he manifested no desire for fresh laurels as a dramatist, but drudged on for his friend Ogilby as a translator from the classics. He died in October, 1666, in St. Giles'-in-the-Fields, London, into which parish he and his wife, who died on the same day, had been driven by the Great Fire of the previous month.

His Literary Descent.—Shirley is the last among the great writers of our old drama—*extremus primorum* by the reckoning of time, but assuredly, and in spite of some half-forgotten obloquy, entitled to a lasting place among them. Although he survived for some years the re-opening of the theatres by which the Restoration was accompanied or preceded, his productivity as a dramatist had come to an end with their suppression. Too much might perhaps be made of the fact that, unlike the D'Avenants and Killigrews, he declined to suit himself to the more exacting requirements and more pronounced tastes of the new generation. His facile powers and receptive disposition, open to the influence of foreign as well as of native examples, would have found no great difficulty in following the critical canons, invented or imported, by which the later Stuart drama regulated its process of decay. And, though he was a poet not only of refined feeling but of earnest purpose, he had in his day too readily given way to license, to have been likely to resist very sternly the current of a "lubrique and adulterate age." Yet he was at least fortunate in the limits of time within which his literary record is actually contained; and under no aspect was he more clearly at the height of his art, than in his unique appreciation of the great qualities of the dramatic period to which he belonged. Shirley was not merely a wellread man but a trained scholar; and his practical experience in teaching, which after the manner of exiles he sought to turn to account in later days of misfortune, must have added to his quickness in the use of his book-learning. He could lay his finger upon a passage in Homer or Horace, and was reminiscent of *La Mort d'Arthure*, as well as of Sidney and Spenser. As will be noticed in connection

with the plots of some of his plays, he was specially familiar with
Spanish literature, of which he had probably imbibed the love at
Oxford, where it continued to be cherished during nearly the whole
of his lifetime. But to his constant and cordial delight in the great
English dramatists, of whom he was an immediate successor or
with whom he was actually contemporary, scarcely a single work
of his fails in one way or another to testify. In the case of *The
Spanish Tragedy* the tribute of repeated quotation is no doubt al-
loyed by ironical intention; but no disrespect is implied by the hack-
neying of words winged merely for a stage-flight. To *Endimion*,
a play which still fascinates by something besides the artificial
graces of Lyly's dialogue, Shirley seems to allude at the opening
of one of his own most brilliantly written comedies (*The Example*).
One of his masques or entertainments (*The Triumph of Beauty*)
treats part of the theme of Peele's *Arraignment of Paris*, and
directly imitates the farcical portion of *A Midsummer-Night's
Dream*. Speaking generally, no other writer of the Elizabethan or
early Stuart periods exhibits a familiarity approaching Shirley's
with the plays of Shakespeare, whom in the pathetic Prologue to
The Sisters he names first among the great masters of the dramatic
art, now forsaken in the sad season of war. His comedies are full
of references or allusions to every kind of figure in the Shakespearean drama—to Hamlet and Polonius, to Shylock, Malvolio,
Falstaff, Pandarus, Parolles and "goodman Verges"; and frequently
the profound sententiousness or the exquisite music of a Shakespearean passage or phrase finds a half-conscious echo in his verse.
Of Jonson he spoke as his "acknowledged master"; but although,
as will be noted, he occasionally sets up a background or introduces
a character modelled upon the master's manner, there was little
that was really congenial to the younger writer in the humorous
creations of the veteran "to whose name wise art did bow." To
Fletcher, on the other hand, he was drawn by what may, on the
whole, notwithstanding indisputable divergence, be termed a close
affinity of genius. He was the author of the address *To the Reader*
prefixed to the first (1647) folio edition of Beaumont and Fletcher,
which was designed as a light of consolation and encouragement in
the midst of gathering gloom; nor is it always easy in the case of

Fletcher's plays to be sure what is owing to the congenial touch of Shirley's revising hand. His indebtedness to Chapman (in *The Ball*) can have been but slight; but the influence of Webster has been rightly traced in what Shirley accounted the best of his tragedies (*The Cardinal*), while a signally effective situation in Thomas Heywood's master-piece must have suggested a passage in one of Shirley's cleverest comedies (*Hyde Park*).

In his masques and other entertainments, he followed the changing fashions of his times. *The Triumph of Peace*, ' offered ' to the King and Queen in 1634 by the four Inns of Court, and intended by its extraordinary splendour to defy the attacks of the puritan censor, then awaiting his sentence in prison, strove to outdo its predecessors in the variety of its anti-masques and the oddity of its characters. Of his later semi-dramatic pieces, *Cupid & Wealth* aimed at little beyond the gracefulness of a private entertainment; *The Contention of Ajax & Ulysses* (ending with the fine 'The glories of our blood & state'), like the companion *Honoria & Mammon* is of hardly more substantial texture than the interludes of our old drama.

His Relation to the Age.—The influences of the age in which he was bred, and which furnished to him the vital experience essential to a national dramatist, were by no means confined to purely literary sympathies or professional traditions. There is no reason for supposing him to have been of gentle birth, and his strenuous insistence upon class ideals is not in itself decisive in favour of such an assumption. But the Oxford college of which he was for a time a member (St. John's), had long been under the marked influence of the Court; and its connection with the great London school whence Shirley proceeded to it (Merchant Taylors') must have heightened the interest of its *alumni* in the controversies of their times, in which religion and politics were closely intertwined. Shirley, accordingly, carries the uncompromising loyalty of our Jacobean and Caroline dramatists to the highest pitch of abstract enthusiasm ever reached by them. Like other members of St John's College, he became (though not during his residence there) a convert to the Church of Rome. He nowhere puts himself forward as a combative Papist; but he loses no opportunity of exhibiting his attachment to the doctrines and practices of the creed professed by him (see *The Wedding; The Grateful Servant; Love in a Maze;* with perhaps, *The Sisters*), and ridicules the popular prejudice against Rome alongside of that against Spain (see *The Bird in a Cage*). He took a lively rather than a deep interest in the course of affairs abroad (see *The Witty Fair One; The Ball; The Opportunity;* and, above all, *The Example*). But, unlike Massinger, with whom he is here and there in literary contact, he seems, before the outbreak of the troubles, to have concerned himself with domestic controversy only when it bore upon the relations between the Court and the art with which he was himself identified (see *The Bird in a Cage*). From first to last he was an enthusiastic adherent of both King and Queen (see especially *The Lady of Pleasure*); although their goodwill towards him is not known to have found expression in material favours.

Career as a Dramatist: General Method.—Under these influences Shirley pursued the singularly even and self-consistent tenor of his career as a productive dramatist. He was gifted with a genuinely poetic temperament, but one that was assimilative and fanciful rather than passionate and profound; and possessed a pleasant wit, together with a humorous perception limited by his own range of experience and observation. The prevailing tone of his mind was serious, and inclined him to prefer forms of composition whose dignity demands a greater expenditure of care. While, accordingly, the dramatic species to which the large majority of his plays belong was mixed to such a degree as to leave very little essential difference between his tragedies and most of his comedies respectively, the tragic element usually preponderates even in plays which cannot be technically classed as tragedies. For the most part these plays fairly correspond to the Attic, which was also the Italian and early Elizabethan, notion of tragicomedy, as resembling tragedies in their outward form and in their principal interest, but containing some comic characters and scenes, and arriving at a 'happy' conclusion. Shirley would appear to have naturally fallen into a preference for this variety of romantic comedy, under the influence of Fletcher and other native, as well as of Spanish, models. In his earliest comedy (*Love Tricks*), which has many marks of youth as well as of scholastic surroundings, and was probably written before he settled in London, he was manifestly copying the Jonsonian comedy of manners, and the *School of Compliment*, which gives its sub-title to the play, is an elaborate humorous device quite after the master's fashion. In his second (*The Brothers*), although he is already trying his hand upon a Spanish plot, and although in some passages the style is already highly ornamented, he had not as yet surely found his proper vein; and in the third (*The Witty Fair One*), of which the action culminates in wild farce, he seems to be on his way back to the extravagance of the native school. But in the far more refined and, in parts, beautiful play of *The Wedding;* in the nobly conceived and finely executed *Grateful Servant;* in those portions at least of *The Changes* which treat a pathetic theme resembling that of its predecessor; and in the bright extravaganza of *The Bird in a Cage*, we have successive examples of the species in which their author excelled. *Hyde Park* in some measure, but far more notably *The Ball*, exhibits a reaction towards the Jonsonian comedy of manners; and *The Gamester* too, though its chief interest is elsewhere, has a realistic background of modern English life. But with the sole unpleasing exception of *The Humorous Courtier*, the remaining comedies of Shirley—*The Young Admiral, The Example, The Opportunity, The Lady of Pleasure, The Royal Master* and *The Constant Maid*—are alike typical of the species of comedy which was most congenial to him, and on his contributions to which, together with his fewer tragedies, his distinctive fame as a standard English dramatist may be said to rest. To his comedies of this class, of which the one here reprinted furnishes a notable example, the observations which follow therefore in especial, though not exclusively, apply.

The Construction of his Comedies.—Shirley has probably been overpraised for the originality of his plots. To speak of his comedies only, and even to waive the question as to whether the resemblances between the main plots of *The Grateful Servant* and *Twelfth Night* are accidental—he expressly claims a Spanish origin for the story of *The Brothers;* the learning of Fitzmaurice-Kelly has traced the plot of *The Young Admiral* to Lope de Vega's *Don*

Lope de Cardona, and that of *The Opportunity* to Tirso de Molina's *El Castigo del Pensèque;* and the most attractive part of the action of *The Royal Master* was, as will be seen, borrowed from Boccaccio. On the other hand, Shirley was incontestably very skilful in the disposition of the materials used by him in the construction of his comedies, and especially in his subordination of the inferior (generally the comic) to the principal interest of the piece. Hence it is rarely difficult to follow without any strain the course of the action in his plays, though invariably made up of at least two, and sometimes, as in *Hyde Park*, and *The Gamester*, of as many as three plots. Ingenious in arrangement and manipulation, he is not particularly careful to avoid self-repetition in the choice of situations and *motifs*. Thus the problem of being in love with two ladies at once meets us both in *The Changes* and in *The Ball;* and his favourite device of a moral *qui pro quo* as well as merely external "shift" (to borrow the Nurse's term in *The Constant Maid*), is illustrated by the chaste Penelope who assumes the part of a wanton lady's maid (*The Witty Fair One*), as well as by the true wife who enacts a *succuba* (*The Grateful Servant*),—in each case *pour le bon motif*. In *The Opportunity* there is a double *qui pro quo;* while in *The Young Admiral* the familiar substitution scheme, which in its crude form is intolerable even in Shakespeare, is for once very charmingly as well as effectively varied.

Shirley's favourite characters are similarly apt to re-appear; and here it would be of interest to speculate on the correspondence or divergence between two artistic ideals and the actual types which came under his ken at the Court of Charles and Henrietta Maria, or in its vicinity. He cherished a strong admiration for Strafford, and we know that when the troubles began they brought out many other examples of the heroism of unselfish loyalty. Shirley may have divined some of these, as we guess them *ex post facto* even from the courtly canvases of Van Dyck. To Shirley the high-minded nobleman or gentleman who sacrifices everything to his duty towards his King was the representative of the truest latter-day chivalry; although the exaggerated form in which the sentiment clothes itself in such plays as *The Grateful Servant* and *The Young Admiral* may be in part due to Spanish influence, and to the un-English sentiment of the equality, or equal insignificance, of all "under the King." But he had other and wider conceptions of true nobility, than are implied either in the Spanish perversion of the principle of loyalty, or in the artificial elaboration of the *punto d'onor*. Passages defining or illustrating Shirley's idea of the true nobleman or gentleman (in the Chaucerian sense of the term) recur in several of his comedies (*Hyde Park, The Ball, The Example*); in one of them a homily on this text brings a would-be sinner to his right mind; in another the noble spirit reveals itself, as in an earlier Lord Kew, beneath the outward habits of the rake. Nor is Shirley afraid of avowing his belief that "honour of blood" is incomplete "without the ornament of knowledge" (*The Lady of Pleasure*). He has an equally lofty conception of "the true lady," whose "beauty spreads over the soul" (*ib.*); but his favourite female type, which he repeatedly introduces, is what must at least be conceded to be a peculiar variety, more familiar to a later age. It may be described as the girl or woman of high spirit, ready to go great lengths in speech and conduct to serve the purpose she has in view, or to give vent to the vitality that is in her; but who remains pure and virtuous. Such are, each in her own way, Penelope in *The Witty Fair One*, Julietta in *Hyde Park*, Lucina in *The Ball*, Jacinta in *The Example*, Celestina in *The Lady of Pleasure*, and (for she may be included), Mrs. Carol in *Hyde Park*, a kind of Beatrix, tamed at last. All these are high comedy figures; and for such Shirley has an unmistakable predilection. Among more conventional types familiar to his comedies may be mentioned his pages, the agile ministers of form or semblance of intrigue (see *The Gamester; The Young Admiral; The Example*); and, perhaps, as remote from one another though probably alike well known to him by experience, the university bumpkin (see *The Lady of Pleasure; The Sisters*) and the compliment-maker, town conversationalist and poetaster (see *Love Tricks; The Humorous Courtier; The Changes*).

His Poetic Style.—Thus, Shirley's comedies show him to have been possessed of more than common instinctive skill, reinforced by a quick use of his exceptional intimacy with the most productive as well as powerful of contemporary dramatic literatures; while he contributed, although in no very signal degree, to the achievements of the English comic drama on its strongest side—characterization. Yet, had he been distinguished by no other qualities, and had he accomplished no other results than these, they would not, so far at least as the evidence of his comedies goes, have entitled him to be ranked among our great dramatic poets of the earlier half of the seventeenth century. His place among his peers he occupies mainly by virtue of a poetic style which by its elevation, wealth, and beauty marks him partner in an inheritance that has fructified in his hands. He was a master in the poetic use of metaphor; and it has been truly said that he was one of those post-Elizabethans— Fletcher being another—to whom the best of the impulse towards poetic imagery noticeable in our drama was communicated after Shakespeare.[1] Yet, figurative and original in the choice of its figures as his diction is, it only exceptionally strains after that kind of effort which we term a conceit; and though he was their contemporary, his poetic style as a rule by no means resembles that of Donne or of other early representatives of the Fantastic School.[2] While his phraseology is often marked by pregnancy and point, yet sheer wit—wit for wit's sake—like that either of Lyly or of Congreve, had no attractions for a writer of his intellectual temperament. As his style was his own, so it had manifestly formed itself without difficulty, and, after being formed, underwent no important modifications during the progress of a long and assiduous literary career. He naturally shrank from any attempt to accentuate its individuality by mannerisms, and showed no anxiety either to improve upon golden traditions, or to force a new silvern departure. Thus ease came to him as a matter of course, and to it were speedily added grace and charm. Moreover, the chosen sphere of his poetic fancy was a world of sun and sweetness. Many other poets—and many English poets among them—have been at home with the flowers of the field and the birds of the greenwood; but none has loved them better than this playwright of the town; and though other phenomena of the natural world (often no doubt

[1] F. I. Carpenter, *Metaphor and Simile in the Minor Elizabethan Drama.*
[2] Cf. Angelina's ridicule of the Scholar's erotic style in *The Sisters;* and cf. Confident Rapture's speeches in *The Example.*

conventional) contribute to suggest the tropes with which he loves to ornament his diction, he derives most of these and of his descriptive touches in general from his favourite trees and flowers and birds. The shadow of the forest, the colour and perfume of rose, marigold and woodbine, the golden sheen of the cornfield, the note of the nightingale and the flight of the birds by land and sea, seem to haunt his pages; and even the stillness of the night presents itself to him as the season when there is

> No whispering but of leaves, on which the breath
> Of heaven plays music to the birds that slumber.

In versification as in diction, no differences of much significance are noticeable between Shirley's earlier and later plays; while in this respect, too, he displays few of those individually distinctive features upon which comparative criticism is entitled to lay stress. He makes one of his characters (in *The Wedding*) declare a preference for "poetical prose" to verse—but it is rhymed verse that is here in question; and there can be no doubt but that rhythmical speech was the form of composition which best commended itself to him. As might be expected from the refined catholicity of his taste, together with his natural predilection for the nearest and fullest, as well as most congenial, example before him, his versification shows a general, but by no means close, resemblance to Fletcher's. It should perhaps be added, that Shirley's blank verse in his earlier plays exhibits a tendency to an excessive use of so-called 'weak endings' (in which the redundant syllable consists of an auxiliary verb, pronoun or the like), and that this transnormal, and by no means effective, habit or trick occasionally reappears in his later work. In general, he is fond of metrical license, whether of earlier or later usage, and is specially addicted to sounding a foot between mute and liquid consonants (*rememb-e-ranced*). But the extremely corrupt condition of their text makes caution very necessary in discussing the metrification of Shirley's plays.

Estimate of " The Royal Master."—The comedy of *The Royal Master* here reprinted, although one of the poet's later works, belongs to a time when he was still in full productivity as a dramatist, and when the presentiment of coming public and personal troubles had not yet arrested the free flow of his fancy. It is thoroughly typical of the dramatic form most congenial to him, and in which he chiefly excelled; and in the conception and treatment of its subject, as well as in manner and style, illustrates not a few of the features adverted to as marking the romantic comedies of this author. The argument is made up of two stories; but so ingeniously and with such seeming ease are they interwoven with one another, that to all intents and purposes they form a single plot. Of these stories the one has a wholly serious interest, rendered intense by the succession of rapid turns in its progress; the other hovers between the pathetic and the humorous, and intermixed with it are for the sake of usage and the groundlings a few rather thinly comic scenes. The principal story, of unknown derivation, is concerned with one of those court intrigues which furnished so many of their dramatic themes to Shirley, Fletcher, Massinger, Webster and other dramatists of their age, and which savour of Italian 'tyranny' in the latter half of the fifteenth and earlier half of the sixteenth century, although the historical original of the 'King of Naples' at whose court the scene of this comedy is laid, lived at least two centuries before. The King, who is a widower, has a sister Theodosia; and for her hand his brother-in-law, the Duke of Florence, is a suitor. Both are favourably inclined towards his suit, but it is opposed with deadly determination by the King's favourite, Montalto, whose ambition aspires to the hand of the Princess for himself. First, he contrives to attract the Duke's fancy to the youthful Domitilla, whom the King had intended to wed the favourite himself. Then, he poisons the Duke's mind against Theodosia, pretending to him that she is contracted to another, and afterwards professing that it is himself with whom she has exchanged vows. But Montalto's wiles are watched by Riviero, a statesman whom he had in former days ousted from the King's favour and as it was believed done to death, but who has now returned in disguise as the Duke's secretary. To him Montalto, in order further to work upon the Duke, asserts the frailty of Theodosia, while seeking to excite her jealousy against the Duke as Domitilla's lover. But Domitilla convinces Theodosia of its causelessness, and after the Duke has accused Theodosia before the King, she nobly vindicates herself to her royal brother of the shameful charge against her. Montalto is plotting the murder of the Duke's secretary, who alone can hold him responsible for the accusation, and he had drawn his dagger at the back of the Duke himself, when a letter from Riviero to the King virtually determines his doom. With much *finesse* the King proposes to him, by way of an extreme favour, to order his temporary arrest, so as to discover his real friends and enemies. Montalto has to walk into the snare with open eyes, and when the test has been applied, he knows, after a moment of delusion, that he is undone. Theodosia and the Duke have found one another; and Montalto's life would pay for his treason, but that it is spared in consideration of Riviero's return.

With this well devised and effectively sustained story of intrigue and counterplot is intertwined the simple romantic tale of the gentle Domitilla's love for the good King. This love springs from the maiden meditation of a guileless heart; though a mere self-delusion, it is at once pleasing and pathetic; and even when it finds itself doomed to disappointment leaves no bitterness behind it. With much tact a natural and satisfactory solution is prepared from the first in the attachment to Domitilla of the lost Riviero's son Octavio, a young courtier whose brightness and buoyancy of spirit are akin to Domitilla's own, and who chivalrously comes forward on her behalf, when the King by testing her virtue applies a painful remedy to her hopeless passion. The coarseness of this last passage—a coarseness which the theatrical adaptation of romance rarely succeeds in altogether avoiding even in times more refined than Shirley's—mars the general effect of the entire episode, the main part of which is distinguished by a kindly humour and even by a certain tenderness of touch.

The Sources in Literature and Nature.—The story of Domitilla and her infatuation is taken from the *Decamerone* where it forms the seventh *novella* of the tenth day, consecrate to examples of that high-mindedness or 'magnificence' of spirit which had so peculiarly strong an attraction for our English poet. The incident is then connected with an historical personage—the Peter of Aragon, who was the first King of his time that held sway in Sicily (from the 'Vespers' of 1282 to his death in 1285), and whose Queen was Constance the daughter of King Manfred. The description, which occurs in the course of Boccaccio's narrative, of Mico of Siena as an excellent *dicitore in rima* of his age, is elsewhere cited as sufficient historical evidence of that personage's literary distinction. The *Decamerone* relates, with its usual graphic simplicity, how Lisa the daughter of Bernardo, a well-to-do Florentine physician settled in Palermo, fell in love with the good King Peter, whom from the window of her father's house she had beheld among his barons on the occasion of a high festival. She never told her love, but concealing it sickened till she seemed near death. It was then that she bethought herself of revealing her irresistible passion to the King before she died; and this desire she with her father's consent entrusted to the accomplished singer and musician Minuccio, whom the King was in the habit of frequently admitting to his presence. Minuccio commissioned the celebrated poet Mico of Siena to write a *canzonetta* expressive of Lisa's love, of her expectancy of death, and of her craving for a sign of recognition before she should pass away. This Minuccio found an opportunity of singing in the presence of the King, who after hearing the song and learning its significance, sent word to the maiden by Minuccio that he would visit her at vesper-time in her father's house. Here the generous kindness of his bearing and his words overcame her anguish, and her desire for death. When he came again, accompanied by his gracious Queen, she willingly agreed, in obedience to his behest, to promise her hand to a suitor of his choice— a gentleman whom he endowed with an estate. At the same time the King declared that henceforth he would be Lisa's knight, and wear her colours in the fray, and this promise in the presence of the Queen he sealed with a single kiss.

This pretty and pathetic story was put into English verse by George Eliot in her poem *How Lisa loved the King* (printed in *The Legend of Jubal, and other Poems*, 1874). Neither the simple theme, nor the light but close-fitting form, suitable rather to the pen of a Leigh Hunt, fitted the great English writer's at once profound and expansive genius; but she treated it with admirable taste and self-restraint, and abstained from any material alteration of the original gracefully avowed at the close of her poem. Was she aware that, many years before, Alfred de Musset had made the same story the subject of one of those dramatic poems in prose, in which he, with rare subtlety, blended the *naïveté* of an earlier age of art with the ironical melancholy of his own poetic genius? *Carmosine* (apparently not printed till 1857, the year of its author's death) is not one of the best known, but far from one of the least charming, of these inimitable water-colours. The changes here introduced leave the story unaltered in substance; but they are signally effective both in accentuating its emotional effects and in softening its primitive asperities; in short, they attest the heightened feeling of the romantic poet and the assured tact of the modern dramatist. The suitor Perdicone who proves fortunate in the end is broken up into two personages, the fatuous courtier Ser Vespasiano and the faithful Perillo; the devoted father, Bernardo, is provided with a foolish spouse, Dame Paque; Minuccio, the agent of the *dénouement*, is invested with the fantastic volubility as well as the instinctive insight of the latter-day troubadour; and above all, Carmosine's broken heart is healed by the womanly sympathy of the high-minded Queen, before the cure is completed by the plain-spoken chivalry of the King in person.

Of the low comedy with which Shirley has here, to a rather slighter extent than is usual with him, diversified the unfolding of his double action, Domitilla's secretary Bombo has almost singly (according to the French expression) to defray the cost. In him the pedant and the booby are humorously mixed, and he makes some honest mirth, though his sallies cannot exactly be described as irresistible. Such as he is, Bombo furnishes a fair, but certainly not more than fair, sample of Shirley's stage fun.

Apart from this rather conventional buffoonery, the characterization in *The Royal Master* is worthy of admiration both for its variety and its discrimination. The *bonhomie* which tempers the dignity of the King, and over which no very dark shadow is cast by his sorrows as a widower, mentioned by him at the beginning and at the end of the play, was probably suggested by the kindly monarch of Boccaccio's *novella;* but a highbred air and a loftiness of soul before which the wiles of cunning collapse distinguish both him and his royal sister, while even her volatile suitor the Duke of Florence is never hurried away into ignobility. Montalto, the chief personage of the action, is drawn with a sure hand and in telling lines—a 'Machiavel' of a subtle and secret sort, versatile in his devices and swift in their execution, while a suitable foil is supplied by the unquestioning servility of his triplet of courtier-creatures. Andrugio, whom at the opening of the play Montalto derides as a dull cipher, proves one of the agents of his ruin. The two most attractive characters of the play, Domitilla and her youthful admirer, Riviero's son Octavio, are such by their real freshness and naturalness; but in the case of each the deeper movements of a loyal and fearless spirit soon reveal themselves under a surface rippled by light-hearted gaiety.

The Royal Master is, even for one of Shirley's romantic comedies, full of passages attesting his love of the beauties of nature, and his practice of ornamenting his poetic diction with metaphors derived from natural objects, or at least from the conventional conception of them. The garden-scene of the second act appropriately enough contains a powerful as well as picturesque passage symbolizing the fate of Theodosia in the ruin spread by a storm over a summer-day; and in the last three acts there is a notable variety of metaphors of the same description, among which may be signalized the striking picture of the comet (IV, i), and that of the fallen forest oak, "the great man's emblem" (V, ii). Theodosia's fair name exposed to suspicion reminds her brother of lovely flowers withered (IV, i); and Montalto's sickening uncertainty in the crisis of his fate is ironically compared by his royal master to the firmness of the rock that defies the insolence of the waves (V, ii). Nor can such passages as these be said to come as a surprise; for in none of his romantic comedies has Shirley more happily sustained the flow of his diction and the harmony of his verse.

Date.—This comedy was licensed by Sir Henry Herbert as Master of the Revels on April 23rd—well omened date—1638. It had been previously performed in Dublin, both in the theatre in Werburgh Street opened in 1635 by Ogilby (see his commendatory verses), and at the Castle before the Lord Deputy, Viscount Wentworth, afterwards Earl of Strafford. The date of its first performance in Ireland is uncertain, as is that of the dedication, written when the play had not yet been 'personated,' and when the

English stage was subject to an interval of silence, on account of a visitation of the plague, known to have terminated by the beginning of October 1637. There is good reason for concluding that Shirley had crossed to assist Ogilby in Dublin early in 1636; unfortunately we remain ignorant of the date of the Prologue to *No Wit to a Woman's*, printed in the 1646 edition of Shirley's *Poems*, where the writer is said to have "two years lived in Dublin."

Previous Editions and the Present Text.—The title of the quarto of 1638, from which the present edition is made, is '*The Royall Master, as it was acted in the New Theatre in Dublin, and before the Right Honorable the Lord Deputie of Ireland, in the Castle. Written by James Shirley. Fas extera quaerere regna.*' It contains no prologue; and Fleay's conjecture, that the *Prologue in Ireland to the Irish Gent* . . . printed in the same volume of Poems was intended for *The Royal Master*, remains unproved. The *Epilogue* is likewise printed in this edition of Shirley's *Poems*, with the title: '*To the never enough honoured E. of St., on New Year's Day at night, after other entertainment,*' and with a different opening line. Since this play has been reprinted but once before, and in a form not easily accessible to the ordinary reader—Vol. IV of the six volume edition of *The Dramatic Works and Poems of Shirley* (with notes by Gifford and additional notes by Dyce), 1833—the General Editor of this series has allowed me to present a modern critical text, although the regulations of the series call for a reproduction of the original quarto. The *dramatis personæ*, and the major part of the stage-directions, are here supplied from Dyce. In the matter of the division of the verse the quarto (Q) has when possible been adhered to; but a certain amount of freedom had to be used in face of a virtually quite arbitrary arrangement; and though Dyce's revision (Dy.), as ever instinct with tact, has been very largely followed, it has been by no means invariably followed, and never where it seems to make insufficient allowance for the fluidity of Shirley's versification.—The commendatory verses in the quarto, by J. Mervyn (two sets), T. I., W. Markham, W. Smith, J. Ogilby and J. Jackson, printed in vol. I of Dyce's *Shirley* with others by F. Butler, D. Cooper and R. Belling, are here without compunction omitted.

A. W. WARD.

THE
ROYALL
MASTER

As it was Acted in the new
Theater in Dublin:

AND

Before the Right Honorable the Lord
Deputie of Ireland, in the Caſtle.

Written by IAMES SHIRLEY.

—Fas extera querere regna

VIGNETTE

LONDON

Printed by T. Cotes, and are to be ſold by John Crooke and Richard
Serger, at the Grayhound or Pauls Church-yard 1638.

DEDICATION.

To the Right Honourable George Earl of Kildare, Baron of Ophalie, and Premier Earl of the Kingdom of Ireland.[1]

My Lord,

It was my happiness, being a stranger in this kingdom,[2] to kiss your lordship's hands, to which your nobleness and my own ambition encouraged me; nor was it without justice to your name, to tender the first-fruits of my observance to your lordship, whom this island acknowledgeth her first active ornament and top-branch of honour. Be pleased now, my most honourable lord, since my affairs in England hasten my departure and prevent my personal attendance, that something of me may be honoured to wait upon you in my absence—this poem. 'Tis new, and never yet personated, but expected with the first, when the English stage shall be recovered from her long silence, and her now languishing scene[3] changed into a welcome return of wits and men. And when, by the favour of the winds and sea, I salute my country again, I shall report a story of the Irish honour,[4] and hold myself not meanly fortunate to have been written and received

The humblest of your lordship's servants

JAMES SHIRLEY.

[1] George Fitzgerald, sixteenth Earl of Kildare, born 1611; succeeded to peerage in 1620; educated at Christ Church, Oxford; was much under the influence of the Earl of Cork to whom he had been transferred as ward and whose daughter he afterwards married. In 1641 he sided with the leaders of the Protestant party in Ireland, and was appointed Colonel of an English foot regiment there. He was one of the sureties of Glamorgan on his liberation from prison, but afterwards acted as governor of Dublin under the Westminster Parliament. He died in 1660.

[2] Ireland.

[3] This may refer, either to the visitation of the plague, or to the beginning of the iron age of the English theatre, which Fleay reckons from 1637 to the present day.

[4] Shirley possibly means to insinuate that Kildare had conferred special lustre upon the Irish peerage—perhaps by rebuilding the castle of his ancestors at Maynooth.

[The Persons of the Play.

KING OF NAPLES.
DUKE OF FLORENCE, *suitor to* THEODOSIA.
MONTALTO, *the* King's *favourite*.
RIVIERO, *a nobleman banished the court, but returned in disguise as the*
    Duke's *secretary, under the name of* PHILOBERTO.
OCTAVIO, *a young courtier, son of* RIVIERO.
ANDRUGIO, *a courtier, friend to* RIVIERO.
GUIDO,
ALOISIO, } *attendants in the court, and creatures of* MONTALTO.
ALEXIO,
BOMBO, *secretary to* DOMITILLA.
IACOMO, } *servants of* SIMPHOROSA.
PIETRO,
Courtiers, petitioners, servants, attendants, etc.
THEODOSIA, *the* King's *sister.*
SIMPHOROSA, *a noble widow.*
DOMITILLA, *her daughter.*
Ladies *attending* THEODOSIA.

THE SCENE: NAPLES, and SIMPHOROSA'S COUNTRY–HOUSE.[1]]

[1] Supplied from Dy.; see Critical Essay, above.

Act I. Scene I. *Naples. The Palace.*

Enter King of Naples, Duke of Florence, Montalto, Octavio, Riviero, Andrugio, Guido, Aloisio *and* Alexio.

Duke. You're great in all that's good.

King.　　　　　　You shew the bounty
　　Of your opinion; my extent [1] in all things
　　Is but to bid you welcome. You'd a sister,
　　The envy of the angels while she lived　　　　　　5
　　Our queen, now made their blest companion.
　　Should we exempt those fair deserts dwell in you, [2]
　　So much we owe her memory.

Duke.　　　　　　　　　Pray, no more!

Riv. [*to* Andrugio]. [3] We must not be too open, truest friend;　10
　　Thy bosom is my sanctuary.

Andr.　　　　　　　When it leaves
　　To be religious for [4] thy safety, may it
　　By an angry flame from heaven be turned to ashes!

Duke. Your nature is too soft; let not the mention　　15
　　Of her that was my sister and your queen
　　Beget another sigh! She was long since blest,
　　Cesaria is in heaven; we're met for joys.
　　You were not framed to be her monument;
　　Sleep let her ashes in the urn contains them!　　20

King. I've done.

　　　　　　Enter Theodosia *and* Ladies.

Duke. Your sister.

King.　　　　　[This] is all the treasure

---

[1] *Query*, intent? But the meaning may be 'the utmost of my purpose.' Dy.

[2] Apart from those fair deserts which dwell in you. Shirley is very fond of the ellipsis of the relative.

[3] Dy.'s hint should not be lost sight of, that in this scene the characters on the stage are separated into little groups.　　　[4] ceases to be devoted to.

Is left me, sir, but cannot be too rich
For your acceptance.   25
Duke.   All my wealth is summed
When she does smile upon me, and her cháracter [1]
In the full glory, when she's named your sister.—
Are you not weary of a guest, dear madam?
Am I still welcome?   30
Theo. ·   Sir, we are
All honour'd in your presence, and though not high
T' [2] your merit, yet your entertainment is
As full of love, as nature can express
To a twin brother; more, I dare presume   35
You shall accuse yourself, if you be less,
A prince in Naples by free use of power
Than your own Florence.
Duke.   Madam, you must be
Less fair and powerful in tongue, if you   40
Expect I should be still a prince; and yet
My ambition will be high, and glorious [3]
Enough to be receiv'd your grace's servant,
For whom I should account my age no travel,
To have my pilgrimage rewarded with   45
Your fair eyes, madam, able to create
Another life and spirit in old nature.
King. How does Montalto like the duke?
Mont. Sir, Naples cannot study an addition [4]
Of fame, beyond what this alliance will   50
Deserve in future story; the excess
Of what is good, nay, excellent in him
Would stock a barren province.
King.   'Tis our happiness.
Mont. [*aside*]. But 'tis not mine; for, though I thus disguise   55

---

[1] description.
[2] On the level of. The contorted string of compliments which follows is quite
in the style of Jacobean and Caroline fine letter-writing. The frequency of weak
endings to the lines is noticeable.
[3] exultant.   [4] title.

My face and tongue, my heart is my own friend,
And cannot wish my ambition supplanted
By any smooth-chinn'd prince alive.—My lords—
Andr. Look how they flock, and fawn upon his greatness!
These are his creatures, by his power placed   60
So near about the king, he can hear nothing
Of his great favourite but what their flattery
And partial tongues convey into his ear.
Riv. Pity, so sweet a nature as the king's
Should be abused by parasites! But I may   65
In time dissolve these court mists that so long
Have hung upon't, and render the king's eyes
Free to distinguish objects, if there be
No witchcraft exercised [1] upon his senses.
First Lady [*to* OCTAVIO]. My lord, you're very pleasant.   70
Oct.   Is it not
Becoming the discretion of a young courtier
To observe times and methods? And when, madam,
Are you for this match?
First Lady.   What, my lord?   75
Oct.   You would not
Be sad at heart to sleep with such a bedfellow
As the duke is?
Second Lady.   How, my lord?
Oct.   Provided   80
Matrimony were not far off; yet, without it,
There are some ladies would excuse their modesty,
And meet, and thank their fate at all adventures,
If no worse man would make their husband of
The honourable order of the night-cap. [2]   85
First Lady. When will *you* marry, my lord?
Oct.   [I?] I'm young;
Yet, when I'm ripe to grapple with a maidenhead,
The lord Montalto, the great court patron,

---

[1] Dy.'s conjecture for the easily explicable misprint of Q, 'exorcised.'
[2] 'Therefore 'tis fit the city, wise men say, Should have a cap called cornucopia.'
R. Davenport, *The City Night-Cap* (licensed 1624, printed 1661), Act IV.

Will help me to a wife.   90
Second Lady.   You're bound to his lordship.
Oct. And so I am, madam, if you knew all.
     I've many obligations to his honour,
     But there is one writ here, whose memory
     Will keep my soul awake.   95
King. Andrugio!
Gui. [*to* MONTALTO]. I do not like their conference.
Mont. 'Las! He has no employment in the State;
     He waits like a dull cipher, and I have
     My spies upon him; if I find him busy,   100
     My power with the king shall soon transplant him,
     Or force him, like Riviero—his old friend,
     But of more brain and faction—to give up
     His ghost abroad.
Aloi.   'Twas just for your own safety.[1]   105
Mont. This is an honest, easy nobleman,
     Allow'd to wear some court formality,
     Walk on the terrace, pick his teeth, and stroke,
     Upon a festival, some golden sentence
     Out of his beard, for which the guard admire him   110
     And cry him up a statesman;[2] he's sent off—
     When he is troublesome, to a phlégmatic clime,
     A dull ambassador.—No! that duke, Guido,
     Is all my fear; but I've contrivèd something
     May rectify my fate.   115
Duke [*to* THEODOSIA].   How much you honour me!
     But you might spare all other entertainments
     And bravery of court; they may affect
     My eyes with wonder, and oblige my just
     Acknowledgement; but all their glories, met   120
     Into one height, hold no proportion
     To inflame my heart, or more express my welcome,

---

[1] Dy. places a comma between 'just' and 'for.'   But the sense is good either way.

[2] 'The Spaniard reserves all passion To express his feeling in occurrences Of State; when in discourse, his tooth-pick still Is his parenthesis.' Shirley, *The Humorous Courtier*, IV, ii.

Than this your free grace, madam, and those hopes
That bless my imagination from your favour.
Theo. I am but what my brother's love and virtue 125
  Will make me; but there's nothing that can move
  With his consent I shall not fly to obey.
Mont. [*to* ALOISIO]. I had rather feed upon his heart.[1]
  [*To the* King.] You promis'd, sir, the duke to hunt this morn-
    ing.
King. I had forgot.—[*To the* Duke.] Will you be pleas'd to try 130
  The pleasures of the forest?[2]
Duke.   I'll attend.
King. Theodosia, you're not for that exercise.—
  Guido! [*Whispers to* Guido, *who goes out.*]
Theo.   I wish all pleasures wait upon you! 135
  My heart must covet your return.
Duke.   And mine,
  To dwell for ever in so fair a bosom.
King. To horse! the morning wastes.
              [*Exeunt all but* MONTALTO, ANDRUGIO, OCTAVIO
                            and RIVIERO.
Mont.   Some policy 140
  Must cure this fear; my bold resolves are fix'd.
  I have made some attempts, and courted her;
  But she has not understood me. I must work
  My countermine, and scatter into air
  His swelling hopes.—Octavio! [*Exit.*   145
Oct.   My good lord.—
            [*As he is going out,* ANDRUGIO *prevents him.*
Andr. Sir, I present this gentleman to kiss
  Your hand; he's the duke's secretary,
  A Roman born, and has a great ambition
  To be known to you, for your father's sake, 150
  With whom he did converse in Rome, and honour,[3]
  Till death concluded their acquaintance.

---

[1] This appears to be in reply to some words from Aloisio, which may, as Dy.
thinks, have dropped out of the text.
[2] Q, 'a forest.'   [3] A zeugma.

Oct.   Sir,
　　Your love and knowledge of my father will
　　Deserve you should be welcome of his son.   155
Riv. He made me his companion many years;
　　No brothers were more chained in their affections.
　　He did impart much of his bosom [1] to me.
Oct. You knew why he left Naples?
Riv.   He did trust me   160
　　With the cause, my lord, and ev'ry circumstance,—
　　The King's minority and Montalto's power,
　　'Gainst which no innocence could plead in Naples.
Andr. Not too loud, sir; you may be heard.
Riv. Your pardon!   165
Oct.   Why should truth
　　Faint at the name of greatness! This colossus,[2]
　　Montalto, is but mortal sure; time has
　　Forgot to use his wings, or nature is
　　Unwilling I should grow to write full man,   170
　　To take revenge upon that politician,[3]
　　Our Prótean favourite.
Riv.   It is my wonder,
　　The king so strangely should continue this
　　Affection to Montalto.   175
Oct.   There's some magic in't.
Riv. Dare none complain?
Andr.   His engines are so plac'd,
　　None can approach the king's ear, at which hang
　　So many flatt'rers to infect it with   180
　　Montalto's praise.
Riv.   Pray give me, sir, this boldness:
　　He that doth lift an axe to strike the root
　　Of any family, cannot be without

---

[1] confidence. A favourite use of Shirley's.

[2] Cf. *Julius Cæsar*, I, ii, 136.

[3] The significance of the term is best illustrated by its use in the title of one of Shirley's tragedies. 'Policy' is the catch-word of Marlowe's *Jew of Malta*, to which 'Machiavel' speaks the prologue. In IV, i, below, the Duke of Florence calls Montalto 'dear Machiavel.'

A thought to wound the branches. You were left,   185
By computation, but an infant, when
Your father's discontents and the strong faction
Of this Montalto made him fórsake Naples,
Which added to your mother's death, the guard
And comforts of your life were taken from you.   190
Having expressed this malice to your father,
A thousand ways he might have sent you to
Another world, and shaken [1] off all fear
Of revenge. How comes it that you live
And visit, sir, the palace with this freedom?   195

Oct. My lord Andrugio's knowledge of you, sir,
Is my assurance of your faith.

Andr.   I'll give
You reasons, at some opportunity,
Not to repent your confidence.   200

Oct.   You have
Supplied my father in your care of me.
I live; why, I am this great lord's favourite,
Courted; his creatures are my honours;
Companion to his pleasures. [2]   205

Riv.   I observ'd
Some gestures very loving to your lordship.

Oct. The king himself, for his sake, gracing me
With title of his bed-chamber.

Riv. [*aside to* ANDR.] 'Tis strange!   210
This news will cool my resolution.

Andr. 'Tis truth; he doth engage him to all favours.

Riv. 'Tis not impossible he may be honest—

Oct. And mean so; but my soul cannot be bribed

---

[1] Dy.'s conjecture for Q, 'taken.'

[2] Dy. has put this speech into better syntactical order by transposing the clauses
in the last three lines, thus:
  Why I am this great lord's [chief] favourite
  Companion to his pleasures; I live courted,
  His creatures are my honours.
Riviero's speech, however, seems to refer to the last clause of the speech as printed
in Q.—Are my honours = wait upon me, as nobles attend a sovereign. Cf. the use of
the term 'honour' in the Dedication, *ante.*

So easily to prostrate my own justice, 215
And leave my father's ashes unrevenged,
Which in my ears groan from beneath the marble,
To keep my thoughts awake.

Andr. We may suspect
This is to catch applause—a trick to win 220
Upon the people, who did love Riviero
And mourn his fate.

Oct. However, I have art
To keep my breast close, and accept his flatt'ries;
Can compliment,[1] and with officious bend 225
Thank his high favours, wear a face of mirth
And prattle with the ladies, as if all
The business I came into the world for
Were but to talk and dance and go a feasting.

Riv. I must presume you want no counsel from 230
My lord, who loved your father, how to manage
Yourself to best advantage of your fame
And honour. Unto both I am a servant.

Andr. My lord Montalto may expect you, sir.

Riv. It is not safe we be observed too much. 235

Oct. [*to* ANDRUGIO]. My lord, you have begun a favour by
The acquaintance of this gentleman; I will
Hope to salute him often by your means.—
[*To* RIVIERO.] You shall not meet a heart more prompt to bid
You welcome, sir. 240

Riv. You too much grace your servant;
I shall present a trouble.

Oct. Come, my lord! [*Exeunt* ANDRUGIO *and* OCTAVIO.

Riv. Montalto's change hath staggered me already.
These favours may be hearty [2] to Octavio, 245
And arguments of penitence. I'll observe,
And sift his close heart; if it prove unsound.
He whets revenge to make the deeper wound. [*Exit.*

[1] This word, always spelt 'complement' in Q is a favourite with Shirley. 'The School of Compliment' is the sub-title of his earliest comedy *Love-tricks*, referring to the scene where a burlesque academy of fine and polite speech is introduced.
[2] sincere.

Act I.　Scene II.　*Simphorosa's Country-house.*

Enter GUIDO, *and* BOMBO *with a book.*

Gui. I would speak with your lady, sir.
Bom. You may.
Gui. Direct me.
Bom. With which of my ladies?
Gui. With both, or one.　　　　　　　　　　　　　　5
Bom. I serve the daughter.
Gui. I would speak with her.
Bom. She is—I know not where.
Gui. What coxcomb's this?

Enter IACOMO.

Gui.　　　　　　　　　　Dost hear, friend? I would speak
　　With my lady Simphorosa.[1]　　　　　　　11
Iac. This way, an't [2] please your lordship.
Gui. Stay; prithee, what fellow's that?
Iac. A servant of my lady's.
Gui. Is he mad?　　　　　　　　　　　　　15
Iac. A little fantastic, but very harmless,
　　And makes my ladies merry.　My young madam,
　　Domitilla, calls him her secretary, for sport
　　And wonder of his good parts.
Gui. What are they?　　　　　　　　　　　20
Iac. He can neither write nor read.
Gui. An excellent secretary!
Iac. But he has been much given
　　To reading, till much poring night and day,
　　And defying spectacles, made him book-blind.[3]　　25
　　He walks and thinks he is wise, and talks upon
　　His old stock.
Gui. Prithee, acquaint my lady! [*Exit* IACOMO.] I' the mean time

---

[1] Printed in Q as prose, for which it was perhaps intended.
[2] Q, 'and.'
[3] Dy.'s inversion of the two clauses as printed in Q.

I'll have more dialogue with him.—[*To* Bombo.] Save you, sir!

Bom. Save yourself, sir; you are, I take't, a courtier.   30

Gui. And you my lady's secretary.

Bom. I am so.

Gui. I hear you are an understanding secretary.

Bom. 'Tis so; I am. How came you by that knowledge?

Gui. We have your fame at court, sir.   35

Bom.   Can you read?

Gui. I hear you cannot.

Bom. Right.

Gui.   Nor write.

Bom.   'Tis true.   40

Gui. What make you with a book? Ha! this is Euclid.

Bom. Euclid? It may be so.

Gui.   Why, these are mathematics.

Bom. I have a chest full of them, in my custody;

　　They were my old lord's, gray when I took charge of 'em,   45

　　But now look spruce and young; there's something in them.

Gui. What, in the name of ignorance, dost thou do with 'em?

Bom. I'm excellent at turning over leaves,[1]

　　By which I keep the worms away—

Gui.   Most learnedly!   50

Bom. I learnt it of my lady's chaplain, sir;

　　Men are not always bound to understand

　　Their library.—But, to omit learning,

　　Not now considered by wise men, what is

　　Your business here, I pray?   55

Gui.   It does concern

　　Yourself. The king has heard of your good parts.

Bom. Sir, as you love me, say you saw me not!

　　I knew I should one time or other be   59

　　Found out for State employments.—Here's my lady! [*Going.*

---

[1] —'my bokes I turne and wynde For all is in them, and no thynge in my mynde.'
See 'Inprofytable bokes', the first section of Barclay's *Ship of Fools*, with which a
man so well-read in our older literature is very likely to have been acquainted.
The touch about the clergyman is not wanting in Barclay; in the woodcut 'the
first fole of the hole navy', who wields a large feather-brush, also wears a fine pair
of spectacles.

Enter SIMPHOROSA *and* DOMITILLA.

I must obscure myself. [GUIDO *speaks apart to* SIMPHOROSA.
Dom.   Why, how now, secretary!
    Whither so fast?
Bom.   You little think—
Dom.   What, prithee?   65
Bom. Nor ever would believe—but 'tis not my fault—
    If the king come in person, I'll not be seen.
Dom. The king!
Bom.   Few words![1] There's one, I know him not,
    Is little better than a spy upon me;   70
    If you look not to me, I'm gone.   [*Exit.*
Dom.   So it seems.
Simph. How? Dine today with us?
Gui.   Such is his royal pleasure.
    He is now hunting with the duke, whom he   75
    Intends to make your guest too.
Simph. My lord, I am not used to entertainments;
    Nor is my house fit for so great a presence.
    To avoid a storm, they might [perchance][2] obey
    Necessity, and take it for some shelter;   80
    But in so calm a day—
Gui.   Madam, although
    You please to undervalue what's your own,
    The king despairs not you will bid him welcome.
    You have no narrow dwelling, and he knows   85
    Your heart is spacious like your fortunes, madam.
    Princes do honour, when they come upon
    Their subjects' invitation; but they love
    Where they invite themselves.[3]

---

[1] This is the Spanish *pocas palabras.* Shirley was fond of Spanish locutions.
See *The Humorous Courtier,* IV, ii (where occurs the opposite *hablar muchas palabras*
abbreviated into *palabras*). Cf. *Much Ado about Nothing,* III, v, and Christopher
Sly's *paucas pallabris* at the beginning of the Induction of *The Taming of the
Shrew.*

[2] Suggested by Dy. to make up the verse.

[3] The first suggestion to Domitilla of the passionate fancy which takes hold of

Simph.   My duty is to   90
  Meet that interpretation though the news
  Come unexpected; now it will, my lord,
  Become me to be thrifty of the minutes,
  Their persons being so near. You will excuse,
  If so short summons do expect my care   95
  To entertain them. My good lord, you've honoured me.
Gui. 'Tis service I am bound to.   [*Exit* SIMPHOROSA.
Dom.   Pray, my lord,
  In your opinion, what should move the king
  To invite himself our guest, and bring the duke   100
  Along with him? He used not to retire
  From hunting with this ceremony.
Gui.   Princes
  Are like the winds, and not to be examined,
  Where they will breathe their favours.   105
Dom.   'Tis confessed
  An honour to us, and I hope you'll pardon
  A woman's curiosity.
Gui.   Shall I
  Deliver my opinion? While the king   110
  In entertainment of the duke is shewing
  The pleasures and the glories of his kingdom,
  He cannot hide that which his Naples boasteth
  Her greatest ornament,—your beauty, madam.
Dom. I thank your lordship; I may now believe   115
  The court's removing hither. Yet this language
  Might do you service to some other lady,
  And I release it willingly. Your compliments
  I know, my lord, are much the worse for wearing.[1]
Gui. You rather will believe yourself worth praise   120
  Than hear it. Though we call it modesty,
  It grows from something like a woman's pride;

---

her.—The sentiment of the last clause of Guido's speech was not always duly appreciated by the subjects thus honoured by Queen Elizabeth and King James I.

  [1] Q, 'much worse for wearing.' Dy., unnecessarily: '[not] much worse for wearing.'

But it becomes you.—Madam, I take leave;
My service to your noble lady mother.
Dom. Mine shall attend your lordship.   125

    [*Exit* GUIDO. *Re-enter* SIMPHOROSA.

Simph.   Now, Domitilla!
 Is my lord gone?
Dom.   Yes, madam.
Simph.   I expected not
 These guests today; they'll take us unprepared.   130
Dom. Not, with our hearts to serve them; and their goodness
 Will éxcuse other want.
Simph.   I know not, daughter,
 But I could wish rather to enjoy ourselves,— [1]
 Not for the cost; those thoughts are still beneath me.   135
Dom. You have no cause to fear, I hope? You're troubled. [2]
Simph. For thy sake, Domitilla.
Dom.   Mine, dear madam!
Simph. It was for thee I chose this quiet life
 Upon thy father's death, and left the court.   140
 Thou'rt all my care, sole heir to all my fortunes
 Which I should see unwillingly bestowed
 On some gay prodigal—
Dom.   I cannot reach
 Your meaning.   145
Simph.   By some hasty marriage.
Dom. You'd have me live a virgin;—a less fortune
 Would serve me for a nun.
Simph.   'Tis not my thought.
 Thou'rt young and fair, [Domitilla,] [3] and though I do not 150
 Suspect thy mind, thus far bred up to virtue,
 I would not have it tempted, but reserved
 For a most noble choice, wherein should meet
 My care and your obedience.
Dom.   You're my mother,   155

[1] that we might be left to ourselves.
[2] Dy.'s emendation of Q, 'You have cause to fear I hope y'are troubled.'
[3] Inserted by Dy., for the sake of the metre.

And have so far by your example taught me,
I shall not need the precepts of your virtue.
And let no thought of me take from your cheerfulness
To entertain the king! We owe him duty,
And that charm will not hurt us.   160
Simph.   This does please me.
Dom. It shall be still my study.
Simph.   I must see
How they prepare; things may want method else.

[*Exit* SIMPHOROSA; *enter* OCTAVIO.

Oct. I kiss your fair hand, madam Domitilla.   165
The king and duke, and all the jolly hunters,
With appetites as fierce as their own hounds,
Will be here presently.
Dom.   I hope they will not
Devour us, my good lord.   170
Oct.   But I would sit and feast,
And feed mine eyes with Domitilla's beauty.[1]
Dom. So, my lord!—Here was a gentleman,
You could not choose but meet him, spake your dialect.
I have forgot his name, but he was some   175
Great lord.
Oct.   Fie! what an ignorance you live in,
Not to be perfect in a great lord's name!
There are few ladies live with us but know
The very pages. Leave this darkness, madam,   180
And shine in your own sphere, where ev'ry star
Hath his due adoration!
Dom.   Where?
Oct.   The court.
Confine such beauty to a country-house!   185
Live among hinds and thick-skinn'd fellows, that
Make faces and will hop a furlong back
To find the t'other leg [2] they threw away
To shew their reverence! with things that squat

---

[1] Line is divided in Q.
[2] As in the common phrase: 'to make a leg.'

When they shall make a curtsey! To court, madam,   190
And live not thus—for shame!—the second [1] part
Of a fond anchorite!   We can distinguish
Of beauty there, and wonder without spectacles;
Write volumes of your praise, and tell the world,
How envious diamonds, 'cause they could not   195
Reach to the lustre of your eyes, dissolved
To angry tears; the roses droop, and gath'ring
Their leaves together, seem to chide their blushes
That they must yield your cheek the victory;
The lilies, when they're censur'd for comparing   200
With your more clear and native purity,
Want white to do their penance in.
Dom.   So, so!
   Have you done now, my young poetic lord?
Oct. There will be no end, madam, of your praises.   205
Dom. And to no end you have spent all this breath.
   Allow all this were wit,—that some did think us
   The creatures they commend (and those whom love
   Hath curs'd into idolatry and verse
   May perhaps do [2] so)—we do know ourselves   210
   That we are no such things,—
Oct.   Is't possible?
Dom. And laugh at your chimæras.
Oct.   You're the wiser.
Dom. If this be your court-practice, let me dwell   215
   With truth and plain simplicity! [3]
Oct.   If I
   Might have my choice, I would live with you, madam,
   A neighbour to this innocence.—Your mother!

Re-enter SIMPHOROSA.

Simph. The king is come already.   220

---

[1] second-rate.   [2] Dy.'s emendation of Q, 'die.'
[3] P. Reyher, *Les Masques Anglais*, p. 233, compares with this attack on the
petty erotic parts that in *The Witty Fair One*, I, iii, and the variation in *The
Sisters*, IV, ii.

Enter King, Duke, Montalto, Guido, Aloisio, Alexio
and Courtiers.

King.   Madam, though you are
So unkind as not to see the court sometime,
The court is come to visit you.
Simph.   You have
Humbled yourself too much, to do us honour.   225
King [*introducing* Duke]. The Duke of Florence.
Simph.   'Tis a blessing that
My roof can boast so great a guest.
King [*introducing* Domitilla *to* Duke]. Her daughter,
Worth your salute.   230
Duke.   She's worth a world.—[*To Montalto.*] My lord,
What is that lady's name?
Mont.   In this you most
Appear a stranger [, sir] [1]; she is the glory
Of Naples for her person and her virtues,   235
That dwell in this obscure place, like the shrine
Of some great saint to which devotion
From several parts brings daily men like pilgrims.
Duke. Her name?
Mont. She is wit, beauty, chastity, and all   240
That can make woman lovely to man's soul;
So far from the capacity of ill,
That virtues in all other of her sex,
Like stains, but set off [2] her perfection;
And when is named all goodness in her titles,   245
The ornament, nay, glory of them all,
Is Domitilla, sir. [3]
Duke.   You speak her high,
And I may guess by your description,
My lord, this lady hath another name: 250
She is your mistress. [4]

---

[1] Inserted by Dy. for the sake of the verse.   [2] Q, 'sit of.'
[3] There seems no obscurity in this: the very best thing about her is herself; none
but herself can be her parallel.
[4] 'Mistress,' as the correlative of 'servant,'—the lady of your affections.   So in

Mont. Not mine; she was created for some prince,
　　And can, beside her virtues, bring a fortune
　　Worth his embrace.
Duke.　　　　　　　What charms are in her looks!　255
Mont. [*aside*]. Are you there, duke?　This meeting was my project;
　　ʼThings may succeed to my ambition,
　　If I do noose your highness.
Simph.　　　　　　　Please your majesty—
King. All things must please here.　　　　　260
Duke.　　　　　　I follow, sir.
Simph. This is a grace I ever must be proud of.　　[*Exeunt.*

Act II. Scene I. *The Same.*

Enter Bombo *with a book, and* Iacomo.

Bom. Have they almost dined?　Stay, stay a little!
Iac. The last course is oʼ the table.
　　Why donʼt you wait? [1]
Bom.　　　　　That were a way indeed
　　To be discovered!　No, the king shall pardon me;　5
　　He has not seen me yet, for all his cunning.
Iac. Whom do you mean?
Bom.　　　　　The king.　Thouʼrt ignorant;
　　Iʼll tell thee after dinner.　Iʼ the mean time,
　　Direct a wandʼring bottle of wine this way,　10
　　And let me alone!　Though I appear not inʼt,
　　I may have a humour to make a masque, if they
　　Stay supper.
Iac.　　　　Thou make a masque?
Bom. I do not say Iʼll write one, for I have not　15
　　My writing tongue, though I could once have read;
　　But I can give, if need be, the design,

The Lady of Pleasure, V, i: ʻYour sex doth hold it no dishonour To become mistress to a noble servant In the now court Platonic way.ʼ—Cf. the Kingʼs speech to Domitilla, *infra*, II, 1, 191–192.
[1] Why are you not in attendance?

Make work among the deal boards, and perhaps
Can teach them as good language as another
Of competent ignorance. Things go not now   20
By learning; I have read, 'tis but to bring
Some pretty impossibilities, for anti-masques,
A little sense and wit disposed with thrift,
With here and there monsters to make them laugh;
For the grand business, to have Mercury   25
Or Venus' dandiprat, to usher in
Some of the gods, that are good fellows, dancing,
Or goddesses; and now and then a song,
To fill a gap; a thousand crowns, perhaps,
For him that made it,—and there's all the wit.   30

Iac. [The wit?] In what?
Bom.   In getting of the money. [1]
Iac. You're witty, signior Bombo. To advance

---

[1] This rather notable passage must be looked upon as a partisan protest, no
doubt honest, and in a sense even generous. Shirley professed himself a follower
of Ben Jonson, though they had not really much in common. (See the dedication
of *The Grateful Servant*.) And (see *Love's Cruelty*, II, ii) he expressly praises the
verse of a masque supposed to be presented in Ferrarese surroundings, as 'speaking
the soul of the immortal English Jonson.' His own masques and entertainments
vary in type; but he seems to have thought it his duty, in accordance no doubt
with the general bent of his genius, to break a lance on behalf of the poetic masque,
as represented by Jonson, against that of which 'painting and carpentry were the
soul,' and which was inevitably fathered upon the professional activity of Inigo
Jones. Jonson's last entertainment of the masque species was originally produced
in 1633; but no masque of his was performed at Court after *Chloridia*, which though
not printed till 1631 is stated to have been presented by the Queen and her ladies
as early as Shrovetide 1630. It was a failure, and is said to have been the occasion
of Jonson's celebrated quarrel with Inigo Jones. This sufficiently explains the references in the text to 'deal boards' and to 'things not going now by learning.' The
device of 'anti-masques' (a term probably corrupted from *antic*-masques, since
the main feature of these episodes consisted of dances generally grotesque and mostly
performed by hired actors) was largely adopted by Jonson himself, whom it particularly suited.—The reference to gods and goddesses can hardly have been intended for the classically-minded Daniel, whose *Vision of the Twelve Goddesses*
had been printed as far back as 1604. Moreover, Venus appears there without her
'dandiprat' (viz. a juvenile attendant of the *Gavroche* type; in which sense it is
applied to Heuresis, Phantastes' page, in the academical drama *Lingua*, printed
in 1607, but probably produced before the death of Queen Elizabeth).—The final
insinuation as to profits has no special application which seems traceable to the
date of *The Royal Master*. On Shirley's own masques see Critical Essay.

The muse, I'll fetch [the] [1] bottle that you talk'd of.

Bom. If there be a superfluous pheasant, it   35
　　Will quell my hunger for a time. I hear
　　Intelligence of an olio; [2] if any
　　Such things may be recovered from the courtiers,
　　That have keen appetites upon hunting-dinners,
　　You shall not [3] need to enquire much after me: 40
　　I shall be hereabouts. [*Exit* IACOMO, *and re-enters with a flask.*]
　　Why, thou hast wings!

Iac. A bottle of rich wine.

Bom.　　　　　　　　　　Thou wert always honest.

Iac. There's asking for my lady's secretary.   45

Bom. I knew't; I am not here.
　　Do they enquire already? Come, I'll pledge thee.　[*Drinks.*
　　What wilt thou say, if somebody be sent for
　　To court?

Iac.　　　　　　I'll drink somebody's health.　　[*Drinks.* 50

Bom. Thou'rt a good fellow, and this courtesy
　　Shall be remembered.

[*A call within.*]　　　　　Iacomo!

Iac.　　　　　　　　　　I'm called.

Bom. Leave, leave your wicker, [4] friend; we'll drink a cup   55
　　When thou art gone. [*Exit* IACOMO, BOMBO *drinks.*]　'Tis
　　very excellent wine.
　　And now I have a stomach like an edge-tool;—
　　But no good comes of idleness. T'other cup!　[*Drinks.*
　　The bottle grows light-headed. How now, friend!   60
　　No dish of meat appear? Nothing to shew
　　The kitchen and the wine-cellar are friends?
　　I would the cook were roasted!—

[1] So Dy. Q, 'a'.
[2] Another form of the Spanish *olla* (hotchpotch).
[3] In Q, Bombo uses the forms 'shannot' and 'wonnot'; but so do his superiors
in the play.
[4] wicker-bottle.

[*Re-enter* IACOMO *with a dish of meat, and* PIETRO *with a flask.*

                              Honest Iacomo!

I was thinking of a brace of cocks just as you came.   65
Iac. I have retriev'd a covey of partridge [1] for you.
Piet. And I a cup of Greek wine. Here's to thee!   [*Drinks.*
Bom. I understand Greek wine; I'll lose no time.   [*Drinks.*
Iac. What's this? A book?
Bom.   No; 'tis my learnèd trencher,   70
Which scholars sometimes eat; [*lays the meat on the cover of the*
                                       book.
         Euclid they call it.
In my opinion, this wing and leg
Is worth all bodies mathematical.
Now let's dispute in Greek! To the king's health! [*Drinks.* 75
Piet.   To me?
I'll pledge.   [*Drinks.*
Iac.   It shall go round.
Bom.   And why d'ye think, my friend,
The king came hither with the duke?   80
Piet.   To dine.
Bom. Thy brains are in thy guts; you shall hear more.
What's this?
Iac.   Potato, bully.
Bom. A cup of wine to clear the passage! [*Drinks.*] So.   85
Here is, as they say, Latin; here is Greek;
And here's, for aught I know, an Hebrew root,
Most learnedly met together.
Iac.   He'll be drunk presently.
Bom. Bottle, in battle 'ray! Present! give fire!   [*Drinks.* 90
So! As you were! [*Sets down the flask.*]—Have they good
    stomachs, [2] Iacomo?
How feeds the king?
Iac.   He was very pleasant with your lady;
But the duke feeds upon her looks.   95

---

[1] Plural, as still used by Pope ('All Worldly's hens, nay, partridge, sent to Town').
[2] appetites.

Bom.　　　　　　　　　　　　My lady's health!
　My lady, little Domitilla's health!　　　　　[*Drinks.*
Piet.　　　　　　　　　　　Well said!—
　About, about! [1]
Bom.　　　　　I am about another,　　　　　　100
　To our rev'rend lady, Simphorosa! [*Drinks.*]—So, so!
　This wine, they say, will make us see things double;
　Here is but one leg visible.—Well, for this favour,
　Gentlemen, if I be forced to live in court,
　I'll make you all, in time.—Who can write　　105
　Or read among you?
Both.　　　　　　None, none; we scorn it.
Bom. You shall have all preferment; trust to me,
　And mark my steps! Here's to the courteous drinker! [*Drinks.*
　Now do I find a noble constitution in me;　　　110
　Now could I leap—would there were [2] any living lady
　In my way now!
Iac.　　　　　　Away! the lords are risen.
Bom. The lords do rise and fall.
Piet.　　　　He's paid [3]—The king will come this way.　115
　　　　　　　　　　　　[*Exeunt* PIETRO *and* IACOMO.
Bom. Ev'ry man go his own way! I'll not see
　The king for all this.

　　　　　Enter GUIDO, ALOISIO *and* ALEXIO.

　　　　　　　　　Friend—
Gui.　　　　　　　　This is
　The lady's secretary; pray, my lords,　　　120
　Be acquainted with him!
Bom.　　　　　　　Do you hear?
　Nobody say he saw me! I will not
　Be seen yet.　　　　　　　　　[*Reels in.*
Gui. Though he be made a spectacle—but leave him!—　125
　'Twas a handsome entertainment o' the sudden.
Aloi. A pretty hunting-dinner. But did you not

---

[1] Pass the bottle!　　　　[2] Q, 'thou wert'; possibly the true reading.
[3] hit (Falstaff 'paid, . . . seven of the eleven' at Gadshill) = dead drunk.

Observe with what intention [1] the duke
Shot eyes on Domitilla?
Alex.   And the king   130
    Applied all his discourse to her. I know not—
    He has made no vow against a second marriage;
    But if he choose at home, and look at beauty—
Gui. She is a very pretty talking lady.
Alex. Very ingenious. [2]   135
Aloi. And with your favour, though she be no court lady,
    She wants no confidence.
Alex.   What if the duke
    Be taken with her?
Gui.   Let him   140
    Be taken a-bed with her; 'tis my opinion
    My lord Montalto will not die for grief on't.
Aloi. They're here.

              Enter Duke, *and* MONTALTO.

Mont.   Your grace is sad; excuse [I pray] [3]
    My diligence to wait on you. I could wish,   145
    If it made no intrusion on your thoughts
    I'd opportunity to express what might
    Not be unworthy of your patience.
Duke. To me?

              Enter King, *leading* DOMITILLA.

Mont. The king . . .   150
    This way leads to the garden; [4] let me have
    The honour to attend you.
              [*Exeunt* Duke *and* MONTALTO; King *comes forward.*
King.   Where's the duke?
Gui. He took that way to the garden, sir,
    With the lord Montalto.   155

    ───────────
    [1] intentness.
    [2] So Gloucester of the little Duke of York: 'O, tis a parlous boy, Bold, quick, ingenious, forward, capable.' *Richard III*, III, i.
    [3] Some insertion of the kind seems called for here.
    [4] Dy.'s felicitous conjecture for Q, 'This way, ladies, to the garden.'

King.   You may remove a little.—[*Exit* GUIDO.
    You have no fear to trust yourself with me?
Dom. I cannot, sir, forget you are the king,
    And, in a wilderness, could have no thought
    With the least prejudice upon your virtue.   160
King. You have the greater innocence at home.
    My intents are fair enough, and you may stand
    The danger of a question; pray, how old are you?
Dom. Although it be not held a welcome compliment
    To our sex, my duty bids me not dispute.   165
    I am fifteen, my mother says.
King.   And are
    You not in love?
Dom.   I must not charge myself
    With so much ignorance to answer, that   170
    I understand not what it means.   I know
    The word, but never could apply the sense,
    Or find it in a passion more than ordinary.
King. Cupid hath lost his quiver, then; he could not
    Be arm'd, and let you 'scape, whose sole captivity   175
    Would be more glory than the conquest made,
    As poets feign, upon the gods.
Dom.   'Tis language
    With which you're pleased to mock your humble handmaid.
King. But this assurse him blind.   180
Dom.   He would deserve
    To lose his eyes indeed, if he should aim
    A shaft at me.[1]
King.   Madam, you have a heart.
Dom. To which no other   185
    Flame can approach, than what shall light it to
    Obedience of your will, and my good mother's.
King. Obedience to my will!   What if it were
    My will that you should love—
Dom.   Sir, I do love.   190

    [1] This recalls the song 'Cupid and my Campaspe played' in Lyly's *Al. and Camp.*
III, v.

King. Love, with the warm affection of a mistress,
    One I'll present a servant? Why that blush?
    The words are not immodest; there did want
    No blood upon your cheek to make it lovely;
    Or does it flow in silence, to express   195
    That which your virgin language would not be
    So soon held guilty of—consent?
Dom.   To what?
King. To love, by my direction, a man
    Whose worth, consider'd, shall deserve thee too,   200
    And in the noblest way invite thy freedom,[1]
    Until the holy priests declare your hearts
    Are knit into one blessing. There's no harm
    In this.
Dom.   Most royal sir, I know not with   205
    What words to say 'you honour me.' How can
    One so unworthy as poor Domitilla
    Be entertain'd within your thoughts and cares
    In this high nature?
King.   Though your mother have   210
    Made both her person and yourself a stranger
    To court, I have had eyes upon your virtues,
    Which, waited on by a most ample fortune,
    I've studied to advance, if you'll accept
    A husband of my choice. What say you, madam?   215
Dom. I have a mother, sir.
King.   She shall think it fortunate
    'Bove expectation. You have not vowed yourself
    To a cold nunnery?
Dom.   Not I, sir.   220
King.   When
    I shall declare how precious he is
    To my own bosom.
Dom.   Royal sir, this language
    Must needs prepare a welcome. I should think   225
    My heart unlike another woman's, not

[1] attract or engage your free choice.

To obey a charm so powerful as your praise;
But when you are considered as my king,
Duty takes off the merit of my will,
And humbles [1] ev'ry thought beneath obedience.   230
King. His name is—
Dom.   Pardon, I beseech you, sir:
Conceal it yet!—[*Aside.*] What gentle spirit walks
Upon my blood?   I dare not look upon him;
My hopes—my fears—[*To the* King.] It is enough, great sir,
That you have one within your thought you would   236
Commend to Domitilla,—one you love,
And precious to your bosom.   Sure you blest him
With such a character?
King.   It was too short. [2]   240
Dom. [*aside*]. My heart is a false prophet.—[*To the* King.] 'Tis a
fate.
Too good and great for Domitilla. [3]
King.   Well,
His name shall be reserv'd; but when it opens
Itself to your knowledge, you will honour it,   245
And thank me, Domitilla.   I' the mean time,
Let the opinion you have of me
Live in your trust; and make room in your heart
To meet the husband I shall bring.   [*Exit.*
Dom. Why may not this be meant by [4] his own person?   250
More wonders have been read in story.   I
Find thick, but amorous tremblings in my heart.
He's king;—why not?   Love has done stranger things
And can lead captive the proud heart of kings.   [*Exit.*

[1] Q, 'humble.'   [2] too short to do him justice.
[3] Perhaps the whole of this speech should be *aside*.   [4] of.

Act II.　Scene II.　*The Same.—A Garden.*

Enter Duke, *and* MONTALTO.

Duke. Here none can reach our voice; be free and clear!
Mont. First, let me kiss your hand, on which I swear
　　To speak all truth; 'tis justice to your person,
　　Your merit, and my faith.　Next, though the secret
　　May both concern and benefit your knowledge, 5
　　I shall desire your pardon.
Duke.　　　　　　　You prepare me
　　For wonder.　If it be an act of friendship
　　To me, it will become me to reward it;
　　Not thanks, nor pardon. 10
Mont.　　　　　　But all truths meet not
　　With charitable ears; there is a déscant[1]
　　That pleases not sometimes, though the best art
　　Present it, if our sense be indisposed
　　To patience and calm hearing. 15
Duke.　　　　　　Do not doubt me!
Mont. 'T will not become me so much as in thought
　　To enquire how long, or with what firm devotion
　　You affect the princess Theodosia.
　　But Naples is more conscious than [2] to doubt 20
　　You bring a welcome treaty in your person
　　And ev'ry voice and heart is busy with
　　The expectation of your marriage;
　　Whilst ev'ry eye, bright with your flame, is able
　　To light a torch to Hymen; virgins have 25
　　No other care than with what flowers, sweet
　　As your own name, to adorn the smiling altars.
Duke. You promised, sir, a secret?
Mont.　　　　　　　It will come
　　Too fast upon your knowledge.　Have you never 30
　　Look'd from the prospect of your palace-window,

[1] comment; discourse.　　　　[2] too well aware of your presence.

When some fair sky courted your eye to read
The beauties of a day; the glorious sun
Enriching so the bosom of the earth
That trees and flowers appeared but like so much   35
Enamel upon gold; [1] the wanton birds,
And every creature but the drudging ant,
Despising providence [2] and at play; and all
That world you measure with your eye, so gay
And proud, as winter were no more to shake   40
His icy locks upon them, but the breath
Of gentle zephyr to perfume their growth,
And walk eternally upon the spring;—
When, from a coast you see not, comes a cloud
Creeping, as overladen with a storm   ·   45
Dark as the womb of night, and, with her wings
Surprising all the glories you beheld,
Leaves not your frighted eyes a light to see
The ruins of that flatt'ring day?

Duke.   This language   50
Carries both mystery and horror. Pray,
My lord, convey your meaning to my knowledge!

Mont. I shall; I had in vain prepared you thus else.
Pardon again the story: Theodosia,
More beautiful than the day I figured by her   55
Is quite o'ercast, and looks through an eclipse
Upon your love; she has no heart but what
Another is possess'd of.

Duke.   Ha!

Mont.   I know.   60
It cannot but afflict your thoughts, that all
Your expectation, ripe, and courted to
The enjoying such a treasure as she is,
Must finish in embracing of a shadow,
Invited to a fable,[3] not a bride   65
That should with joy dwell in your princely arms;

[1] Cf. Shaksp. 2 *G. V.*, II, vii, 29.   [2] care.
[3] to the presentation of the myth of Ixion embracing a cloud instead of Hera.

For Theodosia, without sacrilege,
Cannot be yours; she is contracted.
Duke.   How!
The King of Naples must not, sir, engage   70
Florence to such a mockery.
Mont.   'Tis my duty
To clear his honour in't; he has a pure
Intent to make his sister yours; her close
Though honourable love's design'd without   75
His knowledge, and you will but waste your rage
Upon her destiny, which will bury her
In her own ruins, if your anger make
The king her enemy.
Duke [*aside*].   I do not find   80
My heart in any disposition
To break at hearing of this news; but wish it
Truth to prepare room for another guest;
The fairer Domitilla is here sainted.
Mont. Your excellency—   85
Duke.   Must not be thus affronted,
Montalto, and return with this dishonour.
Was there no cheaper person to be made
Ridiculous in Naples?
Mont.   Calm your blood!   90
I know you must resent it; but let not
Your passion make the world believe you should
Despair to find one apter to your bosom.
The richest beauty in the world your birth
And fortune must deserve, and I should curse   95
My forward duty to your grace—
Duke.   No more!
I have considered better; and although
Your love may merit thanks, yet this intelligence
Will not concern my faith;[1] this cannot be, sir.   100
Mont. My honour is engaged, then, to convince you,
Though with the hazard of my life and fortunes;

[1] affect my trust.

Both which must now depend upon your mercy;
Your breath shall make them bleed or live.

Duke.   What means   105
    Montalto?

Mont.   To translate the power of all
    My stars, and make you lord of my whole fate.
    Theodosia's heart, sir, should be mine, by free
    Gift of herself, who has been pleased to take   110
    My vows in the exchange, which now may boast
    Some time and growth; which could not be a sin
    Against your love, with which all that can spring
    From me deserves no name. Nor dare I take
    Boldness to call her mine, who am a thing   115
    Lighter than air in balance with your grace,
    If you but chide the ambition; and could render,[1]
    Though I commit a rape on my own life,
    All that her love hath promised me.

Duke.   'Tis strange!   120
Mont. But she—let me take freedom to be plain—
Duke. Is not to be reduced, you'll say?
Mont.   Sir, women
    Love not with that safeguard upon their passion.
Duke. She has a wise art to dissemble, then.   125
Mont. 'Tis fear it should arrive at the king's knowledge.
    In whose displeasure she is lost, and not
    A will to mock your grace, for whom there is
    Another wound within her mind—that she
    Should wear a smiling summer in her brow,   130
    Yet frost within her heart; in which, unhappily,
    She comes too near the nature of the adamant,
    Hard to your grace, whom she attracts. But love,
    Your wisdom knows, is in the volume of
    Our fate decreed, whose periods,[2] when they are   135
    By time made known, greatness on earth, that means
    To play the tyrant with us, may have strength
    To punish, not reverse.

----

[1] surrender.   [2] revolutions.

Duke [*aside*].   I am confirmed
    And prosper in my thoughts.   140
Mont. [*aside*].   It takes.
Duke.   My lord,
    You have expressed an act of confidence,
    Which I must not betray, though to my loss.
    It is some happiness to know this early;   145
    We may be expected. You shall find me, sir,
    A prince, but no usurper.
Mont.   I'm your creature.—
    The king.—We build upon your piety,
    Until some little time may call our loves   150
    Out of this silence.

Enter King, Simphorosa, Domitilla, Guido, Aloizio *and* Alexio

King. You understand me, madam?
Simph.   And am honoured.
Duke [*aside*]. Her eyes beget new wonder; I shall be
    Observed.   155
King.   Come, now to horse!
Duke. I shall attend.—Your entertainment has
    Obliged us, madam.
Simph.   'T was not worth such guests;
    But prayers and duty must supply.   160
King [*to* Domitilla].   Now, madam,
    You are a great part of my care; depend·
    Upon me for a husband!
Dom. [*aside*]. Is't not plain?
Duke. Madam, another guest must take his leave,   165
    That here would choose his palace.
Dom.   You are gracious,
    And but encourage more to honour you.
Mont. [*aside*]. I'll creep and kiss thy altar, Love; allow
    Him [1] flame, and knit more charms upon her brow!   170
                                          [*Exeunt.*

                  [1] So Dy. for Q, 'Them.'

Act III. Scene I. *Naples. A Part of the Palace.*

Enter Duke *and* RIVIERO.

Duke. 'Tis thy old quarrel gainst Montalto makes thee
  Incredulous; I dare believe he loves
  Theodosia.
Riv. 'Tis not that I question, sir;
  But that part which concerns her love to him,   5
  Sounds like a plot upon your nature, to
  Secure his own ambition.
Duke.   Why, the princess
  May love; as great a heart has been made stoop.
Riv. Your grace should else in vain court her yourself;   10
  And late your highness thought she met your person—
  A fair design of love—with all the soft
  Behaviour of a princess.[1]
Duke.   But 'tis not
  Impossible a lady should dissemble.   15
Riv. Allow her but the honour she was born with,
  And she'll not stain her blood so much.[2]
Duke.   But love
  Must be obeyed, and prepossession
  Of hearts is a shrewd[3] thing to wrestle with.   20
  I make it my own case; and if I loved
  Another lady better than the princess,
  As every man's not proof against all beauty,
  I think I should be constant too; it would
  Be something to remove me.[4]   25
Riv.   Then, the king?
Duke. He knows not; and I've bound myself in honour
  Not to betray [them].   If they be decreed

---

[1] If she loved Montalto, your own open suit to which only recently you thought
she was, with all her gentle dignity, responsive, would be hopeless.
[2] Her royal instincts alone would save her from so lowering herself.
[3] Dy.'s emendation of 'shrewd,' for Q, 'lewd,' must be accepted.
[4] difficult to make me alter my mind.

To make a marriage, a soft destiny
Attend their loves! 30
Riv. There is some mystery.
But will you rest, and take for granted she
Does love Montalto? If it be a truth,
You're in the same condition when she
Confirms it. 35
Duke. 'Tis not good to be [so] busy
In search of these unwelcome certainties;
There's hope while things are clouded in suspicion.
Riv. But so your jealousy may wound her honour,
Which you may cure by knowledge. 40
Duke. I will think on't.
Meantime, let this dwell in that honest silence
You have profess'd! [1] There is another secret
May follow.
Riv. You must challenge my whole bosom; 45
And I am confident your highness will
Steer all your resolutions by honour,
Which in a prince is sacred.

Enter Servant.

Serv. Sir, the lord
Montalto's coming up. 50
Duke. Then try your art
Upon him, and inform yourself; I'll take
My time to appear. [*Withdraws.*
Riv. I obey.

Enter MONTALTO.

My honour'd lord! 55
Mont. Most noble Philoberto! Where's the duke?
Riv. If you'll but excuse [him] a few minutes—
Mont. 'Tis
My duty to attend.
Riv. How is it with the princess, my good lord? 60

[1] Dy.'s emendation, not quite so convincing as the above, for Q, 'possessed.'

Mont. The princess? She's in health. Why this to me?—
[*Aside.*] He is of inward counsel with the duke,
I must be resolute.
Riv.   I ask, because
His grace intends a present visit to her,   65
And was but now in mention of your lordship,
To bear him company.
Mont. [*aside*].   I like not that.—
He knows he may command my services.
Riv. He will deserve your love. Pray, my lord, tell me—   70
And let us be plain-breasted; you enjoy
The same [1] as I, but with less stock of merit,
The favour of his excellence; how affect you
The present state of things? Will't be a match?
There is loud expectation in the world,   75
And, after all, my master's fond to have it
Proceed; to these,[2] I'm of opinion,
There's no retreating now without dishonour.
Yet, as I'm Philoberto,[3] I much pity
He should through any wound to your affection   80
Perfect his love.
Mont.   He has told you, then, the secret?
And, not to waste more language, I collect,
From what you have express'd, he does resolve
To déstroy me; Montalto must be trod on.   85
Riv. Not so, my lord!
Mont.   Yes; and my heart the ascent
To his hyméneal altar, which must be
Made crimson with the blood of a true lover.
His will be obey'd! Theodosia shall see,   90
To ádvance her, Montalto will go smiling
To his sacrifice; and, after many prayers
That she may live the darling of his heart,

---

[1] Q, followed by Dy., 'The king.' But this gives no sense. His excellence or excellency in the next line is the Duke, whom Montalto addressed by this title in the previous scene.   [2] moreover.
[3] in my private capacity.

I'll change my acquaintance of this world, to be
At peace in my own ashes.   95

Riv.   You will not
Commit a violence upon yourself?

Mont. I shall not need; the thought of her will kill me
With as much silence as I go to sleep;
I only shall bleed inward, and my life   100
Remove itself like a fair apparition,
That vanishes in the eye, and with less noise
Than a calm summer's evening. But when I
Am dead, 'tis not impossible some may
Report, Theodosia was but ravished from me;   105
Fear of a brother's anger, and the trick
Of politic States, that marry to knit powers
Not hearts, did force her to another's [1] arms;
Whilst I, torn from the branch where once I grew,
Travel, I know not whither, in the air.   110

Riv. [aside]. I begin
To think him worth some pity.

Mont.   Into what
Vain thing would the severer apprehension [2]
Of grief transform us? Coward! Let the duke   115
Move with all amorous haste to his delight
And glory in the hope of his fair bride—
Mine by the gift of heaven and hearts; but all
My flowers grow dully on their stalks, and wither.
Let her gay paranymphs,[3] with rosy chaplets   120
Which will take all their colour from their blush,
Attend on Theodosia to the temple;
While, as they go, no rude wind shall be heard,
But so much breath of heaven as gently may,
Lifting their loose hair up, whisper my wrong   125
To ev'ry virgin's ear! Let them be married,

---

[1] Q, followed by Dy., 'Herare's,' which is too mysterious to be entitled to stand. In the next line Q reads 'I once.'

[2] The imagination which exceeds the reality. 'The sense of death' says Isabella in *M. for M.* (III, i) 'is most in apprehension.'

[3] bridesmaids.

Knit hands, and plight a ceremonious faith!
Let all the triumphs waste—let them be wasted,
And light [1] itself bribed with a thousand forms
Of mirth and revels, till the night, grown faint   130
And pale with watching,
Invite to bed. Yet, there, he shall enjoy
But Theodosia's body, and not that
As his fair thoughts expect,—perhaps, the conquest
Of one whom he loved better.   [*Exit.*   135

Re-enter Duke.

Riv.   How was that?
Duke. Now, shall I trust him? If my sense mistake not,
Theodosia may not be a virgin.
Riv.   'T was
His bold conclusion.   140
Duke.   Where is now the honour
You talk of? Durst Montalto charge her with
This stain, without his conscience to assure it?
Riv. Yes, and to me this renders him the more
To be suspected, and I am so far   145
From thinking she affects Montalto, that
I am convinced he loves her not. Can he
Have any noble thoughts of Theodosia
That dares traduce her honour? Think on that!
And can revenge in any lover be   150
A reason to wound a lady's fame? It tastes
Of rank injustice, and some other end
Time will discover. And yet your grace is bound
To have his accusation confirmed
Or hunt this spotted panther to his ruin,   155
Whose breath is only sweet to poison virtue.[2]

---

[1] 'Light' is suggested in the place of 'night' which the printer may have taken from the next line. The text, as Dy. says, must be very corrupt here; though the intentional extravagance of the speech seems to defy correction.

[2] The Greek and Latin passages (from Eustathius, Aelian and Pliny) dwelling on the sweetness of the smell of the panther are cited in Gifford's note to a passage referring to the lusciousness of this animal's breath in Jonson's *Volpone*, III, v.

Duke. What I resolve, enquire not!   [*Exit.*

Riv.   I see through
    Montalto's soul, and have been so long tame
    In mine own sufferings; but this will make   160
    Him ripe for punishment.—Andrugio and
    My son!

Enter ANDRUGIO *and* OCTAVIO.

Oct. I cannot with the wings of duty
    Fly swift enough to prostrate my obedience
    And welcome from a long-supposèd death   165
    My honoured father.

Riv.   Then, I must appear so.

Andr. And let me give a son up to your blessing
    Worthy your best prayers and embrace! 'T was time
    To bring you acquainted; he had else this night   170
    Contriv'd Montalto's tragedy at a banquet,
    For your revenge.[1] His active thoughts I could not
    Counsel to longer patience.

Riv.   Thou hast but
    Prevented me, Octavio; I was weary   175
    Of my concealment.

Oct.   But my joys are wild,
    And will, I fear, transport me.

Riv.   My best friend,
    And my own spirited boy, fear not Montalto!   180
    He's now upon a precipice; his fate
    Stoops with the glorious burden of his pride.
    Things may be worth our counsel; we shall see

Cf. also *Cynthia's Revels*, V, ii ('a tongue steeped in honey, and a breath like a panther') and the passages from Glapthorne and Randolph quoted by Gifford.— It is curious that Dryden should have made no allusion in *The Hind and the Panther* either to this notion, or to the allegorical significance attributed to the panther in the old *Bestiaries*.

[1] It is just possible that Shirley who was very much alive to the occurrences of the Thirty Years' War (see *The Example*, passim; cf. *The Opportunity* III, i), may have been thinking of the murders 'at a banquet' which had preceded the death of Wallenstein in 1634, two or three years before the production of *The Royal Master*.

This prodigy, that would be held a star,
And did so fright us with his streaming hair,   185
Drop like a comet, and be lost i' the air.

Act III.   Scene II.   *Another Part of the Palace.*

Enter MONTALTO *and* THEODOSIA.

Mont. Is't possible the day should be so old,
And not a visit from the duke?
Theo.   While he
Enjoys health, I shall easily forgive
A little ceremony.   5
Mont.   And [he] a lover! [1]
Your grace must chide him!   Other men may have
Excuse for their neglect of time; but he
That loves deserves no pardon.
  Theo.   Judge with charity,   10
My lord; the case may be your own.   You would
Think her a cruel mistress that should doom
Your life to exile, for not payment of
One ceremonious visit.
Mont.   Not where such   15
Perfection were to engage my service, madam.
Pardon the bold comparison; death were not
Enough to punish that rude thought could [2] start from
Your bright idea,[3] or converse with praters [4]
That did not first concern your excellence.   20
I would not be ambitious of a blessing,
But from reflex of yours.
Theo.   You would express [5]
A most officious servant to that lady

---

[1] Q, 'And a lover.' The insertion of 'he' seems called for, and accords with Shirley's metrification.
[2] The omission of the relative in this line and *infra*, before 'Were honour'd in your thought' has the effect of contortion.
[3] image.   [4] idle talk.   [5] show yourself.

Were honour'd in your thought; but the Duke of Florence　25
And I shall make no such severe conditions.
Mont. If he do love you, madam, that will teach him
Above what ceremony prescribes to honour you.
Theo. If he do love?
Mont.　　　　　Your grace's pardon! I　　　30
Speak from an honest freedom, taken from
The assurance of your goodness, that know better
How to distinguish truth. I am not judge
Of his breast, madam.
Theo.　　　　　　I suppose you're not.　　35
Mont. And yet, being [1] a man, another may
Conclude his passions are but such as have
Been read in human nature.
Theo.　　　　　　What infer you
From hence, my lord?　　　　　　　40
Mont.　　　　　Nothing, but that a prince
May be no saint in love.
Theo.　　　　　How's that?
Mont. 'T was in my fear I should displease.
Theo.　　　　　　　You will. [2]　　45
Mont. Not for the empire of the world! I shall
Repent I live, with your suspicion
Upon my humbled soul.
Theo.　　　　　Pray, sir, be free
Touching the duke; I must know all. What is it　50
Makes him no saint?
Mont.　　　　　Madam, he is not dead;
And in his life I see no miracles.
Theo. You talked of love?
Mont.　　　　　No miracles of love.　　55
He loves as other men, that have professed
Devotion to a mistress; but—
Theo.　　　　　What? Speak,
I charge thee by the memory of what

---

[1] he being.
[2] Q, 'your will?'; which, though adopted by Dy. seems to give no sense.

   Thou dost affect most.   60
Mont.   Though it wound myself,
  Be armed, and hear it! How I blush within me,
  To tell your highness Florence has transplanted
  His heart, and all his active thoughts are placed—
Theo. On whom?   65
Mont.   On Domitilla!
Theo.   Ha!
Mont.   I did
  Observe them, madam, at her mother's house,
  Where we were lately feasted after hunting,   70
  How strangely he was taken; how his eyes
  Did wanton with her face, and on her hair
  Tie many golden knots, to keep Love chained.
  But these are but suspicions; he since
  Confessed to me, in hope to win me to   75
  Negociate his affair, how at first sight
  He took in desperate flames, and that she rules
  The intelligence of his soul. I hear, the king
  Hath sent for her to court, which must give, madam,
  A dangerous opportunity to actuate   80
  His ends, with your dishonour. I was unwilling
  To speak this knowledge of his hasty change;
  But all my bonds of piety and faith
  Would have been forfeit to a long [er] silence.
Theo. Shall I be thus affronted?   85
Mont.   We see princes,
  Whom we call gods on earth, in the affairs
  Of love turn men again—[1]
Theo.   For Domitilla!
Mont. That's the dishonour, madam, and infects 90
  My brain to think on't; and as much beneath
  Your grace in all the ornaments of soul
  And person, as she is in blood, if my

---

[1] Quite against Shirley's principles; see the closing lines of *The Opportunity:*—
'Subjects may love as their rude sense imparts, But heaven doth only govern
princes' hearts.'

Impartial thoughts may take so bold commission
To judge between your beauties.   95
Theo.   Is it possible?
Mont. It is too certain, madam. I should be
A villain to accuse the duke unjustly,
Or bring but shadows of a truth. For though
He be unworthy of your love, that dares   100
Thus value your perfections below
That phantom Domitilla, let not passion
Make you too rash in managing a cause
On which depends your fame; compared to which
Ten thousand lives, added to mine, were nothing.   105
Observe him at next visit!
Theo.   I'll study thanks, sir.
Mont. You pay me with a blessing, if my name
But live within your memory.   [*Exit.*
Theo.   This troubles me.   110

Enter King, *and* GUIDO.

King.   Are they both come to court?
Gui. And in those lodgings were prepared.
King.   'Tis well.
And came they cheerfully?
Gui.   Yes, sir; but something   115
I nigh discern like trouble and by starts
In Domitilla; but they're pleased with their
Remove, and wait all your commands.
King.   So! Leave us! [*Exit* GUIDO.
Theodosia, what's the matter? Art not well?   120
Theo. Where is the duke?
King.   I thought to have met him here.
Theo. Is Domitilla come to court?
King.   She is,
By my command, to wait on thee.   125
Theo. To rival me!   [*Exit.*
King.   How's that?
I meant her [for] a wife for good Montalto,

As the reward of his just services.
He knows it not, as he is ignorant   130
For whom I have prepared her. Rival! Strange!
I must know more of this. She ¹ is in nature
Too apprehensive; for, although in love
Suspicion to men a torment be,
There is no fiend to ² woman's jealousy.   [*Exit.* 135

Act III. Scene III. *Another Part of the Palace.*

Enter DOMITILLA *and* BOMBO.

Bom. You may do what you will, madam; [you may] put me
    Into fine clothes, and make an ass of me!
    But should you wrap me in a lion's skin—
Dom. You've ears that will betray what beast you are.
Bom. Pray, madam, tell me in six words of sense   5
    What shall I do here?   I'll not see the king,
    Though he have cunningly devised this trick,
    Only to bring me hither, and betray me
    To offices, make me at least an idol.
Dom. What's that?   10
Bom. An idol in the country, I have read,³
    A thing we call a worshipful, a right worshipful,
    Descended from the house of the Factotums—
    Lord of the soil, and cock of his own dunghill.
Dom. You may be out of fear; you cannot read,   15
    Nor set your name to a warrant.
Bom.   All that's nothing.
    Ignorance ev'ry day comes into fashion;
    And no mean statesmen now, when they do write
    Their names, do for their honours ⁴ so contrive it   20

---

¹ Viz. Theodosia.   ² comparable to.
³ Dy. inserts ''s'=' is' at the end of this line, which is perhaps more satisfactory than the absence of a verb.
⁴ titles.

You can hardly know a nobleman from a mark![1]
Dom. If you be an enemy to all preferment,
    Your best way is to leave the world and turn
    Lay friar.
Bom.   No!   25
    I find no such thing in my constitution.
    Every man is not bound to be religious;
    Men of my bulk and bearing should not fast so.
    I am not given by nature to drink water,
    Or lie without a shirt; I have corns, madam,   30
    And I would make less conscience to undo
    My shoemaker, than walk on wooden pantables.[2]
    I will endure to serve you still and dwell here,
    So you preserve me from the king. 'Tis not
    That I do owe his majesty ill-will;   35
    I could endure him too, upon condition
    He would make nothing of me.
Dom.   Why, he shall
    Make nothing of thee, take my word! Or if
    Thou hast a mind, I'll pray him make thee less.   40
Bom. No, I would be a middling Christian;
    But what will you do here yourself? You'll be
    In [love.][3]
Dom.   With whom, dost think?
Bom.   And cast away   45
    Yourself upon some pageant [4]—one whose wit.
    Must be beholding to another's wool
    To keep it warm; one that can dance and sing
    And wag his feather; or artificial calf-carrier;
    A youth that's sew'd together by his tailor,   50
    And taken o' pieces by his surgeon.
Dom. Why, how now, secretary?
Bom.   I could say more.

---

[1] The pun on 'noble' and 'mark' ought perhaps to be pointed out.
[2] Assuredly another form of 'pantofles,' French *pantoufles*, Italian *pantofole*.
[3] Dropped out in Q.
[4] Thing of wood, that requires decking out with drapery.

Dom. Is this wit natural?

Bom.   You were best say   55
  I got it here at court!   Pray Heaven, I do not
  Lose what I brought!   I had a wholesome wit
  I' the country—ask the parish and the parson;
  For I kept company with those that read
  And learn [ed] wit [1] by the ear.   If any slip from me,   60
  As, when there is a plenty, some will out,
  Here are so many wit-catchers, a lost maidenhead
  Is sooner found, and set upon the shoulders
  Of the right owner.

Dom.   I prithee tell me, Bombo,   65
  And tell me truth, do not you think yourself
  After all this a fool?

Bom.   A fool?   Your servant, madam.

Dom. I'll speak, thou may'st be the king's fool.

Bom.   I thank you;   70
  I tell you, I'll not see the king; or, if—
  Yes, I look like a fool!—I could be angry;
  But then you'd say I were a fool indeed.

Dom. Be not so passionate!

Bom.   Would I'd been a fool!   75
  I would I had!   For my own sake I wish it;
  I should not have been tempted hither then,
  By which I have endangered my good parts,
  To State employment.   But I'll be wise enough.
  He has not seen me yet; not shall not, if   80
  There be a witch in Naples, or a mist
  That will be bought for money, to walk the court in.
  But take your course!   An I were at home again—

Dom. What then?

Bom.   I'd live in the cellar—the wine-cellar.   85

Dom. 'Tis your humility.

Bom. There were some fortification to be made
  Against the court invasions,—countermines
  Of sand and sack; a man might thrust himself

                [1] Q, 'And learn wit now.'

Among the bottles, and defy the world;   90
Be drunk, and not be called out of his sleep
To go ambassador.
Dom.   So, so! [1] Fear not;
Have a strong faith; and thou may'st die i' the country,
For all this.   95

Enter SIMPHOROSA.

Here's my mother! Let your care
Be now, that none may interrupt us!
Bom. I will do anything but see the king.   [*Exit.*
Dom. With pardon, madam, you seem full of thought?
Simph. I'm studying, Domitilla, why the king   100
Should send for us to court.
Dom.   Mother, you cannot
Mention the king in any act of his
That is not glorious, and like himself.
He is the great example of a king,   105
But richer in his soul than state.
Simph.   But why
To us this favour? To call us from those
Cold and obscure shades of retirement, [2]
To plant us here, near his own beams?   110
Dom.   He has
Some meaning in't.
Simph.   It is yet dark to me.
Dom. We shall not stain his court. His sister's but
A lady of more distinction of birth;   115
Yet all that have been princes, came not to
Their state by a descent. The heralds know
Some were not born to purple and to sceptres
That have been queens. Virtue has raised some;
And beauty has had many charms to rule   120
The heart of kings.
Simph.   What's all this, Domitilla?
I hope you are not dreaming of a queen.

[1] Dy. unnecessarily, 'Do so.'   [2] Q, 'of a retirement.'

Such wild interpretation of the king's
Favour to us cannot be made without   125
The forfeits of [our] wits and duties, which
Should teach us to contain our thoughts in their
Own sphere, and not to point them upon objects
Above our level.
Dom. [*aside*].   I betray myself.—   130
When I said beauty had a power to charm
A king, it might acquit me from suspicion
Of any hope to apply them so ambitiously.
You'll grant it just to love the king?
Simph.   Our duties.   135
Dom. And he may where he please place his affection?
Simph. Leave that to her it may concern!
Dom.   And she
That's marked for so great honour, should be mad
To quarrel with her kind fate?   140
Simph.   What's all this
To thee?
Dom.   To me?   Why, mother, is't not possible
A lady not much fairer than myself
May be a queen?   Great princes have [but] eyes [1]   145
Like other men; and I should sin against
What Heaven and nature have bestowed on me,
Should my fate smile, to think my face would be
The bar to such preferment.
Simph.   Leaving this—   150
Which is but mirth, I know—since we are fallen
Into discourse of love, what would you answer
To lord Montalto, if he came a wooing,
And recommended by the king?
Dom.   I would   155
E'en recommend him to the king again.
Simph. Is not his favourite worth your love, if he
Descend to be your servant?
Dom.   As a servant [2]

[1] Q, 'have eyes.'   [2] In the more literal sense of the word.

He may be entertained; and were I queen,   160
Perhaps he should be favourite to both,
And I would smile upon his services,
In imitation of the king, while he
Preserved his modest duty, and his distance.
Simph. [*aside*]. My daughter is transported!—Sure, you are   165
   No queen, sweet Domitilla!
Dom.   'Tis a truth;
   Nor is Montalto yet my favourite.
Simph. [*aside*]. I hope she's not so miserable to affect
   The king, by whose directions I prepare   170
   Her for Montalto.

Re-enter BOMBO.

Bom. A sprig of the nobility, called Octavio,
   Desires access.
Dom.   Admit him!
Simph. [*aside*].   I must let   175
   This passion cool, and leave her.   [*Exit.*

Enter OCTAVIO.

Oct. Welcome to court! Why so! This sphere becomes you,
   Or rather it takes [1] ornament from you.
   Now, Domitilla shines indeed! Your presence
   Doth throw new beams about the palace, madam;   180
   Before, we looked as we had lost our genius.
Dom. You came not from the king with any message?
Oct. I made this haste to tender my own service.
Dom. You have no other suit to me?
Oct.   Yes, madam.   185
Dom.   Speak it!
Oct. And I'll not wander much about. Shall I
   Be admitted a young lover?
Dom. Men must not love till they be one-and-twenty;
   They will be mad before they come to age else.   190
Oct. This law was ne'er decreed i' the parliament

                    [1] derives.

Of Cupid; [1] such a statute would undo
Many sweet virgins like yourself. Yet if
You'll promise to stay for me, I shall think it
A happy expectation. We are both   195
Young; we may choose each other Valentine
And couple, as we grow more ripe, hereafter.
Dom. I'll ask you but one question, my lord;
What would you give to be the King of Naples?
Oct. I dare not think so ambitiously.   200
Dom.   'Tis modest.
What, if I cannot love under a prince?
Oct. Can he be less, whom you will make [so] [2] happy
To boast, in the possession of your fair
Person, a thousand provinces? Those eyes   205
Are able to create another Indies;
All the delights that dwell in blessèd Tempe
Divinely bud and blossom in your cheek;
The treasure of Arabia's in your breath;
Nor Thebes alone, as to Amphion's lute,   210
Stoops to the heavenly magic of your voice,
But all the world.
Dom.   No more of this! These praises
Are made for children, and will make truth blush.
They may fill up where nature is defective;   215
And, were I Queen of Naples, I should punish
Such flattery. But you are young, and may
Outgrow this vanity.
Oct.   You are merciful!
Dom. I shall be ever so to you, Octavio.   220
Let this encourage you to think I love you
In the first place of those who are born subjects!
If you will answer my respects, [3] forbear

---

[1] It is unnecessary to suppose any special allusion here to Massinger's *Parliament of Love* (1624) or to any of the *analoga* to this in our dramatic literature. Massinger's play, as Koeppel has shown, was suggested by the *Aresta Amorum* of Martial d'Auvergne, (who lived from about 1440 to 1508) to which Marston had already been indebted for the climax of his *Parasitaster*.

[2] Q, 'make happy.'   [3] deserve my regard.

To question further.

Oct.   I shall wait sometime,   225
And kiss your hand.

Dom.   And if my power may
Prevail to do you favour with the king,
Make your address![1]

Oct. [aside]. Has not the court transformed her?   [Exit. 230

Dom. Methinks I move upon a state [2] already!
And yet 'tis not the glory of his title
Affects my hope so much; his person's lovely,
And both together make the charm.—I do
Expect his royal presence; how shall I   235
Behave [3] my looks when he declares himself?

Re-enter IACOMO.

Iac. Madam!

Dom.   Admit not every lord to trouble me;
[Aside.] I will take physic;—but I'll be observed.—[4]
You may frame some excuse to ladies, too,   240
That press their visit.

Iac.   'Tis the duke—

Dom.   The duke?

Iac. Of Florence.

Dom.   Princes must not be neglected;   245
That name gives him access. Say, I attend.

[Exit IACOMO.

Enter Duke.

Duke. The acknowledgments I owe your favours, madam,
Late your rude guest, brings me to kiss your hand.

Dom. Your excellence is pleased to interpret fairly
Of our intents.   250

Duke.   And till occasion ripen

---

[1] apply to me.   [2] throne.
[3] Control. So in *Timon of Athens*, III, v (according to the Cambridge Editors),
'with such sober and unnoted passion He did behave his anger.'
[4] The meaning seems to be: 'I will keep my chamber;—but no! I shall be observed.' If so, the line must be supposed to be spoken aside.

My whole discharge [1] for your fair entertainment,
Madam, be pleased to wear these diamonds,
Which, of themselves, betray their want of lustre
And come with an ambition to recover   255
Flame from your smile!
Dom.   It can be no dishonour
To take these from a prince.

Re-enter IACOMO, *who whispers to* DOMITILLA, *and exit.*

                    The king! With wings
I'll haste to meet him!   [*Exit.* 260
Duke.   Gone! And so abruptly!
Her business might allow her breath to thank me
For my rich present; but I'll follow her.
I would not meet the king here. If she prove
Gentle, my heart I consecrate to love.   [*Exit.* 265

Act IV. Scene I. *A Part of the Palace.*

Enter King, *and* DOMITILLA.

King. My pretty Domitilla, now you are
My guest. 'Tis fit, whom I have made my charge,
Should live within my eyes; welcome once more
To court!
Dom.   You're bounty, sir, itself and bind   5
A virgin's prayers.
King.   What, art thou yet prepared
To hear his name I would declare thy husband?

Enter Duke.

Duke. The king!
King.   The duke! [*Aside.*] This but confirms it.   10
Duke [*aside*]. Unlucky fate!   He has spied me!
King [*to* DOMITILLA].   Thou shalt have
                    [1] Full or sufficient expenditure.

A little patience, while the duke and I
Change some discourse in private.
Dom. I obey. [*Exit.* 15
Duke [*aside*]. She is sent off; I hope the king is not
In love with her himself.
King. Now, my lord! What,
Alone? I see you can address yourself
To a handsome lady. 20
Duke [*aside*]. He has prevented me.—
Where I receive [a] favour, I shall never
Want heart to acknowledge [it].[1]
King. That rule binds all.
Duke. It does; but with distinction, to pay— 25
King. But with distinction, to pay
First love to those that best deserve it from us.
Duke. 'Tis justice, sir.
King. This granted, there's another
Whom though[2] you can forget—my sister, sir— 30
Deserves to be remembered.
Duke. You are jealous
That I visit this lady.
King. That were only
To doubt. I must be plain. Florence has 35
Been kind to Naples, to reward us with
Affront for love; and Theodosia must not
Be any prince's mockery.
Duke. I can
Take boldness too, and tell you, sir, it were 40
More for her honour, she would mock no prince.
I am not lost to Florence yet, though I
Be Naples' guest; and I must tell him, here
I came to meet with fair and princely treaties
Of love,—not to be made the tale of Italy, 45
The ground of scurril pasquils, or the mirth
Of any lady, who shall pre-engage
Her heart to another's bosom, and then sneak

---

[1] Q omits 'a' and 'it.'   [2] So Q. Dy., ungrammatically, ' whom,though '.

Off, like a tame despisèd property,[1]
When her ends are advanced.   50
King.   I understand not
This passion; yet it points upon something
That may be dangerous to conclude. Theodosia
Is Naples' sister; and I must not see
Her lost to honour, though my kingdom bleed   55
To rescue her.
Duke.   Now *you* are passionate.
'Tis I must be repaired. My name is wounded
And my affection betrayed. Your sister
That looks like a fair star within Love's sky,   60
Is fallen, and by the scattering of her fires
Declares, she has alliance with the earth,
Not heavenly nature.
King.   Are my senses perfect?
Be clearer, sir! Teach me to understand   65
This prodigy! You do not scorn our sister?
Duke. Not I. As she has title to your blood,
She merits all ambition. She's a princess;
Yet, no stain to her scutcheon,[2] we are parallels—
Equal, but never meant to meet.   70
King.   How's this?
Duke. Truth is my witness, I did mean
No ceremonious love, until I found
Her heart was given from me, though your power
Contract our bodies.   75
King.   Stay, and be advised!
And if your doubts, by some malicious tongue
Framed to abuse my sister and yourself,
Have raised this mutiny in your thoughts, I have

---

[1] tool; instrument.
[2] Q, 'invention,' a printer's blunder. Dy., who suggests 'station' if a substitute
is to be found, describes the line as complete without it, both as to rhythm and
metre. But the rhythm is more in Shirley's usual way with some such insertion;
and the line as printed by Dy., 'Yet no stain to her—, we are parallels,' seems un-
canny. 'Station' would be preferable to my conjecture 'scutcheon,' but for the
consonance with 'stain.'

A power to cure all.   80
Duke.   Sir, you cannot.
King.   Not
    To court thee for her husband, wert possessed
    Of all o'er which our eagle shakes his wings—
    But to set right her honour. And, ere I challenge   85
    Thee by thy birth, by all thy hopes and right
    To fame, to tell me what seditious breath
    Has poisoned her—hear what my sister sends
    By me, so late,[1] time is not old in minutes;
    The word's yet warm with her own breath. 'Pray tell   90
    The duke,' says she, 'although I know not from
    What root his discontents grow, to devote him
    To Domitilla'—
Duke [aside]. How does she know that?
King [continuing]. 'Whose beauty has more spell upon his fancy! 95
    I did contract my heart, when I thought his
    Had been no stranger [2] to his tongue; and can
    Not find within it since, what should divert
    His princely thoughts from my first innocence.
    Yet such is my stern fate, I must still love him;   100
    And, though he frame his heart to unkind distance,
    It hath embracing virtue upon mine,
    And, with his own remove, draws my soul after him.
    If he forget I am a princess, pray
    Let Naples do so too; for my revenge   105
    Shall be in prayers, that he may find my wrong
    But teach him soft repentance and more faith.'
Duke. All this must not betray my freedom, sir.
King. You'll not accuse our sister of dishonour?
Duke. I would not grieve you, sir, to hear what I   110
    Could say; and press me not, for your own peace!
    Fames must be gently touched.
King. As thou art Florence, speak!
Duke.   I shall displease;
    Yet I but tell her brother, who doth press me: 115

---

[1] recently.   [2] Q, 'stronger.'

Lucrece was chaste after the rape; but where
The blood consents, there needs no ravisher.　　　　[*Exit.*
King. I do grow faint with wonder.　Here's enough
　　To blast an apprehension,[1] and shoot
　　A quaking through the valiant soul of man.　　　　120
　　My sister's blood accused!　And her fair name,
　　Late chaste as trembling snow, whose fleeces clothe
　　Our Alpine hills, sweet as the rose's spirit,
　　Or violet's cheek, on which the morning leaves
　　A tear at parting, now begins to wither,　　　　125
　　As it would haste to death and be forgotten;
　　This Florence is a prince that does accuse her; [2]
　　And such men give not faith to every murmur
　　Or slight intelligence that wounds a lady
　　In her dear honour.　But she is my sister;　　　　130
　　Think of that too; credit not all, but ask
　　Of thy own veins what guilty flowings there
　　May tempt thee to believe this accusation!

Enter THEODOSIA.

'Tis she.—Thou'rt come, Theodosia, to my wishes.
Theo. What does distract you, sir?　　　　135
King.　　　　　　　　　　I've done your message
　　To the duke, and find he does love Domitilla.
Theo. Her he shall meet and marry in Elisium.
King. What mean you?
Theo.　　　　　　　　I've shook off my tameness; do not　140
　　Hinder my just revenge; I'll turn their triumphs into death. [3]
King. There is a question of more consequence
　　Thou must resolve; it does concern thee more
　　Than thy own life.
Theo.　　　　　　　You fright me.　　　　145

---

[1] To pervert any imagination.
[2] An inversion.
[3] I have thought it better (though this line has a redundant foot) to keep nearer
to the division of this and the preceding lines than Dy., who has not, I think, here
been as happy as usual.

King.   Are you honest?

Theo. Honest!

King.   I could have used the name of chaste,
  Or virgin; but they carry the same sense.
  Put off thy wonder, Theodosia,   150
  And answer me, by both our parents' ashes,
  Which now are frighted in the urn, and scarce
  Contain'd beneath their marble, while their fame
  Bleeds in my wounded honour: art thou still
  My sister, without stain upon thy chastity?   155
  Tell me, and answer truth; for both our lives—
  Nay, nay; there is no time for thy amaze.
  Hast thou not lost thyself, and been enjoyed—
  I blush to name the way?

Theo.   Never.   160

King.   Again!

Theo. By all the good we hope for, I am innocent
  As your own wishes.

King.   Thou'rt my virtuous sister!

Theo. But by your love, and all that bound [you] to [1]   165
  Be just, now let me know my strange accuser!

King. Thou shall know that hereafter; let thy thoughts
  Live in their own peace, and dispute not mine! [2]   [*Exit.*

Re-enter DOMITILLA.

Dom. [*aside*]. Not speak to me! He frowned too; sure I have not
  Displeased him? Wherefore stays the princess?   170

Theo. [*aside*]. Shew spirit now or never!—Domitilla!
  [*Aside.*] The greatest part of my affliction,
  Let my revenge begin here! [3]

Dom. Your grace does honour your unworthy servant;
  And if I might beseech one favour more,   175
  'Tis but to know what has displeased the king.

  [1] Q, 'bound to.' The pronoun, added by Dy., is necessary; 'binds' would be
preferable to 'bound.'
  [2] In allusion to the term 'the king's peace'—either to his guarantee of the public
security, or to that claimable by persons under his special protection.
  [3] Let my revenge begin here, where the greatest part of my affliction arose.

Theo. Must you, [then,] be of counsel with his passions?
    What hath advanced you to this boldness?
Dom.   Pardon,
    Why does your grace put on those angry looks?   180
    I never did offend you in a thought.
Theo. Cunning dissembler, yes! And 'tis thy death
    Must satisfy; yet, ere I give thee punishment,
    Tell me what impudence advanced thy thoughts
    So high in our dishonour? Was there none   185
    In your own form of blood [1] fit for your love,
    But you must flatter your proud hopes with one
    So much above your birth? Though he in frailty
    Consent to make thee great, darest thou accept it
    And, with my shame,[2] aspire to be his equal?   190
    Disclaim these hopes, and swear never to love him!
Dom. Madam!
Theo. Do; or with this I will secure my fears
    And stand the malice of all other fate. [*Draws a dagger.*
Dom. [*kneels*].[3] Hear me!   195
Theo.   Be brief!
Dom. I know not by what genius prompted, madam,
    To live or die—more happily!—I have no
    Fear of your rage; which is so far from making
    Me sin against my love, it has enlarged   200
    My heart, which trembles not to be love's martyr.[4]
    I can forgive your hand too, if you promise
    To tell the king how willing I die for him—
Theo. The king? Thou lov'st the duke.
Dom.   He's not concerned 205
    In my affection; I have no thought
    Of any prince alive but your own brother.
    Such an example of love's folly have
    My stars decreed me. Yet, if pride and duty

---

[1] order or degree.   [2] to my shame.
[3] Both these excellent stage-directions are Dy.'s.
[4] Possibly in allusion to Robert Chester's allegorical poem, printed, with other verse including a Dirge by Shakespeare, in 1601.

May in one action meet, and be good friends,   210
Both shall assist my last breath, which shall offer
Humbly the king and his affairs to Heaven.
This he will pardon, shall he know it done
By me—more fit to die than live for him.
Theo. [*aside*]. Alas, poor Domitilla! She is wounded   215
As deep as I.—Rise, and forgive my jealousy!
I cannot promise thee to be my sister,
But I will love thee like one. Let us call
A council of our thoughts, and mingle sorrows!
Yet, when we have done all, and tired our breath,   220
There is no cure for love—but love or death.   [*Exeunt.*

Re-enter King, *with* MONTALTO.

King. How will Montalto counsel me? I am
Wild with the repetition.
Mont.   The duke
Lay such a black aspersion on your sister!   225
'Tis blasphemy to honour; but as soon
He may pollute the sun-beams, or defile
The dew of Heaven ere it approach the earth;
Make us believe the rocks of ice do flame,
And may endanger the north-star. My wonder   230
Will make me reasonless; it throws a poison
On your whole family—a stain so deep
And so prodigious, all the blood within
His dukedom will not purge it. Could he find no
Excuse for his revolt to Domitilla   235
But blasting the sweet princess?
King.   Domitilla!
Whom, I must tell you, I already have
Prepared to be thy bride, as an addition [1]
To the reward I owe thy services.   240
Mont. Prepared for me? You are too bountiful.
[*Kneels.*] In you I kneel both to my king and father.
But—my aspiring will be satisfied

[1] a title of honour in addition.

To be your servant still; in your grace I
Enjoy the bride my heart affects. Let me   245
Grow old with duties here, and not translate
My affection, till my weary soul throw off
The burden of my dust!

King.   No more! In this
One act I'll build a monument of my love   250
To thee, and my revenge upon the duke.
Thou instantly shalt marry Domitilla;
Her beauty, blood, and fortune will deserve thee.

Mont. I am your creature; but how this may inflame
The duke—   255

King.   'Tis meant so.

Mont.   But your sister's fame
Were worth your first care; [and] this may be done
With more access of joy when she is righted.
You have been pleased to hear my counsel, sir,   260
And not repented.

King.   What would'st thou advise me?

Mont. The duke is young, and apt to err. You cannot
Preserve your hospitable laws, to affront [1]
Him openly; nor will it be thought prudence   265
To let loose these suspicions to the déscant
Of people's tongues; the air is dangerous.
Let me search the duke's bosom,[2] for the spring
Of this dishonour!

King.   How?   270

Mont.   Mistake me not;
Philoberto is his secret counsellor,
And the receiver of his thoughts. Leave me
To manage this great work! I have a way
To every angle of his heart; meantime,   275
Be pleased to keep your person but retired!
A silent discontent will fright him more,
And arm us with full knowledge.

King.   Wise Montalto!

[1] and at the same time affront.   [2] confidences; private confessions.

I like thy honest counsel, and obey it.   280
But lose no time!   [*Exit.*

Mont.   It never was more precious;
My essence [1] is concerned, and every minute
Brings a fresh siege against Montalto's life.
There's none but Philoberto conscious   285
To my last accusation of the princess;
Then he must be removed. Delays are fatal;
I'll poison him tonight; I have the way.
This done, the duke may follow, or be bribed
With Domitilla's person to quit Naples.   290

Enter GUIDO, ALOISIO *and* ALEXIO.

Gui. My honoured lord!
Mont.   Guido—Aloisio—
Why make I this distinction? You're but one;
To your Montalto have one heart and faith;
Your love and diligence must now be active.   295
Gui. You have deserved us.[2]
Alex. Lord of our fortunes.
Gui. We're your creatures,
Bound by all law and conscience of the court
To serve your ends.   300
Mont.   It is but to wait close
And [to] contrive excuses, if the duke
Desire accéss to the king.
Gui.   This all!
Mont.   Be careful   305
None of his train nor faction be admitted,
In special Philoberto. If he appear,
Present my service and desire to speak with him!
This is no mighty province, gentlemen,
To waste you much; yet this, neglected, will   310

---

[1] existence.
[2] You have deserved this of us. (Cf. below: 'whose honest souls deserve thee').
But the text may be corrupt, as the ellipsis in the next half-line is rather forced.
The words ought perhaps to be given to Aloisio, as each of the three followers must
be supposed to put in his assurance.

Destroy my tall fate, in whose fall you must
Stoop, and be stricken dead with the large ruins.
Gui. Kill us not first by your suspicion!
We look upon you as our destiny;
Prosper, as we are faithful! 315
Mont. You divide me.[1] [*Exit.*
Alex. There is much trouble in his face; howe'er
Let us be firm!—Is not this Philoberto?

Enter RIVIERO.

Riv. My honoured lords!
Gui. We're proud to be your servants. 320
Riv. I'm yours.—Where is the lord Montalto?[2]
Aloi. New
Gone from us, and desires to speak with you,
And is gone either to your lodging or the duke's.
Riv. I've some affairs with the king, and, that[3] despatched, 325
I'll wait upon him.
Gui. We are confident
You will excuse us; we received command
That none should interrupt him.
Riv. I come from the duke. 330
Aloi. His excellence will conster it our duties.[4]
Riv. This was not wont.
Alex. We dare not, sir, dispute
Our master's pleasure.
Gui. Perhaps his cónfessor is with him. 335
Riv. [*aside*]. Perhaps! There is some cunning.—Nay, prefer
The business of the soul! I may presume
[That] he has no long catalogue to account for?
Gui. We[5] have not been of counsel with his conscience;
We do not use to limit his devotions. 340
Riv. 'Tis pious;—and you three by computation

---

[1] You each have a share of me.   [2] In Q this is given to Guido.
[3] Dy., 'those.'
[4] The duke will construe our conduct as imposed on us by duty.
[5] Q, 'You'; but Guido must mean that he and his fellows are not keepers of the king's conscience.

Montalto's knaves, here placed to keep away
Discoveries. In spite of all your subtilties,
The king shall know my mind, and understand
The history of your patron's and your service.   345
Let time speak your reward in your own chronicles!

Aloi. You ['ll] not forget my lord Montalto has
Desire to speak with you? [1]

Riv.   'Tis all my business.
Be careful of your watch, and look about you;—   350
Some weasel may get in else.   [*Exit.*

Gui.   Does he jeer us?

Alex. Let him! His embassy is not performed.

Re-enter Duke *and* MONTALTO.

Mont. You do amaze my understanding, sir,
To réquire I should justify a tale   355
Made to the blemish of so chaste a lady.

Duke. Did not your lordship tell such a story to
Philoberto in my lodgings?

Mont. I dare his malice to affirm 't, and 'tis not
Done like yourself, to sully with one breath   360
Two fames.

Duke.   Shall I not credit mine own ears?

Mont. Dear sir, collect yourself, and let not passion
To Domitilla, whom you may possess
Hereafter, make you so unjust.   365

Duke.   Dear Machiavel!
This will not do; the king shall know your stratagems.

Mont. Go threaten babes! This would exalt my rage;
But I remember you're a guest to Naples;
Nor would I grieve the genius of my country,   370
To place my own revenge above her honour.

Duke. Poor shadow!

Mont. [*draws a dagger at the* Duke's *back*].[2] Now!—'Twill not be
safe.—[*To* GUIDO.] You know
Your charge.   [*Exit.* 375

[1] Q, 'him'; corrected by Dy.   [2] So Q.

Gui. [*to the Duke*]. We're proud to see your excellence
   In health.
Duke.   Where is the king?
Aloi.   A little busy, sir.
Alex. Not yet, I think; [1] he's at his prayers.   380
Duke. I'll add to his litany.
Gui.   It will not need;
   I think his ghostly father can direct him,
   With whom he is in private.
Duke [*aside*].   I know not   385
   How to intepret this; I want Philoberto.
           [*Exit* Duke; *as he goes out, enter* OCTAVIO.
Oct. Your grace's servant!—[*Aside.*] He looks [much] [2] displeased.
Gui. My lord Octavio!
Oct.   Your servant, lords.
Gui. You met the duke?   390
Oct.   His face showed discontent.
Aloi. We sum our fortunes in Montalto's smile,
   By whose commands we have denied the duke
   Access to the king.
Oct.   You have done well; it much   395
   Concerns my lord; his [, yours,] and all our fate
   Depends upon 't. Continue still your care
   And circumspection, and while I'm within,
   Let none be admitted!
Gui.   Let us alone!   400
   A spirit may have the device to enter;
   But if he've so much body as a gnat
   I'll know his errand. Who's this? Oh, it is
   My lady Domitilla's secretary.

        Enter BOMBO, *gaily dressed.*

Bom. Here are so many tricks, and turns, and doors   405
   I' these court-lodgings, I have lost myself.

---

   [1] Dy. supposes some words from the Duke to have dropped out before Alexio's line. But he may be merely improving on Aloisio's information.
   [2] Both in this line and in the second of Octavio's speech below, Q is a syllable short.

Gui. Master secretary!

Bom. 'T was you betrayed me to the king, and caused
My ladies to be sent for, with more cunning
To bring me hither; but all's one. He has   410
Not seen me yet, nor shall not.—
Which is my way out of this labyrinth?

Aloi. Why are you so unwilling the king should see you?

Gui. Or to live in court? Methinks this habit
Becomes you now.—Does it not, my lord?   415

Alex.   He looks
Like a true hero.

Bom.   You're beside the story, sir.
I did read once
That Hero had no upper lip; [1] she was   420
A lady of Leander's lake. [2]

Gui.   A wit!
There's a new word, now, for the Hellespont!
He'll make a subtle courtier.

Bom.   It has undone me.   425

Aloi. Undone thee? How?

Bom. I know not whether it be my wit, or clothes,
Or disposition of the place, or all
Together—but I'm sure I am in love.
I find it by the losing of my stomach.   430
I am most strangely in love.

Gui.   With whom?

Bom.   I know not.

Aloi. Can you not guess?

Bom. I hope 'tis with myself; for I did vow   435
When my first mistress died which was—

---

[1] Dy. emends: 'had no hair on th' upper lip,' which fits in with his arrangement of the verse, and gives a semblance of meaning to Bombo's nonsense.

[2] A 'lady of the lake' a cant term for a courtesan. Cf. *Hudibras*, Part iii, canto I:—'the difference marriage makes 'Twixt wives and ladies of the lakes.' The origin of the expression is disputed. Some think it was suggested by a view of the story of *Sir Launcelot of the Lake* similar to that expressed by Ascham of Arthurian romance in general. Others derive the expression from *lake*, to play or act (O. E. *laike* or *layke*); whence *lakin*, a plaything.

Gui.   [Was] what?
Bom. A dairy-maid that we had i' the country—
    To love no living woman 'bove an hour.
    She was the very cream of all her sex;   440
    Oft have we churned together.
Gui.   And drunk healths
    In buttermilk?
Aloi.   But do you hope you are
    In love with yourself, sir?   445
Bom.   Marry do I, sir.
    Is that so wonderful at court?
Gui.   You're pleasant.
Aloi. Let's be rid on him! [1]
Gui. Come, you shall now speak with the king,   450
    And he shall knight thee. More honours may follow.
Bom. You shall excuse me; put your honours on
    Somebody else!
Gui.   Do you not know what 'tis?   .
Bom. I have not read of late.   455
Aloi.   But you're much given
    To hearing. What is honour?
Bom. Honour a bubble is, that is soon broke; [2]
    A glow-worm—seeming fire, but has no smoke.
Aloi. There's fire and water and [there's] smoke for air! 460
Bom. A painted sun-beam, piece of gilded chaff;
    And he that trusts, leans to a broken staff.
Gui. You should have reconcilèd the four elements
    To the conceit; there was fire, air [and] water—
    Where's the earth?   465
Bom.   Oh, he that leans to a broken staff,
    Shall find that presently!

[1] Q 'on' is worth retaining. The arrangement of the lines ensuing is quite conjectural, and they were probably in part intended for prose. Q reads: 'put your
honour upon.'
[2] This sally is no doubt suggested by Falstaff's: 'What is honour?' *etc. I Henry IV*,
V, i, 135. Falstaff suggested several of Shirley's Shakespearean reminiscences; see
The Example, II, i; *The Lady of Pleasure*, II, ii.

Re-enter King, *reading a paper, and* OCTAVIO.

Gui. The king!
Bom.   King! By your leave, I vanish.   [*Exit.*
King. This paper contains wonder; 't is not possible!   470
Oct. Upon my life, sir, Philoberto can
     Demonstrate these.
King.   The devil has not art
     To abuse us so. This will require some counsel.—

Re-enter MONTALTO.

     He's here.—Montalto!—Leave us!   [*Exeunt* Lords.   475
Mont.   Sir, your pleasure—
King. Is all in thee. Hast met with Philoberto?
Mont. Not yet.
King.   No matter! I have thought upon't,
     And do conclude it best to let things pass   480
  · Yet in a dream. Noise [1] and enquiry may
     Awake suspicion upon innocence.
Mont. You cannot think her guilty, sir?
King.   I am not
     Without some fears; I have collected things   485
     Since we conferr'd, that stagger my good thoughts—
Mont. Of her you cannot, sir. Unthink again
     Whatever would betray her to your jealousy!
     A virgin's monument cannot be more chaste
     I' the temple.   490
King.   Yes, yes; we may be all cozened;
     And, therefore, let her pass among things desperate! [2]
     Yet, were I certain she were spotted thus,
     As 'tis but a young leprosy upon her,
     I could wish heartily my sister timely   495
     Married—not to the duke, that would betray us,
     But to some one, I know not, who could love
     Us both so well, as [to] be that rare friend,

---

[1] Dy.'s conjecture in lieu of Q, 'choise,' which makes no sense.
[2] among insoluble problems.

And save our honours.

Mont.   Do you, then, suspect her?   500

King. Oh, the duke's character had a powerful sense;[1]
And who knows but she may be lost by one
Not fit to make her reparation?—
Could any nobleman be found in Naples
To bind her wound up by so great an art   505
Of secrecy and marriage—but some wind
May listen and convey, I know not whither,
What my sad breath has scattered in the air.—
Thy master has no servant that dare take
One sorrow from him.   510

Mont.   You are, sir, provided
Of more than that can rise to, in my service.[2]

King. Canst thou be so compassionate, to lose
Thy hopes of richer beauty for my sake?
Dar'st thou, with all this knowledge, hide her stain,   515
And marry her?

Mont.   My duty to your majesty
Shall marry me to death. Let not this trouble
The quiet of your heart! I'll take Theodosia,
And think upon her as [3] she had the whiteness   520
Of my good angel.

King.   Thou'rt a miracle!
Teach me but which way I may reward this love!
Till now I had no poverty; thy worth
Will make me everlastingly in debt.   525
What shall I say?

Mont.   Great sir, no more! Your favours
Flow from a bounty, which has only Heaven
Above it.

King.   They're all trifles. Let me see;   530
Is nothing in my power to make thee find
My gratitude? How barren are we! Wealth?

1 Colloquially: the duke had a strong sense of his own.
2 With more than that can amount to, by my service.
3 as if.

Honour?—

Mont.   There's nothing great or good you have not
      Freely possessed me with.   Your favours would—   535
      So mighty have they fallen upon me—rather
      Express a storm,[1] and I had sank beneath
      The welcome violence, had not your love,
      From whence they flowed, enabled me to strength
      And manly bearing.   540

King.   I was improvident
      To réserve nothing;—or it was a fault
      In thee to be so prodigal of merit
      In thy past services.   Canst thou think of nothing
      Worth my addition?   545

Mont.   Nothing, sir.

King.   I have it;—
      And thank my better genius—I have it!
      Such a reward, Montalto, that I dare
      Be honest, yet pronounce: never did prince   550
      Exceed it to his friend.

Mont.   Sir, you amaze me,
      And shame my want of merit.

King.   In the title,
      Let kings peruse the benefit, and study   555
      An imitation to their best-loved creatures.
      They're great as fortune can invent; I'll teach thee,
      A way, Montalto, to know all thy friends
      And enemies.[2]

Mont.   That were a precious knowledge,   560
      Were it in nature.   With your highness' pardon,
      The hearts of men [, sir,] [3] are not to be measured
      With what we reach the stars, or fathom seas.
      Oh, he that's active in a State has more
      Chained to him by the power and strength of office,   565

---

[1] Appear in the form of; resemble.
[2] The meaning seems to be: While with ordinary favourites their good fortune
is the measure of their greatness, I will make you master of your circumstances.
[3] The verse requires some addition like that suggested by Dy.

Than genuine respect; and 'tis not worth
Or person, but the fortunes of a statesman,
That sometimes men adore.

King.   'Tis true; and therefore
I'm proud in this, that I can teach thee look   570
Into men's souls, to know 'em fit for scorn,
Or thy embraces.

Mont.   How may this be done, sir?

King. Almost i' the twinkling of an eye, too.

Mont.   Strange!   575

King. I['ll] seem to frown upon thee.

Mont. _   How, sir?

King. Dost apprehend me? I will counterfeit
That I'm displeased with thee—do not mistake me—
And have it voiced about the court thou art   580
Confined. Dost mark? At this will all thy enemies,
Whose hearts thou canst not see—their tongues before
By thy great power silenced—join in faction,
Complain, discover their whole stock of malice,
Tickling their spleens, that thou art out of favour; 585
Whom I shall hear and smile at. Then all those,
Whose honest souls deserve thee, will rise up,
The champions of thy fame, o' th' other side,
And be so many orators, to make
Thy faith and honour shine. When, this done,   590
The scene is changed, I send for thee; thou comest
With a most glorious train; and then I'll smile,
Take thee again i' the sight of all; discover
'T was but a trick; thy friends keep still thy bosom,
And thou in triumph shoot'st a scorn, with mine,   595
To strike all envy dumb. Is't not a rare one?
I cannot do enough for thee, Montalto.

Mont. You have found out a way, I must confess.
But, with your pardon, I shall be more able
To do you service in the other ignorance   600
Than run [1] a desperate hazard in this knowledge.

                    [1] Q, 'ruin.'

Some hold it sin, and capital enough,
To have the prince's favour; which, once lost,
[Al] though but in suspicion, they may rage,
And, like a torrent, rise to o'erwhelm nature.   605
King. These shall not wound thee.
Mont.   And how other judges
May wrest the actions of a man, employed,
Though ne'er so faithful, to his king and state—
King. I'm confident of thy justice, and decree   610
Thy triumph in't; thy goodness, thus conspicuous,
Renders thee loved, and fit for Theodosia
When she is brightest. The sun never smiled
More cheerful [ly] upon [the] teeming earth,[1]
Than I, to find thee perfect; for I do   615
But seem displeased. Come, I will have it so;
If thou dost love me, no dispute, but let me
Pursue my fancy, meant to do thee honour!—
Who waits?—

Re-enter GUIDO, ALOISIO *and* ALEXIO.

                    Now it begins.—   620
Attend my lord Montalto to his chamber,
Where our will is he be confined until
Our pleasure further known.
Gui.   How's this?
Alex. }
Aloi. }   Confined?   625
King. No ceremony, sir! When that is done,
We ease you of the trouble, too, of waiting.—[2]
You know the way, my lords, to your own lodgings;
From whence, on peril of our anger, stir not
Until we send for you!—Octavio!   630
                    [*Exeunt* King *and* OCTAVIO.
Gui. Do we not dream?
Mont.   Something would creep
Like a dead sleep upon me. I am in

---

[1] Emendations by Dy.   [2] We dismiss you from your office of lord-in-waiting.

A labyrinth;—but hence with coward fear!
I know the worst; grim death can but translate   635
Me hence, and there's an end of death and fate.

[*Exeunt.*

Act V.   Scene I.   *A Part of the Palace.*

Enter Theodosia, Simphorosa, *and* Domitilla.

Theo. Be comforted and counselled, Domitilla;
I have my part in love's affliction.
Simph.   This
I feared; I must acquaint the king.

Enter Iacomo.

                              Where is   5
Your fellow Bombo? His mirth might now be seasonable.
Iac. He's gone, madam.
Simph. Gone! Whither?   8
Iac. Back to the country-house. He heard of my lord Montalto's
disgrace; and the fear of his supplying the place of a favourite
sent him away this morning with all his moveables. The country,
he says, is wholesome, where he will die without fear or wit when
his time comes. He durst not stay to see the king.[1]
Simph. Would we had still been strangers to the court!—   14
Leave us! [*Exit* Iacomo.] My daughter is much bound to your
        grace.
Dom. Is it the king you speak of?   Pray be careful
You speak all goodness of him; he deserves it,
And will, when I am dead.
Simph.   I'll lose no time.   [*Exit.*   20
Theo. I wish it prosper.
Dom. I dare not say the king dissembles with me;
That were a fault beyond my love. But sure
Something he said that made my heart believe
He did not mean me for another; and   25

[1] Q prints the whole of this speech, as if it were verse.

Montalto, whose reward I must be thought,
Is now confined, and under his displeasure.

Theo. He will have more care of his honour, than
    To place thee so unworthily. Montalto
    Has played the cunning traitor with our loves,   30
    If I may trust the noble Philoberto,
    That told me the whole story of his falsehood,
    Which I before suspected.

Dom. And if he should despise me, as 'tis justice,
    Will Heaven be angry if I love him still;   35
    Or will the king call it a treason in me?
    If he do, I can willingly die for it,
    And with my last words pray he may live happy.
    But why am I this trouble to your grace?
    My story is not worth one of your minutes.   40
    Dear madam, pardon me, and teach me how
    To make my time more happy, spent in something
    That may concern your highness; you do love too.

Re-enter IACOMO.

Iac. Madam, the Duke of Florence.
Theo.   How! The duke?   45
Dom. Why does he visit me?—Madam, indeed
    You may believe I love him not.
Theo.   ·   Admit him,
    I prithee, and conceal me, Domitilla!
    I know he comes a wooing to thy beauty;   50
    I prithee let me hear the second part! [1]   [*Withdraws.*
Dom. I shall against my own desires obey you.

Enter Duke.

Duke. The ambition of my eyes cannot be thought
    Immodest, if they ever wish to dwell here;
    They've found their light again. Let no misfortune   55
    Be a second cause to bury me in darkness!
Dom. Your grace's pardon, if my haste to attend

[1] the rest of it.

The king and his commands made me appear
Rude, when I left your excellence.
Duke.   This does more   60
Than satisfy.
Dom.   I know not how I may
Stand guilty in your thoughts, by keeping a
Rich carcanet.[1]
Duke.   You honoured me to accept it.   65
Dom. But with a blush I must remember too,
I did not thank you. There was want of time,
Or manners. I must leave it to your mercy,
And would, by any duty to your grace,
Expiate my error.   70
Duke.   Madam, it is not worth
The mention of this gratitude; your breath
Makes the oblation rich, and me, who am
Encouraged by your virtue to present you
With something of more value than a world   75
Of these poor empty glories. I dare give you
My heart, madam.
Dom.   Bless your grace from such a meaning!
Duke. Can you be cruel to it?
Dom.   I ne'er had   80
The confidence to look upon a wound;
And such a bleeding [2] object as your heart
Would fright my senses.
Duke.   You are more ingenious
Than not to understand that I mean love.   85
I love you, madam, best of all your sex.
Dom. You cannot, sir; you dare not.
Duke.   How!
Dom. You dare not be so wicked, I am sure,
When you remember what you are—a prince.   90
Duke. Is it a sin for princes to love, madam?

---

[1] necklace. A diminutive of the Old French *carcan*, used, according to Littré,
of the iron ring fastening the neck of a criminal to the gibbet.
[2] Q, 'breeding.'

Dom. Or, if you could dispense with so much passion
    To love me,[1] and durst give me what I tremble
    To think you promise, that, that very act
    In which you most advance affection to me,   95
    Would make me think you love me not.
Duke.   Be clearer!
Dom. How should I think his courtship worth my trust
    And meet him with a real change of hearts,
    Who, in his very first attempt on love,   100
    Would blast my honour, and betray me to
    A shame black as the tongue of infamy?
Duke. Would I?
Dom.   And more! For you in this
    Would tempt me to an act, by which I should   105
    Not only wound myself to death of honour,
    But make me guilty of another's blood,
    And kill an innocent lady, whose least tear
    Is worth a thousand lives of perjured men,
    That make a scorn of virtue.   110
Duke.   What lady?
Dom. Have you forgot the princess, sir?
Duke.   The princess!
Dom. In that name you will find yourself again,
    Lost in a mist of passions. Oh, think,   115
    The fames and hopes of two rich countries are
    Engaged upon your faith.[2] Your highness' pardon!
    I find some blushes chide my too much boldness;
    And by a nearer view now of your goodness
    I see my error, to believe you meant   120
    Other than trial of me, or could fall
    To any thought beneath your birth and honour.

---

[1] place your affections so low as to love me.
[2] This is quite in a vein peculiar to Shirley, who in the case of royal personages applied the principle of *noblesse oblige* as in a sense corresponding to his extreme principles of loyalty. Thus at the close of *The Opportunity* the Duchess consoles herself for a personal disappointment by the reflection:
    Subjects may love as their rude sense imparts;
    But Heaven doth only govern princes' hearts.

Duke. But if Theodosia be made another's
    By her own gift, and I at large, with what
    Justice may I be thought then to address   125
    My passions hither!
Dom.   If the princess—which
    I must not think—give your heart back again,
    And that you could quit all your ties with honour,
    My thoughts are all resigned to the king's will.   130
    He must dispose of me, by my own vow
    Without his free consent never to marry.   [*Exit.*
Duke. The king! There 'tis; I thought she was his mistress.
    It is not possible the princess now
    Can pardon my neglect. Montalto's practice   135
    Upon me, and his poisoning of her virtue,
    Will not excuse my shame. I dare not see,
    Whom I have injured, Theodosia.
    I am resolved; this night I'll steal from Naples.

Re-enter THEODOSIA.

Theo. Nay, do not hide your face, my lord; it will   140
    Appear as fresh and lovely to my eyes,
    As when it first presented me your smiles.
    I'm Theodosia still.
Duke.   But I have been—
Theo. Abused. Time will discover, to the ruin   145
    Of his own name, and glory of our loves,
    Montalto's practice to divide our souls.
Duke. You cannot be so merciful; or else
    This sweetness is put on to enlarge my guilt,
    When we are both compar'd. Dare you believe   150
    I can repent, and be revenged?
Theo.   On whom?
Duke. Upon myself, for suffering my eyes
    To wander from this sweetness.
Theo.   You outdo   155
    The satisfaction, if your grace can find
    Me grow again within your heart, where first

My love desired to plant.
Duke.   Oh, let me drown
My blushes in this overflow of charity!   160
But there's an act that justice calls me to,
Before I can be worthy of this peace.
Montalto has played the villain; now I find it,
And from his treacherous heart my sword must force
A bloody satisfaction for thy honour,   165
Poisoned by him.
Theo.   Stay that revenge; shame has
Already sunk him.

                 Enter a Courtier.

Court.   Sir, the king desires
Some conference with your grace—and with you, madam.   170
Theo. I shall attend you, sir; we shall present
Together thus no object to displease him.
Duke. Though I shall blush to see him, I'll wait on you.

                                          [*Exeunt.*

Act V. Scene II. *Another Part of the Palace.*

Enter King, RIVIERO, ANDRUGIO, *and* Petitioners, *who deliver their
petitions to the* King, *and exeunt.*

King. Good Heaven! Upon what human bosom [1] shall
We, that are made your substitutes on earth,
Place secure confidence?   And yet there may
Be malice in complaints. The flourishing oak,
For his extent of branches, stature, growth,   5
The darling and the idol of the wood,
Whose awful nod the under-trees adore,
Shook by a tempest and thrown down, must needs
Submit his curlèd head and full-grown limbs
To every common axe; be patient, while   10
                [1] intimacy; friendship.

The torture's put to every joint, the saws
And engines making with their very noise
The forests groan and tremble; but not one
When it was in its strength and state, reviled it,
Whom poverty of soul, and envy, sends   15
To gather sticks from the tree's wish'd-for ruin.
The great man's emblem![1] I did love Montalto
And would not have him lost, if justice would
Consent, and be a little of his side;
But here are the two plummets weigh him down: 20
His impious practice on the duke, and base
Aspersions on our sister, that defame
Our whole blood, is a loud, loud accusation.
Riv. His conscience dares not, sir, deny 't.
King.   And you   25
Speak here the tragic story of Riviero,
Whose honest soul, for not complying with
His power and ends, chose in a discontent
To make himself an exile; yet pursued,
And by the practice of Montalto poisoned   30
At Rome.
Andr.   This letter, sent to Alvarez,
Whose treacherous physic purged his soul away,
Is too much testimony.
King.   'Tis his character.[2]—   35

Enter OCTAVIO.

Octavio, you come for justice too?
Oct. It were a vain breath to desire it, sir;
Your thoughts are still so conscious of virtue,
They will prevent petition.
King.   Come nearer!   40
Riv. The king is troubled—

---

[1] It is just possible that Shirley in whose writings there are several reminiscences of Spenser, was thinking of the fable of the Oak and the Briar (*The Shepherd's Calendar*, February) though of course the resemblances are superficial only.
[2] hand-writing.

Andr. Where he loved, to find
So much ingratitude.
King. Andrugio!
Riv. [*aside*]. Things are not yet mature for my discovery.[1]   45
King. You observe?—[*To* ANDRUGIO.] Away! [*Exit* ANDRUGIO.]
We may be just, Philoberto;
Yet not destroy another attribute,
Which shows whose representative we are.
Mercy becomes a king; too much can be   50
But thought a sin on the right hand. We are
Resolved.

Re-enter SIMPHOROSA.

Madam, you're welcome.
Riv. I begin
To fear there is some spell upon the king.[2]   55
If, after this, Montalto shall prevail,
Let innocence be stranger to the world
And Heaven be afraid to punish vice!
King. Remove
For a few minutes.   60
Riv. I obey. [*Exit.*
King. You tell me wonders, madam. 'Las, poor lady!
I shall then have enough to reconcile;
She was too hasty to interpret me
Her lover.   65
Simph. If you, sir, apply no cure,
The fond impression may, I fear, endanger
Her sense and life. I urged Montalto, sir,[3]
By your command, before his change of fortune;
But she took no delight to hear him named.   70
King. No, no; nor I. Good Heaven, how I am troubled
How to repair this pretty piece of innocence,
Whom I have brought into a waking dream

---

[1] for me to discover myself.
[2] Riviero naturally supposes the king to have resolved on mercy to Montalto.
[3] Dy. conjectures 'Montalto's suit.' Probable, but not necessary.

Of passion! Something I must do. Pray tell me—
But tell me truth, I charge thee by thy duty   75
To me, to Naples, and to Heaven; or if
There be in woman's faith, or thy religion,
Anything else to make it up a full
And perfect conjuration—

Simph.   You fright me;   80
Without these, not a thought within my heart
But you have power to summon.

King.   Tell me, then,
Is Domitilla virtuous?

Simph.   How, sir?   85

King. Is she exceeding virtuous? [1] Is she most
Divinely chaste? Can she do more than blush
At wanton sounds? Will she be very angry
At an immodest offer, and be frighted
To hear it namèd? Tell me, does she pray,   90
And weep, and would be torn upon the rack,
Ere she consent to stain one virgin thought;
Or dares she more than Lucrece, kill herself
To save her honour, or do something more
Miraculously than all this to preserve   95
Her white name to posterity?

Simph.   I know not
How to reply to these particulars;
But if your meaning be to have me speak
Truth of her modest and pure thoughts, she is   100
All that [a] mother can beseech of Heaven
To bless a child with; of so chaste a soul
And virtuous simplicity—

King.   No more!
I do believe; and will find out a way   105
To make her satisfaction. 'Tis just.—

[1] Is she one of the 'unco' guid'?—The King lightly tests Simphorosa's feeling before he tests that of Domitilla herself. He had previously (see Act II, i) made sure of her not having 'vowed herself to a cold nunnery.'—Lucrece, it may be remarked, would not have 'saved her honour,' in the sense of preserving her reputation, if she had killed herself before the rape.

Say I desire her presence!
Simph.   Now you bless us.
A widow's prayers and tears for this great bounty!

[*Exit.*

Re-*enter* RIVIERO.

Riv. Your sister and the duke, sir!   110
King.   There's new trouble.
Riv. Never [before] so lovingly united.
The pleasant language of their eyes and gestures
Doth speak their hearts at peace.
King.   That would rejoice me. 115

[*Exit* RIVIERO.

Re-*enter* Duke *and* THEODOSIA.

Theo. Take us to your love!
All jealousies are banished, and we both
Breathe from one soul.
King.   My wonder and my joy—
Duke. Your pardon!   120
King.   Take my bosom![1]
Theo.   The misfortune
Kept[2] us at distance was your creature's act.
King. The clouds are now removed.

Re-*enter* RIVIERO.

Riv. [The] lord Montalto, sir!   125
King.   Let music speak
His dear approach!   We sent for him.
Riv.   How's this?
King.   Let me entreat you to obscure your persons
Awhile!   130

[Duke *and* THEODOSIA *withdraw.*

[1] Come to my heart.   [2] Which kept.

Loud music.—*Enter* GUIDO, ALOISIO, ALEXIO, ANDRUGIO, OC-
          TAVIO *and* MONTALTO.

King. My lord, you're welcome to us, very welcome.
    We've kept our word, and find you have not lost
    Your confidence. What a brave armour is
    An innocent soul! How like a rock it bids
    Defiance to a storm, against whose ribs   135
    The insolent waves but dash themselves in pieces,
    And fall and hide their heads in passionate foam!
    How would a guilty person tremble now,
    Look pale, and with his eyes chained to the ground,
    Betray his fear of justice!   140
Mont.   Where should honour
    Shine with his pure and native lustre, but
    Where there is such a king, so good, so great,—
    The example and reward [1] [too]? He must be
    A rebel twice to virtue, that can live   145
    To be convinced [2] of a dishonour near
    Such an instinctive goodness.
King.   Where be all
    His fierce accusers? Call them to his presence,
    Whom all their envies would destroy!   150
Riv. [*aside*].   So, so!
    The king is charmed.
Oct.   They're gone; upon the first
    News of my lord's return they vanished, sir!
Mont. So may all treason fly the brow of innocence!   155
King. 'Tis well said; but they shall not fly their names.
    Read there! Just to our thoughts, they apprehended
    Thee lost in our displeasure.—Where's our sister?—
    And now they came to be revenged, Montalto,
    Upon our favours.   160
Gui.   Right, an't please your grace.
King. There's something may concern your want of grace.[3]—

---

[1] Dy., 'reward. He must be, sir.'   [2] convicted.
[3] Playing upon the word 'grace' in Guido's cringing attempt at applause, the
King suits the action to the word.

Andrugio, Philoberto!   [*Gives them papers.*
Mont. We're undone, Guido, and I see more engines
 Are levell'd at my fate.   165
Riv.   The king would have
 Your lordship péruse this—
Andr.   And these—
       [*They give the papers to* MONTALTO.
Riv. That you may know your friends and enemies.
Mont. Lost! Lost for ever!   170
Riv.   Sir, you know
 You have obliged the princess Theodosia
 And the duke to you, and you may presume
 To use their favours; they are here.

     Re-enter Duke *and* THEODOSIA.

Mont.   'T were better   175
 For me they had no being. I did never
 Expect this, to accuse me for the death
 Of Riviero; but I must obey
 This fatal revolution.   [*Kneels.*
King.   Why does   180
 Montalto kneel?
Mont.   I dare not ask your pardon;
 Only I beg you would put on a brow
 Rough as the cause you have to make it frown;
 And that may strike me dead without more torment.   185
King. Ingrateful man! Am I rewarded thus,
 Not only with my faith abused and subjects,
 But wounding all our honours? [1]
Theo.   Let him find
 Your mercy, sir, for his offence to me!   190
King. I must not, dare not pardon; 'twere a sin
 In me, of violence to Heaven and justice.
Mont. You've been a Royal Master.
King.   Take him hence!

---

[1] The word 'honours' seems here to be used much in the same way as in Act I,
i,= persons closely connected with us; our nobles.

His life [1] will draw a scorn upon the kingdom;   195
Expect the censure of our laws. [*Exit* MONTALTO, *guarded.*]
                                   You, gentlemen,
We only banish from the court.

Gui. ⎫
Aloi. ⎬   You're merciful.
Alex. ⎭

King. Pray, and be honest!   200
Riv. That last will be the greatest penance to them.
                    [*Exeunt* GUIDO, ALOISIO, ALEXIO.

            Re-enter SIMPHOROSA *and* DOMITILLA.

King. My passion would be strong, but here is one
     Come to divert the stream.—How is it with
     The pretty Domitilla? You and I   204
     May change some word in private. [*Takes* DOMITILLA *aside.*
Oct. The king is just, and 'tis within your silence, [2]
     To make Montalto nothing.
Riv.   He will sink
     Apace, without that weight upon him; malice
     Shall have no share in my revenge.   210
King.   And since
     Montalto is become incapable,
     I will not marry thee, that's a thing too common;
     But thou shalt be my mistress,[3]—a preferment
     Above my first intention. Be wise,   215
     And entertain it! Oh, the days and nights
     We'll spend together!
Oct.   The king is very pleasant
     With Domitilla.
King. Come, kiss me, Domitilla, kiss me, now,   220
     Before all these! What needs this modesty?
     Come, let us take in one another's soul!
Dom. Are you the King of Naples?
King.   So they call me.
     And if there be a power within that name,   225

---

[1] His being left to live.   [2] it depends on your not discovering yourself.
[3] I will not marry you to anyone else, but make you my mistress *en titre.*

It shall be thine, to make thee glorious
And great above our Queen; there is no title
Like unto that our heat and blood creates—
A mistress, Domitilla.

Dom.   Are you, sir,   230
In earnest?

King.   Do but thou consent, and I
Will give thee such a proof in my embraces
Of the delight—they will not follow us;
I'll tell thee more i' the bed-chamber.   235

Dom.   I dare
Not understand this language. Can the king
Be impious? How was my opinion cozened!
Sin hath deformed his very shape; his voice
Hath now no harmony.   240

King.   This is but to draw
More courtship from me.

Dom.   Pardon, I beseech you!
I've found my error.

King [*aside*].   Will she yield?   245
Dom.   I did
Consent too soon to my captivity,
Though modesty would not allow me strength
To tell you so; but you have, sir, by what
My fond thoughts never did expect, relieved me,   250
To make me know myself. And now, preserving
That duty which I owe you as my king,
I call love back again, and can look on
Your lusts with a becoming scorn.

King.   You can?   255
Dom. Yes; and were Naples, Rome, and all the wealth
Of Italy laid down, the great temptation,
Thus I would spurn their glories.

King. Come, this is but the trick of all your sex;
We know you can dissemble appetite,   260
As if you were not flesh and blood.

Dom.   Sir, give

Me leave to go, while I have power to pray for you!
Where was I lost? Is there no friend to goodness?
Have I contracted such a leprous form,   265
That I have lost all men's defence and charity?

Oct. Madam, your innocence doth raise in me,
Though young, a willing champion; and with
My safe obedience to the king, I dare,
Armed with the witness [1] of her cause, defy   270
The greatest soldier in the world.

King.   How's this?

Oct. Sir, in a noble cause, if you, to whom
In the first place truth flies as to an altar,
Waive her religious defence, I dare   275
Die for her.

King.   You! So brave? To prison with him!
We will correct your sauciness.

Oct.   You'll grace
My first act, sir, and get me fame, by suffering   280
For so much sweetness.

Dom.   Let not your displeasure,
Great sir, fall upon him; revenge what you
Call disobedience, here!

King.   You owe much to   285
His confidence; nor is there any punishment
Beyond your love and liking of his boldness.
You two should make a marriage with your follies.

Oct. Let Domitilla make Octavio
So blest!   290

Dom.   My lord, you now deserve I should
Be yours, whom, with the hazard of the king's
Anger and your own life, you have defended.
There is a spring of honour here, and to it
I' the presence of the king, his court, and Heaven,   295
I dare now give my heart; nor is 't without

---

[1] So Mrs. Ford, in *M. W. W.*, IV, ii, speaks of 'the warrant of womanhood and
the witness of a good conscience.'—In the text, 'innocence' and 'truth' are treated
as synonyms.

My duty to a promise.[1]

Oct.　　　　　　　　Now you make
　　Octavio happy.

King.　　　　　　'T is to my desires,　　　　　300
　　And I dare wish you joys.　Forgive this practice;
　　—Nay, pretty Domitilla, I did this
　　But to divert more happily thy thoughts
　　Of me, who have not paid yet the full tribute
　　To my Cesaria's dust.　Again let me　　　　305
　　Congratulate thy choice in young Octavio
　　Whose birth and forward virtue will deserve thee.—
　　Brother and sister, love, and wish them happiness!

Theo. May all joys spring within their hearts!

Duke [*beckoning* RIVIERO *forward* [2]]. I must　　310
　　Present this gentleman to be more known to you.

Oct. [*to* RIVIERO]. I hope you are no enemy to this blessing?

Simph. I add, what doth become a most glad mother,
　　My blessing to your loves!

King [*recognizing him*]. Noble Riviero!　　　　315

Riv. I live again by your acknowledgment.

Duke. Sir, you may trust my testimony—Álvarez'
　　Letter is now an argument of his safety,
　　Who is yet living to increase the guilt
　　Of false Montalto.　　　　　　　　　320

King [*to* RIVIERO]. Welcome!　'Tis thy life
　　That hath reversed Montalto's doom, whose sentence
　　Now shall be only banishment.—Our hearts
　　Are full and sprightly; nothing wants but to
　　Perfect with holy ceremony what　　　　　325
　　Your hearts have sealed.　Mirth in each bosom flows;
　　Distraction never had so sweet a close.　　[*Exeunt.*

---

[1] A very pretty touch.　Domitilla, even in accepting Octavio, is constant to the King by keeping the promise which she gave him, *ante*, II, i.

[2] The stage-directions which I have ventured to insert in this passage indicate what must have been the action intended by the author.　The Duke now brings forward the pretended Philoberto; as he moves towards the King, his son asks his approval, Simphorosa adding a mother's blessing; and the king now recognizes him to be Riviero.

Epilogue,

as it was spoken to the Lord Deputy on New-year's day at night,
by way of vote [1] congratulating the New Year.

Our poet doth forget his play. [2]
There is something he would pay,
Due to your greatness, and the day
Which, by a revolution of the sphere,
Is proud to open the new year;   5
And having looked on you, hath hid his face,
And changed his robe with stars to grace
And light you, going to bed, so wait
With trembling lustre [3] on your state.

Shine brighter yet!   You're not the same   10
Clear lamps you were; shine like the name
Of him I bow to; while a flame
Active, and burning here with pure desires,
Shall equal the best borrowed fires.
May health, the bosom's friend, stream through your blood, 15
And know no ebb of the chaste flood; [4]
And though time shift, and years renew,
May yet the spring be still in you!

May she, whom Heaven hath sweetly graced,
And in your noble bosom placed,   20
Whose heart, by only yours embraced,

[1] wish.
[2] In the *Poems* of 1646 this line is changed into: 'Sir, give me leave to court your
stay.'   [3] sconce with lights.
[4] Strafford was seriously ill before leaving Ireland for England in April 1640;
and his illness increased after his arrival in London. Among Shirley's *Poems*
is one congratulating him on his recovery.

Hath made one true and holy Gordian, prove
Fruitful in children, as in love!
And may this fair top-branch,[1] whose early bloom
Doth promise all the fruit can come   25
To virtue and your name, be blest
And live a story to the rest! [2]

All honour with your fame increase;
In your bosom dwell soft peace,
And justice, the true root of these!   30
Wealth be the worst and outside of your fate;
And may not Heaven your life translate,
Till for your ROYAL MASTER and this isle
Your deeds have filled a chronicle!
In all that's great and good, be bold,   35
And every year be copy of the old!

[1] The reference must be to Strafford's only son William, born 1626, upon whom Charles I conferred all the honours forfeited by his father's attainder, on December 1st, 1641. To the second Earl of Strafford Shirley in 1653 dedicated his romantic comedy *The Court Secret*. As has been seen, in the *Dedication* of our play, Shirley applies the term 'top-branch of honour' (head of the peerage) to the Earl of Kildare.

[2] Dy., in the preceding line, 'To virtue, and.' But the wishes expressed in these two lines seem to refer directly to the son.

INDEX

OF HISTORICAL AND CRITICAL MATERIALS

THE following pages contain advertisements of books by the same author or on kindred subjects.

Representative English Comedies

With introductory essays and notes. An historical view of our earlier comedy and other monographs by various writers under the general editorship of

CHARLES MILLS GAYLEY, LITT.D., LL.D., Professor of the English Language and Literature in the University of California.

VOLUME I

FROM THE BEGINNINGS TO SHAKESPEARE

Cloth, 8vo, $2.00 net

The aim of this volume and those which will follow is to indicate the development of a literary type by a selection of its representative specimens, arranged in the order of their production and accompanied by critical and historical studies. So little has been scientifically determined concerning evolution or permutation in literature that the more specific the field of inquiry, the more trustworthy are the results attained, — hence the limitation of this research not merely to a genus like the drama, but to one of its species. What is here presented to the public differs from histories of the drama in that it is more restricted in scope and that it substantiates the narrative of a literary growth by reproducing the data necessary to an induction ; it differs from editions of individual plays and dramatists, on the other hand, because it attempts to concatenate its text by a running commentary upon the characteristics of the species under consideration as they successively appear. It is an illustrated, if not certified, history of English comedy.

CONTENTS

THE MACMILLAN COMPANY

Publishers   64–66 Fifth Avenue   New York

Representative English Comedies

With Introductory Essays and Notes and A Comparative View of the Fellows and
Followers of Shakespeare, under the General Editorship of

CHARLES MILLS GAYLEY, Litt.D., LL.D., Professor of the English Language and Literature in the University of California.

VOLUME II

THE LATER CONTEMPORARIES OF SHAKESPEARE: BEN JONSON AND OTHERS

Cloth, 8vo, $2.00 net

The aim of this series has been stated in the Preface to the first volume: to indicate the development of English comedy by a selection of its representative specimens, arranged, when possible, in the order of their production and accompanied by critical and historical studies. The introductory essay and the special studies in that volume presented an historical view of comedy in England from its beginnings to the time of Shakespeare and his earlier contemporaries. In the present work and its companion, "Fletcher and Others," the comedy of the contemporaries of Shakespeare to the closing of the theatres in 1642 is represented and discussed.

CONTENTS

THE MACMILLAN COMPANY

Publishers   64–66 Fifth Avenue   New York

English Poetry

Its Principles and Progress. With representative masterpieces and notes.

By CHARLES MILLS GAYLEY, Litt.D., LL.D., Professor of the English Language and Literature in the University of California, and CLEMENT C. YOUNG, of the Lowell High School, San Francisco, California.

Cloth, 12mo, $1.10 net

A manual for the general reader who takes an interest in the materials and history of the higher English poetry, and seeks a simple statement of its principles in relation to life, conduct, and art. The introduction on " The Principles of Poetry " aims to answer the questions that inevitably arise when poetry is the subject, of discussion, and to give the questioner a grasp upon the essentials necessary to appreciation and to the formation of an independent judgment.

"The Introduction on 'The Principles of Poetry' should be an inspiration to both teacher and pupil, and a very definite help in appreciation and study, especially in the portion that deals with the 'Rhythm of Verse.' The remarks on the different centuries, in their literary significance and development, are helpful, and the notes to each poem, lucid and sufficient." — HARRY S. ROSS, Worcester Academy, Worcester, Mass.

A History of English Dramatic Literature to the Death of Queen Anne

By A. W. WARD

Cloth, $9.00 net

A SUMMARY OF CONTENTS

VOLUME I — The Origins of the English Drama. The Beginnings of the Regular Drama. Shakespeare's Predecessors. Shakespeare.

VOLUME II — Shakespeare (continued). Ben Jonson. The Later Elizabethans. Beaumont and Fletcher.

VOLUME III — The End of the Old Drama. The later Stuart Drama.

THE MACMILLAN COMPANY

Publishers   **64–66 Fifth Avenue**   **New York**

English Drama of the Restoration and Eighteenth Century

By GEORGE HENRY NETTLETON, Assistant Professor of English in Yale University.

In this volume there is presented for the first time a continuous and comprehensive account, both historical and critical, of the whole period of English drama from the closing of the theatres in 1642 to the height of eighteenth century comedy in Sheridan.   Professor Nettleton includes an account not merely of formal tragedy and comedy, but also of opera, pantomime, burlesque, farce, etc.   He also discusses the development of scenic, operatic, and spectacular stage effects.   In addition to a full study of Restoration drama the following topics are treated : the origin and growth of English pantomime, of ballad-opera and of prose tragedy, the development of personal caricature and satirical farce, the establishment of the formal dramatic censorship, the rise of sentimental drama and the Garrick era. The volume will serve admirably as a text-book for college courses on the drama.

THE MACMILLAN COMPANY

Publishers   64–66 Fifth Avenue   New York